Business
Economics

. . . .

Longman modular texts in business and economics

••••••••••••••••••••

Series Editors
Geoff Black and Stuart Wall

Other titles in this series:

Business Information Technology: Systems, Theory and Practice
Geoffrey Elliott and Susan Starkings

The Macroeconomic Environment
Andrew Dunnett

Management Accounting
David Wright

Financial Accounting (2e)
Christopher Waterson and Anne Britton

Introducing Human Resource Management (2e)
Margaret Foot and Caroline Hook

Quantitative Methods for Business and Economics
Glyn Burton, George Carrol and Stuart Wall

Introducing Organisational Behaviour
Jane Weightman

Marketing (2e)
Elizabeth Hill and Terry O'Sullivan

Business Economics

Second Edition

Win Hornby
The Robert Gordon University, Aberdeen

Robert Gammie
The Robert Gordon University, Aberdeen

Stuart Wall
Anglia Polytechnic University

FINANCIAL TIMES
Prentice Hall

An imprint of **Pearson Education**

Harlow, England · London · New York · Reading, Massachusetts · San Francisco · Toronto · Don Mills, Ontario · Sydney
Tokyo · Singapore · Hong Kong · Seoul · Taipei · Cape Town · Madrid · Mexico City · Amsterdam · Munich · Paris · Milan

Pearson Education Limited

Edinburgh Gate
Harlow
Essex CM20 2JE
England

and Associated Companies throughout the world

Visit us on the World Wide Web at:
www.pearsoneduc.com

First published under the Addison Wesley Longman imprint 1997
Second edition published 2001

© Pearson Education Limited 2001

The rights of Win Hornby, Robert Gammie and Stuart Wall to be
identified as authors of this work have been asserted by the
authors in accordance with the Copyright, Designs and Patents Act 1988.

ISBN 0 273 64603 6

British Library Cataloguing-in-Publication Data
A catalogue record for this book is available from the British Library.

10 9 8 7 6 5 4 3 2 1
05 04 03 02 01

Typeset in 9/12pt Stone Serif by 30
Printed by Ashford Colour Press Ltd, Gosport.

Contents

Companion Web Site

A Companion Web Site accompanies
Business Economics, 2/e
by Hornby, Gammie and Wall

Visit the *Business Economics* Companion Web Site at *www.booksites.net/hornby*
to find valuable teaching and learning material including:

For Students:
- Study material designed to help you improve your results
- Activities designed to further test your understanding
- Annotated web links
- Annotated further reading lists

For Lecturers:
- A secure, password protected site with teaching material
- Extra case studies for download
- PowerPoint slide shows for use in lectures
- An electronic, downloadable version of the Instructor's Manual

Also: This site has a syllabus manager and search functions.

Preface

When we originally wrote this textbook we asked ourselves why yet another textbook in economics? Surely this was an already fairly crowded market place. Why was there a need to produce another offering to students? Three years on, we believe that our original faith in writing a textbook on Business Economics has been vindicated. Our motivation stems from our experience of teaching economics in a business school and our dissatisfaction with many of the existing economics textbooks on the market. In many cases it is still our view that these textbooks provide an excellent underpinning for students who wish to go on and study economics as a discipline in its own right. However, it is our experience that there are a lot of students who are studying economics as part of their course and whose requirements are slightly different. While it is important that these students have an understanding of the way in which economists think about problems, there is less need for a detailed examination of theoretical models. There is more need in our view to bridge the gap into applied areas such as business and to understand the economic background to, and implications of, business decisions. There is also a need to look at practical applications in the areas of business objectives, demand forecasting, costs, pricing and investment decisions and to set these in the economic context within which firms operate. Thus there is a need to blend traditional 'macroeconomic' and 'microeconomic' theory, together with an examination of how business economics can influence such areas as business policy.

There is unfortunately a gap between economics and business. Writing in *The Economic Journal* a decade ago, John Kay summed up this unfortunate divide.

> If you ask most businessmen what they think economics is about their answer will be economic forecasting. They don't think very much of economic forecasting – although they go on thinking they need it – and so they do not think very much of economists. Every day they are concerned to analyse their costs which is done by accountants. They determine their prices. This is the responsibility of their marketing department. They need to interpret the business environment they face – the task of their corporate planners and strategic advisers. The economic input into any of

these functions is minimal. Yet cost, prices, industries and markets are the lifeblood of microeconomics ... economics has almost no influence on business policy and in only a small minority of companies does the chief executive have an economic adviser at all.[1]

This view was echoed by *The Economist*:

> The one group of people to whom most businessmen rarely turn are economists. Big firms ask economists to predict the ups and downs of national economies, but when it comes to finding ways to run their own company better, many managers would sooner consult an astrologer.[2]

These views were simply reflecting the opinions of a number of leading economists from around the world. The reasons are not too hard to find. Although there has been a growth in specialist areas of economics such as Industrial Economics and the more techniques-orientated Managerial Economics, there is arguably an excessive emphasis in much economics on highly mathematical models, with the resulting research often inaccessible and of limited relevance to business. Abstract theorising has tended to dominate economics teaching at both undergraduate and postgraduate levels. Writing in the United States, the well-known economist, William Baumol, was highly critical of much of what went on in university economics departments:

> These days few specialised students are allowed to proceed without devoting a considerable proportion of their time to the acquisition of mathematical tools, and they often come away feeling that any piece of writing they produce will automatically be rejected as unworthy if it is not liberally sprinkled with an array of algebraic symbols.[3]

It was this dissatisfaction with the lack of a strong link between economics and business that prompted us to look carefully at our own teaching. Were we guilty of offering our undergraduate students a series of abstract theoretical models which had little relevance to their careers in business? Our experience of teaching on the MBA and other management programmes, where our comfortable assumptions were challenged by practising managers, reinforced our conviction that there was a danger of our discipline promising more than it appeared it could deliver. This re-examination originally led us to devise a business economics course and to try to produce a textbook around which we could build it.

More recently there has been recognition of this gap in the market. Since the publication of our textbook in 1997, there have been a number of other similar new textbooks in Business Economics which attempt to bridge this divide between business and economics. We believe that our new edition does this in a way that is relevant to students studying business or business-related programmes both here in the United Kingdom and abroad and we have been encouraged by the helpful feedback we have received from users of the first edition.

---

[1] Kay, J. (1991) 'Economics and business', *The Economic Journal*, Vol. 101, January, pp. 57–63.

[2] *The Economist*, 'Quacks and coaches', 17 April 1993, p. 81.

[3] Baumol, W. J. (1991) 'Toward a newer economics: the future lies ahead', *The Economic Journal*, Vol. 101, January, pp. 1–8.

So what then is 'Business Economics'? How would we define this subject area? In our view, Business Economics attempts to bring together economic concepts and business decision-making in order to assist in finding the best solutions to solving business problems. The kind of economic concepts we will be looking at are, for example:

➤ The circular flow of income model of the economy and the theories and principles which inform government macroeconomic policy.
➤ The theories of international trade and the factors which influence the international economic environment within which firms operate.
➤ Theories relating to the structure of economies and how these are changing over time.
➤ The theories of the firm's objectives.
➤ The theories of demand, cost and pricing.
➤ Theories of market structures.
➤ Theories relating to investment decisions and to business strategy, both nationally and internationally.

The areas of business decision-making that we are focusing on are:

➤ How changes in the domestic and international economic environment will impact on businesses and influence their strategy.
➤ How the changing structure of the economy, and in particular the advent of e-commerce, will impact on a whole range of business relationships, creating new models of business behaviour.
➤ How changing objectives affect business behaviour.
➤ How changes to the competitive structure of markets influence decision-making, particularly in areas such as positioning products and services in the market place, and how these factors influence pricing and investment decision-making.
➤ How government can influence the way businesses behave.

Our own starting point is to examine the economic environment within which firms operate. We look at how economists view the way the economy works, the state of the economy, the rate of economic growth, the level of employment and our trading position with the rest of the world. We also wanted to give a flavour of the debates that surround economic policy in as clear and, we hope, as non-technical a way as possible. We analyse these issues in the first three chapters which examine domestic and international economic environment and the key macroeconomic issues facing businesses, such as free trade and international currency mechanisms.

Chapter 4 then deals with the structure of the economy and focuses on the ways in which the different economic sectors have changed in recent years and the factors which have influenced these changes. In particular there is a discussion of the economic effects of the Internet. These first four chapters can be regarded as examining the economic environment within which firms operate. On the other hand, Chapter 5 looks at the ways in which firms and markets are organised, both 'externally' and 'internally', and examines the factors and forces which influence the organisation of business. Chapter 6 looks at the different objectives of firms in theory and practice and examines what economists have to contribute to the debate on the influence of goals, mission statements and targets on actual firm performance. Chapter 7, on demand in theory and practice, analyses the factors which influence the demand for a firm's product or service and gives a brief outline of the methods that firms use to forecast demand, while Chapter 8 examines the role of costs in theory and practice. This is followed by theory and practice of pricing in Chapter 9 and investment in Chapter 10. Chapter 11 looks in detail at some of the economics of business decision-making in the area of corporate strategy as well as examining international business strategy. Finally, Chapter 12 discusses the relationship between government and business and examines those areas of governmental activity which impinge upon the operation of business.

Each chapter commences with a list of objectives. In addition, in order to make this book interactive, there are a number of places in the text where the reader is invited to pause for thought. Interspersed throughout each chapter you will also find a number of boxes in which brief case study examples are given, often drawn from well-known businesses. Guideline solutions to problems and answers to questions are given at the end of the book. At the end of several chapters there are longer illustrative case studies designed to draw together a number of themes from the chapter.

In conclusion, we would like to thank all those students, colleagues and other users of the first edition of the book who helped to make it a success and who kindly wrote to us with their comments and observations. As indicated above, we have tried to incorporate as many of their suggestions as we could into the new edition. We would also like to thank Stuart Wall for his enthusiastic encouragement and for his contribution in writing Chapter 12. Finally we would like to thank our respective wives, Allison and Elizabeth, for their patience and support. Any shortcomings are entirely our own!

Win Hornby and Bob Gammie
January 2001

Acknowledgements

We are grateful to the following for permission to reproduce copyright material:

Table 1.1 from *HM Customs and Excise Annual Report 1997–8*, Table 1.2 from *Economic Trends 1999*, and Figure 12.2 *The Assisted Areas 2000*, being Crown Copyright reproduced with permission of the Controller of Her Majesty's Stationery Office; Tables 1.6, CS9.4.1, CS11.16.1 and Figure 4.3 and Figure CS4.6.2 published by The Economist Newspaper Limited, London, 29 April 2000, 15 May 1993, 19 June 1999, 1 April 2000 and 26 February 2000; Figure 1.2 from *National Income Accounts*; Table CS1.3.1 adapted from HM Treasury *Tax Ready Reckoner* published by Institute for Fiscal Studies, November 1999; Figure 1.4 from *Stability and Growth for Britain: Pre-Budget Report 4479* November 1999, Figure 1.5 from *IFS Green Budget 2000*, Figure 2.2 from *UK Balance of Payment (The Pink Book)* 1998 Edition and Table 4.1 from *Standard Industrial Classification 1992*, published by the Office of National Statistics, Crown Copyright 2000; Figure 2.1 and Table 2.10 from *Annual Report 1999* published by World Trade Organisation; Figure CS3.2.2 from *Britain's relative productivity performance 1980–1997*: a sectional analysis published by The National Institute of Economic & Social Research (O'Mahony, M.); Tables 4.2 and 4.3 from *Annual Report* published by OECD, 2000; Figure 4.2 from *Annual Report* published by International Monetary Fund, 1999; Figure 4.4 from *The World Competitiveness Yearbook 2000* published by IMD International Institute for Management Development, Lausanne, 2000; Table 4.4 from *Schroders Economic Perspective* published by Schroders Plc, First Quarter 2000; Table CS4.5.1 copyright Times Newspapers Limited, London, 12th February 2000; Figure CS4.6.1 from *Blown to Bits: How the New Economics of Information Transfers Strategy* published by Harvard Business School Publishing, Boston (Evans, P. and Wurster, T. S., 2000); Tables 5.4 (Rumelt, R., March 1991) and 11.1 (Hill, Hwang, Kim, Volume 11, 1990) from *Strategic Management Journal* published by John Wiley & Sons Limited; Table CS6.5.1 from *Thomson Financial Extel* published by Datastream International Limited, 1995; Figures 6.11 and 11.1 from *Competitive Advantage: Creating and Sustaining Superior Performance* reprinted with the permission of The Free Press, a Division of Simon & Schuster Inc. (Porter, M.E. 1985, 1998);

Box 7.2 from BMRB/Mintel published by Mintel International Group Ltd., February 1996; Table 7.8 (Sparkes, J. and McHugh, M., Volume 1 No. 11, 1984) from *Journal of Forecasting* published by John Wiley & Sons Limited; Table 8.3 from *European Economy* journal Volume 35, published by the Office for Official Publications of the European Communities, March 1988; Table CS9.8.1 adapted from British Economic Survey published by Pearson Education Ltd., 25th February 1996; Figure 11.2 adapted from *The Growth-Share Matrix* originally published by The Boston Consulting Group Inc., 1970; Figure 11.4 from *Exploring Corporate Strategy (5th edn)* published by Pearson Education (Johnson, G. and Scholes, K., 1999); Table 11.2 from UNCTAD/Erasmus University database, 1999 published by Division on Investment, Technology & Enterprise Development, UN Conference on Trade & Development.

Case Study 5.1 from Moves to Help People to Set Up in Business: Encouraging Entrepreneurs © *Financial Times*, 31 January 1996; Case Study 5.2 from Report on Liability Law to be Published © *Financial Times*, 23 January 1996; Case Study 5.9 from World Trade: 'Japanese Ads Anger Ford's Competitors' © *Financial Times*, 31 January 1996; Case Study 5.10 from Torrid Tales of Tarot Cards and Topless Darts: Raymond Snoddy meets Kelvin MacKenzie and his News Bunny © *Financial Times*, 17 January 1996; Case Study 11.10 from Fiorina moves to put Hewlett-Packard back together © Financial Times, 7 December 1999.

British Broadcasting Corporation for an adapted extract from BBC news page; Blackwell Publishers for an adapted extract from *British Journal of Industrial Relations*, Vol 31, No 1 March 1993 (Gregg, Machin & Szymanski) and *Journal of Industrial Affairs*, Vol 9, No 2 (Reekie and Blight); Boston University for an adapted extract from press clippings service; Chemical Week for extract from the article 'Mercosur economies regain their footing' in *Chemical Week* 13 October 1999 (Kara Sissell); Competition Commission for extracts from the article 'Supply of Groceries from multiple stores monopoly inquiry: issues statement', published 21 January 2000 and 'Supply of groceries from multiple stores monopoly inquiry: remedies statement' published 22 February 2000; Confederation of British Industry for an adapted extract from *CBI Press Release* 27 January 2000; The Economist Newspaper Limited for extracts from the articles 'Choppy waters: Japanese cars in Europe' in *The Economist* 10 December 1994, '3M re-invents itself' in *The Economist* 18 November 1995, 'When the chips are down' in *The Economist* 23 March 1996, 'Let the market take off' in *The Economist* 18 January 1997, 'Is this the end of sticky prices?' in *The Economist* 16 May 1998, 'Price discounting' in *The Economist* 1 August 1998, 'Shopping all over the world' in *The Economist* 19 June 1999, 'Why wages do not fall in recessions' in *The Economist* 26 February 2000 and adapted extracts from *The Economist* 14 May 1994, 29 January 1996, 'Social Security' in *The Economist* 15 August 1998 © The Economist Newspaper Limited, London 1994, 1995, 1996, 1997,1998, 1999, 2000; Elsevier Science Limited for an adapted extract from *Long Range Planning*, Vol 27, No 1 (Brabet and Klemm); Guardian Newspapers Limited for an adapted extract from the article 'Whisper it: Takeovers don't pay' in *The Guardian* 30 November 1999 (Dan Atkinson); Income Data Service for an adapted extract from 'Income Data Support Services Report No 802', February

2000; The Institute for Fiscal Studies for an adapted extract from the 'Institute of Fiscal Studies Green Budget Report 2000'; Kyodo News International Inc for an extract adapted from *Kyodo News Service* January 2000; MCB University Press Limited for an extract from Management Decision 30 April 1995; National Grid Group Plc for an extract from www.nationalgrid.com/uk/activities; National Institute of Economic and Social Research (UK) for an adapted extract from *National Institute Economic Review*, August 1994 (Conyan and Greig); News International Syndication for an extract from the article 'Buying a car on the internet' in *The Times* 12 February 2000 © Times Newspapers Limited 2000 and Pearson Education Limited for an extract adapted from *British Economy Survey* Vol 25, No. 2 1996 (Ison) published by Addison Wesley Longman.

Whilst every effort has been made to trace the owners of copyright material, in a few cases this has proved impossible and we take this opportunity to offer our apologies to any copyright holders whose rights we may have unwittingly infringed.

CHAPTER 1

The domestic economic environment

Objectives

By the end of this chapter you will be able to:

➤ Understand the circular flow of income model of the economy.

➤ Identify the injections and withdrawals from the circular flow of income and assess their impact.

➤ Outline the key objectives of economic policy.

➤ Identify the causes of unemployment.

➤ Examine the factors causing inflation.

➤ Assess the causes of economic growth.

➤ Examine the domestic economic environment within which firms must operate.

Key concepts

Aggregate demand: the total level of demand for goods and services in the economy. It is made up of the expenditure of four sectors; namely, households (consumers' expenditure), business (investment expenditure), government sector (government expenditure) and the overseas sector (exports minus imports).

Cyclical unemployment: unemployment which is a direct result of the slump or depression in the economic cycle.

Deflationary gap: when the level of aggregate demand falls below the full employment level of national income.

Demand deficient unemployment: the level of unemployment created as a result of a deflationary gap.

Fiscal policy: the use of taxation as a means of controlling the economy.

Frictional unemployment: a type of short-term unemployment when people are 'between jobs'.

Full employment: a situation where all those who are seeking employment and who can be employed are employed. This has come to be regarded as being consistent with around 2–3 per cent unemployment.

Income effect: as taxes fall, people become better off. The income effect occurs when they no longer feel the need to work as hard or as long since they can achieve the same level of income with less effort.

Multiplier process: a process whereby increases in investment or government expenditure have a multiple effect on the level of aggregate demand.

Prices and incomes policy: a policy of direct control over wages and prices in which the government sets pay and price norms and creates bodies to 'police' increases above these norms.

Primary objectives of policy: these are the macroeconomic goals of government policy; namely, stable prices, full employment, economic growth and a balance of payments equilibrium.

Public sector borrowing requirement (PSBR): this is the deficit of the central and local government and the deficits of the nationalised industries.

Structural unemployment: this is the name given to unemployment that is the result of changes to the structure of the economy; for example, when there is a decline in the manufacturing sector which is not matched by an increase in employment in other sectors of the economy.

Substitution effect: this refers to the effect of, for example, a cut in taxes on work effort. As a result of the tax cut this results in an increase in the rewards for an extra hour's effort. In other words, there is an increase in the costs of taking additional leisure. The substitution effect says that if people are acting rationally they will substitute extra leisure for additional work.

Technological unemployment: this refers to unemployment created by changes to technology; for example, the decline of the employment of traditional printers in the newspaper industry as a result of changes in the technology of producing newspapers.

Transfer payments: those payments that represent a transfer of income from one group to another; for example, old age pensions, student grants and welfare benefits are paid for out of tax revenues. These payments are thus excluded from the calculation of national income as to include them would result in double counting.

Introduction

The business environment within which an organisation operates is influenced to a very great extent by the way in which the economy is managed. Before we examine the objectives of policy and how governments attempt to achieve these objectives we must first try to understand how the economy works. To do this we will examine what economists call the circular flow of income model.

The circular flow of income model

In order to understand how the economy works we need to construct a simplified model. One of the best-known models is the circular flow of income model. The key components of this model are set out in Figure 1.1.

We can view the economy as consisting of five important sectors. These are

➤ The domestic sector
➤ The business sector
➤ The financial sector
➤ The government sector
➤ The overseas sector

Figure 1.1
**The circular flow of
income model**

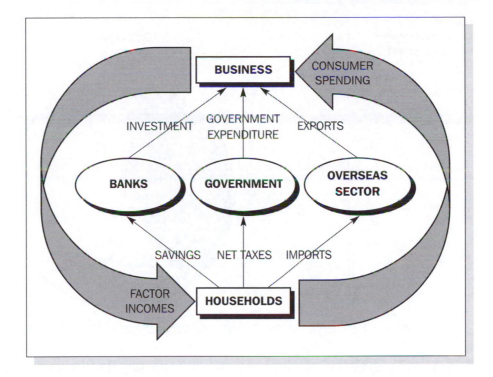

The domestic sector

This consists of households who can be viewed as supplying factors of production such as land, labour, capital and enterprise to the business sector. In return for these factors they receive what are called factor incomes such as wages, salaries, rent, interest, dividends, and profit. Figure 1.2 outlines the main sources of income in the UK in 1997.

As can be seen, about 60 per cent of all income is derived from wages and salaries with the remaining 40 per cent from all other sources of income. The household sector will spend its income either on domestically produced goods or on goods from abroad. If a household buys foreign goods then this is regarded as a leakage or a *withdrawal* from the circular flow of income model. In addition, government can also tax households by direct taxes on incomes or indirect taxes on our spending (VAT). This can also be viewed as a *withdrawal* from the circular flow of income.

PAUSE FOR THOUGHT 1 *Taxpayers have an allowance that they can offset against income tax. In 1999–2000 the allowance for a single person under 65 was £4,335. These allowances are upgraded each year in line with inflation according to statutory provisions unless Parliament intervenes. What would be the effect on the circular flow of income if these allowances were frozen (i.e. not upgraded)?*

Figure 1.2
UK national income by category 1997

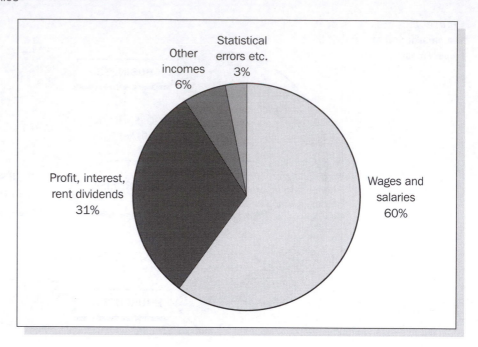

Statistical errors etc. 3%

Other incomes 6%

Profit, interest, rent dividends 31%

Wages and salaries 60%

PAUSE FOR THOUGHT 2   *Over half of all consumer spending is subject to VAT at the standard rate of 17.5 per cent, according to the Institute of Fiscal Studies (IFS 2000) with about 4 per cent taxable at a reduced rate. The reduced rate applies to domestic fuel, which had a VAT rate of 8 per cent but now has a rate of 5 per cent. From the summarised table (Table 1.1) work out what the effect on the circular flow of income would be if the government*

(a) abolished the tax on domestic fuel and power but imposed VAT on books and newspapers

(b) imposed VAT on food

(c) imposed VAT on children's clothing and prescription drugs.

Table 1.1
Estimated costs of zero-rated, reduced-rated and exempt goods and services for VAT revenues, 1998–99

Goods	Estimated cost (£m)
Zero-rated	
Food	8,100
Construction of new dwellings*	2,150
Domestic passenger transport	1,700
International passenger transport	1,350
Books, newspapers and magazines	1,300
Children's clothing	1,000
Water and sewerage services	1,000
Drugs and medicines on prescription	750
Supplies to charities*	150
Ships and aircraft above a certain size	350
Vehicles and other supplies to people with disabilities	150

Table 1.1
Continued

Goods	Estimated cost (£m)
Reduced-rated	
Domestic fuel and power	1,900
VAT-exempt	
Rent on domestic dwellings*	2,750
Rent on commercial properties*	1,050
Private education	950
Health services*	500
Postal services	500
Burial and cremation	100
Finance and insurance*	100
Betting, gaming and lottery	950
Businesses with low turnover	100
Total	26,900

*Figures for these categories are particularly tentative and subject to a wide margin of error.

Source: HM Customs and Excise Annual Report 1997–98.

Households may also decide to save a proportion of their income and this can also be represented as a *withdrawal* of income from the circular flow of income.

PAUSE FOR THOUGHT 3 *The savings ratio (i.e. the proportion of disposable income that is saved by households) is, in normal circumstances, quite stable at around 10–15 per cent. However, in the United States in recent years this ratio has fallen to almost zero across the economy as a whole. Can you explain the factors that may influence the savings ratio and what effect this will have on the circular flow of income in the USA and elsewhere?*

The business sector

Like domestic households, the business sector contributes to the circular flow of income. This sector demands factors of production such as land, labour, capital and enterprise and pays for this by different forms of income. The sector is also responsible for investing in plant and machinery which injects income into the circular flow of income. The amount of investment that is undertaken by the business sector depends on *the costs of borrowing* money and the likely *rate of return* that firms can earn (for details of how this is calculated, see Chapter 10). Future rates of return will be affected by such factors as the initial cost of the capital equipment and the income generated over the life of the asset, whether it is a machine or a factory. Of critical importance to this calculation is *the confidence that the business sector* has about the future. Thus, if businesses are apprehensive about future growth prospects, this can affect not only the amount the sector will invest but also the circular flow of income. Some of this investment is undertaken to replace capital, which has depreciated. Therefore, economists are more interested in the extent to which investment increases faster than the rate of depreciation since this adds to the flow of income in the economy. Equally, firms may decide to retain profits rather than pay them out as dividends. This form of corporate savings can be regarded as a *withdrawal* from the circular flow.

CASE STUDY **1.1**

UK manufacturing grows in confidence

In January 2000 there was an upsurge in optimism amongst the UK's leading manufacturers who claimed that demand was rising for the first time in almost two years despite the high value of sterling, according to the Confederation of British Industry's quarterly *Industrial Trends Survey*.

The survey showed business optimism continuing to rise with 23 per cent of firms being more optimistic and only 14 per cent less optimistic. The balance of +9 per cent compares with +13 in October and +5 in July. In addition, the survey claimed that optimism about export prospects had stabilised for the first time in more than three years, and that total orders had risen over the previous four months for the first time since April 1998 with 30 per cent of respondents indicating that orders were up and 21 per cent saying that they were down. The balance of +9 per cent compared with −5 in October 1999 and −19 in July. Export orders fell slightly but at the slowest rate since October 1996.

In addition, companies said total orders would grow steadily over the first four months of 2000, reflecting expectations that domestic demand would increase and export demand would level off. A balance of +9 per cent anticipate a rise. Firms also said that output rose for the first time since April 1998. Thirty-one per cent said output was up and 20 per cent said it was down. The balance of +11 per cent compares with −1 in October and −14 in July. Companies expect output to continue rising, with a balance of +11 per cent anticipating an increase over the next four months.

Nick Reilly, Chairman and Managing Director of Vauxhall Motors and head of the CBI's Economic Affairs Committee, said:

> *'Manufacturers have taken another step towards recovery. But we should not overstate the extent of the revival because domestic prices and employment continue to fall while investment plans remain weak. Companies are having to run much harder to stand still. Many firms are hanging on by their fingertips and the two-speed economy remains very much in evidence. Exports are stabilising but this is being driven by a rise in world demand. The strength of sterling is still holding back firms as they battle to compete. Another rise in interest rates would restrain economic growth unnecessarily when across the economy there is little evidence of inflation. Moreover, the impact of the millennium is still unclear. The Monetary Policy Committee [of the Bank of England] should keep rates on hold until the trends become more certain.'*

Source: Adapted from CBI Press release, 27 January 2000.

Questions

1   What are the main threats to the upsurge in confidence which the CBI survey indicates?
2   The Monetary Policy Committee did not take the CBI's advice and raised interest rates by 0.25 per cent. How would this affect the business sector and which components of the circular flow of income would be affected?

The financial sector

This sector contributes to the circular flow by the way in which money flows into and out of the sector. Savings are directed via such financial intermediaries as banks and building societies. The level of these savings can be affected by such things as interest rates, the amount of disposable income, and the rate of inflation and consumer confidence about the future.

Figure 1.3 outlines the savings ratio for the USA between 1987 and 1999.

PAUSE FOR THOUGHT 4 *From Figure 1.3 it can be seen that the standard savings ratio in the USA has fallen dramatically from about 10 per cent of disposable income in the 1970s to around 5 per cent by the late 1980s, finally falling to almost zero by the end of the 1990s. What factors could have caused this fall? What are the implications of the fall for the US economy and for the rest of the world? Is this a worry or a benefit for the UK economy according to the model of the circular flow of income?*

The government sector

The government can play an important part in injecting or withdrawing income from the circular flow of income. By raising taxes (*a withdrawal*) and lowering its own spending (*an injection*) it can create budget surpluses or deficits. When the economy is booming there is an automatic tendency for government taxes to increase as consumers spend more (and hence pay more expenditure taxes such as VAT). Companies will also pay more corporation tax, as profits will tend to rise in the boom phase. In addition this will tend to

Figure 1.3
United States personal savings ratio 1987–1998

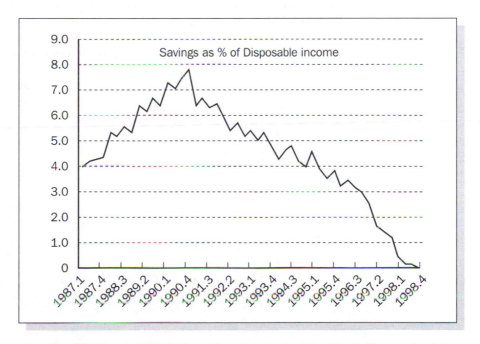

Adapted from P.D. Vujanovic (1999) *Habits and the savings–growth relationship: why US personal savings rates are at historic lows.*

reduce government spending on such things as unemployment or other welfare payments. The reverse, however, is also true when the economy is in a slump. Consumer and corporate taxes will tend to fall while government expenditure on social security will rise. This is known as the 'automatic fiscal stabilisers' and helps to iron out some of the worst of the economic cycles through which the economy runs from time to time. Of course the government can (and often does) try to anticipate this and adjust fiscal policy (i.e. taxes and spending) to take account of anticipated booms and slumps. This is particularly the case if the government is a believer in the Keynesian approach (see Chapter 3).

Figure 1.4 looks at the current budget surpluses and deficits over the last 40 years and clearly illustrates the cycles through which these surpluses and deficits have moved.

More recently the government has been forecasting a budget surplus (see Figure 1.5).

PAUSE FOR THOUGHT 5 *What are the implications of Figure 1.5 for the circular flow of income in the period 1999–2002?*

The overseas sector

The final sector that has an influence on the circular flow of income is the overseas sector. Consumers from other parts of the world can add to the circular flow by demanding goods and services from UK firms. This clearly would represent an *injection* of income into the circular flow. The money that UK consumers spend on foreign imports represents a *withdrawal* of income from the circular flow. Equally, foreign companies investing in the UK would represent an injection into the circular flow whereas the setting up of a UK plant in South East Asia, for example, would represent a withdrawal of income from the UK. These aspects are reflected in the capital account. Table 1.2 shows the vari-

Figure 1.4
Current budget surpluses and deficits as a percentage of GDP, 1966–2000

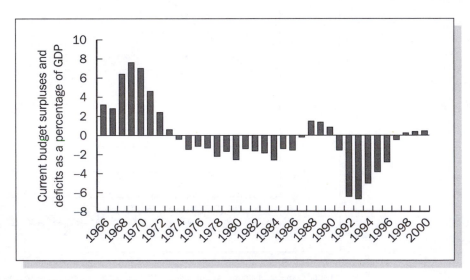

Source: HM Treasury Public Finances Database, December 1999 (Table A2).

Figure 1.5

Government receipts and spending as a percentage of GDP 1996–1997 to 2001–2002

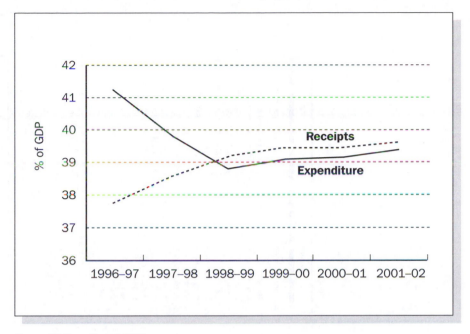

Source: IFS Green Budget 2000.

ous balances on goods and services (the visible account) as well as the balances on interest, dividends, profits and royalties (the invisible account). The capital account looks at the surpluses/deficits of this aspect.

Table 1.2

The balance of payment accounts, £ millions, 1979–1998

Period	Trade in goods	Total services	Current account Visibles	Visibles+Invisibles	Capital account
1979	−3326	–	639	88	–
1980	1329	–	5046	3166	–
1981	3238	–	7072	6549	–
1982	1879	–	4948	4107	–
1983	−1618	–	2323	3299	–
1984	−5409	–	−1068	1209	–
1985	−3416	–	3203	2227	–
1986	−9617	6505	−3112	−2285	135
1987	−11698	6686	−5012	−5583	333
1988	−21553	4330	−17223	−17537	235
1989	−24724	3917	−20807	−23491	270
1990	−18707	4010	−14697	−19513	497
1991	−10223	4471	−5752	−8374	290
1992	−13050	5674	−7376	−10082	421
1993	−13319	6623	−6696	−10618	309
1994	−11091	6528	−4563	−1458	33
1995	−11724	8915	−2809	−3745	534
1996	−13086	8897	−4189	−600	736
1997	−11910	12414	504	6623	804
1998	−20537	12185	−8352	−482	473

Source: Economic Trends 1999.

Figure 1.6 **Some factors affecting the level of aggregate demand**

Aggregate demand

equals

Consumer spending plus **Investment** plus **Government spending** plus **Exports** minus **Imports**

Consumer spending

which depends upon

1. **Disposable income***
   which depends upon
   (a) TAXATION direct
       e.g. income tax and
   (b) TAXATION indirect
       e.g. VAT*

   AND

2. **Savings**
   which depends upon
   (a) THE RATE OF INTEREST*
       and
   (b) THE PROPENSITY TO SAVE

   AND

3. **Consumer confidence**
   which depends upon
   (a) THE 'FEEL GOOD' FACTOR
       and
   (b) DISPOSABLE INCOME*

Investment

which depends upon

1. **The cost of borrowing**
   which depends upon
   THE RATE OF INTEREST*

   AND

2. **The rate of return**
   which depends upon
   (a) THE INITIAL CAPITAL COST
       and
   (b) THE NET CASH FLOW OVER
       THE LIFE OF THE ASSET
       and
   (c) BUSINESS CONFIDENCE

Government spending

which depends upon

1. **The state of the economy***

   AND

   **Government policies
   and commitments***

   AND

   Demographic factors

Exports

which depends upon

1. **The state of
   the world economy**

   AND

2. **The competitiveness
   of the economy**
   which depends upon
   (a) INFLATION RATE*
       VIS-À-VIS OUR COMPETITORS
       and
   (b) WAGES IN RELATION
       TO PRODUCTIVITY †
       and
   (c) EXCHANGE RATES
       and
   (d) DESIGN, DELIVERY, QUALITY
       OF PRODUCTS/SERVICES

   AND

3. **Growth rate of
   UK economy***

Imports

which depends upon

1. **The competitiveness
   of the UK economy**
   which depends upon
   (a) INFLATION RATE*
       VIS-À-VIS OUR COMPETITORS
       and
   (b) EXCHANGE RATES†

   AND

2. **Growth rate of
   UK economy***

Key:
* Factors over which the government has some influence
† Assumes UK remains outside the single currency

| PAUSE FOR THOUGHT 6 | How has the trade in goods affected the circular flow of income? How about services? What effects has the trade on invisibles had on the circular flow? Are we net exporters or importers of capital and what effect does this part of the balance of payments have on the circular flow of income model? |

| PAUSE FOR THOUGHT 7 | 1   From Figure 1.6, which of the main components of aggregate demand would be more easily influenced by the authorities and why do you think this is the case?
 2   If the government decides to (a) reduce the level of income tax, (b) reduce corporation tax, (c) reduce the rate of VAT and (d) reduce interest rates, identify the components of aggregate demand that will be affected. |

Withdrawals and injections

Each of the five sectors mentioned above can create withdrawals and injections, as shown in Table 1.3.

Table 1.3

Injections and withdrawals

Sector	Injection	Symbol	Withdrawal	Symbol
Households			Savings	S
Business	Investment	I	Savings	S
Financial	Investment	I	Savings	S
Government	Government expenditure	G	Government taxes	T
Overseas	• Export of goods/services • Income from overseas investments • Import of capital	X	• Import of goods/services • Income paid out to overseas investors • Export of capital	M

Therefore, to summarise the data in Table 1.3:

Injections (J) $= I + X + G$
Withdrawals (W) $= S + M + T$

and from this it can be seen that for the circular flow of income model to be in equilibrium, then $J = W$. This is not the same thing as saying that savings must always equal investment or that the government must always balance its books; or even that the balance of payments must always be in balance. However, if there is to be an equilibrium in the circular flow, then $W = J$. If for any reason they were temporarily out of balance, then the national income (Y) would rise or fall to ensure that balance is achieved, as shown in Figure 1.7.

At national income level OY_2 households consume CY_2 level of income (i.e. there is no saving or any other form of withdrawal). However, national expenditure is DY_2. Thus $J = CD$ while $W = $ zero. In these circumstances, national income would rise from OY_2 to OY_e. As it does, the level of withdrawals from the circular flow of income will also rise. Conversely, if national income is at the level OY_1, then $BH = $ the level of withdrawals (i.e. the difference between income $OY_1 = BY_1$ and consumer spending, HY_1). Injections J, on the other

Figure 1.7
Equilibrium national income

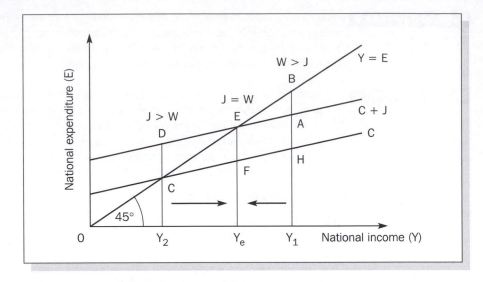

hand, is AH (the difference between C + J and C). Therefore, BH > AH (i.e. W > J). In these circumstances, national income would fall from OY_1 to OY_e. Only when J = W (i.e. at the point E where J = EF and W = EF) will national income reach a stable equilibrium.

Another way of looking at the same situation is to look at the graphs for both withdrawals (W) and injections (J), given in Figure 1.8.

From this diagram equilibrium national income occurs when W = J at income level OY_e where the first J graph (J_1) cuts the W graph at the point A. However, if the government wished to increase national income (let us imagine, for example, that at income level OY_e there was substantial unemployment) then it would be required to raise the J graph from J_1 to J_2.

Figure 1.8
Withdrawals and injections

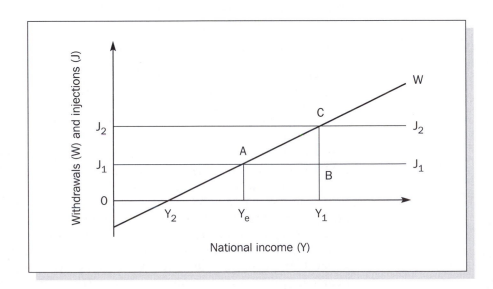

What factors could influence the J graph in Figure 1.8 to move from J_1 to J_2? What, if anything, could the government do to influence this?

However, as can be seen from the figure, the change in J (BC) results in a bigger change in Y (Y_eY_1). This is known to economists as *the multiplier effect*.

The multiplier effect

The multiplier (k) can therefore be defined as follows:

k = Change in national income/Change in injections
= $\Delta Y / \Delta J$
= Y_eY_1/BC
= AB/BC
= tangent of $\angle CAB$
= slope of the W function

Therefore, as indicated in Figure 1.8, the size of the multiplier will be affected by the slope of the W function. The flatter the W function, the bigger will be the size of the multiplier. In other words, the more that people withdraw income from any increase in income, the greater will be the size of the multiplier. Economists use the concept of the marginal propensity to describe the extra income that is saved or taxed or spent on export. Thus a marginal 'propensity to save' of 0.2 indicates that consumers would save 20 per cent of any increase in their incomes. Therefore the more that people spend (and the less income is withdrawn from the circular flow of income) the bigger will be the multiplier.

The multiplier can then be rewritten to reflect this fact:

k = 1/ (1 – mpw)

where mpw is defined as the marginal propensity to withdraw income from the circular flow, and

mpw = mps + mpm + mpt

where mps is defined as the marginal propensity to save, mpm is the marginal propensity to import, and mpt is the marginal propensity to tax, from a given rise in income.

Thus, if mps = 0.2, mpm = 0.15 and mpt = 0.25, then mpw = 0.6 and k, the multiplier, is 1/ (1 – 0.6) = 1/0.4 = 2.5. Therefore, if these were the marginal propensities then an injection of £100 million into the economy would increase the national income by £250 million.

Complete Table 1.4 (the multiplier table) using the formulae:
k = 1/(1 – mpw) *and* ***mps + mpm + mpt = mpw***

Table 1.4
The multiplier

mps	mpm	mpt	mpw	k
0.05	0.05	0.10		
0.10	0.15		0.5	
	0.25	0.15	0.6	
0.30	0.15	0.25		
	0.25	0.35	0.8	
	0.30	0.36		25
	0.25	0.35		100

What do you notice about the results in this table?

CASE STUDY **1.2**

Japanese economy shows signs of recovery

By the beginning of 2000 it was clear that the Japanese economy had stopped deteriorating and begun to recover, with recovery most notable in exports and production, but there were still no signs of a self-sustained recovery in private-sector demand, although the environment surrounding such demand was gradually improving. The Central Bank of Japan (BOJ) therefore thought that it was appropriate for the Bank to maintain its zero-interest-rate policy, since the nation's economy had yet to reach a situation in which deflationary concerns have been eliminated. Under this 'ultra-easy policy' adopted in February 1999, the BOJ steered its target interest rate as close to zero as possible.

The central bank's Policy Board decided at its meeting on 17 January 2000 that the 'zero-interest-rate' policy should be kept intact, as Japan's economy still needed the support of low interest rates.

Although corporate earnings had improved, this had not yet spurred business activity. The income situation for households remained very poor and it was clear that the Central Bank would continue to keep a close watch on the possible effects of the yen's rise since the previous autumn on the economy and prices. There were some signs of recovery in the regions, as well as evidence of marginal improvements in the labour market. However, there were also signs of weakness, including sluggishness in consumer spending, the increasingly limited impact of public spending and the cautious attitude of firms about capital spending in some regions. As for consumer spending, it was argued that it was still falling short of recovery with the exception perhaps being the strong sales of home electronics centring on personal computers. On capital investment, many companies were still cautious about making investments because of excess capacity and concern over the business outlook. Investment was up by some firms, such as those in the information and telecommunications industries. On prices, it was predicted that they would remain stable for the time being, but the downward pressure on prices should also be watched carefully in view of declining income and the lack of clear signs of recovery in private demand.

Adapted from the Kyodo News Service, Tokyo, January 2000.

Questions

1 What does a policy of zero rates of interest mean and what are supposed to be its intended effects?
2 Using a 45-degree diagram, similar to Figure 1.7, explain the intended outcome of this policy.
3 Explain why the multiplier process has failed to take off in Japan.

CASE STUDY **1.3**

Tax revenue ready reckoner and the 2000 Budget

At the time of the Budget, the Treasury publishes what it calls the tax revenue ready reckoner which gives estimates of the effects of various tax changes. Table CS1.3.1 gives the data.

Table CS1.3.1

Direct effects of illustrative changes in taxation to take effect April 2000

	Cost/yield (Non-indexed base) 2000–01 (£m)
Income tax	
Rates	
Change starting rate by 1p	390
Change basic rate by 1p	2,650
Change higher rate by 1p	720
Change basic rate in Scotland by 1p	240
Allowances	
Change personal allowance by £100	560
Increase starting-rate limit by £100	290
Basic-rate limit	
Change basic-rate limit by 1%	140
Change basic-rate limit by 10%:	
increase (cost)	1,250
decrease (yield)	1,600
Allowances and limits	
Change all main allowances, starting- and basic-rate limits:	
increase/decrease by 1%	460
increase by 10% (cost)	4,400
decrease by 10% (yield)	5,000
Corporation tax	
Change main rate by 1 percentage point	1,100
Change smaller companies' rate by 1 percentage point	160
Capital gains tax	
Increase annual exempt amount by £500 for individuals and £250 for trustees	25
Inheritance tax	
Change rate by 1 percentage point	60
Increase threshold by £5,000	40
Excise duties*	
Beer up 0.3p a pint	30
Wine up 1.3p a bottle (75 cl)	10
Spirits up 6.4p a bottle (70 cl)	5
Cigarettes up 3p a packet (20 king-size)	60
Petrol up 0.5p a litre	115
Derv up 0.5p a litre	95
Change insurance premium tax (both standard and higher rates) by 1 percentage point	235
VAT	
Change both standard and reduced rates by 1 percentage point	3,175

Table CS1.3.1
Continued

	Cost/yield (Non-indexed base) 2000–01 (£m)
VAT coverage	**1999–2000**
Extend VAT to:	
food	7,800
domestic and international passenger transport	3,550
construction of new homes	2,750
books, newspapers, etc.	1,300
water and sewerage services	950
children's clothing	110
prescriptions	650

Source: HM Treasury Tax Ready Reckoner, November 1999.

Questions

1 In 2000 it was estimated that the Chancellor had about £7 billion extra to spend or to reduce taxes. Suppose that you were the Chancellor and you wanted to devote about half of this total to cutting taxes (i.e. £3.5 billion). Using Table CS1.3.1, work out a budget that would reduce taxes by this amount.

2 What would be the effects of your tax cuts?

3 What are the possible dangers if the Chancellor spends or reduces taxes by £7 billion?

The aims of macroeconomic policy

The remainder of this chapter looks at the main aims of government economic policy and at the current controversies that surround the conduct of macroeconomic policy.[1]

The macroeconomic environment is determined by the way in which the government attempts to achieve the four main aims of economic policy. Since the end of the Second World War every government has committed itself to these objectives, although the weight which successive governments have attached to each objective has varied over time. The four objectives are:

1 Full employment.

2 Stable prices.

3 Economic growth.

4 A balance of payments equilibrium.

Table 1.5 gives the data for the UK economy for the period 1979–2000.

Table 1.5

The UK economy: key economic indicators

Year	Growth: % change in real GDP	Inflation: % change in RPI*	Unemployment (millions)	Current account as % of GDP
1979	2.8	13.4	1.1	−0.6
1980	−2.1	18.0	1.4	1.5
1981	−1.1	11.9	2.2	2.8
1982	1.7	8.6	2.5	1.7
1983	3.7	4.7	2.8	1.2
1984	2.0	5.0	2.9	0.5
1985	4.1	6.1	3.0	0.6
1986	3.8	3.4	3.0	−0.2
1987	4.6	4.1	2.8	−1.2
1988	4.5	4.9	2.3	−3.5
1989	2.1	7.8	1.8	−4.4
1990	0.6	9.5	1.6	−3.3
1991	−2.4	5.8	2.3	−1.3
1992	−0.5	3.7	2.8	−1.6
1993	2.0	1.6	2.9	−1.6
1994	3.6	3.8	2.6	−0.9
1995	3.7	4.2	2.3	−1.2
1996	2.3	2.5	2.1	−0.1
1997	3.5	3.1	1.6	0.8
1998	2.2	3.4	1.4	0.0
1999	1.5	1.6	1.3	−1.4
2000	2.4	2.2	1.3	−2.4
Averages	**2.0**	**5.9**	**2.2**	**−0.7**

*RPI inc. mortgages
Source: Goldman Sachs (1999) *The Economics Analyst.*

ACTIVITY 1.1

The aims of macroeconomic policy

1   Using the data from Table 1.5 plot on a graph economic growth and unemployment against each year from 1979 to 1996. On a separate graph plot inflation against the current account balance. From the data in Table 1.5 and your graphs above can you detect any significant relationships between the key economic objectives as indicated?

2   How easy has it been for the government to achieve these objectives simultaneously?

Achievement of economic objectives

As can be seen from Activity 1.1, it has been difficult for governments to achieve these objectives simultaneously. Governments have often had to 'trade off' one objective in order to achieve others – a problem that is illustrated in Figure 1.9.

PAUSE FOR THOUGHT 10

Before reading on, why do you think that it has been difficult to achieve these four objectives? What is the relationship between full employment and stable prices and between economic growth and the balance of payments? Why is it difficult to achieve a balance of payments and full employment? What do you think is the relationship between economic growth and stable prices?

Figure 1.9
The trade off in economic objectives

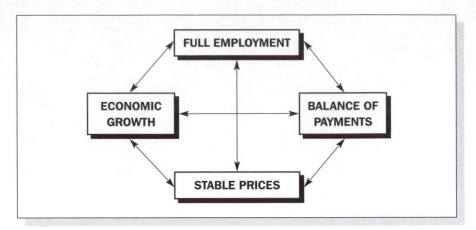

Full employment

Full employment has come to be defined as being consistent with around 2–3 per cent unemployment in advanced industrialised countries. Unemployment occurs where human resources are available for work, but are unable to find it. A number of types of unemployment are often identified.

➤ *Frictional unemployment* occurs because at any one time there will always be some people who are between jobs, or who are temporarily out of work for one reason or another.
➤ *Seasonal unemployment* occurs because demand for some goods and services varies with the times and seasons – for example, ski instructors or people employed as Santa Claus over the Christmas period.
➤ *Cyclical unemployment* occurs because of changes in the level of demand in times of recession or slump. Some workers will find that their jobs are among the first to feel the effects of such a downswing in the so-called business cycle. Some occupations seem to be more vulnerable than others in this respect; for example, construction workers are often the first to notice the effects of recession as firms postpone or delay capital projects and house building. This type of unemployment is a feature of the Boom–Bust cycle that dogged the UK economy over the past 30 or 40 years.
➤ *Structural unemployment* is caused by changes in the pattern of demand; for example, the decline of jobs in the manufacturing sector is often referred to as de-industrialisation (see Chapter 4).
➤ *Technological unemployment* refers to job losses resulting from changes in technology. For example, new technology completely revolutionised the way that newspapers were produced in the late 1980s, with the effect that a number of skilled print workers were made redundant. Car production has also been transformed by automated and robotic technologies and major changes in electronic/telecommunication technologies have had a dramatic effect on employment in areas such as television, banking and retailing.

PAUSE FOR THOUGHT 11 *Make a list of the different types of unemployment outlined above and give three examples of each type.*

The measurement of unemployment

The way in which unemployment is measured has aroused a considerable degree of controversy in recent years.[2] It has been calculated that the way in which unemployment is measured has been changed more than 30 times since 1979, although government ministers claimed at the time that only nine of these changes have had any significant impact on the unemployment total.

Unemployment is the measure of how many people are out of work in the economy. It is usually expressed as a percentage of the total workforce, on a monthly basis. There are several ways to measure unemployment, and they vary from country to country. In the United Kingdom, the government traditionally has counted the number of people who are claiming unemployment benefit – the so-called claimant count.

PAUSE FOR THOUGHT 12 *Before reading on, what are the problems in using the claimant count as the basis for measuring unemployment?*

But this leaves out those people who are not eligible for unemployment benefit but who may also be looking for jobs. It also leaves out the unemployed who are on special training schemes. In April 1998 the Labour government decided to publish *Labour Force Survey* (LFS) as a guide to unemployment figures. This measures the whole workforce, and then attempts to find all those who are seeking jobs, not just those who are receiving benefit. This method is recommended by the International Labour Organisation (ILO) and gives a more internationally comparable figure for unemployment. The government issues these ILO figures monthly instead of four times a year. The new number includes anyone who is actively available to start work within the next two weeks and has looked for work in the last four weeks or has already found a job but is waiting to start. The previous figures counted only those out of work and claiming unemployment benefit. By using this definition of 'unemployed', the figures should show that unemployment is much higher than the previous monthly figures indicated – as much as half a million higher.

PAUSE FOR THOUGHT 13 *Before reading on, identify the advantages and disadvantages of each of these measures.*

Advantages and disadvantages of different methods

It is argued that the claimant count gives the more precise figure for monthly unemployment as it is based on numbers collected by the government. This, however, has been widely criticised as being misleading. The old methods, as mentioned above, have had more than 30 changes in 20 years – and each time the change indicated a lower total. The Labour Party, when in opposition, complained about the method and promised to change the system once in power. For example, the previous methods excluded teenagers and anyone over 55 years old. The *Labour Force Survey* will be more consistent over time, but as it is based on a statistical survey it is therefore subject to sampling error. Because of this, the LFS is published on a rolling three-monthly basis and does not include all those who want jobs but are not actively seeking them (over 2 million in the winter of 1998).

1   *What sectors of the economy or particular products or services are vulnerable to technological change in the next few years?*
   2   *Can you speculate on what new products or services might begin to 'take off' in the early years of the new century?*

Stable prices and inflation

There are a number of different measures of inflation.[3] Firstly, there is the retail price index (RPI) which measures the average price level across a whole range of goods and services. These goods and services are weighted according to their importance in the average consumer's 'shopping basket'. If you can imagine that the shopping basket is worth £1,000, then Figure 1.10 gives the weighting factors, and it can be seen that about £100 out of the £1,000 in the shopping basket is spent on alcohol and tobacco.

1   *Suppose that there was a 10 per cent increase in housing costs. What impact would this have on the overall RPI?*
   2   *Apart from housing costs, which prices in which categories of expenditure have the biggest impact on the RPI?*

Figure 1.10
The Retail Price Index weighting factors 1999

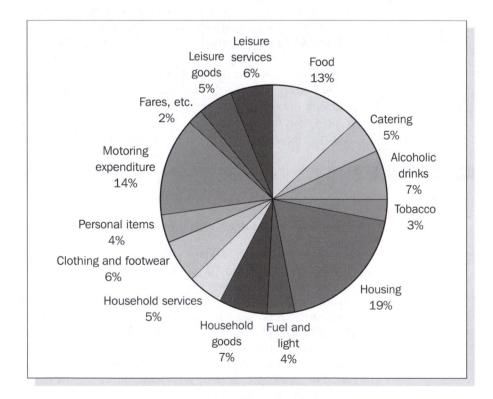

In addition to the RPI (sometimes referred to as the headline rate), two other measures are used. The second is called RPI-X, which takes out the distorting effects of changes in mortgage interest payments. Internationally, this is the most common method of calculating inflation. A rise in interest rates to curb inflation increases headline inflation in the short run as mortgage interest payments increase. Hence, RPI-X is sometimes called the underlying rate and is used as the government's target for inflation.

The third measure is called RPI-Y. This is inflation excluding mortgage interest payments and indirect taxes. Another key distorting effect results from indirect taxation. Value added tax rates rarely change, but new taxes on alcohol, tobacco and fuels may distort the inflation index figures. Measuring RPI-Y is most useful around December and January when budget duty increases come into effect.

The stability of prices can be affected by a number of factors which can be grouped under three main headings:

1 Demand factors
2 Cost factors
3 Monetary factors.

Demand inflation

Inflation can be defined as 'too much money chasing too few goods' and/or 'too many jobs chasing too few workers'. Figure 1.11 illustrates the situation.

The inflationary gap can be eliminated by bearing down on the components of aggregate demand. There are two principal weapons that governments can use to 'solve' the inflation problem, viz.:

➤ *fiscal policy*, involving changes in government spending and/or changes in taxation
➤ *monetary policy*, i.e. controlling the money supply or varying interest rates.

Figure 1.11
Inflationary gap

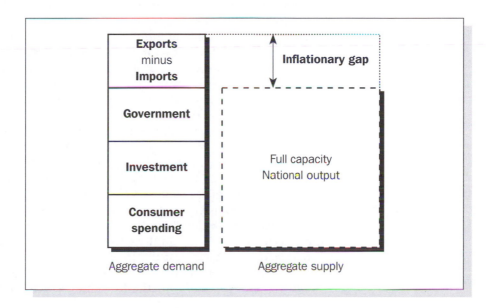

The aim of both of these policies is to bring aggregate demand more into line with aggregate supply or the productive potential of the economy.

PAUSE FOR THOUGHT 16 *Using Figure 1.11, outline the policy measures that could be used by the authorities to reduce an inflationary gap.*

Cost inflation

In the immediate post-war period, demand factors appeared to be the most significant cause of, and cure for, inflation. However, in the 1970s a number of other factors related to cost began to play a more significant role. For example, in 1972 the Organisation of Petroleum Exporting Countries (OPEC) raised the price of a barrel of oil by 400 per cent, and inflation became rampant. It was clear that demand management techniques were simply not capable of coping with this type of cost–push inflation. It is true that raising taxes and cutting government expenditure would eventually have worked, but this would only have been achieved by raising unemployment to extremely high levels. The Labour government at the time was unfortunately overwhelmed by the problem, and inflation hit 24 per cent by 1975. The effects on the government were devastating, as they were unable to control the inflationary forces that were unleashed. As the price of oil rose, so too did the cost of producing products which were derived from oil. Further, the costs of transport, energy and distribution also rose rapidly. Coupled with the decision to float the currency (for more details, see Chapter 3) the government experienced severe balance of payments difficulties, with the official gold and foreign exchange reserves in danger of running out. This prompted the government to introduce a prices and incomes policy to try to maintain price stability. This type of policy required the government to set up bodies to review all requests for increases in both wages and prices. It meant that these bodies were charged with the task of determining whether price increases were 'fair' and whether demands for pay increases were justified. In some cases the prices and incomes policies were 'voluntary' in that the recommendations of such bodies did not have the backing of the law. In other instances, the policy had statutory force, such as when the government imposed a pay and prices 'freeze'. However, with trade union militancy increasing in the face of rising prices, the government found that it was almost impossible to make such policies work and were forced to accept the intervention of the International Monetary Fund (IMF), who insisted on a massive dose of monetary medicine. Eventually, the Labour government found itself using all three conventional weapons in order to solve the inflation crisis; namely, deflationary fiscal policy, IMF-imposed monetary policy and a prices and incomes policy. Denis Healey, the then Chancellor of the Exchequer, was thus forced to introduce a series of measures which caused real wages to fall significantly but which also resulted in a rise in unemployment. Thus the UK had the worst of all worlds, with inflation still continuing to rise along with rises in unemployment. Stagflation (inflation coupled with a stagnant economy) was now rampant. Naturally enough, the trade unions did not take kindly to this, especially from a Labour government, and they exacted their revenge in the so-called Winter of Discontent of 1978/9. The Labour Party eventually lost the 1979 election and remained out of office for the next 18 years. This episode in our recent economic history demonstrates the various cost factors at work and the difficulties of controlling them.[4]

PAUSE FOR THOUGHT 17 *From the section above, identify as many cost–push factors as possible.*

Monetary theory

This episode heralded the introduction of a new Conservative government, which believed that the main cause of inflation was monetary. It is important to stress that these monetary theories pre-dated the 1979 Conservative government. Indeed, as we have seen, the first serious attempt to use monetary measures to solve inflation was introduced by a Labour government under Denis Healey. Even before that, Milton Friedman in the USA was writing about the importance for governments to control the money supply.[5]

The crux of this view stems from the classical theory of money. Simply stated this says that the following equation must hold:

$$MV = PQ$$

where M is the quantity of money circulating in the economy, V is the velocity of circulation of a given unit of money, P is the average price level and Q is the volume of goods and services an economy produces in a given time period.

PQ is Price × Quantity for the economy as a whole. In other words, it corresponds to the nominal value of national output or national income. It is therefore possible to derive V, the velocity of circulation of money, by dividing money national income by a suitable measure of the money supply, and there are several measures that can be used.

M0

M0 equals notes and coins in circulation in the private sector *plus* private sector non-interest bearing sterling sight deposits *plus* Bankers' operational balances with the Bank of England.

M2

M2 equals M0 *plus* private sector interest bearing retail sterling bank deposits with banks and building societies.

M4

M4 equals private sector non-interest-bearing sterling sight bank deposits *plus* private sector interest-bearing sterling sight deposits *plus* private sector time bank deposits (including sterling certificates of deposit) *plus* private sector holdings of building society shares and deposits and sterling certificates of deposit.

This enables us to calculate various measures of the velocity of circulation (V). However, according to the monetarist view, the velocity of circulation is comparatively stable over a period, no matter which definition of the money supply one cares to take. Thus if we can regard V as stable, then this implies that there is a direct relationship between M, the money supply, and both P (the average price level) and Q (the volume of goods and services the economy is capable of producing). If we further assume that Q is capable of growing at a predictable rate, then we have a direct link between M (the money supply) and P (the average price level). Figure 1.12 gives the relationship between the money supply and price inflation for the period 1994–2000 using quarterly data.

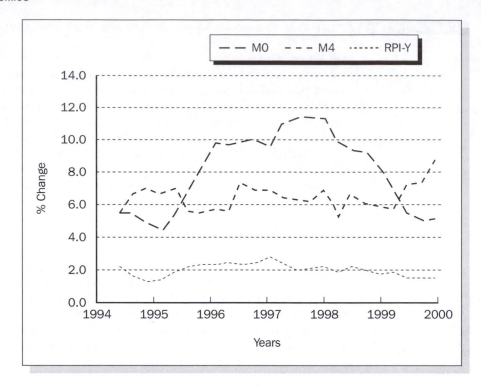

As can be seen, there is not much of a direct relationship between the two variables. Nevertheless, in spite of this apparent lack of support from the empirical evidence, the UK government still pursued the monetarist experiment from 1979 until about 1985. During that period the cornerstone of economic policy was the medium-term financial strategy (MTFS), which set monetary targets for the next three- or four-year period.

The results of pursuing monetarist policies were mixed and subsequently governments have abandoned attempts to control the money supply as the principal weapon in controlling inflation, preferring instead to pass responsibility for the control of inflation to the Bank of England and its monetary policy committee (MPC). In 1997 Gordon Brown set the MPC the inflation target of 2.5 per cent. The committee, which is independent, meets once a month to review a range of economic indicators and to set interest rates. While the announcement of an inflation target is no guarantee that the government will not be tempted to tinker with the economy for political reasons, it does at least ensure that there is some principle or objective by which to guide policy.

The government has therefore given much more independence to the Bank of England in the formulation of monetary policy. The Bank, it can be argued, is now totally independent.[6] Gordon Brown, the first Chancellor of the Exchequer in the Labour government of 1997, has gone much further than any of his predecessors in allowing the Bank of England a more independent voice. The Bank periodically publishes its own inflation report and offers the Chancellor independent advice on interest rates and exchange rate policy. The minutes of the monthly meeting between the Chancellor and the Governor of the Bank of England are now published and allow the public to see the kind of information and advice that the Chancellor is receiving. In those circumstances it is more difficult for the government to manipulate monetary policy for purely political purposes.[7]

PAUSE FOR THOUGHT 18 *Examine the case for giving the Bank of England independence in framing monetary policy. What are the dangers in this and how would you aim to overcome them?*

Economic growth

The third key objective of economic policy is to achieve a fast rate of economic growth. Only by achieving economic growth can a society improve the economic well-being and living standards of its citizens. Before discussing the causes of economic growth it is important that we define the meaning of the term.

Economists usually define economic growth as the percentage change in real national income per head. Growth figures are therefore based on national income statistics and, as a result, suffer from all the imperfections of those statistics. For example, not all incomes are necessarily taken into account in these statistics. Some income is deliberately excluded because its inclusion would result in some 'double counting'. This is the case with so-called *transfer payments*. (This does not refer to the exorbitant prices paid by football clubs for the services of rather indifferent strikers!) Transfer payments refer to such things as students' grants, old age pensions and social security pensions, which are transferred from one section of the community to another via the tax and benefit system. It would be 'double counting' if transfer payments were included in the national income figures as the gross incomes used when calculating national income already include the tax element which funds these payments. However, some income is *not* declared, and this forms part of the 'black economy'. The black economy is almost impossible to quantify because of the very nature of the problem. Economists have attempted to put a figure on this with estimates ranging from 2 to 10 per cent of GNP. In addition, payments in kind, whereby goods and services are exchanged for other goods and services, also fail to be captured in the national income statistics. Taxation can distort the picture, especially expenditure taxes such as value added tax (VAT), which will tend to exaggerate the true size of the value of our national output. A similar argument applies to subsidies, which will have the opposite effect.

The way that national income is made up (i.e. its composition) can also have an effect on living standards. Imagine a situation in which two countries have identical national income per head figures but the first country spends 50 per cent of its income on defence while the second spends an equivalent amount on hospitals, schools and help for those below the poverty line. The national income per head figures will simply fail to detect any such differences although common sense tells us that there is bound to be a difference in the well-being and living standards of the two countries concerned. Similar arguments apply to the ways in which a country spends its income. In northern Europe central heating is much more prevalent and so national income statistics will be affected by such expenditure. In some parts of the world central heating is simply not needed to keep the population warm, yet the absence of such spending may result in those countries having an apparently lower national income per head.

It should also be remembered that the GNP per head figure is an average and takes no account of the way in which income is distributed. Thus an economy may experience significant rates of growth while at the same time inequalities in income may also grow. It can therefore be difficult to extrapolate from growth figures to living standards if these differences in income distribution exist.

Finally, if a large proportion of national income is exported it can be difficult to infer that increases in national income per head necessarily result in improved living standards.

Despite these difficulties, international league tables of economic growth involving national income are still published. Table 1.6 illustrates the pattern of economic growth around the world.

Table 1.6
International growth league table showing percentage change in GDP in 1994 and 1999

Country	1994	1999	Country	1994	1999
China	11.8	8.1	Italy	3.7	2.1
South Korea	9.3	13.0	France	3.6	3.2
Brazil	9.2	3.1	Germany	3.3	2.3
Malaysia	8.9	10.6	Holland	3.3	4.6
Singapore	8.7	7.1	Denmark	3.0	2.0
Thailand	8.4	6.5	Israel	2.9	3.0
Taiwan	7.0	6.8	Spain	2.8	4.0
Australia	6.4	4.3	Switzerland	2.6	3.0
Argentina	6.0	0.1	Austria	2.5	3.8
Canada	5.6	3.0	South Africa	2.1	2.1
Hong Kong	5.5	8.7	Hungary	2.0	5.9
Philippines	5.1	4.6	Belgium	1.7	4.5
Poland	5.0	6.2	Greece	1.1	3.7
India	4.7	5.5	Japan	0.9	0.0
Czech Republic	4.7	1.0	Sweden	0.4	3.4
Mexico	4.0	5.2	Portugal	−0.7	n.a.
USA	4.0	4.6	Venezuela	−3.3	−4.5
UK	3.9	3.0	Turkey	−8.9	−3.4
Chile	3.9	3.9	Russia	−14.0	7.3

Source: *The Economist*, 29 April 2000.

The table shows the figures for two years only and should therefore be treated with some caution. Nevertheless, it is interesting to note that the 'go–go' economies, where growth rates exceeded 6 per cent per annum, are mostly to be found in the Far East, with South Korea topping the table in 1999 with a phenomenal 13.0 per cent per annum. Some argue that the reason some countries can experience such fast rates of growth reflects the fact that these countries start from a relatively low economic base in terms of the GDP per head. However, in the case of the so-called 'tiger economies' of Hong Kong, Malaysia, Singapore and South Korea, the base level is not far behind that of the rest of the world's economies, with a GNP per head comparable with, and in some cases exceeding, the so called 'mature' economies. The middle-ranking economies (i.e. those whose growth rates were between 4 and 6 per cent) are a mixed set of economies, while most of the more mature economies of Western Europe fall into the next category of growers (i.e. those whose growth rates were between 2 and 4 per cent). Interestingly Japan, traditionally considered to be a model of economic rectitude, has had a disappointing period with a sluggish economy barely able to achieve any measurable increase in its economy in 1994 and with growth for 1999 negligible. Finally, those in the 'relegation zone' of our league table are undergoing very significant upheavals. It is perhaps not entirely coincidental that those economies that actually shrunk in 1994 are also experiencing political upheavals of some kind (e.g. Turkey and Russia). By 1999, while the Russian economy had improved, Turkey and Venezuela were still experiencing severe economic dislocation.

PAUSE FOR THOUGHT 19 *Why do some economies grow faster than others? Before reading on, make a list of such factors.*

The growth rate of an economy can be affected by a number of factors, some of which have been identified as:

1 The quantity of the resources available.
2 The quality of the resources available.
3 The attitude of managers and workers.
4 Government policy.

Availability of resources

It is always possible for an economy to grow as a result of acquiring additional resources. West Germany's post-war economic miracle was helped by the influx of immigrant workers in the 1960s and, in Britain, the discovery of a new resource (North Sea oil) undoubtedly helped the economy to grow in the early 1980s when there was a very deep recession. (There is a view which links the two events, namely, the slump in manufacturing with the discovery of North Sea oil, but that will be considered later – see Chapter 4.)

PAUSE FOR THOUGHT 20 *Before you read the relevant section on this point, can you explain how the discovery of North Sea oil could have a damaging effect on the competitiveness of our manufacturing sector? (Hint: It links in with the effect of the discovery of oil on our exchange rate.)*

Quality of resources

As well as the quantity of resources available to an economy, one should also consider the quality of the resources available – in particular, the amount of investment that is undertaken in replacing outdated capital equipment and in developing new products that take advantage of technological developments. As well as the investment in plant and machinery, it is argued that investment in people is just as crucial to an economy's growth prospects. The appropriate kind of training is necessary to ensure that the economy has the requisite skills on which to call. The proportion of the workforce that is educated beyond school-leaving age can also have an influence, as can the type of education. The education system in the United Kingdom has been criticised for encouraging an 'anti-industry' and, in particular, an 'anti-manufacturing' attitude among school leavers. The UK's international competitors, it is claimed, are more sympathetic to the merits of vocational education. These criticisms are beginning to have less force than they had a decade ago, but they still persist.

Attitudes

The attitude to risk-taking can also be said to have an effect on the growth prospects of an economy. If entrepreneurs are encouraged to set up on their own and take risks, they may create business growth in areas that had not been considered previously. Martha Lane Fox and her partner set up the LastMinute.com web-based company selling last-minute deals on holidays, tickets for the theatre and sporting events. They saw an opportunity to develop a market that no-one at the time saw. They had the audacity to venture into an area of business that no-one else had spotted. Another example is Richard Branson who saw an opportunity to compete in the airline market in a way that few others would have believed possible. He also saw an opportunity to compete in the Cola drink market with the development of Virgin Cola. This sort of attitude creates added value for his business while at the same time adding to the country's economic growth.

Government policies

Governments can help or hinder economic growth by their own policies. In the past governments have been criticised for failing to provide the kind of stable economic climate in which firms can take long-term economic decisions (see also Chapter 12). The 'stop–go' cycle actually inhibited long-term growth because the economic environment was continually changing. A period of economic growth in which exports and investment are the main 'engines' of growth is likely to be more sustainable than a short consumer boom in which demand is artificially stoked up to levels that outstrip our ability to produce. The inevitable consequence of this type of growth is usually a balance of payments crisis and a run on the currency or an alarming reduction in our foreign exchange reserves (see section below on the balance of payments and exchange rates). Thus a well-managed economy can be a considerable advantage in securing sustainable economic growth. More recently, for example, the government has attempted to raise productivity by offering tax incentives for small firms to undertake Research and Development.[8]

However, while it is true that these factors play a significant role in the growth process it has been difficult to establish a direct 'cause-and-effect' relationship between each factor and economic growth. Does it follow, for example, that if an economy invests more then faster economic growth will automatically follow? Unfortunately, the answer is that it all depends! It depends, for example, on the quality of the investment decisions, rather than simply the volume. There is no simple relationship between the volume of investment and economic growth.

When an analysis of the main components of investment is conducted, one may discover for instance that a large proportion may be devoted to research and development of weapons systems for the defence industry or that investment in housing may form a significant proportion of a country's investment stock. The type of investment obviously has implications as to whether long-term economic growth is likely to be achieved. Thus a quantitative analysis that ignores these qualitative aspects is unlikely to give a definitive answer to the question of what causes economic growth. Similarly, simply increasing expenditure on education may not by itself necessarily increase economic growth. Again, qualitative aspects of the type of expenditure in education will play a part. There is, in fact, a strong scepticism about the economic benefits of educational expenditure. The 1960s and 1970s saw a significant expansion in expenditure on higher education in Britain, yet there was no noticeable improvement on our economic performance during that time. A closer examination of the ways in which this money was spent indicates that, unlike our international competitors, a large proportion of educational spending went on 'student maintenance' (i.e. students' living expenses) rather than directly on the educational process as such. While this expenditure is important, other countries found different ways of using their education budgets which laid greater emphasis on investing in the educational process itself. Again, simply looking at absolute numbers may mask a number of important qualitative issues.

Conclusions

In this chapter we have examined a simple model of how the domestic economy works and assessed the aims of economic policy. We will discuss in more detail the fourth objective (viz. achieving a balance of payments) in the next chapter. However, we have seen how difficult it has been for governments of all political persuasions to achieve these objectives simultaneously.

Notes

1 For a good website on this topic see www.bized.ac.uk/virtual/economy/
2 For details see the BBC's webpage at:
   news2.thls.bbc.co.uk/hi/english/biz/the_economy/economy_reports/
3 For a good survey of the way to measure inflation and the RPI visit the Office of National Statistics webpage at: www.ons.gov.uk/data/cpgi/rpiguide.htm
4 For an insider's view of the difficulties of that period, see Healey, D. (1989) *The Time of My Life*, Michael Joseph, London, esp. ch. 19, Managing the Economy.
5 Friedman, M. (1968) The importance of monetary policy, *American Economic Review*, Vol. 58, March, pp. 1–17.
6 For an interesting analysis of how independent the Monetary Policy Committee is, see 'Bank at a crossroads as Whitehall rattles sabre: Independence would be better guaranteed if members were not eligible for reappointment', *The Independent*: London; May 30, 2000; Sarah Hogg.
7 For interesting evidence of the relationship between central bank independence and the control of inflation, see Posen, A. (1994) 'Why Central Bank Independence Does Not Cause Low Inflation' in *Finance and the International Economy*, No. 7, Amex Bank.
8 For details of this see The Institute of Fiscal Studies, *The Green Budget 1999*, London, or visit the IFS website at www.ifs.org.uk

References and additional reading

Curwin, P. ed. (1994) *Understanding the UK Economy*, Macmillan, London.

The Economist (1994) 'A bad case of arthritis', 26 February, pp. 92–3.

Ferguson, P.R., Ferguson, G.J. and Rothschild, R. (1993) *Business Economics: The Application of Economic Theory*, Macmillan, London, esp. ch. 13, pp. 249–67.

Friedman, M. (1968) 'The role of monetary policy', *American Economic Review*, March, Vol. 58, pp. 1–17.

Gough, J. (2000) *Introductory Economics for Business and Management*, McGraw-Hill, London, esp. ch. 12, pp. 307–44.

Griffiths, A. and Wall, S. (1997) *Applied Economics*, Longman, London, esp. ch. 19, pp. 468–90; ch. 20, pp. 492–519; ch. 24, pp. 602–28; and ch. 27, pp. 697–710.

Holden, K., Matthews, K. and Thompson, J. (1995) *The UK Economy Today*, Manchester University Press, Manchester.

Layard, R., Nickell, S. and Jackman, R. (1994) *Unemployment: Macroeconomic Performance and the Labour Market*, Oxford University Press, Oxford.

Perman, R. and Scouller, J. (1999) *Business Economics*, Oxford University Press, Oxford, esp. ch. 14.

Posen, A. (1994) 'Why Central Bank independence does not cause low inflation', *Finance and the International Economy*, No. 7, Amex Bank, New York.

Rifkind, J. (1995) *The End of Work?*, G.P. Putman & Sons, London.

Sloman, J. (2000) *Economics*, Financial Times, Prentice Hall, London, esp. chs. 13–22.

CHAPTER 2

The international economic environment

Objectives

By the end of this chapter you will be able to:

➤ Analyse the theory of international trade.
➤ Assess the case for and against free trade.
➤ Analyse the economics of trading blocs.
➤ Understand the structure of the balance of payments.
➤ Evaluate economic strategies for restoring equilibrium in the balance of payments.
➤ Understand and analyse the factors that influence exchange rates.
➤ Examine the international economic environment within which firms must operate.

Key concepts

Balance of current account: is the difference between exports and imports of goods and services.

A common market: has all the features of a customs union (see below) but in addition there are a number of other features which attempt to create a single market such as common or harmonised taxes, common regulations and laws governing employment and trade, free movement of labour and capital as well as goods and services, no special treatment (by way of subsidies or special procurement policies of a country's home industries), a close co-ordination of macroeconomic policies and a single currency (or at least an agreed rate of exchange between currencies of member states).

A customs union: occurs when each member state has no tariff barriers with other member states but the member states adopt a common external tariff against non-member states.

Direct investment: occurs when, for example, a Japanese car company sets up a plant in the UK or a UK company builds a factory overseas.

A free trade area: occurs when the member states agree to lower tariff barriers between one another in an attempt to create free trade, but each member of the free trade area is free to set its own external tariff against non-member states.

Portfolio investment: occurs when foreign individuals or companies buy shares in UK companies, or UK residents or companies buy shares in foreign companies.

Trade creation effects: occur when, by reducing tariff barriers, new trade is undertaken which would not otherwise have taken place.

Trade diversion effects: occur when, by having barriers against non-member states, a country may divert trade away from a low-cost non-member state to a high-cost member state.

Voluntary export restraints: are policies designed to limit the exports from one country to another. They are 'voluntary' in the sense that one country agrees to limit its exports to the other. The extent of coercion is, however, a matter of debate. For example, Japan may agree to limit its export of cars to European markets because it fears worse retaliation if it does not agree to such limits. The extent to which such restraints are voluntary is thus a matter of interpretation.

Introduction
....

This chapter looks at the way in which the international economy impinges on business decision-making. We look first at the theory of international trade and at the advantages of free trade. We then examine the balance of payments accounts and finally explore the theory of exchange rates.

Why do we engage in international trade and what are the advantages for us as a nation by trading with other countries? What are the limitations on free trade? What are the advantages and disadvantages of various forms of preferential trading arrangement? What factors influence exchange rates? These are just some of the questions that will be discussed in this chapter.

The economics of international trade
....

The basic theory of international trade

The basic theory of international trade revolves around the principle of comparative advantage. In order to illustrate how this works, let us imagine that there are two countries in the world, Alpha and Beta, and that they each have two types of resource available to them, namely labour and capital. Let us also assume for the sake of simplicity that both countries have the same amounts of labour and capital. In addition, they can each produce two different products – cars and computers. The production possibilities are set out in Table 2.1.

Table 2.1
The production possibilities (absolute advantage)

Country	Output of cars	Output of computers
Alpha	1,000	100
Beta	500	400

The table illustrates that if Alpha puts all its resources into the production of cars it can produce 1,000 per annum; alternatively, if Alpha devotes all its resources to the production of computers it could produce 100 computers per annum. In the case of Beta, if it specialises in the production of cars it could produce 500 per annum or if it specialised in the production of computers it could produce 400 per annum. In this case we say that Alpha has an absolute advantage in the production of cars (because it is twice as efficient as Beta at car production) and Beta has an absolute advantage in the production of computers (because Beta can produce four times the number of computers with the same resources).

Another way to look at the same situation is to introduce the idea of opportunity cost; that is to say, what the country concerned would have to give up in order to produce one more unit of the good in question. If Alpha wanted to produce one more computer they would have to sacrifice 10 cars (1,000/100).

On the other hand, the opportunity cost for Beta is considerably less at 1.25 cars for an extra computer (500/400). It will clearly be to everyone's advantage to specialise in the products in which they have an absolute advantage and to trade with one another – Alpha trading its cars for Beta's computers. If we assume that before trading each country used half its resources in the production of each product then the production possibilities would be as shown in Table 2.2.

Table 2.2
Production possibilities before trading (absolute advantage)

Country	Output of cars	Output of computers
Alpha	500	50
Beta	250	200
Total	750	250

By specialising along the lines indicated, it is clear that everyone benefits. The situation after specialisation is given in Table 2.3.

Table 2.3
Production possibilities after specialisation (absolute advantage)

Country	Output of cars	Output of computers
Alpha	1,000	0
Beta	0	400
Total	1,000	400

The world has gained 250 cars and 150 computers as a result of specialisation. The two countries can agree a trading price and both of them will be better off. Let us say that they agree to trade with one another at the rate of 500 cars from Alpha for 200 computers from Beta, then both can gain from trading. Table 2.4 sets out the position after trading.

Table 2.4
The position after trading (absolute advantage)

Country	Output of cars	Output of computers
Alpha	500	200
Beta	500	200
Total	1,000	400

If we now compare the situation before and after trade, then it is clear that country Alpha gains 150 computers and country Beta gains 250 cars. However, to some extent it is fairly obvious that there will be advantages to specialisation and trading if one country has an absolute advantage in the production of one product and the other country has the absolute advantage in the production of the other. But what if one country has an absolute advantage in both products in our model? Let us examine the situation as outlined in Table 2.5.

Table 2.5
Production possibilities (comparative advantage)

Country	Output of cars	Output of computers
Alpha	1,000	400
Beta	500	100

This illustrates the new production possibilities if each country were to devote all its resources to the production of either cars or computers. It is clear that Alpha is now more efficient at producing both goods, and it is not immediately obvious why they should trade with Beta who are unable to match the efficiency levels of Alpha.

PAUSE FOR THOUGHT 1 *Can you give any reason why Alpha should trade with Beta? How might you persuade the politicians in Beta that it is not advisable to erect tariff barriers against Alpha's cars and computers?*

The figures in Table 2.5 reveal that although Alpha has an absolute advantage in the production of both products it has a comparative advantage in the production of computers. Although Alpha is twice as efficient as Beta in the production of cars, it is *four times* as efficient in the production of computers. Therefore, according to the principle of comparative advantage, Alpha should specialise in the production of computers and trade these for the cars that Beta produces.

> A country has a comparative advantage (in a two-product model) in that product for which its absolute advantage is greatest or its absolute disadvantage is least.

The reasons can be made clearer by referring to the opportunity costs of producing cars and computers in both countries. The production of an extra car in Alpha, for example, costs 0.4 computers (400/1,000) while in Beta it only costs 0.2 computers (100/500). In other words, Beta has a lower opportunity cost in car production than Alpha, and therefore has a comparative advantage in car production even though it has an absolute disadvantage in both products.

Similarly, Alpha has a lower opportunity cost than Beta in computer production. The production of an extra computer in Alpha costs only 2.5 cars (1,000/400) while in Beta it costs 5 cars (500/100).

> A country has a comparative advantage (in a two-product model) in that product for which it has a lower opportunity cost than the other country.

It can be shown that for specialisation according to comparative advantages and trade to benefit both countries, the trade must take place on 'terms' or 'relative prices' in between the limits set by the respective opportunity cost ratios.

Therefore, provided the two countries agree to trade at a price between these two limits, at say 1 car to 0.25 computers, there will be a gain. Alpha will be able to import the cars at a price that is lower than it could itself produce and Beta will gain because it can sell cars at a price above the opportunity cost of production.

It will be useful to follow through the arguments presented above using our example in Table 2.5. Let us suppose that as before (absolute advantage example) both countries devote half of their resources to the production of cars and computers. The situation will be as outlined in Table 2.6.

Table 2.6
The position before specialisation (comparative advantage)

Country	Output of cars	Output of computers
Alpha	500	200
Beta	250	50
Total	750	250

Now let the two countries specialise according to the law of comparative advantage. The situation now is as indicated in Table 2.7.

Table 2.7
The position after specialisation (comparative advantage)

Country	Output of cars	Output of computers
Alpha	0	400
Beta	500	0
Total	500	400

Now let us suppose that the two countries decide to trade at a price of 1 car for 0.25 computers, i.e. on terms of trade in between the limits set by the respective opportunity cost ratios. Suppose, therefore, Alpha sells Beta 50 computers in return for 200 cars. We can now examine the position after trading, and this is set out in Table 2.8.

Table 2.8
The position after trading (comparative advantage)

Country	Output of cars	Output of computers
Alpha	200	350
Beta	300	50
Total	500	400

As can be seen, Beta is better off than before. It has the same number of computers as it would have had if it had produced them itself. However, it has increased its volume of cars from 250 to 300 so it is clearly better off from specialising and trading. There would have been no advantage to be gained from erecting tariff barriers against trade with Alpha. What about Alpha? Is it better off? In order to assess this we need to do the same 'before and after' comparison by looking at Tables 2.6 and 2.8. Alpha clearly benefits by now having an extra 150 computers as a result of specialising and trading. The problem is that it has 300 fewer cars. At first sight this would appear to be a worse deal. However, in order to get a common measure with which to evaluate this we can use the opportunity cost concept to convert to a common standard. In the case of Alpha, it costs 2.5 cars to produce an extra computer (1,000/400 from Table 2.5). Therefore gaining 150 computers is worth the equivalent of 375 cars. The loss of 300 cars from trading is more than compensated by the extra computers because Alpha values computers more than cars (in terms of the opportunity costs of production). Both countries thus benefit from specialising and trading even though one of them, Alpha, has an absolute advantage in the production of both products.

ACTIVITY **2.1**

From the following table identify the country that has a comparative advantage in a product and calculate the likely gains from specialisation and trading as illustrated above.

Country	Output of cars	Output of computers
Gamma	400	200
Omega	600	300

PAUSE FOR THOUGHT 2   *Before reading on, what are the limitations of the theory of comparative advantage?*

The limitations of the theory

There are obvious limitations to the theory. For example, it is assumed that wage levels are the same in both countries and that there are no differences in the labour costs per unit of output. It is also assumed that demand for the two products in question is equally strong in both countries. If, for example, there is no real demand for cars in Alpha then there is a problem about setting a trading price that both countries can benefit from. No account is taken of the transport costs and it is assumed that any differences in efficiency, and hence competitiveness, are not wiped out by exchange rate movements. If there are wild fluctuations in the rates of exchange between Alpha and Beta then this can alter the competitive advantage and reduce the gains from trading. In addition, there are some disadvantages from over-specialisation, especially with goods that are regarded as strategically important. It may not be wise to rely exclusively on imported goods to meet domestic demand and industries which are allowed to run down as indicated by the law of comparative advantage may never be able to recover again.

Real world complications

In the real world (as opposed to the models of international trade of the text-books) there is a lot less specialisation than the theory implies. For example, there is a lot more 'intra-industry' trade with countries both exporting and importing the same product. In addition, in the real world there are likely to be diminishing returns from increasing specialisation. This means that more and more resources are consumed to produce a given increase in output. In other words, by switching labour and capital to, say, the production of cars, the output increases but at a diminishing rate. This means that the opportunity costs of producing the cars increases and is not constant as was implied in the basic model. In the real world there are considerable political pressures to pro-tect domestic firms from free trade. Politicians are reluctant to espouse the cause of free trade if it is going to cost jobs. Equally, business managers are just as guilty. In a survey of 11,700 managers in 25 countries conducted by the Harvard Business Review and quoted in *The Economist*,[1] 83 per cent of British managers supported the idea of free trade. Eighty per cent also supported the idea that governments should actively assist domestic firms in international markets. While South Korean managers were in favour of protection, the survey found that Japanese businessmen were more in favour of free trade than their European or American counterparts, very much contrary to the experience of those who have done business in Japan.

In spite of what might seem an encouraging picture from the Harvard study, the rise in protectionism has increased in recent years. Six arguments are advanced to justify protectionism and these can be summarised as:

1   The cheap labour argument.
2   The 'anti-dumping' argument.
3   The 'level playing field' argument.
4   The 'infant industry' argument.
5   The strategic industry argument.
6   The balance of payments argument.

The cheap labour argument

It is argued that cheap foreign imports are destroying domestic industries and hence depressing living standards. Therefore trade barriers are necessary to pre-vent low-wage countries from flooding the markets of developed countries. If it costs $16 an hour to employ a worker in the United States and only $1 an hour to employ a worker in China, then free trade will threaten the prosperity of the rich nations.

PAUSE FOR THOUGHT 3   *Can you give any counter-arguments to the 'cheap labour' arguments advanced above?*

The evidence supporting this proposition is, however, extremely weak. If it was the case then one might expect world trade to be dominated by low-wage economies, but this is clearly not the situation. This is because low wages are often associated with low productivity. It is labour costs per unit of output which are the key to competitive advantage and not just wages alone (for details of this argument see pages 98–99). If there are differences in labour costs per unit of output then free trade will tend to result in an equalisation of these unit costs as demand increases in the low unit cost country (thereby driving up wages and hence unit costs), whereas demand will fall in the high unit cost country (depressing demand and lower wage costs). This counter-argument has received powerful support in a paper by Stephen Golub, an economist with the Federal Reserve Bank of San Francisco.[2] Golub argues that the so-called unfair advantage of low-wage developing countries is nothing of the sort. In 1990, for example, manufacturing wages in Malaysia were only 15 per cent of those in America. However, comparing productivity levels, Golub found that productivity levels in manufacturing industries in Malaysia were also on average 15 per cent below those in the United States. In other words, unit labour costs were roughly the same in both countries. Indeed according to Golub's calculations the average unit labour costs were in fact higher in countries like India and the Philippines. Furthermore, the fear that improvements in productivity in the so-called 'tiger economies' of South East Asia as a result of technological innovation and transfer would leave the rich countries struggling to compete, also seems to have been unfounded. Theory and experience suggest that rising productivity is often matched by rising wages and a stronger exchange rate. For example, over the last 20 years South Korea, which has seen the biggest rise in productivity, has also seen the biggest rise in real wages.

The 'anti-dumping' argument

If goods are being 'dumped' on domestic markets by foreign imports then it is argued that measures must be taken to prevent this. There is a strong case for selective intervention to protect industries where 'dumping' takes place. Dumping occurs when a good is sold at a price well below its real cost of production. Under the rules of the General Agreement on Tariffs and Trade (GATT) a country could retaliate against the country concerned if it could be shown that the dumping significantly affected employment in the industries concerned. Inside the European Union cases of dumping can be referred to the European Commission. For example, in 1997 there were 56 goods including CD players, photocopiers and dot-matrix printers which are the subject of anti-dumping orders. In addition, according to one authoritative source, the number of 'anti-dumping' cases investigated by GATT rose from 176 in 1983 to 254 by 1993, an increase of almost 50 per cent in ten years.[3]

The 'level playing field' argument

The 'level playing field' argument implies that protective tariffs retaliate against those countries who are protectionist. In other words, if other countries have protectionist measures then it is necessary to have the same measures to protect your own industries, otherwise the competition will be unfair. In recent years this argument has been extended to look at the way some countries regulate (or, to be more accurate, fail to regulate) product and labour markets or to offer the same levels of environmental protection. Also if countries have vastly different regulatory regimes in areas such as competition policy then the playing field is said to be uneven. These types of dispute are likely to become more frequent as national economies become more integrated and as competition for direct foreign investment intensifies. The danger, according to those who subscribe to the level playing field argument, is that competition will drive standards down, that multinational companies will seek out those countries with the laxest of standards of labour, product and environmental protection, and that some form of harmonisation in national standards is required. Tariffs and other protectionist measures are therefore seen as a legitimate weapon for the richer nations to use on the poorer nations in order to get the latter to conform to the standards of the former. However, in a recent paper by the economist Jagdish Bhagwati[4] from Columbia University in New York, it was argued that the attempt by richer nations to impose common conditions on the poorer nations would not make the playing field more even. The imposition of extra costs on the economies of the poorer nations would be less, not more, likely to obtain a level playing field. Nor was there evidence that there was a 'race to the bottom' in terms of standards by incoming multinational companies. More often than not (but with one or two well-publicised exceptions which clearly damaged the reputations of the companies concerned) foreign multinational companies actually raised the standards in product and labour markets.

The infant industry argument

It is generally accepted that there are strong arguments for protecting new industries. New industries, particularly in developing countries, may need to be protected from the full rigours of international competition if they are to be successful. The difficulty is in knowing when these infant industries are sufficiently 'grown up' to be able to compete. The danger is that once established it may not be so easy to remove the protective barriers.

The strategic industry argument

There may be a number of industries which are regarded as too important to lose in the battle for international markets. It is often argued that no self-respecting country could allow industries crucial to its national defence to go out of business. In addition, certain industries are regarded as strategic and companies within them are regarded as national champions. In developing countries, for example, governments are often determined to create strong national car companies. In Indonesia, President Suharto in 1997 planned to promote a national car firm by awarding tax breaks and reliefs from tariffs on imported parts. This damaged the exports of cars to Indonesia and a number of countries, in particular Japan, planned to bring a case before the World Trade Organisation. Indonesia defended its actions under the key strategic industry argument.

The balance of payments argument

If a country is suffering from a fundamental problem in its balance of payments insofar as it cannot reconcile full employment with a balance of payments, it may be forced to consider some form of protection for its industries in order to restore the balance. Unfortunately, it is not likely to find much favour for this as a long-term solution to its trading problems, and its international trading partners are likely to tolerate such protectionist measures as only a temporary situation.

Forms of protection

There are a number of policies that governments can pursue in order to protect their industries. Until recently, the most common method was a tariff which is essentially a tax on imported goods. The tax may take the form of a lump sum tax or an ad valorem (a percentage on the value of the goods imported). The use of tariffs, however, was restricted by the General Agreement on Tariffs and Trade (GATT). Its successor, the World Trade Organisation (WTO), also has the aim of reducing tariffs world wide (see pp. 46–51 for further details).

As well as tariff barriers of the kind described above, there has been a rise in recent years in the incidence of non-tariff barriers as a means of protecting home industries. Quotas which are restrictions on the volume (or in some cases the value) of imports can also be used. In some cases import quotas are 'agreed' between the respective governments. The reason why such agreements are reached is often to prevent a full-scale trade war breaking out between the two countries. Thus the Japanese government has in the past agreed to restrict its exportation of cars to the USA and Europe in order to avoid more draconian measures on its exports. These are known as voluntary export restraints and there is the implicit threat that if these are not accepted then 'official' government backed quotas will be imposed in their place. In extreme cases an embargo is placed on certain goods (in effect a zero quota), but this is normally done for political reasons to isolate the country concerned (e.g. banning oil imports from Iraq or banning companies from investing in Cuba when governments in these countries were pursuing what were regarded by other countries as unacceptable policies).

Other more subtle measures, such as subsidising exports, can be used to protect a country's home-based industries. These may take the form of state-sponsored subsidies such as regional development assistance or export credit guarantees which protect the exporter from default by overseas buyers. This type of assistance can have a damaging effect on free trade but because these subsidies are often 'hidden' it is more difficult for such organisations as the WTO to police them. Exchange controls, abolished throughout Europe as a result of the creation of the single market, have also been used in the past by a number of countries to restrict foreign trade. Also it should not be forgotten that countries can use devaluation of their currencies as a means of restoring the competitiveness of their exports and restricting imports. This policy is, however, likely to provoke competitive devaluations, which is why there is pressure for some sort of exchange rate mechanism to prevent this from happening.

Finally, one of the biggest areas that prevent free trade relates to the rules and regulations concerning trading with other countries. These rules are often drawn up for other reasons (e.g. to ensure that imported products meet certain health and safety standards), which makes it expensive for firms to comply with the rules and hence to deter them from trading. Sometimes the rules are deliberately applied in such a way as to discriminate against imported goods. In one celebrated example the Thai government used an anti-smoking campaign to justify taxes and restrictions on imported cigarettes – but not on those domestically produced![5]

Nevertheless, in spite of the arguments for greater protectionism, the law of comparative advantage has been used for many years by economists to justify arguments for freeing up trade and reducing trade barriers and while there are obvious limitations to the theory it still has powerful support. Golub,[2] in the study referred to above, found that there was a negative correlation between the ratio of US–Japanese unit labour costs and the ratio of US–Japanese exports. In other words, in the industries where the unit labour costs in the USA were low in comparison to those in Japan, the USA would have a comparative advantage and hence the ratio of US–Japanese exports in those industries would be high. The reverse was also found to be true, thereby giving powerful support to the predictions of the theory of comparative advantage. In short, in spite of all its shortcomings and the pressures to move away from the free trade world of the theory, empirical evidence appeared to support the theory.

However, while trade between nations is important, with companies exporting and importing from one another, a significant amount of the world trade is now conducted by multinational companies locating in foreign markets. The United Nations Commission on Trade and Development estimated in 1996 that the sales of multinational firms' foreign affiliates are now about $5 trillion a year, roughly the same as world cross-border trade.[6] Thus trade through foreign direct investment is becoming increasingly important in a wide number of industries from cars to banking and telecommunications. We will look at why firms become multinational organisations and the different types of international business strategy in more detail in Chapter 11, but now let us turn our attention to trading blocs and examine the arguments for and against these types of trading arrangement.

The economics of trading blocs

A world of totally free trade is, as we have seen, far from the present situation in the international economic environment. There are powerful forces which act as a constraint on unfettered free trade. In reality, the world is dominated by a number of trading blocs and we examine the advantages and disadvantages of each of the different kinds of trading arrangement.

Essentially there are three different types of trading arrangement. These are:

➤ A free trade area
➤ A customs union
➤ A common market.

In a *free trade area* the member states agree to lower tariff barriers between one another in an attempt to create free trade, but each member of the free trade area is free to set its own external tariff against non-member states. In a *customs union* there are similarities with a free trade area insofar as each member state has no tariff barriers with other member states, but unlike a customs union the member states must adopt a common external tariff against non-member states. Finally a *common market* has all the features of a customs union but, in addition, there are a number of other features which attempt to create a single market, such as

➤ Common or harmonised taxes.
➤ Common regulations and laws governing employment and trade.
➤ Free movement of labour and capital as well as goods and services.

➤ No special treatment (by way of subsidies or special procurement policies of a country's home industries).

➤ A close coordination of macroeconomic policies.

➤ A single currency (or at least an agreed rate of exchange between the currencies of member states).

PAUSE FOR THOUGHT 4 *Before reading on, what are the advantages and disadvantages of a free trade area and a customs union?*

Each of these different types of preferential trading arrangement has its own advantages and disadvantages. There are basically two types of economic effect with each of these types of arrangement. The first, known as the *trade creation effects*, occurs when, by reducing tariff barriers, new trade is undertaken which would not have taken place before. If two countries previously had very high tariff barriers against one another then there would be a tendency for the low-cost producer to lose out to a high-cost producer. By having a free market, trade will be created from the low-cost producer to the high-cost producer. Consumers in the high-cost country will benefit and the increasing competition will stimulate the high-cost producers to become more efficient. These then are the trade creation effects. However, counterbalancing these effects are *trade diversion effects*. By having barriers against non-member states, a country may divert trade away from a low-cost non-member state to a high-cost member state. In the case of the free trade area, generally speaking, the bigger the free trade/customs union area then the more the trade creation effects will outweigh the trade diversion effects. At the extreme, if all the world were a customs union, there would be only trade creation effects and no trade diversion effects. On the other hand, if only two countries formed a customs union and had high common external tariff barriers against the rest of the world, there would be very few trade creation effects and large trade diversion effects.

In addition to these effects (known to economists as *static* effects because they are essentially 'once and for all effects' which are unlikely to be repeated) there are also dynamic effects. These are effects which, in opposition to 'one-off' static effects, cause changes in the way economies operate over a period of time. The dynamic effects are such things as:

➤ *Economies of scale*, where, for example, as a result of the creation of a larger market, companies merge or develop production techniques which enable them to produce more at a lower unit cost (for more details see Chapter 8).

➤ *Increased competition*, which occurs when there are reductions in the trade barriers which act as a spur to firms to reduce costs.

➤ *Improved terms of trade*, which occur where the bargaining power of the customs union is greater than any of the individual countries that form the union. This ensures that the members of the customs union receive the benefits in terms of lower costs of imported goods.

All of the above may be said to be *dynamic benefits*. On the other hand, there are a number of dynamic factors which can give rise to *dynamic disbenefits or costs*. For example:

> *Resource transfers.* Resources may flow from those countries that are unable to compete to those that are able to benefit. This can cause areas to depopulate and result in severe regional imbalances between member states. 'Nothing succeeds like success', but equally nothing fails like failure and there can be situations where regions suffer from a downward spiral of economic activity.

> *Monopolisation and cartelisation.* If cross-border mergers and acquisitions take place without proper safeguards, then there is a danger that markets could become very concentrated. Consumers may find that their choice is restricted or that prices within the customs union are kept artificially high by the abuse of this monopoly power. (For further details see Chapter 9).

There are a variety of examples of these types of preferential trading arrangements usually involving a number of smaller trading nations. For example, in 1995 a common market was formed between Argentina, Brazil, Paraguay and Uruguay called MerCoSur (see Case Study 2.1). In 1993 the Asian Free Trade Area was set up with the objective of reducing internal tariffs among member states to a maximum of 5 per cent by 2008. In the same year, there was established the North American Free Trade Area consisting of the USA, Canada and Mexico. There is a programme with the aim of reducing tariffs to zero between these three countries by 2009. However, unlike the European Union, there are no plans to harmonise taxes or macroeconomic policies, or indeed currencies. As can be seen from Case Study 2.1, this can often cause problems.

CASE STUDY **2.1**

MerCoSur economies regain their footing

Brazil's recession, a downturn in commodities, and meagre capital flows in 2000 have tested South America's fragile economies. Brazil's devaluation of the real in January 1999 also heightened trade tensions between Brazil and Argentina, the two largest economies in the Southern Cone Common Market (MerCoSur), which also includes Paraguay and Uruguay. Still, economists expect Brazil and Argentina to outperform its Andean Pact neighbours – Colombia, Venezuela, Ecuador, Peru and Bolivia whose political and economic turmoil has reduced investment.

Experts forecast moderate growth for Latin America as a whole in 2000. The International Monetary Fund (IMF; Washington) estimates that GDPs of countries in the region, including Mexico, will grow 2–3 per cent on average in 2000 (see Table CS2.1.1).

Table CS2.1.1
MerCoSur growth forecasts 2000

Country	1999	2000
Argentina	−3.0	1.5
Brazil	−1.0	4.0
Chile	−0.4	5.5
Colombia	0.0	2.6
Ecuador	−7.0	1.5
Peru	3.0	5.5
Uruguay	−2.0	2.5

Source: IMF (1999).

'Most countries have touched bottom and are starting to recuperate', says Arturo Porzecanski, chief economist/Americas at ING Barings (New York). However, GDP growth in South America remains two to three points below levels forecast prior to the 1997 global financial crisis.

Brazil has fared better than economists expected since the January 13 currency devaluation. Brazil's GDP will slip an estimated 0.5–1 per cent this year – nowhere near the 4–5 per cent decline many economists had projected. But economists say recovery and growth in Brazil hinge on the implementation of fiscal reforms.

Brazil's devaluation has also affected commerce in Argentina, whose currency, the peso, is the only major South American currency pegged to the dollar. Manufacturers, particularly Argentine producers of automobiles and other durable goods, have been hit hard by higher production costs and a dwindling demand for their products in Brazil, Argentina's biggest export market. Argentina's economy will contract approximately 3 per cent this year, though IMF predicts a 1.5 per cent GDP increase in 2000; optimistic Argentine officials forecast 3.5 per cent growth for 2000.

Tension about the trade imbalance with Brazil escalated in September when Argentina threatened to place import quotas on Brazilian shoes, clothes and textiles. Officials have since resolved that dispute, but analysts say the tensions reflect a structural imbalance that must be rectified to preserve MerCoSur.

'MerCoSur cannot go on with the differential in currencies and economies between Brazil and Argentina', says Rina Quijada, managing director/Latin America at CMAI (Houston). 'It will be bumpy for the next six to eight months and they will have to make some adjustments. But they want to keep it together. They've already put so much work into it.'

The Argentine peso is overvalued, but presidential hopefuls have vowed to maintain the exchange rate. Investors are waiting for the outcome of Argentina's October presidential elections before making any bets on the economy.

In September 1999, currency readjustments are under way elsewhere in South America. Last month, Chile eliminated its currency trading band and Colombia let its peso float. Chile's GDP will grow an estimated 3.4 per cent in 1999 but is expected to decline slightly, 0.4 per cent, by 2000.

Meanwhile, inflation and political upheaval have stalled investment in Venezuela. Despite an upswing in oil prices – on which Venezuela depends for more than 70 per cent of its GDP – the nation's GDP is expected to shrink as much as 7 per cent in 2000. 'The business climate has deteriorated sharply despite rising oil prices', Porzecanski says.

Other Andean countries also show signs of weakness. Escalating violence linked to guerrilla insurgencies and the drug trade have discouraged investment in Colombia. 'Colombia and Venezuela are a bit of a cancer for the region right now', says Jorge Mariscal, chief strategist/Latin American investment at Goldman Sachs. Colombia last month negotiated a $6-billion aid package from multilateral agencies, which will require implementation of fiscal reforms.

Ecuador defaulted in September 1999 on a $96-million Brady bond payment[7] and became the first country to default on the bonds.

Source: Kara Sissell (1999) MerCoSur economies regain their footing, *Chemical Week*, New York, 13 October.

Questions
1   What have been the major problems with MerCoSur according to the case study?
2   What are the biggest threats to the continued success of this customs union?

The best-known customs union is, of course, the European Union which was originally established in 1957 as the European Economic Community (EEC) of six member states (Belgium, France, Italy, Luxembourg, Netherlands and West Germany, as it was then known). In 1973 the UK, Denmark and Ireland joined the EEC followed by Greece in 1981, Spain and Portugal in 1986 and Sweden, Austria and Finland in 1995.

Although falling short of a United States of Europe with a federal European structure, there are a number of European institutions which affect the way individual member states are governed. For example, the *European Commission* is responsible for administering existing policy and proposing new policies. There is also the *European Council of Ministers*, which consists of the senior ministers of each member state. This body receives proposals from the European Commission and has the power to decide on all European matters. There is also the *European Parliament* where the Members of the European Parliament (MEPs) can debate Europe-wide issues. In theory, the European Commissioners and the European Council of Ministers are answerable to the European Parliament. In practice, this power is often more theoretical than real. However, in 1999 the European Parliament, alarmed at what it saw as waste and incompetence, threatened to bring the European Commission's proceedings to a halt by refusing to grant the Commission the necessary finance to carry on its work unless there were serious moves towards reform. As a result of this threat a number of commissioners resigned, the President of the European Commission was replaced and a reform package was agreed. Selected statistics of some European economies are given in Table 2.9.

Table 2.9
European economies: selected statistics

Country	Growth (% change GDP 1999)	Inflation (% change p.a. May 2000)	Unemployment (% rate 2000)	Balance of payments Current account as % of GDP forecast for 2000
Austria	+3.8	+1.9	4.5	−2.3
Belgium	+4.5	+2.2	11.3	+4.1
Britain	+3.1	+3.0	6.2	−1.9
Denmark	+2.0	+3.1	5.9	+0.7
Finland*	5.9	+2.2	10.6	n.a.
France	+3.3	+1.3	11.3	+2.4
Germany	+3.3	+1.5	10.6	−0.5
Greece†	+3.5	+5.5	10.0	n.a.
Ireland†	+10.5	+1.5	10.2	n.a.
Italy	+2.1	+2.5	11.7	+1.2
Luxembourg†	+3.7	+1.3	3.6	n.a.
Netherlands	+4.2	+2.1	3.4	+4.4
Portugal	+3.5	+2.4	6.8	n.a.
Spain	+4.0	+2.9	16.6	−1.5
Sweden	+3.4	+1.1	5.3	+2.3

Source: Adapted from *The Economist*, 9 June 2000 and *Trends In Europe and North America*, United Nations Statistical Year Book 1999.

* Data for growth 1997
† Data for 1997

The World Trade Organisation

The World Trade Organisation (WTO) is the international body dealing with the rules of trade between nations. At its heart are the WTO agreements, negotiated and signed by the bulk of the world's trading nations. These documents provide the legal ground-rules for international commerce. They are essentially contracts, binding governments to keep their trade policies within agreed limits. Although negotiated and signed by governments, the goal is to help producers of goods and services, exporters and importers to conduct their business.

The WTO's main purpose is to help trade flow as freely as possible. In addition one of the WTO's most important functions is to serve as a forum for trade negotiations. A third important side to the WTO's work is to settle disputes between nations.

The WTO was established on 1 January 1995, but its trading system is half a century older. Since 1948, the General Agreement on Tariffs and Trade (GATT) had provided the rules for the system. Over the years GATT evolved through several rounds of negotiations.

The latest and largest was the Uruguay Round, which lasted from 1986 to 1994 and led to the creation of the WTO as GATT had mainly dealt with trade in goods. The WTO and its agreements now cover trade in services, and in traded inventions, creations and designs (intellectual property). As a result of the WTO and its predecessor, the GATT, international trade has grown significantly as illustrated in Figure 2.1 and Table 2.10.

Figure 2.1

Growth in the volume of world merchandise trade and GDP, 1990–1999

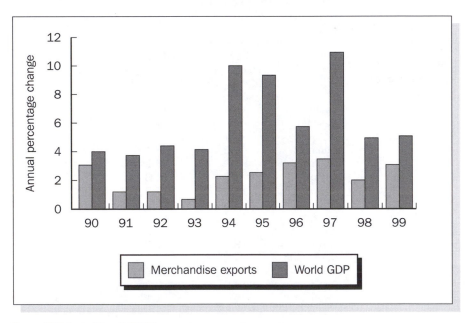

Source: WTO Annual Report (1999).

Table 2.10

Growth in the value of world merchandise trade by region, 1997–1999

(billion dollars and percentage change)

	Exports (f.o.b.)				Imports (c.i.f.)			
	Value	Annual percentage change			Value	Annual percentage change		
	1999	1997	1998	1999	1999	1997	1998	1999
World	5,460	3.5	–1.6	3.5	5,725	3.5	–0.8	4.0
North America	934	9.2	–0.7	4.0	1,281	10.3	4.4	11.5
Latin America	292	10.2	–1.2	6.0	329	18.5	4.8	–4.0
Mexico	137	15.0	6.4	16.5	148	22.6	13.9	13.5
Other Latin America	156	7.2	–6.2	–2.0	181	16.4	–0.1	–14.5
Western Europe	2,349	–0.6	3.4	–0.5	2,437	–0.3	5.9	0.5
European Union (15)	2,176	–0.5	3.8	–0.5	2,233	–0.5	6.3	1.0
Extra-EU(15) trade	799	1.8	–0.3	–1.5	851	–0.3	6.2	2.5
Transition economies	212	4.1	–4.6	–1.5	211	6.5	–1.8	–13.0
Central/Eastern Europe	101	6.3	9.5	0.0	129	5.6	10.8	–2.0
Russian Federation	74	–0.4	–15.9	0.0	41	6.7	–19.8	–30.5
Africa	113	1.9	–15.5	8.0	132	5.5	1.2	0.5
South Africa*	27	6.2	–9.0	1.5	27	9.5	–9.3	–8.5
Major fuel exporters**	41	–0.1	–31.4	24.0	30	9.6	–0.8	5.5
Middle East	169	4.7	–22.4	22.0	152	8.1	–3.2	4.0
Asia	1,390	5.4	–6.1	7.5	1,201	0.4	–17.8	10.5
Japan	419	2.4	–7.8	8.0	311	–3.0	–17.2	11.0
China	195	21.0	0.6	6.0	166	2.5	–1.5	18.0
Asia (15)†	371	5.1	–3.5	9.5	292	–3.1	–30.9	15.5

* Beginning 1998, figures refer to South Africa and no longer to the Southern African Customs Union.

** Angola, Algeria, Congo, Gabon and Nigeria

† Indonesia, the Republic of Korea, Malaysia, Philippines and Thailand

Source: WTO Annual Report (1999).

Sometimes the WTO has mixed success as Case Study 2.2 illustrates.

CASE STUDY 2.2

The beef over bananas

The trade war between America and Europe over bananas, and a looming clash over hormone-treated beef, expose big weaknesses in world trade rules. America's patience with the European Union snapped on 3 March 2000. The reason? The EU's failure to amend to America's satisfaction its banana-import rules. These favour fruit from ex-colonies in the Caribbean distributed by European firms over Latin American bananas distributed by American ones. America's response: a knockout blow to imports of 14 European products. But the move does more than threaten to cut off America's supplies of Parma ham and Belgian waffles. It also signals a crisis of confidence in the World Trade Organisation (WTO), the supposed arbiter of world trade disputes.

The immediate worry is that hostilities will break out on other fronts too. America is fuming about the EU's ban on hormone-treated beef. It is unhappy with Europe's reluctance to embrace genetically modified food. It is angry over European subsidies for Airbus, Boeing's rival in aerospace. It is concerned that an EU directive on data-privacy and proposed rules on aircraft noise discriminate against American firms. It is peeved that the EU has asked the WTO to rule against its sanction-imposing 'Section 301' legislation. In the background, there is huge resentment that the EU is doing so little to stimulate demand, leaving America as the sole locomotive of the world economy and chief bearer of the 'burden' of imports from struggling emerging countries.

A worse fear is that the WTO seems incapable of enforcing its rules. After all, the WTO has twice told the EU that its banana regime is illegal. But it has not been able to bring the EU into line because its rules on compliance are so unclear. America is stretching WTO rules too. It has imposed immediate sanctions that are equivalent to 100 per cent duties on a range of European products. It will, however, refrain from actually collecting these until the WTO produces its delayed assessment of the damage done to America by the EU's banana regime.

Legal shenanigans aside, this underlying flaw in the WTO could yet prove fatal. If countries feel that the WTO does not work, they will be tempted to bypass or ignore it. Big powers such as America and the EU may prefer to act unilaterally. Smaller ones might gang up, or curry favour with bigger powers to pursue their claims. The predictability and fairness of a rules-based system could be lost. In its place would be an arbitrary one based on power. Almost inevitably, there would be more protection and more trade wars.

The WTO's dispute-settlement mechanism is meant to have teeth. Its key strength is that countries cannot veto WTO rulings against them. They have the right to appeal once; if they lose again, they have 15 months in which to fall into line with world trade law. If they do not comply, the plaintiff can demand compensation or impose retaliatory sanctions.

Until recently, the system had been surprisingly effective. It has dealt with 163 disputes since the WTO was set up in 1995. America has brought the most cases, 53 in all, closely followed by the EU, with 43. America and the EU are also the most common defendants, the United States in 29 cases, the EU in 26. Developing countries have used the system too, both against each other and against rich countries. Most cases have been settled without the need for arbitration. And when the WTO has been called on to adjudicate, no government has yet defied any of its rulings.

Thus America amended petrol standards when the WTO judged that they discriminated against Venezuelan products. It obeyed the WTO by lifting restrictions on Costa Rican underwear. And Japan is reforming its discriminatory alcohol taxes after losing a case brought by America, the EU and Canada. Indeed, the big worry was that the system was too strong, not too weak. That was encouraging countries to use the WTO's enforcement powers to pursue objectives that may have stretched beyond its remit. America tried to use the WTO to compel Japan to enforce its antitrust rules. The EU complained to the WTO about America's Helms–Burton act, which penalises companies investing in Cuba, but later reached a bilateral settlement. And, urged on by trade unions and green groups, America wants the WTO to impose tough and enforceable labour and environmental standards on developing countries.

Such fears now look premature. In the banana case, America first complained to the WTO about the EU's regime in September 1995. Two years later, the WTO ruled for the second time that the regime was illegal. The EU was given 15 months to comply, and on 1 January it enacted some minor changes to its rules. Neither America and its Latin American co-plaintiffs, nor most independent observers, think that the EU's new regime is legal. But the EU says they cannot be sure until the WTO has ruled again, which it will do by 12 April. Even that may not be the end of it. If the WTO finds against the EU for an unprecedented third time, the EU could tinker with the rules yet again and ask the WTO to repeat the process. The EU might never have to comply in full.

The precedent is dangerous. The EU has already hinted that it will not lift its ban on hormone-treated beef from America, by 13 May as the WTO requires. Canada is refusing to rescind restrictions on foreign (mostly American) magazines. If it cannot win justice from the EU and Canada, America is unlikely to respect a WTO ruling against its ban on shrimps from countries which use nets that trap turtles.

One solution would be for the WTO to stipulate what countries must do in order to comply with its rulings. But America and the EU are against the WTO's taking on such a prescriptive role. John Jackson, an expert on WTO law at Georgetown University in Washington, DC, suggests instead that an independent arbitrator could rule quickly on whether a country has complied. That could be a winner. Both America and the EU, a bit more circumspectly, claim that they want the rules on compliance to be clarified. America says it is keen on change as soon as possible, perhaps once the WTO's review of its dispute-settlement procedures concludes in July. But such protestations should be taken with a pinch of salt. The EU is not obliged to exploit the loophole in the rules. Indeed, the ambiguity in the rules about compliance may be deliberate. America and the EU may want to hold other countries to account without binding their own hands too tightly. If so, tightening the rules would merely ensure that they are flouted more regularly.

The real problem is that America and the EU are not always willing to accept that the writ of the WTO can trump domestic political considerations. Sometimes, as in the banana case, this is because old-fashioned lobbies are too strong. In other cases, such as the rows over hormones in beef or genetically modified foods, there is genuine popular disquiet at the intrusion of the WTO into sensitive matters that were once exclusively domestic. Trade rules need to be strong enough to deter protectionism. But they also need to be flexible enough to cope with the most difficult cases without testing the system to destruction.

Source: The ISP Clippings Service of the University of Boston Economics Department at http://econ.bu.edu/isp/s99/153.htm

Questions

1 Why has the dispute about bananas threatened the WTOs credibility?
2 The case refers to an underlying flaw in the WTO's rules which 'could yet prove fatal'. What is it and how could it be avoided?
3 What evidence is there to support the proposition that the WTO had been an effective organisation?
4 'The big worry was that the system was too strong not too weak.' What is the evidence to support this assertion?
5 'America and the EU are not always willing to accept the writ of the WTO.' Why?

In addition the WTO has been criticised by a number of groups for favouring the interests of the larger industrialised nations and multinational businesses at the expense of the developing countries. As one webpage put it:[8]

Increasing poverty and cuts in social services while the rich get richer, low wages, sweatshops, meaningless jobs, and more prisons, deforestation, grid-locked cities and global warming, genetic engineering, gentrification and war: Despite the apparent diversity of these social and ecological troubles, their roots are the same – the global economic system based on the exploitation of people and the planet.

PAUSE FOR THOUGHT 5 *Why are the critics so vehement in their condemnation of the WTO?*

While there are serious criticisms of the way the WTO has operated, a number of countries see advantages from membership as the following case illustrates.

CASE STUDY **2.3**

China to join the World Trade Organisation

After a 14-year wait, in May 2000, US firms last week came closer than ever to securing access to Chinese industries long protected by Peking. By a 237 to 197 vote, the House of Representatives approved permanent normal trade relations (PNTR) with China. US business applauded the vote, while Chinese firms braced for an onslaught of foreign competition.

Once China joins the World Trade Organisation (WTO) British investors could also ride a multi-billion dollar surge in the annual world exports of goods and services to China. Hawking everything from insurance to brandy, foreign businessmen look to the WTO to remove many of the bureaucratic obstacles and state monopolies that have dogged them since China opened its doors in the late 1970s.

Although China's WTO application did not hinge on PNTR, the vote smoothed the entry process and boosted those reformers in Peking committed to resolving the painful legacy of China's command economy. Supporters of PNTR were helped by the Sino–EU agreement signed in Peking last Friday, China's last big hurdle to WTO membership. Only Switzerland, Mexico, Costa Rica, Guatemala and Ecuador are still to conclude bilateral agreements.

A recent report by consultants Roland Berger suggests that following WTO accession, direct foreign investment in China may jump to $100bn (£68bn) a year by 2005, up from $40bn last year, though other analysts are more cautious. As the Chinese market is bloated by over-supply of up to two-thirds of industrial products, and price deflation continues, an investment boom like the early 1990s is unlikely.

Investors in China are under growing pressure to show results. WTO entry may only buy a little more time to prove their China plays.

Besides benefiting from tariff cuts on many items, companies from WTO member countries will enjoy improved access to restricted sectors such as telecommunications and insurance. 'Foreign companies have been unable to invest in areas like mobile telephony in the past, but have spent many years positioning themselves for entry', said telecoms consultant Patrick Horgan of APCO China in Peking.

'There has been a lot of activity identifying partnerships for the best sectors, and this will only increase over the next few months.'

Insurance has for years been a prime example of China's very political economy. Peking bestows operating licences on a country-by-country basis as a reward for 'good' behaviour. While US insurers stole a march in the early 1990s, Peking denied British brokers a single licence out of displeasure over Chris Patten's democratic reforms in Hong Kong. With the territory safely returned to China, Royal & Sun

Alliance and Prudential were rewarded for their patience and expensive demonstrations of 'good citizenship'.

To secure WTO membership, Peking has promised to rely instead on 'prudential criteria'. Recently, it started another scramble for influence with the gift of seven licences for as yet unspecified European brokers. CGU and Standard Life wait anxiously in the wings, with rivals from France, Italy, Germany and Holland.

The US Congress vote on PNTR capped months of stormy debate over trade relations with China. On the other side of the Pacific, Chinese domestic media have stifled dissenting opinion ever since Communist party leaders fully committed the People's Republic to WTO entry. Amid the cheers at China's progress towards accession, Han Deqiang has sounded a lonely voice of opposition. Although some industries in China are doing better than others, overall Chinese enterprises are not yet ready or strong enough to compete', said Dr Han, author of the controversial book *Collision* on the problems WTO may bring. 'Even an outstanding enterprise like Hai'er, the fridge maker from Shandong, is still a "little brother" in world trade terms.'

China's inefficient state-owned enterprises, in sectors like automotive, oil and steel, are expected to shed over 11 million workers into a crowded labour market. China's farmers, the majority of the population, may be hit even harder. 'When urban Chinese start to enjoy America's cheap wheat, corn and beef, nearly 900 million Chinese farmers will suffer bitterly', Dr Han told the *Independent on Sunday*. 'Our tiny, family-based farming units stand absolutely no chance of competing with large, modern and well-equipped US farms.'

In contrast, many private enterprises hailed PNTR. 'We look forward to WTO, as we need to expand overseas', said Li Xiaodong of the New Hope Group, one of China's leading private firms. 'With WTO, we expect less obstruction on imports and exports, reduced costs of raw materials, and cheaper prices for our customers, the ordinary people.'

In recent years there has been grudging acceptance from the Communist Party of the important role played by private firms in the national economy. 'WTO should bring less protection for state-owned companies and more equal treatment for enterprises like ours', said Mr Li.

Trade with China is also set to increase, with tariffs plunging by an average of 40 per cent on over 150 products made in Europe. That was good news for Scotch whisky and French brandy, where tariffs fell from 65 to 10 per cent. 'This is very low by international standards so imports will definitely increase', said Wang Yancai from China's Alcoholic Drinks Industry Association. 'This increases the pressure on Chinese alcohol companies, which can no longer rely on government support but must compete by themselves.'

Only with China's WTO accession will foreign firms gain rights that Chinese companies enjoy in Europe and the US – importing, distributing and wholesaling without relying on layers of middle men. But WTO entry will come too late for Bass, which is selling its stake in a remote brewery. In a sobering lesson to all companies lured by the China dream, Bass found most consumers unwilling to pay top dollar for a foreign brand.

Source: Calum MacLeod (2000) *The Independent*, London (UK); 28 May 2000; p. 5.

Questions

1 Is China's entry into the WTO good or bad?
2 What dangers are there for China and how might these be overcome?

Balance of payments

As discussed in Chapter 1, there are four key objectives of macroeconomic policy. The final objective of macroeconomic policy, which can affect the economic environment in which firms operate, concerns our international economic position with the rest of the world. In short, it concerns achieving a 'satisfactory' outcome in terms of the balance of payments and a stable exchange rate. The balance of payments accounts are set out in two main parts:

1 The current account.
2 Transactions in external assets and liabilities.

Since these figures follow the basic principles of accounting and use double entry book-keeping conventions, the accounts must of necessity balance. This means that every transaction must have both a credit and a debit item. This, of course, is different from saying that the balance of payments is always in 'equilibrium' or that the UK is invariably performing 'satisfactorily' in its external trade. For example, if a British company exports goods to a German company then there will be two transactions that will show up in the current account of the balance of payments. First, the British company will receive a positive flow of currency which will show up as a credit on the visible part of the current account of the balance of payments. However, this will be matched by a reduction in the sterling account of the German firm. In other words, there will be a reduction in the liabilities of the UK as sterling is transferred from the German company's sterling account to the UK firm's account. The same transaction is simply viewed in two different ways. A technical balance in the accounts is, in this sense, a statistical inevitability.

The main part of the balance of payments accounts which receives the most attention from the media and from City analysts is that part which is known as the balance of current account. This part of the account consists of two main parts. The visibles relate to the export and import of goods (known as the balance of trade) and the invisibles refer to the export and import of services.

The invisible part of the accounts consists of the profits, interest, dividends, royalties earned and income received from selling our services abroad (e.g. banking, insurance, investment advice and tourism to name a few) less the profits, interest, dividends and royalties that we pay out to foreign companies that do business in the UK. It is clear that the UK benefits from the export of capital when, for example, a British company sets up in France because any profits and dividends that are earned will be 'repatriated' to the UK. It therefore would not make sense to limit overseas investment, as there are corresponding returns that can be earned throughout the time the firm operates overseas. Equally, foreign companies will 'repatriate' profits and dividends to their parent companies as a result of the import of direct investment into the UK. Traditionally, the visible part of the accounts have been in deficit (i.e. we tend to import more goods than we export) as can be seen in Table 2.11. In only three of the previous 20 years has the UK earned a surplus on the visible part of its balance of visible trade.

Table 2.11
Balance of visible trade (£m) 1979–1999

Period	Exports of goods	Imports of goods	Balance of trade
1979	40,849	44,175	−3,326
1980	47,493	46,164	1,329
1981	51,034	47,796	3,238
1982	55,657	53,778	1,879
1983	60,984	62,602	−1,618
1984	70,565	75,974	−5,409
1985	78,291	81,707	−3,416
1986	72,997	82,614	−9,617
1987	79,531	91,229	−11,698
1988	80,711	102,264	−21,553
1989	92,611	117,335	−24,724
1990	102,313	121,020	−18,707
1991	103,939	114,162	−10,223
1992	107,863	120,913	−13,050
1993	122,039	135,358	−13,319
1994	135,260	146,351	−11,091
1995	153,725	165,449	−11,724
1996	167,403	180,489	−13,086
1997	171,783	183,693	−11,910
1998	164,092	184,629	−20,537
1999	165,204	191,815	−26,611

Source: www.statistics.gov.uk/statbase/tsdataset.asp

On the other hand, our invisible balance is usually positive, signalling the fact that the UK is a net beneficiary of a thriving banking, insurance and investment centre as well as benefiting from the stock of direct investment of UK companies overseas. The extent to which the current account is in balance depends on the extent to which the positive invisible balance (Table 2.12) outweighs the negative visible balance.

Table 2.12
Balance of invisible trade (£m) 1979–1999

Period	Export of services	Import of services	Invisible balance
1979	13,955	9,990	3,965
1980	15,002	11,285	3,717
1981	16,281	12,447	3,834
1982	16,922	13,853	3,069
1983	18,767	14,826	3,941
1984	20,944	16,603	4,341
1985	23,635	17,016	6,619
1986	24,784	18,279	6,505
1987	26,906	20,220	6,686
1988	26,723	22,393	4,330
1989	29,272	25,355	3,917
1990	31,188	27,178	4,010
1991	31,426	26,955	4,471
1992	35,428	29,754	5,674
1993	40,039	33,416	6,623
1994	43,507	36,979	6,528
1995	48,687	39,772	8,915
1996	52,900	44,003	8,897
1997	57,543	45,129	12,414
1998	60,869	48,745	12,124
1999	63,826	52,712	11,114

Source: www.statistics.gov.uk/statbase/tsdataset.asp

Another important part of the accounts relates to what used to be known as the capital account and refers to the export and import of capital investment. There are two kinds of capital investment: portfolio investment – whereby foreign individuals or companies buy shares in UK companies, or UK residents or companies buy shares in foreign companies; and direct investment – where, for example, a Japanese car company sets up a plant in the UK or a UK company builds a factory overseas. The import of capital represents a transfer of real resources and can be seen as being of benefit to the economy. The export of capital represents a transfer of investment overseas and is a reduction in real resources to the UK economy.

| PAUSE FOR THOUGHT 6 | *If the export of capital represents a transfer of resources out of the UK should the government consider ways of limiting such overseas investment? Are there any likely benefits from overseas investment by UK firms? Are there any disadvantages?* |

The capital account (Table 2.13) indicates the balance between the export and import of capital.

Table 2.13
Balance on capital account (£m) 1986–1999

Period	Capital account
1986	135
1987	333
1988	235
1989	270
1990	497
1991	290
1992	421
1993	309
1994	33
1995	534
1996	736
1997	804
1998	473
1999	788

Source: www.statistics.gov.uk/statbase/tsdataset.asp

Finally we can examine the extent to which foreign companies invest in the UK (and the extent to which UK companies invest abroad). We measure this by foreign direct investment (fdi). When one examines the data from Figure 2.2, a trend begins to emerge. Leaving aside the portfolio investment and focusing instead on the balance between the direct investment overseas by UK firms and the direct investment in the UK by overseas firms, there has been a significant inflow of direct investment into the UK since 1994. The increase has been almost four-fold from £6.1 billion in 1994 to £23.2 billion in 1997. This reflects the favourable economic environment for foreign companies in the UK. However, from 1991 there has been a similar explosive growth in direct investment abroad by UK firms, from £9 billion in 1991 to £36.3 billion in 1997, reflecting the increasingly global market place in which UK firms operate. (For further details see Chapter 11.)

Figure 2.2
UK foreign direct investment, £ millions, 1987–1997

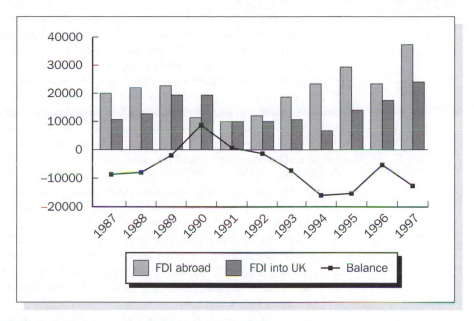

Source: UK Balance of Payments (The Pink Book) 1998 edition.

PAUSE FOR THOUGHT 7   *Why has there been a significant inflow of foreign direct investment (i.e. foreign companies setting up plant in the UK) in recent years? What do you think are the attractions of locating in the UK?*

In recent years Japanese car companies have located outside their home base in Europe. The UK has been a main beneficiary of this trend and this has had a significant impact on our balance of payment accounts. As well as providing a welcome boost to the UK capital account, it has also clearly benefited the UK's current account as a very large part of our output has been exported. In addition, the import side of the accounts has also benefited since the UK is no longer required to import Japanese cars. There is still the question, however, of how long this trend can continue – as Case Study 2.4 illustrates.

CASE STUDY **2.4**   **Japanese aircraft carriers**

Jacques Calvet, the head of France's PSA which makes Peugeot and Citroën cars, once described Japanese factories in Britain as 'aircraft carriers' off the coast of mainland Europe. Although voluntary export restraints[9] limit the market share that Japanese car companies can gain in Europe to single figures, the plants set up in Britain by Nissan, Honda and Toyota are designed to get round such trade barriers. The British plants, which have to date cost £2.5 billion to set up, help the Japanese car makers to overcome the effects of a strong yen which makes it more difficult to sell in overseas markets. But while European car makers feared that the Japanese had found a way of overcoming the trade barriers that the Europeans had erected, the recent figures suggest that the Japanese are not having things all their own way. While European car sales grew by 5 per cent in 1994, Japanese car companies have seen their sales slump by nearly 7 per cent. Their capacity, which was expected to reach 600,000 vehicles in 1994, barely reached 400,000 and their market share, which was 12.5 per cent in 1993, fell back to only 11 per cent in 1994.

Toyota's factory in Burnaston in Derbyshire failed to reach the productivity levels of Japanese factories, operating at 20–30 per cent below the plants in Japan. Nissan, by contrast, has managed to equal and in some instances surpass the productivity levels of equivalent operations in Japan and in 1992 made £28.9 million profit. However, profits fell to just £2.8 million in 1993 as a result of the slump in the European car market. In 1994, it is forecast to make a loss of around £10 million and has cut production from nearly 240,000 to 205,000. Production has switched from the Primera model to the Micra which tends to operate on smaller profit margins thus masking what could be an even greater fall in profitability. Honda plans to double its production to 100,000 vehicles at its Swindon plant, but its market share is only a fraction of that of the other Japanese car makers operating in Britain and it has still to regain its position in the car market after its split with Rover. Mazda has signed a deal to build and sell models in Europe, but this is really a special case as it is 25 per cent owned by Ford and it is likely that Ford will build the models (based on the Fiesta) in its existing UK plant. Therefore, all is not well with the Japanese 'invaders'.

There are a number of reasons why all has not gone quite according to plan. Although the plants must have at least an 80 per cent local content rule under EU regulations, many key parts are still imported. With the yen continuing to be strong, this has added to the costs of production. For example, both Toyota and Nissan have seen the cost of key components like gearboxes, clutches and axles rise by as much as 25 per cent in sterling terms in the last 12 months. In addition, the rising costs of the imported parts have made the task of meeting the 80 per cent local content rule more difficult to meet. To overcome this, Japanese companies are having to consider expensive options such as setting up new axle plants in the UK. Also because of the restrictions in the European markets, Japanese companies have been forced to use local companies to make components and they have often struggled to meet the legendary Japanese standards on quality. In addition, Japanese companies have had problems in setting up dealer networks and are having to redirect their marketing efforts away from selling low-volume, high-margin cars like Toyota's Celica and MR2 sports car range to higher volume, low-margin models. Unfortunately, this is proving more difficult in the depressed market conditions that are now prevailing. Finally, the biggest increase in the European car market in 1995 is likely to occur in France and Germany where the government is heavily subsidising its own car companies and where the Japanese firms are at their weakest owing to the protectionist measures adopted against them by these governments.

These problems have, however, provided a much-needed breathing space for 'local' European car manufacturers. They have improved their own productivity records by, in some cases, aping Japanese production techniques, reaching levels of almost 90 per cent of their Japanese rivals. After 1999, however, when it is expected that the existing barriers against Japanese companies are likely to be removed, Europe is likely to feel the full blast of competition with some analysts estimating that Japanese market share will rise to around 30 per cent by the year 2000. For this reason the 'aircraft carriers' are unlikely to go away.

Adapted from *The Economist*, 10 December 1994.

Questions

1 In what ways has the Japanese invasion benefited Britain's balance of payments accounts? Using the framework of the accounts identified in the text illustrate the way each part of the accounts is affected.

2 What benefits has the invasion had on indigenous (i.e. European) car manufacturers?

3 The British government has adopted a more liberal view of Japanese car companies setting up in the UK than have their European counterparts. In your view, which approach is best?

While it must always be true that the balance of payments must balance, this is only true in the narrow accounting sense. The balance of payments can and often is out of equilibrium. This refers to the situation where we import more than we export at the full employment level of national income. The situation is demonstrated in Figure 2.3.

Figure 2.3

Balance of payments disequilibrium

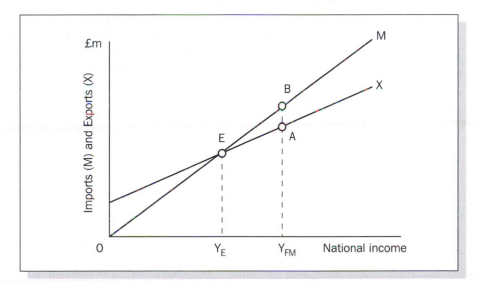

The figure shows that the balance of payments is in equilibrium at point E where exports equal imports. This corresponds with a level of national income of OY_E. The full employment level of national income is however at OY_{FM}. Thus the government is faced with the uncomfortable choice of either reducing the level of national income (thereby increasing unemployment and sacrificing economic growth) or living with the balance of payments deficit.

Clearly, the latter option could only be sustained in the short run. A government could always finance such a deficit by running down its foreign exchange reserves and that is precisely what these reserves are for. However, if this deficit persists then more radical measures are required.

There are three possible ways in which a balance of payments deficit can be 'cured' although it has to be said that each is not without its own particular costs. The three methods are known as 'the 3Ds' and are as follows:

1 Direct controls.
2 Deflation.
3 Devaluation.

Direct controls

Direct controls involve the government introducing controls to limit the volume of imports. This can take the form of quantitative measures such as import quotas on the volume of goods and services imported or it can take the form of an import tariff which is a tax on imported goods. By raising the price of imported goods in relation to domestic goods it is hoped to encourage domestic consumers to switch away from these imported goods to home-produced ones. Both import quotas and import tariffs suffer from the major drawback that the government may be unable to introduce them because of our trade agreements with our international partners. The Single European Market effectively rules out such measures as far as Britain's European partners are concerned and other obligations, like Britain's agreements under the World Trade Organisation (WTO), rule out any unilateral action on its part against the UK's other international trading partners. Failure to observe these treaty obligations is in any event likely to rebound on the UK as other countries would be likely to retaliate against its goods and services. Even if the UK could impose such measures it is by no means certain that they would work anyway. If the imported goods in question were not being produced by UK firms or it was extremely expensive for them to do so, then either UK consumers would still spend money on importing the goods (thereby resulting in the taxes imposed going to the government with a subsequent fall in aggregate demand in the economy) or resources would be diverted to producing these goods and away from producing those things in which we have some expertise.

Deflation

Deflation involves raising taxes and reducing government expenditure in a way that is designed to lower the level of aggregate demand in the economy. The aim of such measures is to reduce the level of consumer spending and hence the level of imports. In addition, by lowering demand in the economy it is hoped that this will reduce the price level in the domestic economy and hence improve the competitiveness of our own exports. This was the approach that was consistently followed in the 1950s and 1960s when the UK economy was faced with periodic balance of payments problems. The 'downside' of this approach is all too familiar. The internal objectives of macroeconomic policy (namely, economic growth and full employment) are sacrificed in order to achieve an external balance. In addition, the approach lacks precision in that all consumer spending is affected, whether this involves expenditure on imports or not. Deflation has a kind of 'scatter-gun' approach which tends to hit those sectors which are not directly in the firing line. In terms of Figure 2.3 deflation reduces the level of national income, thereby moving more towards OY_E. The 'trick' for the government to pull off would be to lower the M curve at all levels of income (reducing Britain's propensity to import, to use economists' jargon) and at the same time increase its propensity to export (i.e. raising the X curve) so that both graph lines intersect at OY_{FM}. Deflation as a weapon often fails to achieve these 'shifts' so that when the government aims to restore full employment and achieve faster economic growth the same disequilibrium problems re-emerge. It is for this reason that the balance of payments constraint bedevilled economic policy for decades.

Devaluation

A more radical approach is to devalue the currency in terms of other currencies, thereby improving the competitiveness of our exports while at the same time increasing the costs of importing. This, on the face of it, represents a way of shifting the X and M curves so that a balance can be achieved at full employment. Before examining the case for such an approach it is necessary to look at the basic theory of exchange rates.

Exchange rates: Theory and practice

The exchange rate is no more than a price. It is the price of one currency in terms of another. Like most prices it is determined by the forces of supply and demand, and these prices are made on the computer screens of millions of dealers in foreign exchanges around the world. To illustrate the basic theory let us imagine that there are only two countries in our world, the UK and Germany. The rate of exchange between these two countries is determined by the factors in Figure 2.4.

The demand for sterling (£) comes from our exports. As UK firms require to be paid in sterling, German companies will go to the foreign exchange markets and demand sterling for which they will exchange Deutschmarks (DM). Similarly, if a German company wishes to set up a plant in the UK (the import of capital into the UK) they will require £ to do this and again will demand £. UK imports from Germany, on the other hand, require UK firms and customers to pay in DM. This necessitates UK companies supplying £ in exchange for DM. Similarly, a UK company wishing to set up in Germany (the export of capital) will supply £ and receive DM in exchange. As with the demand for most goods the higher the price one is required to pay the less the demand. Equally, the higher the price, the more willing are people prepared to supply. The relevant supply and demand diagrams are given in Figure 2.5.

The diagram indicates that the market-clearing rate is 2.50DM/£. Let us assume that at this rate of exchange there is an equilibrium in the balance of payments and that the export of goods and services to Germany (and the

Figure 2.4

Operation of foreign exchange markets in a two-country world

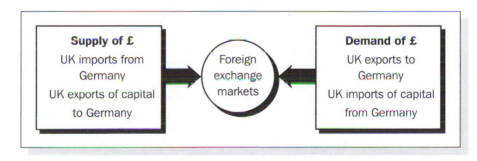

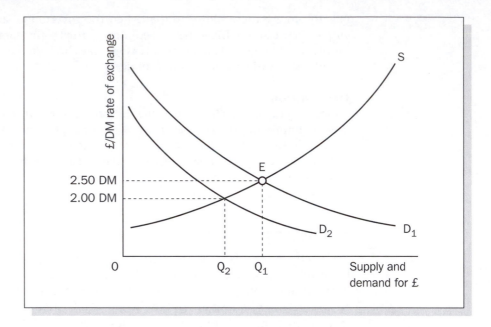

Figure 2.5
**Supply and demand
in foreign exchange
markets**

import of capital from Germany) exactly matches the import of goods and services from Germany (and the export of UK capital to Germany). Under these conditions there is no tendency for the rate to move and providing that price levels, growth rates and the level of interest rates remain the same this situation can continue indefinitely. However, suppose that our inflation rate starts to rise faster than the rate in Germany and, as a consequence, our goods become less attractive to German consumers. This will have the effect of reducing our exports and the demand curve for £ will shift to the left to D_2. As can be seen from the diagram the exchange rate has now fallen to 2.00DM/£. A number of consequences of this will now occur.

First, German consumers will only have to part with 2DM to purchase £1 of UK goods, a 20 per cent reduction in price which makes the purchase very much more attractive than before. Alternatively, a UK product, which was selling in Germany for 100DM, would previously have yielded a sterling price of £40 (100DM/2.50). Now it returns a sterling price of £50 (100DM/2.00). Either way, UK exports have now become an attractive proposition. (In reality, UK exporters would probably compromise between passing all the benefits on to German consumers and taking all the profit themselves by charging a DM price of say 90DM and yielding a sterling price of £45 (90DM/2.00).)

On the import side, it would work in the reverse direction. UK consumers would find that they are now required to pay a higher price for importing German goods. A Mercedes car, which might have cost £30,000 to import, would have required a British consumer to find 75,000DM at the old exchange rate. This is the price it is assumed that the German car company charges for its cars in the UK. To pay this price of 75,000DM will now require £37,500 (75,000DM/2.00), an increase of 25 per cent in the sterling price. By this process, UK exports will rise and UK imports will fall until the balance is restored again.

Before reading on, what are the possible drawbacks of this apparently simple method of restoring a balance of payments?

The first danger is that a devaluation of the £ (or a downward float, as in our example) will increase inflation. There are two ways in which this might occur. First, the cost of imported goods has risen. If these are, for example, component parts in the production process then the rising costs will feed through as either increased prices or lower profit margins. Secondly, the price of finished goods will also rise, and if these form a significant part of consumer spending then consumers will find that their real spending is adversely affected. Workers may seek pay rises to compensate, with consequent losses in UK competitiveness.

The second adverse effect may in fact be experienced on the side of the balance of payments that is expected to do well, namely exports. If the economy is already operating at or near full capacity then the boost in demand for exports (caused by the fall in the £ price of UK goods abroad) may simply add to the inflationary pressures. Thus any advantage that is gained from the devaluation may quickly be eroded.

The third disadvantage concerns the demand for imports as a result of the changes in price (the elasticity of demand, to use economists' terminology; see Chapter 7 for further details). If the demand is not very responsive and, as a result of a 25 per cent increase in the £ price of the Mercedes quoted in the section above, demand falls by only 1 per cent, then paradoxically the situation could get worse as the import bill, instead of falling as the theory predicts, will in fact rise.

The fourth disadvantage concerns the role of the expectations in the foreign exchange markets. If buyers of £ feel that the exchange rate has still not yet reached its market clearing level, or if they doubt the government's ability to pursue policies designed to correct the imbalance in the trading position, they may continue to sell £ and retreat into buying 'safer' currencies. This can set up dangerous forces which are sometimes difficult to stop. Government action to prevent a run on a currency (for example, by raising interest rates to encourage foreigners to buy £) can often exacerbate the situation with each move being regarded by the market as a panic measure resulting in a further reduction in confidence and a further wave of selling. Although this process will eventually peter out, the damage may well have been done by that time.

Finally, devaluation is only likely to work if other countries are prepared to accept it. If, to return to our two-country example, the German authorities were to resist attempts to allow the £ to fall by devaluing their own currency then no gains would be achieved from allowing the price of £ to fall. This competitive devaluation would in effect render the policy useless.

For these reasons it has been argued that devaluation by itself is unlikely to be the panacea that the simple theory would imply.[10] Because of this, attempts have been made to introduce systems which allow a degree of flexibility in exchange rates while at the same time attempting to retain the stability that fixed exchange rates offer. One such system is the Exchange Rate Mechanism (ERM), as indicated in Case Study 2.5.

CASE STUDY **2.5**

Does devaluation provide a 'free lunch'?

In 1992 Britain was forced to leave the Exchange Rate Mechanism. Since our departure from the ERM the £ has fallen in value by 16 per cent. Sweden also abandoned its policy of linking its currency, the krona, to the ECU and watched as its value fell by 24 per cent. Spain experienced the first of its four devaluations within the ERM and the peseta fell by 22 per cent while Italy's currency, the lira fell by no less than 34 per cent.

As a consequence of these upheavals the exports of these countries have soared on average by over 10 per cent in the past two years whilst the rest of Europe achieved export growth of about half that rate. Inflation, instead of soaring as was predicted, was lower in 1994 for the devaluing countries concerned than in 1992. Thus devaluation seemed to be a resounding success with little evidence of the 'downside' that was predicted. Indeed, the experience of Britain, Sweden, Spain and Italy would appear to undermine the case for ERM and the move towards a single currency. Devaluation, it seemed was a costless option – a 'free lunch' in fact.

The answer to this apparent paradox lies in an analysis of the circumstances in which devaluations are likely to work. Devaluation is only likely to work if a number of conditions apply. First, there must be spare capacity otherwise the increased demand for exports will simply feed through to higher prices. Secondly, workers must be prepared to accept lower real wages because if they do not then the competitive effects of devaluation will simply be eroded in higher pay. Thirdly, if imports form a very small proportion of a country's national income the effects of higher import prices will be much more muted than if imports form a significant percentage of GDP.

When we examine the situation with the '1992 devaluers' we discover that some, if not all, of these factors were present. Their economies had just been through a deep recession so there was a significant level of spare capacity. In addition, in order to try to keep within the mechanism all the countries concerned had pursued very tight monetary policies, so tight in fact that had they remained in the ERM mechanism then some argue that inflation would have been negative. In other words, they were already pursuing policies which were bearing down very heavily on inflation and hence the inflationary impact of devaluation was more than offset. Finally, consumer confidence and competition in the depressed home markets of the 'devaluers' meant that producers had little scope for passing on the imported price increases.

However, these special combination of circumstances are unlikely to persist indefinitely and there are already signs in all the economies that they are reaching full capacity (as a result of the boost to aggregate demand that their economies received from the boom in exports). In addition, there are signs that inflationary pressures are beginning to build as producer prices rise (an early warning signal of inflation to come).

Adapted from *The Economist*, 25 March 1995.

Questions
1   Is it better for a country to be inside a mechanism that ensures that its exchange rate is stable or should the country have total freedom of action to devalue (or revalue) its currency?
2   Why is devaluation not a 'free lunch'?

Fixed or floating exchange rates?

There has been much debate about the merits of fixed or floating rates of exchange. The arguments in favour of one system are often 'mirror' images of the arguments against the other. While floating rates allow exchange rates to adjust to changing economic circumstances, they introduce uncertainty into international transactions. On the other hand, fixed rates introduce certainty but at the cost of flexibility. The arguments for and against fixed and floating rates are summarised in Tables 2.14 and 2.15.

Table 2.14

Arguments for and against fixed exchange rates

For fixed rates	Against fixed rates
➤ Certainty	➤ Encourages speculation
➤ Stability	➤ 'One way' bet
➤ Confidence	➤ Government required to 'defend' £
➤ Anti-inflationary	➤ Internal objectives (growth, full employment) sacrificed
➤ Reduces speculation	➤ Can't cope with sudden shocks
➤ Encourages 'responsible' macroeconomic policies	➤ Can't cope with countries growing or inflating at different rates
➤ Encourages trade	

Table 2.15

Arguments for and against floating exchange rates

For floating rates	Against floating rates
➤ Allows automatic adjustment	➤ May make matters worse depending on elasticity of demand
➤ Reduces speculation ('two way' bet)	➤ Uncertainty
➤ Internal/external objectives not in conflict	➤ Lack of confidence
➤ Can handle sudden shocks	➤ Adversely affects trade
➤ Can handle countries inflating or growing at different rates	➤ Increases transactions costs
	➤ Inflationary
	➤ Encourages 'irresponsible' macroeconomic policies

Those economists who are in favour of flexible or floating rates of exchange argue that, far from encouraging speculation, floating rates deter speculators because rates can go down as well as up (the so-called 'two way' bet) as opposed to the 'one way' bet with fixed rates. At the present moment the UK government is pursuing a policy of allowing exchange rates to find their own level in the foreign exchange markets. However, if the UK government were ever to join a single currency the rates would be fixed. (For details see Chapter 3.)

Conclusions

This chapter has looked at the three important topics in international economics. Firstly, we have examined the theory of international trade and looked at the advantages and disadvantages of free trade. Secondly, we have examined the balance of payments accounts and looked at ways of correcting balance of payments deficits. Finally, we have looked at the way exchange rates are determined and the economic impact of fixed and floating rates. The next chapter looks at some of these macroeconomic issues in more detail.

Notes
········

1 *The Economist*, 11 May 1991.
2 Golub, S. (1995) 'Comparative and absolute advantage in the Asia Pacific Region', Federal Reserve Bank of San Francisco, Workiing Paper, quoted in *The Economist*, November 1995, p. 142.
3 *The Financial Times*, 25 November 1993.
4 Bhagwati, J. (1996) 'The demands to reduce domestic diversity among trading nations', in J. Bhagwati and R. Hudec (eds) *Fair Trade and Harmonisation: Prerequisites for Free Trade*? MIT Press.
5 Quoted in *The Economist*, 7 October 1995, p. 142.
6 Quoted in *The Economist*, 14 September 1996, p. 108.
7 A debt instrument designed in the late 1980s by the US Treasury to restructure sovereign debts and discourage defaults.
8 www.agitprop.org/artandrevolution/wto/index.html
9 For further details of voluntary export restraints, see Chapter 11.
10 See *The Economist* (1996) 'A much devalued theory', 20 January, pp. 82–3.

References and additional reading
···

Curwin, P. ed. (1994) *Understanding the UK Economy*, Macmillan, London.

The Economist (1998) 'Euro Brief: Eleven into one may go', 17 October, pp. 113–14.

The Economist (1998) 'Euro Brief: The merits of one money', 24 October, pp. 135–6.

The Economist (1998) 'Euro Brief: Euro Towers or Fawlty Towers?', 31 October, pp. 99–100.

The Economist (2000) 'The Debate that will not die', 17 June, pp. 33–4.

Gough, J. (2000) *Introductory Economics for Business and Management*, McGraw-Hill, London, esp. ch. 12.

Griffiths, A. and Wall, S. (1997) *Applied Economics*, Longman, London, esp. ch. 19, pp. 468–90; ch. 20, pp. 492–519; ch. 24, pp. 602–28; and ch. 27, pp. 697–710.

Holden, K., Matthews, K. and Thompson, J. (1995) *The UK Economy Today*, Manchester University Press, Manchester.

Perman, R. and Scouller, J. (1999) *Business Economics*, Oxford University Press, Oxford, esp. ch. 16.

Sloman, J. (2000) *Economics*, Financial Times Prentice Hall, London, esp. chs 23 and 24.

CHAPTER 3

Macroeconomic issues

Objectives

By the end of this chapter you will be able to:

➤ Evaluate the contribution of Keynesian, monetarist and New Classical theories to the achievement of full employment.

➤ Understand the conflicts between the key objectives of economic policy and evaluate the concept of the Phillips curve.

➤ Understand the role that rational expectations play in economic policy.

➤ Analyse what is meant by 'supply-side economics'.

➤ Evaluate what is meant by the 'new economics'.

➤ Examine the case for and against the UK's entry into the single European currency.

Key concepts

Adaptive expectations: a situation where people's expectations about the future are based on the immediate past.

Aggregate demand: the total level of demand for goods and services in the economy. It is made up of the expenditure of four sectors; namely, households (consumers' expenditure), business (investment expenditure), government sector (government expenditure) and the overseas sector (exports minus imports).

Deflationary gap: when the level of aggregate demand falls below the full employment level of national income.

Demand deficient unemployment: the level of unemployment created as a result of a deflationary gap.

Equilibrium real wage: a situation where the level of wages (adjusted to take account of price inflation) is such that the demand for labour exactly matches the supply of labour in a given market.

Fiscal policy: the use of taxation as a means of controlling the economy.

Full employment: a situation where all those who are seeking employment and who are able to be employed are employed. This has come to be regarded as being consistent with around 2–3 per cent unemployment.

Income effect: this results in the worker striving to make up for the loss of earnings through higher taxes by working longer and harder.

Keynesian school: those economists who believe in the theories of John Maynard Keynes. They believe in active intervention in the economy, mainly by fiscal policy, to influence the level of aggregate demand.

Monetarists: the term given to those economists who believe that there is a strong correlation between the money supply and the rate of price

increases. The principal economist whose theories underpin this view is
Professor Milton Friedman.

New classical school: economists who believe in the effectiveness of market-
orientated policies particularly in labour markets. Unemployment according
to this view is caused by inefficiency in operations of the labour market.

Non-accelerating-inflation rate of unemployment (NAIRU): the level of
unemployment which will result in a stable rate of inflation, sometimes called
the 'natural rate of unemployment'. Attempts by government to reduce
unemployment to below this level will result in a faster rate of inflation.

Phillips curve: the relationship between the level of unemployment and the
rate of growth wages (and hence prices). It appeared to show that there was
a stable relationship between unemployment and prices and that
governments could choose different combinations of the two.

Public sector borrowing requirement (PSBR): this is the deficit of the
central and local government and the deficits of the nationalised industries.
It is the amount of money that the government is required to borrow. This
term has been replaced by the term **public sector net borrowing
(PSNB)** which measures essentially the same thing.

Rational expectations: this concept applies to the situation whereby
people's expectations are based on all available information about the state
of the economy. People therefore do not use any 'rules' to guide them (e.g.
expectations about this year's level of inflation are based on last year's level
plus x per cent) since this leads to systematic errors. Instead they forecast
the future correctly on average. Unforeseen events will often mean that
people's expectations are wrong, but they are just as likely to overestimate
as to underestimate.

Substitution effect: this is when the worker, faced with higher income taxes,
works less and takes more leisure (i.e. substitutes the now relatively cheaper
'leisure' for the more expensive 'work'). The two effects combine to result in
either more or less effort from workers as a result of higher taxes on
incomes.

Supply-side economists: economists who believe that government measures
should focus on improving the ability of the economy to increase the
supply of goods and services. They take the view that this is best done by
making markets (both for goods and services and for factors of production)
work more efficiently. Thus they are in favour of removing any barriers to
this objective (e.g. the monopoly power of trade unions and state
industries; welfare benefits which make it better for people to refuse to
work; minimum wage legislation and wages councils). They are in favour of
measures which improve work effort (e.g. tax cuts) and also increase
productivity (e.g. education and training).

Introduction
··················

In this chapter we will look at a number of important contemporary macroeconomic issues that impinge upon the economic environment in which firms
operate. We will look at some of the current debates in this area and evaluate
the impact that these will have on the business environment. The first issue,

which draws on material from Chapter 1, is a domestic one, and looks at whether governments can create full employment. The second major issue, which draws on material from Chapter 2, is an international one and looks at whether it is a good idea for the UK to join the single European currency.

Issue 1: Can governments create full employment?

The Keynesian solution

What factors affect unemployment? Can and should governments do anything about achieving full employment? One controversial theory states that there is what is called a demand deficient type of unemployment. The debate surrounding this type of unemployment centres on the question of whether governments can in fact create full employment by manipulating the level of demand in the economy. This school of thought, which was influential for almost 40 years in the post-war period, is described as the Keynesian school, named after the economist John Maynard Keynes. According to this school of thought, governments have a responsibility to ensure that the aggregate demand in the economy is kept at a level that consistently maintains the full employment of the labour force. Aggregate demand refers here to the total spending on the goods and services produced in the domestic economy and includes elements such as consumer spending, investment, government spending and spending on UK exports. If aggregate demand falls below the level consistent with having around 2–3 per cent unemployment (full employment), the government should, in this view, take the necessary action in order to ensure that any deficiency in demand is removed and full employment is maintained.

The main factors that influence aggregate demand were set out in Chapter 1 in Figure 1.6. In addition, a number of the main influences on the components of aggregate demand are also listed. The Keynesian view is that in order to maintain full employment the government should use fiscal policy (government spending or taxation policy) in order to boost demand. Failure to do so will result in demand deficient unemployment. The task of government is seen to be relatively straightforward. First, the government will estimate the 'gap' between the current level of aggregate demand in the economy and the level of aggregate demand needed to give a 'full employment' level of national income and output. Having identified this gap – known as the deflationary gap – the authorities 'prime the pump' by injecting the appropriate amount of demand by a combination of tax cuts and increases in government expenditure. As indicated in Chapter 1, they are not required to inject the whole amount because of a process known as the multiplier effect, whereby an initial increase in aggregate demand results in a much larger eventual increase in aggregate demand (for details, see page 10). Take, for example, extra government spending on health care under which more nurses and doctors are employed. Any increases in their incomes are then passed on in increased consumer spending, which eventually becomes income for other people who, in turn, will spend a proportion of that new income. This will become income for yet another group of people, and so on. So, if the authorities know the size of the 'gap' (say, £20 billion) and they are able to estimate the size of the multiplier (say 2), then it becomes a relatively straightforward matter (in theory at least) for the government to pump £10 billion into the economy in a combination of tax cuts and expenditure increases in order to close the 'gap'.

The monetarist critique

The Keynesian view of unemployment has, however, been challenged by an alternative school of economic thought. This school comprises those who are loosely identified as monetarists and their key objection to this view of unemployment is that they do not believe that governments can have any significant effect on the level of unemployment. These criticisms gained force in the late 1970s when it became apparent that the so-called Keynesian demand management policies were simply not working. A number of reasons were suggested for the failure of Keynesian policies.

First, it was clear that the authorities did not have as much knowledge and information about the state of the economy as they might need to estimate with any certainty the size of the 'deflationary gap' – (this gap being the shortfall in demand below the level needed for full employment output). Most of the data on which to base such a judgement was unfortunately out of date, usually by as much as three to six months in the case of figures for economic growth. Therefore, when the Chancellor had to make his Budget decisions he would be working with imperfect information.

Secondly, it was well known that fiscal policy changes usually took some time to be effective. The time lag was often as much as 6 to 18 months before the effects were fully felt.

The combination of these two things often had unforeseen consequences. In effect, the government would make changes based on a situation which was six months out of date, and the results of the changes were not felt until a year to 18 months later. It is little wonder that commentators described policy at this time as being either 'too little too late' or 'too much too late'. Steering the economy in this manner can be described as like driving a car down a road in the Alps with the front screen blacked out and with only the rear view mirror to direct the driver. In addition, the brakes and accelerator do not work instantaneously and the steering wheel has a delayed action! Keeping the car (economy) on track is obviously difficult in these circumstances and it is perhaps no surprise that demand management policies came to be regarded as an ineffective way of maintaining full employment.

However, critics had a far more damaging set of criticisms to make of Keynesian theories. They argued that even if the government had perfect knowledge and that the policy weapons worked instantaneously, it was not possible for the authorities to create jobs in the way described. First, it was pointed out that cutting taxes and increasing government spending has the effect of increasing the government's public sector borrowing requirement (PSBR),[1] i.e. the difference between public spending and tax revenue. A higher PSBR increases the calls on the money market to lend the government money in order to finance this deficit. The effect, it was argued, would be to 'crowd out' private investment and consumption. The mechanism is that money markets would only lend more if they were offered higher interest rates, which would then discourage private sector investment and consumption. An extreme version of 'crowding out' claims that for every £1 of extra government borrowing, private consumption and/or investment will fall by the same amount, thereby leaving aggregate demand unaltered.

Rational expectations and the Phillips curve

In addition to the 'crowding out' effect, critics introduced the concept of rational expectations. This concept has to a large extent undermined the key principles of the demand management school of thought. To understand its significance it is necessary to look at some theory of labour markets. In 1958 a New Zealand economist, Bill Phillips, published a paper that was to dominate thinking about economic policy for a generation. Based on data taken over a long period (from 1861 to 1957), he discovered a relationship between the level of unemployment and the rate of change of money wages (and hence inflation).[2] This relationship, which became known as the Phillips curve, appeared to offer convincing proof that the government could 'trade off' lower unemployment for higher rates of inflation. Figure 3.1 outlines the relationship.

This indicates that as unemployment rises from U_1 to U_2 so inflation falls from P_1 to P_2 and vice versa. However, the Phillips curve relationship has not held up too well. In the UK the relationship seems to have begun to break down by about 1968 and, in the USA, by about 1970. There appears to have been a shift in the Phillips curve to the right, as illustrated in Figure 3.2.

As the curve moves to the right, a given level of unemployment is associated with a higher level of inflation. The explanation of this phenomenon is provided by the role of expectations (Table 3.1).

Figure 3.1

The Phillips curve

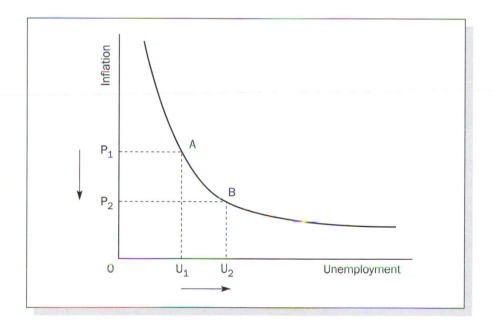

Figure 3.2
Shift in the Phillips curve

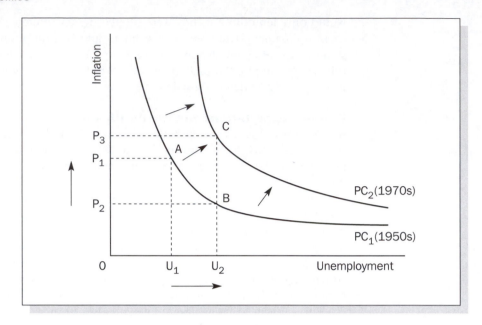

Table 3.1
The role of expectations

Time period (t)	1	2	3	4	5	6	7	8
A Actual rate of inflation %	0	2	4	8	10	6	4	2
B Expected rate of inflation (based on previous time period)	0	0	2	4	8	10	6	4
C Divergence from expectation (A − B)	0	2	2	4	2	−4	−2	−2
D Expected rate of inflation based on rational expectations	0	0	4	5	12	6	8	1
E Divergence from rational expectations (A − D)	0	2	0	3	−2	0	−4	+1

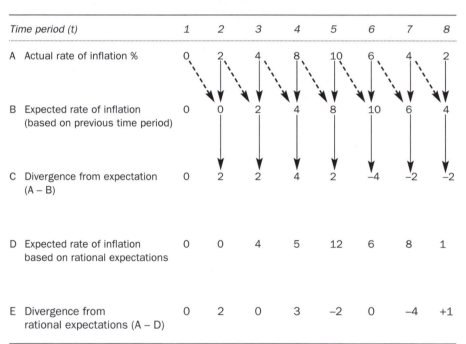

Many believed that the explanation for the breakdown in the Phillips curve relationship lay mainly with the concept of rational expectations. In essence, what this meant is that the government can 'fool some of the people some of the time but it can't fool all of the people all of the time'. People will, it is claimed, predict the future correctly on average. Imagine the situation where there is substantial unemployment so that the government decides to raise the level of aggregate demand. This reduces unemployment but raises inflation from, say, 2 per cent to 4 per cent. The increase in employment will only be permanent as long as workers do not try to compensate for the increase in inflation by raising their wages in line with the new and higher rate of inflation. If workers base their expectations about inflation on last year's price rises then there will always be a chance that real wages will fail to adjust. It follows that if inflation is increasing, then many wage claims for this year will be lower than the increase in this year's prices. Real wages will therefore fall and the extra employment can be maintained over time. There will be a tendency for real wages to lag behind changes in prices when inflation is accelerating, giving a boost to employment. In short, employment can only be expanded if workers willingly accept a reduction in their real earnings. Table 3.1 illustrates the point about expectations.

This illustrates the situation known as *adaptive expectations*, where workers are applying a rule (namely, that expectations about this year's inflation rate are based on last year's rate). This clearly results in a systematic error being made by workers. They literally do not learn from their mistakes but are fooled all of the time. Rational expectations stem from the belief that such behaviour is irrational. Workers will clearly not go on making the same mistakes time after time. Instead they will learn to take account of past errors and look at all available information about future prospects in the economy. Government action, which in the past has resulted in higher rates of inflation, will form part of the information around which workers will base their expectations. Of course they will not always guess correctly and will occasionally make mistakes. The difference here, however, is that the mistakes will be more random, so that there will be no tendency for workers to either consistently over-predict or under-predict next year's rate of inflation. The key question is how quickly will workers adjust their expectations? If, as is argued by some critics, the adjustment of expectations by workers is almost instantaneous, then there simply is no possibility that government action can create permanent employment. At the very moment that the government announces a reflationary package of tax cuts and increases in government spending, workers will accurately anticipate higher inflation next year and will immediately demand and receive large pay awards in anticipation that these will be needed to maintain the real wage. Real wages will remain unaltered.

The situation, however, is not simply just as before. What in effect has happened is that the economy now experiences a higher rate of inflation but with the same level of unemployment. There is, in effect, no trade-off between unemployment and inflation. In short, the new Phillips curve is a vertical straight line, as illustrated in Figure 3.3.

Therefore, it is argued, the government cannot create jobs by simply pumping money into the economy.[3]

However, before looking at the neo-classical school it is interesting to examine the most recent data on unemployment to see if there is any evidence to support the contention that there is no trade-off between unemployment and inflation. The data for the period 1989–1999 is given in Figure 3.4.

Figure 3.3
No trade-off between unemployment and inflation

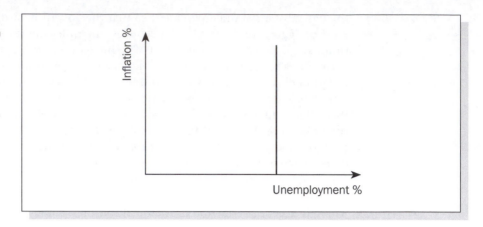

Figure 3.4
Phillips curve 1989–1999

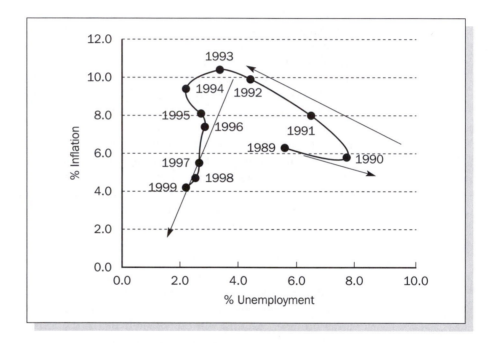

Interestingly, from 1989 to 1993 there appears to be a kind of Phillips curve relationship in operation. As unemployment rises, inflation falls and vice versa. However, as we move from 1993 to 1999 we discover that there appears to be a leftward shift of the curve, which is the exact opposite of the effects we have been discussing above.

PAUSE FOR THOUGHT 1 *Before reading on, why do you think that unemployment and inflation have fallen over the last five years?*

One possible explanation appears to be that as the rate of inflation has fallen, so expectations of higher rates in the future have been revised downwards. This is therefore having a beneficial effect with the government able to run the economy at lower levels of unemployment without incurring an upsurge in inflation.

The neo-classical school

What is the explanation of this new phenomenon? If Keynesian demand management policies are not the way to increase employment, what, if anything, can governments do to solve the problem of unemployment? The answer lies more in the area of the microeconomics of the labour market, according to a school of economists known as the neo-classical school. They believe that governments can influence the rate of unemployment by either reducing or increasing the flexibility of labour markets. Labour markets are described as being 'rigid' if certain factors are having an undue influence on the way the markets operate.

These factors may be listed as follows:

➤ Trade unions.
➤ 'Insiders' versus 'outsiders'.
➤ Imperfect information.
➤ Minimum wage.
➤ Taxation.
➤ Welfare benefits.

Trade unions

Trade unions can affect the way in which labour markets operate because they act as monopoly suppliers of labour, able to raise wages above the 'market clearing' rate. Figure 3.5 illustrates the point.

The equilibrium real wage at which supply and demand are balanced is given by the level RW_E in Figure 3.5. However, if trade unions are able to push real wages to the level RW_1 then the effect is to reduce the demand for labour to OL_1, leaving a gap between supply and demand of L_1L_2. Thus the aggressive behaviour of trade unions can damage jobs, so the argument runs. The evidence to support this proposition is mixed. Those countries where the level of unionisation has been low have, in the past few years, experienced faster rates of job creation. This has been the case in the United States where unionisation

Figure 3.5

Trade unions and the labour market

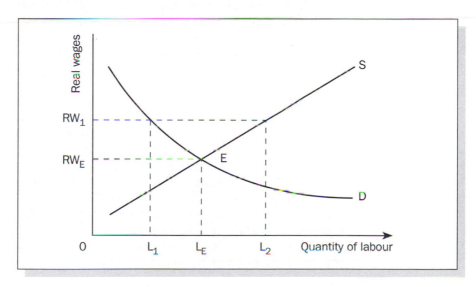

is only around 15 per cent. In contrast, in European economies where the level of unionisation is much higher, the rate of job growth has been slower in recent years.[4] It is for this reason that governments have sought to limit the power of trade unions to influence labour markets by banning the closed shop and reducing their legal immunities, as in the case of strike action.

'Insiders' versus 'outsiders'

The second reason for rigidity in the labour market is a phenomenon known as the 'insider–outsider' theory of labour markets. This theory has been developed to take account of the situation where high levels of unemployment co-existed with high rates of inflation. In theory this should not happen, as a large pool of unemployed workers should cause real wages to fall, thus increasing the demand for labour and reducing the levels of unemployment. While it is acknowledged that inflation may be caused by factors other than pressure on wages (such as 'cost–push' factors), it was often difficult to explain away periods of inflation which coincided with high levels of unemployment. The 'insider–outsider' theory suggests that the labour market is, in fact, a dual market, which is split into those workers who have the requisite skills (insiders) and those who have not (outsiders). If workers have been out of work for any significant length of time it becomes more difficult for them to re-enter the labour market. In effect, they are outside the labour market and, more importantly, do not exercise the same influence on real wages as those workers who do have the relevant skills. Employers are more likely to employ workers who have been unemployed for only short periods because they will still possess many of the relevant skills and it will cost the employer less to reintegrate them into the labour force. Thus it is possible to have intense competition between firms for those who are currently employed (or who have been recently unemployed) while at the same time a significant proportion of the labour force remains unemployed. Wage inflation together with high levels of long-term unemployment can therefore be seen to co-exist. The solution is to try to retrain the long-term unemployed and thereby encourage them to develop the skills that are going to make them employable. Only then can they be regarded as 'insiders' and place downward pressures on wages by effectively increasing the labour supply. Of course this may be a slow process. However, only by focusing on the 'micro' level of the labour market will government action be successful, according to this theory.

Imperfect information

A variation of this view is provided by imperfect information about the quality of labour that is being purchased by employers. This theory states that employers have no real information about the true level of the skills they are purchasing. They do know, however, that those workers who are highly skilled tend to be those who have received a better education and who have undertaken training to acquire the necessary skills. These workers will have a certain minimum level of wages – often determined by market conditions – below which they will be unwilling to work. Thus a worker who is familiar with the latest computer software in, for example, accounting will be in demand and thus will have a certain 'market price' or minimum wage below which it would not be sensible for an employer to offer if he or she wishes to retain (or capture) the worker's services. It is argued that even if there is generally an excess of supply over demand in the labour market, firms will then be reluctant to reduce wages for certain categories of worker for fear of losing what they perceive to be their best quality workers. It is argued that the market mechanism in this case operates in a one-way direction. It raises wages when there are particular skill shortages, but does not reduce real wages when there is an excess supply of labour. The fear is that 'if we pay peanuts we will employ monkeys'.

Minimum wage

A further source of rigidity is the existence of a minimum wage. Theory suggests that fixing a minimum wage at a level which is above the market clearing rate will in effect cause unemployment. We can usefully return to Figure 3.5 but this time interpret the real wage level RW_1 as the government-imposed legal minimum wage and we can then see the likely consequences. By imposing a minimum wage that is greater than the level that would be determined by the market, an unemployment gap has been opened up (L_1L_2). In these circumstances it is difficult to see what the attraction of minimum wage legislation can be. There is little doubt that if a level is fixed for the minimum wage that is seriously at odds with market wage rates, then unemployment will be an inevitable consequence.

However, the situation is often not quite as simple as described above. One of the effects of raising wages, especially at the bottom end of the income scale, is that it will add to aggregate demand. This in turn can have the effect of pushing the whole demand curve for labour (D in Figure 3.5) to the right. In these circumstances there are likely to be two effects, each operating in the opposite direction. One effect is to raise the costs of employing labour; this can be viewed as an employment-destroying measure. The other effect is to increase the demand for labour (by raising the level of aggregate demand); this can be seen as a labour-enhancing measure. It is difficult to say, with any precision, which of these two effects will be the stronger at any one time and much will depend on the actual level at which the minimum wage is set.

In France, for example, the minimum wage rose from around 40 per cent of the national average in the 1970s to about 50 per cent in the mid-1980s. Unemployment among young workers in France (generally regarded as among the lowest paid) in the same period rose from 4 per cent to more than 20 per cent. In the United States, by contrast, youth unemployment fell when the minimum wage was reduced from about 40 per cent of the national average to 30 per cent.[5]

PAUSE FOR THOUGHT 2

1 *Outline the case for and against a minimum wage in the UK.*
2 *What do you understand by the expression 'increasing the flexibility of the labour market'?*
3 *Outline the various measures that can be used to increase labour market mobility.*

In the United Kingdom the introduction of a national minimum wage appears to have been implemented without serious economic effects as the following case illustrates.

CASE STUDY **3.1**

Minimum wage, minimum impact?

A report published in early 2000 by Incomes Data Services (IDS) argued that fears about the economic impact of the national minimum wage (NMW) had proved groundless. The IDS report in effect supported the views of such bodies as the Low Pay Commission (LPC), which argued that there should be an increase in the wage to a new rate of £3.70 from April 2000.

The IDS report team reached five important conclusions from this research. These were:

➤ The NMW did not bring a sharp upwards step in average earnings in the spring of 1999.
➤ The predicted job losses did not occur. In fact over 1999 there were major job gains in the services sector.
➤ The trend in youth pay is to pay adult rates from age 18.
➤ The NMW had very little impact on differentials.
➤ Compliance with the level of £3.60 was relatively straightforward.

The report went on that, contrary to some predictions when it was first introduced, the minimum wage did not lead to a sharp upward trend in average earnings in the spring of 1999. Predicted job losses also failed to materialise. The IDS reports that there were major job gains in the services sector as a result of broader economic conditions. The new statutory minimum pay had 'very little' impact on differentials, according to the IDS analysis, and most parts of industry found the new minimum wage regulations relatively straightforward.

The study concedes that it has not 'all been plain sailing'. In some sectors such as the riding-school sector, the system of 'working pupils' who traditionally did not receive wages has had to be rethought and charitable bodies have had problems in defining who is an employee and who is a volunteer. The issue of tips in restaurants was also problematic, with a number of major chains changing their pay arrangements.

These problems aside, IDS concludes that the introduction of the rate 'has been relatively orderly and many of the earlier worries about job loss, the disruption of pay structures and the impact on differentials have been found to be groundless.'

The research group comments that many organisations think the minimum wage should be increased annually and were surprised that no such mechanism was set by the legislation. However, commenting on the success of the NMW, the Trade and Industry Secretary, Mr Stephen Byers said:

The introduction of the National Minimum Wage has been a tremendous success. It has been instrumental in taking some 1.5 million people out of the trap of poverty wages without having an adverse impact on employment.

Michael Portillo, the new shadow Chancellor, also ended the Conservatives' opposition to the minimum wage. But he left the Tories with room for manoeuvre by promising that although the minimum wage would not be abolished in the short term, it would be continuously reviewed.

Adapted from Income Data Services Report No. 802, February 2000.

Questions

1   Why do you think there has been so little adverse economic impact of the minimum wage?

2   Why do you think the Opposition has dropped their objections to the minimum wage?

Taxation

A further factor, which can affect the efficient operation of the labour market, is the tax system. Higher taxes introduce distortions and rigidities by affecting both the supply of labour and the demand for labour. For example, higher rates of income tax reduce the amount of 'take home' pay a worker receives, and can have two effects. The first effect may result in the worker striving to make up for the loss of earnings by working longer and harder. This is known as the income effect because workers are working more to regain lost income. The second effect, however, works in exactly the opposite direction. Imagine that a worker is paid £10 per hour and the tax rate is 25 per cent. In effect, this worker is receiving £8 after tax for supplying an extra hour's effort (and giving up an extra hour's leisure). If income tax rates are now raised to 50 per cent, then the worker will receive only £5 after tax. In other words, leisure is now cheaper; an extra hour of leisure only costs £5 of income foregone, instead of the £8 before the tax increase. The substitution effect is when the worker works less (takes more leisure), i.e. substitutes cheaper leisure for work.

Which of these two effects is the stronger depends on different circumstances. It is difficult to give a definitive answer. In the United States, when the Reagan administration cut taxes in the 1970s, it was discovered that total tax revenues received by the federal government actually increased. The suggestion here is that lower rates of income tax resulted in a strong substitution effect as workers worked harder in response to the extra rewards for doing so.[6] In other words, they substituted work for the now dearer leisure, since each hour of leisure represented more income forgone after the tax cuts.

Higher taxes, on the other hand, can provoke workers to push for higher real wages to compensate. In addition if the authorities attempt to raise revenue by increasing payroll taxes (e.g. increasing employers' national insurance contributions), then there is a danger of increasing the costs of employing labour and raising the level of unemployment. Generally, costs of employing labour tend to be higher among the UK's European partners but are lower outside Europe. In Italy, for example, it is estimated that employers' costs in 1994 are roughly about 37 per cent of gross income, in France 25 per cent, in Britain 15 per cent, in the United States 7 per cent and in Japan about 5 per cent.[7] This helps to explain Britain's insistence on an 'opt out' of the Social Chapter of the Maastricht Treaty, which, critics argue, is a recipe for creating unemployment.

Welfare benefits

Finally and controversially, it is argued that a government that is too lax with the social security system and pays 'overly generous' unemployment benefit distorts the labour market. The suggestion here is that people will lack the incentive to seek work if they can be just as well off on the dole (i.e. receiving unemployment benefit). In addition, the system of means-testing benefits can have the unintended effect of reducing a person's entitlement to benefit as they enter employment after a period out of work, almost £1 for £1 in some cases. This is a severe disincentive to seek a job and it is not unknown for the 'effective' marginal rates of tax to exceed 100 per cent for those workers who just creep into the tax net and lose means-tested benefits as they enter employment. This 'unemployment trap' is a very severe disincentive to work. The controversial solution advanced by those who subscribe to this view is to argue for cuts in benefit and to tighten up the rules for unemployment benefit in such a way as to 'encourage' more people to seek jobs. One way to estimate the extent of the problem is to calculate the 'replacement rate' (i.e. the ratio of unemployment benefit to wages). In the United States, for example, the replacement rate averaged 36 per cent in 1990 compared with 75 per cent in Holland and just 16 per cent in Britain. The higher the replacement rate, the less the incentive to take a job as opposed to remaining unemployed.

'Welfare to work' scheme

In 1997, in an effort to remove a barrier to entering the labour market, the Labour government introduced a 'Welfare to Work' scheme designed to help unemployed people get off state benefits and back into employment. Under this scheme, people under 25 years of age who had been unemployed for more than six months and were claiming jobseekers' allowance will be helped to obtain work or undergo training. The options were:

➤ Employers would receive financial incentives of £60 per week for six months to take on young people who have been unemployed for at least six months.
➤ Work with the voluntary sector paying a weekly wage equivalent to state benefit.
➤ Work with a government authorised environmental task force on full benefit.
➤ Full-time study for young people without qualifications on approved courses without loss of benefits.

The option of remaining on full benefit while refusing to take part in the scheme was removed.

PAUSE FOR THOUGHT 3   *What are the arguments for and against the 'Welfare to Work' scheme?*

Supply-side economics

All of these factors – namely, trade unions, imperfections in the way the labour markets operate, minimum wages, taxes and social security systems – have the effect of raising the 'non-accelerating-inflation rate of unemployment' (NAIRU): in other words, the rate of unemployment required to keep inflation steady. Sometimes NAIRU is referred to as the 'natural' rate of unemployment, which is somewhat misleading by giving the impression that there is nothing that anyone can do about unemployment, in much the same way it is argued that one can do very little about natural disasters. This is, of course, nonsense. For this reason, the rather cumbersome term NAIRU is used instead. It has been estimated that NAIRU is higher in Europe than in either the USA or Japan. One study calculates that NAIRU for Europe is around 8 per cent, with the comparable figures for USA and Japan being 6 per cent and 2 per cent respectively (Layard *et al.*, 1994). Put another way, unemployment must rise to 8 per cent in Europe, for example, before inflation can be prevented from increasing year-on-year. The more rigid the labour market, in terms of the six factors listed on page 173, the higher this NAIRU will tend to be. On the other hand, the less rigid (i.e. the more flexible) the labour market is in terms of these six factors, the lower the NAIRU will tend to be.

PAUSE FOR THOUGHT 4   *What recommendations would you make if you were a neo-classical economist for solving unemployment? How could you systematically reduce an economy's NAIRU?*

Those economists who focus on trying to improve the flexibility in the labour market (thereby reducing the NAIRU) are often referred to as 'supply-side' economists. The emphasis in recent years has been much more on these supply-side policies than on the demand management techniques that were favoured in the immediate post-war period. Indeed, it has become fashionable to argue that the solution to unemployment was essentially to be found in the microeconomics of the labour market rather than in the macroeconomics of demand management.

PAUSE FOR THOUGHT 5   *What is the distinction between microeconomic solutions to unemployment and macroeconomic solutions referred to above, and why is the former alleged to be better than the latter?*

CASE STUDY **3.2**

New millennium, new paradigm, new economy?

In the past the great problem for governments of all political persuasions has been to try to reconcile the four main objectives of economic policy (economic growth with stable prices, full employment and a balance of payments). This has proved to be quite difficult as the data from Table CS3.2.1 indicates. However, as the century drew to an end a number of economists detected that there had perhaps been a significant change in the way the economy was working.

In the late 1990s the UK economy enjoyed a period of sustained economic growth. In addition it has also managed to have low inflation. This view, that the UK had finally managed to combine economic growth with low inflation, was hailed by a number of economists as 'the New Paradigm' or more colloquially the 'goldilocks economy' (neither too hot nor too cold!).

For example, Mervyn King, deputy governor of the Bank of England, was quoted in late 1999 as saying 'Growth with low inflation is likely to be with us for some time.' And in his pre-Budget statement in November 1999, Gordon Brown, the chancellor, revised upwards the Treasury's estimate of Britain's long-term growth rate from 2.25 per cent to 2.5 per cent.

The main cause of this optimism has been the speed with which the economy had bounced back in 1999–2000. GDP was virtually flat in the last quarter of 1998 and the first quarter of 1999. This led a number of economists to predict that we were heading for a recession. Table CS3.2.1, which is based on data published just before the 1999 budget, shows just how pessimistic the independent forecasters were at that time with 70 per cent of the Treasury's panel of 31 forecasters predicting a recession (either a hard landing or 'global meltdown' in 1999–2000).

Table CS3.2.1

Growth forecasts: three scenarios for 1999–2000

Soft landing	+2 to +1% growth	30% chance?
Hard landing	+1 to 0% growth	50% chance?
Global meltdown	Less than 0% growth	20% chance?

Source: Based on information from the Treasury (1999).

However, in the second quarter of 1999, official statisticians reaffirmed that the economy grew by 0.5 per cent (Figure CS3.2.1). So slight was the slowdown, and so strong had the recovery been, that economists, who a few months prior to this were forecasting recession, were now looking for signs of inflation, and were forecasting increases in interest rates within a few months.

Nevertheless, by the beginning of 2000, inflation seemed to be under control. The retail price index (RPI) had risen by only 1.3 per cent in 1999. The Bank's target measure of inflation, RPI-X, which excludes mortgage-interest payments, was only 2.2 per cent, below the target rate of 2.5 per cent. And there were few signs that inflation was about to rise sharply.

Underlying this were a very good set of conditions in the labour market. The government's preferred measure of the rate of unemployment, 'ILO unemployment', which is based on a survey of households, was only 6.0 per cent in 1999, the lowest since records began in 1984. Under the older 'claimant count' of the number on jobless benefits, the rate was 4.3 per cent, the lowest since March 1980. In previous economic cycles, wages had been bid up at far higher levels of unemployment than this. This time, it appeared that wages had been subdued.

Figure CS3.2.1

The three scenarios 1999–2000

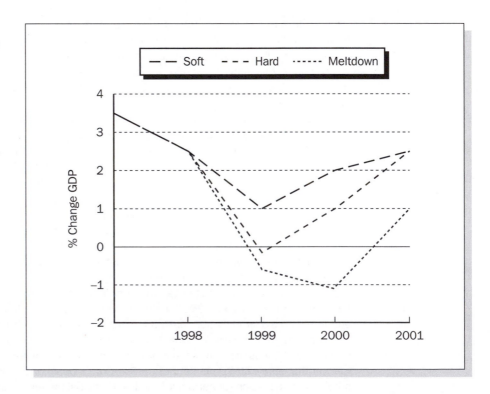

Some argued that there were similarities in all this between Britain's economy and America's. It seemed that, as a result of the Conservative government's labour-market reforms, the rate of unemployment consistent with stable inflation had fallen in Britain, as it has in America. However, some economists argued that there was scant evidence in Britain for hailing this phenomenon the 'new paradigm' that commentators detected in the United States. Britain's growth performance in recent years, it was claimed, had been solid, but much less impressive than America's. Whereas in America, some economists claim that productivity has markedly improved, in Britain there has been no productivity miracle. Since the mid-1990s, Britain's output per worker has grown by less than 2 per cent a year and compares unfavourably with our major international competitors (Figure CS3.2.2).

Even so, some questions remained. Why had Britain been able to reduce unemployment so far without pushing inflation up? And now that the economy was growing, how long could growth without inflation last? Economists advanced a number of possibilities.

One possibility is that *low inflation feeds on itself*. When inflation is in double figures – as it was in 1990, the last time the labour market looked anything like as tight – wage claims are likely to be correspondingly high. Now inflation was low, and expected to remain so. One of the Bank of England's proudest boasts was that trade unions' expectations of RPI inflation one year ahead, compiled by Barclays Bank, had tumbled from over 8 per cent in the early 1990s to 2.5 per cent in 1999. This would certainly accord with the views of those who believed in the concept of a 'rational expectations augmented Phillips curve'.

Figure CS3.2.2
**Productivity:
international
comparisons**

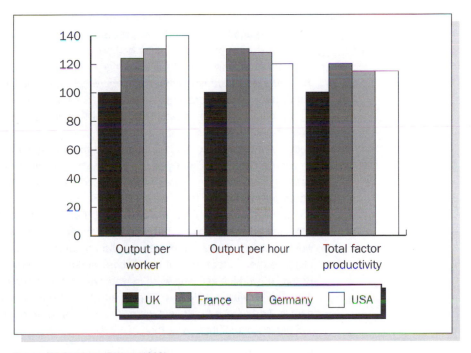

Source: IFS The Green Budget (1999)

A second and equally important possibility was the fact that it was argued that *labour was not as scarce as the unemployment figures implied*. In 1999, in fact, unemployment had not fallen much – by 53,000 on the ILO definition. Yet employment has risen by 347,000. The other 294,000 workers did not count as unemployed a year ago. They were looking after their children, or did not qualify for unemployment benefit, or were simply not looking for work. But they had been drawn into work because there are jobs and money around. This pool of employable people, it was believed, had held down the bargaining power of those in work and allowed firms to fill jobs without, as often happened in the past, bidding wages up.

The third possibility, *the change in the duration of unemployment*, had also helped to hold down wages. Those in jobs face less competition from the long-term unemployed than those who have been out of work for only a few months. (This is the so-called 'insiders versus outsiders' concept – the insiders being those in a job, the outsiders being those long-term unemployed.) According to this concept, absence from work blunts skills and the ability to adapt to office or factory routine. But after more than seven years of economic growth, broken only a brief interruption in the winter of 1998, long-term unemployment has been tumbling. By 2000, government schemes to help the long-term unemployed back to work were also beginning to help. From 1997 to 1999, the number of people unemployed (on the ILO measure) for over a year had fallen by more than 250,000. The number out of work for less than six months had barely changed. By 1999 it comprised 56 per cent of the total, up from 36 per cent in 1995.

Whether the coincidence of high growth and low inflation can persist depends, in the short run, according to economists, largely on three things:

➤ *Import prices*. Britain's low inflation rate in 1999 was principally because of a high pound and low commodity prices. But by the end of 1999 the pound had levelled off and commodity prices had begun to rise. This, it was argued, would feed into retail prices and then into wage inflation.

➤ *The strength of the economic recovery*, which will determine companies' demand for labour. Consumer demand in 1999 was strong even in the period of slow economic growth. In late 1999 the GDP figures prompted some economists to speculate that the rate of growth would increase in the rest of the year because in the second quarter companies met rising demand by running down stocks. To build them up it was argued that they would have to produce more. Faster growth would ultimately strain the economy's capacity.

➤ *The supply of labour*. There was a view that there was still, in 1999/2000, some slack to be taken up. It was thought that many firms did not sack workers when the economy slowed, but held on to them in the belief that the slowdown would be brief. These companies, so the argument ran, should be able to increase their output without hiring more workers. Moreover, the proportion of Britons of working age who were in work was actually lower in 1999, at 74 per cent, than it was in 1990, at 75 per cent: the difference was about 370,000 people. And the 78.8 per cent who were either in work or seeking it was 1.8 percentage points lower than in 1990.

What about the position in the long run? Further increases in labour supply would help to keep wage pressures in check in future business cycles. The government believes that its New Deal for the young unemployed and over-50s is already helping to encourage work. It expects that the Working Families Tax Credit, which began in October 1999, will do the same. But it still remains to be seen whether the new millennium will bring a new model of how the economy works or whether the old relationships of high growth and high inflation and of boom followed by bust would reassert themselves. These are tough nuts to crack: for example, employment and activity rates for men of all ages are several percentage points lower than they were at the start of the decade. It is argued that if only we could sort these out, then the British economy would have still more room to grow without creaking at the seams.

Source: Authors, and also based on information from *The Economist*, 28 August 1999.

Questions

1 Economists measure the rate of growth in the economy by Gross Domestic Product (GDP). How would you describe the rate of economic growth in the UK? How does our growth rate compare with other countries? (*Hint*: Have a look at http://www.unece.org/stats/trend/trend_h.htm and also the latest edition of *The Economist* [webpage: www.economist.com] for the main economic indicators for the main industrialised countries. Check the data for GDP growth over the past year for USA, Japan, Germany, Italy and France; also check out the growth data for the emerging markets such as China, the Far East and Russia.)

2 The rate of inflation is measured in two ways: by the Retail Price Index and by a variation on this called RPI-X. What is the difference between these two measures? What factors can cause inflation?

3 How does the UK's rate of inflation compare with other countries? (*Hint*: Do a similar analysis from the same data sources as for Question 1.)

4 The Bank of England has been given much more independence in framing monetary policy and has been set a target for the rate of inflation of 2.5 per cent. How does it attempt to reach this target? How can it try to control the rate of inflation? Is it a good idea in your view for the Bank of England to be given this independence?

5 There are two ways of measuring unemployment. What are these and why should there be a difference in total number of unemployed produced by these two measures? What are the principal causes of unemployment?

6 Using the same data sources as in Questions 1 and 3 above, compare the UK's unemployment rate with other countries. What measure of unemployment appears to be used in these comparisons?

7 It is often thought very difficult to have fast growth and low unemployment without also having inflation. In America some economists claim that they have 'cracked' this problem and are able to achieve these goals simultaneously (the 'new paradigm' reference in the case study). What reasons are given for the apparent good fortune with reconciling these objectives in the UK?

8 Can fast economic growth and low inflation persist in the UK?

9 What are the latest government forecasts for the economy and how have these been revised? (For more details visit the Treasury's webpage [*www.hm-treasury.gov.uk/e_info/forc/comp/main.html*]. You will need to download a free Adobe Reader to see the document if you do not already have one on your system. It will tell you how to do this!)

Issue 2: Should the UK join the single currency?

One of the key issues which will dominate the economic debate in the next few years will be whether or not the United Kingdom joins the Economic and Monetary Union (EMU) and adopts the proposals for a single European-wide currency. The outcome of this debate will undoubtedly affect the environment within which business in the United Kingdom operates.

The plan to create an economic and monetary union was devised by Jacques Delors and is known as the Delors Plan. This plan has three stages.

➤ *Stage 1*: The creation of a single market.
➤ *Stage 2*: The convergence of European economies with the harmonisation of economic and monetary policies of the member states.
➤ *Stage 3*: The creation of a single currency and a single European Central Bank.

A timetable was agreed for each stage and criteria were set out in the Maastricht Treaty for determining when 'convergence' had been achieved. All the member states signed up, agreeing to both the timetable and the conditions. (The United Kingdom, however, was granted an opt-out, which left the UK free to decide nearer the time whether or not it was going to join in Stage 3, i.e. full Economic and Monetary Union.)

Stage 1 was achieved in 1994 with the signing of the Single European Act, the aim of which was the removal of all tariff barriers between member states. This was designed to open up the whole European market and permit the free movement of goods and services between member states. It also allowed for the free movement of capital (with the abolition of exchange controls) and labour (by the mutual recognition of national professional qualifications) between countries in the EU.

However, it was recognised that a major barrier to a 'Europe without frontiers' was the existence of separate currencies. This increased the transaction costs of doing business in Europe by increasing the exchange rate risks. For example, suppose a UK manufacturer was selling to Germany at, for example, £90 a unit (after taking account of production, marketing, transport and distribution costs). Now imagine that this same UK manufacturer decided to sell the product in Germany for, say, £100. The company could reasonably expect that there would be a £10 per unit profit. However, this would depend on movements in the exchange rate. If at the time the firm received the order it quoted a price on the basis of the prevailing exchange rate (let us assume it was 2.50DM/£) then the DM price would be 250DM. If, however, by the time payment was due the rate had changed to 3DM/£, then the sterling price would have fallen to £83.33 (250DM/3DM). The firm would therefore be trading at a loss. In reality the firm would try to 'hedge' against this exchange rate risk by using such devices as the forward exchange market and currency options. However, there is a cost involved in doing this both in cash terms and also in the time and effort in monitoring exchange rate movements. It was for this reason that it was felt desirable to move towards a single currency as a means of removing what was seen as a serious barrier to trade.

It was also recognised that this could not be achieved in one step and that there should be a process of harmonisation of economic and monetary policies leading to the convergence of the EU economies before the step was taken to adopt the single currency. This represented Stage 2 of the process. This stage was to commence on 1 January 1994 with the creation of a new European Monetary Institute (EMI) and was to seek to obtain 'a high degree of sustainable convergence'. These were enshrined in the Maastricht Treaty of 1991.

The Maastricht conditions for convergence were as follows:

1 Price stability: this was defined as a rate of inflation no more than 1.5 per cent above the average of the three best performing countries.
2 Government finances: there were two reference values, one relating to the size of the government's overall national debt position which was fixed at 60 per cent of GDP, the other relating to the government deficit (or public sector borrowing requirement) which was fixed at 3 per cent of GDP.
3 Interest rates: this was measured by examining long-term interest rates and should not exceed 2 per cent above the average of the three best performing countries.
4 Exchange rate movements: these should not have exceeded the agreed margins for more than two years.

The Maastricht Treaty required the EMI to specify by 31 December 1996 the framework for the creation of the European System of Central Banks (ESCB). The treaty also set a date for the beginning of the third stage, the creation of a single currency based on the European Currency Unit (ECU) – to be called the 'euro'. The ESCB was the precursor of a European Central Bank, which will ultimately have the right to issue currency throughout the EU.

The European central banks were to cooperate in order to keep exchange rates within certain narrow bands (±2.25 per cent in the case of all members except the UK and Spain who were allowed margins of ±6 per cent). Thus the exchange rate mechanism was seen as a way of reducing exchange rate movements prior to the creation of the single currency. The UK joined the mechanism in 1990. However, it gradually became clear that the decision to enter was causing severe strains and the UK was forced to come out of the mechanism two years later in November 1992.

However, after a period from 1994 to 1998 when there was some doubt as to whether there would be a convergence of the European economies, in January 1999 eleven countries, known as the Euro 11,[8] joined the single currency. It is planned to introduce euro notes and coins by January 2002 and for national notes and coins to be withdrawn by July 2002.

The arguments for and against entry

ACTIVITY **3.1**

The single currency: you decide
Before you read on you should read the references given in note 9 on page 89 and visit the Euro's webpage at www.hm-treasury.gov.uk. After you have done this you are required to prepare the case for and against a single currency.[9]

The arguments for and against entry are summarised in Table 3.2.

Arguments for	Arguments against
Entry into a single currency will: ➤ Reduce transaction costs ➤ Eliminate exchange rate uncertainty ➤ Increase trade ➤ Increase inward investment ➤ Improve competition and efficiency ➤ Lower inflation and interest rates	The single currency will result in: ➤ Surrender of economic (and political) sovereignty ➤ One 'size' of monetary policy fits all ➤ Convergence becoming difficult to maintain ➤ Regional imbalances ➤ Failure to cope adequately with sudden economic shocks ➤ A 'United States of Europe'

Arguments for entry

Those in favour of the euro argue that the single currency will reduce the cost of exchanging one currency for another. It has been estimated that if you left the UK with £100 and travelled to all the capitals of Europe and exchanged the £100 sterling into local currencies but spent nothing, by the time you returned to the UK you would have only £26 left. By eliminating exchange rate uncertainty a single currency will promote international trade. Investment into the UK by foreign companies will also be encouraged. In early 2000 the strength of the pound in relation to the euro made it difficult for foreign companies based in the UK to compete with their European competitors. A number of these companies believed that this was damaging the UK's position as a home to foreign direct investment and threatened to locate in continental Europe. This was putting pressure on the government to accelerate the timetable for joining. (See Case Study 3.3 on page 88.)

A further argument concerned the increased competition and efficiency that would be brought about as a result of the greater transparency in pricing and in wage costs. Companies would no longer be able to 'hide' their price increases by pricing in the local currency. A further point of the argument was that consumers would be more able to compare prices with a single currency and would therefore be more prepared to shop around to get the best bargains.

Finally, because it would not be possible to restore competitiveness to the economy by devaluation, the UK would be forced to take corrective action to keep inflation down. In the longer term this would mean that interest rates would also be lower. Proponents further argued that the European Central Bank would be responsible for keeping inflation under control free from political interference.

Arguments against entry

The principal argument against entry concerns the loss of economic (and some argue political) sovereignty – that is to say, the ability to fix our own interest rates according to the circumstances that prevail in the UK economy. Critics of the single currency argue that 'one size will not fit all'. For example, the economic circumstances of an economy in a euro zone which is booming are bound to be different from an economy in slump. However, member governments will be unable to influence the rates set by the European Central Bank. For example, at the time of entry the economy of Ireland was booming and interest rates were set at around 9 per cent, reflecting the circumstances of the Irish economy at the time. On entry into the euro, Ireland was forced to cut its interest rates to 3.5 per cent which clearly did not suit its circumstances. The effect was to let loose an inflationary boom, which the central bank in Ireland could do nothing to prevent.[10]

Regional imbalances between the richer nations and regions of Europe and the poorer ones become a severe problem in a monetary union, particularly if there is not a political mechanism to redistribute resources from rich to poor regions in Europe. In a fully federal state the federal government performs this function but few national governments seem willing to surrender this sort of power, according to critics. Therefore, it is argued that an economic union without a political union would be doomed to failure.

Finally, critics argue that a single currency cannot cope with what economists call 'asymmetric shocks'. Suppose that one country (say Portugal) in a currency union is more heavily dependent on trading with other non-member countries (say Latin America) than with member states (for example, Finland). If there is a recession in Latin America this will have a bigger impact on Portugal than on Finland. This is an asymmetric shock and a currency union which has these different trading patterns will find it difficult to cope with these types of shocks unless the economies, including the trading patterns of the member states, converge. Critics argue that the UK economy does not converge with the Euro 11 .

Within months of setting up the euro (€), the new currency came under severe pressure and plummeted in value.[11] Meanwhile the UK government maintained its position of waiting until the five economic tests were fulfilled before joining. These tests, which were set out by the Chancellor of the Exchequer in October 1997, are listed below together with the Treasury's evaluation of the position as far as the UK is concerned.

The five tests

The government has indicated that the UK will only enter the single currency when we meet the five economic tests. These 'tests' were set out in October 1997 by the Chancellor Gordon Brown and remain the present government's position (January 2001).The five conditions are:

1 *Convergence*: Are business cycles and economic structures compatible so that we and others could live comfortably with euro interest rates on a permanent basis?
2 *Flexibility*: If problems emerge, is there sufficient flexibility to deal with them?
3 *Investment in UK*: Would joining the EMU create better conditions for firms making long-term decisions to invest in the UK?
4 *Financial services*: What impact would entry into the EMU have on the competitive position of the UK's financial services industry, particularly the City's wholesale markets?
5 *Employment and growth*: In summary, will joining the EMU promote higher growth, stability and a lasting increase in jobs?

In evaluating the UK's position in relation to each of these tests, the Treasury conducted an appraisal, as set out in Table 3.3.

Table 3.3

The Treasury's evaluation of the UK's position in relation to the five tests

Test	Treasury view (1997)
Convergence	Not yet
Flexibility	Not yet
Investment	More needs to be done
Financial services	More preparation
Employment and growth	Risks in going in too early

Source: Based on data from the Treasury (1997)

However, it is fairly clear that entry into the single currency will depend more on political factors than on an evaluation of the economic case.

CASE STUDY **3.3**

Economic and political pressure mounts on government to join the euro

Tony Blair faced renewed pressure to launch an early campaign for Britain to sign up to the euro as a cabinet ally called on the government to start 'making the case' to join, and a think tank said the UK economy was converging with Europe's.

Trade Secretary Stephen Byers used an interview with the *Daily Mirror* to say that once in every generation the argument for positive engagement in Europe needed to be made. 'I guess in my generation it's going to be over whether or not we join the single currency', he said. 'We do have to be putting the case both for Europe and the euro.'

Mr Byers' comments threaten to reignite cabinet tensions over the single currency. Chancellor Gordon Brown is widely seen as wanting to keep the issue out of public debate until after the next general election. Mr. Byers' remarks came within hours of a report from the Organisation for Economic Co-operation and Development which found the business cycles of the UK and Europe coming into line, interest rates getting closer and structural reform in Euroland gathering pace.

In its regular analysis of the UK's economy, the OECD said that in some respects the UK would soon be more like Euroland than some of the European single currency zone's existing members. 'In sum, on several scores, even as an "out" the United Kingdom is projected to be as close, or even closer, to the economic centre of gravity of the euro area than some of the current "ins"', its report said. Economic convergence is at the heart of the government's key tests on whether to join the euro.

Source: http://news.bbc.co.uk/hi/english/uk_politics/newsid_784000/784023.stm

Question

Should the issue of the UK joining the single currency be left until after a general election in the UK?

Conclusion

Finally, Gunde (2000) puts the single currency debate into some sort of perspective when he comments:

> Perhaps the real perspective on EMU and the € needs to be its role as part of the New Economy characterised as it will be by 'e-everything' and a business environment rapidly transformed by many new changes…of which EMU is only a part.
>
> (Gunde (2000): 37)

Notes

[1] This term has been replaced with the term public sector net borrowing (PSNB) which measures essentially the same thing.

[2] For details see the original paper: Phillips, A.W. (1958) 'The relationship between unemployment and the rate of change of money wage rates in the United Kingdom 1861–1957', *Economica*, vol. 24, pp. 283–99.

[3] For an alternative view on the rational expectations theory, see Kaletsky, A. (1995) 'The bunkum of rational expectations', *The Times*, 19 October, p. 29. He makes a comparison between the damage done to economies from following the recommendations of rational expectations theorists and the devastation of a war!

[4] For more details see *The Economist* (1994) 'Labour pains', 12 February, pp. 80–1.

[5] There is a lot of controversy surrounding the debate about the effects of the minimum wage and in particular its impact on employment. For more details of the debate see *The Economist* (1995) 'Minimum wage, maximum fuss', 8 April, p. 109, and *The Economist* (1994) 'The minimum wage debate', 10 September, p. 90.

[6] For an evaluation of the supply side debate, see *The Economist* (1996) 'The supply-siders ride again', 24 August, p. 74.

[7] *The Economist* (1994) 'A bad case of arthritis', 26 February, pp. 92–3.

[8] The Euro 11 were Austria, Belgium, Finland, France, Germany, Ireland, Italy, Luxembourg, Netherlands, Portugal and Spain. Britain and Denmark opted out, Sweden stood aside and Greece aspired to join.

[9] For this activity you may wish to consult the following sources: *The Economist* (1998) 'Eleven into one may go', 17 October; *The Economist* (1998) 'Euro Towers or Fawlty Towers', 31 October; *The Economist* (1996) 'Farewell, EMU?', 3 February, pp. 13–14; *The Economist* (1993) 'Europe's monetary future', 23 October, pp. 25–7; *The Economist* (1995) 'Europe learns its alphabet', 9 December, pp. 19–21; *The Economist* (1992) 'The case against EMU', 13 June, pp. 23–5.

[10] In theory the Irish Government should have used fiscal policy to correct this by raising taxes and cutting spending. However, in 2001 they did the reverse, thereby provoking serious criticism from their European counterparts, who threatened to publicly censure them. It is this sort of 'meddling' by other countries in Europe that critics of the Euro fear would happen if the UK joined.

[11] For an interesting evaluation of the first year of the euro, see *The Business Economist*, vol. 31, No. 1, 2000. The whole issue is devoted to a detailed evaluation of the first year of operation.

References and additional reading

Breedon, F. (2000) 'The first year of the single currency', *The Business Economist*, Vol. 31, No. 1, pp. 11–19.

Curwin, P. (ed.) (1994) *Understanding the UK Economy*, Macmillan, London.

Friedman, M. (1968) 'The role of monetary policy', *American Economic Review*, March, Vol. 58, pp. 1–17.

Griffiths, A. and Wall, S. (1997) *Applied Economics*, Longman, London, esp. ch. 19, pp. 468–90; ch. 20, pp. 492–519; ch. 24, pp. 602–28; and ch. 27, pp. 697–710.

Gunde, L. (2000) 'One year on has business taken to the single currency?', *The Business Economist,* Vol. 31, No.1, pp. 28–37.

Holden, K., Matthews, K. and Thompson, J. (1995) *The UK Economy Today*, Manchester University Press, Manchester.

Layard, R., Nickell, S. and Jackman, R. (1994) *Unemployment: Macroeconomic Performance and the Labour Market*, Oxford University Press, Oxford.

Posen, A. (1994) 'Why Central Bank independence does not cause low inflation', *Finance and the International Economy*, No. 7, Amex Bank, New York.

Sloman, J. (2000) *Economics*, Financial Times Prentice Hall, London, esp. ch. 25.

CHAPTER 4

The structure of the economy

Objectives

By the end of this chapter you will be able to:

➤ Understand what is meant by the 'structure of the economy'.

➤ Measure the structural changes that have taken place in the UK economy.

➤ Define what is meant by 'de-industrialisation'.

➤ Identify the reasons for structural change in an economy.

➤ Critically discuss the importance of the manufacturing sector in the economy.

➤ Evaluate the 'cures' for de-industrialisation.

➤ Define the e-commerce sector and assess its economic impact.

Key concepts

De-industrialisation: the process whereby there is a decline (whether measured by output or employment) in the manufacturing sector either absolutely or relative to other sectors in the economy.

Disintermediation: the term to describe the removal of a stage in the value chain.

E-commerce: can be defined as any trade that takes place using the Internet through a buyer visiting a seller's webpages and fulfilling a transaction there.

Externalities: benefits (or costs) which accrue to one sector as a result of the activities of another sector.

Input measure: the percentage of total employment or capital that a given sector utilises.

Output measure: the percentage share of GDP that is accounted for by a given sector.

Primary sector: consists of those activities that can be regarded as relating to our natural resources – for example, farming, fishing, mining and the extraction of minerals.

Production industries: these relate to the manufacturing sector, excluding the construction sector but including the extractive industries of coal, oil and gas.

Re-intermediation: a term to describe the introduction of a further stage in the value chain.

Relative unit labour costs (RULC): this term is used to measure wages in relation to productivity between a number of different countries.

Secondary sector: relates to the manufacture of goods and involves the production of products using the inputs from the primary sector. The manufacturing sector is the main part of the secondary sector and includes, for example, the construction industry and utilities such as the gas, water and electricity industries.

Standard Industrial Classification (SIC): a system for classifying different industries.

Tertiary sector: includes all the services provided by both the private objectives sector (e.g. banking, insurance, tourism, distribution) and the public sector (e.g. health, education, local government and defence).

Introduction

In the previous chapters, we looked at the economic environment in which firms operate. This chapter focuses on the way in which the economy is structured and analyses the shifts that have taken place in the various sectors of the economy. The chapter looks at the way the UK economy has changed in relation to the UK's international competitors and attempts to explain these changes and discuss their implications. Should the government be concerned about the changing structure of the economy and should they do anything about it? Finally the chapter looks at the expanding e-business sector and examines the implications of the changes brought about by the explosion in the 'knowledge economy'.

Structure defined

It is normal in the United Kingdom to use the Standard Industrial Classification (SIC) to define the structure of an economy. This is set out in Table 4.1.

Table 4.1
The Standard Industrial Classification

Classification	Sector
A	Agriculture, hunting and forestry
B	Fishing
C	Mining
D	Manufacturing
E	Electricity, gas and water supply
F	Construction
G	Wholesale and retail trade; repair of motor vehicles, motor cycles and personal household goods
H	Hotels and restaurants
I	Transport, storage and communication
J	Financial intermediation
K	Real estate, renting and business activities
L	Public administration and defence; compulsory social security
M	Education
N	Health and social work
O	Other community, social and personal service activities
P	Private households with employed persons
Q	Extra-territorial organisations and bodies

Source: Standard Industrial Classification (1992).

Each sector is assigned a letter and from this it is possible to categorise each of the firms and organisations as belonging to a given sector. The national income statistics can then give a breakdown of the contribution of each sector to the total gross domestic product (GDP). Thus, for example, it is possible to categorise economies into three sectors:

1   The primary sector.
2   The secondary sector.
3   The tertiary sector.

➤   The primary sector consists of those activities that can be regarded as relating to our natural resources, for example, farming, fishing, mining and the extraction of minerals.
➤   The secondary sector, on the other hand, relates to the manufacture of goods and involves the production of products using the inputs from the primary sector. The manufacturing sector is the main part of the secondary sector and includes such things as the construction industry and utilities such as the gas, water and electricity industries.
➤   The tertiary sector includes all the services provided by both the private sector (e.g. banking, insurance, tourism, distribution) and the public sector (e.g. health, education, local government and defence).

In addition, statistics are occasionally produced which refer to the production industries. These relate to the manufacturing sector excluding the construction sector but including the extractive industries of coal, oil and gas.

In measuring the extent of structural change in an economy it is normal to measure this in one of two ways. First, we can measure a sector's significance by an output measure (namely, the percentage share of GDP that is accounted for by that sector). Secondly, we can use an input measure (namely, the percentage of total employment or capital that a given sector utilises). As there are some difficulties in obtaining accurate figures on the capital inputs used by each sector and because of the interest in employment and unemployment, it is more normal to find statistics relating to employment.

PAUSE FOR THOUGHT 1   *What differences would you expect in the results of measuring structural change in the two ways outlined above? How, for example, would the different measures (i.e. input and output measures) affect the way you might assess the importance of the chemical industries sector and the hotel and tourism sectors? (Jot down a few pointers before you read on!)*

Using input and output measures to gauge structural change will, of course, give different answers. Those sectors which are relatively labour intensive, but which have a poor record of labour productivity, will tend to be overestimated in significance if one uses an input measure. Similarly, those sectors which have low labour inputs but show significant increases in productivity will have their significance undervalued using an input measure. There is also a complication when using the percentage share that a sector has of total GDP. Should one use current or constant prices?

What difficulties do you envisage in measuring the significance of a sector using current prices as opposed to constant prices (which adjust for the different rate of price increases in each sector)?

Imagine a sector which has shown significant technological advances (e.g. computers). Measured in current prices, it may appear that as prices have fallen so the value of that sector's output has decreased. Equally, take a sector where there is intense competition both at home and abroad. Again, the use of current prices which have been kept low because of competition may give a false impression of the true worth of a given sector's contribution to the total GDP. Using constant prices eliminates the influence of price variations in the calculation and focuses instead on volume or quantity changes.

Even here it is not always possible to capture the true nature of the structural changes that may have taken place over a period of time, especially if there have been significant qualitative changes to accompany the quantitative ones as measured by output. It is clear that in the area of electronic business (e-business) there has been not only a quantitative change but a very dramatic qualitative one as well. In addition, the real cost per unit of computing power has dropped dramatically. Unfortunately, the national income statistics are not sufficiently sophisticated, nor the methods of analysis sufficiently advanced, to capture all such nuances of structural change.

PAUSE FOR THOUGHT 3 *Can you identify three reasons why constant prices may diverge from current prices? In the 1970s, OPEC kept oil prices high. What effect would this have on the way in which we measure structural change then and subsequently?*

PAUSE FOR THOUGHT 4 *How do you think the Internet will affect the structure of the economy?*

CASE STUDY **4.1**

The output of higher education

In the national income statistics the output of the non-market service sector (e.g. higher education) is calculated on the basis of the costs of inputs. These will include, for example, the salaries of the lecturers and administrative support staff that operate in a university. The cost of equipment and resources used by universities to support students (library books, periodicals, etc.) is also included in such figures.

The government has encouraged universities to increase access to higher education by setting a target for the 'participation rate'. This represents the proportion of young adults who go into higher education. In the UK the figure was roughly 22 per cent, although there were significant regional variations. (In Scotland, for instance, the figure was closer to 30 per cent.) The target set was to be 40 per cent by the year 2000. The universities began to increase access by a variety of methods and started to expand their provision for groups of the population who had previously been under-represented in higher education. In addition, the universities began to offer courses in a variety of different and innovative ways (open learning, distance learning, part-time, etc.) and to give students credit for prior learning whether in another educational institution or in their workplace. A number of universities strengthened their links with local further education colleges by designing courses which linked directly into degree programmes. Therefore the breadth and diversity of provision of higher education in the UK underwent a very significant 'sea-change' in a comparatively short time. Thus the numbers going into this sector expanded rapidly. Government resources in the form of grant in aid to the universities did not, however, keep pace with this expansion and the 'unit of resource' (i.e. the amount per student received by each university) fell in real terms. Staff–student ratios increased dramatically, reaching 1:25 or 30 in some university departments. As well as the expansion in numbers the government set up various bodies, e.g. the Quality Assurance Agency (QAA), to examine and assess the quality of such provision. These bodies assessed the teaching quality in the universities and also evaluated their procedures for maintaining quality of provision. Their findings seemed to suggest that, on the whole, this significant expansion had been achieved with no discernible diminution of academic standards.

Questions

1 Explain the problems of measuring the contribution of the higher education sector to the economy in the light of the above.

2 How might you overcome the difficulties highlighted above to get a more accurate measure of the sector's importance? Is the concept of 'value-added' relevant here and how might you go about measuring the 'value added' of a university?

Structure measured
....

Table 4.2 gives the percentage shares of GDP of the various sectors (an output measure of structural change) between 1987 and 1997 for some of the main economies of the world, while Table 4.3 gives the percentage distribution of employment by sector (an input measure of structural change).

The figures indicate that in every economy in the table, manufacturing has declined in importance. In the UK in 1997, for example, manufacturing accounts for only 18.8 per cent of GDP compared to 21 per cent in 1987.[1] In the United States the figure for 1997 is 18.2 per cent compared to 19.8 per cent in 1987,[2] while in Japan the figure is 24.3 per cent in 1997 compared to 28.1 per cent in 1987.[3]

Meanwhile the service sector of all the major OECD countries has expanded in the last decade. Typically the service sector accounted for around 60–65 per cent of GDP a decade ago. The current figure for the share of the service sector is around 70 per cent for the major advanced economies of the OECD.

PAUSE FOR THOUGHT 5 *What, if anything, is worrying about this shift in employment patterns across the world? Where are the manufacturing jobs going and should governments do anything about it?*

As can be seen from the tables, the shift to the service sector is almost universal among the mature economies of the world. It is this structural shift that has caused there to be a debate among economists about the role of the

Table 4.2

Sectoral contributions to GDP

Country	Agriculture		Industry Total		Manufacturing		Services	
	1997	1987	1997	1987	1997	1987	1997	1987
Australia	3.2	4.1	26.2	31.0	14.0	16.1	70.6	64.9
Austria	1.4	3.2	30.4	32.7	19.8	22.7	69.2	64.1
Belgium	1.1	1.9	27.6	29.5	18.4	20.4	71.3	68.6
Canada	2.4	2.7	26.0	30.5	14.4	17.0	71.6	66.8
Czech Republic	4.1	4.5	37.5	45.0	23.7	20.3	58.4	50.5
Denmark	3.6	3.8	24.3	24.6	17.2	16.3	72.1	71.6
Finland	3.5	5.9	30.2	32.5	22.4	22.5	66.3	61.6
France	2.3	3.9	26.2	29.6	19.3	21.4	71.5	66.5
Germany	1.3	1.4	29.7	34.6	23.6	28.9	68.9	64.0
Greece	12.0	13.8	20.0	25.1	11.9	15.5	67.9	61.1
Iceland	9.4	10.1	21.6	25.7	13.1	15.7	69.0	64.2
Ireland	5.1	8.6	39.3	34.4	NA	NA	55.6	57.0
Italy	2.6	4.1	30.5	34.1	20.1	23.4	66.9	61.8
Japan	1.9	2.8	37.9	40.4	24.3	28.1	60.2	56.8
Korea	5.7	10.0	42.9	42.8	25.7	21.4	51.4	47.2
Luxembourg	1.0	2.1	24.0	32.0	15.4	23.3	75.0	65.9
Mexico	5.6	7.3	26.1	29.5	10.8	21.9	68.4	63.3
Netherlands	3.1	4.0	27.1	28.2	17.8	18.0	69.8	67.8
New Zealand	7.4	6.9	26.9	28.0	18.5	18.4	65.6	65.1
Norway	2.0	3.4	32.1	38.6	11.1	13.2	65.9	58.0
Portugal	3.9	7.3	35.2	36.6	25.3	27.4	60.9	56.1
Spain	3.5	5.5	25.6	35.3	17.8	25.0	70.9	59.3
Sweden	2.0	3.0	27.5	30.7	15.5	21.8	70.5	66.3
Switzerland	3.0	3.6	33.6	35.6	23.5	25.8	63.5	60.8
Turkey	14.5	17.8	31.3	33.1	21.5	21.8	54.2	49.1
United Kingdom	1.7	1.7	27.5	32.2	18.8	21.0	70.5	66.1
United States	1.8	2.0	26.5	29.7	18.2	15.5	71.4	68.3

Source: OECD Labour Market Statistics (1999)

NA: Not available

manufacturing sector in mature economies. Does manufacturing matter? Before examining this question we must first look at the main causes of structural change in an economy.

Structural change: the reasons

According to one authoritative source (Griffiths and Wall, 1999) there are five main reasons why the structure of an economy may change:

1 Maturity.
2 Low wage competition.
3 Supply-side changes.
4 'Crowding out'.
5 Productivity changes.

The maturity argument suggests that as economies mature and as people become better off so they demand more services (banking, insurance, health care, restaurants, holidays). There is therefore a change in their pattern of

Table 4.3

Civilian employment

Country	Agriculture, forestry and fishing (%)		Industry (%)		Services (%)	
	1997	1987	1997	1987	1997	1987
Australia	5.2	5.7	22.1	28.2	72.7	66.1
Austria	6.5	8.8	30.3	37.7	63.2	53.7
Belgium	2.6	3.0	26.0	28.8	71.4	68.2
Canada	3.8	4.7	23.2	25.3	73.0	70.0
Czech Republic	5.8	12.0	41.8	47.5	52.5	40.5
Denmark	3.7	5.7	28.8	28.2	67.5	66.0
Finland	7.1	10.4	27.5	31.2	65.5	58.4
France	4.6	7.0	25.8	30.0	69.6	62.8
Germany	3.2	4.2	38.5	40.4	58.3	55.4
Greece	20.3	27.0	22.0	28.0	58.0	45.0
Hungary	8.0	NA	39.4	NA	57.0	NA
Iceland	8.5	10.8	25.4	31.8	65.9	57.8
Ireland	10.4	15.3	28.4	27.0	61.7	57.0
Italy	6.8	10.5	32.0	32.8	61.2	56.8
Japan	5.3	8.3	33.1	33.8	61.8	57.9
Korea	11.0	21.7	31.0	32.8	57.7	45.5
Luxembourg	2.8	4.1	25.8	33.1	71.3	62.7
Mexico	23.2	NA	22.7	NA	54.1	NA
Netherlands	3.7	4.9	22.2	28.8	74.1	66.3
New Zealand	8.5	10.9	23.8	27.4	67.8	62.8
Norway	4.8	6.7	23.7	27.0	71.6	66.3
Poland	20.6	NA	31.9	NA	47.5	NA
Portugal	13.7	22.2	31.5	34.9	54.8	42.9
Spain	8.4	15.0	30.0	32.5	61.7	52.5
Sweden	2.8	3.9	26.0	29.7	71.3	66.3
Switzerland	4.9	5.7	29.3	36.8	65.9	57.5
Turkey	41.9	47.1	23.4	21.9	34.7	31.0
United Kingdom	1.9	2.3	26.8	32.9	71.3	64.8
United States	2.7	3.0	23.9	27.1	73.4	69.9
G7	3.7	5.1	28.1	30.0	68.2	64.9
EU-15	5.0	7.7	29.8	32.4	65.2	60.0
OECD 1999	8.2	NA	27.7	NA	64.1	NA

Source: OECD Labour Market Statistics (1999).
NA: Not available

demand from manufacturing to services and this is reflected in the output and input measures of sectoral change. The analogy is drawn with the switch from agriculture to industry in the late nineteenth century in the UK. Data from Liesner (1985) shows that all mature economies experienced the same structural shift away from agriculture, albeit at different rates and from different starting positions. In Japan, according to Liesner, 68 per cent of the labour force were employed in agriculture in 1900. By 1990, this number had fallen to 7 per cent. In the USA the corresponding figures were 44 per cent in 1900 and 3 per cent by 1990, while in the UK the relevant figures are 19 per cent and 2 per cent. Therefore, so the argument runs, there will be a similar shift from manufacturing to services as these economies mature.

This argument, however, is seriously flawed in a number of important respects. First, it is simply not true that the shift was from agriculture to manufacturing, as described above. As Brown and Julius (1994) point out, over this period the shares of employment in manufacturing did not show a corresponding rise. In the USA, the share of manufacturing employment peaked at 27 per cent of the labour force in 1920 (when 30 per cent still worked in agriculture) and then fluctuated between 21 and 26 per cent for the next 60 years. The UK, which was more industrialised, had around 33 per cent of its workforce in manufacturing in 1900 and this figure remained more or less the same until 1960. In neither country was there a systematic tendency for unemployment to rise in the period 1900–60 despite the rise in the labour force and the shrinkage of farm jobs. Brown and Julius observed that the displaced agricultural workers and the new entrants into the labour force went into service sector jobs, and have been doing so for most of this century in the so-called mature economies. Furthermore, they believe that, left to market forces, there is little reason to suppose that manufacturing employment will not follow a similar path over the next 50 years to that followed by agricultural employment over the last 50 years. Rising productivity and technological change, together with the continued change in the pattern of consumer spending, lead them to conclude that manufacturing employment will continue to fall across the OECD countries, reaching levels of 10 per cent or below in the next 30 years. The largest falls in manufacturing will be felt in those countries where manufacturing employment is still comparatively high (Germany at 32 per cent, Japan at 24 per cent and Italy at 22 per cent). If the manufacturing prowess of the developing countries continues at its present rate, Brown and Julius (1994) believe that even their projections may be too modest.

Persuasive though these arguments are, the recent data published by the OECD (1993) would tend to cast some doubt on this thesis. When the share of manufacturing output is measured in constant prices, the USA actually shows an increase from 19.4 per cent in 1970 to 20.4 per cent in 1989, reflecting the faster rate of productivity in US manufacturing in the period. A similar picture emerges in the case of Japan where the figures (in constant 1985 prices) rise from 25.1 to 30.6 per cent by 1989. While it is true that there is a decline in the percentage share of GNP coming from manufacturing in other mature economies in the period 1970–90, these declines are much more modest than in the UK, the very opposite of what Brown and Julius are suggesting. In Germany, for instance, the decline is from 35.2 to 30.4 per cent and in Canada from 19.3 to 16.7 per cent. In the UK there is a 7.4 per cent shift in the share of manufacturing output from 27.5 per cent in 1970 to 20.1 per cent in 1990. In short, there must be some other explanation at work.

The second argument relates to low wage competition from third world countries. It is convenient to blame others for engaging in 'unfair' competition and for stealing markets by paying below subsistence wages. If workers are paid £10 an hour in Country X and £1 an hour in Country Y, it is argued that no one will produce anything in Country X. The so-called 'cheap labour' argument is fundamentally flawed because it assumes that international competitiveness depends only on relative wages. In actual fact, firms pay less attention to the wage rates they pay their workers than to labour costs per unit of output, or wages adjusted for productivity. If workers in Country X are more productive because of superior know-how, better infrastructure, sounder management, or a

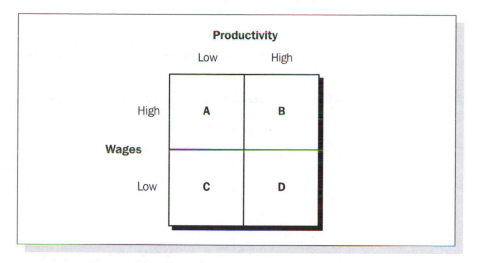

Figure 4.1
Wages/productivity matrix

larger stock of capital (human, financial and physical) such superior productivity can more than offset the effects of higher wages. So this argument really misses the point. The problem is not *low wages per se*, but *wages in relation to productivity*. The matrix in Figure 4.1 helps set out the various possibilities.

In quadrant A (high wages and low productivity) a country's labour costs per unit of output are rising and it will be difficult for its manufacturing industries to compete in international markets (Germany in the 1990s, for example). In quadrant B (high wages and high productivity) unit labour costs are stable. This is the normal combination for mature economies such as the USA and to some extent the UK. In quadrant C (low wages and low productivity) unit labour costs are again stable and do not pose too much of a threat to the manufacturing sectors of the mature economies. This combination is the usual pattern for third world countries. In quadrant D (low wages and high productivity), the unit labour costs are declining and countries in this situation will derive considerable competitive advantages. It was often the case that the so-called 'Tiger economies' of South-East Asia displayed the characteristics of countries in quadrant D. (More recently, however, with the arrival of some companies from South-East Asia into the UK, it has been argued that the reason that the UK economy has become attractive is that it has shifted from quadrant B to quadrant D.)

Thus an economy which has low wages but low productivity may not pose any serious threat to an economy which has low wages but high productivity. The key factor in determining how great a threat a competitor is to your manufacturing industry is the relative unit labour costs (RULC). Thus a high-wage economy which can also boast a high level of productivity in manufacturing can just as easily match a low-wage, low-productivity economy. The declining economies are those in which wages do not match productivity. Interestingly, the IMF publishes data using RULC in manufacturing and the results are not always what one might expect (see Figure 4.2).

Figure 4.2

Relative unit labour costs in manufacturing in a common currency

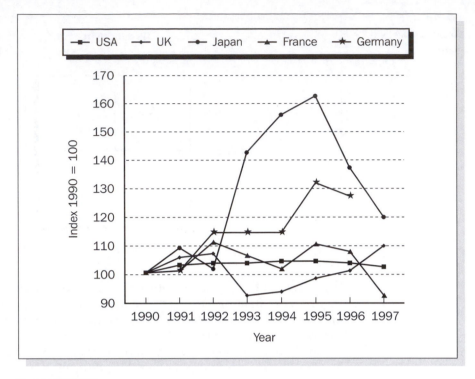

Source: IMF (1999).

For instance, if we look at the USA (what we might call a 'star' economy according to the above classification, i.e. high wages and high productivity) then we discover that its RULC has in fact increased by 2.1 per cent since 1990. Japan, on the other hand, actually experienced a rise in its RULC of 20.5 per cent in the same period with the increase peaking at 63 per cent in 1995. The German economy, long thought to be a model economy, experienced a significant rise in its RULC of 26.8 per cent by 1996. The UK economy, in contrast, experienced a modest 9.5 per cent rise in its RULC having fallen by 8.2 per cent in 1993.[4] So much for stereotypes!

PAUSE FOR THOUGHT 6 *From the data in Figure 4.2, which economies appear to be the 'stars' in recent years?*

The essential point here is that the low-wage argument cannot be used in a serious way to explain the significant shifts in the structure of economies. Important though the third world is, it is still a very small part of world trade and hence we need to look elsewhere for explanations of the structural shifts.

CASE STUDY **4.2**
· · · · · · · · · · · · · · ·

New Labour, old problems

In the spring of 2000, the United Kingdom government was facing a number of crises in the manufacturing sector. In Scotland there was the prospect of the closure of the Govan shipyard as the order book ran out. The shipyard was hoping to win an order from the Ministry of Defence to build RORO (Roll On–Roll Off) ferries. However, the order was to be won instead by a German shipyard, provoking an angry reaction from the workforce who felt let down by the government.

In the car industry it was announced by their owners BMW that the Rover plant was to be sold or shut down.[5] The effect on the West Midlands economy was likely to be devastating. Not only would there be a loss of jobs at Rover but it was estimated that about 19,000 jobs in the supply industry would also be lost. Meanwhile Ford, the American car giant, was about to announce that after almost 60 years in the UK it was planning to shut down its plant at Dagenham.

At this time the pound was at its highest level against the euro for a number of years and a number of economists were warning that there could be a re-run of the process of de-industrialisation of the early 1970s when a high pound cause a sharp decline in manufacturing. There was also intense pressure on the government to do something about the plight of these key manufacturing sectors. In addition there were calls for the government to intervene in the foreign exchange markets and to bring down the level of the pound so that UK firms could be competitive abroad. This posed a severe problem for 'new' Labour, as it wanted to appear to be 'business-friendly'.

Adapted from *The Economist*, 29 April 2000, p. 31.

Questions

1   What is the economic case for government intervention to help the manufacturing sector?
2   What are the arguments against such intervention?
3   Should the government manage the exchange rate in order to assist manufacturing?

Structural change: the debate

The issue of 'de-industrialisation' has been around for almost 30 years. In the UK a controversial book sparked off the debate (see Bacon and Eltis, 1976).

The Bacon and Eltis thesis was straightforward. If the UK continued to have the same level of structural change in the late 1970s that it had in the immediate post-war years, then we were heading for disaster. In particular it was feared that if the economy should ever pick up there would be no significant manufacturing base left in the UK and we would be subjected to high inflation as the demand for manufacturing goods outstripped our capacity to supply. In addition, there would be an almost constant balance of payments crisis as imports of manufactured goods exceeded the export of such goods. This would result in a permanently deflated economy as successive governments attempted to restore the balance with the subsequent loss of jobs. Moreover, Bacon and Eltis pointed out that at the time of their book the biggest growth sector was in the public sector where services like health, education and welfare were all growing rapidly. This was imposing severe burdens on the government's finances with a larger than expected public sector borrowing requirement (PSBR) and consequent rise in interest rates (see page 68 in Chapter 3).

The debate was given further impetus by a controversial view which argued that the decline of manufacturing was related to the discovery of North Sea Oil. As a result of the discovery of oil in the North Sea, sterling had become a petrocurrency, demanded for the strength of its newfound resource base. Thus, the £ was probably at a rate much higher than it might have been had we not discovered oil. The effect of this 'artificially' high £ was to price our exports (which were predominantly from the manufacturing sector) out of world markets. Consequently, there was a significant 'shake-out' of employment from the manufacturing sector and into the service sector. The implications of this proposition were equally controversial. Some politicians dismissed the theory on the grounds that it implied that we should never have discovered the oil in the first place (or that having discovered it we should have left it under the sea!). Others felt uncomfortable as the message of this theory seemed to imply that governments should do nothing because, as oil began to run out, the process would go into reverse with the exchange rate declining and the competitiveness of our manufacturing exports restored to their former level. Thus market forces it seemed could be relied upon to restore our competitiveness, with the re-emergence of a strong manufacturing sector being the inevitable consequence. The issue was again raised in the late 1970s and early 1980s, first by an important contribution by Singh (1977: 113–36) and then by Thirwall (1982: 22–37) and the House of Lords (1985). Finally, the debate has been brought up to date by an influential contribution by two economists, Richard Brown and Deanne Julius (1994), who have examined the role of manufacturing in the New World Order. Why then does manufacturing matter?

Does manufacturing matter?

The crisis at Longbridge, followed by the threatened closure of another of the most famous industrial sites in the world, Ford at Dagenham, are the tip of an iceberg which is heading towards British manufacturers. It is not just these two, central though they have been in Britain's long industrial history, and it is not just car manufacturers, vital though they are to Britain's economic prosperity, that are suffering. It seems that barely a day passes without an announcement by yet another inward investor or prominent industrialist that they are looking to lay off workers, slim down production or move abroad. More than 40,000 jobs have been lost in clothing manufacture in the past year alone. The British managers of Rover, Nissan, Mathmos, Vauxhall, Toyota, Ford, Mitsubishi, Peugeot and Renault have all – in their own different ways – expressed severe concerns in recent months at their ability to continue operating in Britain.

Now is a critical time for the whole European car industry. It is thought that production across the continent needs to fall by a quarter as the market reaches saturation. When Labour came into government it promised a new dawn. It did not promise carnage in manufacturing, and it is small wonder that it is worried about voters in Labour heartlands turning out in elections. Tony Blair's reputation is vanishing almost as fast as jobs in manufacturing. Unless he takes action to deal with the exchange rate, his Government may disappear too. There are 120 parliamentary constituencies where two-fifths of the jobs are in manufacturing industry – at the moment, all are held by Labour.

Source: Michael Heseltine, 'Wake up Blair our industry is dying, *The Times*, 3 May 2000.

PAUSE FOR THOUGHT 7 *Before reading on, do you agree with Michael Heseltine that we should do more to protect the UK car industry?*

The case for manufacturing rests on the links between fast economic growth and a strong manufacturing base. Those who believe that manufacturing is special (the Manufacturing Is Special School, or MISS to use the acronym of Brown and Julius) rest their case on the simple fact that the high growth developed economies (e.g. Japan and Germany) have been those with a large and buoyant manufacturing base. According to Brown and Julius, three main arguments are put forward to explain this:

1   Manufacturing jobs have higher productivity and higher wages; hence a shift to the service sector reduces the growth of GDP and incomes.
2   Manufactured goods have a higher export content; thus a shift to services creates a balance of payments constraint on faster growth.
3   The manufacturing sector possesses 'externalities' that create spin-off growth and jobs in other sectors, for example, through economies of scale and greater rate of technical progress.

Unfortunately, the arguments are not as straightforward as is suggested above. For example, it is argued that according to the latest figures, labour productivity in the service sector grows more slowly than in the manufacturing sector. (The data suggests that the growth in productivity was 0.9 per cent per annum in the service sector of the seven largest of the OECD countries compared to 3.1 per cent per annum in manufacturing between 1979 and 1990.[6]) However, there is considerable doubt about the accuracy of such information and what in fact it shows. For example, the data fails to capture the improvements in the quality of the services provided. The output of non-market services, such as higher education, is calculated as the costs of inputs thereby excluding by definition any improvements in quality or productivity (see Case Study 4.1 earlier).

However, what is important is not so much the average productivity of each sector but what is happening at the margin. Many of the recent changes in service sector jobs are both high value and highly paid[7] and eventually it is likely that prices and wages in manufacturing will be in long-term decline. Thus, as resources are shifted at the margin it is likely that in the future they will move from low value added and low productivity manufacturing jobs to high value added and high productivity service jobs. It is therefore by no means obvious why a strong manufacturing sector is necessarily associated with strong economic growth.

The second argument of MISS is that services have a low export content and also a low income elasticity of demand (for details of the definition of this concept, see pages 185–7 in Chapter 7). Therefore, according to this aspect of the theory, if a country experiences de-industrialisation then its share of world markets will decline and its demand for imports will rise as people turn to foreign markets to satisfy their demand for manufactured goods. This in turn will necessitate a significant degree of deflation in order to restore the balance which, in turn, will adversely affect domestic output and growth.

This implies that services are, according to Brown and Julius, the 'wrong' goods. However, this is far from clear. Services are already an increasingly important part of world trade and the trade in services is in fact growing faster than the trade in manufactures. For example, if one looks at the current account transactions of the major industrial nations between 1983 and 1992, exports grew by 128 per cent and imports by 125 per cent while service exports grew by 160 per cent and service imports by 179 per cent.[8] In addition, it is argued that, increasingly, services are being provided by foreign direct investment in order to overcome trade barriers. This has implications for the profits, interest and dividends of such overseas service providers. In other words, the service sector's activities will affect all parts of a country's balance of payments accounts.

The third strand to the MISS relates to what are known as 'externalities' – namely, that large capital intensive firms are the means whereby new technology and hence new jobs are generated throughout the economy. Industries such as the car and chemical industries are classic examples where both product and process technology have transformed the economy. However, it is simply no longer the case that the main engine for technological innovation is being driven solely by the manufacturing sector. The communications industry is one area where technological developments are literally creating new industries before our eyes. It is fashionable to talk about the 'Information Superhighway' and the 'Knowledge Economy' but it is clear that the interaction of hardware manufacturers with software engineers and information providers is creating tremendous opportunities for value-added activities in industries that simply did not exist five years ago. (For further details, see the section below on e-commerce.)

In addition, large corporations are looking towards contracting out services that were formerly undertaken in-house, such as marketing; or, in the case of major oil companies such as British Petroleum and Conoco, their finance function to a major accountancy firm. In short, breakthroughs in technology and improvements in productivity are now just as likely (and some would argue even more likely) in the service sector. Thus there is no automatic link between manufacturing and the growth of an economy.

Cures for de-industrialisation?

Nevertheless, in spite of these arguments that there is no intrinsic reason why manufacturing should be regarded as special, the 'myths' about manufacturing persist. As *The Economist* points out:[9]

> There is something tempting about the idea that every economy needs a manufacturing base, and that it deserves special (preferably generous) attention from government. This is a strong theme of [the] annual conference of the Confederation of British Industry (CBI); it occupies an obligatory paragraph or more in the economic platform of Democratic candidates for [the] American presidential election; it is the justificatory clause in every demand for an industrial policy in the European community.

However, as the article concludes it is right to worry about whether people are capable of creating wealth but not about whether there is a factory down the street. Any attempt by governments to try to spot 'winners' and to subsidise these industries in some way or to give them favourable tax treatment is likely to be doomed. Governments' record in respect of this type of policy has been particularly poor as the experience of the Industrial Reorganisation Corporation in the 1960s illustrates. That is not to say that governments have no role to play in the process. Their role, however, is much more of an enabling one. They can do this in one of three ways:

1 To provide the education and infrastructure necessary to put the workforce in a position to create wealth.
2 To avoid doing things which will unwittingly obstruct the process, for example with excessive taxation, with over-regulation and constant changes to macroeconomic policy.
3 To implement policies designed to improve the economy's overall productivity.

Case Study 4.3 illustrates this type of approach.

CASE STUDY **4.3**

Productivity and the role of government

In its Pre-Budget Report in 1999, the UK government focused on policies to increase productivity. It pointed to Britain's 'productivity gap' of 40 per cent with the USA and 20 per cent with France and Germany (see Figure CS3.2.2, page 81). This gap was measured using output per worker. But output per worker can vary for a number of reasons, not all to do with differences in productivity levels. For example, if workers work longer hours, or if there are a larger number of unemployed people, in one country, then output per worker will be higher, but this does not reflect a higher level of productivity. What do these different measures tell us about the extent to which Britain faces a productivity gap? Alternative measures tell quite a different story. If we take into account differences in hours worked, our productivity gap with the USA falls to 20 per cent. Allowing for differences in the amount of other inputs used, such as the use of plant and machinery, the gap falls to around 12 per cent. Accounting for differences in the age and quality of this machinery, the gap narrows even more. When we look at trends over time, we see that productivity levels have become much more similar in the four countries than they were several decades ago.

The Pre-Budget Report also highlights the low levels of investment in research and development (R&D) and physical investment in Britain compared with other industrialised countries. This is a worrying feature of our economic performance. However, before implementing policies aimed at increasing investment levels, it is important to understand why investment levels are low. They are, in part, due to low levels of government investment.

In the Pre-Budget Report, the government announced its intention to consult on several policy options aimed at increasing productivity and investment levels. The main proposals were concerned with increasing fiscal incentives for R&D, particularly for small firms; making permanent increased capital allowances for small businesses; changes to the tax treatment of venture capital and possible tax incentives for corporate venturing; and possible changes to the structure of tax-advantaged employee share-ownership schemes.

What impact will these new policies have, and would they be effective at increasing investment levels? Several of them may have merits in their own right, and improving the effectiveness of existing fiscal incentives is always welcome. However, they are unlikely to lead to large-scale increases in investment or productivity levels in the near future. They are mainly aimed at small firms, which do not account for a large share of investment. If we do not face a large productivity gap with the USA, but rather have lower levels of investment, then policies to correct these shortfalls could take a generation or longer to have an impact.

Source: Authors

Questions

1   What factors cause improvements in productivity?

2   Is there a 'productivity gap' in the UK and, if so, how could it be reduced?

3   Why are critics sceptical about the effects of some of the governments proposals?

CASE STUDY **4.4**

Industrial policy in Finland

Finland is faced with severe economic problems which have sparked off an intense debate about industrial policy. The main issue centres on how to create a new competitive production structure as internationalisation and economic integration change national comparative advantage and undermine traditional success industries.

The new approach stems from the basic idea that strengths and weaknesses tend to be firm-specific, and that linkages between firms are significant factors in growth. The strategy focuses on those things which the government believes are going to have the greatest impact, such as technological and human skills and the industrial infrastructure. In addition, open and competitive markets and market mechanisms are also vital for growth. However political judgements and choices as well as the 'invisible hand' of the market mechanism have important effects on economic development. The strategy takes into account that:

➤   competitive advantage is created, not inherited;

➤   technology and skills are the main factors underlying growth and the capacity to change;

➤   new opportunities will come from technologies meeting stricter environmental requirements;

➤   subsidies to firms must be cut;

➤   European integration and increased competition will be crucial in shaping the new industrial structure.

This strategy recognises that industrial policy is making a 'come-back', but in a changed form. It should promote business, not direct or subsidise individual firms. It should be active and market oriented, not a 'hands-off' approach.

Adapted from OECD Report (1993), p. 22.

Questions

1   Can you outline examples of where the government might assist markets to work more effectively?

2   What do you understand by the expression 'political judgements and choices' and what role do you believe that they may play in industrial policy?

3   What is the distinction between a 'hands-off' policy and an active and market-orientated one?

Figure 4.3

The e-commerce matrix

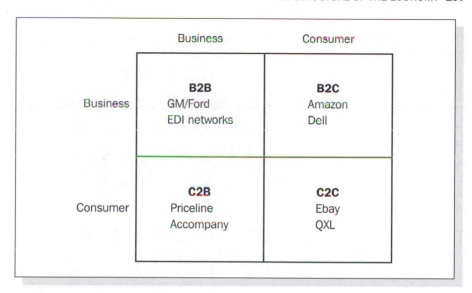

Source: *The Economist*, 1 April 2000.

E-commerce
••••••••••••••••

In the last few years we have seen the emergence of a new sector, the e-commerce sector. E-commerce can be defined as any trade that takes place through the Internet through a buyer visiting a seller's webpages and fulfilling a transaction there. There are normally two parties to these transactions, namely businesses and consumers, and this can result in a number of different business models and relationships, as set out in Figure 4.3.

B2B networks

By far the biggest of these areas is the business-to-business relationship (the so-called B2B networks). The size of this market is forecast to grow globally to around $4 trillion by 2004.[10] Business-to-business transactions dominate e-commerce, accounting for 70–85 per cent of the total, according to the OECD. Only 30 per cent of households in 11 OECD countries surveyed had a home computer in 1997.[11] The data from the IMD in Figure 4.4 illustrates this.

Examples of this type of business relationship are General Motors, Ford and Daimler Chrysler who, in February 2000, joined forces to create the largest virtual market to date. In effect these car companies have combined to create a market which will buy some $300 million worth of components from a huge number of individual suppliers. The effects of this move are quite dramatic.

PAUSE FOR THOUGHT 8 *Before reading on, outline what you think might be the advantages for car companies of using the Internet to buy their components.*

Supporters of this vast B2B network argue that this virtual market will bring a number of benefits. Firstly, it will reduce the procurement costs for car companies by forcing suppliers to have very competitive prices. The Internet will enable

Figure 4.4

PC ownership per 100 people 1999

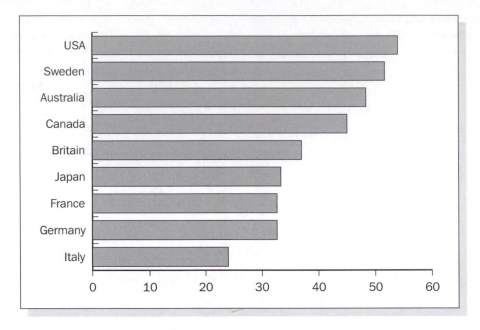

Source: The World Competitiveness Yearbook 2000, IMD.

buyers in the car companies to surf the net for the cheapest supplies from any part of the world. It will therefore greatly increase the buying power of the car companies. In one study by Brookes and Wahhaj (2000) it was estimated that the costs of procurement in the car industry could fall by as much as 14 per cent. Secondly, it will also help the suppliers because by 'surfing' this virtual market they will also be able to gauge the demand for components by car companies. It is also claimed that the exchange will help to reduce the need to hold large stocks (inventories), because the virtual market should ensure that the demand for components is smoothed out, as there will be less volatility in demand.

PAUSE FOR THOUGHT 9   *Are there any disadvantages of such a virtual market?*

A number of other companies have also set up similar virtual markets on the Internet. In February 2000 Sears Roebuck, the American retailer, and the French retail outlet Carrefour set up a retail consortium called GlobalNetXchange estimated to result in $80 billion worth of annual purchases. These kinds of exchanges have a number of advantages according to Steven Kaplan and Mohanbir Sawhney.[12] In markets where there are only a few firms, and where market power is already fairly heavily concentrated, it is easier to increase market power via such virtual markets because they can achieve critical mass very quickly. Hence there is little difficulty in persuading sellers (suppliers) to join such a virtual market: to be outside is to lose business. These are called 'hubs'. However, in other more fragmented markets there is, according to Kaplan and Sawhney, more opportunity for third party exchanges, such as the stock exchange which brings together buyers and sellers. This type of model is more of an exchange and is known in the jargon as 'intermediation'. Which models apply to which industries depends on the extent of concentration and fragmentation.

Identify a number of sectors of the economy and try to find out if they are concentrated, with a few large firms dominating, or fragmented, with a large number of smaller firms. Which sectors are more suitable for hubs and which for exchanges?

Before reading on, do you think that the creation of these B2B virtual markets makes a barrier to entry to new firms? Will the Internet increase or diminish the optimum size of firms?

It has been argued that the costs of setting up these new types of market will act as a deterrent to new firms entering the market and hence lead to a less competitive market structure in many sectors. However, as Coase[13] has pointed out, firms exist to reduce transaction costs. Firms may expand and grow for the following reason: as demand for a firm's product or services increases, there will be a tension between that firm undertaking all the tasks itself or deciding to use the market and buy in the services of other firms. For example, a car company could decide to undertake the production of each component itself or it could decide to allow other firms to supply the items. The decision will depend upon the balance of costs and benefits between using the market (externalisation) or undertaking these tasks in-house (internalisation). As the Internet has the potential to reduce such transaction costs, it favours externalisation.[14] This means in effect that the optimum size of firm has been reduced as a result of the Internet. The Internet can be seen as a means of increasing the transparency of transactions between businesses. It makes it easier for buyers and sellers to compare prices and increases the information flow (approximating to perfect information assumed in the model of perfect competition[15]).

B2C networks

Perhaps the best-known example of a business to consumer network is Amazon.com which provides an online service for people wanting to buy books and poses a real threat to high street book stores.

Visit the Amazon.com website and type in the name Hornby. How many books have been published by authors with this name?

These business-to-consumer markets offer a variety of advantages to consumers and firms alike. Firstly, consumers can browse these markets from the comfort of their own homes and can order directly from the retail outlet. Secondly, it becomes easier to compare prices and offers consumers a bewildering choice. Thirdly, it allows firms to capture data on consumers. Not only can the Internet capture the number of 'hits' a page receives but it can also indicate how long the consumer spent on the website ('stickability' in the jargon) and also where the consumer has come from and goes to from the website. This gives firms trading on a C2B network invaluable information and so allows them to market directly on the basis of this 'real time' market research. Fourthly, from the firm's point of view, trading electronically means that there can be significant cost savings in terms of the physical buildings, working capital and other associated overhead costs such as rent rates and insurance. High street retailers, for example have the advantages of location, but the disadvantages of the overhead costs that go with such a position.

For instance, book retailing on the web offers a number of key cost advantages. Books can be very slow-moving items so there is a need to carry lots of stock at any one time, thus tying up a lot of working capital. In addition, booksellers trading online get paid faster than more traditional booksellers and this gives online traders a considerable cash-flow advantage over more traditional outlets. There are also considerable advantages to be obtained through economies of scale and scope. Firms trading online can very quickly scale up their marketing effort at minimal extra cost. They can therefore double in scale without doubling their marketing effort.

PAUSE FOR THOUGHT 12 *Before reading on, what are the disadvantages of buying/selling on the Internet? Are some goods and services more amenable to e-commerce than others?*

From the point of view of the seller there are some arguments which identify the costs of trading on the Internet. Firstly, there is the question of reliability. If you plan to set up a webpage for trading it must work, and making sure that it is reliable can be very expensive. Secondly, firms have also to ensure that once their site is operating they can fulfil the demand. To fail in either of these aspects is likely to expose the firm to serious consequences.

Buying via a website obviously offers none of the social interaction that some consumers associate with shopping. Some shoppers enjoy the thrill of impulse buying as a result of 'browsing' round a store. Websites with search engines require you to have at least some idea of what you are looking for. In addition, it is recognised that there are some goods that people want to see and touch before they purchase. In some countries there is a strong tradition of feeling and smelling fresh produce before purchase and clearly the Internet cannot do that.[16] Analysis by the Boston Consultancy Group[17] indicates that such things as computer hardware and software, travel, music, videos, books, and such financial services as the buying and selling of shares, are very popular types of purchase on the net, accounting for about $30 billion of sales in 1999. These are called 'low touch' items, in contrast to food, wine, groceries, clothes and shoes, which can be regarded as 'high touch' items. However, even these distinctions are beginning to break down.

C2B networks

In the spring of 2000 a number of organisations such as the Consumers' Association and Virgin began to look at the car market as ripe for the creation of consumer-to-business networks. There were a number of reasons which prompted the creation of these C2B businesses. Firstly, consumers were becoming increasingly angry at the disparities in prices charged for cars in the UK and overseas, particularly in Europe. The distribution of cars was the subject of a Competition Commission investigation which, at the time, believed that there were certain anti-competitive practices and price discrimination policies that required investigation.[18] Secondly, the Consumers' Association believed that it could now use the Internet to put customers in contact with sources of new cars on the continent and so undercut the traditional car retailer. Similarly, a number of other websites opened up which offered consumers some very tempting bargains, as the case study below illustrates.

CASE STUDY **4.5**

Buying a car on the Internet

In April 2000 Sir Richard Branson launched one of the first 'virtual car showrooms', bypassing the traditional showrooms. Sir Richard is exploiting the rapidly growing demand for e-commerce, as well as consumer anger at the high price of buying a new car in Britain compared with on the Continent.

The cars, all right-hand drives, will be shipped into the country. On average, they will be 22 per cent cheaper than in the high street, Virgin said. In some cases, the savings would be even greater. A Fiat Bravo, with a manufacturer's list price of £14,092, will sell for £9,034, a saving of 36 per cent. A Ford Focus Ghia saloon, with a £14,320 list price, will be sold by Virgin for £9,745, a reduction of 32 per cent. A typical saving is on the Renault Clio 1.4RT, which is now listed as £9,975. Virgin is to sell it for £7,461, 25 per cent lower (see Table CS4.5.1).

The cost of British cars is one of the main complaints about 'rip-off Britain', and the increased focus on the issue has been blamed for a plunge in new car registrations of 10.6 per cent in March 2000. Virgin Cars will use techniques that the company says are borrowed from the 'lonely-hearts' industry. Customers will be invited to enter their requirements on size, price and petrol consumption. The website, which will contain car reviews, will then suggest four suitable models. Customers will pay a 15 per cent deposit.

Sir Richard, speaking about the scheme for the first time, said:

'We will demystify the process. It could take mere minutes to find the car you want and to buy it. The industry needs shaking up because prices are way too high and service can be mediocre. It is ripe Virgin territory. I believe that we can shake it up. The Internet is the biggest business revolution to emerge in the last 50 years and it will change people's lives like no other invention'.

Virgin Cars is the latest transport venture by Sir Richard, a pioneer of low-cost transatlantic air travel. He said that his new aim was to make buying cars easy and more transparent. The Virgin Cars website would offer 95 per cent of the models currently on the road, he said. Insurance, service, and loan agreements would be included in the package, with the prices listed separately.

Sir Richard said that he would bring transparency to car pricing. Many car showrooms now include insurance and after-care service as part of the overall price of the car, without specifying their contribution to the total. Virgin Cars will break down the costs, including tax, delivery and, if applicable, finance, insurance, and service. Sir Richard said: 'The service will begin with buying the car, including finance options, and will extend right through to running the vehicle. We will even recommend outlets for replacement tyres and batteries.'

The company has created 100 jobs at a centre in Watford which will service the new customers. Orders could also be lodged by telephone or fax, Sir Richard said. Operators would be trained to give advice and answer technical questions. They would be independent, not linked to any specific manufacturer. For customers who want to make the buying of the car an adventure, Virgin will offer a package including a weekend mini-break to Europe, complete with hotel, and they will find their new car waiting at the seaport or airport.

Sir Richard said he believed he had seen the future. 'Within ten years, I think that 50 per cent of cars will be bought through the Net. There will be competition but we hope to be the major supplier. An Internet service takes the power from commerce to the customer.'

Since the first speculation that the Branson machine was moving into cars, there have been 12,300 registrations on the Virgin website. The company will expand into France and Germany and all other EU markets next year. An initial £10 million has been invested. Despite its move into importing, Virgin is adamant that it is not selling Britain short. After the Competition Commission's investigation into car retailing and distribution during the next 18 months, Virgin Cars would buy cars directly from British factories, the company said.

In May 1996 the low value of sterling appeared to make car prices in Britain among the cheapest in Europe. By May 1998 they were perceived to be among the most expensive. An EU survey in 1999 confirmed that the UK was the dearest country for 57 out of 73 popular models. Last year the Consumers' Association confirmed that manufacturers had been placing obstacles in the way of people who wished to buy cars more cheaply from Europe.

Table CS4.5.1
Virgin Cars prices on the Internet

Manufacturer/Model	Specification	Manufacturer list price	Virgin Cars price	Savings (£)	(%)
Alfa Romeo 156	2.0 Twin Spark 16v	£20,024	£14,378	5,848	28
BMW 3 series	318i Convertible	£24.420	£21,063	3,367	14
Ford Focus	1.6i Ghia Saloon	£14,320	£9,746	4,575	32
Fiat Bravo	1.8 16v 115 HLX	£14,092	£9,034	5,058	36
Mercedes-Benz A Class	A140 Classic	£14,315	£10,479	3,838	27
Nissan Micra	1.0 GK NCVT	£9,905	£7,380	2,626	25
Vauxhall Astra	1.6 8v Envoy Hatch	£11,825	£9,071	2,754	23
Renault Espace	2.0 16v RT X 7 seats	£21,020	£15,881	5,139	24
Renault Clio	1.4 RT	£9,975	£7,481	2,514	25
Volkswagen Golf	2.2 V5	£18,720	£14,603	4,117	22

Source: *The Times*, 12 February 2000.

Questions

1 Why have Richard Branson and the Consumers' Association become involved in car retailing?
2 What are the limitations on buying a car via the Internet?
3 How have traditional car distributors retaliated?

C2C networks

The final type of relationship is the consumer to consumer network. In this type of relationship consumers are put in touch with other consumers through a kind of virtual auction system. The best-known examples of these types of network are Ebay and QXL (see www.ebay.com and www.qxl.com). For example, you might be a golfer (as are two of the authors) and you might want to purchase a graphite-shafted driver. By accessing QXL's website you can get access to the sports sections and join an online auction for just such a club. The bidding, which in this example began at £20, goes up in increments of £5 and you have until a given date to make your bid. You can also observe the auction in process online and intervene at any point. In addition to buying you can also sell, so QXL brings together a whole host of buyers and sellers. In addition, you can access comments by other buyers who have bought a product from the same seller.

CASE STUDY **4.6**

New business models and the Internet

In late 1999, two consultants, Philip Evans and Thomas Wurster, working for the Boston Consulting Group, published a report which attempted to assess the impact of the Internet on retailing (Evans and Wurster, 1999). They devised a methodology for assessing the web's effects on the retail sector. Their methodology highlighted three main factors (Figure CS4.6.1) which they described as

➤ Reach
➤ Richness
➤ Affiliation.

'Reach' they define as the size of your audience while 'richness' refers to the ability of a retailer to tailor and customise the goods and services that the retailer can provide. Finally, 'affiliation' is defined as the extent to which a retailer responds to a customer's interests. So if customers bought French wine they might also be interested in French cheese or perhaps they might also be interested in buying a book on French wines and the art of wine tasting. This is 'affiliation'. In the 'real' world of retailing, as opposed to the virtual one, these three things often have to be traded off.

Figure CS4.6.1
Internet effects on retailing

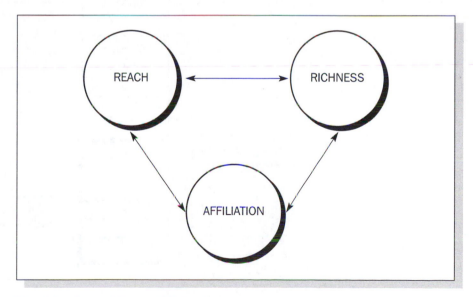

Adapted from Evans and Wurster (1999) by authors.

In order to achieve 'reach' a retailer may have to sacrifice 'richness'. It is quite difficult to achieve a global spread as a retailer and at the same time obtain the kind of customisation of services that are often required to appeal to the local market. However, with the Internet all these things become possible. Even quite small retailers can achieve a global reach while at the same time giving customers the feel of responding to their individual needs with a customised service.

In addition, the Internet opens up the possibilities of redefining the value chain by removing stages from the process ('disintermediation' in the jargon) or introducing new stages into the value chain ('re-intermediation'). Figure CS4.6.2 illustrates the situation.

This illustrates the normal value chain from manufacturer through distributor to consumer. The Internet can eliminate stages by allowing the manufacturer (or distributor) to set up his or her own website and deal directly with the consumer. Alternatively, new e-retailers can be set up (of which Amazon.com is one of the better known) in direct competition to existing retailers. New stages can also be added to this chain by the creation of portals such as Yahoo, AOL or Freeserve which offer consumers the choice of different outlets online. Different companies choose different business models. For example, Dell computers were among the first to sell directly to consumers (originally by telephone but now via the web). Travel agents and record shops are being 'disintermediated' as consumers go directly online to buy holidays and tickets. Amazon.com also sells videos and CDs. There are also possibilities of publishing books directly onto the web for consumers to download after paying online, thus eliminating both traditional publishers and bookstores. Some economists believe that further business models will emerge such as 'navigators'

Figure CS4.6.2
Value chain and the Internet

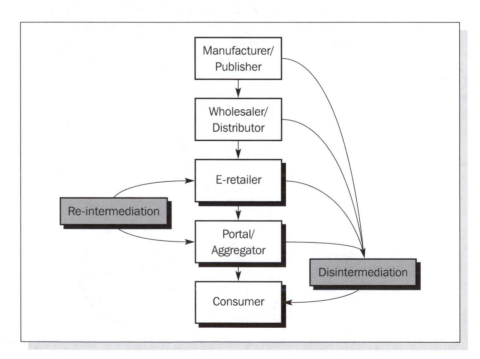

Source: *The Economist*, 26 February 2000.

who will help consumers to find what they want on the web, and 'infomediaries' who will help to look after consumers over such issues as payment security and issues surrounding privacy, thereby creating completely new sectors of the economy.

One example of 'infomediation' applies in the road haulage industry. It is a well-known phenomenon in the road haulage industry that while outbound journey loads are likely to be full, there is usually not much to carry on the way back. The problem is that there has been no mechanism to link up potential buyers of lorry space with empty containers. One answer was to set up a new organisation, National Transportation Exchange (NTE), which uses the Internet to connect shippers who have loads they want to move cheaply with fleet managers who have space to fill.

NTE helps to create a spot market by setting daily prices based on information from several hundred fleet managers about the destinations of their vehicles and the amount of space available. It then works out the best deals. When a deal is agreed, it issues the contract and handles payment. The whole process takes only a few minutes. NTE collects a commission based on the value of each deal, the fleet manager gets extra revenue that he would not otherwise have had, and the shipper gets a bargain price, at the cost of some loss of flexibility.

When NTE was first set up in 1996 it used a proprietary network, which was expensive and limited the number of buyers and sellers who could connect through it. By moving to the web, NTE has been able to extend its reach down to the level of individual lorry drivers and provide a much wider range of services. Before long, drivers will be able to connect to the NTE website on the move, using wireless Internet access devices.

Adapted from *The Economist*, 26 February 2000.

Questions

1 What are the disadvantages of trading on the Internet?
2 Can you find other examples of 'disintermediation', 're-intermediation', 'navigation' and 'infomediation'?

Economic effects of the Internet

There have been a number of attempts to identify the economic effects of the Internet, and these can be analysed into two broad categories:

➤ Supply-side effects.
➤ Demand-side effects.

Supply-side effects

The supply-side effects can be summarised as, firstly, reducing firms' production costs, and, secondly, increasing efficiency and/or reducing the profit margins of suppliers. The Internet can therefore result in all of these things and hence increase an economy's capacity for producing more with the same resources. British Telecom, for example, have estimated that procuring goods and services online will in effect reduce their costs of processing a transaction by about 90 per cent. It has also been calculated that the costs of processing a transfer between bank accounts in America is about $1.27 by bank teller, 27 cents if done by a machine and just about 1 cent by the Internet. A recent piece of research from the investment bank Schroders on the effect of Internet buying on the retail price index (RPI) in the UK has estimated that it will have the effect of lowering future inflation by 0.59 per cent per annum from what it would otherwise have been. While it is estimated that Internet sales account for about 1 per cent of final sales in the UK[19] the impact on prices is therefore marginal. However, as more consumers get 'wired' and use the Net for purchases, the effects will be much greater. The table from Schroders (Table 4.4) indicates that if about 10 per cent switch from traditional food retailers to e-retailers for their purchases, then this alone will cause prices in this area to fall by 0.27 per cent.

Table 4.4
**Impact of
e-commerce on
inflation**

Sector	Weight in RPI-X	Estimated deflation (%)	Internet substitution (%)	Impact on RPI-X
Food	13.0	5	10	−0.07
Household goods	9.0	15	20	−0.27
Household services	1.8	20	20	−0.07
Clothing and footwear	5.5	5	15	0.04
Leisure goods	4.6	10	20	−0.09
Leisure services	3.3	8	20	−0.05
Total	**37.2**	**9**	**16**	**−0.59**

Source: Schroders, Economic Perspective, January 2000.

As regards improving productivity, Goldman Sachs estimates that B2B commerce will result in a permanent increase in output by about 5 per cent per annum amongst the rich countries of the world. They further estimate that about half of this increase will come within a ten-year period, implying an increase in GDP growth of about 0.25 per cent.[20]

Demand-side effects

In addition to these supply-side effects there are a number of demand-side consequences to consider. Firstly, if as a result of the lower inflation the economy can grow faster before it overheats, then this can have the effect of boosting aggregate demand. Secondly, there is also a possibility that the higher growth of the economy as a whole will have a beneficial effect on stock market prices, thereby increasing consumers' wealth. This in turn can have an effect on consumer spending. There is some evidence from the USA that the stock market boom of the late 1990s fuelled consumer spending. The question of whether the demand-side effects outstrip the supply-side effects cannot be answered from an analysis of theory alone. It is essentially an empirical question which can only be answered by observing what happens in practice. If, for example, supply-side effects outweigh demand-side effects then the Internet will mean that an economy can produce more goods and services at a lower cost. If, on the other hand, demand-side effects are stronger, then the effects of the Internet will be to fuel inflation. At the present moment the consensus among economists is that the former is more likely than the latter.

It should also be noted that the demand-side effects, however, are not necessarily all one way. Profits of companies may be squeezed as a result of the Internet as competition increases and barriers to entry to markets are reduced. Some dot companies in the new economy will inevitably go bust and some shareholders may experience a decline in their wealth.[21]

Other effects

There are a number of other effects of the Internet which should also be taken into account. For example, the Internet may put pressure on governments to reduce taxes as consumers are free to shop in low tax countries from the comfort of their own homes. In addition, the Internet can also help developing economies where reductions in transactions costs reduce the optimal size of firms. Furthermore, it may also affect the business culture of a number of companies. The close ties between companies and their suppliers which exists in Japan, for instance, because of the cross-holding of shares, is threatened by the existence of the Internet. Thus the Internet, and the new relationships and business models that will be developed in the future as a result of the impact of e-business, may undermine what has been hailed as the strength of Japanese businesses.

Conclusions

This chapter has examined the ways in which the structure of the UK economy has changed. There has been a shift, in most of the mature economies of the world, away from traditional manufacturing towards the service sector. A number of reasons are given for this phenomenon of deindustrialisation. Since the 1970s there has undoubtedly been a loss of competitiveness in the UK manufacturing sector and this has caused a rise in unemployment and a deterioration in the balance of trade in UK manufacturing. The picture has recently become slightly more encouraging as far as the competitiveness of the United Kingdom economy is concerned. However, as discussed in this chapter, it is by no means clear that the government should intervene to 'prop up' the manufacturing sector. What is important from an economic point of view is that the economy should grow, with the question of the composition of our GDP being of secondary importance. Finally, there was an analysis of the economic impact of the Internet on the structure of business. The new emerging relationships between businesses and between customers and business and the new business models created by the Internet were assessed.

Notes

1. The comparable figure for 1970 in the UK was 28 per cent.
2. The comparable figure for 1970 in the USA was 25 per cent.
3. The comparable figure for 1970 in Japan was 35 per cent.
4. IMF Annual Report (1999).
5. At the time of writing there appeared to be two competing bidders, Alchemy and Phoenix, for the Rover company.
6. OECD (1994).
7. KPMG (1993) *Report on Manpower Requirements in the UK Economy*, KPMG, London.

[8] IMF (1993) *World Economic Outlook*, IMF, Washington, DC.

[9] *The Economist* (1994) 'The manufacturing myth', 19 March, pp. 98–9.

[10] Quoted in *The Economist*, 'Internet economics', 1 April 2000, p. 78.

[11] E-Commerce Forum, *OECD Observer*, 7 January 2000.

[12] Kaplan, S. and Sawhney, M. (2000) 'B2B E-commerce hubs: towards a taxonomy of business models', *Harvard Business Review*, May.

[13] Coase, R. (1937) 'The nature of the firm', Economica, vol. 4, pp. 386–405.

[14] Indeed this is often the argument which is used by firms who wish to 'outsource' some of their activities.

[15] For more details see Chapter 5.

[16] Anecdotal evidence tends to suggest that European consumers are far more likely to be 'high touch' as far as fresh products are concerned compared to their Anglo Saxon counterparts.

[17] Quoted in *The Economist*, 'Survey of E-commerce', 26 February 2000, p. 12.

[18] For details of this investigation visit the Competition Commission's webpage at: www.competitioncommission.gov.uk.

[19] *Scotland on Sunday*, 20 February 2000.

[20] Quoted in *The Economist*, 1 April 2000, p. 78.

[21] In the spring of 2000 a number of prominent dot com companies experienced spectacular falls in value as the stock markets around the world began to correct, prompting fears of a stock market crash which would trigger a world-wide recession.

References and additional reading
••

Bacon, R. and Eltis, W. (1976) *Britain's Problem: Too Few Producers*, Macmillan, London.

Brookes, M. and Wahhaj, Z. (2000) *Procurement Costs and the Internet*, Goldman Sachs, New York.

Brown, R. and Julius, D. (1994) 'Is manufacturing still special in the New World order?, *Finance and the International Economy*, No. 7, Amex Bank, New York.

Crainer, S. (1995) 'The Home Office', *Business Life*, March, pp. 77–80.

The Economist (2000) 'A survey of E-commerce', 26 February.

The Economist (2000) 'Seller beware', 4 March.

The Economist (2000) 'Internet economics: a thinker's guide', 1 April.

Evans, P. and Wurster, T. (1999) *Blown to Bits*, Harvard Business School Press.

Griffiths, A. and Wall, S. (1999) *Applied Economics*, Longman, London.

House of Lords (1985) *Report from the Select Committee on Overseas Trade*, HMSO London.

Liesner, T. (1985) *Economic Statistics 1900–1983*, The Economist Publications, London.

OECD (1993/1994) *Industrial Policy in OECD Countries*, Annual Review, OECD, Paris.

Singh, A. (1977) 'UK industry and the world economy: a case of deindustrialisation?', *Cambridge Journal of Economics*, Vol. 1, No. 2, June.

Thirwall, A.P. (1982) 'Deindustrialisation in the United Kingdom', *Lloyds Bank Review*, no. 144, April.

World Economic Outlook (1993) *A Survey by Staff of the International Monetary Fund*, Washington, DC.

CHAPTER 5

Organisation of firms and markets

Objectives

By the end of this chapter you will be able to:

➤ Identify the main types of business structure that operate.

➤ Understand the advantages and disadvantages of each type of structure and the reasons for changing from one type to another.

➤ Identify the different types of market structure that exist in the business world and the impact of market structure on an organisation.

➤ Understand the different methods of internally organising a firm and why different internal structures have been arrived at. Structure (perfect competition/monopoly, etc.) is assumed to directly affect the firm's conduct (pricing/investment behaviour, etc.) which in turn influences the firm's performance (whether productive/allocative efficiency, etc., is achieved).

Key concepts

Allocative efficiency: where allocation of resources is optimal; no one can be made better off without someone being made worse off. Sometimes called 'Pareto Optimal' or 'First Best' resource allocation. Marginal cost pricing is a necessary condition.

Limited liability: distinction is made between what belongs to the business and to the individual; exposure is limited to value of shares held.

M-form: an organisational structure based on operating divisions, thought more appropriate to large-sized firms.

Partnership: a business in which responsibility for ownership is normally shared between 2 to 20 partners. Unlimited liability still applies.

Private limited company: ownership based on shares held, with limited liability. Cannot advertise the sale of their shares or obtain a full Stock Exchange listing. Company name ends with Ltd (limited).

Productive efficiency: using the most efficient technical means of production; usually linked to average total cost (ATC) being a minimum.

Public limited company (plc): as for private limited company, but full Stock Exchange listing possible, with benefits of easier transfer of shares but responsibilities for disclosure of more information, etc. Company name ends with plc.

Sole proprietor (trader): a business with only one owner; subject to unlimited liability.

Structure–Conduct–Performance (SCP): an approach whereby the *market structure* (perfect competition/monopoly, etc.) is assumed to directly affect firm *conduct* (pricing/investment behaviour, etc.) which in turn influences firm *performance* (whether productive/allocative efficiency, etc. is achieved).

U-form: an organisational structure based on functional units, thought more appropriate to small and medium-sized firms.

Unlimited liability: no distinction made between what belongs to the business and what is owned by the individual.

Introduction

Analysis and investigation of decision-making in the business environment must take into consideration a number of influential and competing factors, at both the macroeconomic and microeconomic level. At the level of the individual organisation, a number of questions need to be answered about the organisation of the business, involving both the legal requirements and the internal structure of the organisation. This chapter will look at each of these factors.

The organisation of business

Four main types of organisation will be examined: sole proprietorships, partnerships, private limited companies and public limited companies.

Sole proprietor

This is a business with only one owner. It is, and always has been, the most common type of business organisation in terms of the number of firms. However, the contribution of sole proprietors to total output is relatively small. This is because the nature of a firm that is owned by a single person does not lend itself to a prolonged and rapid growth in size. If this were to take place it would usually follow that there would be a change to one of the other forms of business organisation outlined in this chapter. This is because growth for the sole trader will run up against problems inherent in the concept of unlimited liability and in access to adequate sources of funds.

Unlimited liability means that there is no distinction between what belongs to the business and what is owned by the individual. In the eyes of the law there is no difference at all as regards ownership. Thus, in the case of bankruptcy, all the possessions of the owner can be seized and sold to pay the debts of the firm. The owner can be left with nothing at all, not even his home, car or clothes!

The other major problem for the sole trader is in raising sufficient funds to finance investment in the firm. Funds for investment can take many forms: retained profit, bank borrowing, ordinary shares, preference shares and debentures, hire purchasing, leasing and factoring.

The first method, retained profits, is available to all firms that have been trading profitably for a period of time. The destination of any profit in a sole proprietorship is either re-investment back into the firm or funds paid out to the owner. The owner can therefore choose to put profits back into the business to finance expansion and growth or take profits for purposes of personal or family consumption. The availability of retained profits depends on the trading performance of the company in previous years and on the owner's attitude towards investment in the firm. The most prevalent method of raising money, however, is through bank borrowing, as is evident from the data in Table 5.1.

Table 5.1

Primary source of funding for small firms (%)

Bank	73
Other	8
Family and friends	4
Government agencies	4
Credit union Co-op	3
Building societies	2
Other individuals	0.5

Source: *Small Businesses and Banks – An Interbank Comparison*, The Forum of Private Business (1989).

Clearly, bank borrowing provides almost three-quarters of the funding of small firms. Bank borrowing can take two forms: an overdraft and/or a loan. An overdraft is an agreement between a firm and its bank that allows the firm access to a certain level of funds as, and when, they are required at an agreed rate of interest. A loan is where a firm borrows money from the bank and agrees to repay this in regular instalments over a period of time. Banks generally work on the principle that the larger a firm, the less risk is attached to providing finance to that organisation, and consequently the amounts that can be raised by bank borrowing for sole traders are somewhat limited. In addition, the rate of interest is usually higher for smaller amounts borrowed. In effect, money is a commodity and the more that is required the cheaper it will be, which is simply an economy of scale through bulk buying. However, it is often difficult when starting up in business to persuade banks that the business will succeed – a notable example being Anita Roddick, founder of The Body Shop, who in 1976 could not persuade a bank to lend her £4,000. However, a hallmark of the Thatcher years (1979–90) was the encouragement given to small businesses (see also Chapter 12, especially Table 12.2). Four of the most important initiatives are: (i) the Enterprise Allowance Scheme, which pays the unemployed setting up a business £39 a week for the first year of the business, (ii) the Loan Guarantee Scheme, which indemnifies (guarantees repayment in case of default) small and medium-sized bank lending to small firms, (iii) the Enterprise Initiative, which subsidises the provision of management consultancy services, and (iv) a concessionary rate of corporation tax for small businesses.

It is inappropriate to talk here about shares and debentures as these methods are not available to sole proprietors. However, sole proprietors may use hire purchase, which allows them to defer payment over a period of time, but is normally accompanied by a relatively high rate of interest. Alternatively, leasing is a possibility depending on the nature of the business. This avoids high initial capital expenditure on a capital item that may have a high rate of obsolescence or is possibly only of use in certain periods of the year. The final strategy to be considered here is factoring the debts of the company. This is quite a simple method of decreasing the risk of non-payment from customers and of ensuring a regular cashflow situation by selling off customer debts to a specialised finance company which will purchase these at a value less than they are worth. For example, if a sole trader is owed £1,000, this can be sold to a factoring company for £950. This will guarantee the firm 95 per cent of the money owed to it in the short term, resulting in an improved cashflow position to pay salaries and bills. The factoring company may be able to recoup 100 per cent of the debt in the longer term, thus making £50 profit.

The spectre of unlimited liability, together with problems in attracting adequate and inexpensive finance, is not a particularly attractive proposition. This raises the question of why so many sole traders do actually exist! The answer lies partly in the ease of setting up and commencing operation. In effect, there are no legal formalities that need to be undertaken to commence business (other than industry-specific undertakings, such as licences). Another obvious benefit is the absence of any need for complex and bureaucratic management structures. The owner is charged with all strategic decision-making responsibility, with little or no need for the employment of specific managers to run the business. The tax implications are also straightforward in that the profits of the business determine the tax liability that must be paid.

CASE STUDY **5.1**
··················

Moves to help people to set up in business

The aim of this case study is to examine, from a non-UK perspective, measures that might facilitate business start-up, and then to examine their applicability in Britain.

When Mr Gunther Rexrodt presented his government's package on jobs and investment, the first thing he focused on was how to strengthen the entrepreneurial spirit in Germany. Mr Rexrodt, the Economics Minister, believes that Germany's culture of self-reliance, initiative and independence is underdeveloped. Indeed, he pointed out that an average of four jobs are created when a business starts up. These new businesses, whether they be in the Handwerk (the crafts and trades sector) or the Mittelstand (Germany's small and medium-sized company sector), are still considered the backbone of the country's economy. Mr Rexrodt said that new business start-ups needed the opportunity to find backing from financial institutions. The cabinet agreed that DM1 billion (£446 million) should be made available as venture capital through banks and other financial institutions. Venture capital is hard to find in Germany, and many medium-sized companies rely entirely on family investment. The cabinet also proposed that a further DM1 billion be made available for companies which are fundamentally competitive but are experiencing temporary liquidity problems. The aim is to provide a kind of safety-net to make Germans less averse to risk-taking and to encourage them to branch out on their own. Ministers also favour the use of tax breaks to encourage entrepreneurship. Those prepared to take the risk of setting up a company would be given income, trade and company tax concessions over a three-year period, or the possibility of setting off investments against tax. The Handwerk would be subject to less red tape and 'superfluous' regulations would be scrapped to encourage individuals to set up in business.

Adapted from *Financial Times*, 31 January 1996.

Questions

1   The aim of the measures that are outlined above is to assist in the setting up of small and medium-sized businesses in Germany. Is the setting up of a small business in the UK a difficult task? What needs to be done before commencement of operations? Is there a need for assistance and clarification as in the case of Germany?

2   What help is currently given in the UK to individuals who would like to set up business as a sole trader?

3   Critically evaluate the measures outlined above. Which of these would you suggest should be introduced in the UK? Examine the practicalities of your ideas.

A partnership

This is similar in many ways to the sole trader described above, in terms of both the advantages and disadvantages that have been identified. The most significant difference between the two is in the number of owners of the company. For the sole trader there is only one, whereas in a partnership the responsibility for ownership is normally shared between at least 2 and at most 20 partners. Of the two main disadvantages cited for the sole trader, that of unlimited liability still remains. For example, if the partnership goes into liquidation, all the partners are liable for the debts of the firm. If one partner makes a catastrophic error of judgement plunging the firm into bankruptcy, all the other partners must share in the blame for this and may have to sell their private assets to meet the debts. This type of business structure does, however, overcome one of the main negative points of operating as a sole trader in that, almost by definition, if funds are being provided by a number of individuals there is greater accessibility to larger amounts of capital. Further, where external finance is required, banks and other financing institutions are usually more ready to lend, and appropriate collateral for such loans is easier to acquire for a partnership.

A significant advantage of partnership is the pooling together of partners with skills in different areas within the umbrella of one organisation. In contrast, the sole trader must buy in specialised knowledge in any instance where he or she cannot provide this. Indeed, the rationale behind the formation of the partnership may be the channelling together of complementary skills – as, for example, where two sole traders join together to form a partnership in order to allow access to a wider geographical market and to significantly reduce administrative overheads; or where one trader, who has a reputation for a specific type of service, joins with another niche trader to form an organisation offering a more comprehensive range of services.

Traditionally, partnerships have been the organisational structure that has been associated with the professions (doctors, dentists, accountants and architects, for example), the hallmark of which is to provide a sense of duty and care to their customers. The scenario that the professional firms are trying to avoid is one whereby a disgruntled client sues the partnership, which could then result in enormous damages that have to be met. Bearing in mind that the concept of unlimited liability exists, any award made in a court of law would be binding on, and may mean bankruptcy for, the individual partners. This is obviously a worst-case situation, but is seen as a method of ensuring the highest level of 'workmanship' from such professionals as accountants, solicitors, medical and dentistry practices, architects and quantity surveyors.

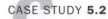 CASE STUDY **5.2**

Report on liability law to be published

This case study will examine the debate on whether to change the liability law as it currently stands in the UK. It questions the logic for such a law, and the safeguard that it provides for members of the public.

The government will this week announce that it is to publish a Law Commission report on the reform of the law of liability as it affects professionals such as accountants, solicitors, surveyors, architects and doctors. In August last year, the government said it was considering legal reform that could free thousands of professionals from the threat of crippling court actions for negligence. It asked the Law Commission to investigate the feasibility of reforming the law of joint and several liability. Mr Ian Brindle, senior partner of Price Waterhouse and a campaigner for reform, said: 'It's another move forward. Let's get it out in the open. Then we can have an understanding of the issues. It is encouraging – at least it sounds like a door opening, not a door closing.' Such a reform would be a victory for a wide range of professionals who are exposed to potentially devastating legal action in cases of alleged negligence. Under the principle of joint and several liability, such professionals can be compelled to pay all the damages in an action, whatever their degree of negligence. So if a company fails because of fraud, the auditor can be sued for the total amount of the creditors' losses, even if the directors were the negligent party and the fraudsters have been caught. The government has been under pressure for some time to reform the law. US legislation was reformed to allow for 'proportionate liability' – by which the degree of damages awarded matches the degree of negligence. Accountants in the UK have argued that unless the government moves towards reform quickly, the litigants in multinational disputes may start taking UK auditors to court rather than US or European auditors.

Adapted from *Financial Times*, 23 January 1996.

Questions
1 Who will be the winners if there is a change in the liability legislation?
2 As a corollary to Question 1, who may potentially lose out if the laws were changed?
3 Make a list of the advantages and disadvantages of a change to the laws as being suggested by the accountants. Explain why you think it is, or is not, a good idea.
4 Do you agree with the system that has been implemented in the USA and should it be used in the UK?

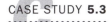 CASE STUDY **5.3**

KPMG ends secrecy on partnerships

The aim of this case study is to examine why a firm has changed from one type of business form to another, after many years in its old format.

KPMG has become the first big accountancy firm in the UK to publish 'plc-style' financial results – ending more than a century of secrecy surrounding the major partnerships. The firm, which has 8,000 staff and 600 partners, is unlikely to be followed by its competitors among the so-called Big Six firms – at least in the short term.

KPMG has moved to full disclosure because it would have had to reveal financial results for its audit business next year as it is turning into a limited liability company.

The firm decided that it should disclose results for the whole business in the UK – and hopes financial transparency will give it a competitive edge in a tight market. Gerry Archer, head of audit at KPMG, is clear about the advantages of incorporation and of full disclosure and he believes it will help to attract the best staff to KPMG.

The profession has long argued that extensive auditor liability would ultimately damage the quality of people representing audit firms because candidates would prefer safer careers. 'I believe incorporation has important long-term benefits, it gets rid of the risk that your personal assets can be taken away from you.' He also believes that to be competitive auditors need to do more than simply assure clients of the quality of the service they are providing. 'To be highly regarded people need to understand you, and that is why financial transparency is going to be important.' When KPMG announced its decision last year to meet the threat of rising litigation and help to promote itself as the leading audit firm, it seemed likely that the others would follow suit. Now they seem more likely to register offshore. Ernst & Young has said it will publish fuller results even if it is registered in Jersey. The other firms look set to hold on to confidentiality for some time. National Westminster Bank is one client who has welcomed the move to greater transparency. KPMG hopes that publication will show it to be a business of substance.

Questions

1   The last sentence in the case study indicates that KPMG wishes to make itself a 'business of substance'. How does it aim to do this by simply changing its legal form?

2   The accountancy profession has grown faster than any other in the UK over the last 20 years. How does this equate with the argument that people will not want to enter the profession if they face losing all their personal assets?

3   There is a view that the litigious society that now exists in the USA, and increasingly so in the UK, will drive all firms away from unlimited liability status. If this were to take place what would be the advantages and disadvantages to the consumer?

Private limited company

A private limited company is a firm that has issued a number of shares. Ownership of a share means ownership of part of the company. This format of corporate structure entitles those who possess these shares to limited liability, which is the most significant difference between this structure and those examined above. Thus, if for any reason a legal case was brought against a private limited company, the owners of the shares are not liable to pay out any money from their own individual assets for any resulting damages. The company has, in the eyes of the law, a separate legal identity, resulting in the shareholders' own wealth being retained in the event of bankruptcy.

The raising of finance is again a major concern, though in this instance it is notionally easier than for the sole trader or partnership. New shares can now be issued to realise money for investment, in addition to the other forms of capital funding that are also available to sole traders and partnerships. The reason that these limited companies are referred to as private is that their shares are not freely available to the general public, as they would be in the case of a public limited company (see below). Consequently, it is often difficult to procure a shareholding in one of these firms. A prospective buyer cannot simply call his stockbroker and arrange to purchase a certain number of shares in the company. Shareholders of a private company initially subscribe by private arrangement, and can only transfer shares with the agreement of the company, resulting in membership being kept within a select group of people. In general this restriction on finance is the main determinant of the size of these companies, which tend to be small and medium-sized organisations. If, however, a private company wished to expand beyond the resources available by the agreed arrangement, it would have to change its constitution to that required by a public company. It could then apply to the Stock Exchange to have its shares quoted and allow free transferability.

The private limited company is also not required by legislation to disclose as much information about the company as is a public corporation, for example in terms of accounting information and details of its directors. Nevertheless, it does have to submit an annual return to the Registrar of Companies which is open to inspection by any member of the general public.

Public limited companies

The concept of the public limited company (plc) is similar to that of the private limited company, in that it also has a legal identity independent of the people who created it or who currently hold shares of ownership. The transfer of these shares is the main difference between these two organisational forms. Public limited companies can invite the general public to subscribe to their shares. There is also an unrestricted right for shareholders to transfer shares to anyone who offers them a price that they are happy to accept. A public limited company must have plc at the end of its name, while private companies must end with Ltd (Limited).

A plc will have its shares quoted on the Stock Exchange. UK firms are normally quoted on the London Stock Exchange, although there is a much smaller exchange located in Birmingham. In the majority of European countries there is one stock exchange for the country, normally located in its financial capital. The main advantage of such a quotation is that it allows the shares to be traded in large volumes. Consequently, ownership of shares in this type of firm can be increased or decreased at any time, depending on the perceived desirability of the shares. If it is judged that a company is about to win a major contract, for example, the perception of the market is likely to be that the company is going to report higher profits in the future. This will increase the attractiveness of this firm to prospective share buyers. The demand for these shares will therefore increase, together with their value. The opposite scenario would apply to the company that has just missed out on a large contract. The perception of the market may then be that this company will experience reduced profitability in the future, hence ownership of these shares would not be as desirable as before. The holders of these shares may therefore decide to sell them, thereby increasing supply and reducing their price. This type of activity involving the purchase and sale of shares can take place very quickly, with much of the process now being computerised. This can in turn lead to very rapid rises and falls in the share price of firms. However, it is this ease of purchase and sale that makes share ownership in this type of firm so attractive and which provides such firms with access to large sums of capital.

The owners of the three other types of business structure analysed above are normally those individuals who are actively involved in the day-to-day operations of the company. This is not usually the case for public limited companies because the number of shares in these firms runs into millions. Indeed, the number of shareholders can total hundreds of thousands, ranging from large financial institutions which can own a significant percentage of the overall shares, to individuals who may only own one or two shares. All are owners of the firm, irrespective of the size of their shareholding, and all have equal rights to vote on the strategic direction of the firm (assuming ordinary shares are involved). It is obvious that the daily operation of a firm that required consensus by its owners could not be achieved in the case of a plc because of the diversity of ownership. To allow the firm to trade, the shareholders will therefore elect a Board of Directors to look after the strategic decision-making of the business. They in turn will recruit managers to implement these decisions in terms of day-to-day operations. The performance of the Board will be analysed and discussed by the shareholders at the Annual General Meeting. However, the views of the vast majority of smaller investors in the company are usually either not heard or ignored.

It follows from this analysis that the ownership of the business and the control of its operations may be in the hands of two separate groups of people. This can lead to discretionary behaviour by those in control of operations (the agents), who may then channel resources into areas that may not lead to the wealth maximisation of the owners (the principals). The section on internal organisational structure below presents a fuller examination of this particular issue. The only option for a disappointed shareholder would be to sell his or her shares, which might have the effect of depressing the share price because of the increase in share supply. If the share price was to fall far enough, then the firm may become the target for a takeover bid, other firms seeing this firm as a bargain. The market perspective is that although the price of the shares is low, this is mainly because of bad management, thus the company has the potential to perform much better if it had new management in place. Incumbent management will be aware of the risk of takeover in the event of a collapse in the share price, which may act as a mechanism for ensuring that they perform to the satisfaction of their shareholders.

Public limited companies must disclose more information about their operation than any of the other types of business structure. A legal requirement under the Companies Act stipulates the type of information they must provide, including the names of directors, the salaries they are paid and detailed company accounts.

CASE STUDY **5.4**

Does who owns what matter?

The aim of this case study is to look at the importance of organisational form and the impact of this on the profitability of firms.

Much of industrial economics is concerned with the interactions between the firms that make up an industry. For example, comparisons are drawn between monopoly, perfect competition and oligopoly. A feature of this type of analysis is that it treats the individual firm in a very simple manner. In particular there is no explicit attention given to the organisational form of the enterprises concerned. Yet, in practice, there is an enormous variation of enterprise types in most economies. One in particular that does not receive much attention is that of worker ownership. In one sense, the employee-owner is already prevalent in the UK: both the sole trader and the manager who owns a small proportion of the shares of a public corporation are workers with ownership rights. Moreover, the government has instituted employee share ownership plan (ESOP) legislation to encourage firms to adopt a significant element of worker ownership into their structures. Such firms do exist at present, although they are not widespread. Well-known examples include Baxi (a leading gas boiler manufacturer) and the National Freight Corporation.

Production requires more than just bringing together a set of inputs. The inputs have to be organised, and even for the simplest of activities there is generally a variety of organisational structures that could, in principle, be adopted. Consider, for example, a coach service that requires one coach and one driver. If we focus on the ownership structure, who should own the coach? One obvious possibility is that the driver should own the coach or at least be directly involved in hiring the coach from another individual. Another possibility is for the coach to be collectively owned by a group of shareholders, which may or may not include the driver. Which would be the best? This can be considered from two positions when we take both incentives and risk into consideration.

If incentives are analysed first, it is imperative that the coach is treated with care – since poor driving can generate costs (mechanical repairs) that far outweigh any benefits (time saved from fast driving). If the driver hires a coach from another individual, will the driver have as much incentive to maintain the coach as he would have if he owned it? The obvious answer is no, thus in this case the ownership structure has an important impact on the incentives of the driver towards maintenance and longevity of the coach. The point is simply that if the driver owned the coach rather than hired it, he or she would bear all the costs of reckless driving, and so would have the greatest incentive to drive in an efficient manner.

If we now turn to risk, it is possible to state that most people are risk averse – they would generally prefer £1,000 with certainty to an even chance of winning £2,000 or nothing. This is reflected in the fact that in many circumstances individuals are prepared to pay to insure themselves against risk, or to take action to spread their risks as far as possible. Thus, from the driver's point of view, a disadvantage of owning the coach is that it carries an element of risk. Some risks can be insured against (e.g. an accident) but others cannot (e.g. a downturn in the demand for coach travel). Leaving aside incentive effects, a more efficient arrangement in the face of these uninsurable risks might be to have the coach owned by a wealthy individual or group of individuals for whom ownership of the coach is only a small part of their portfolio of investments. They may, for example, have other investments in car manufacture or airlines, the values of which may increase if the demand for coach travel declines. Their overall exposure to risk is less than that of an individual with all, or most, of his or her capital invested in the coach.

In many instances, overall efficiency will require a compromise between the need to provide incentives and the need to spread risk. Thus, the driver of the coach and, more generally, employees (including managers) may own a proportion of the shares in the firm.

Questions

1   There is a claim above that most individuals are 'risk averse'. Consider this characteristic carefully and suggest whether or not it is likely to lead to different decisions being taken based on ownership (i.e. if you are the owner of a firm, do you take less risky decisions rather than more risky ones which might result in a major strategic error and the loss of the business?).

2   If individuals are employees of large firms, will they be more or less willing to implement riskier strategies due to the limited liability of the company and the knowledge that their salary is unlikely to be affected?

3   If the workers are part-owners of the company you might expect them to be more highly motivated and productive as they will share in the profits of the firm. Is this likely to be a long-term phenomenon or to wear off in a couple of years, with the workers going back to the levels of productivity they had achieved before?

CASE STUDY **5.5**

Brands Hatch takes fast track to the city

The aim of this case study is to examine the reasons for a private company changing itself into a public limited company through a flotation on the stock market.

The race is on, the chequered flag is in sight, and the trophy is there for the taking. Brands Hatch, one of the world's most famous motor-racing circuits – steeped in history and the virtual birthplace of British Motorsport – is to go public in a float that is likely to value it at about £40 million.

The plan to transform Brands Hatch into a broad leisure venue is the brainchild of its Chief Executive. Aiming to turn the circuit into a family attraction in the vein of Alton Towers – and only an hour's drive from London – the company expects to raise about £8 million of new capital to repay debts and provide funds for expansion. The management believe that the expansion will revolve around 'rides' in high-speed machines.

One option is to dispense with the flight simulator by thrusting virgin pilots into a light aircraft and at 2,000 feet talking them down for an emergency landing. An experienced pilot will be with them. Brands Hatch Leisure operates the Nigel Mansell Racing School and offers 4-wheel-drive and off-road training and corporate entertainment. The biggest revenue earners are the motorsport events. Profits last year are thought to have been between £1.5 million and £2 million on sales of about £11 million, and strong growth is expected in 1996. Supporters believe it to be a well-run business that is more than just a brand name and has immense potential.

The firm will spend some of the £8 million raised in expanding into corporate entertainment and the 'adrenalin pumping' leisure activities markets. The marketing will include a Brands Hatch cartoon character, flood-lit carting, and merchandising. The conference facilities and grandstand will be upgraded to make Brands Hatch more appealing.

Adapted from *The Sunday Times*, 6 October 1996.

Questions

1 Why has this particular company decided that they must change from being a private limited company to a public limited company?
2 Examine the added reporting responsibilities incumbent upon the Chief Executive of a plc compared to that of a private company.
3 Discuss what other strategic alternatives were available to this company.

CASE STUDY **5.6**

Changing ownership

The aim of this case study is to examine how a firm has developed over time and how in order to grow it has been forced to change its ownership structure, primarily to generate finance for expansion.

Jessops is a retail photography business that plans to float on the London Stock Exchange. The current ownership of the firm is dominated by the incumbent management team which account for around 40 per cent of the share capital with the balance being held by financial institutions. The company have, as yet, not disclosed the proportion of the organisation to be floated. The listing is expected to value the company at more than £100m. The firm was started in 1884 as a chemist shop and has for many years been a key organisation for enthusiastic photographers. The company has been expanding rapidly, largely through acquisitions, since a management buyout from the owning family four years ago. The rate of growth can be demonstrated with a simple comparison of the number of stores it now has – 190 – compared to the number pre-buyout, which was approximately 70.

The strategic direction as outlined by the company is to raise the number of stores it owns to around the 400 mark. It operates in a market place where the competitors are somewhat diffuse. On the one hand it could be argued that its main rivals are broader retailers such as Dixons, Argos, Boots and John Lewis. However, there are some 600 independent photography retailers in a section seen as ripe for consolidation.

To date the company has acquired the chain of Techno shops from Carphone Warehouse earlier this year. The company has been broadening its horizons in an attempt to extend its appeal to the more casual photographers. Jessops is also a leading supplier of own-label products including film, inks, paper and accessories, which it exports to 34 countries. That business, which has given the company visibiltiy overseas, is viewed as a potential springboard for the establishment of a network of stores in continental Europe.

Questions

1 Examine the market in which Jessops operates and identify the key features associated with it.
2 Discuss the possible future for Jessops if it retained its current structure of ownership.
3 Discuss some of the potential pitfalls of the current plans as outlined in the case study.

CASE STUDY 5.7
....

Norwich leads float of insurers

The aim of this case study is to examine a situation when a specific case of ownership is being classed as somewhat outdated and a trend towards floating on the stock market is now seen as being inevitable. One of the main outcomes of this is likely to be a substantial increase in the volume of shareholders in the UK.

A decade later than planned, the British may finally be becoming a nation of shareholders. Norwich Union's decision to go public will result in the creation of a new stock market company with almost 3 million investors. The flotation of the Alliance and Leicester, Halifax and Woolwich building societies will create banks with as many as 12 million shareholders between them. Even with some overlap, it is probable that the existing total of 10 million private shareholders could soon be more than doubled.

Demutualisation,* not privatisation, is swelling those ranks. Building societies have already started abandoning mutual status. Now, with the first of the mutual life insurers† to float, it looks as though the insurance industry will soon follow suit. Already in the wake of Norwich's decision, there is speculation within the industry that Scottish Widows, Scottish Amicable and even Standard Life, the sector leader, may eventually move on to the stock market.

Founded in 1797, Norwich Union will mark its bicentenary by bringing to a close the mutual ownership of the past two hundred years. It has been studying the option of floating for almost two years, but the decision to convert into a public limited company was made only last month. It has done so because it believes it has outgrown its mutual structure. Technically, it is owned by holders of its 'with-profits' life policies. But Norwich has grown since its days as a simple life fund, particularly since 1990. As well as being a leader in general insurance, pensions, unit trusts and personal equity plans, it has £40 billion under its fund management and as many as 5 million customers. But the ownership of these different businesses by people who bought its life policies was starting to look odd.

For the 3 million members of the life fund, the float will bring free shares in the listed company. With a market value of about £4 billion, enough to make it an automatic member of the FTSE 100 index once it is floated, members could collect shares worth £500 on average. That should be enough to ensure the support of all but a small minority. At the same time Norwich will raise about £2 billion of fresh capital. Analysts believe it will get a warm welcome on the market as it has consistently outperformed the market.

Adapted from *The Sunday Times*, 6 October 1996.

* In terms of building societies, they were originally owned by those who invested their money in them. Demutualisation describes the transformation from this structure into public limited companies.
† Mutual life insurers are firms that are owned by those individuals who have life insurance policies with the company. The policy is part ownership of the firm.

Questions

1 Explain what is meant by 'the ownership of these different businesses by people who bought its life policies was starting to look odd.'
2 Can you identify the probable gainers and losers in transforming the company into a plc?
3 The trend of moving away from mutual ownership would appear to be just beginning. Do you think that all similar firms in the industry will follow the trend set by Norwich Union?

CASE STUDY **5.8**

Windfalls or rates – the dilemma

The aim of this case study is to examine the specific case of demutualisation and some of the implications in this industry of changing ownership structure. It also highlights the difference between the long term and short term from a somewhat different perspective.

A long-standing argument of the pro-mutualisation lobby is that just because a building society promises you a windfall on changing its status does not mean it is best for you in the long term. The evidence is clear from a host of ex-building societies – when they convert into banks, they are usually forced to raise mortgage rates in order to be able to raise the funds to pay dividends to shareholders – something mutuals do not have to worry about. A new range of terminology has been developed to accommodate these ownership changes. The phrase 'mutuality gap' has been coined to describe the difference between the mortgage rates offered by those that have remained building societies and those that have converted into banks listed on the Stock Exchange. A good example of this are the standard variable rates at Abbey National and Halifax are currently at 7.74 per cent, compared to a rate of 7.29 per cent at the Nationwide which has already defeated two attempts by carpetbaggers to force it to convert and pay windfalls. A consequence of this differential is that it would take just one year for a £725 windfall to be eroded by the effects of a higher rate on a £150,000 mortgage. On a more typical mortgage of £80,000, it would take about two years.

The trend, however, appears set to continue with the Bradford & Bingley being the latest building society that seems set to join the Stock Exchange. If members of this society agree to the proposed demutualistaion, then they will be set to receive windfalls of 250 shares each. This will be paid to both savers and borrowers regardless of how long they have been with the society or how much they have invested or borrowed. Interestingly, the society has already started behaving like a bank in anticipation of acceptance by its members and has moved its mortgage rate to 7.64 per cent.

Abbey National was the first building society to convert into a bank in 1989 and also recommended that its members vote in favour of demutualisation. As with the Bradford & Bingley, Abbey also paid a flat amount of shares to borrowers and savers – everyone got 100 each. A spokesman for Abbey National said:

> Our shares are now worth £9.17, meaning that people who have held on to their shares have nearly £1,000 today. When we became a listed company, we made 5.6m new shareholders. Of those 3m are still shareholders. While a plc has a different group of shareholders, we are still in a competitive market. The reality is that we have to stay competitive, we couldn't be one point above the others on mortgages just to pay dividends to shareholders. We are a business and we have to be among the best.

Questions

1 Why do individuals keep their mortgages with banks when, by and large, they can get a better rate with a building society?

2 Why do members of building societies vote for a change in ownership structure when the evidence suggests that they will be worse off?

3 Discuss why some building societies have opted to remain as member-owned organisations.

Firms or industries

This chapter has concentrated its analysis at the level of the firm, examining different types of organisational structure and highlighting the positive and negative aspects of each type. However, much of the research and modelling in economics concentrates at a broader industry level and on factors external to the firm, with little focus on trying to explain why one firm in an industry differs from another. Yet the business is vitally interested in finding out, at the firm level, how to achieve sustainable competitive advantage over the firm's rivals within the industry. A number of issues will now be examined, starting with the structure–conduct–performance (SCP) model at the broad industry level and then progressing on to more recent developments at the firm level, involving internal company structure.

Structure–conduct–performance

The famous economist of the nineteenth century, Alfred Marshall, whose work is responsible for much of the present study of microeconomics, chose not to concentrate on the firm as the basis of his analysis. Instead he used 'the representative firm' as a basis, indicating that firms were on the whole largely similar and that their behaviour was mainly triggered by exogenous factors. Firms were not regarded by Marshall as being distinctive and unique entities that could gain advantages over other firms within the boundaries in which they operated. The emphasis was instead on the setting within which all the firms in an industry operated. Marshall's view is concisely expressed in the following quotation from a later economist, J.S. Bain, who followed in his footsteps:

> I do not take an internal approach, more appropriate to the field of management science, which could inquire into how enterprises do and should behave in ordering their internal operations and would attempt to instruct them accordingly . . . my primary unit for analysis is the industry or competing group of firms, rather than the individual firm or the company wide aggregate of enterprises. (Bain, 1959: 7–8)

The so-called structure–conduct–performance (SCP) paradigm or viewpoint was developed on the assumption of a causal relationship between the structure of a market and the conduct of those firms within the market, thereby influencing economic performance (see Table 5.2).

Table 5.2
Traditional causal SCP model

Stage 1	Stage 2 (determined by Stage 1)	Stage 3 (determined by Stage 2)	Stage 4 (determined by by Stage 3)
Basic conditions	Market structure	Conduct	Performance
Costs	Market concentration	Business goals	Efficiency
Demand	Product differentiation	Business strategy	Equity
Technology	Barriers to entry	Competitive	Employment
	Vertical integration	practices	
	Conglomerate diversification		

> *Structure* is used to describe the characteristics and composition of markets and industries in an economy, in other words the environment within which firms in a particular market or industry operate.

> *Conduct* refers to the behaviour (actions) of the firms in a market or industry, such as setting a price, deciding budgets for advertising expenditure, research and development, and so on.

> *Performance* involves aspects such as whether or not firms are enhancing economic welfare, e.g. are they producing the right goods in the right quantities as efficiently as possible?

This particular model of industrial analysis is rather simplistic and somewhat flawed. If we examine the following two scenarios based on the information in Table 5.3, this will become clear.

Table 5.3
Structural characteristics of two markets

	Market structure	
Structural characteristics	Perfectly competitive market	Oligopolistic market
Number of firms	Many firms each with a small share of the market	Few firms with similar market shares
Number of buyers	Many	Few
Nature of the product	Homogeneous	Differentiated
Entry barriers	Low	Substantial

If the perfectly competitive market is examined first, what can be deduced about conduct? Individual firms will be unable to influence the price (i.e. price takers) and will have no desire to spend money on advertising, R&D, etc., as such firm expenditures will have no effect on long-run price, merely serving to reduce firm profitability in the long run. Therefore, price will tend towards marginal cost that will result in production being allocatively efficient in the long run. The suggestion here is that empirical analysis of conduct is not necessary, as market structure, in itself, determines firm conduct in the industry and the performance of all firms in the long run will be virtually identical. Allocative efficiency is said to occur in perfect competition since consumers are charged exactly what it costs to produce the marginal unit. Here marginal cost pricing is seen as necessary for creating an economy which is 'Pareto Optimal', in the sense that no one can be made better off without someone else being made worse off. Conduct in the perfectly competitive market, with price = marginal cost = average cost in the long run, will also result in production being productively efficient. Here costs per unit of production are as low as is technically feasible. In other words, the perfectly competitive market structure results in firm conduct which yields a performance which is both allocatively and productively efficient.

The situation in the oligopolistic market, where there are a small number of equal-sized firms, is rather different. Such a market structure suggests that firm conduct, involving aspects such as price strategies and advertising, will be decided collectively to avoid unnecessary and destructive competition (such as price wars). The result of this will tend to be a higher price and a lower level of output compared with those experienced in a perfectly competitive market.

However, collusive behaviour is not guaranteed to occur in the market place (indeed, explicit collusion is illegal!) and firms may in practice compete for larger market shares. Price may then be kept closer to the perfectly competitive level as a result of this competitive conduct of firms within an oligopolistic market structure. All this suggests that individual firm conduct is an essential component in the overall analysis, irrespective of the general oligopolistic nature of the market structure.

The traditional viewpoint of SCP analysis, where market structure is exogenously determined, is also somewhat questionable as it would intuitively appear that firm conduct and performance can both impact upon structure! For example, if firms engage in merger activity then this will alter the number and size distribution of firms in the market (i.e. market structure); again, if firms engage in substantial innovation and advertising, then this will impact upon the level of entry barriers in an industry and therefore on market structure. In this case the result will be to make the industry more monopolistic or oligopolistic as new firms find it more difficult to enter. On the other hand, if firm conduct and performance results in high profits being generated in an industry, then this will attract entry, again resulting in a change in the structure of the overall industry.

Thus, a more realistic interpretation and representation of the SCP approach is presented in Figure 5.1, which shows interaction between the component parts and not just a simple, one way, causal flow.

Figure 5.1

A more realistic representation of the SCP approach

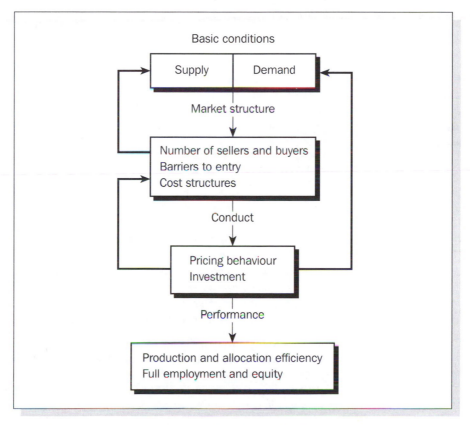

Source: *Economics and Business Education*, Vol.1, Part 1, No. 2 (1993).

As is evident from Table 5.2, many of the factors examined there are external to the firm, and the performance measures in that table are not those that would be of practical interest to the management or owners of the firm. Rather, the performance measures are those that would more likely concern the policy-makers in an economy, involving issues such as efficiency, equity and employment. Nevertheless, the more realistic approach of Figure 5.1 still does not answer the fundamental criticism attached to the SCP approach as it ignores the ability of the individual company to make decisions which might enable it to gain a sustained advantage over its rivals. This is because it does not concern itself with actual business decision-making, but with what is known as *corporate strategy*. This has developed more and more as a science over the last 30 years, with the major role in this being taken by Michael Porter (see Porter, 1980). He, and those following him, showed little concern for the SCP approach traditionally heralded by economists, arguing that business decision-makers are likely to place little emphasis on ownership, industry or cyclical effects in comparison to those factors that are specific to that particular firm (as can be seen from the evidence presented in Table 5.4). In an analysis of a large sample of American firms, Richard Rumelt found that the industry in which the firm operated explained only 8.3 per cent of the variance of profits. Even if cyclical factors are included which might relate to the industry in which the firm operates (e.g. construction is most affected by the business cycle), only just over 16 per cent of the variance of profits can be explained. Of much more significance in explaining profit performance is the nature of the business unit rather than the industry as a whole. (See Case Study 5.9.)

Table 5.4
Contribution to the variance of profits across business units (%)

Factors in profit performance	Contribution (%)
Corporate ownership	0.8
Industry effects	8.3
Cyclical effects	7.8
Business unit specific effects	46.4
Unexplained factors	36.7

Source: Rumelt (1991).

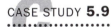 CASE STUDY **5.9**   **Ford infuriates competitors with Japanese adverts**

The aim of this case study is to examine how the performance of established (or incumbent) firms in a particular market over a period of time can influence the prospects of new firms entering into that market, in an attempt to win market share from established firms. This is an example of the structure of an industry being altered by the profit performance of the incumbents.

Japan is renowned for providing obstacles to new firm entrants from overseas into its own markets where Japanese firms are already well established. Some progress in capturing market share has been made by overseas car manufacturing but Ford, the US car manufacturer, has provoked an unseemly argument with its European competitors in consensus-conscious Japan by taking out advertisements in the main newspapers suggesting that rival vehicles are overpriced. 'Why is golf expensive in Japan?', Ford asks in an advertisement featuring the popular Volkswagen Golf perched on a golf tee. Ford admits that the play on words is intended to suggest that the rival Volkswagen Golf is as highly priced as is the playing of golf in a country with famously expensive green fees.

European manufacturers have missed the joke, said a spokesman. 'It's absolutely infuriating. Ford has only just started to invest in the Japanese market while European car companies and other US companies have worked hard to develop the market. And here somebody comes in at the last moment and throws that at us.' According to the Ford advertisements, European cars such as the VW Golf allegedly cost more in Japan than in Europe. The Golf, according to Ford, is ranked in the lower–medium class of cars, but in Japan costs more than the Ford Mondeo, which is ranked above it in the medium class. The Ford Mondeo 'is the first European car to be introduced into the Japanese market at the same price as it sells in Europe... Ford is different from those manufacturers who suddenly put up their prices when they sell cars in Japan', the advertisement says.

Volkswagen in Japan said the price comparisons did not take into account the equipment offered. In Germany, air conditioning, airbags and an anti-lock braking system were not necessarily included in all VW cars, it said. The squabble reflects the increasingly fierce competition between importers in Japan. Imported vehicle registrations in Japan rose for the third consecutive year and reached a record 388,162 units last year, with car imports up 31 per cent to a 10 per cent share of the market.

Adapted from *The Financial Times*, 31 January 1996.

Questions

1　The Ford campaign has caused widespread anger from other manufacturers. Why?
2　Why do you think that Ford have not entered the Japanese market before now? Is this a case of performance determining conduct, i.e. Ford have witnessed other firms entering the market, making large profits and are now copying them?
3　What is the downside of the strategy outlined in Question 2?
4　How do you think other firms will respond to Ford's adverts?
5　Will this increase in competition lead to a reduction in profit for all firms in the Japanese market?
6　If profits are reduced by Ford entering the market, what strategies may be adopted by the competing car firms?

Corporate strategy

In the last 20 years, there has been a marked move away from the SCP approach and towards a more company-based approach; there has also been an increasing concern with incentive structures, with principal–agent problems, and with games and interactions between small groups. These are precisely the types of issues that do matter to individual firms. The focus is on what makes them different (Kay, 1993).

It is not the aim of this section to examine corporate strategy in depth or how it has developed. It is, however, important to be aware that business economics and corporate strategy should not operate in isolation from each other. Indeed, the foundation of all corporate strategy is based on economic principles.

In the study of business economics the firm is not treated as the traditional 'black box', with a set of inputs going in one end resulting in outputs coming out the other end as products for sale. The study of the individual firm and its decision-making processes is of fundamental importance to business economics in explaining both firm and industry behaviour. It is the conduct of individual firms, through strategic decision-making, that creates competitive advantages and allows access to markets that may appear to be closed as a result of the barriers erected by incumbents. Case Study 5.10 has been included as an example of how entry into a market can still occur despite seemingly high entry barriers.

CASE STUDY 5.10

Torrid tales of tarot cards and topless darts

The aim of this case study is to examine how, through creating a specific individual product, a firm can create a significant and permanent niche for itself in a competitive market.

Mr Kelvin MacKenzie, the former editor of *The Sun* and the Head of Broadcasting for the Mirror Group, finds it difficult to stop laughing at the brilliance of his television news innovation – the creation of a News Bunny. As Alison Comyn reads the news on Live TV, the News Bunny is sitting around in camera shot, drinking tea or answering the telephone. Mr MacKenzie would have liked the rabbit to be able to give a 'thumbs up' for good news stories and 'thumbs down' for bad news – but the television regulators would not accept that. 'It is hilarious. You can't watch the news because you laugh so much', said Mr MacKenzie. The News Bunny is just one of a series of ideas dreamed up to make Live TV fun, get it noticed and, perhaps, help it find an audience. Mr Mackenzie's other two innovations so far are topless darts every night at 11pm, and its very own soap opera, Canary Wharf, a torrid tale of the life and loves of a television station a bit like . . . Live TV. Live TV will involve a £30 million investment over three years and is now available in about 1.1 million cable homes in the UK. It is cable exclusive and not available via satellite. It cost around £6 million to set up and this year's losses are likely to total around £8 million. Its income comes largely from subscription rather than from advertising. The cable operators, eager to differentiate their product from those of BSkyB, pay Live TV 25p per subscriber each month. Mr MacKenzie believes the channel will break even by its third year and is not at all disheartened by the general scornful reaction to his channel.

Adapted from *The Financial Times*, 17 January 1996.

Questions

1   The case illustrates how innovation can create a niche in the market place for a new entrant to the industry. This may entice other firms to move into the market place in competition with Live TV. Is this behaviour consistent with the traditional SCP paradigm?

2   Why do you think the decision was made to move into this particular market?

3   Live TV wound up its operation within a year of its commencement, citing inability to secure a viable audience with the finances they had available. Discuss the view that the only real barrier to entry is availability of financial resources, and that all other barriers can be overcome if an organisation has the required amount of capital.

Internal organisational structure
....

The modern corporation is often characterised as being a large multiproduct organisation that operates in oligopolistic markets. Typically, expansion of such an organisation means that new sources of funding must be secured, often with the result that the original owners have to surrender part of their holding in the company to those new investors putting finance into the business. This follows from the fact that financial input into an organisation is largely secured by means of the transfer of at least some of the ownership of the firm, as in the case of individuals purchasing shares in companies that have been newly floated on the stock market. Individuals and institutions often invest money in the company by purchasing one or more shares of the company, which results in their becoming part-owners of the firm in question. They can then, at least theoretically, become involved in the decision-making of the company through participation in the annual general meeting and in the election of the directors who will actually run the company. In return for this investment, they will also receive financial reward in terms of dividends, a yearly payout to each shareholder based on the profits made in the year. They may also benefit from capital appreciation if the value of the shares they purchased increases. This may be because the company is doing particularly well in comparison to its competitors or because of particular events, such as securing a new contract that indicates future enhanced profitability.

As the ownership of the company is spread over a wide number of people, the directors and managers of the firm are given the responsibility of running the business, answering to the shareholders at the end of each year. The owners of the company (the shareholders) cannot exercise immediate control over company decisions, whether they be operational or strategic. As a result, two groups are created: the first consists of those who provided the capital (the owners) and the second is represented by professional managers with little or no financial stake in the company.

It has been claimed that a conflict of interest may exist between the owners (the shareholders) and those responsible for the operation of the corporation (the managers). Managers, being a separate and distinct group, may have objectives that differ from those of shareholders. The shareholders may want to maximise profits and thereby their dividend returns, whereas managers may wish to pursue a number of other aims. These aims come under the umbrella of managerial theories of the firm and include growth, sales revenue (turnover), managerial status and market dominance. For example, some studies suggest that managerial salaries are more closely correlated with sales revenue or firm growth than with pure profit performance, giving managers incentives to follow these non-profit objectives. These models argue that the separation of ownership and operational decision-making (control) could therefore result in the risk-takers (the shareholders) earning less than the maximum achievable. Shareholders might only become aware of underperformance when profits fall below some previously acceptable threshold. In other words, they might not become aware of any profit-related problem within the company until after the event, and then there is very little they can do about it as the options they then face are extremely limited. For example, the shareholdings are likely to be spread far and wide, making it difficult to get together a large enough group of shareholders to influence and change management strategies. In fact, incumbent managements have been able to survive such challenges by enlisting the support of relatively small proportions of shareholders. In the end, the shareholders are faced with little choice: they can either keep their shares or sell them.

However, this analysis fails to incorporate the way in which the internal organisational structure may affect corporate performance. The suggestion here is that the way in which a company organises its operations can have an impact on its results. The appropriate structure will be determined by the size and complexity of the organisation involved. The goal of that organisation will be achieved through appropriate monitoring of management. There are two basic organisational forms: the U-form and the M-form.

The unitary, or U-form, of internal structure

The U-form of organisational structure is thought to be the best method for small and medium-sized firms, and is illustrated in Figure 5.2. The main characteristics of the U-form are:

1 Organisation is based on the functional units within the firm, with separate departments for marketing, finance, sales, etc. The number and type of department will obviously depend on the nature of the industry in which the firm operates. This will allow the firm to benefit from specialisation and division of labour.
2 The firm will be controlled by a chief executive who has ultimate responsibility and control for all aspects of the business, from both a day-to-day and longer term strategic perspective. All information generated by the divisions is passed to the Chief Executive who uses it in the strategic and decision-making process.
3 The divisions are run by a layer of middle management (heads of divisions, etc.) who report directly to the chief executive. Their capacity for discretionary behaviour is limited because of their lack of decision-making opportunities, even in day-to-day operational matters. In effect, they have to implement the decisions that are made by the Chief Executive and report directly back to him on the impact and result of putting these decisions into practice.

Figure 5.2
The unitary or U-form internal structure

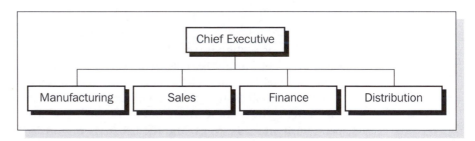

As long as the firm that operates this particular organisational structure remains relatively small, the Chief Executive can monitor the actions of the division heads effectively. However, as the firm increases in size, the U-form structure may become totally inadequate to deal with the volume of information generated by the system. The Chief Executive will not be able to cope with the vast amount of data that will pass across his or her desk, and things will probably start to get a little out of control. If the system is maintained and no delegation of decision-making authority takes place, this will cause problems in the monitoring and appraising of corporate performance. A number of these issues are as follows:

1 As the firm increases in size and becomes more diverse in its products and markets, the greater is the propensity for the Chief Executive to become overwhelmed by information and this will result in (s)he being unable to assimilate the information or act on it as effectively as before.
2 The functionally based structure means that the Chief Executive has to devote excessive time to daily operating decisions. This may have a negative impact upon the quality of the strategic decisions that are made and could result in the loss of important business opportunities that will ultimately have a negative impact on profit or other firm goals.
3 Problems with monitoring performance may enable the divisional managers to follow their own objectives, which may not be profit. For example, the manager in charge of the sales division may have the goal of building up his or her salesforce, thus increasing that person's status and power within the organisation.

The financial performance of a firm that is growing in size will ultimately suffer as the firm becomes too big to be effectively run through a U-form structure, restricting the ability of the owners to regulate middle management. This results in those managers having a significant degree of freedom in which they can pursue their own particular aims, which may well be different from those of the organisation. Consequently, increasing size leads to the classic problem of separation of ownership and control.

The multidivisional, or M-form, of internal structure

The M-form, illustrated in Figure 5.3, is a structure that is more suitable for large firms. Firms will often adopt this form to pursue profitability.

The key features of an M-form firm are as follows:

1 The functional divisions are replaced by quasi-autonomous operating divisions, which operate like independent firms within the organisation. The managers of these divisions have a large degree of responsibility for the operational aspects of the business, but have little impact on strategic matters.
2 An additional layer of management is introduced – the élite staff. This acts as a buffer between the operating divisions and the head office or chief executive. An important function of the élite staff is to reduce the information that is passed on to the Chief Executive. This is achieved by providing head office with an overall picture of company performance, while filtering out excessive operational detail. This process allows head office to concentrate on strategic matters such as long-term planning and financial control.

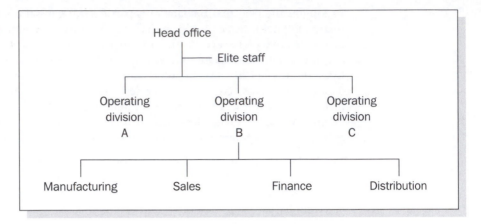

Figure 5.3

The multidivisional or M-form of internal structure

3 The divisions must meet performance targets set by head office. These are profit-orientated and are based on an accurate appreciation of each division's capabilities. The élite staff are responsible for monitoring the division's performance and ensuring that targets are achieved.

4 There is more likely to be an effective monitoring and reward system. Divisional managers who achieve or better their targets are rewarded by promotion or improved remuneration packages. Managers who do not succeed will not only forgo these benefits but will also find their jobs at risk.

5 The élite staff and head office are more likely to have a commitment to some form of profitability objective. They are less likely to set, or try to achieve, non-profit-related objectives.

We have now reviewed the two main structural forms for internal organisation of firms. However, a number of derivations of these forms of internal organisation are outlined in Table 5.5.

Table 5.5

Derivations of U- and M-form structures

Name	*Description*
Holding companies (H-form)	A divisionalised enterprise where the divisions are often linked with the parent company by means of a subsidiary relationship. No internal control apparatus.
Transitional multidivisionals (M-form)	A firm in the process of adjusting to a traditional M-form. This may be the existing firm learning about the new structure or a newly acquired part being integrated into the organisation.
Corrupted multidivisional (M̄-form)	This is where the traditional M-form is in place but the head office and/or chief executive has become involved in the day-to-day operations of the firm.
Mixed (X-form)	A divisionalised firm in which the divisions may be a combination of all the above forms identified.

Source: Weir (1995: 27).

The evidence relating to the nature of firms employing each structural type, and the consequent impact on performance, suggests that there is a clear link between the size of a firm and its internal structure. This evidence is in line with what is suggested above, i.e. small firms generally adopt the U-form, and large firms generally adopt the M-form. However, the relationship with profitability is not quite so clear, with no real evidence that large M-form firms exhibit superior profit-related performance. Thus, the adoption of the M-form structure does not automatically ensure superior profitability, as can be seen in Table 5.6.

Table 5.6
Profitability and organisational type (%)

Profit by size of firm	U-form	H-form	M´-form	$\bar{M}$-form	M-form
Above-average profit:					
– medium	50	100	60	50	100
– large	25	25	56	59	47
Below-average profit					
– medium	50	0	40	50	0
– large	75	75	44	41	53

Source: Weir (1995: 30).

In fact 53 per cent of large M-form firms achieve below-average profit, and Weir suggests a number of possible explanations for this. First, there may be ineffective monitoring of divisional managers which fails to identify discretionary behaviour. Secondly, the élite staff may not be committed to the profit-maximising objective. Thirdly, the reward system related to profit performance may be insufficient to meet the ambitions of the division heads who therefore pursue other, less-profit-related goals. Fourthly, allocating funds to projects and divisions expected to yield the highest returns may not actually achieve this end.

Conclusions
....

This chapter has analysed the structure of a business from a legal perspective and outlined the advantages and disadvantages of each type of business structure, starting with the 'smallest', the sole proprietorship, and finishing with the largest, the public limited company. In this case, the term smallest relates to the number of employees and turnover. If the number of firms were to be used as the basis for classification, it is evident that there are a far greater number of sole proprietorships than any other type of business structure in the UK, and indeed this is the case in every other country in the world, irrespective of the stage of economic development in which they find themselves. Thus, research and assistance for this sector is hugely important to the economic prosperity of countries. The chapter then examined the structure–conduct–performance (SCP) model of industrial organisation, together with more recent developments placing less emphasis on the industrial context and rather more on the need for analysing decision-making at firm level. The chapter concluded by investigating (a) the internal structure of firms and (b) how this could impact on the profitability of firms. Indeed, the evidence suggests that the size of the firm and the consequent internal structure adopted could have significant implications for the profitability of the company.

References and additional reading

Bain, J.S. (1959) *Industrial Organisation*, John Wiley, New York, pp. 7–8.

Clarke, R. (1989) *Industrial Economics*, Basil Blackwell, Oxford, esp. ch. 1, pp. 2–4.

Ezzamel, M. and Watson, R. (1993) 'Organisational form, ownership structure and corporate performance: a contextual analysis of UK companies', *British Journal of Management*, Vol. 4, pp. 161–76.

Ferguson, P.R., Ferguson, G.J. and Rothschild, R. (1993) *Business Economics: The Application of Economic Theory*, Macmillan, London, esp. chs 2 and 3, pp. 7–41.

The Forum of Small Business (1989) *Small Businesses and Their Banks – An Interbank Comparison*.

George, G.D., Joll, C. and Lynk, E.L. (1992) *Industrial Organisation: Competition, Growth and Structural Change* (4th edn), Routledge, Chapman & Hall, London, esp. ch. 5, pp. 129–58.

Hill, C.W.L. (1985) 'Internal organisation and performance: some UK evidence', *Managerial and Decision Economics*, Vol. 6, pp. 210–16.

Kay, J. (1993) 'Economics in business', *Economics and Business Education*, Vol. 1, part 1, No. 2, Summer, pp. 74–8.

Porter, M. (1980) *Competitive Advantage*, The Free Press, New York.

Rumelt, R. (1991) 'How much does industry matter?', *Strategic Management Journal*, Vol. 12, No. 3, March, pp. 167–85.

Weir, C. (1995) 'Organisational structure and corporate performance: an analysis of medium and large UK firms', *Management Decision*, Vol. 33, No. 1, pp. 24–32.

Williamson, O.E. and Bhargava, N. (1972) 'Assessing and classifying internal structure and control apparatus in the modern corporation', in Cowling, K. (ed.) *New Developments in the Analysis of Market Structure*, Macmillan, London.

CHAPTER 6

Business objectives

Objectives

By the end of this chapter you will be able to:

➤ Distinguish between mission statements, goals and objectives.
➤ Understand the classical economic theory of profit-maximisation.
➤ Review and understand alternative economic models of business objectives.
➤ Critically evaluate the relevance of the various models of business objectives for a modern business organisation.

Key concepts

Behavioural theories: the group of theories that focus on the actual behaviour of firms. These theories stress the interaction between subgroups within organisations which often leads to compromises between different goals and 'trade-offs' between conflicting objectives.

Goal: a statement which seeks to set out the general direction in which an organisation will seek to set its policies.

Managerial theories: the group of theories which suggest that managers seek to maximise objectives other than profit (e.g. sales revenue or growth).

Managerial utility: the satisfaction that managers receive from pursuing their own goals or objectives.

Minimum profit constraint: the minimum level of profit required to keep shareholders satisfied with the current directors and managers.

Mission statement: a statement which seeks to outline an organisation's basic philosophy, its core beliefs and its value system.

Objectives: a statement which quantifies a specific target which an organisation seeks to achieve within a given time period.

Profit maximisation principle: the principle states that a firm will maximise profit when output is expanded to the point where the marginal (or extra) revenue generated from that output matches the marginal (or extra) costs of producing it.

Satisficing behaviour: behaviour of organisations which results in them delivering certain minimum satisfactory levels of performance.

Introduction

In this chapter we consider the various types of statements relating to the direction in which the firm seeks to set its policies. Certainly the goals and objectives set can influence the price and output policy of the firm. As we shall see, there are ranges of maximising and non-maximising goals and objectives available to the firm. Particular problems may arise when different groupings within the firm pursue separate, and often conflicting, goals and objectives.

Mission statements, goals, objectives

Mission statements have been described by one humorist as 'a long awkward sentence that demonstrates management's inability to think clearly' (Adams, 1996). However, most organisations, whether they are in the public sector or the private sector, have 'objectives'. Sometimes, these 'objectives' are called 'mission statements' or goals of the organisation, with the word 'objective' being reserved for more precise or quantifiable statements.

A personal example may help to illustrate the difference in terminology. One of the authors recently took up golf. His mission was to find some way of exercising and relaxing. The goal was to master the game of golf. The objective was to reduce his handicap to below 20 by the end of the season (an objective which was achieved with a struggle!).

However, in order to see the distinctions between mission statements, goals and objectives, the following examples are drawn from three well-known companies.

PAUSE FOR THOUGHT 1 *What are the similarities and the differences between the mission statements, objectives and goals of the three organisations in Case Study 6.1 below?*

CASE STUDY **6.1**

Mission statements, goals and objectives
The Body Shop

Mission Statement
'The Body Shop walks its talk. We think profits and principles go hand in hand. We are against animal testing in the cosmetics industry. We campaign for human rights all over the world. We are committed to establishing trading relationships with indigenous people around the globe, and we seek alternative ways of doing business.'

Goals
'A major reorganisation within the Group is already having the desired effect of changing the emphasis from a business which is becoming production led to one that will be retail led ... [which] will have a crucial effect on our future strategy.'

Objectives
'In the coming year, the supply company will continue to drive costs down ...'
'The aim of each and every department is to increase market share in the UK and abroad.'

Source: The Body Shop Annual Report, 1993.

Sainsbury's

Mission Statement

'To discharge the responsibility as leaders in our trade by acting with complete integrity, by carrying out our work to the highest standards and by contributing to the public good and quality of life in the community.'

Goals

'To provide unrivalled value to our customers in the quality of the goods we sell, in the competitiveness of our prices and in the range of choice we offer.'

Objectives

'Over the next three years we expect group capital expenditure to remain steady in real terms at around 1988/89 level.'

Source: Sainsbury's Annual Report, 1989.

Saatchi & Saatchi

Mission Statement

'To become the leading creative agency everywhere it operates. The 'nothing is impossible' mentality is encouraged and rewarded.'
'Globalise or die.'

Goals

'To improve our financial position
To dispose of non-core businesses
To delegate operational issues to operational management.'

Objectives

'Our objective is to achieve a 10 per cent trading margin.'

Source: Saatchi & Saatchi Annual Report, 1993.

The Body Shop is well known for having a well-defined and widely publicised mission, as indicated in Case Study 6.1. Since the company's inception, Anita Roddick has been highly visible in promoting the company's philosophy of 'profits and principles'. Nevertheless, the company has indicated a more clear-cut goal; namely, to change itself from a production-led business to become one which is more retail led, by which it means that it needs to produce cosmetics that will sell, rather than create exotic cosmetics which customers do not want. There is a recognition in the goals of The Body Shop of a need to reorientate its focus. This resulted from two disappointing results (1992 and 1993) and in response to increased competition from other firms, anxious to emulate and imitate The Body Shop's success in 'environmentally' friendly cosmetics. The more specific objectives relate to costs and market share, and although no precise figure is put on these objectives they can be regarded as measurable insofar as performance in both these areas can be assessed.

In the case of Saatchi & Saatchi (see Case Study 6.1), the company also has a grand vision. Using its 'nothing is impossible' philosophy, it aimed to become the world's biggest (and most creative) advertising agency. Its expansion proceeded at breath-taking pace, as it expanded its network world wide. 'Globalise or die' became its watchwords after Maurice Saatchi read a famous article (Levitt, 1983) in the *Harvard Business Review* on the development of global markets.

However, a succession of ill-advised takeovers, coupled with a downturn in the world economy and a decline in revenue from advertising in a number of key markets, combined to push the company to the brink of extinction. Thus, in the 1993 Annual Report the company recognised the need to set itself some clear-cut goals; namely, to improve its financial position and to sell off 'non-core' unessential businesses. This gave it a focus which the 'Nothing is impossible', 'Globalise or die' mission does not. At an operational level Saatchi & Saatchi aimed to achieve a 10 per cent trading margin by ruthlessly cutting costs and maximising revenue opportunities. Subsequent events proved that this objective was in fact impossible to achieve in 1994. (For more details of this case, see Case Study 6.5 in the appendix to this chapter.)

However, as this example illustrates, the objective is measurable and has consequences if it is not achieved in a way that mission statements and, to a lesser extent, goals have not.

Finally, just how useful are mission statements? Case Study 6.2 indicates the results of some recent research.

CASE STUDY **6.2**

The usefulness of mission statements

In 1991, three lecturers in strategic management – Klemm, Sanderson and Luffman – carried out an investigation by postal questionnaire of the extent and usefulness of mission and objectives statements in a sample of 150 large industrial and finance companies in the UK taken from the Times 1000 Index.[1] The results are given in Table CS6.2.1.

Table CS6.2.1

	Mission statements (%)	Objectives statements (%)
No significant value	11.7	0
Management efficiency	29.4	78.2
Better leadership	62.7	63.0
Improved staff morale	50.9	41.3
Improved staff efficiency	25.4	54.3
Customer and supplier links	29.4	13.0
Attracted investment	15.6	27.9
Improved public image	43.6	27.9
Other	17.6	13.0
Respondents	51	46

Note: Respondents could choose any number of alternatives.

Managers appeared to see the mission and objectives statements as more useful internally than externally despite the fact that the actual words seem to focus on customers and shareholders. The mission statement, which was seen as a symbol of leadership, was more likely to be revised when new managers were appointed than when there was a change in the business environment. In terms of improved 'efficiencies', there was more support for the sharper focus of objectives statements.

Adapted from Brabet, J. and Klemm, M. (1994) 'Sharing the vision: company mission statements in Britain and France', *Long Range Planning*, vol. 27, no. 1, pp. 84–94.

Theories of business goals and objectives

Economists, it has to be said, have not normally made such fine distinctions between goals and objectives in the way described above but have instead tended to use these terms almost interchangeably. Nevertheless, we can identify five schools of thought:

1 Classical profit maximisation theory.
2 Managerial theories.
3 Behavioural theories.
4 Structure–conduct–performance paradigm.
5 Principal–agent theory.

The profit maximisation principle

Traditionally economists have assumed that the main goal of a business is profit maximisation and that if the firm is acting rationally, it will respond to 'supply signals' (e.g. changes in its costs) by adjusting either its pricing policy or its output or both. According to this theory of business behaviour, the firm is essentially a 'black box'. It assumes that:

➤ There is no division between ownership and control and the manager who makes the decision is also the owner of the business.
➤ The firm knows with a high degree of certainty its revenues and its costs. In other words, the firm will be able to gauge accurately the effects of raising and lowering its price on its sales revenue and the effect of expanding or contracting its output on its costs.
➤ The firm is assumed to be producing one product for which no joint costs are incurred. In other words, there are no problems associated with the allocation of fixed costs between different products.
➤ Finally, the firm 'acts rationally' and it essentially pursues a single objective; namely, profit maximisation to the exclusion of all others.

It is easy to criticise these assumptions as being quite unrealistic, but before we discard the theory entirely let us consider an example.

The case of the Maxiprofit Shirt Company

The Maxiprofit Shirt Company produces a very smart sportshirt which has proved very popular. Its has both fixed costs (rent, rates, insurance, heating, lighting, administrative staff costs) and variable costs (e.g. labour cost, material costs) as set out in Table 6.1.

The average costs are simply calculated as:

$$\text{Average (unit costs)} = \frac{\text{Total cost}}{\text{Output}}$$

Table 6.1

Maxiprofit Shirt Company

(1) Output shirts/week	(2) Total fixed costs (£)	(3) Total variable costs (£)	(4) Total costs (£)	(5) Average costs (£)	(6) Marginal costs (£)
0	1,000	0	1,000		
					2.00
100	1,000	200	1,200	12.00	
					3.00
200	1,000	500	1,500	7.50	
					5.00
300	1,000	1,000	2,000	6.66	
					8.00
400	1,000	1,800	2,800	7.00	
					12.00
500	1,000	3,000	4,000	8.00	

The marginal cost (or extra cost) of producing one more unit of output is calculated as:

$$\text{Marginal (extra) cost per shirt} = \frac{\text{Change in total cost}}{\text{Change in output}}$$

For example, the marginal cost of producing the extra 100 shirts per week (which raises total output to 300) is the total cost of producing 300 shirts (namely £2,000) less the total cost of producing 200 shirts (namely £1,500), i.e. £500. Thus the extra cost is £500/100 = £5.00 per shirt. The profit maximisation principle simply states that the firm goes on expanding its output until the marginal cost of producing the additional output equals the marginal (or extra) revenue generated from the sale of that output. Imagine that the company sells its shirts for £8.00 each.

We can now construct a table of marginal costs (MC) and marginal revenues (MR) (see Table 6.2).

Table 6.2

Marginal cost/ revenues

Output	Marginal cost	Marginal revenue	
100		8.00	MC<MR
	3.00	8.00	MC<MR
200	(4.00)	8.00	MC<MR
	5.00	8.00	MC<MR
300	(6.00)	8.00	MC<MR
	8.00	8.00	**MC = MR**
400	(10.00)	8.00	MC>MR
	12.00	8.00	MC>MR
500		8.00	MC>MR

Note: Figures in brackets are the estimated marginal costs.

Because marginal cost is calculated between output levels, it is conventional to indicate that marginal cost relates to 150, 250, 350 units, etc. At output levels of 300 and less, the marginal revenue (£8.00) exceeds the marginal cost and hence adds to profit. At output levels of 400 and greater, the marginal cost exceeds the marginal revenue and hence reduces profit (Figure 6.1). Only at 350 units of output does marginal revenue = marginal cost (Figure 6.2). The profit here is at the maximum attainable (see Table 6.3).

Table 6.3
Maxiprofit Shirt
Company profit/loss

Output	Total revenue (£)	Total cost (£)	Profit (£)
100	800	1,200	−400
200	1,600	1,500	+100
300	2,400	2,000	+400
400	3,200	2,800	+400
500	4,000	4,000	0

Figure 6.1
Profits/loss

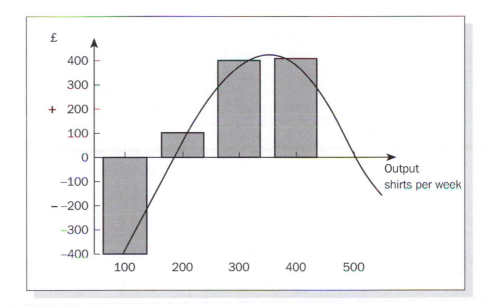

Figure 6.2
Marginal cost/revenue

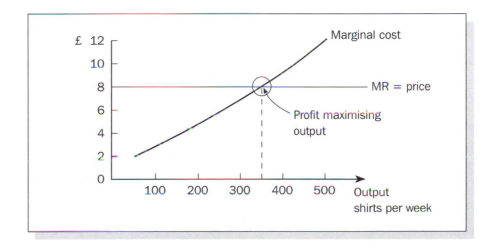

PAUSE FOR THOUGHT 2 *Suppose the price of the shirts were to fall to £5.00. How many would Maxiprofit produce in a week?*

PAUSE FOR THOUGHT 3 *What is the most efficient level of output for Maxiprofit to produce in a week and why does it not always produce at its most efficient level of output?*

For a good illustration of the profit maximisation principle in practice, see Case Studies 6.7 and 6.8 on BP in the appendix to this chapter.

Criticisms of the traditional model

As indicated above, it is not difficult to criticise this model of business behaviour. The two major grounds for criticism are:

1 Organisational.
2 Operational.

On *organisational* grounds it is argued that there is a division between ownership and control. The majority of major companies are not owned by owner-managers. Managers own very few shares in their companies, according to the pioneering work of Berle and Means (1932) in the USA and Florence (1961) in the UK. The modern business corporation is seen as run by managers who may pursue quite different objectives. Although the extent of this division between ownership and control has been questioned (Nyman and Silbertson, 1978), there is a consensus that non-profit goals are likely to be more important for firms. This has led to the development of the so-called managerial theories of the firm.

The second objection is on *operational* grounds and hinges on the criticism that firms do not actually calculate marginal costs and marginal revenue. Hence, it is argued, they cannot therefore operate as the conventional theory suggests. In a variety of surveys, it has been demonstrated that firms price their products in ways not envisaged by the profit maximisation theory. (For more details of these empirical studies, see pages 176–77.)

Managerial theories of the firm

Because of the division between the owners (shareholders) and the managers, it has been argued by a number of economists that managers are more likely to pursue non-profit goals such as sales revenue (or turnover) maximisation (e.g. Baumol, 1959) or growth maximisation (Marris, 1964). It has also been argued that managers may be more interested in pursuing the maximisation of their own personal goals (described as 'utility' or satisfaction) and that the personal goals of managers will be linked to the number of staff that they manage or the size of the budget they control or the 'perks' that they are able to acquire (Williamson, 1964). Collectively these theories are referred to as managerial theories and would appear to add significantly to the realism of the traditional theory of the firm. Each of these alternative models of business goals, however, acknowledges that the managers cannot totally ignore the wishes of the shareholders and that it is necessary for them to ensure that dividends are paid and a reasonable level of growth in the value of the shares is maintained. In short, the manager's freedom is constrained by the necessity of earning a satisfactory level of profit known as the minimum profit constraint.

For details of how the division between owners and managers affects business objectives, see Case Studies 6.5 and 6.9 in the appendix to this chapter.

Sales revenue maximisation

According to Baumol (1959), managers are more motivated by the growth of sales revenue (or turnover) rather than profit, because the managers' remuneration is often linked to this performance variable rather than some profit-related goal. The shareholders, it is argued, are more interested in profits growth and in shareholder returns (in the shape of dividends and capital gain). Managers, on the other hand, will have other priorities. Once a satisfactory profit is made, managers are much freer to pursue growth in sales.

This proposition has recently received interesting support from the following empirical study carried out by Conyon and Gregg (1994) on the relationship between executive pay and company performance.

CASE STUDY 6.3

Executive pay and company performance – Mr Kipling's recipe?

Early in 1995, the issue of executive pay shot to the top of the political agenda. The public debate that it provoked was based round some highly publicised pay awards that were received by the top executives of the recently privatised utilities. For example, Cedric Brown at British Gas was awarded a pay rise of 75 per cent, taking his salary to £475,000.

Nor did company bosses appear to require to succeed in order to receive handsome pay-offs. In August 1994, Peter Davies, the departing co-chairman of Reed Elsevier, a publishing firm, departed £2 million better off. Four directors ousted from Tiphook, the financially troubled transport firm that lost £331 million in 1993, shared compensation of around £4 million. Finally, Peter Sherlock resigned as chief executive of NFC, a road-haulage firm, with a reported pay-off of £750,000, two years after a hasty exit from Bass, the brewer, with a £395,000 'golden good-bye'.

It appeared as if Kipling's words about 'meeting triumph and disaster and treating those two impostors just the same' was fast becoming the maxim by which top British managers were paid!

Interestingly, the literature on the relationship between executive pay and performance is not extensive. One recent study sheds interesting light on this question. Conyon and Gregg (1994) considered the determination of top directors' pay during the 1980s using data from 170 companies between 1985 and 1990. Conyon and Gregg found in their sample that:

➤ Directors' pay rose by 10 per cent per annum in real terms, the equivalent of a real increase of 77 per cent from 1985 to 1990.

➤ The real growth of earnings of employees in the same firms was 2.6 per cent per annum or 17 per cent over the period.

➤ While the growth in top directors' pay was positively related to sales growth, it was only weakly related to total shareholder returns and not at all to current accounting profit.

➤ The growth in executive pay was systematically higher among enterprises that expanded by takeover activity rather than through internal growth.
➤ The growth in sales after takeovers was substantially higher than profits or returns to shareholders. Hence managers seeking to enhance their own pay or their marketability were likely to be keener on mergers than shareholders.
➤ Finally, the authors argued that these results 'raise questions as to whether effective control of managerial pay setting by shareholders is in place'.

Adapted from Conyon and Gregg (1994).

In Figure 6.3 total revenue rises as the firm sells more output. However, after a certain point (OQ$_3$) in order to sell more, the price cuts required fail to generate additional revenue. The total cost curve rises as additional output is produced and begins to rise steeply as capacity constraints are reached.

At output levels below OQ$_1$, the firm makes a loss as a result of high (fixed) costs and low output and sales. Profits are maximised at output OQ$_2$ and if the firm were a profit maximiser there would be no incentive to expand output beyond that level. However, in the case of the firm in Baumol's (1959) model, he argues that managers have an incentive to expand beyond output OQ$_2$. In essence, Baumol is saying that the drop in profits (from X to Y in the diagram) hardly affects either shareholders or managers, whereas the increased output from Q$_2$ to Q$_3$ greatly enhances sales revenue and, therefore, the manager's position (not to mention his remuneration). Provided the level of profits does not fall below the minimum level to keep the shareholders happy, then the managers are free to pursue extra sales revenue.

Figure 6.3
Baumol's model of sales revenue maximisation

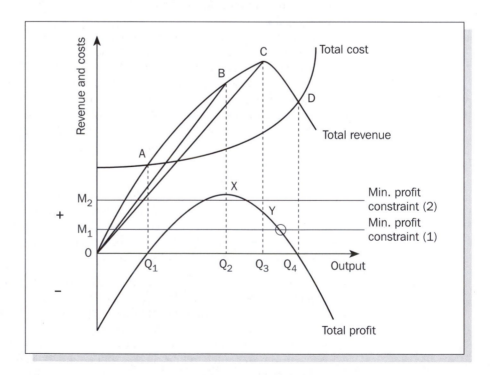

If, on the other hand, shareholders demand a higher level of profit performance from the company, then managers will have to respond. The minimum profit constraint now becomes OM_2 and managers would be forced to reduce output from OQ_3 towards OQ_2. However, given the hitherto comparatively passive nature of shareholders, managers normally have a considerable degree of freedom and discretion.

Growth maximisation

The Marris model is essentially a variation on this theme. The primary goal according to Marris (1964) is the growth of the company (normally measured by the growth of the assets over which managers have control). Again there is empirical support for the view that managers' salaries, career prospects and marketability in the executive labour market are all enhanced if they have had responsibility in managing a large growing company.

In this model, it is argued that there is a relationship between growth (G) and profit (P); the nature of that relationship is shown in Figure 6.4.

When the growth of assets is negligible, it is argued that profits are likely to be low. Initially, as the firm grows, so do profits because the company may be able to gain some advantages of scale as well as creating synergies within the organisation. Eventually, at a given rate of growth (OG_3), the firm attains maximum profit (OP_1). However, for reasons similar to those outlined by Baumol, Marris argues that managers will gain more satisfaction from the extra growth of the company than from the reduction in profit. Thus, there is an incentive for managers to look for further opportunities to increase the size of the company. More acquisitions may be sought. More of the profits of the company may be retained for expansion. However, after a certain point (OG_3) these additional growth opportunities are delivered at some cost. The firm's managers may diversify away from their core business, or they may decide to expand domestically with domestic multisite operations and/or internationally with the acquisition or creation of an overseas company. All of these moves will increase costs. Provided, however, that managers can ensure that shareholders

Figure 6.4

Marris growth model

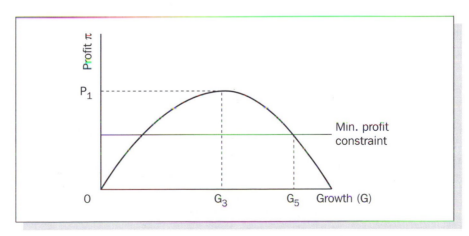

are kept happy, they are free to pursue these expansionist goals. If, on the other hand, shareholders become dissatisfied with the company's profit performance and require higher returns than the minimum profit, the constraint is raised and managers are required to switch their emphasis from growth of assets to profits once more.

The main point about Figure 6.4 is that managers can come under pressure from growing either too slowly or too quickly. Shareholders can in theory remove those managers who fail to deliver at least the minimum level of profit. If managers pursue a reckless policy of growth (i.e. beyond OG_5 in the diagram) they can be removed. Indeed, as the Saatchi & Saatchi case illustrates, this is exactly what happened to Maurice Saatchi. Between 1989 and 1993 the profitability of Saatchi was such that shareholders became more and more dissatisfied as the share price slumped. The expansion of the company had moved it into areas where it had little or no expertise or where it acquired companies at a premium price that failed to deliver an adequate return (see Case Study 6.5 in the appendix to this chapter).

Managerial utility maximisation

According to Williamson (1964), managers are likely to pursue their own satisfaction or utility, subject to obtaining a satisfactory level of profit. A manager's satisfaction will depend upon his or her power, status and influence. These in turn will depend upon three things.

The number of staff the manager controls

Other things being equal, managers will derive greater satisfaction from controlling a larger group of staff than a smaller group. However, the degree of satisfaction and utility will diminish the more staff a manager has directly under his or her control (see Figure 6.5).

After OS_1, the extra satisfaction achieved is in fact *negative*. The stress and pressure of managing a huge number of staff may in fact result in less satisfaction for a manager after a given point.

Figure 6.5
Utility and staff

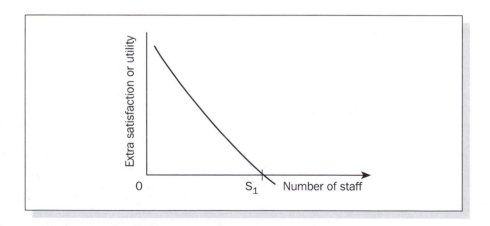

Figure 6.6
Utility and budget

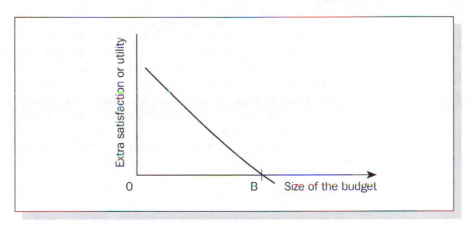

The size of the budget that the manager controls

One of the ways in which a manager's status is measured is by the size of the budget he or she commands. In most organisations managers require clearance before spending certain sums of money. At the very top of the organisation the senior executives may have very large budgets and have considerable discretion. At the other end of the spectrum a head of department may find that he or she cannot spend more than £1,000 without reference 'up the line'. However, even the budget a manager controls may be subject to diminishing marginal utility (or satisfaction – see Figure 6.6).

After OB, the manager's satisfaction may actually be negative. This is because of the extra responsibility and pressure on the manager to be accountable for the enlarged budget. A manager with a £1,000 budget is unlikely to bankrupt the organisation if he or she makes a mistake. However, a budget of millions of pounds is significant and when a manager moves into this league, the costs of making a mistake are magnified. Figure 6.6 implies that managers would prefer to avoid budgets greater than OB.

The size and amount of 'perks' managers enjoy

'Perks', or non-pecuniary remuneration, can often be a significant element of a manager's recompense. This may extend to a company car, private health

Figure 6.7
Utility and perks

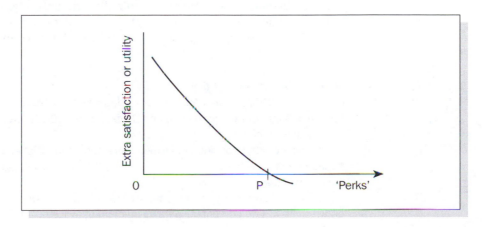

insurance, tax free expenses, foreign travel, business social events (e.g. golf tournaments, new product launches in exotic locations). A manager's status and power tends to be measured by such things, but for reasons similar to budgets and staff the extra satisfaction gained from 'perks' is also subject to diminishing marginal returns (Figure 6.7). Indeed there may come a point where extra perks may result in the manager having less satisfaction. This may come about because of envy or because of tax complications or because it may result in a backlash by influential shareholders.

Beyond OP, managers' satisfaction declines. The model thus states that

$$U = f (S, I_d, P)$$

Maximise U subject to π_{min} where

      U = managerial utility or satisfaction
      S = staff
      I_d = discretionary investment (or budget)
      P = perks
      π = profit
  π_{min} = minimum profit to keep shareholders satisfied.

In order to maximise U, managers will go on 'consuming' staff, budgets and perks up to the point where:

$$\frac{MU_S}{£S} \; = \; \frac{MU_{Id}}{£I_d} \; = \; \frac{MU_P}{£P}$$

That is to say, if the extra satisfaction achieved per £ spent on staff, budgets and perks were identical, then managers would be unable to reallocate money between these three categories and increase their overall utility or satisfaction.

This theory has a number of interesting implications. First, it implies that managers are not necessarily cost-minimisers, constantly on the lookout to cut costs. Indeed, it indicates that there are some costs that managers may actively enjoy incurring. Secondly, there may be an incentive for managers to incur some of these management costs as this will also reduce the reported profits of the company and hence the company's tax bill. Managers can thus feel doubly satisfied by incurring these additional costs. The theory goes some way to explaining such phenomena as 'empire building' and 'gold plating'. It also helps to explain the familiar phenomenon of chief executives who lavish millions of pounds on extravagant headquarters, as illustrated in Case Study 6.4.

CASE STUDY **6.4**

Maximising Attali's utility

On 25 June 1993, Jacques Attali stepped down as the first president of the European Bank for Reconstruction and Development (EBRD) after mounting criticism of his extravagance.

It emerged that considerable expenditure had been lavished on the EBRD headquarters, and there were other expenses that were investigated by a special audit committee.

Mr Attali had three company cars. He had extensive use of an EBRD credit card on which he ran up personal expenses amounting to £20,000. The report of the audit committee on the bank's over-spending underlined the idiosyncratic style of management of Mr Attali. The report focused on the £66 million cost of refitting the bank's London headquarters.

> Expensive marble was bought to replace the marble already there.
> Special expensive carpets were purchased.
> A specially designed high-tech suspended ceiling was built.
> Chairs were ordered at a cost of £1,000 each.

The report was not just confined to the spending on the headquarters. It looked at the much criticised use of special chartered flights. In a masterly piece of understatement, the report said: 'The committee is of the view that the bank's frequent use of chartered aircraft for travel to destinations well served by scheduled airlines was inappropriate.' Mr Attali, however, left defiantly and is quoted as saying: 'I know of no action that I have taken that in any way could be worthy of reproach.'

Based on information from *The Economist*, 24 July 1993, 10 July 1993, 3 July 1993, 12 June 1993 and *The Banker*, 4 August 1993.

Questions
1   What are the implications of the case of Mr Attali's utility?
2   Can such expenditures ever be justified?

Behavioural theories of the firm

In the discussion so far the goals or objectives of the firm have been identified as profit, or sales revenue or growth, or indeed the manager's own utility or satisfaction. The key assumption in all these theories, however, has been that there has been some objective to be maximised. Maximisation has been assumed to be the main goal in the firm.

This view of how firms behave has been challenged, first by Simon (1959) and then, subsequently, by Cyert and March (1963). Simon's contribution is interesting because he suggests that firms are not maximisers at all. Most managers of firms are what he describes as 'satisficers'. Figure 6.8 indicates the behaviour of a 'maximiser' while Figure 6.9 illustrates 'satisficing' behaviour.

The maximiser is continually seeking ways of improving performance, and even when objectives are achieved, looks to achieve improvements. The satisficer, on the other hand, settles for what is achieved. If the target is to achieve 3 per cent growth in sales or a 15 per cent return on capital employed, there is no drive to seek a better performance. The objective having been achieved, the manager tends to leave well alone and seeks the 'quiet life'.

If objectives are not achieved then two responses are possible. First, the manager may argue that the circumstances in the market place were difficult and that the performance, while not meeting the objectives, was nevertheless creditable. In other words, there is an implicit downward revision of objectives. This is likely to be the preferred route if profits are such as to keep shareholders happy. If, however, profits fall below the minimum profit constraint, then managers may be forced to take corrective action, but will only do so until the original objective has been achieved.

Figure 6.8
**Maximising
behaviour: the
decision-making
process**

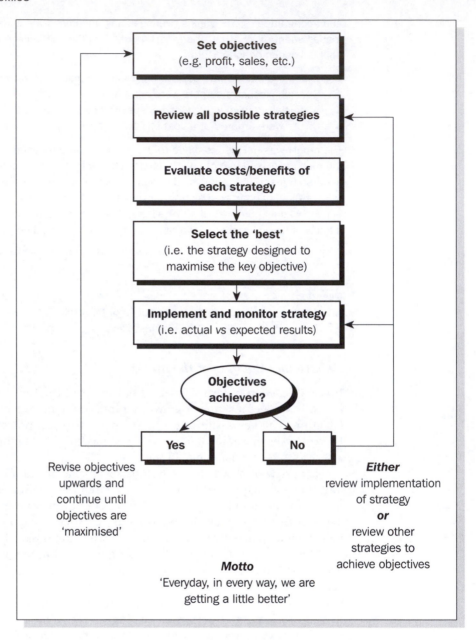

Set objectives
(e.g. profit, sales, etc.)

Review all possible strategies

Evaluate costs/benefits of
each strategy

Select the 'best'
(i.e. the strategy designed to
maximise the key objective)

Implement and monitor strategy
(i.e. actual *vs* expected results)

Objectives
achieved?

Yes

No

Revise objectives
upwards and
continue until
objectives are
'maximised'

Either
review implementation
of strategy
or
review other
strategies to
achieve objectives

Motto
'Everyday, in every way, we are
getting a little better'

PAUSE FOR THOUGHT 4 *In what circumstances are firms more likely to be satisficers than maximisers?*

Cyert and March, on the other hand, believe that firms pursue multiple objectives or goals which they list as:

➤ Profit goals (e.g. rate of return on capital employed).
➤ Sales goals (e.g. growth of turnover or market share).
➤ Production goals (e.g. to achieve a given level of capacity or to achieve a certain unit cost of production).
➤ Financial goals (e.g. to achieve a sustainable cashflow).
➤ Inventory goals (e.g. to ensure a sufficient level of stock).

Figure 6.9
Satisficing behaviour: the decision-making process

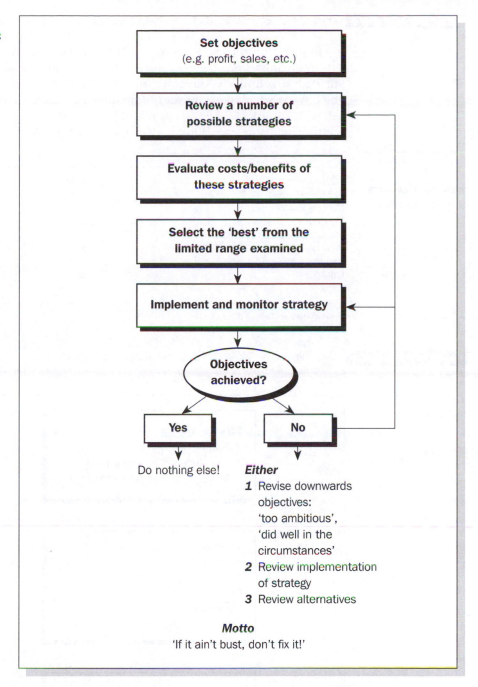

Within the organisation different groups will pursue different priorities. In order to achieve success the firms' managers have to compromise and 'trade off' some goals or objectives against others. For example, a single-minded pursuit of production goals can obviously conflict with sales goals (if the production levels exceed market demand), inventory goals (if the unsold production piles up in warehouses), financial goals (if the firm's cash is tied up in unsold output) and profit goals (if, in order to sell the output, prices are slashed to below cost).

PAUSE FOR THOUGHT 5 *Outline the possible conflicts between sales goals and profit goals.*

In short, it is the internal group and informal coalitions that spring up from within organisations that are important in determining which objectives are pursued. It is unlikely, therefore, that the single-minded pursuit of a single objective is what characterises the manner in which a modern corporation behaves. Empirical support is provided by a recent study of the objectives of Scottish companies (see Hornby, 1995 and Table 6.4 below).

Table 6.4
Important objectives of top Scottish firms

Objectives	Number	Per cent
No single objective	23	29.9
Maximising profit	22	28.6
Maximising sales revenue	1	1.3
Increasing shareholder value	11	14.3
Target rate of return on capital employed	7	9.1
Other	13	16.9
Total	77	100.0

Source: Hornby (1995)

PAUSE FOR THOUGHT 6 *Why might it be difficult to test behavioural theories?*

Figure 6.10
SCP model

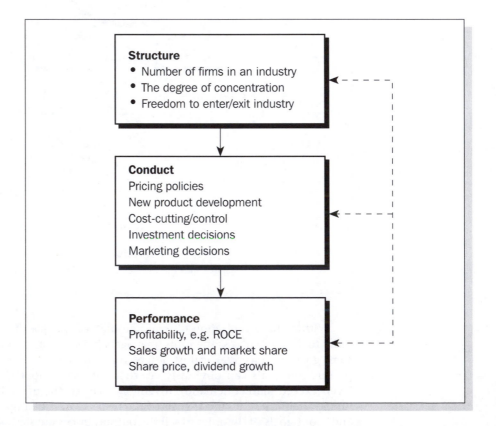

Structure–conduct–performance paradigm

There is a further school of thought which is relevant to the discussion of firms' behaviour. This may be called the structure–conduct–performance paradigm (SCP) or the industrial organisation school (Figure 6.10). The economists most principally associated with this school are Mason (1939), Bain (1956), and Scherer (1980). More recently, this model has been developed by Michael Porter (1980) and has become known as Porter's 'five forces' model, although its antecedents can be clearly seen in the SCP industrial organisation theories listed above.

The traditional SCP model indicates that the structure of an industry affects the conduct of firms within it, which ultimately influences the performance of these firms. In highly concentrated industries dominated by a few firms, companies may seek to avoid price competition and seek instead to erect barriers to entry. Firms may choose, therefore, to maximise joint profits rather than individual profits (for a more detailed discussion see Chapter 9). Conversely, it is argued that firms in more competitive markets will set prices at or near costs. Because of the fear of entry firms will not seek to earn abnormal profits. More recently, it has been argued that the process is a little more complex than the simple SCP model suggests. Cable (1994) argues that performance can clearly affect structure. Those firms which perform unsuccessfully may fail to survive, either going out of business or being swallowed up in takeovers. Equally, highly successful firms may encourage others to break into their market. Thus performance can affect structure.

These ideas have been popularised by Porter in his 'five forces' model (Figure 6.11). As Porter explains:

Figure 6.11
Porter's 'five forces' model

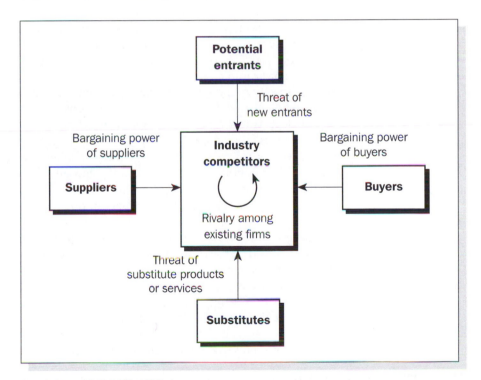

Source: Porter, M. E. (1985, 1988).

the goal of competitive strategy for a business unit in an industry is to find a position in the industry where the company can best defend itself against these competitive forces or can influence them in its favour. Structural analysis is the fundamental underpinning for formulating competitive strategy (Porter, 1980).

PAUSE FOR THOUGHT 7 *Take an example of an industry (e.g. food retailing) and identify the strength of the five forces identified in Porter's model.*

Principal–agent theory

Principal–agent theory considers the relationship between the owners of the firm and the managers and also the relationship between the managers and those they manage.[2]

The simplest version of this model assumes that the principals (the owners or shareholders of the firm) delegate to the agent (the manager) the responsibility for selecting and implementing an action. The agent receives a reward from the principal with the principal receiving what is left after payment of the compensation. The major problem is for the principal to negotiate a contract specifying the agent's reward given that the two parties may have different interests.

For example, a contract which guarantees the agent an income irrespective of the outcome means that there is no incentive for the manager to take risks. On the other hand, a contract which pays the agent entirely according to the profit earned may mean that there is now a coincidence of interest but the agent may be unwilling to sign such an agreement since the risks are too high.

In addition, concepts such as 'moral hazard' and 'adverse selection' are introduced to principal–agent theory. Moral hazard occurs when the principal and agent share the same information up to a point where the agent chooses a particular action. The principal, on the other hand, is only able to observe the outcome. For example, for a shareholder it is impossible to draw up a contract that will specify every action in every situation that may confront a manager. The shareholder therefore cannot hope to observe the manager's daily actions. Nevertheless, these actions will clearly affect the outcome and, hence, the rewards. This is moral hazard. Secondly, there is the concept of adverse selection. Adverse selection occurs when the agent (the manager) is privy to information to which the principal (the owner) is not. Thus although both the action and the outcome are observed, the principal cannot judge whether the agent acted optimally. Only the agent has the necessary information to evaluate that.

One way to try to overcome the obvious differences in objectives between principal and agent would be to try to devise contracts which bring about a coincidence of aims. The rise of share options bonus schemes as a means of rewarding top executives is one obvious way. Another possible mechanism exists through the threat of takeover. Managers, it is argued, are kept in check and honour their contracts with existing shareholders because they fear for their jobs in any takeover. The threat of takeover as a mechanism for controlling managers is, however, greatly exaggerated and managers are often adept at concocting devices to thwart takeover bids (e.g. poison pills, green-mailing, golden parachutes).

PAUSE FOR THOUGHT 8 *What do you think poison pills, green-mailing and golden parachutes are?*[3]

Figure 6.12
Principal–agent relationships

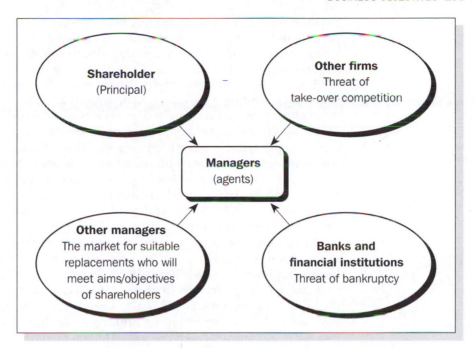

Yet another control mechanism is the threat of bankruptcy. The agents are constrained from taking actions which will put their own jobs in jeopardy. The banks and other financial institutions can also play a part and have a relationship with managers. Finally, there exists a market for managerial talent, albeit an imperfect one. If managers are not performing, they can be sacked.

As can be seen in Figure 6.12, there are therefore a variety of control mechanisms and relationships in this model. As Strong and Waterson (1987) argue:

> Thus rather than one contract between principal and agent, control over managers in fact involves a nexus of (partly implicit) contracts between these various interest groups and management involving multiple principals and perhaps multiple agents. Managerial behaviour is not determined by shareholders alone.

Business objectives in practice

There have been a number of studies which have attempted to evaluate the extent to which companies are profit maximisers. As long ago as 1939 two economists, Hall and Hitch, cast doubt on the traditional classical assumptions of profit maximisation when they questioned a small sample of firms on how they priced their products (Hall and Hitch, 1939). They discovered that few firms had even heard of the concepts of marginal cost and marginal revenue and hence they argued that it was not possible for firms to maximise profits without knowledge of such concepts. However, a more thorough and rigorous survey was conducted by Shipley (1981). This survey of 728 firms in the UK attempted to define what was meant by 'profit maximisation'. Shipley defined as true profit maximisers those firms who claimed both to maximise profits and to regard profit as being of overriding importance. He concluded that only 15.9 per cent of his sample were true profit maximisers as he had defined the term. Using a similar methodology, Hornby (1959) found that 24.7 per cent of respondents in a small sample of 77 top Scottish companies could be defined as profit maximisers using the Shipley definition. These results may appear somewhat disappointing given the importance that economists attach to the principle of profit maximisation. However, it may be that managers may not always recognise their behaviour as profit maximisation even though they may behave in this fashion. It has been suggested that setting a target rate of return, and being prepared to review this target upwards when it is achieved, is behaviour consistent with the notion of profit maximisation. When managers are asked to describe the way in which objectives are set and projects are evaluated, they often describe behaviour that would be regarded by economists, but not by the managers, as consistent with notions of profit maximisation.

In addition, firms may place greater emphasis on long-term profit maximisation. For example, in Shipley's survey almost 60 per cent gave priority to long-term profits as opposed to only 20 per cent who emphasised short-term profitability. The problem is to identify the behaviour that is consistent with the firm's objective of long-term profit maximisation. The danger is that almost any type of behaviour, including running losses in the short term, may be thought to be consistent with the goal of long-term profit maximisation.

A more plausible explanation is that firms are *not* maximisers; they are 'satisficers', to use Simon's terminology (see Simon, 1959). In the study by Hornby in 1995 he found that almost 30 per cent of firms had no single objective and that 51.9 per cent of the sample of top Scottish companies could be defined as 'satisficers'. This result is borne out by a subsequent study by Hornby and Macleod (1996) which indicated that 55.5 per cent of the major Scottish computer firms regarded themselves as 'satisficers' while only 3.7 per cent were true profit maximisers. There was some evidence that, in this industry at least, maximising sales revenue was regarded as a significant objective with 63 per cent citing this as a significant influence on their pricing policies.

Conclusions

This chapter has dealt with the objectives that firms have set themselves. It has looked at the traditional economic theory of profit maximisation that economists have used for decades in order to predict how firms will behave. It has also looked at alternative managerial and behavioural theories and briefly at the empirical evidence to support each of these theories. Managers are likely to pursue multiple objectives, with profits being a significant objective.

Appendix

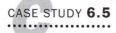

CASE STUDY **6.5**

Ownership and control, and business objectives – the case of Saatchi versus Saatchi

The conventional wisdom has it that the modern business corporation is owned by its shareholders but run and managed by directors and managers. As shareholders are widely dispersed both geographically and in terms of their individual holdings, managers are left free to run the business and to pursue their own goals and objectives. However, in 1995, there was a dramatic example of the exercise of shareholder power which challenged this conventional view – although it is a case not without controversy.

The Economist (14 January 1995), for example, described the boardroom mutiny which saw Maurice Saatchi resign as company chairman as 'long overdue', and went on: 'It was another excellent sign that the big shareholders of big companies are at last beginning to live up to their responsibilities as owners.'

On the other hand, the chairman of Dixons described the events as 'one of the worst examples of corporate governance I have ever witnessed'.

Such a sudden removal of a chairman by shareholders is rare in Britain, although it is more common in the United States where shareholder power has removed the bosses at General Motors, IBM and American Express.

The major issue at stake in this case centred around who owns companies and how should they exercise their power. In Britain, shareholders have not normally exercised such direct control as removing the chairman and it is interesting to note that the main spokesman for the institutional shareholders was David Herro, an American fund manager and director of international investments at Harris Associates which held 9.8 per cent of Saatchi & Saatchi stock, and is its largest shareholder. This followed news in October 1994 that the American company General Electric had raised its stake to 5.02 per cent. Other large American shareholders were media mogul Laurence Tish and Fidelity, the world's largest mutual fund group, and it was rumoured then that the American shareholders were ready to strike.

Herro was unrepentant and summed up the mood of the major institutional shareholders. 'We feel the company is tremendously undervalued. These brothers [Maurice and Charles Saatchi] destroyed this company.'

He is reported to have recommended that the chairman 'be taken out and shot!'.

The rise and fall of Saatchi & Saatchi is set out in Table CS6.5.1.

Table CS6.5.1
Profit/loss table

	1989	1990	1991	1992	1993
Sales (£'000)	4364	4354	5072	3973.5	4279
Operating profit (£'000)	44.1	63.9	(22.5)	(577.4)	33.9
Return on sales (%)	1.0	1.5	(0.4)	(14.5)	0.8

Source: Thomson Financial Extel (1995).

Globalisation became Saatchi & Saatchi's guiding principle in the 1980s: 'Globalise or die', to quote Saatchi & Saatchi's Annual Report. Inspired by the writings of Professor Levitt of Harvard University,[4] Maurice Saatchi set about creating a global advertising agency. By the end of the 1980s, Saatchi & Saatchi had achieved its mission. It was, however, to 'reap the whirlwind' of this expansion. Its problems are clearly identified in the table. John Kay describes the problems Saatchi & Saatchi created for themselves at this time:[5]

> Saatchi & Saatchi began with a reputation that was unmatched in its business and a creative team that was almost equally admired. These are characteristic assets of the highly successful professional service firm. The firms it bought were firms which had precisely these assets themselves. Its largest acquisition, Ted Bates, was itself one of the largest and most respected advertising agencies

in the United States and had no need of the Saatchi label. It already enjoyed an equivalent reputation in its own market and there was never any suggestion that it would trade under the Saatchi name. International customers did not bring their business to the new merged agency. They took it away, fearing conflicts of interest as the enlarged concern was often already handling the accounts of its competitors. Ted Bates was worth less to Saatchi & Saatchi than to almost any other purchaser. Saatchi already had those things which made Bates valuable and they were worth less not more under Saatchi ownership. But in the grip of the strategic objective of internationalisation, Saatchi paid a large premium to gain control of that and other businesses. For a time, the inherent weaknesses of the strategy were concealed by the growth in the underlying earnings of the businesses and the capacity of the Saatchi share price to drift upwards on a cushion of hot air. Eventually earnings faltered and the hot air escaped. The company was left with a mountain of debt and a collection of businesses that while sound in themselves were not worth the prices that had been paid for them.

Not surprisingly, the share price collapsed – quite dramatically. Anyone who bought a share in 1987 would have paid more than £50. At the time of Maurice Saatchi's departure the share price was £1.50.

Subsequently, three further resignations from key people, Jeremy Sinclair (deputy chairman), David Kershaw and Bill Muirhead, caused ripples of panic among investors. A major problem with any advertising agency is that the assets (i.e. the creative people the agency employs) can simply walk out the door and take influential clients with them. Although contractually this can be made difficult, it is often very hard to enforce restrictions. One commentator who foresaw the creation of a new Saatchi agency and the pirating of key executives, said: 'This is the advertising industry... it is business as usual' (quoted in *The Economist*, 14 January 1995).

In addition, a number of influential clients, including British Airways, the Mirror Group and Dixons, either cancelled their contracts with Saatchi & Saatchi or threatened to do so. A spokesman for Hewlett Packard voiced the concerns of many: 'We are obviously concerned and are watching the situation to see if they are delivering the goods. If accounts managers [at Saatchi & Saatchi] are looking to move, we have to look to our good fortune' (quoted in *The Sunday Times*, 15 January 1995).

The unease among key managers and major clients spread to another group of loyal shareholders who saw the price of shares plummet still further and wipe even more millions from the value of the company. These shareholders threatened to sue the remaining directors. So not everyone was cheering this example of thrusting shareholder power. As one analyst put it: 'People buy stocks to sell them at a higher price. If you do not like the way a company is being run, why did you buy it? I do not know why a company should be made to jump through a hoop just so somebody can sell it when the price goes up' (quoted in *The Sunday Times*, 15 January 1995).

Based on information from *The Economist*, 6 and 14 January 1995; *The Sunday Times*, 15 January 1995; *The Money Programme*, BBC, 15 January 1995.

Questions

1   Is this the 'worst example of corporate governance ever seen'?
2   Should a group of shareholders have the right to remove a company chairman even if this is going to damage the share price for the remaining shareholders?
3   Has the growth of American institutional shareholders been helpful in your view?
4   What, if anything, does this case illustrate about managerial theories of the firm?
5   What ultimately happened to Saatchi & Saatchi?

CASE STUDY 6.6

Directors' pay – a national lottery?

A further study carried out by Gregg, Machin and Szymanski in 1993 investigated what they described as 'the disappearing relationship between Directors' pay and Corporate Performance'. Their 1992 survey, based on the relationship between the remuneration of the highest paid director and the economic performance of approximately 300 companies over the 1980s and early 1990s, revealed:

➤ The rate of growth of directors' remuneration was very high (about 20 per cent per annum on average).

➤ Directors' remuneration was very weakly linked to corporate performance, after adjusting for size, the state of the economy, etc.

➤ Any such links (between executive pay and company performance) broke down after 1988, when the very high pay awards received by top directors in the recession period up to 1991 appeared to be unrelated to the performance of their companies.

➤ It appeared that corporate growth was an important determinant of the change in directors' remuneration (it was estimated that a 50 per cent increase in sales growth resulted in a 10 per cent increase in directors' remuneration, other things being equal).

➤ Finally, the results of this research called into question the effectiveness of current systems of pay determination for top company directors.

The authors argued:

the findings ... should be a cause of concern to both shareholders and public policy-makers. Shareholders should clearly be concerned since the failure to set incentives in ways that align the interests of directors with those of shareholders is likely to reduce shareholder returns. From a public policy perspective, the fact that it is not performance but size that is the more important determinant of directors' compensation suggests that directors may well pursue mergers and acquisitions regardless of their economic merits. It seems important that an independent method of setting the pay awards of top directors (i.e. not partisan remuneration committees on which directors of other large companies decide the going rate) is introduced.

Adapted from Gregg, P., Machin, S. and Szymanski, S. (1993) 'The disappearing relationship between directors' pay and corporate performance', *British Journal of Industrial Relations*, Vol. 31, No. 1, March.

Questions

1 In what ways could executives' salaries be brought more into line with company performance?
2 'It seems important that an independent method of setting the pay awards of top directors is introduced.' What methods could be used and why is it the case that the present method seems so inadequate?
3 What relevance does principal–agent theory have to this case?

CASE STUDY 6.7

Profit maximisation – the case of BP (1992)

In 1992, Sir David Simon took over the running of British Petroleum (BP). When he took over the company, BP was described as 'demoralised, heavily in debt and losing money'. Three years later, Sir David was being hailed as 'Britain's most impressive industrialist' in a poll of leading industrialists.

This was achieved as a result of a ruthless pursuit of profit maximisation. While other managers talked about 'downsizing, outsourcing and empowerment', BP practised it with a vengeance. Since 1992 BP has slashed its workforce from 112,000 to 60,000. The organisation has been slimmed down with whole layers of management removed. Businesses which no longer formed part of BP's 'core activities' of oil, gas and chemicals, such as food and minerals, were sold off. The results of this reorganisation were impressive. By 1994, BP was making more profit per barrel of oil than any other oil major. Upstream costs (i.e. the cost of getting oil out of the ground) had been drastically reduced largely as a result of using sophisticated technology (e.g. three-dimensional seismic surveying). In addition downstream activities such as refining, which were traditionally poor at contributing to BP's profits in the past, began to improve. In January 1996, BP announced that it was going to sell about 30 per cent of its refining capacity world wide. This represented something of a departure for BP as it shifted the company's key objective from size to profit.

This approach is not without its critics both within the company and outside it, and there is no denying that the new strategy represents a sizeable risk. About 70 per cent of BP's profits came from its upstream activities in 1994. However, BP is unusual in that it is highly dependent on a limited number of oil and gas fields. Around 80 per cent of BP's oil and gas comes from North America and Britain and, furthermore, much of this comes from just a handful of large but mature oil fields in Alaska and the North Sea, both of which are nearing or are just past their peak. Although BP is opening up new areas for exploration and development these are mainly in areas where political stability is not very prevalent, for example in places such as Colombia, Azerbaijan and Algeria. The other problem is that by slashing expenditure on upstream activities BP has made it more difficult to reduce the costs of extraction in these less promising areas. Between 1991 and 1994, for example, upstream investment expenditure fell from $4 billion to $2.5 billion.

One analyst, Richard Gordon of the Petroleum Finance Company in Washington, DC, reckons that BP will not replace its existing reserves at a fast enough rate to compensate for the declining reserves of its existing fields and hence could face problems beyond the next decade. Size is not everything but it can help, as BP's major rival Royal Dutch/Shell has discovered. Shell's approach is in stark contrast to the approach adopted by Sir David Simon as it operates in over 130 different countries and undertakes a number of projects which, at the time, on the face of it, do not appear to yield a high return. Size, it seemed, was for Shell a goal in itself. This strategy offered Shell the opportunity to diversify and to throw up deals which eventually became money-spinners.

There is little doubt that BP's strategy has worked. By focusing on profit at the expense of size BP has hauled itself back into profitability. The real test is still to come, however, as BP moves towards the next millennium.

Adapted from *The Economist*, 20 January 1996.

Questions

1   Compare and contrast the objectives of BP and the Royal Dutch/Shell oil companies.

2   What are the risks associated with BP's strategy?

CASE STUDY **6.8**

Business objectives: the case of BP (1998)

In 1998 with the price of Brent Crude at its lowest level in real terms for 25 years, the oil industry was experiencing harsh times. The biggest industrial merger ever, between British Petroleum and Amoco, heralded a new era of consolidation in an industry where mergers had been scarce of late.

BP, whose American wing is based around the Ohio part of Rockefeller's Standard Oil empire, paid $48 billion to acquire Amoco, which was created from Standard Oil of Indiana. Although this represents a 15 per cent premium over Amoco's pre-bid value, the merger was applauded as a good fit: BP, it was argued, was generally better at the upstream part of the business (finding and extracting oil); Amoco at the downstream business of refining, distributing and marketing the stuff. Amoco's stronghold is the United States – hitherto a weak spot for BP. And the Chicago-based firm beefs up BP's gas and petrochemicals divisions.

As these empires are meshed together, it was claimed that there should be plenty of savings. Sir John Browne, BP's boss, who will also head the new company, has a flair for cutting costs: BP's workforce now has fewer than half the 112,000 people it had in 1992. Some 6,000 of the 99,000 jobs at the new BP Amoco are already earmarked to go; managers' bonuses will be tied to producing $2 billion in annual pre-tax savings by the end of 2000. Businesses that are not number one or two in their segments are likely to be sold.

All the same, Sir John promised much more than mere cost-cutting. He described both BP and Amoco as being 'at the top of the second division'. The deal put the new BP Amoco in a first division of 'super majors', alongside Exxon and Royal Dutch/Shell. The new firm will on some counts be these firms' equal: it will, for instance, have more oil and gas reserves than Exxon. More important, the merger puts BP in a different league from all the other companies in the business.

As a competitive tactic, this worked well, and for a time the oil industry was buzzing with gossip about further consolidation involving BP's former peers, such as Chevron, Mobil and Texaco. BP's bosses even speculate that the news may have caused a frisson of pain in Shell House, where its old enemy had been concentrating on overtaking Exxon.

Yet the question of whether the oil industry is charging in the right direction remains unanswered. Having left the Middle East long ago, all the majors are heavily dependent on giant fields that were discovered decades ago, many of which (particularly those in North America and Europe) are starting to decline.

The great task for today's oil firms is to replace these 'crown jewels'. In recent years a mere handful of fields containing more than 500m barrels have been discovered, in contrast with dozens of big new discoveries in previous decades. Deep-water reserves, such as those in the Gulf of Mexico and off the coast of West Africa, are expensive to extract. Russia, which sits on 5 per cent of the world's proven oil reserves, is prickly. in 1997 BP took a 10 per cent stake in Russia's Sidanco; it also reported a $20m loss due to problems there. The Caspian, where both BP and Amoco have struck deals, is stuck in a tortuous geopolitical argument over the route of pipelines from the area.

Then there is natural gas: demand is growing more rapidly than demand for oil, in part because burning it produces less pollution. Amoco has large reserves of gas. In 1988 it bought Dome Petroleum, a Canadian gas firm, for $4.2 billion. But transporting gas is difficult and it has no international spot market, forcing producers to find long-term buyers before any big investment in a gas field, which can be a long process.

BP thinks the merger will help it to deal with these difficulties. Simply by having a broader range of countries, it should be less vulnerable than most to upsets in any one place: Shell's problems in Nigeria made only a small dent in its performance. 'Your appetite for risk is a function of how much capital you have', one senior figure stresses. 'Now we can afford to make bigger bets.' Both BP and Amoco have often had to go into partnership on big oil deals; now they can bid alone. There is also a growing tendency by governments to demand that oil companies do more than just extract oil; they have to build infrastructure as well—once again pushing up the cost. BP and Amoco also say that they will reconsider the liquefied natural gas industry that they have shied away from in the past.

In all this, Sir John is careful to talk about size being an 'outcome, not an aim' and stresses his willingness to sell businesses as well as enter them. He is adamant, however, that scale does matter in some areas — and even in the fashionable business of knowledge. He claims that BP 's profit growth has partly stemmed from transferring expertise (in drilling technology, for instance) around the company; now these skills, built at great expense, can be put to work across a much wider group at little extra cost.

The same logic would presumably apply to Amoco's flair for retailing. But the case for size and creativity within a super major remains unproven. BP's return on capital employed – the main benchmark of profitability amongst big oil firms – was 14 per cent in the 12 months to the end of June, well above Shell's figure of 10 per cent (Amoco scored even lower at 9 per cent). Shell is even now starting a restructuring drive that may clamp back on investment. As for Exxon, its 14.5 per cent return has been achieved more by returning its capital to investors through share buybacks than by using it to grow bigger.

Moreover, the oil industry's future may turn on two things where nimbleness may count for more than size. The first is the long-awaited introduction of other forms of energy – a development where large reserves of oil may actually prove a handicap. The other, more immediate possibility is the re-entry of western firms to the Middle East. This is the real prize in the oil industry, both because of the Middle East's reserves and because it still costs less than $2 a barrel to extract oil there.

Furthermore, while OPEC, which is dominated by Middle Eastern producers, owns three-quarters of the world's proven reserves, it currently produces only 41 per cent of the world's annual oil supply. This means that as non-OPEC supplies begin to dwindle, or are made uncompetitive because of the low oil price, the importance of the Middle East is likely to grow. So far, winning deals in the Middle East seems to depend in larger part on the political astuteness and lobbying skills of oil bosses than on the size of their capital base. French oil firms, such as Total and Elf, have had a head-start in negotiating deals in Iran and Iraq because their government is more friendly to these regimes. Even the best-organised oil firms can be undermined by politicking.

Adapted from *The Economist*, 15 August 1998.

Questions

1 Have BP's objectives changed from 1992, in your opinion?
2 'Size is an outcome, not an aim.' What does this mean, and do you believe it?
3 Does size matter in this industry, and if so why?

CASE STUDY 6.9

The division between owners and managers

It is frequently argued that managers take a long-term view of the companies they run while shareholders are supposed to be more concerned with short-term gain. This view of the different objectives of owners and managers found powerful support from management gurus such as Peter Drucker and Michael Porter in the 1980s and early 1990s. For well over a decade this view went largely unchallenged.

In 1995, however, two pieces of research rather turned this comforting notion on its head. At the annual meeting of the American Academy of Management held in Vancouver in August 1995, two papers suggested that it is often investors and not managers who take the long-term view. In a study of 135 randomly selected manufacturing firms by two academics from the University of Texas, Rahul Kochlar and Partiban David found that the institutional investors are often responsible for encouraging research and development in firms in which they have a substantial holding. Those investors who have close links with the firms in which they have investments – for example, the banks – tended on the whole not to press the management to innovate. In addition, many managers believe that they have the long-term interests of the companies they manage at heart because they are always looking for ways of combining their talents with those of other companies to gain the benefits of 'synergy'. 'Synergistic companies' believe in the power of mergers to create long-term wealth for shareholders.

Unfortunately, the results of these mergers have nearly always been disappointing, depressing the share price and adversely affecting profitability. 'The higher the price paid for the acquired company the greater the losses for the shareholder' seems to be the general rule. All of which prompts the question 'if mergers are so bad why do managers persist in pursuing them as an important part of their strategy?' To help to answer that question, two academics from the University of Columbia, Matthew Hayward and Donald Hambrick, suggest that the prime motivation is 'managerial ego'. Their conclusion is based on the results of research into 106 publicly traded American companies involved in acquisitions costing $100 million or more between 1989 and 1992. They conclude that four things motivate managers to pay 'over the odds' for companies.

First, they put it down to inexperience. New managers are anxious to make their mark and hence tend to rush into deals in order to give the impression that they are doing something positive. Secondly, after a period of successful trading managers may begin to have an overinflated sense of their own organisational abilities. This often goes with a cash mountain which appears to 'burn a hole' in their pockets. Thirdly, the authors found that a powerful driving force for mergers was the managers' self-esteem as measured by their salary in relation to their peers. One sure-fire way to acquire such esteem is, according to Hayward and Hambrick, to manage a bigger operation and a quick way to do this is to 'go the acquisition route'. Finally, according to the research, the most important factor is self-publicity. Hayward and Hambrick estimate that each favourable story about a company boss that appears in the press adds on average a 5.4 per cent premium to the price paid for a company takeover.

The conclusion from all this seems to be that if a company has experienced a recent upsurge in growth, and has just appointed a new manager with a high salary and glowing profiles in the business press, watch out for a spate of ill-judged takeovers with the company paying over the odds and the share price plummeting!

Adapted from *The Economist*, 12 August 1995.

Questions

1   What is the conventional wisdom about the objectives of shareholders and managers?

2   How does the new research referred to above fit in with managerial theories of the firm and in particular Oliver Williamson's Managerial Discretion Model?

CASE STUDY **6.10**   **The diminishing importance of size**

The 1980s saw a swing away from size as a major goal of firms as more and more large companies experienced difficulties. Companies like IBM and General Motors, which in the 1980s were hailed by management gurus as the model firms of the future, were savaged in the 1990s as the business equivalent of prehistoric dinosaurs. As smaller companies such as CNN in the television news media market and Microsoft in the computer business showed, being small and nimble on your feet was the way to be in the mid-1990s. It was calculated by David Birch at the Massachusetts Institute of Technology that, in the last decade, eight out of ten new jobs were being created by small firms.

The reasons for the growth and development of the small business were not hard to find. The liberalisation of the capital market with increasing competition between capital providers for business coupled with the introduction of microtechnology has helped to reduce the barriers to entry in a number of markets. Markets, too, are fragmenting, resulting in the growth of firms serving particular market niches. Thus 'flexibility' became the watchword and superseded 'economies of scale' as the driving force for firms.

Recently, this view has been challenged by Bennett Harrison, a professor at Carnegie-Mellon University in the United States. His case is supported by four propositions. Firstly, the case against big business has been overstated. While it is true that IBM and Daimler-Benz have run into trouble, there are numerous examples of big firms that continue to prosper, such as Coca-Cola, McDonald's and Toyota. The biggest challengers to big businesses are other big businesses and in spite of the need for flexibility, economies of scale are still very important in giving firms a competitive edge.

Secondly, a large number of big firms have restructured or 're-engineered' themselves as a result of the traumas they faced in the recessionary times of the late 1980s and early 1990s. Firms such as ITT and AT&T which sprawled across a whole range of industries have discovered the wisdom of focusing on 'core competences' and have decided to 'stick to the knitting', to use the graphic phrase of one management guru. Thus firms such as Xerox and Hewlett Packard and 3M are now discovering that it is possible to be both 'big and lean'.

Thirdly, the job-creating potential of small firms has been greatly exaggerated according to recent research published in 1994 by the National Bureau of Economic Research, which calculates that, in the United States between 1973 and 1988, plants with more than 100 employees created about 75 per cent of all new jobs while those with more than 500 employees created more than 50 per cent of the total. Small firms with less than 100 employees therefore created comparatively few jobs. In addition, small firms were also responsible for a far higher proportion of job losses than larger firms, and were less likely to use sophisticated technology.

Fourthly, many small firms rely very heavily on large firms for their survival. This trend has been accelerated by the process of 'contracting out' activities from the larger firms to smaller businesses which often places the smaller firms at the mercy of their bigger customers. Indeed, such are the relationships and the contractual arrangements that are prevalent with contracting out that it is argued the small firms cannot in reality be regarded as truly independent.

It is in relation to this last trend that one begins to see that the distinction between small and large firms is becoming very 'fuzzy' and blurred. Larger companies are thus trying to imitate the flexibility of small firms by creating smaller, more autonomous units within their organisations. For example, Asea Brown Boveri, the Swedish–Swiss engineering company, has split itself up into 1,300 independent companies and 5,000 autonomous profit centres. To counteract their weak bargaining power, smaller firms are seeking alliances and partnerships and forging longer term relationships with the larger firms. In America, small software companies aim to extend their influence and range by seeking out partners of a similar size whose strengths complement their own.

The result of all this re-invention and re-engineering is that it is often very difficult to define a company as 'big' or 'small'. Take Benetton, for example. It is clearly a 'big' company operating across international frontiers with a huge following and a worldwide reputation to match. And yet, judged in terms of its core business, it is really a series of small local businesses working to the Benetton formula. Similarly, Nike can be viewed as a large multinational or as a series of small locally orientated firms working to the Nike prescription. Indeed it has been argued that such firms are really 'fluid networks' rather than single entities who 'add value by co-ordinating activities across geographical and corporate boundaries'. Size therefore becomes more difficult to pin down with firms being simultaneously both 'big' and 'small'!

Adapted from *The Economist*, 14 May 1994.

Questions

1   What factors, according to the article, have lowered the barriers to entry into markets?
2   Why is it argued that 'flexibility is more important than economies of scale'?
3   Outline the case against the 'small is beautiful' school of thought.
4   Why is size 'all in the mind'?

Notes
....

[1]   See Klemm, Sanderson and Luffman (1991).
[2]   For a detailed discussion see Strong and Waterson (1987).
[3]   For help, read Cable (1994), p. 24; see also Gilman and Chan (1990), pp. 26–37.
[4]   See Levitt (1983), pp. 92–102.
[5]   See Kay (1993), pp. 12–13.

References and additional reading
....

Adams, S. (1996) *The Dilbert Principle*, Harper Business, New York.

Bain, J.S. (1956) *Barriers to New Competition*, Harvard University Press, Cambridge, MA

Baumol, W.J. (1959) *Business Behaviour, Value and Growth*, Macmillan, London.

Berle, A. and Means, G. (1932) *The Modern Corporation and Private Property*, Macmillan, London.

Brabet, J. and Klemm, M. (1994) 'Sharing the vision: company mission statements in Britain and France', *Long Range Planning*, Vol. 27, No. 1, pp. 84–94.

Cable, J.R. (1988) 'Organisational form and economic performance', in Thompson, S. and Wright, M. (eds) *Internal Organisation, Efficiency and Profit*, Philip Allan, Oxford.

Cable, J.R. (ed.) (1994) *Current Issues in Industrial Economics*, Macmillan, Basingstoke.

Coase, R. (1937) 'The nature of the firm', *Economica*, Vol. 4, pp. 386–405.

Coase, R. (1988) *The Firm, the Market and the Law*, University of Chicago Press, Chicago.

Conyon, M.J. and Gregg P. (1994) 'Pay at the top: a study of the sensitivity of top director remuneration to company specific shocks', *National Institute Economic Review*, August, pp. 83–91.

Cunningham, D. and Hornby, W. (1993) 'The pricing decision in small firms: theory and practice', *Management Decision*, Vol. 31, No. 7, pp. 46–55.

Cyert, R.M. and March, J.G. (1963) *A Behavioural Theory of the Firm*, Prentice-Hall, New York.

Earl, P.E. (1995) *Microeconomics for Business and Marketing*, Edward Elgar, Aldershot, esp. ch. 6, pp. 144–55.

Fama, E. and Jensen, M. (1983) 'Separation of ownership and control', *Journal of Law and Economics*, Vol. 26, pp. 301–26.

Florence, P. (1961) *Ownership, Control and Success of Large Corporations*, Sweet & Maxwell, London.

Gilman, R. and Chan P.S. (1990) 'Mergers and takeovers', *Management Decision*, Vol. 28, No. 7, pp. 26–37

Griffiths, A. and Wall, S. (1996) *Intermediate Microeconomics*: *Theory and Applications*, Longman, London, esp. ch. 5, pp. 205–49.

Griffiths, A. and Wall, S. (1997) *Applied Economics*, Longman, London, esp. ch. 3, pp. 53–68.

Hill, C.W.L. (1984) 'Organisational structure: the development of the firm and business behaviour', in Pickering, J.J. and Cockerill, T.A.J. (eds) *The Economic Management of the Firm*, Philip Allan, Oxford.

Hornby, W.B. (1995) 'Economics and business: the theory of the firm revisited: a Scottish perspective', *Management Decision*, Vol. 33, No. 1, pp. 33–41.

Hornby, W.B. and Macleod, M. (1996) 'Pricing behaviour in the Scottish computer industry', *Management Decision*, Vol. 34, No. 6, pp. 31–42.

Jensen, M. (1983) 'Organisational theory and methodology', *Accounting Review*, Vol. 50, pp. 319–26.

Kay, J. (1993) *Foundations of Corporate Success*: *How Business Strategies Add Value*, Oxford University Press, Oxford.

Klemm, M., Sanderson, S. and Luffman, G. (1991) 'Mission statements: selling corporate values to employees', *Long Range Planning*, Vol. 24, No. 3, pp. 73–8.

KPMG Peat Marwick (1993) 'A study of the top 100 companies in Manchester', quoted in *The Financial Times*, 4 June 1993.

Levitt, T. (1983) 'The globalisation of markets', *Harvard Business Review*, No. 1 (May–June), pp. 92–102.

Marris, R. (1964) *The Economic Theory of Managerial Capitalism*, Macmillan, London.

Mason, E.S. (1939) 'Price and production policies of large scale enterprises', *American Economic Review, Paper and Proceedings*, Vol. 29, Part 1 (supplement), pp. 61–74.

Milgrom, P. and Roberts, J. (1993) *Economics, Organisation and Management*, Prentice-Hall, London.

Nyman, S. and Silberston, A. (1978) 'The ownership and control of industry', *Oxford Economic Papers*, March, Vol. 30, pp. 82–9.

Pickering, J.F. and Cockerill, T.A.J. (1984) *The Economic Management of the Firm*, Philip Allan, Oxford.

Porter, M. (1980) *Competitive Strategy*, Free Press/Collier Macmillan, London, pp. 4–5.

Reekie, W.D. and Crook, J. (1987) *Managerial Economics*, Philip Allan, Oxford, esp. ch. 3, pp. 49–84.

Scherer, F.M. (1980) *Industrial Market Structure and Economic Performance*, Rand McNally, Chicago.

Shipley, D. (1981) 'Pricing objectives in British manufacturing industry', *Journal of Industrial Economics*, Vol. 39, June, pp. 429–43.

Simon, H.A. (1959) 'Theories of decision-making in economics', *American Economic Review*, June, Vol. 49, pp. 56–65.

Strong, N. and Waterson, M. (1987) 'Principal, agents and information', in Clarke, R. and McGuinness, T. (eds) *The Economics of the Firm*, Philip Allan, Oxford.

Williamson, O.E. (1964) *The Economics of Discretionary Behaviour*, Prentice-Hall, New York.

Williamson, O.E. (1975) *Markets and Hierarchies and Anti-Trust Implications*, Free Press, New York.

Williamson O.E. (1985) *The Economic Institutions of Capitalism*, Free Press, New York.

CHAPTER 7

Demand in theory and practice

Objectives

By the end of this chapter you will be able to:

➤ Identify the various stages in creating a demand model.

➤ Derive a demand curve.

➤ Understand and apply the concept of elasticity of demand.

➤ Identify the factors affecting price elasticity.

➤ Assess the dangers and the pitfalls in using demand models.

➤ Evaluate alternative techniques for forecasting demand.

➤ Assess the extent to which the techniques discussed are used in industry.

Key concepts

Coefficient of determination (R^2): a measure of the closeness of fit between the regression line and the actual data. R^2 is the percentage of the total variation 'accounted for' or 'explained by' the regression line.

Correlation (R): a measure of the closeness of fit between the regression line and the actual data ($R = \sqrt{R^2}$).

Cross-sectional data: data gathered on a number of items at a single point of time.

Dependent variable: that variable which is seen as being influenced by one or more other variables.

Elasticity: a measure of the responsiveness of demand to a range of variables. Separate measures exist for price, cross and income elasticities of demand.

Independent variables: one or more variables which are seen as influencing some other (dependent) variable.

Least squares line: sometimes also called the line of best fit (*see* Regression line).

Multiple regression analysis: where more than one independent variable is on the right-hand side of the demand function.

Regression line: that line (or curve) which 'best fits' the data, in the sense of minimising the sum of squared deviations from the line.

Simulation: an attempt to capture economic reality in terms of 'models', consisting of a set of equations.

Time series data: data gathered over a specified period of time.

Introduction

At some point in the operation of a business, it will be necessary for the managers of the business to make some estimate of the demand for the firm's product or service. They may employ a variety of techniques from the 'rule-of-thumb' techniques (i.e. last year's figure plus a percentage) to more sophisticated methods using statistical techniques and computer simulations of the market. Most businesspeople remain profoundly sceptical of the validity of a lot of economic forecasting and regard economists as little or no better than astrologers at predicting the future. However, it is still a fact that no business can hope to survive without some view of the likely future demand for its output.

In this chapter we will first deal with demand theory in order that an insight can be gained into the way that economists look at demand forecasting. The chapter will outline the economic principles that underline this important area of business economics. The second part of the chapter will look at one of these techniques, regression analysis, in some detail as it draws on the theory of demand. Finally, we will look at a variety of other forecasting techniques before examining the ways in which businesspeople in fact forecast demand.

The theory

In order to understand the principles involved, it will be helpful if we look at a simple example.

Imagine that we wish to create a demand forecasting model for computer games. In order to undertake this task, we need to follow a number of separate steps in our process of building a model of the demand for this product. These can be divided into a number of stages.

PAUSE FOR THOUGHT 1 *What other factors might play a part in the demand for computer games? How would you incorporate these into the demand forecasting model?*

Stages in demand modelling

Stage 1: Identify the key variables

A number of variables can be identified as having an effect on the demand for computer games. For example, the price of the computer game, the disposable income of the consumers of the game, the level of advertising, the price of personal computers or games consoles on which the game will run, together with the price of competitive products which may be regarded as having a bearing on the demand for computer games (e.g. cassettes, compact discs). These factors are listed in Table 7.1 and an appropriate symbol is assigned to each.

Each of these factors can be given a symbolic representation as follows:

$$Q = f(P, Y, P_{hc}, A, P_{cp}, \ldots)$$

All that this means is that the quantity demanded (Q) is a function (f) of the factors identified. The precise relationship between Q and the other variables is what we will examine in the next section.

Item	Symbol
Price of the product	P
Disposable income	Y
Advertising	A
Price of home computers; consoles	P_{hc}
Price of competing products	P_{cp}

Stage 2: Specify the form of the model

We are now required to specify the form that any equation linking these variables will take. Very often we simply do not know with any certainty what the correct form should be, as this only becomes apparent when we test alternative formulations. There are a number of possible forms that an econometric demand forecasting model can take, but, basically, there are three main specifications:

1 *Linear*, e.g.
   $$Q = a + b_1 P + b_2 Y + \dots \text{ etc.}$$
2 *Non-linear*, e.g.
   $$Q = a + b_1 P^2 + b_2 Y^2 + b_3 A^2$$
3 *Logarithmic*, e.g.
   $$Q = aP^{b1}Y^{b2} \quad \text{or}$$
   $$\log Q = \log a + b_1 \log P + b_2 \log Y$$

where Q = quantity demanded (measured in volume terms, e.g. thousands per annum), $b_1 \dots b_n$ are the coefficients telling us the impact on the dependent variable (both direction and size) of any change in each independent variable, P = price, Y = income, A = advertising, etc., and a = constant parameter.

In the absence of any evidence to the contrary, we will assume that, in our example, the equation takes the linear form:

$$Q = a + b_1 P + b_2 Y + b_3 P_{hc} + b_4 A + b_5 P_{cp}$$

We can now set up a number of hypotheses (often called *a priori* hypotheses because they represent what we believe to be the relationships between variables before we actually have the necessary evidence to support our views). These hypotheses specify the relationship between the dependent variable (i.e. Q, the quantity demanded) and the independent variables (i.e. price, income, advertising, etc.). These are listed in Table 7.2.

Variable	Beta coefficient	Relationship	Sign
Price	b_1	Indirect	−ve
Income	b_2	Direct	+ve
Price of home computers	b_3	Indirect	−ve
Advertising	b_4	Direct	+ve
Price of CDs	b_5	Direct	+ve

The terms 'direct' and 'indirect' indicate the relationship between the dependent variable (quantity demanded) and the independent variables (price, income, etc.) and how these are expected to be linked. Thus, for example, we would normally expect that as the price of the computer games increases then so the quantity demanded would fall, assuming that there are no other compensating changes in any of the other variables (what economists refer to as 'other things remaining equal', or the 'ceteris paribus' assumption). Thus the two variables of price and quantity demanded are said to be indirectly related and the beta coefficient in the demand forecasting equation (b_1) should be negative (indicating that as price rises so the demand falls).

In the case of income and the quantity demanded, the expected relationship is a direct one – that is to say, as income rises we would expect that the quantity demanded would also rise. The beta coefficient (b_2) in our demand forecasting equation would therefore be positive.

PAUSE FOR THOUGHT 2	*What is the relationship between the demand for the computer game and (a) the price of personal computers and (b) the price of a potential competitor product, e.g. compact disc or cassette? What would you expect the signs to be of the beta coefficients b_3 and b_5?*

Stage 3: Gather the data

The next stage is to gather the data. In many instances this is the hardest part of the exercise. You must first decide on how you are going to measure certain key variables. For example, how should you measure income? Is it disposable income, average earnings or GDP? There is no single right answer here. Equally, something as apparently unambiguous as price can be subject to a number of different ways of measurement. Is it price with VAT or without? Is it actual price or is it a price index? Should it be measured in real terms or in nominal money-of-the-day terms? Is the important factor affecting demand the price level or the change in the price level? Each of these practical questions needs to be resolved before you can start to put the numbers into a computer for analysis.

Sometimes, in fairness, the forecaster really does not know which definition to use and will try a variety of different ways of measuring the same thing. Which of the various alternative measures will eventually be chosen often depends on how well they work in correctly forecasting demand!

PAUSE FOR THOUGHT 3	*1 What is the difference between a nominal price and a real price?*
	2 How would you calculate a real price increase?
	3 Can the nominal price rise but the real price fall, and if so how?
	4 Can you find any recent examples of where this might occur?
	5 What is the difference between the price level and changes in the price level?

Data can be gathered in basically two different ways:

1 *Time series data.* In this case data is gathered over a period of time. For example:

Year	Q	P	Y	P_{hc}	A	P_{cp}
1980	..	..	..	..	..	..
1981	..	..	..	..	..	..
...	..	..	..	..	..	..
1995	..	..	..	..	..	..

2   *Cross-sectional data.* The data is collected at one point in time but uses different sections of the population to get the information. Thus it may be possible to gather data by area. For example:

Area	Q	P	Y	P_{hc}	A	P_{cp}
1	..	..	..	..	..	..
2	..	..	..	..	..	..
...	..	..	..	..	..	..
10	..	..	..	..	..	..

In this case each of the numbers in the first column (1, 2, 3, ..., 10) represents a geographic area.

There is often a debate about whether time series data or cross-sectional data is 'best'. If the time series data extends over a very long period then it can be argued that it will be more difficult to rely on the results of such an analysis as so many other factors will have changed in the intervening period. The relationships identified may no longer be reliable and valid. Cross-sectional data is obviously not affected to the same extent by these sorts of problem. However, the representativeness of the population remains the biggest problem with cross-sectional data. Are the areas chosen a good sample of the total population? In short, there is no absolute guarantee with either type of data that you will get reliable forecasts, and very often the decision about which type of data to use is governed by totally practical considerations such as the way in which the information was gathered and published in the first place.

Once the data has been input into the computer we are ready to run what economists call a regression analysis.

Stage 4: Run the regression analysis

To understand the principles of regression, let us look at a simple two-variable model. Let us imagine we have a series of data from 1990 until 1996 which gives information on sales (measured by volume) and advertising (measured in £ millions). Let us further assume that we have adjusted the data to take out the effects of inflation. We can see the data below and let us imagine it looks like the accompanying graph (Figure 7.1).

Figure 7.1
Sales and advertising, 1994–2000

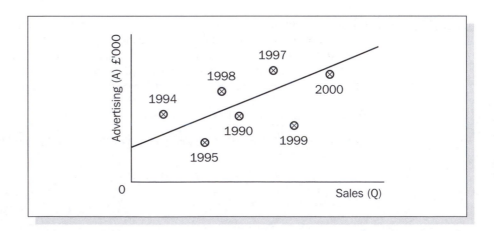

This is assumed to be a linear function which takes the form:

$Q = a + b_1 A$

In order to get an equation that fits this we use a technique known as ordinary least squares (OLS). However, most computers have installed a simple computer package which undertakes regression analysis and gives the answer quickly without the need to undertake tedious calculations.

Stage 5: Interpreting the results

Imagine we have put in our data, we have used the regression command in the relevant computer package and the computer has printed the forecasting equation as follows:

$Q = 3.7 + 0.4A$

where Q is the quantity demanded (measured by volume), and A is advertising (measured in £'000 per annum).

We can now use this equation to predict sales volume if we know the level of advertising in any future year. For example, if we estimate that advertising in 2001 is, say, £10,000 then we can 'plug' A = 10 into our predictor equation and forecast the likely level of sales. Thus:

$Q = 3.7 + (0.4 \times 10)$
$= 7.7$ (or 7,700 units per annum).

We can begin to use the model to interpret certain things about the product. Imagine that we have run the model through the computer. Because we have included more than one variable in the model, we use the technique known as multiple regression analysis (MRA). The technique is similar to OLS regression analysis except that there are now several variables. Suppose our predictor equation is as follows:

$Q = 100 - 10P + 0.01Y - 0.25P_{hc} + 50P_r + 0.1A$

If we know what the estimated values are for each of the independent variables then we can predict the sales for computer games. This is set out in Table 7.3.

Table 7.3
Predicting sales

Independent variable	Estimated value of the independent variable	Parameter	Estimated effect on demand
Constant	100	100	100
Price (P)	£10	−10	−100
Income (Y)	£10,000	+0.01	+100
Price of home computers (P_{hc})	£200	−0.25	−50
Price of records (P_r)	£2	+50	+100
Advertising (£'000)	£500	+0.1	+50
Total demand			+200

From this table we can predict the demand for computer games, given assumptions about the size of the independent variables. We are also in a position to derive a demand curve, as can be seen below.

Derivation of a demand curve

Let us assume that all other factors apart from price are as shown in Table 7.3. By 'plugging' the values into the predictor equation we arrive at the equation:

$$Q = 300 - 10P$$

PAUSE FOR THOUGHT 4

1 *Given the above equation, what is the maximum price that could be charged (i.e. the price above which nothing would be bought)?*
2 *Suppose the firm decides to give the product away, what is the maximum number that the market would take?*

We can now construct the relevant demand schedule (Table 7.4).

Table 7.4
Demand schedule

Price (£)	Quantity ('000)	Total revenue (£)
0	300	0
5	250	1,250
10	200	2,000
15	150	2,250
20	100	2,000
25	50	1,250
30	0	0

From Table 7.4 we can construct a demand curve (see Figure 7.2).

Figure 7.2
The demand curve

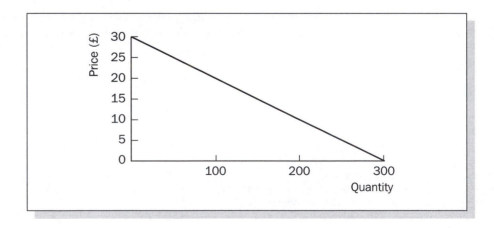

Elasticity of demand

Economists use the term *elasticity* to describe how responsive the quantity demanded is to changes in, for example, price or income or advertising. The central assumption in using this concept is that we observe the responsiveness of demand to changes in, say, price by assuming that all other things remain equal. There are a number of key elasticity concepts, some of which are set out Table 7.5.

For example, if the price is said to be price inelastic, this means that the proportionate change in the quantity demanded is less than the proportionate change in the price. A 5 per cent increase in the price resulting in a 1 per cent drop in the quantity demanded of the product implies a product where the demand is said to be price inelastic, i.e. having an elasticity value of less than 1. Similarly, if the demand for the product rises more quickly than the rise in disposable income, then the demand is said to be income elastic (i.e. the demand is very responsive to a change in income and has an income elasticity value greater than 1). Finally, a product may be described as having a high advertising elasticity of demand if a small percentage change in the level of advertising causes there to be a large percentage change in the level of demand.

Table 7.5
Elasticity concepts, symbols and formulae

Concept	Symbol	Formulae	Expected sign	Size
Price elasticity	E_p	% change in Q / % change in P or $(dQ/dP) \times P/Q$	−ve	$E_p > 1$ elastic $E_p < 1$ inelastic
Income elasticity	E_y	% change in Q / % change in Y or $(dQ/dY) \times Y/Q$	Normally +ve	$E_y > 0$ normal goods $E_y < 0$ inferior goods
Cross-elasticity	E_x	% change in QA / % change in PB or $(dQA/dPB) \times PB/QA$	+ve substitutes −ve substitutes	$E_x > 0$ $E_x < 0$
Advertising elasticity	E_a	% change in Q / % change in A or $(dQ/dA) \times A/Q$	+ve	$E_a > 0$

Price elasticity and the revenue rules

There are a number of important implications to the concepts of price inelastic and price elastic demand. These are to do with the revenue that results from a price increase/decrease. The rules are:

1   When demand is price inelastic, then price and total revenue move in the same direction.
2   When demand is price elastic, then price and total revenue move in opposite directions.

In order to see how this works out in practice we need to return to the demand schedule in Table 7.4. Total revenue is simply the price multiplied by the quantity demanded. Thus it can be seen from the table that as the price increases the total revenue increases at first, reaches a peak at £2,250 and, as the price continues to rise, the total revenue falls again. This is because initially the quantity demanded does not respond by as much as the initial rise in price. In effect, the demand is said to be price inelastic. To see how to calculate the elasticity from the table we use what is referred to as the 'arc' formula. This is because the calculation of percentages can be ambiguous.

PAUSE FOR THOUGHT 5 *What is the percentage change in price when it increases from £5 to £10? Now do the same calculation for a change in the opposite direction. Why should there be a difference in the answer for the same price change?*

Because of the 'percentage fallacy' (i.e. the answer you get in calculating a given percentage depends on the starting point), the 'arc' formula has been devised. Box 7.1 illustrates the way the formula works. It is directly equivalent to the calculation of percentages.

Box 7.1
···········

The calculation of elasticity values: the 'arc' formula

Because of the ambiguity created by using percentage changes, economists use what is known as the 'arc' formula for calculating elasticity values. To illustrate how this works, imagine that in 1999 the demand for widgets was 10 million per annum and the price was £2 each. In 2000 let us suppose that the price rose to £4 and, other things being equal, the demand fell to 8 million.

We can use the following formula, which will give us an unambiguous answer:

$$e_p = \{(q_2 - q_1)/(q_2 + q_1)\} \times \{(p_2 + p_1)/(p_2 - p_1)\}$$

where e_p = price elasticity of demand
q_2 = the new quantity demanded in 1995 (in millions)
q_1 = the original quantity demanded in 1994 (in millions)
p_2 = the new price in 2000 (£)
and p_1 = the original price in 1999 (£)

Thus the calculation is as follows:

$$e_p = \{(8{-}10)/(8{+}10)\} \times \{(4{+}2)/(4{-}2)\}$$
$$= (-2/18) \times (6/2)$$
$$= -0.33.$$

Demand is inelastic with respect to price and hence total revenue falls as price falls.

Question

Suppose that the price in 1999 had been £4 and that the number sold was 8 million but that in 2000 the price was dropped to £2 and, other things being equal, the demand rose to 10 million. What is the price elasticity of demand now?

This clearly demonstrates the important revenue rules. When the demand is inelastic (i.e. with a numerical value less than 1, ignoring the sign, which in the case of price elasticity is always negative), revenue rises with price. However, when the demand is elastic, with a numerical value greater than 1, the revenue decreases as price rises.

Factors affecting price elasticity

There are a number of factors that can affect the price elasticity of demand.

The availability of substitutes

In 1997 a number of research studies indicated that a 10 per cent increase in price would result in a 7 per cent fall in petrol use. The demand for petrol, which has few substitutes, is therefore inelastic. Conversely, the greater the number of substitutes the more elastic the demand curve is likely to be. As the number of competing products increases, consumers will be more sensitive to small changes in price, as Case Study 7.1 illustrates.

CASE STUDY **7.1**

Cola war takes the fizz out of Cadbury profits

Cadbury Schweppes, the UK confectionery and soft drinks group, admitted in September 1995 that it had become the victim of the high street cola wars with its joint venture with Coca-Cola in Britain suffering its hardest six months in its history.

The group is considering escalating the price war in cola to boost sales volumes after the recent entry by supermarket giants such as Sainsbury and Tesco, using cola produced by Cott Corporation, the Canadian Group. In addition, Richard Branson announced the introduction in 1995 of his own brand of cola, Virgin Cola, also manufactured by Cott.

'Every Tom, Dick and Harry is launching an original American cola now', said managing director of Cadbury Schweppes, Derek Williams.

The competitive conditions resulted in a 2 per cent drop in profits and a fall in the earnings per share from 12.89p to 11.72p.

'The company has fought its way through the hardest six months in its history', reported David Wellings, the chief executive.

Adapted from *The Times*, 7 September 1995.

Another factor that can influence the price elasticity of demand is the length of time over which the adjustment takes place.

The time period under consideration

The longer the time period the greater the opportunity for consumers to adjust their demand.

CASE STUDY **7.2**

The price of oil

In the early 1970s the Oil Exporting and Producing Countries (OPEC) raised the price of oil from about $5 a barrel to over $20 almost overnight. The effect on western economies was devastating, resulting in a massive transfer of spending power. The results were far reaching. As well as plunging economies into recession it also had a major impact on inflation and the balance of payments. At this time, the UK had yet to realise the tremendous potential of the oil beneath the North Sea. In the short run it was simply impractical for users of oil (householders, industry, electricity generators and other consumers) to find alternative sources. The effect was greatly felt on the import side of our balance of payments, which showed a deficit of £3.5 billion in 1974. Thus in the short run demand was inelastic and hence as prices rose so did the revenue that was earned by OPEC.

However, with the passage of time demand was able to adjust. The higher price for oil prompted the search for alternative energy sources and swung the balance in favour of nuclear power (a process hastened by the difficulties the government had with the miners throughout the 1970s). In addition, the higher price of oil gave fresh impetus to the search for oil in the North Sea. Exploration activity in the sector was closely linked to the price of oil on world markets. Consumers began to replace existing systems which relied on oil with other energy sources (e.g. gas). Thus as time passed so the demand for oil from OPEC began to subside.

The importance of the item or product in a consumer's budget

The greater the importance of this in a budget, then the more responsive will consumers be to a small change in the price and hence the more elastic the demand.

CASE STUDY **7.3**

The demand for beer

Two economists, Reekie and Blight, attempted to use multiple regression analysis to forecast the demand for beer. Using quarterly data stretching back over a 15-year period they were able to obtain 60 data observations. Their demand equation used the following predictor variables:

1 P_b the real price of beer (i.e. the price of beer in relation to the rate of inflation).
2 A_b the real level of advertising on beer (i.e. the level of advertising in relation to an advertising index of TV and press).
3 A_a the real level of advertising on other alcoholic drinks.
4 Y_r the real level of personal disposable income.
5 P_c the real price of other alcoholic drinks.
6 W the daily mean temperature.
7 S a seasonal factor to reflect the higher consumption of beer in the summer months and at Christmas.

The results of their analysis are as follows:

$$Q = 3.18 - 1.355P_b + 0.004A_b + 0.019A_a + 0.057W + 0.085Y_r + 0.371P_c + 0.019S$$
$$ (0.287) \quad (0.64) \quad (0.32) \quad (2.66)* \quad (5.84)* \quad (0.10) \quad (0.173)$$

t-ratios are in brackets. * indicates the statistically significant variables. $R^2 = 0.57$

Adapted from Reekie, W.D. and Blight, C. (1982) 'An analysis of the demand for beer in the United Kingdom', *Journal of Industrial Affairs*, Vol. 9, No. 2, pp. 45–49.

Questions

1 Can you identify the variable whose sign is not what you would have expected?
2 Are there any other variables that you might have included in the demand equation?

3 Why do you think that the two economists used real prices and real incomes in their model?

4 Can you explain the apparently perverse result with the variable which measures the real level of advertising of competing products?

5 What might explain why the model fails to predict a higher level of the variation in demand?

Problems and pitfalls of using multiple regression analysis

There are a number of problems associated with this technique. The key points are given below.

Data problems

One of the main problems that a forecaster can encounter concerns the collection of appropriate data. In a number of cases there may simply be insufficient data on which to build a reliable model. For example, it may only be possible to go back five or ten years to get figures on the demand for a given product. If, however, our demand equation contains four or five variables, then there is likely to be a very wide margin of error. Statisticians have a rough rule of thumb that there must be at least two more observations than variables for a regression model to be reliable. However, it would be most unwise to try to forecast the demand for a product on the basis of a model which had just five years' data and three predictor variables (e.g. price, income and advertising). It would be rather like trying to predict the result of a general election on the basis of a sample of five voters! However, if the product is relatively new then this may militate against using this technique as the basis of forecasting. One way round this data problem would be to use quarterly, monthly or even weekly data if it is available. Unfortunately, this is often not the case.

Another associated problem with data is that the multiple regression technique requires the forecaster to make estimates of the values of the independent variables (i.e. the price, income, advertising, etc.). So paradoxically, in order to forecast demand the forecaster is obliged to forecast these other variables as well. As these subsidiary estimates may themselves be subject to wide variations, it is perhaps not surprising that the technique is shunned by business people.

Measurement problems

There are often difficulties in how one might go about measuring particular variables. For instance, in Case Study 7.3 on the demand for beer, all the economic variables are expressed in terms of relative real values (i.e. the price of beer relative to the general retail price index). This is a perfectly defensible way of measuring price but it is only one of a number of possible methods. One could, for example, have measured price by taking the percentage change in the price index of beer; in other words, measuring the movement in the price rather than its absolute level. Either way is defensible, but would clearly give a different result. Similarly, when one comes to measure income, there are numerous ways in which this can be done from using real personal disposable income, as in the beer case study, to using gross domestic product (GDP).

Specification problems

What form the demand equation takes is not something that can be known with any certainty before the research has been conducted. The examples quoted so far in this chapter have all been linear models, but very often this will not be the case and there will be a non-linear relationship between the variables, and this can only be found by 'trial and error'. If, for example, it appears that one formulation of the model is producing poor results, then an alternative formulation will be tried to ascertain if this will produce better results.

Identification problems

The identification problem refers to the fact that when the forecaster is trying to forecast demand over a long period of time there may be supply-side changes which are happening simultaneously. In other words, what may be observed is not a relationship between demand and price, but an interaction between supply and demand which appears to show an inverse relationship between price and demand.

PAUSE FOR THOUGHT 6 *Why might the identification problem be less apparent with demand models which use cross-sectional data?*

As can be seen from Figure 7.3, what we have in this instance is not a single demand curve but a series of demand curves and a series of supply curves intersecting to give a series of prices. Thus it becomes hard to identify the demand curve in this situation. Unfortunately, this problem may be prevalent in those demand models which are based on data gathered over a long period of time where there have been significant shifts in the supply side. With cross-sectional data this is much less likely to be the case as the data will have been collected at a given point in time and there is therefore less likelihood that there will have been large supply-side changes.

Figure 7.3
Identification problem

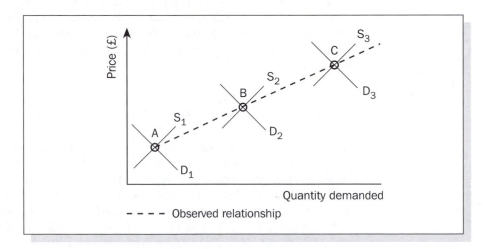

Technical problems

A number of problems of a technical nature, known as the 'residuals' or forecasting errors, are associated with all forecasts. With any forecast there will be a difference between what the model predicts and what actually happens in practice. The forecaster is hoping, however, that there will be no systematic bias in these errors so that the model is not producing persistent forecasting errors. One of the ways in which this can be checked is to look at how the model might have predicted the immediate past, and to compare the forecast results with the actual. While forecasting 'history' might seem a particularly useless exercise it does have the advantage of doing a 'dry run' to evaluate the residuals. If there is any systematic bias in these residuals (for example, the forecasting errors get bigger over time or display some sort of cyclical pattern) then the model is said to be suffering from autocorrelation.

Another problem can arise when there is a correlation between the so-called independent or predictor variables. For example, income and the level of advertising often move in the same direction over a period of time. It becomes very difficult, therefore, to disentangle the effects of these variables, especially as they are likely to be highly correlated one with another. When this occurs the model is said to be suffering from multicollinearity. This can usually be suspected if you discover that a model has a high coefficient of determination (R^2), but none of the independent predictor variables is statistically significant. The computer programs that enable the forecasters to use multiple regression analysis cannot distinguish the separate effects of two independent variables that are themselves highly correlated.

Alternative techniques of forecasting demand

In addition to the econometric methods outlined above there are a number of alternative techniques that can be used to forecast demand. The main alternatives are surveys, managerial techniques, market experiments, statistical techniques and barometric techniques.

Surveys

There are a number of different types of survey that are used to forecast demand. The three principal ones are:

1 Surveys of consumers.
2 Surveys of the salesforce.
3 Surveys of experts.

Surveys of consumers

There are a number of organisations that undertake market research on behalf of firms who wish to be able to forecast the demand for their product or service. The polling organisations will often include in their questionnaires questions about the reasons why consumers purchase a particular good and from this information profiles of consumers can be built up that enable the firms to identify the factors that influence the demand or, alternatively, help firms to identify areas where the demand for their product or service is weak and hence assist them to refocus their marketing strategy. Specialist publications such as Mintel provide firms with the necessary market intelligence based on the results of large sample surveys. An example is given in Box 7.2.

Box 7.2

Impulse Ice Cream survey: attitudes regarding Impulse Ice Cream in relation to frequency and type of purchase, February 1996

	Buy as an occasional treat %	Buy more frequently than previously %	Prefer scoop/soft ice cream %	Tend to buy frozen confectionery %
All	47	10	39	14
Men	48	8	34	13
Women	46	12	43	14
15–19	47	1	27	30
20–24	45	7	31	10
25–34	57	9	29	15
35–44	55	15	40	11
45–54	47	9	43	12
55–64	38	7	47	12
65+	38	15	48	13
AB	51	9	34	16
C1	52	13	40	15
C2	47	8	38	13
D	41	9	40	11
E	37	12	43	12
London	47	13	36	14
South	43	21	39	23
Anglia/Midlands	41	10	42	9
SW, S Wales	56	5	30	9
Yorkshire, N Wales	50	11	37	18
North West	51	4	39	16
Scotland	47	14	54	12
Pre-family	48	4	23	20
Family	56	13	41	12
Empty nesters	48	10	39	11
Post-family	38	12	48	12

Base: 1,023 adults

Source: BMRB/Mintel.

PAUSE FOR THOUGHT 7   *Before reading the next section, can you think of any advantages that surveys might have over econometric techniques?*

The advantages of surveys

There are several advantages with this technique of forecasting demand. In the first instance, such surveys are ideally suited to forecasting the demand for new products. Statistical techniques such as trend analysis (p. 200) and econometric methods such as multiple regression analysis require firms to have a run of past data on which to make a forecast. In addition, such techniques are often conducted at a high level of aggregation; in other words they deal with the demand for generic categories of product or service rather than the specific brand of a particular firm. For example, the demand forecasting model for beer deals with beer as a whole rather than a particular brand or label. Surveys overcome these difficulties by being much more focused. They are particularly suited to estimating the demand for products new on the market for which no data previously exists.

PAUSE FOR THOUGHT 8	*Before you read on, can you identify some of the weaknesses of surveys of consumers as a method of forecasting demand?*

The disadvantages of surveys

There are a number of disadvantages with using consumer surveys. In the first place they can be extremely costly to mount. The sample size needs to be large enough to produce meaningful results and this can increase the costs and the time needed to undertake the analysis. In a number of cases firms may share the costs by adding some questions to an already devised questionnaire of a reputable polling organisation. In this way some of the costs of administering the survey can be shared between a number of clients. The second danger to be aware of is the representativeness of the sample and the time frame within which the research has been conducted. For most reputable polling organisations this is not usually a problem. However, even with the most respectable polling firms there can be problems. For example, at the 1992 General Election several of the polling organisations got the forecasts of the results wrong largely because of hitherto undetected flaws in their sampling techniques which systematically overrepresented Labour voters and underrepresented Conservative voters. Minority parties continue to complain that their support is also underpredicted because their support is often concentrated in particular areas and 'representative' sampling will underrecord the strength of their support, particularly in general elections. So it is important to pay particular attention to the size of a sample and the methods of sampling used to draw it up. For example, it is obvious that surveys conducted on the internet will have an automatic built-in bias towards those in the higher socio-economic groups who are more likely to have access to the internet.

The timing of the survey can also be a crucial factor in the reliability of the forecast. Surveys conducted on consumers' eating preferences between, for example, beef and other products immediately before news reports of the outbreak of BSE or 'mad cow' disease are clearly going to be unreliable.

Surveys of the salesforce

One way of overcoming the costs and the delays that can occur from using surveys of consumers is to use surveys of your salesforce instead.

PAUSE FOR THOUGHT 9 *Before reading on, can you identify several advantages and disadvantages in using a survey of your own salesforce as a method of forecasting demand?*

The advantages of salesforce surveys

There are several advantages to this technique of forecasting demand. For example, it is obviously quicker to survey your own salesforce than it is to conduct a big consumer survey. It will obviously be less costly as the survey can be conducted via telephone, fax or even video-conferencing and the results obtained almost instantly. In addition a company's salesforce should be in close touch with the firm's main customers and prospective customers and should therefore be more sensitive to the factors that could influence demand in the short term. By being close to the market place the results should be more reliable, so the argument runs.

The disadvantages of salesforce surveys

The counter-argument is that there can be a bias in the way in which such surveys are conducted. The members of the salesforce are not neutral observers of the market place. Very often they are paid by results or have an element of their pay which is performance related and hence linked to growth in sales, usually above a given target. If targets are set which are based on surveys of the salesforce, and if payment by results is linked to these targets, then it is fairly obvious that there will be an incentive for the salesforce to consistently present the situation as one of apparently low growth in demand so that modest targets are set. These targets will then be easily met and in many cases exceeded, giving rise to substantial bonus payments. It is likely that the senior managers of the firm will eventually realise this (perhaps having been 'fooled' once before) and hence build in an extra 'growth' factor to take account of this bias. This may result in the salesforce realising that a growth factor is being built in and, subsequently, adjusting their own forecasts downwards. So the process goes on with the actual forecast bearing little resemblance to reality. It could work in the opposite direction with a consistent bias upwards in the forecasts, especially if the salesforce wish to appear to be dynamic and ambitious. The speed and cost of this method, therefore, need to be offset against reliability.

Surveys of experts

One way to overcome the problem of respondents having a vested interest in the outcome of their responses is to go outside the firm and conduct a survey of so-called experts. For example, if one wanted to forecast the level of exploration activity in the North Sea one could seek the views of a number of independent experts in government, research institutions (e.g. the Institute of Fiscal Studies), the research departments of large investment banks and stockbrokers (e.g. Goldman Sachs), oil economists, consultants and the academic world. On the basis of these views a consensus can be arrived at on, for example, the number of new exploration wells that will be drilled.

The advantages

The obvious advantage for this technique is its alleged objectivity and independence. Those making the forecast have an incentive to get it right since their reputations are at stake. They are knowledgeable about the market but have no direct commercial involvement in its primary activities. So the forecast should be reliable. In a variation of this technique the results of the survey of experts are often relayed back to the participants, who are offered the opportunity to review and revise their own forecasts in the light of the emerging consensus. Those experts whose forecasts are significantly out of line with the consensus are asked to explain their reasons, and these can be taken into account before arriving at a final verdict on future demand. This variation is known as the 'Delphi technique'.

The disadvantages

The problem with this method of forecasting demand is that there is no clear basis on which the forecasts are made. Consensus may be reached but it may be the result of all sorts of dubious and widely varying assumptions about the factors that will influence a given market. Indeed, the Delphi technique has been derided by some critics as producing a consensus based on ignorance!

PAUSE FOR THOUGHT 10 *You are given the task of forecasting the demand for out-of-town shopping. What techniques might you employ and what are the advantages and disadvantages of each?*

Managerial techniques

There are a number of methods that can be described as managerial techniques and which derive from an area known as management science or decision-making theory. A detailed description of all these techniques goes beyond the scope of this book, but four of them will be discussed here: decision tree, scenarios, simulation modelling, and programme evaluation and review techniques (PERT).

Decision trees

Decision trees have been widely used in operations research but not so often in forecasting demand. Nevertheless, they form an important technique for attempting to forecast the future course of a business. Figure 7.4 gives an example.

From the figure it can be seen that the company has decided to research and develop a new AIDS drug and to launch it onto the market. Before it embarks on the project the company would have to make some sort of forecast of the likely outcome. The decision tree is a tool which helps the company to make such a decision. At each stage it will have to estimate the probability of success. For example, the company may discover that it cannot develop a safe drug to prevent AIDS and that after several years it has to withdraw from this market. Alternatively, it is able to discover a drug which, in the laboratory, can inhibit the onset of AIDS. The probability of success may be based on previous new drug developments or on the experience of other similar companies working in the field – although as this is such a new field it may be difficult to get reliable estimates of this. The second stage is the commercial development of the drug. It is one thing for a drug to work in laboratory conditions, but it requires to be developed and produced commercially. There may therefore be a risk that the company is unable to develop the product commercially. However,

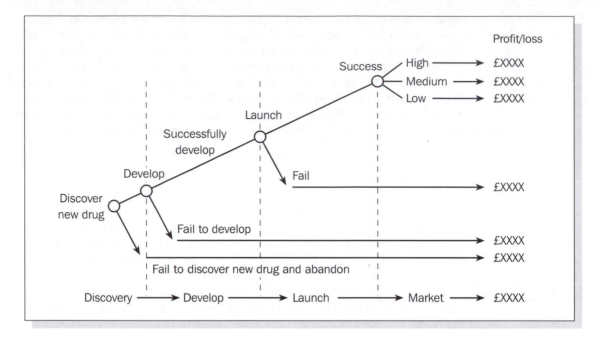

Profit/loss

Figure 7.4

Decision trees

let us assume that the chances are more than 'evens' and the company proceeds to launch the product on the market place. How it is received can also depend on the state of the market at the time of launch. If there are no competitor products, and it has been established that the drug has no known side-effects, then the demand can be described as 'high', estimates of the likely annual sales can be made, and net income or profits can be calculated over the likely product life-cycle of the drug. Furthermore, the likely returns can be calculated (see Chapter 10 for a discussion of the investment appraisal techniques used). Equally, there might be competitive drugs on the market and other firms may draw sales from this company. In this case we could describe the demand as 'medium' and calculate the returns accordingly. Finally, the demand may turn out to be much less, perhaps owing to the development of a completely new type of treatment that does away with the need for drugs altogether. The demand is therefore 'low'. The size of the likely annual profits will depend on the relevant costs and revenues, and probabilities can be assigned to each separate stage of the process. In our example let us suppose that the chances of successfully finding an AIDS drug are put at 5 per cent (probability, $p_1 = 0.05$). Then let us assume that the chances of developing the drug commercially are thought to be very good at, say, 90 per cent (probability, $p_2 = 0.90$). Finally, let us also assume that the chances of the demand being high are also thought to be quite good, say 40 per cent (probability, $p_3 = 0.40$). Then the chances of all three things happening are calculated by multiplying the three probabilities together. Thus the chances of 'the golden scenario' where everything goes just right is $p_1 \times p_2 \times p_3$ or $0.05 \times 0.90 \times 0.40$, which equals 0.018. According to this estimate there are 18 chances in 1,000 of all the stages in this decision being right. If we assume that there is a 30 per cent chance of a 'medium' level of demand then the chances of making a profit will be 0.018 + (0.05 × 0.90 × 0.30) which equals 0.0315 or approximately 32 chances in 1,000 that this project will make a profit. Whether the firm decides to undertake this project depends upon the likely rewards and their attitude to the risks involved.

The technique has some merit insofar as it helps to systematically identify the key factors that will affect a business decision. However, it is hedged around with a number of difficulties, the most obvious of which is the assignment of probabilities to different stages in the decision-making process. In many cases it will not be practical to determine the probability of success as there will be no previous data on which to make an estimate.

Scenarios

This technique, which is borrowed from the area of business strategy, can also be used to forecast the demand for a product. For example, a company might be thinking about breaking into a market in the former Soviet Union. It has to estimate the likely demand for its product against a very uncertain economic and political background. It can estimate the effect of different 'scenarios' on its market prospects. As well as trying to gauge the political climate, and whether or not the region has the political stability for the company to be able to do business, they may have to make assumptions about the likely rates of exchange, the tariff barriers, the attitude of the government to the import of 'foreign' goods and the likely state of the local economy. On each of these questions the forecasters can make assumptions and estimate the effect of these on their market share. The company may have what it considers to be the most likely scenario but prepare plans for a sudden change in the position (the worst-case scenario or the 'doomsday' scenario). Thus the use of scenarios allows for the development of contingency planning. While this technique helps businesses to come to terms with uncertainty, it is by no means a precise technique that can give an unambiguous answer. The likelihood of a given scenario will itself be the subject of much debate and even when there is agreement about the likelihood of a particular set of circumstances occurring there can still be room for considerable diversity in terms of their impact on the demand for the company's product.

PAUSE FOR THOUGHT 11   *What impact do you think that the Internet and the development of multimedia computer software may have on the way that higher education is delivered and how might this affect the demand for higher education? Construct a number of possible scenarios from the point of view of a company that is currently producing textbooks.*

Simulation modelling

Most of the simulation models that have been developed for economic forecasting have been macroeconomic models. These are based on a series of equations (using multiple regression analysis) to determine the relationship between key economic variables such as the link between changes in income tax rates or interest rates and consumer spending. In some of the more sophisticated models (such as the Treasury's model) there can be up to 400 such equations. It is then possible using these models to forecast the likely outcome of certain policies. These can be 'modelled' and the outcomes, according to the simulations of the computer model, assessed. In some cases these macroeconomic models can be used to feed into regional models that can in turn be used to predict the likely effect of changes in macroeconomic policy on certain regional industries. However, it is comparatively rare for simulation models of this type to be used at the level of an individual industry or firm, for example, and even rarer for the technique to be applied at the level of an individual brand or product. It is also important to bear in mind that no matter how sophisticated the simulation model it will inevitably have to simplify the real world. There is therefore a danger that the forecasts will fail to take account of these complexities. For example, a cut in tax rates may be assumed to increase consumers' disposable income and hence increase their propensity to spend. Ordinarily this might not be too unrealistic, but if consumers decide to increase their savings because they are uncertain about the future, or they feel that there is a decided lack of the 'feel-good' factor, then the predictions about increased consumer spending will have proved false. The real world and real consumer behaviour can prove difficult to capture in a few equations.

Programme evaluation and review technique (PERT)

This managerial technique attempts to forecast the likely outcome by speculating on different 'states of the universe'. To help understand how this operates, an example can be used. Imagine that a company is about to launch a new computer operating system and wants to predict the likely demand for this product. However, clearly the demand will depend on a number of factors, any combination of which can be described as the likely 'state of the universe'. For example, the take-up rate of the new package will depend on the ability of existing PCs to run the program. It may be estimated that there could be three possible 'states':

1   An optimistic state in which 70 per cent of existing users switch to the new package.
2   A 'most likely' state whereby 50 per cent of existing users switch to the new software.
3   A pessimistic state whereby only 30 per cent of existing users switch over.

In addition, it may be possible to calculate the likely growth in demand for personal computers. Again there will be several possible 'states': an optimistic state which predicts 20 per cent growth; a most likely state which predicts 10 per cent growth; and a pessimistic state with only 5 per cent growth in the total market.

Finally, the company can make a judgement based on its estimates of what proportion of the new sales it will obtain with three possible 'states' being outlined: an optimistic 'state' in which it takes 70 per cent of the new sales growth; a most likely 'state' in which it takes 50 per cent; and a least likely 'state' in which the company takes only 10 per cent of the new sales.

On this basis the company is able to work out its most optimistic forecast (i.e. it takes 70 per cent of existing users of PCs, the market grows at 20 per cent per annum and the company takes 70 per cent of this growth). If, for the sake of illustration, the current market is 200 million PC users, then the calculation of the most optimistic 'state of the universe' is straightforward. It is

$$(200 \times 0.7) + 0.7(200 \times 0.2) = 168 \text{ million units.}$$

In the case of the most pessimistic 'state of the universe' the company would take only 30 per cent of the existing market, the growth in demand would be only 5 per cent in the next year and the company would only take 10 per cent of this new market. The calculation would now be:

$$(200 \times 0.3) + 0.1(200 \times 0.05) = 61 \text{ million units.}$$

The most likely 'state' will be somewhere in between, say, at around 100 million units.

On the basis of these types of calculation the company can decide whether to proceed. For example, if it costs the company £199 per package to produce and if it sells the software package for £200, then it makes £1 per package. If we assume that the research and development costs are £150 million, then 150 million unit sales becomes the breakeven output. Given that the most optimistic 'state' PERT forecast is 168 million, this may cause our company to reflect on the wisdom of proceeding, or to look more closely at the economics of the project.

There are, however, some difficulties with this technique. The most obvious is that it is not always easy to assign values to the various 'states', nor is it obvious that each state has an equal probability of occurring. The technique therefore is not as precise as is implied in our example and there is a great deal of uncertainty surrounding its application in reality. Nevertheless, it does have the merit of trying to be systematic in the way in which it highlights the various possible outcomes.

Market experiments

Using a market area to test a product is another method whereby a business can make a forecast of the likely future demand. It enables the firm to do a 'dry run' before a full-scale nationwide launch. Valuable lessons can be learned on how consumers react to the product and changes can be introduced before it is too late to do anything about it. This technique is often used by car manufacturers before the major launch of a new model and panels of consumers are given the opportunity to comment on the car's style, design and specification which provides feedback to the designers and the people who have to market the car. Hollywood moguls about to launch a major film will often use test marketing to gauge the audience reaction to a film and will use the feedback that they receive to change the ending of the film or to reshoot scenes to which the audience reacted unfavourably. (In January 1996, it was reported that a number of scenes from the John Cleese film 'Fierce Creatures', a sequel to 'A Fish Called Wanda' and starring the same cast, had to be reshot as the feedback from a test marketing audience in the USA who had seen a version of the film, found it difficult to understand the Cleese/British sense of humour and laughed in all the wrong places!)

There are, however, a number of difficulties with this technique. In the first instance it is important that the test market area or audience is seen as representative. If it is not, then it obviously becomes difficult to extrapolate the feedback received from such market experimentation. Another difficulty with the technique is that by test marketing the product before launch it will reveal the firm's hand before a national launch. This can often result in rivals engaging in 'spoiler' tactics, either by launching similar products or by trying to distract attention from an imminent product launch by arranging a diversionary advertising campaign to distract consumers.

Statistical techniques

There are a number of statistical techniques that can be used to forecast the demand for a product or service. The most frequently used method is one of time series forecasting. The first and crudest way is simply to extrapolate the recent trends observed in the data. Table 7.6 gives the data for the intake of students and the total enrolments of students in a University Business School. The task would be to use this data to forecast intake and total student numbers for 2000.

Table 7.6
Intake and total student numbers, 1991–1999

	1991	1992	1993	1994	1995	1996	1997	1998	1999
Intake	194	204	224	236	323	330	365	333	407
Total	507	532	564	686	779	933	1,014	1,076	1,140
Percentage change intake		5.2	9.8	5.3	36.8	2.2	10.6	–8.7	22.2
Percentage change total		4.9	6.0	21.6	13.5	19.7	8.7	6.1	5.9

The percentage change year-on-year is calculated for both the intake figures and the total student numbers. Averaging out the growth rate over the nine-year period reveals that the average growth rate was 10.4 per cent for intake and 10.5 per cent for total student numbers. Applying this to the data yields a 'prediction' that intakes for 2000 will be up by 10 per cent to 450 and that the total student numbers will be up by a similar percentage to 1,250.

It is not difficult to see that such naive extrapolation is unlikely to prove very accurate, although it has to be said that such considerations do not appear to deter people from using this method! There are all sorts of reasons for assuming that the past is not a very good guide to the future as far as forecasting student numbers is concerned.

PAUSE FOR THOUGHT 12

1 *Why do you think that the method of simple extrapolation of the data on student numbers is unlikely to yield very reliable forecasts of student numbers for 2000?*

2 *Does the data provide any sort of guide to future demand for places at the University's Business School?*

At one time, students were funded largely by grants. Gradually, however, these were replaced by student loans. In addition, universities were encouraged to expand their intakes in the early 1990s in response to government policy to increase the 'participation rate' of students going into higher education. Since 1994, however, there has been pressure on universities to 'consolidate' their numbers, especially in the business and management fields. So 'the past is very much a different country' and the factors which governed growth rates then clearly do not apply now.

More sophisticated methods using time series can be used, although they all suffer from the basic weakness of assuming that the future will be much the same as the immediate past.

Barometric techniques

It is sometimes possible to use one set of data to predict another set. For example instead of using past numbers of students to forecast future numbers, one technique would be to seek to use some other variable which might be seen as a barometer of future demand. This might be described as a 'leading indicator' of demand. One such variable might be the birth-rate 18 years prior to the date of the forecast. If you want to know the population of 18 year olds who might form the basis of the future demand for places in higher education, then looking at the birth-rate 18 years previously might give you a starting point. The demand for soft furnishings may also be linked to the number of new houses completed and sold. Likewise the demand for Cable TV may be linked to the number of new houses completed in a given area one year before.

PAUSE FOR THOUGHT 13   *Can you think of other examples of barometric indicators which could be used for forecasting purposes?*

While this technique is helpful it suffers from a number of drawbacks. It is often difficult to determine the time lag between the change in one variable and the change in the forecast variable. How long will it take, for example, after the upturn in the housing market for the demand in soft furnishings to increase? Is it six months, a year, or longer? Also, although it may be possible to determine the direction of the change it is often difficult to predict the magnitude of the change in the forecast variable.

Who uses what?
....

Finally, let us look at who uses the various methods of forecasting in their business. A number of studies have been done to try to establish those methods that are the more prevalent. Two in particular are worth reporting. The first was conducted in the USA by Wheelwright and Clarke (1974); the second in the UK by Sparkes and McHugh (1984). The results are given in Table 7.7. Table 7.8 outlines the different methods used by British managers.

Table 7.7
Methods of forecasting demand, USA and UK

Method	Wheelwright and Clarke (%)	Sparkes and McHugh (%)
Salesforce estimates	67	n.a.
Expert opinion	77	72
Customer surveys	48	57
Statistical methods	65	58
Time series methods	24	11
Econometric methods	70	10

Table 7.8
Techniques for forecasting used by British managers

Business area	Executive assessment	Trend analysis	Moving averages	Surveys	Exponential smoothing	Regression correlation
Market share	32	17	12	6	0	0
Production/ stock control	10	3	8	0	2	0
Financial planning	20	3	3	0	1	0
Total	**62**	**23**	**23**	**6**	**3**	**0**

Total sample (N) = 65
Source: Sparkes and McHugh (1984).

Conclusions

This chapter has identified a number of different techniques that economists use to forecast the demand for products and services. The main technique which is based on demand modelling is called econometric forecasting. However, the main conclusions to emerge from the research outlined above into the different forecasting techniques used by businesspeople are:

1 British firms used econometric techniques and sophisticated time series techniques far less than their American competitors.
2 British firms displayed a lack of knowledge of specific techniques.
3 The most popular technique used by British firms was 'Executive Assessment'.

The case studies in the appendix look at examples of companies attempting to forecast the demand for their products and services.

Appendix

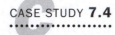

CASE STUDY **7.4**

Forecasting the demand for a new product – Windows 95

In August 1995, Bill Gates, the President of Microsoft, launched Windows 95, the latest version of Microsoft's operating system. This new system was Gates' answer to the challenge posed by Apple Macintosh's 10-year-old operating system which, although not as popular in terms of market share, was regarded as the leader in terms of user-friendly applications. The new operating system offered consumers a number of advantages. First, it updated the previously clumsy Windows operating system which had not been changed since 1990. Secondly, it was more user friendly with files having the appearance of normal files instead of the usual computerspeak (for example, files could be labelled 'Letter to Mum' instead of 'MUM.TXT'). Thirdly, the program was easier to use in conjunction with other add-ons such as sound cards or CD-ROMs. And finally, consumers were able to run more than one program at a time. For example, you could print the text of a document while designing graphs or doing spreadsheet calculations.

Armed with all these extra features, you could be forgiven for thinking that Microsoft were going to 'clean up'. However, the company was being unusually shy in making its predictions of the demand for Windows 95 as there were a number of 'imponderables' which made forecasting the demand for this new product particularly difficult. This did not stop a number of other forecasters from making their own predictions. These are listed below and give the estimates of the number of software packages sold from August to December 1995 (in millions):

Dataquest	29.0
Computer Intelligence Infocorp	22.5
International Data	20.0
INTECO	14.0

As can be seen there is a considerable divergence in the forecasts between the main forecasters. To a large extent this reflects the fact that there are a large number of uncertainties associated with this market.

The big problem with Windows 95 is that to operate effectively it requires a lot of power in the PC. Although Microsoft claim that it can run on a personal computer with as little as 4 megabytes of computer memory the new program needs at least 8 megabytes and preferably 16 megabytes. According to Computer Intelligence Infocorp, in 1995 out of a total of 202 million PC 'platforms', 39 per cent did not have the capacity to run Windows 95, having less than 3 megabytes of memory, while 22 per cent had memory between 4 and 7 megabytes, barely enough for the package to run effectively. Thus it was estimated that only 39 per cent had the necessary memory capacity to run Windows 95 without upgrading their PCs. Therefore if almost two-thirds of consumers wanted to use Windows 95 the choice confronting them was either to buy a new PC or to upgrade their existing PC by adding more memory chips. The difficulty with the latter option is that there is a world-wide shortage of memory chips and the costs of upgrading are therefore quite expensive. It has been calculated that the cost of 'beefing up' a PC to run Windows could be between £700 and £1,400. However, 1995 saw an explosion in PC sales and industry forecasters were sceptical that after such an initial outlay consumers would be all that willing to splash out such sums on upgrading operating systems which tend to be 'invisible' and less exciting than multimedia software. Also the corporate market may prove a tougher nut to crack for Windows. Corporate buyers who account for over two-thirds of all PCs installed world-wide are more concerned about the compatibility between the new package and existing software. In addition, there are the added costs of staff training to consider and a general reluctance to buy the very first version of the new package, fearing that there may yet be some 'bugs' to iron out. Hence they are sticking with their existing Microsoft applications software for the immediate future. According to a forecast by the head of Compaq's commercial operations, Bruno Didier, he expected only about 40 per cent of the corporate market to be using the new software by 1996, while INTECO, another forecasting body for the industry, estimated that about 20 per cent of corporate users will be adding the program to their old machines by the end of 1995. A number of analysts argued that industry may even ignore the product altogether and go instead for the 'industrial-strength' of Windows NT, which promises better networking facilities, more reliability and faster processing power. Microsoft acknowledged this possibility by bringing in a 'user interface' which will link Windows 95 and Windows NT together. This, according to industry sources, will mean that the two operating systems will become virtually the same from the user's perspective.

Another feature of the market will be the role played by the companies who write the software applications. In 1990, when Microsoft's previous operating system, Windows 3.0, was launched, a number of companies chose to write software programs either for the existing Microsoft operating system MS-DOS, or for competing operating systems such as IBM's OS/2. They lost out comprehensively and companies like LOTUS and Word Perfect never really recovered from this. This time the software companies do not need to be econometric whiz-kids to forecast the way the industry is likely to go and they will almost certainly write new applications software packages to run on Windows 95 and Windows NT. This time it is not a case of backing the right operating system but of writing the best software.

Based on information from *The Economist*, 8 July and 26 August 1995.

Questions

1   Why is there such a wide variation in the forecasts of demand for Windows 95?
2   The market for the product is clearly segmented. What factors influence the demand in each of these sectors?

CASE STUDY **7.5**

The National Grid and forecasting demand

The National Grid carry out demand forecasting to calculate the expected demand and to ensure that they have enough scheduled generation available. They take into account the individual demand forecasts of suppliers, network operators, directly connected customers and, in certain cases, generators. They also refer to information sources such as weather forecasts (changes in weather conditions affect the short-term forecasts; for example, the peak winter demand can increase by up to 400 MW with a 1°C fall in temperature), television schedules, TV pick-ups (see Table CS7.5.1) and an equivalent day's demand profile from previous years and plan for rare events, such as the solar eclipse in the UK in August 1999.

The forecasting is done for both short-term operational and longer-term planning purposes, thus enabling them to schedule and despatch generation to meet the expected demand on a day-ahead basis and to ensure in the longer term that the transmission system is developed to cope with the demands of the future. To make sure that security standards are met, over 600 predictive studies are carried out each week. These studies are computer models of the power system and are a snapshot of a particular point in time. The number of studies carried out has dramatically increased over the last few years because the power system is being driven ever harder by the National Grid as they strive to bring down costs.

The effects of television audience habits on electricity load on the National Grid system have been observed for a number of years. Popular television programmes inhibit normal domestic electricity consuming habits during the course of the programmes, only to release this activity at commercial breaks and at the finish of the programme. These sharp transient increases in electricity demand occurring at these release times are known as 'TV pick-ups'.

Research in the 1960s indicated switching on of kettles (which each take two or three kilowatts) occurred during commercial breaks and at the end of programmes. Also when darkness falls during the evening people will generally switch their lights on during breaks between television programmes.

Table CS7.5.1
Top ten highest pick-ups since 1990 (in date order)

Date	Actual pick-up (MW)	Programme title
04 July 1990	2,800	World Cup Semi-Final: England v West Germany (End of Extra Time)
01 April 1991	2,000	Coronation Street
28 April 1991	2,200	The Darling Buds of May
12 May 1991	2,200	The Darling Buds of May
02 September 1992	1,800	Coronation Street
03 September 1992	1,800	Eastenders
07 September 1992	1,800	Coronation Street
05 April 1994	1,900	Eastenders
18 April 1994	2,200	Coronation Street/Eastenders (combined pick-up)
30 June 1998	2,100	World Cup 1998: England v Argentina (Half Time)

Television pick-ups reflect increased activity after a programme, but there are rare occasions when an event attracts such a large audience that they actually depress demand. This situation also has to be managed, with generation being reduced back to a point where it is in balance with the lower demand. This situation was clearly demonstrated during the funeral of Princess Diana when normal activities ceased as over 31 million people sat down to watch the television coverage and electricity demand was well below normal throughout. At times, demand plunged by 1,000 MW in a matter of seconds, and prompt action by National Grid control staff was needed to keep the system operating normally. Other notable TV pick-ups are shown in Table CS7.5.2.

Table CS7.5.2
Other notable pick-ups

No.	Date	Channel	Programme title	Actual pick-up (MW)
1	22 January 1984	BBC1	The Thornbirds	2,600
2	16 January 1984	BBC1	The Thornbirds	2,200
3	29 July 1981		Royal Wedding: Charles & Diana	1,800

On 11 August 1999, National Grid experienced a record increase in demand for electricity following the solar eclipse. As life returned to normal, demand jumped by 3,000 MW – the equivalent of meeting the demands of an additional four million people. This was the largest rapid increase in demand that had been experienced on the National Grid system and it occurred in just under 30 minutes. However, they had planned for this and ensured that there was sufficient power in reserve, so it did not cause any problems.

At 10.30 am, as interest in the eclipse picked up, electricity demand throughout England and Wales was 35,500 MW. By 11 am, this had dropped by 500 MW and at 11.15 demand was at its lowest point, at 33,150 MW. As the sun reappeared and people returned to their homes, offices and factories, electricity demand swiftly increased and within minutes reached 36,150 MW – a rise of 3,000 MW.

About 1,000 MW of the increase was in relation to television pick-up – the audience switching on kettles for a cup of tea as life returned to normal. The rest was due to the big switch back on as people returned to their normal activities in homes and offices and factories. The new record beats one that was set back in 1990. This 2,800 MW increase occurred in approximately 15 minutes following the television coverage of England's penalty shoot-out defeat in the World Cup football semi-final against West Germany.

Source: The National Grid webpage: www.nationalgrid.com/uk/activities/

Questions

1 Construct a demand forecasting model for the demand for electricity at a given hour of the day. What factors could upset this demand forecasting model and how would you attempt to minimise the risks of getting the forecast wrong?

2 What are the consequences for the National Grid of getting the demand forecasts wrong?

References and additional reading
....

Earl, P.E. (1995) *Microeconomics for Business and Marketing*, Edward Elgar, Aldershot, esp. ch. 3, pp. 34–66.

Ferguson, P.R., Ferguson, G.J. and Rothschild, R. (1993) *Business Economics: The Application of Economic Theory*, Macmillan, London, esp. ch. 9, pp. 143–70.

Griffiths, A. and Wall, S. (1996) *Intermediate Microeconomics: Theory and Applications*, Longman, London, esp. chs 1 and 2, pp. 1–101.

Reekie, W. D. and Crook, J. (1987) *Managerial Economics*, Philip Allan, Oxford, esp. Part II, pp. 85–98.

Sparkes, J. and McHugh, M. (1984) 'A survey of forecasting techniques', *Journal of Forecasting*, Vol. 3, No. 1, pp. 37–42.

Wheelwright, S.C. and Clarke, D.G. (1976) 'Corporate forecasting: promise and reality', *Harvard Business Review*, Vol. 54, December.

CHAPTER 8

Costs in theory and practice

Objectives

By the end of this chapter you will be able to:

➤ Understand the ways in which the word 'cost' is used in economics as opposed to its everyday usage.

➤ Identify what is meant by both fixed and variable costs.

➤ Distinguish between total, average and marginal costs and revenues.

➤ Identify and distinguish between diminishing average and marginal returns.

➤ Define and identify both economies and diseconomies of scale.

➤ Understand the significance of isoquant and isocost lines and be able to identify the point at which a firm can minimise cost within the constraints under which it is operating.

Key concepts

Diseconomies of scale: increased size raising the long-run average total cost via various inefficiencies related to size, e.g. managerial problems.

Economies of scale (EOS): increased size reducing the long-run average total cost. Applies to the long-run time period where all factors of production are variable. Here the proportions in the factors of production need not be varied. We then speak of scale economies, e.g. where doubling all factor inputs more than doubles output, etc.

External economies: scale economies due to growth in size of the industry of which the plant or firm is a part. Often related to geographical concentration.

Firm (enterprise) economies: economies due to the growth in size of the institutional unit (firm or enterprise).

Fixed costs: costs that do not vary with output in the short run. Sometimes called indirect or overhead costs.

Internal economies: scale economies due to the growth in size of the plant (establishment) or firm (enterprise) itself.

Isocost: combination of the factors of production that can be purchased for a given expenditure.

Isoquant: combination of the factors of production that are required to produce a given output under present technology.

Law of variable proportions: applies to the short run, where adding more units of a variable factor to a fixed factor changes the proportions in which the factors are combined. Can be broken down into 'laws' of increasing returns and diminishing returns, respectively.

Long run: that period of time over which all factors are variable.

Minimum efficient scale (MES): the point at which scale economies are exhausted, i.e. the long-run average cost curve is at a minimum.

Opportunity cost: the next best alternative forgone.

Short run: that period of time over which at least one factor of production is fixed.

Technical economies: economies due to the growth in size of the productive unit (plant or establishment).

Variable costs: costs that vary with output in the short run. Sometimes called direct costs.

Introduction

Economists use the word 'cost' in a different way from its everyday use. The economic cost of production for a firm is the opportunity cost of production, i.e. it is the value that could have been generated had the resources been employed in their next best use. Although an opportunity cost often involves physical output, it is convenient to talk about the pound equivalent of opportunity costs. When the opportunity cost of an activity is calculated in money terms, the question that is being answered is: what value of output did we forgo to produce this?

There are, in fact, a number of economic costs that form part of the production process but which the manufacturer does not actually pay for. Common examples of these include depreciation and the 'goodwill' associated with brand names. The economic cost of depreciation is the difference between the purchase price of a fixed asset (a piece of machinery, for example) and the second-hand value of the asset. The difference between the two figures represents the monetary value of the opportunity cost of continuing to hold the asset. Goodwill can accrue for a firm trading over a number of years when it produces a brand that has become a household name. The brand then has a value attached to it that could be realised if sold to a competitor. The opportunity cost of not selling this brand name can be regarded as the opportunity cost of the interest forgone on the potential sales value of the brand name.

Accountants, on the other hand, measure historical cost rather than economic (opportunity) cost. This particular method values the factors used in the production process at the prices that have been paid for the items in question.

Costs can be broken down in a number of different ways that can facilitate decision-making in the firm. Economic definitions of cost are often textbook based, with no real application of ideas involving opportunity cost being made in practice. However, there are times when the economic definition of cost is being utilised but where the operator is unaware of this fact, as we shall see below.

The short run and the long run

In simple terms, the short run is an undefined period of time, when some of the factors used in production are fixed and some of them are variable. Put another way, the short run is a period of time in which at least some of the factors of production can be regarded as fixed. The length of the short run will differ from industry to industry. A time period often used for the short run is one year, mainly because firms often plan and budget for a 12-month period. However, in practice the short run may be quite different from this. Suppose, for example, that a factory owned by a firm is operating at full capacity yet is still not meeting the current demand for its product. It may then decide to erect a new building. This, however, will obviously take time and a great deal of planning; in some cases it may take several years – for the nuclear industry it may take a decade or more. It follows that the short-run time period, in which at least one factor of production is fixed, will vary in length from industry to industry. The long run can then be defined as an indefinite period of time in which all factors used in production are variable. In our previous example, the long-run time period will be over a decade for the nuclear industry, but might be a year or less for a small machine-shop-based industry, such as knitwear.

Fixed costs and variable costs

The *fixed* costs of a firm are those costs that do not vary with the level of output in the short run. As can be seen from column 2 in Table 8.1, fixed costs do not change as the number of units produced increases. An example of a fixed cost might be the rent on premises. The rent of premises is usually agreed, and a contract negotiated, for a specified period of time, often 12 months or so.

The *variable* costs of a firm are those costs that do vary with the level of output in the short run. As can be seen from column 3 in Table 8.1, variable costs rise as the number of units produced increases. An example of a variable cost might be raw materials, or energy, or labour costs. It may be that increasing output in the short run requires the use of more raw materials in the production process, using machinery and buildings for longer periods (thereby raising electricity, gas and other 'energy'-related costs) and paying overtime rates to labour. All these additional costs are the direct result of changes in the level output in the short run, and therefore are often referred to as direct costs.

If, for example, a pizza home delivery firm were faced with an increase in demand, there would be a subsequent increase in the basic ingredients required to produce the pizzas. Extra packaging would be needed and there may be a need to recruit additional kitchen staff as well as delivery agents. This may facilitate the need for new uniforms and possibly the purchase of a new van. Thus the increase in demand raises the level of output and causes these (variable) types of cost to increase.

The calculation of average costs is relatively simple. In Table 8.1, column 5 contains the data for the average fixed costs (AFC). This is derived by dividing the total fixed costs by the level of output. Thus, at 6 units of output, the calculation is as follows: £500/6 units = £83 (rounded to the nearest whole number). It is obvious from the table that average fixed costs decrease as the level of output increases. This is simply a feature of fixed costs and follows from the fact that in the short run, by definition, fixed costs do not alter. As the production level increases, these fixed costs are spread over a greater number of units, thus the average fixed cost per unit will fall. A simple conclusion to draw from this would be that if production is zero, these costs will still be incurred. Consequently, the higher the level of output, the lower the fixed cost per unit. Figure 8.1 shows the average fixed cost falling continuously as the level of output increases.

Average fixed cost (AFC) = Total fixed cost/ Total output

Table 8.1

Costs – a breakdown

(1) Output per month (units)	(2) Total fixed costs (£)	(3) Total variable costs (£)	(4) Total costs (£) (2)+(3)	(5) Average fixed costs (£) (2)/(1)	(6) Average variable costs (£) (3)/(1)	(7) Average total costs (£) (4)/(1)	(8) Marginal costs (£)
0	500	0	500				
1	500	400	900	500	400	900	400
2	500	600	1,100	250	300	550	200
3	500	750	1,250	167	250	417	150
4	500	1,200	1,700	125	300	425	450
5	500	1,800	2,300	100	360	460	600
6	500	2,700	3,200	83	450	533	900
7	500	3,800	4,300	71	543	614	1,100
8	500	5,200	5,700	63	650	713	1,400
9	500	6,900	7,400	56	767	822	1,700
10	500	8,700	9,200	50	870	920	1,800

Note: Data rounded to nearest whole number.

In Table 8.1 the total variable costs are shown in column 3 and the average variable costs (AVC) are calculated in column 6. The data contained in column 6 is found using the same approach as outlined for average fixed costs; that is, if the total variable costs are divided by the level of output, then the average variable costs are determined. For example, at 6 units of output, the average variable cost is calculated as follows: £2,700/6 units = £450.

Average variable cost (AVC) = Total variable cost / Total output

The data in column 6 of Table 8.1 has been plotted in Figure 8.1 to give an indication of the normal trend associated with average variable cost (AVC). It can be seen that for the AVC curve there is an initial high value, followed by a decline and then a steady rise upwards. It can be deduced that there is a certain level of output (here 3 units) at which the average variable costs are at the lowest level achievable for a firm. One possible target for managers of a firm is to seek to operate at the level of output for which variable (or running) costs per unit (AVC) are at their lowest point. (In the next section, we consider how the firm might operate where total costs per unit, ATC, are at their lowest point.)

PAUSE FOR THOUGHT 1	What do you consider are the advantages to a firm in terms of its strategic decision-making capabilities in identifying the variable and fixed components of its overall costs, and of calculating averages for these?

Figure 8.1
Average costs

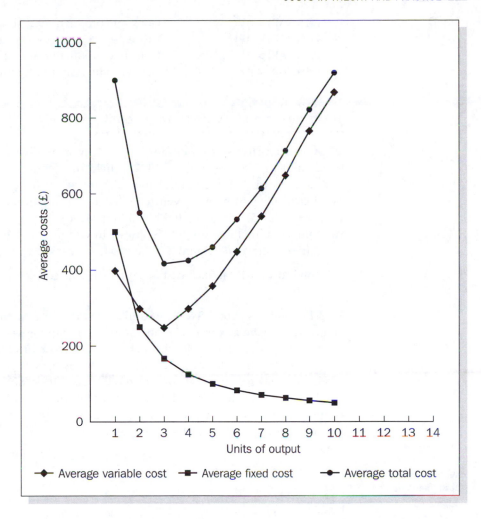

If the firm is covering all its variable (running) costs, then it is at least making some contribution to the fixed costs it has already incurred. In the short-run time period it is then worth continuing in production. In other words if the price of the product (average revenue) is greater than the average variable cost, then the decision might well be to continue production. Of course, if price (average revenue) is less than the average variable cost, then the firm might well consider closing down since continued production is merely adding to the firm's indebtedness and making no contribution to covering the fixed costs already incurred.

In the long run, of course, the firm must cover all its costs of production, both fixed and variable. Arguably, a certain level of profit ('normal' profit) will also be needed if the firm is to continue committing its (scarce) resources to that product in the long run. This 'normal' level of profit is often regarded as a cost of production in the long run; if the firm does not achieve it, it will move its resources elsewhere.

Price (AR) > AVC   Continue production in short run
Price (AR) < AVC   Cease production in short run
Price (AR) > AFC + AVC   Continue production in long run
Price (AR) < AFC + AVC   Cease production in long run

Total costs and average total costs

We have seen that it is important that a firm break down its costs into both fixed and variable categories as this can help the decision-making process. We have also noted that it is of fundamental importance to consider costs in total, as all costs have to be met eventually by the firm, whether they are fixed or variable. Total cost is generated by adding together total fixed costs and total variable costs. In Table 8.1 this is shown in column 4 by summing column 2 (total fixed costs) and column 3 (total variable costs).

Total cost = Total fixed cost + Total variable cost
TC   =   TFC   +   TVC

The total cost, total fixed cost and total variable cost curves are shown in Figure 8.2 to give a comparison of the relationship between the three curves over a range of outputs. Obviously, the total fixed cost element remains the same, whereas the total variable cost component rises steadily over time once production has begun. Total cost is simply the addition of this (constant) total fixed cost to total variable cost at any level of output. It is clear that the difference between the curve representing total cost and that representing total variable cost is simply the total fixed cost element.

Figure 8.2
Total, fixed and variable costs

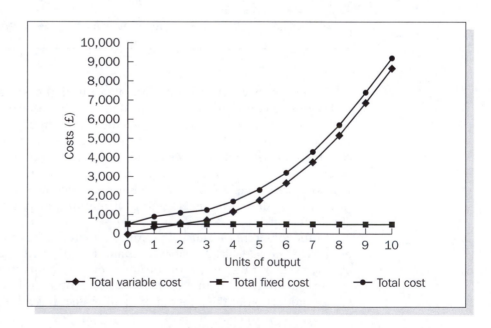

Average total cost is the sum of average fixed and average variable cost. This follows from our earlier definition:

$$TC = TFC + TVC$$

$$\text{Average total cost (ATC)} = \frac{\text{Total cost (TC)}}{\text{Total output (Q)}}$$

$$ATC = \frac{TFC + TVC}{Q}$$

$$= \frac{TFC}{Q} + \frac{TVC}{Q}$$

$$= AFC + AVC$$

In Table 8.1 we also find average total cost (ATC) in column 7 by dividing total costs in column 4 by total output in column 1. Thus, for 6 units of output,

ATC = AFC + AVC, i.e. ATC = 83 + 450 = £533.

In terms of Figure 8.1 we add the AFC and AVC curves vertically to get the ATC curve. Notice that the ATC and AVC curves get closer and closer together as output increases. This is because we are adding (vertically) a progressively smaller AFC to AVC as output increases.

PAUSE FOR THOUGHT 2 *Consider a number of industries in your area. Identify whether they have a major fixed component associated with their cost structures, and estimate the length of the short run and long run in these industries.*

Marginal cost
· · · · · · · · · · · · · · · · ·

Marginal cost is the addition to total cost of producing one more unit of output. Mathematically this is calculated as follows:

$$MC = \Delta TC / \Delta Q$$

where ΔTC = change in total costs, and ΔQ = change in output.

When marginal cost is expressed mathematically it appears rather complex, which is somewhat misleading as it is a very simple concept. Using Table 8.1 again, in calculating the marginal cost of producing the sixth unit of production, the only relevant data in this calculation relates to the total cost before it was produced and the total cost after it was produced. Thus:

Total cost for 5 units of production = £2,300
Total cost for 6 units of production = £3,200

It can be seen that the additional cost, the marginal cost, of producing the sixth unit of production was £900.

Total, average and marginal revenues
· ·

The analysis in this chapter to date has concentrated on the cost side of the equation. The other side of this is the revenue that a firm generates in order to pay these costs. What is left after a company has deducted its total costs from its total revenue is known as its total profit. Thus:

Total profit = Total revenue – Total costs

However, it is possible to calculate and analyse revenues using similar techniques and terminology to that applied when costs were examined above.

The total revenue of a firm is the total amount of money received by a firm for the sale of any given level of output.

Total revenue = Total quantity sold × Price per unit

In the calculation of average revenue, the aim is to find the average amount of revenue from each unit sold. If the selling price is constant for the output, then this is a needless calculation. This becomes clear from the formula:

Average revenue = Total revenue/ Total quantity sold

It is a simple mathematical exercise to deduce that if the selling price per unit is constant then average revenue will equal price (in which case when drawing the average revenue curve, you will be drawing the demand curve). However, it is not difficult to think of examples where this is not the case, one of the most obvious being that of air travel. There may be 150 people on a plane, but they are likely to have paid a variety of prices for the same journey based on whether or not they have fulfilled a certain number of criteria. For example, the price may vary depending on when the seat was booked, duration of stay (i.e. does it include a Saturday night), whether it is a single or return ticket, etc. In this type of circumstance the calculation of the average revenue per paying passenger is different from price and is an important guide to trends over a period of time.

Marginal revenue is the addition to total revenue from selling one more unit of output. For example:

Total revenue for selling 9 units = £9,000
Total revenue for selling 10 units = £10,000
Then the marginal revenue for selling the 10th unit is £1,000.

PAUSE FOR THOUGHT 3 *The analysis of marginal cost and marginal revenue is important in economic analysis. A great many people actually consider the marginal unit without realising it. For instance, consider the marginal costs facing a couple that already have a 1-year-old little girl and are about to have another baby in the next month. Assume it is another girl and attempt to estimate the marginal costs associated with this second child. Would these be more or less if the couple were to have a boy?*

Marginal costs and revenues (benefits)

Marginal costs and revenues (benefits) are of huge importance in the economic analysis of decision-making. It can be deduced from what we have said above relating to these two concepts that the most advantageous position for the company is the level of output at which marginal cost is equal to marginal revenue (or benefit). Only where marginal cost (MC) equals marginal revenue (MR) is total profit maximised.

If we consider the scenario where marginal revenue is greater than marginal cost, i.e. where the revenue received from selling a unit is more than the additional cost of producing it (MC < MR), then it is clear that this is profitable for the company and production could in fact be increased up to the point where the cost of producing the unit is equal to the money received from selling it (MC = MR). Beyond this point the additional cost would be greater than the addition to total revenue (MC > MR), thus it would be unwise to produce beyond where MC = MR (see Case Study 8.1).

CASE STUDY **8.1**

The concept of marginal costs and benefits

The aim of this case study is to further explain what is meant by marginal analysis and the difference between this and examining a situation from an 'average' perspective.

The concepts of marginal costs and benefits are central to much economic analysis, so it is worth being clear about their meaning. The basic idea is that marginal cost and benefit refer to the change in total costs or benefits that comes about as a result of some specified small change. So, the marginal cost of water pollution is the extra cost that would be imposed by a small increase in the level of water pollution; the marginal benefit from increased spending on the health service is the extra benefit that would derive from the small increase in spending and health care. It is crucially important to distinguish between marginal costs and benefits on the one hand, and average costs and benefits on the other. If offered the choice between buying one bar of chocolate at 30p and two similar bars for a total cost of 50p, the marginal cost of the second bar is just 20p (the increase in total cost from 30p to 50p), while the average cost of each of the two bars is clearly 25p. This distinction may seem obvious, but it is surprising how often it is overlooked.

Questions

1   Do you think that hospital administrators are aware of the marginal benefit to patients of increased spending? Explain your answer?
2   In a multi-product firm, which possibly makes five or six products on the same production line, what are the implications for marginal analysis?
3   In practice, strategic decision-making is often based on an average cost and revenue basis. Why do you think this might be the case?

The example below explains how basing a decision on marginal cost as to which hospital to use can be more efficient than basing a decision on average cost.

In Figure 8.3 we assume, for simplicity, that two hospitals, A and B, have identical average and marginal cost curves. We can see that although each hospital treats a different number of patients, they each have the same average cost C in a situation where Q_A treatments take place in hospital A and Q_B treatments take place in hospital B, and therefore both hospitals would charge the same price if this was based on average costs. However, an efficient allocation of resources (patients) would be one that encouraged hospitals to base prices on marginal costs. This would allow hospital A to charge a lower price than B, since scale economies are available to A which would reduce average costs with extra treatments (unlike hospital B where average costs would increase with extra treatments).

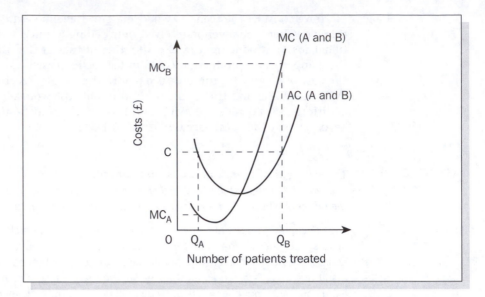

Figure 8.3
Problems with average cost pricing

This lower price would then attract patients to hospital A which can provide treatment at a lower (average) cost than hospital B. Therefore, the regulation in the current internal market for the health service which insists on average cost pricing does not permit the market for health care to send appropriate signals to patients. Resource allocation would then be inefficient where patients (or their agents) choose the identically priced hospital B rather than A. In summary, a marginal cost pricing principle would be more appropriate than an average cost pricing principle in this example.

CASE STUDY **8.2**

Marginal analysis

The aim of this case study is to provide an example of a classic application of marginal analysis to a situation that occurs across the entire university sector in the UK.

The intake of MBA (Master of Business Administration) students is a matter of some debate in business schools throughout the UK. The government provides no financial assistance to students who wish to embark on this particular course of study. Nor do they provide any money for the business schools. Thus, it is in effect a private transaction between the academic institution and the individual. The government takes no active role in the allocation of funds, and is consequently not in a position to limit places in the way that it does for undergraduate courses in the area of business and management. It is therefore up to each university to try to attract as many students into these courses as it can.

MBA programmes, and their like, are seen as fundamental sources of income. The advantage to each university of student recruitment of this type is that all costs and revenues are based on a marginal analysis. If costs are looked at first, the main prerequisites for offering and delivering a programme such as this are that there are qualified lecturers and suitable accommodation to teach MBA students. A university will normally possess both of these resources, the costs of which will be met whether or not the MBA course runs (up to a certain level of intake of course!). Thus, there are no major additional costs to the university of running the programme, except for minor costs such as heating and lighting, extra photocopying and paper costs, etc. which are likely to be minimal, say £50 per annum per student. If each student is charged £10,000 it becomes clear that this is a lucrative niche market for the university sector to be in. The strategy based on these figures would appear to be obvious – recruit as many students as possible. It may be that after a certain number are recruited a part-time lecturer may be required to assist with some of the teaching, but based on a marginal profit per student of £9,950 (MR – MC = £10,000 – £50). It would appear that significant increases in the marginal cost of each MBA student could be absorbed before making this an uneconomic proposition. The only problem is, of course, that in the long run any excess supply in the market place will lead to a downgrading of the MBA qualification, a lower return on such qualifications and a consequent drop in the demand for places for MBA courses. However, at the moment this is only a distant worry and it will be addressed as and when it occurs. The MBA is a 'golden goose' at the moment and the university sector is doing its best to slay it!

Questions

1. At what point would it be uneconomic to take on any more students?
2. In the long run, would it be better to increase or decrease the price of the MBA in order to preserve its longevity?
3. Is there an argument, based on the marginal concepts that have been examined in this chapter, for the university sector to offer more and more courses on this basis? Is this good for the UK as a whole? List some possible advantages and disadvantages.

CASE STUDY **8.3**   A marginal application

The aim of this case study is to show how, using different techniques of analysing the same data, different answers can be arrived at that may result in decisions being altered accordingly.

The importance of examining the relationship between marginal cost and marginal revenue (benefit) is that it allows decision-making to be made on the basis of setting marginal benefit equal to marginal cost, without having to worry about the accurate measurement of total benefits and costs. The use of the marginal idea distinguishes economic approaches to decision-making from much popular discussion that tends to focus on averages. A good example is that of road safety. A debate might arise from data on expenditure on road safety measures (e.g. crash barriers on motorways) and estimates of the number of lives saved. Suppose that £20 million of such expenditure is estimated to have saved 50 lives in the last year. The policy question might then be how much should we spend next year?

It is easy to see the line of argument that might be taken in popular debate in newspapers and elsewhere: the question posed might then involve whether lives are worth £400,000 each (£20 million divided by 50). People may differ in their responses to this question, but if they think that saving a life is worth at least £400,000, they will tend to argue that we should spend more on road safety.

However, this approach makes the mistake of focusing on averages rather than on the margin. The real question to ask is: how many lives would be saved at the margin by increasing expenditure on road safety?

In order to answer this question, the following data needs to be considered:

Expenditure (£m)	Lives saved
5	25
10	40
15	48
20	50

This additional information shows that expenditure on road safety suffers from diminishing marginal benefit (i.e. the more that is spent, the less the benefit that is gained from the additional spending). So the last £5 million spent saves only two lives at a cost of £2.5 million each; put another way, the marginal cost of saving a life increases sharply with the total number of lives saved.

Once the issue is seen in marginal terms, the debate as to whether lives are 'worth' £400,000 is arguably irrelevant. At the margin, in a situation when £15 million is already spend on road safety, the real question is whether we are willing to spend an extra £2.5 million per life saved. If we are, then we should maintain or increase our expenditure, if not we should only maintain or reduce our expenditure.

Adapted from *Economic Review*, 13 February 1995.

Questions
1 What other information would be needed before making a decision on whether to increase or decrease spending on road safety?
2 Do you think that the marginal benefit will continue to decrease as expenditure on road safety is increased? Explain your answer.

Time horizons
....

A firm is no different from an individual when assessing the future. An individual will plan for things that are going to happen in the next two to three days with a reasonable degree of certainty, even though some circumstances may alter. Take, for example, the context of planning the family budget for one month. Certain things will be the same each month and can be predicted with a reasonable degree of certainty, such as mortgage repayments that are often altered only once a year. Although over time much of the family budget will change, in the short term payments can be regarded as fixed. This perspective can be translated into the business environment when considering the costs the firm can expect to remain unchanged in the short term. These can include rent and business rates, for example, which have been set outside the company and are determined for a definite time period. However, if a firm would like to produce more output in the next two weeks, depending on the industry in which it is involved, some costs are likely to change. For instance, it may need to hire more employees in order to increase output, which would have the obvious effect of increasing the total labour costs of the firm, but leave costs such as the rent or business rates unchanged as these are not linked to the level of output.

There are two time horizons that businesses must concern themselves with: the short run and the long run. There is no definition in terms of weeks, months or years to indicate the duration of these two periods; they are firm and industry specific and will be determined by production factors. In the short run at least one factor that is used in the production process cannot be altered. For example, a manufacturing firm may want to expand its production. It can get more raw materials, it can get present employees to work longer hours or even hire more staff, but it has a fixed factory size. Thus in the short run, the expansion of output is not limited by the availability of raw materials or of employees, but it is limited by the size of the factory. Here the factory is the fixed factor.

The long run, on the other hand, is a period of time during which there are no fixed factors of production, i.e. all factors can be changed. If, in our example, it will take two years to build a new factory, then the long-run time period is two years onwards.

The law of variable proportions

In the short run, we can only change some of the factors of production. As we change these variable factors, the proportions in which the variable and fixed factors are combined must change. The effect on output of changing the input of variable factors can be explained in terms of the law of variable proportions. This law can be broken down into two component laws. These are the law of increasing returns and the law of diminishing returns. We take each in turn.

➤ *The law of increasing returns*: This law states that as more units of a variable factor are added to a fixed factor, output will at first rise more than proportionately.

➤ *The law of diminishing returns*: This law states that as more units of a variable factor are added to a fixed factor, there will come a point when output will rise less than proportionately. When this happens we say that the firm experiences diminishing returns.

Putting these two laws together gives us *the law of variable proportions*. This states that as more units of a variable factor are added to a fixed factor, output will at first rise more than proportionately. However, as more units of the variable factor are added, output will, after a certain point, rise less than proportionately.

Average and marginal product

When discussing the law of variable proportions or its component laws we often make use of the concepts of *marginal product* and *average product*. These are measured with respect to a specific type of input, usually labour.

The marginal product of labour is simply the change in total output when one more worker is employed. The average product of labour, on the other hand, is simply total output divided by the total number of workers employed. The relationship between total, average and marginal product is illustrated in Table 8.2.

It can be seen from the table that up to the employment of the fifth worker marginal product is rising. When marginal product is rising, the firm is said to be experiencing increasing marginal returns.

Table 8.2

Relationship between total, average and marginal product

No. of workers	Total product	Average product	Marginal product
1	2	2.0	2
2	5	2.5	3
3	10	3.3	5
4	22	5.5	12
5	42	8.4	20
6	62	10.3	20
7	77	11.0	15
8	86	10.75	9

With the employment of the sixth worker the situation changes, because marginal product is constant. Here we say that the firm is experiencing constant marginal returns. With the employment of the seventh worker marginal product begins to fall. In these circumstances we say that the firm is experiencing diminishing marginal returns.

The ideas of increasing returns and diminishing returns are illustrated in Figure 8.4, which is based on the data in Table 8.2. Notice that marginal product begins to diminish before average product. Marginal product starts to fall after the sixth worker is employed, but average product only starts to fall after the seventh worker is employed. In terms of Figure 8.4, as long as the marginal product is above the average product, average product will continue to rise. This is true even when marginal product is itself falling. It must follow that the marginal product curve intersects the average product curve at its highest point, since as soon as marginal product is below average product, average product falls.

We can therefore say that diminishing marginal returns set in after the sixth worker employed, but diminishing average returns set in after the seventh worker employed.

This idea of diminishing marginal returns is a nice theoretical concept, but the practical limitations of the idea should also be highlighted. In the complex world of business today very few firms make only a single product. Consequently, the availability of marginal data is limited, from both an output and a cost perspective. Additionally, production has switched from its labour-intensive foundations to being fundamentally capital-intensive today.

What if demand for the product is consistently above what can be made in the existing factory? If the management perceives that the demand for the product is sufficiently long-lasting it may decide that a new factory should be built. Thus in the long term no factor is fixed, as all variables that are inputs into the production process can be altered eventually. The law of diminishing returns is clearly based on firms operating in the short run where at least one factor of production is fixed.

Figure 8.4
**Increasing and
diminishing returns**

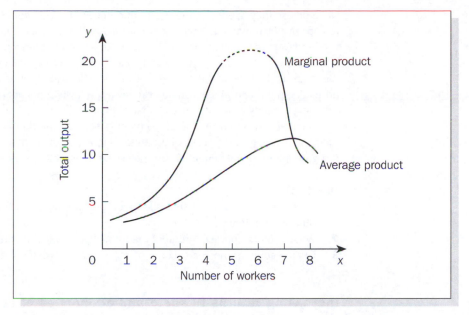

Note: Values for marginal product are plotted at the mid-points of the ordinates on the *x* axis.

An interesting question to pose based on the long-run perspective where all inputs can be altered, is what happens to output if a firm increases all its inputs by the same proportion? This introduces the concept of returns to scale, and principally the idea of economies of scale. For some firms increased scale, or size, reduces costs, while for other firms increased scale might lead to inefficiency and waste.

CASE STUDY 8.4

Marginal environmental analysis

The aim of this case study is to use marginal analysis to look at an issue that is occupying more and more time in the headlines, namely pollution.

The analysis of the costs associated with pollution is an area that lends itself to marginal analysis. In many cases the marginal costs and benefits associated with any particular pollutant will vary greatly with the level of that pollutant, so that calculations based on average data may be seriously misleading. A simple example might be the case of a factory pumping waste material into a river. At low levels of output the river may be able to 'effectively carry' the pollution without harmful effects. However, at some point the output of pollutant exceeds the 'carrying capacity' of the river, and at this point the marginal social cost of an extra unit of pollutant may become extremely high (and much higher than the average cost per unit of pollutant). Yet at still higher levels of output of the pollutant, the marginal social cost may again be rather low (and much lower than the average cost) since the damage has already been done and any additional pollution may not make the situation much worse.

These simple observations about marginal cost tell us something about appropriate policy responses that would not be so obvious if we thought only about average costs. Policies aimed at environmental protection are unlikely to be worth while unless they operate in the region of output of the pollutant in which the pollution is imposing high marginal social costs. It follows that policies aimed at reducing the highest levels of pollution may not be sensible since the marginal benefits of such policies (that is the reduction in social costs of pollution) are likely to be small at those levels. Policies that are most likely to be effective in terms of environmental protection are those which focus on reducing the level of pollution below the critical 'carrying capacity' where the social cost reductions available are at their greatest.

Another way of making the same point is that we can do the most good by focusing policy in those areas of greatest marginal significance – i.e. where we get the greatest marginal benefit for our policy expenditure.

Questions

1 What does the marginal analysis tell us that we might not have been aware of otherwise in this case?

2 What does the phrase 'greatest marginal significance' mean?

3 Outline some of the social costs of pollution in the case of a river.

Increasing returns to scale and economies of scale

In the long run there are no fixed factors of production. All factors are variable, and firms are therefore able to adjust their input of all factors of production. When firms change the input of all factors of production, we say that there has been a *change in the scale of production*. There is no longer the need, as in the short run, to change the proportions in which the various factors are combined.

When firms change the scale of production this will almost certainly change productivity. When an increase in the input of all factors of production leads to a more than proportional increase in output, we say that the firm has experienced economies of scale. For example, if the firm increases the input of labour, capital and land by 10 per cent and output rises by more than 10 per cent, the firm has experienced *economies of scale*. On the other hand, when an increase in the input of all factors of production leads to a less than proportional increase in total output, we say that the firm experiences *diseconomies of scale*. Thus, if the firm increases the input of land, labour and capital by 10 per cent and output rises by less than 10 per cent, then we say that the firm has experienced diseconomies of scale.

Great care must be taken to distinguish between an increase in productivity that has occurred as a result of an increase in the use of variable factors only, and an increase in productivity that has occurred because of an increase in the scale of production. Increasing returns and diminishing returns refer to short-run changes in output, that is, changes in output when the firm has at least one fixed factor. Economies and diseconomies of scale refer to long-run changes in output, that is changes in output when there are no fixed factors.

For simplicity, economies of scale are sometimes defined as an increase in the scale of production that leads to a fall in the average cost of producing each unit. Diseconomies of scale, on the other hand, are defined as an increase in the scale of production that leads to an increase in the average cost of producing each unit.

The economies of scale can be either internal or external. *Internal economies of scale* are obtained through the growth of the firm itself. *External economies of scale* are obtained through the growth in the size of the industry as a whole. They are important when the industry is heavily concentrated and are outside the direct control of business itself.

Internal economies of scale

Technical economies

Large firms are able to make more use of the division of labour; for example, with a small output it may not be possible to employ one person wholly on one process or part of a process. However, as output rises a greater degree of specialisation is possible. As workers specialise on particular activities their productivity often increases: 'practice makes perfect'. Adam Smith showed that a pin factory could produce many more pins if each person concentrated on a particular activity (drawing the wire, cutting the wire or sharpening the head) rather than trying to undertake all the various activities. It is this specialisation which is called the division of labour.

The firm can also make more use of machinery. For example, a machine may only be used for two hours per day in a small firm, but may be fully used in a large firm. This will save the 'cost' of having expensive machinery lie idle. Larger specialised machinery can also be used which produces more output per hour. It may even be possible for the whole process to be undertaken in the form of a production line (mass production). This would not usually be possible in a smaller firm with only a limited output. It is often said that specialisation is limited by the extent of the market.

Benefits may also occur for large firms due to increased volume; for example, if a container is doubled in size its surface area increases four times but its volume increases eight times. There are, therefore, savings to be made in using larger containers, which will cost relatively less per unit of volume than the smaller ones. Larger lorries (juggernauts), aircraft and blast furnaces are further examples of the benefits that can be obtained from extra size. The 'running costs' of a 4-tonne lorry are less than twice those of a 2-tonne lorry.

Research and development (R & D) is also possible in a larger firm and this could lead to an improvement in the quality of the goods produced and a reduction in costs through better ways of producing the goods.

Management economies

Larger businesses are able to appoint qualified staff who are specialists in a particular area. The small firm is likely, of necessity, to have a work force of 'jack of all trades'. Management costs will not necessarily increase in proportion to the growth in size of the firm. For instance, you may be able to double the size of the firm without doubling the managerial staff. This will reduce management costs per unit of output.

Marketing (trading) economies

Marketing economies can be viewed in terms of buying and selling. When a business buys its raw materials, it is likely to obtain preferential treatment, perhaps in the form of a discount if it is making a bulk purchase. A larger business is in a stronger position to secure good discounts because it could threaten to go elsewhere if it was not satisfied with the terms, and this threat would be a financially powerful one because of the size of its order. When selling the product, specialist sales personnel can be appointed, who can often obtain larger orders with no extra time and effort than that needed to obtain a smaller order. Administration, transport, advertising and packaging costs can then also be spread over large orders. For example, the packaging costs per item are likely to be less for 1,000 items than if 10 items were packed.

Financial economies

Most firms need to borrow money to finance their business. Large firms are able to obtain their finance from banks more easily and more cheaply, borrowing at lower interest rates. A bank will more readily give a loan to a well-known company than to Joe Smith who is just starting up a window cleaning business. The larger firm is also likely to have more assets to offer to the bank as security for the loan.

Risk-bearing economies

Large producers can spread their risk so that they do not have all their 'eggs in one basket'. They can obtain their supply of raw materials from different sources and this will allow them to safeguard against shortages. Larger firms can also produce a wide range of products; for example, Hillsdown Holdings plc owns Smedley's Food Ltd, Chivers Hartley Ltd and Premier Beverages as well as upholstered furniture, house building and office furniture companies. You will probably have a number of its products in your kitchen since its brand names include Typhoo tea, Olde English recipe marmalade and Haywards Pickles. If there is a fall in the demand for one of the products, losses can be offset by profits from sales of the others.

External economies of scale

As the industry in an area grows, it may mean that certain processes can be done better by a specialist (ancillary) firm. In the West Yorkshire woollen industry, firms specialised in making textile machinery. The same specialisation has occurred in the motor vehicle industry; for example, Lucas has specialised in the production of car lamps and electronics for the major car assemblers in the Midlands. The individual firm can often buy cheaper and better quality components and services from these specialist firms.

Other benefits may also follow from an industry developing in a particular area, enabling individual firms to gain advantages:

➤ *Better training*: As local colleges offer courses for the main industry of the area, a pool of skilled labour will eventually develop, to the benefit of individual firms.
➤ *Better transport*: The road and rail networks often improve as an industry develops in an area, e.g. the Millennium Dome in Greenwich.
➤ *Better commercial services*: Banks and insurance companies will become expert, having special knowledge of an industry's needs.

Similar firms in an area will require up-to-date information on such things as raw material supplies and foreign government regulations. There may be a free flow of such information between firms. Firms may also group together to make a joint contribution to R&D, whereas they may not be able to afford to undertake independent research. This will save individual firms both time and money.

PAUSE FOR THOUGHT 4

There are now many cities in the UK that have two, three, four or even more universities. Consider a city where there are two universities that offer some similar courses, but in other cases there is no overlap. Identify some of the economies of scale that might evolve from a merger between the two establishments. What disadvantages may accrue from a merger such as this?

CASE STUDY **8.5**

The knowledge revolution

The aim of this case study is to identify how, in attempting to create organisations that will result in economies of scale, diseconomies of scale can arise. The case will examine how the development of a field of expertise entitled 'knowledge management' is attempting to eradicate these potential diseconomies and will ultimately assist in strategic decision-making.

The knowledge management market is a new and rapidly expanding phenomenon in the business world of today. Experts in the field believe that visual retrieval technology has the greatest potential with the most common view being that the distinction between text and image, such as video and TV, will disappear. The demand for expertise such as this is almost entirely from large organisations, with firms involved in knowledge management currently delivering mostly departmental solutions for large organisations.

One of the commonest challenges for those providing knowledge management services is to persuade people to share. A simple solution to this is that if the software will let you do it automatically, then you do not even realise that you are sharing the knowledge. 'Autonomy' is one of the foremost systems in this field. It was installed within the Virtual University at BAe Systems. The company was of the view that it required to put in place a 'one stop shop for information' and set up a trial on some 300 websites. Subsequently the package has now been 'embedded in the management development framework of the business'.

Other developments include features such as pattern-recognition technology and concept highlighting. This gives the user blocks of text from relevant web pages, and highlights in red those things that are of personal interest to the user. At the hub is a reasoning engine that updates itself every hour. BAe links that to 10 or 12 news feeds, providing 10,000 to 15,000 stories per day, plus 300 specified Internet sites. The system invokes a five-star grading system; it randomly selects colleagues interested in the same management issues, in effect creating 'virtual networks – enabling the knowledge economy'. This allows the construction of communities of common interest within large organisations. A quote from a satisfied customer highlights the usefulness of this type of software: 'We've transformed an organisation that's been very product-based in terms of networking and infrastructure, towards a much more service and e-business solution focus.'

The use of knowledge management systems can also be extended into recruitment, matching the personal agents of a new employee with the specific expertise of existing personnel. This has the potential to accelerate the induction process and identifies even more importantly whom within the organisation they should be talking to as a first priority.

It is also possible to link the software to the Lotus Beta product Quickplace, where it trawls the content within the online discussions – often spread across several countries – and looks for information that might be useful for feeding into best practice. A fine example of the benefit of embracing this methodology is within one large firm that employs 2,500 employees world wide. It is clear with a firm of this magnitude that managing content becomes very important. Recently, the company imported 36 gigabytes of old information acquired over five years ago in Logical Australia and categorised it. 'Tens of thousands of documents were categorised over a weekend! It tells you what you didn't know you had.'

A KPMG survey concluded that nearly two-thirds of organisations complained that they were suffering from information overload. Previously, those who ascended the corporate ladder had the social skills to get on with people. In today's world, it will be those who can master the new technology remotely and then deploy it to the benefit of the enterprise collectively who will succeed in the new global economy.

Question

Examine why the embracing of knowledge management systems is especially useful in the business world of today.

Constant and decreasing returns to scale

Constant returns to scale

In this instance the percentage increase in all inputs is identical to the percentage increase in output, e.g. if all inputs are increased by 10 per cent then the subsequent increase in output will be 10 per cent. In relation to the average cost per unit produced, constant returns would imply that the change in scale of the firm's operations has had no impact on the average cost of production.

Decreasing returns to scale (diseconomies of scale)

Decreasing returns to scale occur when the percentage increase in all inputs is greater than the subsequent percentage increase in output, e.g. if all inputs are increased by 10 per cent, but output only increases by 5 per cent. This is also defined in terms of the average cost per unit produced. When an increase in the scale of production leads to a higher cost per unit, then diseconomies of scale are said to occur.

There is a view that diseconomies of scale do not occur in some production processes, irrespective of the level of output. However, the most often cited example as to why diseconomies of scale do sometimes exist is bureaucratic inefficiency. As size increases beyond a certain point, operations tend to become more difficult to manage. There is a risk of the business becoming top-heavy with management, which can lead to inefficiencies. For example, there may be an increase in the time needed for the decision-making process as the chain of command becomes more extensive and the procedural elements involved become more formal. The management of the firm may then become less responsive to the business environment in which it operates. In recent years a number of privatised firms in the UK have responded to this problem by removing entire layers of management and deleting their job category from the organisational hierarchy (de-layering).

It has also been argued in the past that large firms are more likely to face problems with organised labour (i.e. unions) than perhaps are small firms. However, with the many reforms that have been made to trade union legislation, this threat is no longer as significant as it once was (see Chapter 12). Indeed, it could be argued that small firms with specialised staff may be more at risk from employee dissatisfaction than the large firms of today.

Minimum efficient scale

Minimum efficient scale (MES) refers to the level of output at which scale economies are exhausted; i.e. the long-run average cost (LRAC) curve is at a minimum. This is output Q* in Figure 8.5. The cost gradient represents the increase in average costs as a result of the production unit (or institutional unit) being only a specified percentage of the optimum size. Here the information relates to the (percentage) increase in average output costs where the production unit is only half the MES for that branch of manufacturing industry. An important summary of studies concerning economies of scale in the UK, USA and Germany (Pratten, 1971) is presented in Table 8.3. The study covers various branches of manufacturing industry and provides information about the minimum efficient scale (MES), cost gradients and the nature of the various types of economies of scale (EOS) in general. The table lists various branches of industry ranked by the importance of the economies of scale observed in that industry.

Figure 8.5
Minimum efficient scale (MES) and cost gradient at $\frac{1}{2}$ MES

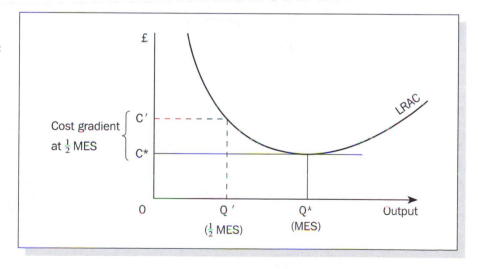

We can see some broad trends and patterns in Table 8.3. Economies of scale (EOS) are clearly larger in transport equipment, chemicals, machinery and instrument manufacture (office machines, electrical equipment, etc.) and in paper and printing. These sectors account for some 55 per cent of industrial production, and 65 per cent of industrial employment in the European Union. They are sectors where demand has been growing strongly and which have a high technological content. By contrast, economies of scale are clearly smaller in food, drink and tobacco, textiles, clothing, leather goods and timber. These sectors have been characterised by relatively stagnant demand and low techno-logical content of products.

Table 8.3
Minimum efficient scale (MES), cost gradients, and other economies of scale (EOS)

NACE Code	Branch	Cost gradient at $\frac{1}{2}$ MES	Remarks
35	Motor vehicles	6–9%	Very substantial EOS in production and in development costs.
36	Other means of transport	8–20%	Variable EOS: small for cycles and ship-building (although economies are possible through series production level), very substantial in aircraft (development costs).
25	Chemical industry	2.5–15%	Substantial EOS in production processes. In some segments of the industry (pharmaceutical products), R&D is an important source of EOS.
26	Man-made fibres	5–10%	Substantial EOS in general.
22	Metals	>6%	Substantial EOS in general for production processes. Also possible in production and series production.
33	Office machinery	3–6%	Substantial EOS at product level.
32	Mechanical engineering	3–10%	Limited EOS at firm level but substantial for production.
34	Electrical engineering	5–15%	Substantial EOS at product level and for development costs.
37	Instrument engineering	5–15%	Substantial EOS at product level, via development costs.
47	Paper, printing and publishing	8–36%	Substantial EOS in paper mills and, in particular, printing (books).
24	Non-metallic mineral products	>6%	Substantial EOS in cement and flat glass production processes. In other branches, optimum plant size is small compared with the optimum size for the industry.
31	Metal articles (castings)	5–10%	EOS are lower at plant level but possible at production and series production level.

NACE Code	Branch	Cost gradient at $\frac{1}{2}$ MES	Remarks
48	Rubber and plastics	3–6%	Moderate EOS in tyre manufacture. Small EOS in factories making rubber and moulded plastic articles but potential for EOS at product and series production level.
41–42	Drinks and tobacco	1–6%	Moderate EOS in breweries. Small EOS in cigarette factories. In marketing, EOS are considerable.
41–42	Food	3.5–21%	Principal source of EOS is the individual plant. EOS at marketing and distribution level.
49	Other manufacturing	n.a.	Plant size is small in these branches. Possible EOS from specialisation and the length of production runs.
43	Textile industry (carpets)	10%	EOS are more limited than in other sectors, but possible economies from specialisation and the length of production runs.
46	Timber and wood	n.a.	No EOS for plants in these sectors. Possible EOS from specialisation and longer production runs.
45	Footwear and clothing	1%	Small EOS at plant level but possible EOS from (footwear) specialisation and longer production runs.
44	Leather and leather goods	n.a.	Small EOS.

Source: European Economy (1998).

The final column of Table 8.3 provides a guide as to the nature of the general economies of scale available in that branch of manufacturing industry, including both technical and non-technical economies.

CASE STUDY **8.6**

What happens when companies combine?

The aim of this case study is to examine why a merger between two companies can produce both economies and diseconomies of scale.

Takeovers and mergers are often in the news. In both cases the effect is to take two independent companies and to make one. There is no doubt that mergers and/or takeovers can create very large enterprises. An example of a proposed large merger was that between the French car producer Renault and the Swedish car producer Volvo, abandoned at the last moment in December 1993. This combination, as you can see from Table CS8.6.1, would have created the sixth largest car producer in the world.

Table CS8.6.1
Top ten car producers' performance, 1992

Ranking	Company
1	General Motors
2	Ford
3	Toyota
4	Volkswagen
5	Nissan
6	Renault + Volvo
7	Fiat
8	Chrysler
9	Peugeot Citroën
10	Honda

It is therefore important to understand the motivations for combining and to examine what makes such a combination profitable. One source of profit is the elimination of inefficiencies. It is often thought that the biggest potential source of inefficiencies lies in the management, or perhaps mismanagement of a firm's assets. If an inefficient management is replaced by an efficient one, profits will be higher. The management that is being accused of inefficiency seldom agrees with the charge, so that combinations of firms motivated by the desire to obtain managerial efficiency are often takeovers, rather than mergers.

A second source of profits that arise from companies combining their productive capabilities is in economies of scale. Both manufacturing industry in general and car production in particular are thought to be characterised by falling average costs of production as output increases (see Table CS8.6.2).

Table CS8.6.2
Economies of scale in car production

Output per year	Index of unit average costs (cars)
100,000	100
250,000	83
500,000	74
1,000,000	70
2,000,000	66

Source: Rhys, G., 'Competition in the car industry', *Developments in Economics*, 9.

The suggestion is that the average cost is a minimum (i.e. MES) only when output is as large as 2 million per unit. At this level of output, average costs are some 34 per cent smaller than for a firm producing only 100,000 cars a year.

Larger firms, therefore, have a natural cost advantage over small firms. This might be true both of the assembly of cars, and of the production of the component parts. If Volvo, for example, specialises in the assembly of cars and, therefore, frees a part of Renault's productive facilities to specialise further in engine production, the consequence of the merger of Renault and Volvo might be a combined company that enjoys a lower unit cost than its constituent parts.

In the case of the combination of Renault and Volvo, Renault claimed that the total cost of savings due to merger would have been of the order of FF30 billion (about £4 billion at the time) by the year 2000. That would have been sufficient to double the combined companies' profits from now to the year 2000. Perhaps, not surprisingly, the majority of commentators on the proposed merger were somewhat sceptical!

Adapted from *Economic Review*, 11 March 1994.

Questions

1   The merger between the two firms was abandoned before it was completed. Why do you think this may have been the case?
2   Can you think of any diseconomies of scale that may have resulted if the merger had taken place?
3   In the case study it is suggested that the projected savings were rather on the high side. Why do you think that these projections were so optimistic?

Producing at least cost
·······························

It is difficult to imagine that a product can be made in only one way. Different management teams facing the same situation might make a decision relating to the production process that another group of individuals may disagree with. Technological developments have resulted in new possibilities for the process of manufacturing a huge variety of goods, the car industry being a well-cited example of this. In the early days of manufacture this was a very heavily labour-intensive industry which has now become increasingly dominated by robotics technology. This has been a general world-wide trend in the last 20 years, as all manufacturing industry has reduced the volume of labour that it has employed. The replacement of labour by machinery (capital) has also been the case in the service sector, with banking being a familiar example. Research has shown that the majority of customers are now more comfortable dealing with various types of banking technology than they are when face-to-face with tellers inside the bank itself. It is a common sight for a large queue to form outside the bank, with people waiting their turn on an automated cash dispensing machine, while the interior of the bank is not busy at all. This use of automated machinery has resulted in large-scale redundancies within the banking industry, allowing firms to reduce costs through the substitution of capital for labour and ultimately through achieving a more efficient allocation of factor inputs.

PAUSE FOR THOUGHT 5   *The trend towards the substitution of machines for employees is something that is set to continue. What are the implications of this for young people of today and in the future?*

Substitutability of capital and labour

The banking and car industry examples that were analysed above both indicate an increasing tendency towards the substitution of labour by machines (capital). The advantages to the firm are numerous: machines are more reliable in terms of productivity, with no union disagreements, no absenteeism, no period of training, etc. This may well result in substantial cost savings. Usually firms need a combination of both people and machines (i.e. both labour and capital).

If this can be optimised, i.e. the best possible combination found, then costs can be minimised and profit can be increased.

A hypothetical example has been constructed below to examine this concept. The figures in Table 8.4 show different combinations of labour and capital needed to produce 100 units of output. It is evident that if we select a process requiring only a skeleton staff (Method (e)), then a great deal of capital is required; whereas at the other end of the scale if a highly labour-intensive process is chosen (Method (a)), then a much smaller level of capital input is required. The question is: what is the best combination of labour and capital?

Table 8.4

Combinations of capital and labour to produce 100 units of output

Method	Number of workers (L)	Cost per unit of labour (£000s)	Units of capital (K)	Cost per unit of capital (£000s)
(a)	50	1	10	2
(b)	35	1	15	2
(c)	20	1	22	2
(d)	10	1	35	2
(e)	6	1	50	2

Figure 8.6

Isoquant line analysis

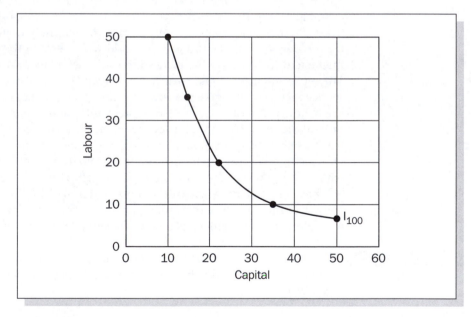

Isoquants

The data in Table 8.4 are expressed graphically in Figure 8.6. The curve joining the five points shown is known as an *isoquant*. An isoquant line is a line of constant quantity (iso – constant; quant – quantity). This shows the different combination of inputs capable of producing a given level of output in a technically efficient way.

Figure 8.7

Isoquant line for different levels of output

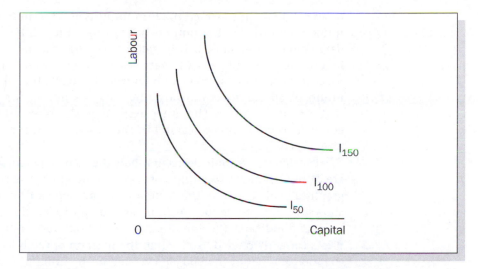

The isoquant line shows the most efficient range of production possibilities that the firm faces in order to produce a given level of output. If a combination of inputs were chosen that fell below this line, then the output would be less than the 100 units required. For example, 20 units of capital and 20 units of labour is a combination of inputs which is insufficient to produce 100 units of output. If a combination of inputs were chosen above the line then it would be possible to make the 100 units, but this would not be as efficient a way as those combinations of inputs on the line. In effect, resources would not be utilised to their full capacity by such a combination, e.g. machines would not be operating at full capacity, or there may be too many employees for the available machines. For example, 50 units of capital and 10 units of labour is a combination of inputs which is excessive for producing 100 units of output. We can see that 100 units of output could be produced using 35 units of capital and 10 units of labour or 50 units of capital and 6 units of labour, in each case using less of one factor of production and no more of the other.

The isoquant shown here is for the production of 100 units of output, and if a firm wished to increase or decrease its level of output, a new isoquant line would be drawn above or below that constructed for 100 units. An example of this can be seen in Figure 8.7.

To produce a higher level of output, e.g. 150 units, in a technically efficient manner will require more of at least one factor of production, possibly both. This will give an isoquant line above and to the right of the existing isoquant.

To produce a lower level of output, e.g. 50 units, in a technically efficient manner will require less of at least one factor of production, possibly both. This will give an isoquant line below and to the left of the existing isoquant.

Isocosts

The other important aspect of this particular problem is to identify what combination of factor inputs a firm can purchase given the budget constraint that it is working under. One of the main elements in decision-making is the financial situation in which the firm finds itself. This, in turn, will have some influence on the level of output that can be achieved. If we again utilise the data contained in Table 8.4, it is clear that the costs per unit of capital and labour are constant over the various combinations in which they may be used. If the firm has a production budget of £50,000 then it can afford a maximum of 50 employees at any one time, assuming that it makes a zero investment in capital. The other extreme position would be to employ the equivalent of 25 units of capital in the process, with the labour force dropping to zero.

The different combinations of inputs that can be purchased for a given cost are displayed on an *isocost* line (iso – constant; cost). The isocost lines can be graphically illustrated in the same way as the isoquant lines. Thus, Figure 8.8 shows the isocost line for this firm based on a £50,000 budget available to the firm, and indicates the combinations of labour and capital available at the prices currently quoted. Notice that the position of the isocost line is given by the total amount of the budget available to the firm but that the slope of the isocost line depends on the relative price of the factor inputs.

As in the case of the isoquant analysis, if one of the parameters alters then this will result in the construction of a new isocost line. This is the case in Figure 8.9 where the firm has potentially secured increased financing that will allow it to increase its budget from £50,000 to £100,000.

Another possible scenario that will require a new isocost line is the change in the price of the inputs relative to each other. Suppose the cost for each unit of capital employed is increased from £2,000 to £4,000 with the budget remaining the original amount of £50,000 and the labour cost still £1,000 per unit. This will have the impact of altering the slope of the isocost line, as can be seen in Figure 8.10. Instead of £50,000 purchasing 25 units if spent entirely on capital, it can now only purchase 12.5 units. This obviously will affect the rate at which capital can be substituted for labour. We might expect that a rise in the cost of capital relative to labour will make more labour-intensive production processes increasingly desirable for the firm.

Figure 8.8

Original isocost line

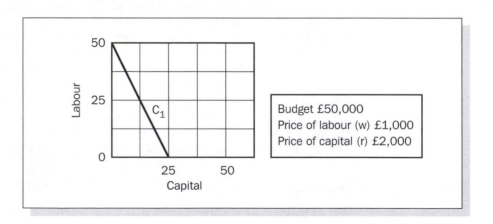

Figure 8.9
**Original and budget
increased isocost
line**

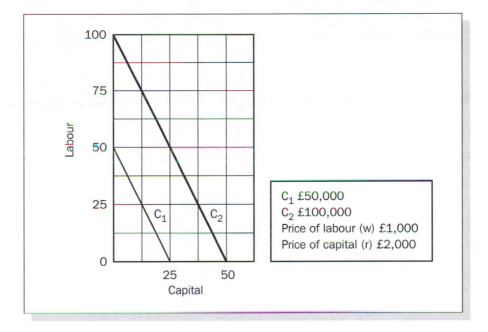

Figure 8.10
**Changes in relative
factor price**

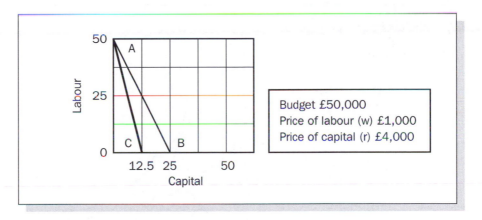

The relevance of this type of analysis for strategic decision-making is that it can help explain the combination of inputs used by the firm in its production process. In Figure 8.11 there are three isocost lines (AB, CD and EF) and one isoquant line (I_1). The isoquant line indicates the quantity of output that the firm wishes to produce, and the various combinations of labour and capital required to produce it. Each isocost line indicates the various combinations of labour and capital that can be purchased for a given sum. The further away from the origin an isocost line is, the greater the budget available to the firm to spend on factor inputs. The fact that each isocost line is parallel to the others indicates that the relative price of labour and capital remains unchanged. The isoquant line I_1 intersects various isocost lines at three separate points X, Y and Z, each of which can be considered in turn. Points X and Z can be analysed together as they are both on the same isocost line (EF). Both are feasible options for the

Figure 8.11

Finding the least-cost combination of inputs

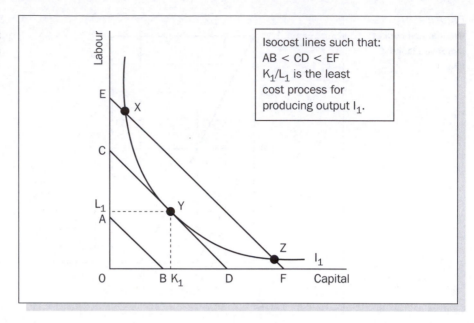

Figure 8.12

An alteration to the optimum after a relative price change

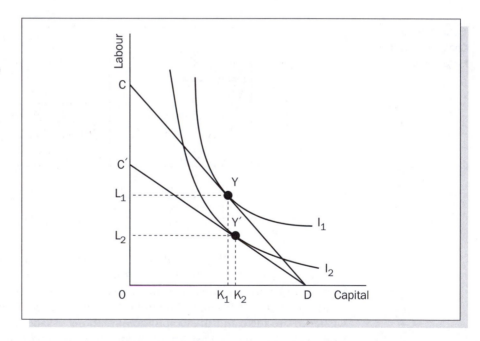

company in terms of producing output level I_1. However, the input combinations of labour and capital corresponding to points X and Z would be more expensive than that corresponding to point Y. At point Y output I_1 can also be produced by the input combination of L_1 labour and K_1 capital. This combination of capital and labour is preferred to either point X or point Z, because it is a less expensive way of achieving output I_1. This is because isocost line CD is nearer to the origin than EF. The third isocost line in the diagram (AB) is irrelevant to the analysis here in that the isoquant line (I_1) does not touch AB at any point. So, although it offers even lower cost combinations of factor input, the required level of output I_1 cannot be reached. *Thus, a firm will operate at least cost when the isoquant and isocost lines are tangential.* This will occur at a single point, assuming a constant relative price between the factors of production (in this example, capital and labour).

The slope of the isocost line indicates the rate of substitution between the two factor inputs. If the price of one of the inputs changes, then we have already noted that the slope of the isocost line will also change (see Figure 8.10). It is evident that this may have an impact on the combinations of labour and capital used by the firm if the change in cost is significant. Figure 8.12 illustrates an example of such a situation, where the cost of the labour input has increased, altering the slope of the isocost line. If the same amount is now spent entirely on labour, less can now be purchased than before. The isocost line pivots from CD to C'D.

If CD is the original isocost line and C'D the isocost line following the rise in labour costs, then from the diagram it can be seen that the isoquant line I_1 does not cut the new isocost line. This indicates that with the budget currently available to the firm it cannot produce the same level of output as it could prior to the increase in the price of labour. It must either produce less or increase its budget. Assuming that the budget is fixed, the firm is faced with the former strategy. Thus, a new isoquant line (I_2) has been constructed which just touches the new isocost line C'D at Y', using L_2 labour and K_2 capital input. This indicates a substitution of (now cheaper) capital for (now more expensive) labour in the production process.

PAUSE FOR THOUGHT 6   *Much of the analysis and evidence has indicated the desirability of using machines rather than hiring labour. Can you think of any advantages that humans would have over machines in the production process? In what circumstances in Figure 8.12 might you expect labour to be substituted for capital when a firm has a fixed budget?*

Conclusions
....

The analysis of costs is fundamental to effective decision-making. Managers need to be aware of both the fixed and variable elements in their costs and the specific length of time represented by the short run and the long run for their activities. It can also be useful for the firm to be aware of the difference between average and marginal analysis. This will help managers to be more aware of what the figures that have been calculated actually mean when they are making decisions.

The industry in which a firm is operating, and the technology associated with that industry, will clearly influence the combination of capital and labour to be used in production. However, the relative price of labour and capital and the size of the budget to be spent on factor input will also be important. The capital/labour ratio is usually consistent across firms operating in the same industry, especially in industries with a greater degree of competition, where all firms must operate at minimum cost to maintain margins and profitability.

References and additional reading
•••

Cook, M. and Farquharson, C. (1998) *Business Economics*, Financial Times Publishing, London.

Earl, P.E. (1995) *Microeconomics for Business and Marketing*, Edward Elgar, Aldershot, esp. ch. 7, pp. 156–202.

Ferguson, P.R., Ferguson, G.J. and Rothschild, R. (1993) *Business Economics: The Application of Economic Theory*, Macmillan, London, esp. chs 4–6, pp. 42–105.

Maurice, S.C., Thomas, C.R. and Smithson, C.W. (1992) *Managerial Economics* (4th edn), Irwin, Boston, esp. ch. 10, pp. 334–59; ch. 11, pp. 370–403.

McGuigan, J.R., Moyer, R.C. and Harris, F.H. (1996) *Managerial Economics* (7th edn), West, New York, esp. ch. 8, pp. 294–311; ch. 9, pp. 328–38.

Pratten, C.F. (1971) *Economies of Scale in Manufacturing Industries*, Cambridge University Press, Cambridge.

Reekie, W.D. and Crook, J. (1987) *Managerial Economics*, Philip Allan, Oxford, esp. ch. 7, pp. 181–218.

CHAPTER 9

Pricing in theory and practice

Objectives

By the end of this chapter you will be able to:

➤ Identify some of the factors that influence price setting under different types of firm objective and market situation.

➤Understand the nature of price determination and price stability within an oligopolistic market structure.

➤ Understand the nature of collusion, both explicit and tacit, within an oligopolistic market and how this allows firms to move to their most profitable output level.

➤ Be aware of the circumstances in which it will be profitable to charge different prices for the same product (i.e. price discrimination).

➤ Identify that firms in an oligopolistic market are faced with a large number of different strategies that may result in permanent disequilibrium in the market.

➤ Relate game theory to the operation of an oligopolistic market.

Key concepts

Barometric price leadership: where some firm (often small) is widely used by other firms as the 'barometer' of the market. Other firms tend then to follow the prices set by this firm which is presumed to be close to market developments.

Cartel: a formal type of collusion.

Collusion: where firms act together, formally or informally, to influence price and/or output.

Games: used in oligopoly models to try to predict action/reaction of rivals. Games can use various strategies and can be expressed using values for different outcomes (payoffs).

Kinked demand curve: a model used to help explain price rigidity or 'stickiness' said to be observed in oligopoly markets.

Oligopoly: a market dominated by a few large producers.

Price discrimination: setting different prices for identical units of a good or service.

Tacit collusion: an informal type of collusion.

Zero-sum game: a 'game' where any benefit to one can only be made by an equivalent loss to another.

Introduction

Setting the price of a good or service is one of the most important areas of decision-making in any business. Yet, due to the multidimensional nature of pricing behaviour, it is a highly complex process and can lead to the success or failure of many firms. Essentially, the pricing decision does not rely on any single subject discipline but rather encompasses many different theoretical aspects such as accounting, economics and marketing. What is nearly always true is that the price of a good or service will have a minimum level determined by the costs incurred in production and sales, and a maximum level which will be determined by the prevailing market conditions.

Determining costs

The determination and analysis of costs has been the domain of accountants since the beginning of this particular profession. It is important that we briefly consider how they allocate costs to certain products that, to some degree, will influence price. No critique of these methods is provided here, merely a synopsis of the main points of each. Traditionally, two main approaches have been identified to determine which costs are relevant for inclusion in making pricing decisions: full (absorption) costing and contribution costing. However, a more recent development is activity-based costing which differs significantly from the more tried and tested methods. The difference will become evident in reviewing the main features of each method.

Full (absorption) costing requires, in theory, that all business costs are applied to products or services. Costs therefore include direct costs allocated to a given product as well as a proportion of indirect (overhead) costs absorbed according to some unit of business activity, typically business hours. Often an estimate is made as to likely output (say two-thirds of capacity) in order to calculate the cost base on which the percentage mark-up can be applied. Alternatively, using a *contribution costing* approach, the cost element within the price is calculated by considering only those costs that directly relate to output, with no consideration of overhead costs at this stage. *Activity-based costing*, on the other hand, differs from conventional costing in its treatment of overhead costs, including only those that are related to the production process but which are relatively independent of production volume.

Firm objectives

We noted in an earlier chapter that firms may have different objectives. The rise of the limited liability company has led to a separation between ownership (shareholders) and control (managers). Owners are often thought to have profit as a long-run objective. Managers are often thought to be more interested in sales revenue (turnover) since salaries, perks and status are more closely related to company turnover than to pure profit performance. Consequently it is hypothesised that the output of a pure sales revenue maximising firm will be higher than that of a pure profit maximising firm. A higher output will, given a downward sloping demand curve, usually mean that a lower price will be set on the market.

A firm which is more interested in sales revenue than profit will be likely to use a higher proportion of capacity output in seeking to estimate the cost base on which the mark-up is to be applied. Again a higher proportion of capacity output will usually imply a lower cost base, and therefore lower price for any given percentage mark-up.

Market conditions

Neo-classical economic theory suggests that the price of a good or service is influenced by market conditions. Most industries in developed countries throughout the world could be said to be imperfectly competitive, with the vast majority being classified as oligopolistic. For a market to be called oligopolistic it must possess three characteristics:

1   Supply in the industry must be *concentrated* in the hands of relatively few firms, as for example in an industry where the four largest firms hold 80 per cent of output. There may, however, be a large number of much smaller producers that make up the remaining 20 per cent of the market share.

2   The industry must possess significant *barriers to entry* that will deter other firms from moving in to take advantage of the abnormal profits which characterise an oligopolistic market. This may be in the form of technological barriers, high start-up costs, product proliferation or any other major hurdle that might deter new firm start-up in an industry.

3   Firms must be *interdependent*. The actions of one large firm will directly impact upon other firms in the industry. In perfect competition firms are independent, in that they cannot influence the market as individual firms. If they alter output or price this will not affect the price or quantity sold of other firms. However, in an oligopoly the action of one firm will directly affect the price and/or quantity sold of other large firms. If a firm decides to cut price, consumers are likely to switch to this firm from another supplier to take advantage of the reduced price. This is then likely to lead to retaliatory behaviour in the form of matching price cuts by the competing firm. The obvious disadvantage of this is that, assuming costs stay the same, profit margins will have been reduced.

Firms in an oligopoly recognise this interdependence and this recognition will impact upon their decisions. No firm can afford to ignore the actions and reactions of other firms in the industry. It is therefore impossible to estimate the effect of a change in the firm's price or output without first making some assumption about the reactions of other firms. Depending on the nature of these assumptions, different predicted outcomes will be arrived at. History has shown that firms can react rather unpredictably, and not as one might expect in a certain set of conditions or circumstances. Indeed the element of surprise is a key tool in generating competitive advantage.

CASE STUDY **9.1**

The price of Tequila

The aim of this case study is to highlight how different factors can combine to change the price of a product dramatically. It will also examine the roles of a number of players – namely the consumer, the manufacturer and the supplier of raw materials – and how each has a part to play in price determination.

Tequila is the fastest growing seller on the world spirits market. It is made from the pared hearts of the blue-tinged agave cactus. A price boom has boosted the price of blue agave to £1 sterling a kilo – 10 times what it cost just over a year ago. In a region where rural labourers are lucky to earn £20 a week, truckloads of agave can be worth thousands of pounds. Prices have been forced up by an acute supply shortage that coincided with a surge in international demand that has seen exports double in five years.

The agave pinas are cooked in giant steam ovens, then crushed to release their sweet liquor, which is fermented for a week, then double-distilled. Ageing takes place in white-oak barrels. There is no disguising the quality of a product, which has an earthy flavour that has captured the imagination of drinkers everywhere. 'Aromas of salt, minerals and licorice', *New York Times* wine critic Eric Asimov wrote of one of the finer products.

The distillers have raised the image of tequila by applying rigorous rules of origin whose acceptance by the European Union has displaced copycat brands from within the EU that had resulted in the image of the spirit being somewhat tarnished. It is obvious that blue agave can be grown in other regions, but regulations state that only local produce can be used in the authentic tequila recipe. The consequence of these rules, which are strictly applied, is that the distillers have come a little unstuck in terms of the volume that is required to satisfy demand, but the fallout from this is distinctly lucrative for the distillers. However, there are additional market features that have come into play. The first relates to the very nature of the agave plant, which is rather unpredictable and temperamental, and can take up to eight years to mature. Thus, in a period where demand for tequila was not so buoyant, the farmers turned to other, faster ripening and maturing produce. The second major issue is that of a disease which has afflicted the agave plant and thus reduced the yearly crop. The third major concern is the lack of planning in relation to the amount of agave that is planted. There are no agreements between farmers. Consequently, supply and demand are not in equilibrium. The result is a series of boom-and-bust cycles accompanied by wildly gyrating prices.

The farmers blame the distillers, citing that a few years ago they were losing money hand over fist and that the distillers took full advantage, offering no support at all. However, an agreement has now been reached, after the big distillers went on strike by refusing to buy agave for a month. Prices have now been fixed at 60p a kilogram, and farmers have been offered long-term aid in return. Industry experts believe that it could take years for supplies to stabilise. Meanwhile, prices seem certain to rise for consumers the world over.

Questions

1 What type of pricing are the distillers operating here?
2 Which group(s) are suffering as a result of these price increases?
3 Is a hugely inflated price for tequila sustainable in the long run?

Non-price competition

The majority of the analysis in this chapter will concentrate on the impact of a change in the level of prices on market share and profitability. An important characteristic of oligopoly that must be examined is that of non-price competition. This is often used in preference to price competition because of the potential damage to all firms in an industry as a result of a price war. Firms are all too aware of this and so a policy of price stability is often pursued. Firms will then concentrate their strategic policy on non-price competition in order to entice customers from their rivals. Examples of this include advertising campaigns.

If a firm in the industry were to introduce a new advertising campaign and increase its market share, this may result in other firms in the industry countering with a campaign of their own. However, this could have the effect of increasing the size of the market as a whole, which would be of benefit to all the firms in the industry. It is unlikely that the aim of an advertising campaign would be to force rivals out of the market. This is an extremely risky strategy that might backfire with strong retaliatory tactics from other firms. More realistically, an advertising campaign would be seen as a method of achieving small increases in market share and profits and of increasing the barriers to entry of the industry, thus deterring new firms from taking some of the existing firms' market share.

PAUSE FOR THOUGHT 1   *Consider a number of television advertising campaigns that are currently ongoing. Make a list of the products that are being promoted. An interesting exercise is then to identify who owns the brands being advertised and to consider the nature of these industries in terms of their market structure.*

Another non-price tactic that may be employed by oligopolists is the creation of strong brand images which, although difficult to create, have a number of advantages once established. A powerful product image will result in a product being perceived to have relatively few substitutes. The firm can then charge what is in effect a premium price for the product. Put another way, the establishment of a strong brand image makes demand for the product less price elastic, so that a rise in price causes few customers to switch to other suppliers. This will result in the firm increasing revenue and therefore profitability from a price rise, without reducing demand for the product to any significant extent. In addition, it becomes a more difficult proposition for the other competing firms in the market to launch a new product that can effectively compete with an existing product with a strong brand image. (See Case Study 9.2.)

CASE STUDY **9.2**   **Competition under oligopoly – the Hoover free flight promotion**
This case study looks at the way in which one firm in an oligopolistic market attempted to increase its market share using non-price competition.

Companies such as Hoover, Hotpoint, Philips and Electrolux produce appliances such as washing machines, refrigerators, dishwashers, tumble dryers and vacuum cleaners. The market for such 'white goods' is dominated by a few firms and is an example of an oligopolistic market structure. In recent years there has been growing interest by firms in the use of free gifts as a means of attracting new customers, or maintaining existing customers. This has been particularly true of promotions involving free air miles or air tickets.

Households tend to purchase products such as vacuum cleaners only when their existing appliances have irrevocably broken down or perhaps when they are moving house. The market for such products is therefore by nature rather static, a situation not helped by economic recession. Given these factors, Hoover launched a free flight promotion in 1992 as a means of stimulating demand and gaining market share at the expense of its competitors' products. Customers who spent a minimum of £100 on the purchase of one of their products qualified for two free return flights to one of six European destinations. This was subsequently extended to include US destinations. In reality consumers had to spend at least £119, since that was the price of the cheapest Hoover product, namely a vacuum cleaner.

The aim of any promotion is to expand the sale of the product, increasing revenue and strengthening brand loyalty by means of non-price competition. As far as Hoover was concerned, the free flight offer was successful in persuading the customer to purchase the product. This could have been achieved by a reduction in the price of the product providing that the price elasticity of demand was favourable. This response has been extensively used in the past, particularly in times of recession, and although still practised it is now somewhat less popular. The problem with reducing the price is that it creates a degree of uncertainty in the market and the possibility of stimulating a price war. It may also cause the customer to question whether a lower price means lower quality and this could be potentially damaging for the product's image.

The Hoover promotion was successful in terms of the level of demand that it generated, but it created a number of major difficulties. First, additional labour had to be employed and the factory had to be placed on seven-day working in order to meet the increased demand for appliances. Secondly, it soon became apparent that consumers were buying the product for the free flight offer rather than for the product itself. This was hardly a policy aimed at improving brand loyalty. Thirdly, and arguably the most problematic area, the offer exceeded all expectations and ultimately proved to be a costly promotion. Hoover found it difficult and expensive to cater for the demand for free airline tickets for which its customers were eligible. With hindsight, Hoover could have possibly made the offer more restrictive. For example, they could have set the point of eligibility at £200 rather than £100, or offered one free ticket instead of two. In many promotions the customer has to apply for the offer of a free gift and this often involves them in having to make additional purchases such as hotel accommodation or restaurant meals. This would have proved to be an additional cost to the customer and could ultimately have acted as a deterrent to taking advantage of the free flight offer.

In recent years it is certainly the case that non-price competition in the form of promotional activity incorporating offers such as the use of free air miles, air tickets or holidays have become more popular. However, any promotional activity includes an element of risk for the company, while the benefits, if achieved, are ones of increased product sales and a strengthening of brand loyalty. One of the most precious assets any company possesses is the brand name of its products, which in most instances has been built up over many years. Therefore, in planning any promotional activity the effect of the promotion on the brand name must be given careful consideration.

Adapted from S. Ison, 'Competition under oligopoly: the case of Hoover', *British Economy Survey*, Vol. 25, No. 2, 1996.

Questions

1   In what respects was the Hoover free flight campaign a success and in what respects was it a failure?
2   What, if any, long-term damage do you think this offer will do to Hoover?
3   Do you think that the 'free-offer' type of strategy has any long-term effect on the market share of firms in an industry?

PAUSE FOR THOUGHT 2   *As a consumer would you prefer simply to see a reduction in the price of the goods that you are purchasing rather than have it linked into some special offer or other promotional campaign? Can you think of five special offers that you have actually taken advantage of? If not, why not?*

Oligopoly, collusion and price

There is obviously a risk that if firms in an oligopolistic market compete against each other on a price basis, then this may result in a price war. This can be very damaging for the firms involved in the industry and difficult to stop once it has started. Suppose an industry has three large firms (firms A, B and C) controlling 75 per cent of the market, and that firm A reduces its price by 5 per cent, then a number of customers of firm B and of firm C are likely to take advantage of this and purchase from firm A. This will result in firm A increasing its market share to the detriment of the other two firms. The obvious response is for firm B and firm C to also cut price by the equivalent amount to try and entice their lost customers to return. However, firms B and C may decide that to lure customers away from firm A they will have to reduce price by an amount greater than the initial price reduction of 5 per cent. Thus, firm B and firm C drop their price by 7 per cent. Consequently, they get back their original customers plus perhaps some of those that were originally buying from firm A. This will reduce the market share of firm A to below that which it held before any price cutting. Firm A is then faced with the dilemma of how to increase its market share. Does it decrease its price again?

The problem that this highlights is that once this type of strategic behaviour has started it is difficult to find a solution to avoid the ensuing price warfare unless the firms decide between themselves that, in order to protect the profit margins and overall profitability of the firms in the industry, they agree a strategy on pricing. The other solution is either that a firm withdraws from the market place because it can no longer achieve profitability in the price-cutting environment in which it finds itself, or there is a spate of merger activity in the industry which reduces the number of competing players.

If the firms decide to collude with each other and agree to limit competition between them, damaging price wars can be avoided. They may agree on a number of things in addition to price, such as setting output quotas, limiting product advertising, restricting product development or agreeing to segment the market in such a way as to provide a designated niche for each firm.

PAUSE FOR THOUGHT 3 *There have been a number of mergers recently in the financial services industry, particularly insurance companies. Examine why this phenomenon is taking place, and speculate whether it is likely to continue or not.*

A formal collusive agreement is called a *cartel*. This will reduce the uncertainty in the market so that the industry will, in effect, act like a monopoly. Cartels are illegal under restrictive trade legislation in the UK, unless the firms involved can provide evidence that their agreement is in the public interest. Firms can, however, keep within the law by becoming involved in *tacit collusion*, which does not involve a formal agreement between firms. Participants in an industry can, through various mechanisms, avoid price wars and other forms of profit-reducing strategic behaviour. A number of methods of setting price in an oligopoly using tacit collusion will now be examined.

PAUSE FOR THOUGHT 4 *The prices at competing petrol filling stations are usually very similar. Why do you think this is the case? Examine how different firms try to attract you to use their pumps. Evaluate, in your opinion, the success or otherwise of these campaigns.*

Dominant firm price leadership

In an industry there may be one firm that is recognised by the others within the industry to be, in simplistic terms, 'the leader'. This is usually the largest or dominant firm in the industry. When this firm has decided upon a price, or a change in the current price, then the other firms in the industry will follow that price movement. The main flaw in this particular model is that it makes the assumption that the firms that are not dominant, 'the followers', will be content to remain as such, and that they will also be happy to continue with the market share that they currently have. They may, however, decide not to follow the price rise initiated by the dominant firm in an attempt to raise their own market share. This, however, risks incurring the wrath of the largest firm in the market that, almost by definition, will have the greatest financial resources with which to respond. This threat of retaliatory action by a powerful competitor may indeed be sufficient to prevent the rebellious behaviour outlined. (See Case Study 9.3.)

CASE STUDY **9.3**

Miles more: a shake-up in UK domestic flights

The aim of this case study is to look at a specific sector of the UK domestic air passenger industry, which for many years was largely dominated by one large company that set the price, that the others largely followed. It would appear to have been a case of tacit collusion, via dominant firm price leadership.

Historically, air travellers between London and Scotland have had a choice of which airline to use, but not much choice over the cost of the ticket. Though they offer a range of restricted fares, the main carriers which run flights between London and Scotland charge exactly the same for an unrestricted business ticket: £234 for a return flight of about 400 miles. That is about 25 per cent more than a similar journey between New York and Boston in the United States, and not much less than the cost of an advanced-purchase ticket from London to New York and back.

Now a number of budget airlines are trying to disrupt this arrangement with much lower prices. If they succeed, they could not only expand travel dramatically between London and Edinburgh and Glasgow, but also show the way for more and cheaper air travel on other routes within the British Isles.

Ryanair, a Dublin-based airline, now fly between Prestwick airport 35 miles south of Glasgow, and London's Stansted airport, the capital's third airport, 35 miles north-east of the city centre. Ryanair offers return fares of between £59 and £99. Easyjet fly from Glasgow and Edinburgh to Luton, 33 miles north of London. Easyjet is offering single fares from £29 to £59. A number of the established carriers have already responded, introducing a restricted £58 return fare.

British Airways, however, is sticking to its existing fares, a sign that it does not expect to lose many customers to the newcomers. It may be right. Business people might be willing to tolerate the no-frills, cheap and cheerful service of the new airlines – as their counterparts have done in America – but many of them are unwilling to fly to or from any London airport except Heathrow, and would feel stranded if they landed at Luton or Stansted.

Yet even if some businessmen continue to pay high fares to fly into Heathrow, lower fares to other airports could dramatically boost traffic volumes. Ryanair has shown that there are plenty of people eager to fly if the price is right. In 1994, it started flying between Prestwick and Dublin for between £55 and £75 return, undercutting Aer Lingus's Dublin–Glasgow fares of £69 to £186. Travel industry sages doubted that both services would survive. They have been proved memorably wrong.

In the last month of its monopoly, Aer Lingus flew 5,700 passengers on the route. Twelve months on, it carried 6,400 passengers, while Ryanair carried 11,400. Much the same thing happened on the Dublin–Manchester route after entry by Ryanair. The picture is much the same as when Ryanair began flying the London–Dublin route: passenger numbers more than doubled over the next eight years (after a decade of little growth).

Adapted from *The Economist*, 5 November 1995.

Questions

1   Oligopolistic theory would suggest that if other firms in the industry cut prices then British Airways should also reduce their price. This has not been the case.
    Suggest reasons for BA's choice of strategic direction in this niche of their market.
2   If British Airways were to cut price dramatically, it could force smaller competitors out of the market altogether, which would also act as a deterrent for potential entrants in the future. Why do you think they have not adopted this strategy?
3   Which industry is really suffering from this increase in volume of air travellers?

Barometric firm price leadership

This is a variation on the dominant firm leadership, where the firms in an industry are led by a firm that has emerged over time as the most reliable guide to changing market conditions. The industry will be using this firm as a barometer to predict the future conditions in the market place. The firm that is being used as the barometer may, of course, change over time.

Average cost pricing

This is an alternative to having an established leader in the industry. In this instance there would be an accepted industry norm for setting price. For example the 'rule of thumb' may simply be to add a certain percentage for profit on top of average costs. Such a pricing policy may be a relatively simple way of setting price in circumstances where the firm lacks full knowledge concerning demand and cost curves. In using this method firms do not have to take into consideration precise information as to marginal cost or revenue when determining their price. Instead, if there is an increase in the level of average costs, this will simply be passed straight on to the consumer through the same increase in the level of price. For example, if average costs were to increase across the industry by 5 per cent, then all firms in the market would raise their price by 5 per cent. It is interesting to assess some of the implications of using this particular tool for setting price.

If this 'rule' is strictly enforced then the price will remain largely unaltered through all phases of the business cycle. This is because the price is based on costs estimated at some notional level of output, say two-thirds of capacity, rather than costs related to actual output. Changes in demand will then be largely irrelevant to pricing policy, with only changes in the cost of production leading to changes in price, not changes in the demand for the product caused by boom or slump during a complete business cycle.

However, it is also evident that the costs of production will change over different levels of output (see Chapter 8). The traditional U-shaped average cost curve indicates that average total costs fall initially as output increases, helped by the fact that fixed costs are spread over a greater number of units. Average total costs then level off over a period of output before rising again due to diseconomies of scale. Nevertheless, if the cost base for the pricing policy was based on *notional output* rather than *actual output*, there is no necessity to change price as demand and actual output varies. Therefore, if the economy is experiencing boom conditions then output will increase, resulting in actual average costs falling, which will lead to an increase in profit margins for firms if price is not reduced, as it is unlikely to be. If a recessionary economic period was being experienced, the subsequent reduction in demand for the product might result in actual average costs rising, leading to a decrease in profit margins.

In oligopolistic industries price setting may differ from this stylised version of average cost pricing, at least in recessionary periods when prices might rise to retain the profit margin as actual average costs rise.

An example of this was the London Brick Company, with a market share of 40 per cent. This company had not used its market power to raise prices in times of high demand, but had been able to raise its price during a recession to recover profitability. This was probably achievable in this case because of the very large market share in the hands of one individual firm. More generally, the ability to raise price in a recessionary period may depend upon firms in the industry acting as a single cohesive unit in order to prevent buyers switching to price-cutting firms. If there are a small number of firms involved, making a homogeneous product, then the likelihood of this type of unified action is increased.

It must be noted that average cost pricing does not, in itself, determine the actual price charged; this is dependent upon the mark-up that is added. The level of the mark-up will depend on the goals of the firms involved, which might affect the target rate of return on capital that firms are trying to achieve. Indeed, it has been argued that the percentage mark-up tends to rise in situations when firms find it easier to make profits (e.g. boom) and fall in situations when firms find it difficult to make profits (e.g. recessions). In other words, the 'rule of thumb' of average cost pricing might be a device to achieve profit maximisation in situations of change and uncertainty.

Price benchmarks

In certain industries there are accepted levels of price increases that are often invoked when prices are set to rise. There are a great many examples of this in consumer goods that end in the price suffix of .99. In these instances if costs rise (for example), then a good that was previously charged at £12.99 is often subsequently priced at £13.99. The compact disc industry is a particularly relevant example of this and has been selected for detailed examination in Case Study 9.4.

CASE STUDY **9.4**

The price of compact discs

This case study looks at a specific oligopolistic market, identifying a number of price-setting practices that appear, on the face of it, to give the consumer little choice than to pay more than they would intuitively expect.

In 1991, £1,218 million worth of vinyl records, pre-recorded cassettes and compact discs (CDs) were sold in the UK, with CDs accounting for £617 million (51 per cent) of total sales. This equated to sales of 73 million CDs sold, which rose to 85 million in 1992. This trend is expected to continue throughout the 1990s.

There has been a great deal of debate on the nature of the CD market and whether the consumer is being charged a fair price. Two questions that have been raised relate to whether they are priced too high in absolute terms, and whether they are too high in relation to the USA. In Table CS9.4.1 a number of illustrative examples give an insight into the UK versus US price differential example.

Table CS9.4.1
CD retail prices

New York dollar (and sterling equivalent) price and UK price
(Exchange rate £1 = $1.54)

'Diva', Annie Lennox	New York $11.99 (£7.78), London £10.99
'The Body Guard', Whitney Houston	New York $11.99 (£7.78), London £10.99
'Lady in Satin', Billie Holliday	New York $13.99 (£9.07), London £11.99

Adapted from *The Economist*, 15 May 1993.

The reason put forward by the CD industry for the high absolute price of their product in the UK is that there are a number of different factors that have to be taken into consideration when determining the price of the good; namely, costs of manufacture, marketing, discount and distribution, design and packaging, the finding and development of new talent, the artist and overheads. The industry argues that it operates in a high-risk environment, where innovation and investment are required to be funded from company profits in order to ensure a continuing stream of new developments. The industry is oligopolistic in nature with four main companies who hold 70 per cent of the market (PolyGram, EMI, WEA/Warner and CBS/Sony). Given the nature of the product, in that each CD is intrinsically a unique item, the producer has a monopoly position for each CD and is thus able to charge a price the market is willing to bear. In addition, there are a number of smaller firms who would find it uneconomic to continue if prices were reduced.

A second argument to explain the relatively higher UK price is that due to population differences, a greater volume of CDs are produced and sold in the USA, allowing costs to be spread over a much greater number of units. This will reduce the average cost per CD, which will result in a lower price in the USA (while allowing for the same profit margin) than in the UK per CD sold. The counter to this argument was that the UK is part of the Single European Market which has an estimated population of 340 million, compared to only 249 million in the USA.

Another possible reason for the price differential is that the major record companies and retailers are operating as effective cartels preventing real price competition in the industry. There is, however, no evidence of formal collusion. The five major UK retailers that control 54 per cent of the market are Virgin, Our Price, Woolworth's, HMV and WH Smith. They can possibly be criticised for not using their power to insist on the record companies reducing their prices.

Questions
1 Consumers in the UK appear to be prepared to pay the price that the CD firms are charging for their product. Is this simply a case of demand and supply fundamentals with the firms charging the equilibrium price?
2 What type of price-setting methods are apparent in this particular market?
3 Is there evidence of average cost pricing being employed in the case of the UK market?

Price discrimination

One of the reasons for the price of compact discs being different in the two markets (home and overseas) may in fact be totally unrelated to costs. It may, instead, be more closely related to the existence of different price elasticities of demand for the product in markets that can be readily separated. When a firm charges different prices to different consumers for exactly the same product (good or service), it is said to be engaging in *price discrimination*. In fact, two conditions are necessary if price discrimination is to occur:

1 Producers must be able to prevent consumers transferring from the dearer to the cheaper market. Such barriers to transfer might include geographical distance, border tariffs, legislation, time (e.g. peak period pricing), etc.
2 Each market in which price discrimination occurs must have a different price elasticity of demand from the other markets.

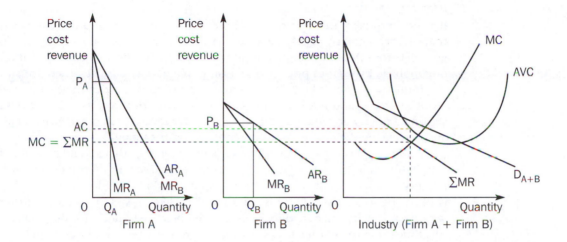

Figure 9.1

Price discrimination

It can be shown that, if these two conditions hold, then only by charging different prices in the respective markets can profits be maximised. In fact, for the level of industry (whole) output at which MC = MR, then this industry output should be allocated among the separate markets so that MC for the whole output = MR in each separate market. This will imply lower prices for markets with higher price elasticities of demand, and higher prices for markets with lower price elasticities of demand. This can be seen in Figure 9.1.

It follows that in the case study on compact discs, if price elasticity of demand could be shown to be higher in the USA than in the UK and barriers to transfer exist, then a price discriminating policy would predict that profit maximising companies would charge a lower price in the USA than in the UK for an identical product.

For simplicity we have a duopoly, with two firms (A and B) making up the industry. If we sum the firm MR and AR curves horizontally, we obtain the industry MR and AR curves. Profit maximisation occurs where MR for the industry = MC for the industry (i.e. $MR_{A+B} = MC_{A+B}$) at output Q_1. Now there is no better (from the point of view of profit) allocation of this output than to equate MC for industry output (C) with MR in each separate market, i.e.:

$$MC_{A+B} = MR_A = MR_B$$

This gives outputs Q_A and Q_B respectively and prices P_A and P_B. Notice that price is lower in the market (B) with the higher price elasticity of demand. You should be able to see that any other allocation of the (industry) profit-maximising output Q_1 must reduce industry revenue and, with industry total costs unchanged, must reduce industry profit. For example, one extra unit than Q_A sold in market A and one less unit than Q_B sold in market B will add less to revenue in A than is lost to revenue in B. If industry revenue falls with costs unchanged, industry profit falls. Only when MC for whole output = MR in each separate market can industry profit be a maximum. If price elasticities are different in the respective markets, then this will in turn imply the setting of different prices in those markets.

Price stability

It is not surprising that a frequently noted feature of oligopolistic industries is that of price stability, mainly because it is a logical and rational strategy for oligopolists to follow in maximising profitability. It has been shown that if an oligopolistic firm raises price it risks losing market share if the other firms in the industry do not follow suit. The outcome of raising price might then be reduced profits and market share. Conversely, if a firm lowers price, it risks starting a price war, which might result in lower revenues as other firms retaliate by reducing their prices, resulting in lower profits for all.

It would appear that changing price is not a strategy that should be entered into lightly. If a firm raises price, it loses market share and suffers reduced profitability; if it reduces price, other firms respond and again reduced profitability is likely. Hence, price stability is commonplace. The next section gives further reasons as to why price stability might be the preferred option for oligopolists, this time using the so-called 'kinked-demand' model. (See Case Study 9.5.)

PAUSE FOR THOUGHT 5 *Can you think of three products that you regularly purchase for which the firms involved are operating in an oligopolistic market? Do you agree with the view that prices in these markets are stable and there is little price competition? Do you think this is fair on you as a consumer? Who gains, and who loses from price stability?*

CASE STUDY **9.5**

Is this the end of sticky prices?

The aim of this case-study is to examine the nature of price movements and to demonstrate how, for some products, price movements will occur more readily than for others. The context that the example here is set in incorporates the Internet into this analysis. Some analysts say that the Internet is ushering in a world in which prices change at the click of a mouse. It is clear that there will indeed be plenty of exceptions.

As shares are bought and sold, the prices on trading screens flicker red and black. Most other prices are far less jumpy. Petrol-pump prices don't change every time the oil price moves, holiday prices and standard hotel rates are fixed for months, and doctors seldom alter their fees. Some claim that the Internet could change all that. Prices could flick at the click of a computer mouse. And, they argue, the economy would run more efficiently as a result.

Will the Internet really make prices more flexible? The answer depends on why prices fail to fluctuate with every shift in supply and demand now. Simply put, prices change only when the cost of leaving them unchanged becomes bigger than the expense of adjusting them. In financial markets, prices move all the time because the cost of quoting the 'wrong' price can be huge. If market-makers failed to raise prices when they were too low, for instance, they would make hefty losses because they would be obliged to sell unlimited amounts of securities on the cheap. And on a market stall, a fruit trader who didn't lower prices when they were too high would have to throw away unsold produce at the end of the day.

The Internet is unlikely to increase the cost of leaving prices unchanged. It will not make petrol perishable or make it more expensive to sell holidays at less than cost. But it will make it cheaper to change some prices. Electronic price-tags can be altered almost costlessly. Digital holiday brochures do not need reprinting. And the Internet makes finding out and comparing prices much easier. Rates for hotel rooms in Honolulu can now be checked from a laptop in London. That, some argue, will make booking a room more like buying shares, where investors plump for the broker quoting the best price, which changes all the time.

For many goods, they may be right. Most people would buy the latest Madonna CD, John Grisham thriller or even their electricity from the supplier with the lowest prices; who the retailer is barely matters. In those cases, keener competition may make prices adjust faster to swings in supply and demand. But the Internet is unlikely to make all prices more flexible, especially because it may often be more efficient for prices to change irregularly. Sticky prices are likely to survive in at least three cases: when the quality of a product is hard to assess; when consumers dislike frequent price changes; and when a market is dominated by a few firms that are wary of altering the amount they charge.

First, consider firms that compete on quality as well as price. Consumers often find it difficult to judge how good their product is; and making a mistake may be costly. It can be hard to know how good a hotel is until you've stayed there; and a sleepless night in a lousy hotel before a big meeting is best avoided. So customers who have stayed in a hotel they like may return, even if rivals of the same standard are offering cheaper rates – especially as on a repeat visit they may know which side of the hotel is less noisy, and the manager may remember to book them a good table for dinner.

But if prices have risen since their last visit, they may reconsider. This may be why hotels that are nearly full rarely raise their rates for the night, as you might otherwise have expected. And half-empty hotels may be reluctant to cut room prices, because raising them again when demand recovers could drive away repeat customers as well as bargain hunters. That in turn could hurt their reputation – and hence how much new business they are likely to get (they may, of course, have different seasonal or weekend rates). Similarly, doctors are unlikely to cut their fees when demand is slack during the summer or raise them when patients flock to them in winter.

Firms may also keep prices stable because they are providing insurance to customers who dislike volatile prices, especially when buying expensive things. Customers choosing a holiday do not want prices to change while they are deciding where to go; and they will be loath to book months in advance if the price of their holiday might fall sharply a few days later.

Companies rarely fix both prices and quantities, though, because it would make their profits too risky. So consumers who value fixed prices usually have to accept that firms may ration access to the good. Thus a travel agency may guarantee the price of a holiday, but with the proviso that the charter flight can be cancelled if not enough people book.

That may seem less efficient than deals where the desired quantity is always available and access is rationed by price, but perhaps not. Fixed-price contracts give firms, which generally know more about market conditions than consumers, an incentive to be truthful rather than misrepresent the levels of supply and demand. If doctors did not fix their fees, they would have an incentive to say they were in huge demand – and that you needed to see them urgently. And a hotel that varied its prices a lot would have an incentive to pretend it was nearly full, to get customers to pay more. In this way, sticky prices can improve the flow of information about the market.

Even when assessing the quality is straightforward, and consumers have no reason to object to flexible prices, prices may stay sticky if competition is lacking. Take petrol, which is sold by a handful of big companies. As there are only a few providers in the retail market, each will consider its rivals' likely response before changing prices. A petrol company may thus be reluctant to raise prices if it expects its rivals to try to steal a march on it by leaving their prices unchanged. And it may also be wary of cutting prices, because it may gain nothing but earn lower profits if others follow suit. If each firm reasons in this way, prices may change infrequently. When prices are fixed for too long, of course, supply and demand may get badly out of kilter. In that case, hotels, holiday companies, doctors, petrol retailers and the like will decide to alter their rates, fees and so on. In times of high inflation, too, prices may change more often. But the Internet is unlikely to spell the end for sticky prices.

Source: *The Economist*, 16 May 1998.

Questions
1 Why do prices move instantaneously in some markets but 'stick' in others?
2 What impact will the Internet have on prices according to the case study?
3 Why are 'sticky prices' likely to remain?

CASE STUDY **9.6**

Pricing strategies in highly competitive markets
This case study looks at the strategies employed in one specific market that has developed into a regional oligopoly. It looks at the link between the theoretical view of pricing behaviour and how things really work in practice using an actual example.

The industrial distributor market is highly competitive. This industry supplies firms with machinery they require in their production. Firms in this industry do not make anything, they simply distribute machinery, made by the manufacturers, to those firms who have purchased it for their factories. In effect, they are middle-men between the manufacturers of machines and the users of these machines. The nature of competition in the market has developed in the form of a number of localised oligopolies. Many sellers supply products that are partial substitutes for one another, so market entry is relatively easy and prices are interdependent with other suppliers. This is limited only by the extent to which product and service differentiation can create an element of monopoly power. This leads to the situation where some aggressive forms of competition and, in particular, price competition are rife and likely to leave the whole industry worse off from the standpoint of profitability. Price cuts are quickly and easily matched by rivals, and consequently lower revenues result for all firms.

The first of these market factors, which leads to difficult competitive conditions for industrial distributors, is that of numerous and equally balanced competitors. When firms are numerous, mavericks, who habitually believe that they can cut prices without being noticed, are inevitable. Also, while the majority of firms remain as local organisations of approximately the same size, this tends to prolong retaliatory moves. There is a trend towards merger by industrial distributors, which potentially could prove beneficial to the whole industry, if price leadership emerges to impose discipline on the market.

Slow industry growth is another characteristic of the market. Industrial distributors are dependent on derived demand from manufacturing industry, so the de-industrialisation of the UK from the mid-1970s has depressed growth rates and price cutting has been used to buy market share. Economic recession serves only to exacerbate this problem. Unstable competition is also likely to result from a lack of differentiation. As the trend towards industrial product standardisation accelerates, brands begin to lose their identity and choice by buyers is largely based on price and service. Pressure from substitute products increases and a quasi-perfectly-competitive situation starts to emerge. The market fixes price at levels which preclude any supernormal profits and cost inefficient distributors are forced out of the market.

Significant benefits can accrue to any firm able to differentiate its product and services to reduce substitution effects and reduce its cross-elasticity of demand, thereby opening up the possibility of proactive pricing practices.

Finally, high exit barriers are probably intensifying price competition among industrial distributors. Thus, we can see that the competitive conditions under which industrial distributors are operating are likely to lead to a requirement for astute tactical pricing decisions, and in particular a highly discerning discounting policy. The skill with which such decisions are undertaken is likely to be a significant determinant of performance in a market where price competition is unstable and survival rests upon the narrowest of margins.

Adapted from *Management Decision*, 30 April 1995.

Questions

1   If you were brought into one of the firms in the industrial distributor market, what advice would you give them on how to increase their market share?
2   Do you think that mergers are inevitable in a market such as this?
3   Who is in fact benefiting from the way in which this market has developed?

Non-collusive oligopoly – the kinked demand curve

Early models of oligopolistic behaviour were first introduced by Cournot in the middle of the nineteenth century, based on the belief that a firm's actions were determined by the perceived reactions of other firms in the market, Later, Paul Sweezy, one of the most influential writers in the 1930s, sought to explain why prices in oligopolistic markets did not fall more quickly during times of major recessions. He put forward a rationale for this based on the following suppositions:

1   If a firm increases its price, it does so unilaterally; the rest of the industry will not follow, resulting in the first firm losing out on market share as customers will change over to those firms that are now charging a relatively lower price.
2   If a firm decreases its price, this will provoke a price cut by all the other firms in the industry to avoid losing market share to the firm with the lower price.

The demand curve that faces a firm (see Figure 9.2) under these conditions is characterised by a kink at the current price (P). Thus, at prices greater than P, the demand curve is relatively elastic, meaning that any change in price above

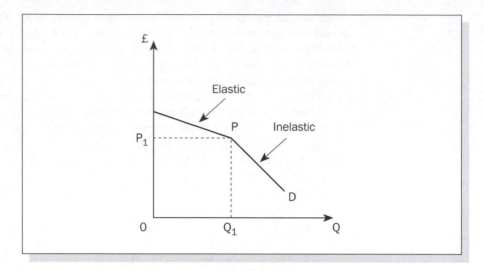

Figure 9.2
The kinked demand curve

P will result in a significant decrease in the quantity demanded from that firm if, as assumed, other firms do not follow suit. Conversely, the slope of the demand curve below P is relatively inelastic, which would indicate that any reduction in price would not result in a large increase in sales as all other firms react with a retaliatory price cut. The end result is that all firms charge a lower price, so that the firm initiating the price cut achieves little extra demand. The implication of this kink is that firms will be unwilling to change price, because a price change will simply mean that profits are reduced. A price rise with a relatively elastic demand will reduce revenue and profit; a price fall with a relatively inelastic demand will also reduce revenue and profit. Price stability would then seem an attractive option for the firm.

The main criticism of this model is that it does not try to explain how the initial price is arrived at. Price stability may be generated by other factors such as the individual firm's wish for a period of quiet trading in the market place to ensure continuity of revenues and cashflows. However, despite its simplicity, the kinked demand model is a useful first step in explaining stability in an oligopolistic market.

| PAUSE FOR THOUGHT 6 | *It would appear that the kinked demand curve is a useful explanatory tool in that it does appear to answer the question relating to why prices do not fluctuate wildly in an oligopoly. However, of what use is it in assisting strategic decision-making in a competitive environment?* |

CASE STUDY **9.7**

Phones war may cut bills

The aim of this case study is to look at the situation in an industry which has periously operated in a monopoly situation in the UK, and to examine one of the consequences of increasing competition.

Telephone bills could be cut by up to 50 per cent this week thanks to an explosive price war between British Telecom and AT&T, the American telecoms giant. BT is introducing a reduced charge tariff on Tuesday which it claims will save residential users up to 25 per cent on their bills. In conjunction with BT's existing special offers, such as the Premier Line discount scheme, which can save 15 per cent, and its Friends and Family scheme, which can save 10 per cent on calls to five nominated numbers, the total reduction could be 50 per cent.

AT&T, which entered the market in June, has pre-empted the move with a new tariff launched tomorrow. It claims its scheme will save up to 20 per cent against BT's rates, and is more flexible for those who call a wide variety of people and make regular international calls. Phillipa Rogers of AT&T said: 'To make the maximum savings with BT you need to pay £24 a year for its Premier Line service, and full use of its Friends and Family scheme which allows only discounts on five regularly used phone numbers. It is expensive and restrictive.'

According to AT&T, its new scheme will be cheaper than BT's for anybody whose phone bill regularly exceeds £90 and who makes regular calls abroad. However, it admits that BT is still cheaper for local UK calls. The BT cuts reduce the cost of a basic national evening call from 5.85p to 4.65p a minute, and to 3.29p at weekends. Daytime calls fall to 8.8p from 9.8p. However, AT&T will charge just 3p a minute for national evening calls and 6p a minute daytime.

The domestic AT&T service is free but its Country-Call plan, which gives discounts on international calls, costs £16 a year. Even with BT's reduced international rates, AT&T says it is still cheaper for most long-distance calls. To gain access to AT&T's system, customers simply register by calling 0800-143 143, then dial 143 before each call they make.

Adapted from *The Sunday Times*, 6 October 1996.

Questions

1   Why do you think AT&T, a huge American company, chose to enter the UK telecommunications market in the first place?
2   Why do you think that AT&T started a price war after entry, when oligopolistic theory suggests price stability in a market structure such as this?
3   What do you think will happen to this market in (a) the short run, and (b) the long run? You should consider price, possible further new entry into the market, continuing price competition and market shares.

Game theory
·················

The behaviour of a firm, when an oligopoly is not acting under any form of collusive agreement, has been the subject of much debate by economists. Further developments following on from the kinked demand curve have sought to rationalise and explain firm behaviour using game theory. This examines the best strategy a firm can adopt for each assumption it might make about its rival's behaviour. In other words, it is a way of analysing strategic interaction and was invented by John van Neumann in 1937.

Strategies of a game

In all games, be it football, basketball or golf, players will determine a strategy that they perceive will result in their achieving the best possible outcome. In these sports, the aim of the strategy will be to win (although in some cases it may be to limit defeat, which is also a useful concept in oligopoly games). Strategies in game theory refer to the broad pattern which guides the 'player' in seeking to influence all the possible variables involved in the 'game'. This would include behaviour relating to price, output, advertising and product enhancement. Players can increase, decrease or hold each of these variables constant, depending on the strategy being developed by that particular player.

Payoffs in the oligopoly game

In game theory the score of each player is called the *payoff*, which represents the profit and loss of each player. These profits and losses are determined by the constraints the players face, and the strategies they pursue. Constraints come from the *technology* available, from *customers* who determine the demand level in the industry, and from the *costs* that face the oligopolists.

The prisoner's dilemma

The best-known example of game theory is *the prisoner's dilemma*. This highlights some of the main features of the operation of game theory and how it leads to the prediction of the behaviour of players. This will now be described using two hypothetical prisoners.

Jim and Michael have both been arrested for robbing a bank. They are interviewed separately and they are each told of the three scenarios they face:

1 If they both confess they will each be given three years' imprisonment.
2 If only one of them confesses, and his accomplice does not, the confessor will receive a short sentence of just one year, while his accomplice will receive a 10-year sentence.
3 If neither of them confesses, they will only be tried for the lesser offence of car theft, which carries a two-year prison term.

The prisoner's dilemma is a game with two players, each of whom has two possible strategies: to confess to the bank robbery or to deny the charge. Thus, because there are two players, each with two possible strategies, there are four possible outcomes:

1 Neither player confesses.
2 Both players confess.
3 Jim confesses, but Michael does not.
4 Michael confesses, but Jim does not.

Each prisoner can work out exactly what will happen to him – his payoff – in each of these four situations, and this is shown in Table 9.1.

Table 9.1

Prisoner's dilemma payoff matrix

	Jim's strategies	
	Confess	Deny
Confess	**Jim 3 years** *Michael 3 years*	**Jim 10 years** *Michael 1 year*
Deny	**Jim 1 year** *Michael 10 years*	**Jim 2 years** *Michael 2 years*

Michael's strategies

The payoff matrix shows all the possible gains and losses for each player and every possible action by the other player. Each square indicates the payoff for each player, depending on the strategy selected by both. The dilemma is based on the consequence of confessing or not confessing. What should each of them do? They cannot discuss tactics with each other, but they are both faced with the same scenarios: if I deny and my accomplice also denies, then we will both get two years. However, if I confess I may only get one year, in the knowledge that if my accomplice also confesses then we will each get three years in prison. The resolution to this situation involves finding the game equilibrium.

The equilibrium for this type of game is called *a Nash equilibrium*. This situation occurs when X selects the best possible outcome taking the action of Y into consideration, and, conversely, Y selects the best possible outcome taking the action of X into consideration. In this particular example, the Nash equilibrium occurs when Jim makes the best choice of strategy after taking Michael's choice into consideration, and when Michael makes his best choice of strategy given Jim's choice. Let us now examine the possibilities that each is facing and the best strategy available to each at this point.

Jim's viewpoint

Possibilities

1 If Michael confesses, then Jim's best strategy is to also confess as he will get three years as opposed to 10 years.
2 If Michael does not confess, it would still be the best strategy for Jim to confess, as the outcome then would be one year rather than two years.

Strategy for Jim
Thus, irrespective of the strategy employed by Michael, Jim should confess.

Michael's viewpoint

Possibilities

1 If Jim confesses, Michael's best strategy would also be to confess as he will get three years as opposed to 10.
2 If Jim does not confess, it would still be the best strategy for Michael to confess, as the outcome then would be one year rather than two years.

Strategy for Michael

Again, irrespective of the strategy employed by Jim, Michael should confess.

Each prisoner is aware that in this situation, irrespective of the actions of the other, the best strategy is to confess. If they adopt this strategy then they will each receive a prison term of three years, which is the equilibrium of the game. The prisoner's dilemma is a specific type of Nash equilibrium called a *dominant strategy game*. In this instance the strategy taken is the same regardless of the action taken by the other player. In effect the strategy arrived at is the same for both players.

A simple zero-sum game

For the purposes of simplicity of explanation, let us assume that the scenario being examined is one of market share under duopoly, where the gains of one firm are exactly matched by the losses of the other. The implication of this is that as one firm wins, the other will by definition lose, as they have the total market (100 per cent) to share between them. This is called a zero-sum game. The payoff matrix for this example is contained in Table 9.2 and relates to the production of two firms involved in the manufacture of Good Soup and Anderson's Soup. The matrix shows percentage changes in market share if Good Soup was to introduce Tomato, Oxtail and Noodle soups, and Anderson's Soup was to respond with either Broth, Chicken, or Minestrone. For example, if Good Soup was to introduce Tomato flavour, and Anderson's Soup was to respond with Broth, then Good Soup would gain 5 per cent of the market. If, however, Anderson's Soup chose to respond with either Chicken or Minestrone, then the situation would be that Good Soup would lose some market share (1 per cent and 4 per cent respectively).

Table 9.2

A simple zero-sum game

Matrix of Good Soup's gain (+) or loss (−) of market share (per cent)

		Anderson's Soup			
		Broth	Chicken	Minestrone	Minimum
Good Soup	Tomato	+5	−1	−4	−4
	Oxtail	+3	+1	+9	+1
	Noodle	+4	−2	−6	−6
	Maximum	+5	+1	+9	

Each firm might expect the other firm to instigate the most damaging strategy in response to the one it chooses. Based on this assumption, Good Soup should adopt a strategy that chooses the best out of the worst possible options available to it. From the data in Table 9.2, it is evident that if Good Soup introduces Tomato, the worst possible outcome is for Anderson's to respond with Minestrone. If Good Soup introduces Oxtail, the worst outcome would be if

Anderson's responds with Chicken, and for the introduction of Noodle, the worst outcome in Good Soup's terms would be if Anderson's responds with Minestrone. Good Soup can then choose the best of these worst possible outcomes to generate what might be termed the 'bottom line'. In a zero-sum game such as this, this is known as *the maximin strategy*.

Conversely, suppose Anderson's respond to Good Soup's strategies by choosing the strategy for itself that will minimise the impact of Good Soup's policy. This is called *the minimax strategy*. Here Anderson's is selecting its retaliation strategy in terms of that which gives the worst of Good Soup's best possible outcomes. (The strategy of choosing the policy which has the best possible outcome is called *a maximax strategy*.)

In Table 9.2, the column marked 'Minimum' indicates the minimum benefit in terms of market share that Good Soup could expect for each of the three flavours. The maximin strategy for Good Soup is to choose the best of these minimum benefits, i.e. Oxtail soup (+1 per cent). From Anderson's perspective, it will be looking to minimise the best outcome that Good Soup can achieve. The row marked 'Maximum' indicates the maximum benefit in terms of Good Soup's market share of its introducing any one of its three flavours in the market. For example, if Good Soup introduces Oxtail and Anderson's Soup retaliates with Minestrone, then Good Soup increases its market share by 9 per cent. The minimax strategy of Anderson's is to choose the Chicken flavour for its retaliation, since this is the worst of Good Soup's best possible outcomes.

Hence, if Good Soup launched its Oxtail flavour onto the market, then Anderson's would respond with Chicken. This would result in Good Soup increasing their market share by 1 per cent and Anderson's declining by 1 per cent. In this situation, both the firms recognise that neither can do better than this combination, even if they had been aware of the choice of flavour each were going to launch in advance.

In this 'game' we have the respective strategies as maximin (Good Soup) and minimax (Anderson's). It would be difficult to assume a maximin strategy for Anderson's when the payoff matrix is only expressed in terms of Good Soup's outcomes!

CASE STUDY **9.8**
· · · · · · · · · · · · · · · · · · ·

A non-zero-sum game

The purpose of this case study is to look at a more complex decision-making environment using game theory as a basis for arriving at the best possible solution for both firms.

Two firms, Metal Trades Ltd and Building Supplies Ltd, who are the two main producers of specialist roof timbers, have formed a cartel to control the market. The figures in Table CS9.8.1 show the profits that each firm can expect under varying assumptions about whether the other firm maintains or breaks the cartel agreement (i.e. it cheats). This is a non-zero-sum game, thus there is an incentive for both firms to try to achieve a maximin position in order to get a net advantage over each other.

It can be seen from the table that, logically, if there was complete trust between the two companies and they were happy to maintain the agreement, they would both earn £5 million profit (Scenario A). However, if Metal Trades keeps to the agreement but Building Supplies does not, Building Supplies will gain by obtaining £6 million profit instead of £5 million (Scenario C). In the meantime, Metal Trades' profits will have fallen from £5 million to £2 million. When Metal Trades realises this it will also break the agreement because it can raise its profits from £2 million to £4 million (Scenario D). Taking the other perspective, if Building Supplies Ltd were to stick to the agreement, but Metal Trades Ltd decides to cheat, then Metal Trades' profit will rise to £6 million, while Building Supplies' will fall to £2 million (Scenario B). In turn, Building Supplies will break the agreement as it can raise profits from £2 million to £4 million (Scenario D). Therefore, under these conditions there is an incentive for both firms to cheat. The long-term outcome of this is that they will both end up with profits of £4 million, while if they had persevered with the agreement they would have enjoyed profits of £5 million.

The same conclusion can be arrived at by using the maximin approach. The maximin criteria for Building Supplies is obtained by choosing the best of the worst outcomes. For example, if Building Supplies maintains the agreement, then we can see that its profits can be £5 million or £2 million depending on whether or not Metal Trades maintains the agreement or not. Similarly, if it breaks the agreement then its profits will be £6 million or £4 million, depending on Metal Trades' reaction. The two worst outcomes for Building Supplies are £2 million and £4 million, with the higher of these being the maximin solution. Repeating the exercise, for Metal Trades to find the worst outcomes as £2 million and £4 million, with the best again being £4 million. Therefore the final solution to this problem is that both companies will follow the maximin approach and break the cartel agreement. This will lead to Scenario D with both companies earning £4 million each, in contrast to £5 million each if they had maintained the agreement.

Note that both firms could adopt a maximin approach to this game, since we have the payoff matrix expressed in terms of each firm's outcomes.

Adapted from *British Economy Survey*, 25 February 1996.

Table CS9.8.1
Cartel game

Building Supplies Ltd – BSL (profits £ million)		Metal Trades Ltd – MTL (profits £ million)	
		Maintain agreement	*Break agreement*
	Maintain agreement	A MTL 5 BSL 5	B MTL 6 BSL 2
	Break agreement	C MTL 2 BSL 6	D MTL 4 BSL 4

Questions

1 What other factors would the firms in this industry need to take into consideration before making their decisions?
2 Does game theory take the 'attitude to risk' of the players into consideration when assessing outcomes?

A disequilibrium game

The games that have been analysed to date have all arrived at a definite solution, which has led to stability in the market as a result of arriving at a set of strategies that have determined an equilibrium. The complexity of the business world leads to many games that do not have a set of strategies that result in equilibrium. A simple example of this would be if a certain move by one firm resulted in a strategy change by another. The analysis to date has only analysed the market in which a duopoly exists, which unfortunately is rather simplistic, even if it is useful for explanatory purposes. Game theory identifies that there are a large number of different outcomes in an oligopolistic setting: if there were three firms with six policy options available to them, then the number of possible solutions would be 1,296!

In Table 9.3 a more complex game is illustrated. The firm, Golden Roast, is a coffee manufacturer. Golden Roast has a number of different strategies available to it in relation to price, advertising and product development. It faces competition in the industry from six other companies who will respond to any changes made in these variables by Golden Roast. Obviously this will have some impact on the profit of Golden Roast and it is the Golden Roast profit figures that are quoted in Table 9.3 (£m). There is an implicit assumption that these can be calculated by Golden Roast.

Table 9.3

A disequilibrium game – profit possibilities for Golden Roast (£m)

Strategies for Golden Roast	U	V	W	X	Y	Z
			Other firms' responses			
1. Cut price	200	120	−10	20	60	160
2. Increase advertising	80	100	40	60	50	120
3. New product launch	180	30	60	50	40	100

The question that the firm has to answer is as follows. Based on the information calculated in the payoff matrix, which solution should Golden Roast choose: 1, 2 or 3? It depends largely on the risk profile of the management of the firm. If it decides to opt for a safety first option (maximin), it will choose the strategy that increases advertising, as the worst possible outcome from this is that profit will be £40 million, which is higher than the worst possible outcomes from 'cut price' (−£10 million) and 'new product launch' (+£30 million). Thus the best of the worst possible outcomes for Golden Roast is to choose an increase in advertising.

However, if the risk profile of the management of the company is not risk averse, they may decide to go for something a little more aggressive. In this case they might look for the strategy that is going to give them the highest possible profit outcome. From Table 9.3, the strategy that they would then choose would be that of cutting price, which would generate profits of £200 million. It is, however, possible with this maximax strategy (best of the best outcomes) that losses of £10 million could also be generated, based on the response of the other firms in the industry to this move by Golden Roast.

The alternative to selecting one of these polarised risk positions is to choose a strategy that does not maximise profit but is better than the worst possible scenario, i.e. it generates more profit than the £40 million risk averse position but less than the pro-risk position of £200 million. This will be a compromise strategy and here might involve the launch of a new product, where the maximum profit is only £20 million less than that of the pro-risk strategy, but where the minimum profit is only £10 million less than the risk averse strategy.

PAUSE FOR THOUGHT 7 *Game theory has been the subject of much debate and research by economists. What role, if any, do you think it has for businessmen in making strategic decisions for their business which will probably be operating in an oligopolistic market?*

CASE STUDY 9.9

Indiscriminate pricing

The aim of this case study is to demonstrate how in certain situations companies can often find it profitable to vary their prices according to customers' willingness to pay. (Interestingly, however, this is not always the case as is evidenced below.)

'NO DISCOUNTS, we promise' may sound a strange sales pitch. But Saturn, a division of General Motors, swears by its no-haggle policy. Retailers such as Bloomingdale's offer a similar commitment – 'everyday low pricing' – rather than frequent sales and discounting. And firms such as Procter & Gamble and General Mills have tried to eliminate money-off coupons. Why do some companies find it worth while to pledge to charge everybody the same price?

Most firms, after all, prefer not to. Varying prices to match customers' readiness to pay is usually a more profitable strategy. Airlines, for instance, charge free-spending businessmen more than price-conscious tourists. They make bigger profits from businessmen and get more tourist passengers than if they had a single price for everybody.

Airlines would, of course, lose from this if many businessmen chose to fly economy instead. So they make cheap seats narrower and more uncomfortable, and they impose restrictions on tickets that are more likely to deter businessmen than tourists. Any company that sells at different prices in different countries faces a similar dilemma. Most cheered when the European Court recently outlawed 'grey imports' – so that British supermarkets may no longer import cheap Levi jeans from Bulgaria and sell them at a discount to normal British prices.

Yet even if firms can discriminate successfully, and so boost initial profits, they could still end up worse off if rivals retaliate. A branded-cereal maker that offers too many coupons may steal sales from a maker of own-label cereals, provoking price cuts for all customers that hit both firms' bottom lines. To deter such competition, the branded-cereal maker may pledge not to offer discounts. In effect, the branded cereal would cede the most price-sensitive segment of the market to the own-label cereal, in the hope that the own-label firm will keep its prices up. That would allow the branded-cereal company to support its prices, and hence profits, in the less price-sensitive sector of the market.

In some cases, a commitment not to offer discounts may not boost profits. Take America's long-distance telecoms firms. They offer big incentives to each other's customers to induce them to switch provider. But that in turn means they have to cut prices for existing clients, so as not to lose them. As a result, all firms make lower profits than if none had offered discounts. And no firm has an incentive to commit itself unilaterally to uniform pricing, since that would not prevent rivals coming after its clients. Nor can firms get together to agree not to discriminate, since cartels are illegal; besides, each firm would have an overwhelming incentive to cheat.

Yet in some cases, companies can credibly pledge not to offer discounts, without colluding with their rivals, as a new paper by Kenneth Corts of Harvard Business School explains. This occurs when each firm would like to offer discounts to the other's clients but only a single group of consumers can be targeted.

Consider a department store. Some of its customers are impatient buyers who would rather pay full whack, say, for a suit than wait for the sales. Others are bargain-hunters, willing to wait so as to pay less. If the department store wants to pinch custom from discount retailers whose low prices attract bargain-hunters, it may hold sales more often. But the discounters may retaliate with their own price cuts, leaving both with lower profits. So it may be profitable for the department store to promise not to hold sales more than, say, twice a year, if at all. Such a commitment can be effective because, whereas the department store can aim its price cuts at bargain-hunters, the discounter cannot offer price cuts to impatient buyers without offering discounts to all its clients.

There are other reasons why firms may wish to offer a single price to all. Some are keen to point out that 'everyday low pricing' leads to smoother sale patterns than seasonal sales, reducing costly production spikes or stockholding and distribution bottlenecks. A 'no-haggle' policy may appeal to customers who dislike being expected to bargain with shifty car dealers. And guaranteeing the same price to all may tempt customers of big-ticket items such as cars to buy now, rather than wait to see if prices fall.

Should competition watchdogs worry about price discrimination – or a lack of it? Not usually. In the telecoms case, both consumers and the economy are unambiguously better off, since price discrimination spurs price cuts for everyone, which encourages people to call more. As for airlines, they may earn higher profits by discriminating. But consumers are not necessarily worse off, since businessmen pay more and tourists pay less. And since price discrimination should encourage more people to fly, the economy as a whole ends up better off.

Commitments not to discriminate are a trickier antitrust problem. Last September Procter & Gamble agreed – without admitting wrongdoing – to pay $4.2m to settle antitrust charges brought by New York state's attorney general over its elimination of coupons. The trustbusters apparently believed that the consumer-health giant was colluding with rivals, because eliminating coupons 'only works if everybody goes along with it'.

But that is not necessarily true, according to Mr Corts's theory. And in the absence of collusion, there should be no antitrust worries – companies are not, after all, obliged to offer coupons. Consumers who are miffed at not getting them can always shop elsewhere. The problem, if there is one, is more one of presentation. 'Everyday low pricing' sounds good, but consumers are often paying more than they would with frequent discounting. Perhaps Procter & Gamble should have replaced its 'no-coupon' policy with a 'no-haggle' pledge instead.

Source: The Economist, 1 August 1998.

Questions

1 What do you understand by the term 'price discrimination' and what is the economic rationale for such a policy?

2 Explain why firms make more profit by varying prices for the same product/service.

3 '… even if firms can discriminate successfully and so boost initial profits they could still end up worse off'. In what circumstances could this occur?

4 'In some cases a commitment not to offer discounts may boost profits.' Discuss the rationale behind this statement. What relevance does the kinked-demand curve have here?

5 Should competition watchdogs worry about price discrimination? Explain your answer in detail.

CASE STUDY **9.10** **The price of air?**

One effect of the merger between British Airways and American Airlines has been to highlight the question of takeoff and landing slots. A dispute arose between the British government and the European competition commissioner, Karel Van Miert, over how many slots British Airways would have to give up at Heathrow to enable the authorities to allow what, on the face of it, would be a monopoly-creating merger between two airlines. The British government appeared prepared to allow the merger to take place if British Airways gave up 168 slots (84 flights in and out of Heathrow) to other airlines. This was felt to be sufficient to offset the 60 per cent market share that the combined airline would have on transatlantic flights. The EU commissioner, however, argued that this was insufficient and that British Airways should give up more. Furthermore the airline should be forced to give them away free.

The question of buying and selling slots at airports is in some ways a strange concept. What is it that is being bought and sold? Essentially it is space (airspace if you like) and you could be forgiven for thinking that this must be free. Not so, it is a scarce commodity and as such could command a price. At least it could if the EU rules allowed it, which currently (January 1997) they do not.

How then are these important takeoff and landing slots allocated? At the present moment they are allocated by the airport authorities and the charges levied do not reflect the costs of providing them or the different levels of demand. (For example, the highest demand at Heathrow is for the takeoff and landing slot first thing in the morning to allow business travellers a full day's work in the capital or to make onward connections to foreign destinations.) However, this method of allocating slots can adversely affect the structure of competition across Europe as each airport authority tends to favour its own national carrier. For example, according to 1995 figures published by Morgan Stanley, Alitalia, the Italian airline, has about 70 per cent of all the slots allocated at Rome airport, Lufthansa has 60 per cent of the slots at Frankfurt airport, while Air France, Swissair, KLM and SAS have around 50 per cent of the slots at Paris, Zurich, Amsterdam and Copenhagen respectively. Ironically British Airways benefits least from this method of allocation as it has about 40 per cent of the slots at Heathrow, although it does also have about 30 per cent of the slots at Gatwick. This procedure further reduces the competition by a system of what is known as 'grandfather rights' whereby slots allocated to an airline in one season are retained by it indefinitely provided it uses them.

From an economic point of view this is quite senseless. Incumbent airlines are therefore able to repel any competition. The system effectively does away with consumer choice as there is no way that an inefficient airline providing a poor service can be replaced provided it continues to use the slot. Equally it is difficult for airlines to respond to the customers' wishes to fly by a different route to a given destination. This can be frustrating as passengers are often force to fly to hub airports whether they want to or not. (This is a big bone of contention, for example, for Scottish customers who are often forced to fly to London before flying on to other foreign destinations rather than flying directly from a Scottish airport.) The system is therefore one big barrier to entry as new airlines are not able to get convenient slots at hub airports such as Heathrow.

How could things be organised differently? One way which could be used and which ties in with some of the ideas encountered, is to allow some sort of pricing mechanism to operate and to allow airlines to buy and sell slots among themselves in much the same way as oil companies will sell off blocks of the North Sea that they have been allocated.

In this way the most popular slots would be sold to the highest bidder and it is argued that these would be the most efficient airlines. If inefficient airlines paid over the odds and tried to pass the increase on to passengers, then there would be a reaction from the customers and they would switch to other airlines. Thus it would be in the best interest of the airlines to do their sums carefully before bidding. Too high a bid and they would stand no chance of making a profit and eventually be forced to give up the slot; too low a bid and they will not even be given the chance to fly. In addition each slot could be allocated on a time basis (say for two years) after which time slots are reallocated.

However, an even better way would be for the governments of Europe to scrap the present system and auction off the slots themselves to the highest bidder. In this way the government would get the benefit. The governments could also hold the ring if they wished to prevent the monopolisation of key slots by big airlines. They could also use some discretionary powers to allocate slots to smaller carriers in order to create some competition for the 'big boys'.

Adapted from *The Economist*, 18 January 1997.

Question

What are the problems with a system of auctioning air slots to airlines? Outline some of the difficulties associated with selling airspace.

Empirical evidence on oligopoly pricing

This chapter has shown that the determination of prices in an oligopolistic market is a complex issue and this conclusion is supported by the results of a large number of studies in this area. Probably the best-known piece of research in this area has been conducted by Hall and Hitch. They interviewed 38 businessmen and found that average cost pricing with a 'normal' mark up was the most common pricing procedure. The same finding has appeared from more recent studies conducted in the USA and the UK. The main reason put forward for the large-scale implementation of this rather simplistic pricing method is that it is a method of setting price which does not require a great deal of information, and is consistent with a firm attempting to achieve long-term profit maximisation.

There is, however, a body of evidence that indicates that a minority of firms are involved in other price-setting methods (see Hall *et al.*, 1996). These include price discrimination and dominant firm pricing. The degree to which the market is, or is not, competitive has also been found to have a significant impact on the ability of firms to unilaterally alter their price.

The evidence relating to the playing of hypothetical games under controlled and monitored environments is, on the whole, consistent with the predictions based on oligopoly theory. These games are normally structured around a number of players who are asked to select a price for a product, given a specific payoff matrix. The aim is to try to identify whether some form of tacit collusion will be arrived at by the players. The results have suggested that the greater the number of players in the game, the lower the prices and profits, which suggests that the more competitive the industry, the more difficult is the implementation of tacit collusion. It has also been found that the more information players receive about their rivals' reactions to their strategies (and vice versa), the higher the prices and profits in the industry. This would tend to suggest that an agreeable result for all participants can be reached more easily with a greater amount of available information, which is not altogether unexpected. However, these experiments involving game playing can easily be criticised as being too simplistic to correspond to real business behaviour and decision-making.

Conclusions

We have seen that the nature of the market can influence the type of pricing policy adopted. In more competitive markets, firms may have little or no control over price. They may then be 'price-takers' or at least 'price-followers'. However, as well as the nature of the market, the objectives pursued by the firm can also influence price-setting behaviour. A profit-orientated firm is more likely to charge a higher price, for example, than is a firm whose primary objective is sales revenue (turnover) or market share. Oligopolistic market structures are the type most frequently found in the business world. Indeed it would not be inaccurate to say that most markets are in fact oligopolistic in nature. These markets are dominated by a small number of interdependent firms who compete against one another. Theorists have developed models to explain firm behaviour, an early influential model being that of the kinked demand curve. This suggests that firms will have considerable incentives to keep prices relatively stable. Further developments in the theorising of oligopoly behaviour have resulted in game theory, which attempts to explore the reactions of one player to changes in strategy by another player. Non-price competition is common in oligopolistic markets, mainly because it is less risky as a strategic choice than is alteration of the price level. Collusion, whether explicit (which is unlawful) or tacit (which is not), is a ploy that may enable oligopolistic firms to move to their most profitable output level. It is clear from this chapter that the complexity of strategic decision-making is such that any economic modelling of an industry is always likely to be somewhat oversimplistic in nature.

References and additional reading

Cunningham, D. and Hornby, W. (1993) 'The pricing decision in small firms: theory and practice', *Management Decision*, Vol. 31, No. 7, pp. 46–55.

Earl, P.E. (1995) *Microeconomics for Business and Marketing*, Edward Elgar, Aldershot, esp. chs 8 and 9, pp. 203–97.

Ferguson, P.R., Ferguson, G.J. and Rothschild, R. (1993) *Business Economics: The Application of Economic Theory*, Macmillan, London, esp. chs 10 and 11, pp. 171–218.

Griffiths, A. and Wall, S. (1996) *Intermediate Microeconomics: Theory and Applications*, Longman, London, esp. chs 6, 7 and 8, pp. 250–378.

Griffiths, A. and Wall, S. (1997) *Applied Economics*, Longman, London, esp. ch. 6, pp. 124–42 and ch. 9, pp. 202–18.

Hall, S., Walsh, M. and Yates, T. (1996) 'How do UK companies set prices', *Bank of England Quarterly Bulletin*, May.

Hornby, W.B. (1995) 'Economics and business: the theory of the firm revisited: a Scottish perspective', *Management Decision*, Vol. 33, No. 1, pp. 33–41.

Hornby, W.B. and Macleod, M. (1996) 'Pricing behaviour in the Scottish computer industry', *Management Decision*, Vol. 34, No. 6, pp. 31–42.

Reekie, W.D. and Crook, J. (1987) *Managerial Economics*, Philip Allan, Oxford, esp. ch. 9, pp. 241–91.

CHAPTER **10**

Investment in theory and practice

Objectives

By the end of this chapter you will be able to:

➤ Understand the differences between non-discounting and discounting methods of investment appraisal and the advantages and disadvantages of each.

➤ Calculate the average rate of return and the payback period for a number of projects.

➤ Calculate the net present value (NPV), the internal rate of return (IRR) and a profitability index (PI) on a number of projects and use these measures to evaluate the optimum combination of projects for a given budget.

➤ Assess the cost of capital and be aware of the factors that can influence its cost.

➤ Distinguish between risk and uncertainty, identify the different types of risk and be able to take account of these factors in evaluating projects.

Key concepts

Average rate of return: the estimated total return on a project over and above the initial capital outlay is expressed as a percentage of that initial capital outlay. This is then expressed as an average (per annum) by dividing by the number of years of the project.

Discount factor: the factor by which a future value is multiplied to give a present value. This is often expressed as $1/(1 + r)^n$, where r is the rate of discount (as a decimal) and n is the number of time periods.

Discounting: the process of expressing a future value (or stream of values) in terms of the present.

Internal rate of return (IRR): that rate of discount (r) which must be applied to the estimated future returns on a project in order to make NPV = 0.

Net present value (NPV): this is the present value of the estimated future returns on the project minus the initial capital outlay.

Payback period: the time period necessary for the total returns on the project to pay back the initial capital outlay.

Profitability index (PI): This index measures the ratio of gross present value of future cash flows to the original outlay.

Risk: the estimated probability of particular outcomes occurring. Risk can be insured against. Risk is broken down in this chapter into market risk, technological risk, factor cost risk and political risk.

Uncertainty: possible outcomes which may occur but whose estimated probabilities are largely unknown. Uncertainty cannot be insured against.

Introduction

At some point in every business's life the managers will be required to evaluate a particular project. In order to do this they will need to use a number of techniques to appraise each project, to determine either which of various competing projects should be given priority or whether to proceed with any given investment. This chapter will outline the main techniques involved in investment appraisal.

PAUSE FOR THOUGHT 1 | *Outline the factors that you think would make a project viable. What costs are associated with a given project? What benefits?*

Investment appraisal techniques

Appraisal techniques can be divided into basically two groups:

1 Non-discounting techniques.
2 Discounting techniques.

In order to illustrate the nature of each of the techniques let us imagine that you are the manager of a widget factory and that you are about to investigate whether to make an investment in a new computer enhanced widget toolmaker, which you estimate will cost you £100,000. The machine will have an economic life of five years, by which time you will be expected to replace it. Because the machine is much better than the previous technology, you estimate that initially you will be able to sell more widgets more profitably. This is because the firm's widgets will now be more accurately designed than those of its competitors, thereby increasing sales volume and sales revenue. Furthermore, the widgets will now be cheaper to produce because the new machine can produce more widgets per unit of input of labour and raw material. In addition, because of the enhanced quality of the widgets produced you expect that in the next few years your company will be able to charge a premium price. In time, however, the competition will catch you up and hence towards the end of the five-year period your profitability will be eroded.

You estimate that the net income (revenue – cost) that your company will receive is likely to be as follows:

Year	1	2	3	4	5
Net income (£)	38,000	30,000	23,000	22,500	21,500

However, at the same time you are being lobbied by another group of managers within your company. They argue that the widget market is not where the future lies. They believe that the company should instead switch to the manufacture of gizmos. Although they have a similar product life-cycle they are thought to be a better bet. The capital cost of a machine to manufacture gizmos is also estimated at £100,000. It will, however, take time for a profitable market to establish itself. After much research the gizmo team come up with a net income flow over the life of the project as follows:

Year	1	2	3	4	5
Net income (£)	5,000	57,000	60,000	12,000	1,000

PAUSE FOR THOUGHT 2 *Which of these competing projects would you recommend? Do you buy the gizmo machine or go for the machine producing widgets? Before reading on, make a preliminary assessment.*

Non-discounting techniques

These techniques simply take the figures for capital outlay and net cash flows over the life of the project as given, making no adjustment for the timing of the income stream. Such techniques often calculate one or other of the following:

➤ An average rate of return (ARR).
➤ A payback period (PBP).

In the case of the widget project, the calculation of an average rate of return is straightforward. The capital outlay today (Year 0) is £100,000. The total returns earned over the life of the project are £135,000. Therefore the project earns a return of 35 per cent above the initial capital cost (£135,000 minus £100,000 divided by the initial capital outlay of £100,000). This averages out at 7 per cent per annum over the five years. The gizmo project also has a similar average rate of return. Although the returns are initially much lower in Year 1, they build up much more quickly before falling off again. Nevertheless, the total returns are exactly the same for both projects as is the average rate of return.

$$\text{ARR} = \frac{(\text{Total return} - \text{Initial capital outlay})}{\text{Initial capital outlay}} \times 100 \div \text{Time period of project}$$

The payback period is also very straightforward to calculate in both cases. The payback period represents the time it takes to repay the initial capital outlay. In the case of the widget project £38,000 is paid back at the end of Year 1, £68,000 is paid back at the end of Year 2, £91,000 is paid back by the end of Year 3, and £113,500 at the end of Year 4. Thus the payback period is between three and four years (if one assumes that the income is spread evenly throughout the year, then the actual payback period is 3.4 years). In the case of the gizmo project £5,000 is paid back at the end of Year 1, £62,000 is paid back at the end of Year 2, and £122,000 is paid back at the end of Year 3. Thus the payback period is between two and three years. (Using the same assumptions about the income being evenly spread throughout the year, the actual payback period is 2.6 years.) This would seem to point to the fact that the gizmo project is superior as the initial capital is paid back at a quicker rate. However, in neither of these two methods is the timing of the net income flows taken into account. £1 received today is valued just the same as £1 received in five years' time.

Discounting techniques: net present value

In looking at the flow of income over the life of a project it is often advisable to take account of the time dimension of these income flows. This aspect is important for the following reason. If as a manager you receive the income sooner rather than later, you will be able to re-invest that money and hence make a better return than if you are required to wait a number of years. This is a factor which is important irrespective of whether there is any inflation. Clearly, if there is a high rate of inflation then the real value of the income received in five years' time will be worth less than it is today. However, discounting has nothing to do with the rate of inflation. Even in a world where no inflation exists it would still be necessary to discount the net income flows. Discounting is linked to the concept of the opportunity cost of money. If as a manager you are required to wait five years to receive £1,000 then there will be a cost to you in terms of what you are required to give up in the way of lost interest on that sum. Discounting offers the manager a technique for valuing a given sum of money which is received some time in the future. For example, if you had £100 and decided to invest it at an annual rate of 10 per cent, at the end of the first year you would receive £110. An alternative way of looking at this is that £110 received in one year's time has a present value of £100 discounted at 10 per cent. In order to work out the relevant *discount factor*, the formula is as follows:

Present value (PV) = $V_n \times$ Discount factor

where V_n is the value of income received in time period n.

The *discount factor* is given by the formula

$1/(1 + r)^n$

where r is the rate of discount (expressed as a decimal, i.e. 10 per cent = 0.10) and n is the number of years over which you are discounting.

Thus, to calculate the discount factor over one year at 10 per cent, the calculation is as follows:

$1/(1 + 0.10)^1 = 0.909$

Therefore £110 received in one year's time is worth at the present day £110 × 0.909 = £100. If, however, you had had to wait two years before you received £110, then the discount factor would be:

$1/(1 + 0.10)^2 = 0.826$

In this case the £110 would now be worth only £110 × 0.826 = £90.91.

Thus the technique of discounting allows managers to value the future flows of income received at today's value.

Table 10.1 gives the discounted cash flow (DCF) calculations for both projects. The first column gives the years starting with the present year (Year 0) when £100,000 is spent on each of the two projects. Columns 2 and 3 give the non-discounted cash flows (NCF) for widgets and gizmos respectively, while column 4 calculates the discount factors for a discount rate of 10 per cent. Columns 5 and 6 give the discounted cash flows for both projects. As can be seen, the sum of the discounted cash flows gives the net present value (NPV) of both the widget and gizmo projects (£5,337 and £5,549 respectively). On this basis, and taking no other factors into account, it would appear that the gizmo project offers a marginally higher NPV than widgets.

Table 10.1
Widget and gizmo projects (10 per cent discount rate)

Year	NCF (Widgets)	NCF (Gizmos)	Discount factor	DCF (Widgets)	DCF (Gizmos)
0	−£100,000	−£100,000	1.000	−£100,000	−£100,000
1	£38,000	£5,000	0.909	£34,545	£4,545
2	£30,000	£57,000	0.826	£24,793	£47,107
3	£23,000	£60,000	0.751	£17,280	£45,079
4	£22,500	£12,000	0.683	£15,367	£8,196
5	£21,500	£1,000	0.621	£13,350	£622
Sum	£35,000	£35,000		£5,337	£5,549
NPV	£5,337	£5,549			
IRR	12.32%	12.35%			

PAUSE FOR THOUGHT 3 *What other factors might you take into account before deciding on the relative merits of these two projects ?*

Discounting methods: internal rate of return

The internal rate of return (IRR) is the rate of discount which when applied to a given cash flow yields a NPV equal to 0. It therefore represents the rate of return the project earns, taking account of the time factor of the cash flows. This rate of return which is earned internally (hence the name internal rate of return) can then be related to the costs of borrowing, or the opportunity costs of using the capital outlay in another way. In the example of widgets, it is calculated that the internal rate of return is 12.32 per cent. This is calculated by a process of iterations. A 'guess' is made that the IRR will exceed 10 per cent since we know that at a 10 per cent discount rate there is a positive NPV (£5,337 in the case of the widget project, £5,549 for gizmos). If a higher rate of discount is chosen then the NPV values will be less. For example you should try using 15 per cent rate.

PAUSE FOR THOUGHT 4
1 *What is the NPV for widgets and gizmos if the discount rate is 15 per cent?*
2 *You should do the calculation as before only using a 15 per cent discount factor before checking your answer against Table 10.2.*

Table 10.2
Widget and gizmo discounted net cash flows (15 per cent discount rate)

Year	NCF (Widgets)	NCF (Gizmos)	Discount factor	DCF (Widgets)	DCF (Gizmos)
0	−£100,000	−£100,000	1.000	−£100,000	−£100,000
1	£38,000	£5,000	0.870	£33,043	£4,348
2	£30,000	£57,000	0.756	£22,684	£43,100
3	£23,000	£60,000	0.658	£15,123	£39,451
4	£22,500	£12,000	0.572	£12,864	£6,861
5	£21,500	£1,000	0.497	£10,689	£497
Sum	£35,000	£35,000		−£5,596	−£5,743
NPV	−£5,596	−£5,743			

As can be seen from Table 10.2 the NPV values are now negative for both projects. This implies that the internal rate of return for both projects must lie somewhere between 10 and 15 per cent. In fact, the true value of IRR is given in Table 10.1. This implies that the rate of return for widgets is 12.32 per cent while it is 12.35 per cent for gizmos.

Another measure that can be employed is called the *profitability index* (PI). This index measures the ratio of the gross present value of future cash flows to the original outlay. This is a useful measure when managers have to evaluate the profitability of projects which have different capital outlays and must normally exceed unity in order for the net present value to be positive. It measures the efficiency of each project per £1 spent. In our example, since the capital outlays are the same then the merits of this index are less obvious and in fact it will give us a similar answer (in terms of which project is preferable). The profitability index for widgets is £105,336/£100,000 = 1.05336 and for gizmos the index is £105,549/£100,000 = 1.05549. Therefore, there is a marginal advantage in favour of gizmos over widgets. In some cases, however, the ranking of projects obtained by using the NPV method may not coincide with the ranking obtained from the PI. Table 10.3 gives an example of what can happen when ranking projects using NPV and PI.

Table 10.3

Project ranking using NPV and PI

Project	Outlay (£)	NPV (£)	PI	NPV ranking	PI ranking
A	50,000	8,000	1.16	4	6
B	25,000	15,000	1.60	2	1
C	25,000	10,000	1.40	3	2
D	50,000	16,000	1.32	1	3
E	25,000	6,000	1.24	6	5
F	25,000	7,000	1.28	5	4

If the capital budget is just £50,000, then according to the NPV criteria the best project is D, which yields the highest NPV of £16,000. However, according to the PI criteria, the best two projects are B and C which, between them, yield a combined NPV of £25,000. This is the best combination and gives a better 'value added' than any other possible combination of projects.

PAUSE FOR THOUGHT 5 *Before reading on, can you calculate the best combination of projects when the capital budget is (i) £75,000 and (ii) £100,000?*

If the capital budget is £75,000, then according to the NPV method projects B and D yield a total NPV of £31,000, while the PI method indicates that B + C + F yield a total NPV of £32,000. Only in the case of a capital budget of £100,000 do both methods yield the same combination of projects (B + C + D) with a combined NPV of £41,000. This indicates that if there are a number of competing projects with different capital outlays it is advisable to calculate both NPV and PI measures to get a complete picture before making a final decision.

The results of these techniques are summarised in Table 10.4. On the basis of the various techniques identified it would appear that the gizmo project offers the best returns. However, it can be seen that there is not much to choose between them and it would not take very much for the balance of advantage to shift.

Table 10.4
Summary of the results

Technique	Widgets	Gizmos
Average rate of return (ARR)	7% per annum	7% per annum
Payback period (PBP)	3.32 years	2.63 years
Net present value (NPV@10%)	£5,337	£5,549
Internal rate of return (IRR)	12.32%	12.35%
Profitability index (PI)	1.05336	1.05549

PAUSE FOR THOUGHT 6 *What factors might cause a manager to choose the widget project over the gizmo project even though it appears that it is 'inferior'?*

The cost of capital

In the examples we have used so far we have avoided explaining how managers determine the appropriate rate at which to discount the relevant cash flows. The cost of capital is the discount rate that is used by firms to calculate the net present value of projects and the rate firms use should reflect the cost of raising finance. In deciding which projects to undertake, the profit-maximising firm will equate the internal rate of return (i.e. the rate of discount on the cash flows of a given project that yields a net present value of zero) with the cost of financing the project.

It will undertake only those projects which yield a rate of return at least equal to this cost, other things being equal. The cost of capital can therefore be seen as the opportunity cost of investing in the best alternative project. Having said that, it is nevertheless difficult to estimate what this actually is in practice. If a firm is borrowing money from a bank then it might use this as the basis of evaluating its projects. Some, however, object to this because it assumes that the next best alternative to using the money is to reduce a debt. If the firm used the money to lend on to the money market then a different rate would apply as there is usually a difference between lending rates and borrowing rates. Also the cost of capital will vary depending on the source of the capital, with a different rate applying to different sources of capital. For instance, there is a difference in the costs of debt finance (borrowing) and equity finance (shares) due largely to the fact that interest charges arising from borrowing (debt finance) can be offset against the prevailing rates of corporation tax. In addition, it is traditionally argued that the gearing ratio (the ratio of debt to equity) also can affect the cost of capital. Highly geared companies (with more borrowing than shares) are a greater risk than lower geared companies since the debenture holders who lend money to the company have a prior claim on the profits than the equity shareholders. Thus, a highly geared company that experiences a fall in its profits is seen as a greater risk than a lower geared company with the same profits. Although this view has been challenged by Modigliani and Miller in a famous paper, their challenge rests on a number of highly restrictive assumptions which takes us beyond the scope of this book. (Interested readers are advised to refer to the Modigliani–Miller paper, 'Dividend policy, growth and valuation of shares', *Journal of Business*, October 1961.) Thus the calculation of the cost of capital is by no means straightforward.

Suffice it to say that the firm has only three principal source of funds, namely, retained profits, equity (i.e. the issuing of shares for which it is required to pay a dividend) and finally debt finance (i.e. borrowing for which it is required to pay interest which can be offset against its corporation tax and hence is normally less costly). The actual cost of finance will therefore depend on the cost from each source and the proportion of finance raised from each source. To return to our example, imagine that our company finances the

Table 10.5

The funding of the widget and gizmo projects

Source	Amount (£)	Cost (%)
Profits	50,000	10
Equity	30,000	15
Debt	20,000	12
Total	100,000	11.9

widget project as shown in Table 10.5.

Thus the cost of capital is calculated as a weighted average of the costs of the alternative sources of funding.

PAUSE FOR THOUGHT 7 *What would the cost of capital be if the company decided not to use retained profit at all but used equity and debt finance in equal proportions to finance this project?*

Risk and uncertainty
....

Definitions of risk and uncertainty

The distinction between risk and uncertainty is said to be that while risk is insurable uncertainty is not. Undoubtedly, one of the factors that can play a part in the decision is the degree of risk associated with each project. If one project is perceived as less of a risk than another then other things being equal a manager will prefer that project whose returns are more certain (i.e. less risky). Risk analysis is therefore an attempt to quantify the likelihood that a given set of returns will be received. In order to quantify this a manager may estimate the probability of receiving a given cash flow. This may be based on previous experience of similar projects in the past or it may simply reflect the manager's judgement of the risks involved. For example, it is not unreasonable to assume that returns which are going to be received in the immediate future are more likely to occur than those received in the more distant future. In other words if we take the cash flows for widgets we might assume that as it is a market with which the firm is already familiar and in which it has already established its name then there is less risk associated with this project than with the more unfamiliar gizmo project. Thus the probabilities of obtaining the cash flows identified above are as shown in Table 10.6.

Table 10.6
The probability of receiving the relevant cash flows

Year	Widgets	Probability	Gizmos	Probability	ECF (Widgets)	ECF (Gizmos)
0	−100,000	1.00	−100,000	1.00	−100,000	−100,000
1	38,000	0.90	5,000	0.80	34,200	4,000
2	30,000	0.85	57,000	0.75	25,500	42,750
3	23,000	0.80	60,000	0.70	18,400	42,000
4	22,500	0.75	12,000	0.65	16,875	7,800
5	21,500	0.70	1,000	0.60	15,050	600
					10,025	−2,850

As can be seen, this significantly alters the relevant cash flows. Now that we have incorporated the relevant risk factors it would appear that the balance of advantage has shifted towards the widget project. In other words, there appears to be less risk with this project. The expected cash flows (ECFs) for each project reflect the total of the weighted cash flows (weighted by the probabilities that are estimated for receipt of these). The difficulty is, of course, to estimate the relevant probabilities and it would only take a small shift in the risks involved to alter the decision in this case.

PAUSE FOR THOUGHT 8 *What would the relevant cash flows be for the widget project if the manager takes a more pessimistic view of the future? Calculate the ECFs for widgets if a lower probability is chosen for each year of the project. (Take as your starting point that the chances of obtaining the cash flow in year 1 are estimated as no more than 70 per cent, i.e. the probability is 0.7 and the chances are less as time goes by.)*

Types of risk

There are a variety of different types of risk which can influence investment decisions. These can be classified as follows:

1 Market risk.
2 Technological risk.
3 Factor cost risk.
4 Political risk.

Market risk

There is always going to be a risk that the market conditions will change and that this will affect the economics of a particular project. At the macroeconomic level the economy may experience a particularly severe slump. This can obviously affect sales and cash flows over the life of the project. Or, alternatively, the structure of the market may change with an increase in the competition and the degree of product differentiation. There may also be a change in the product's life-cycle with the product reaching the maturity stage in a shorter time span than was originally envisaged at its launch. Businesses may misjudge the market demand for a given product, overestimating the extent to which consumers will accept the product or service. Consumers' tastes may also change to such an extent that previously safe markets may simply disappear or new market opportunities open up which are seen as a threat to established products.

For example, market conditions in the offshore supply industry have altered dramatically in the early to mid-1990s. Oil companies, who are the major customers, wanted to drive down costs as the real price of oil failed to rise in line with the ever-increasing costs of extracting oil from the more marginal oil and gas fields of the North Sea. They launched a programme to reduce their costs (the so-called CRINE initiative – Cost Reduction in the New Era). They entered into new partnering arrangements with offshore suppliers which totally transformed the competitive structure of the industry. Small supply companies were forced to become part of larger consortia bidding for longer term contracts. The nature of the contracts was also transformed with the risks (and rewards) involved in any given project being shared among the partners in the consortium. New strategic alliances were formed which altered previous competitive arrangements. In addition, the rules applying to the Single Market meant that the oil companies were forced to put out to a much wider tender work which had previously been regarded as exclusively the preserve of UK- or Scottish-based companies. Thus, in a very short space of time the risks associated with this market were transformed.

Technological risk

Changes in technology, whether they are associated with new products or new processes, can also pose significant risks to businesses. The research and development involved is also a very risky undertaking with no guarantees that the process or product will find a market or indeed if the R&D expenditure will in fact yield anything of value. Pharmaceutical companies spend significant sums of money on trying to develop new drugs not all of which reach the marketplace.[1] In the fast-moving world of computers and information technology technological risk is extremely high. Apple Macintosh was generally regarded as being the industry leader in producing user-friendly software which was the precursor to the current 'Windows' software that is now dominated by Bill Gates's Microsoft. However, they lost their technological edge (indeed, they did not so much lose it as gave it away by selling the rights to Bill Gates). Since that moment Apple's fortunes have been in decline and a succession of chief executives have struggled to keep Apple at the forefront of this industry. IBM too suffered at the hands of the all-powerful Microsoft and failed to realise the significance of the development of the desktop PC in the 1980s. IBM, widely regarded by most analysts at the time as almost indestructible, suffered hugely as consumer tastes followed the changes in technology and rendered a large part of IBM's product portfolio redundant. Belatedly, IBM realised its mistake and it has been running hard to catch up ever since.

PAUSE FOR THOUGHT 9 *What other examples of technological risk can you identify which have affected the way a given market operates? Can you give one example of technological innovation which has affected products and one which has affected processes?*

CASE STUDY **10.1** **When the chips are down**

Throughout the 1990s the semiconductor business seemed like a 'licence to print money'. Demand for 'chips' which drive today's personal computers soared, as did the power of the chips themselves. In addition, the price of these wonders of technology also rose. A world-wide price war in the 1980s forced many American companies out of the basic memory chip end of the market and into the more lucrative and higher value-added microprocessor end of the business. One group of analysts calculated that the profit margins for chip-makers rose from 16 per cent in 1990 to nearly 60 per cent by 1995. By 1996, the number of chips sold rose by 40 per cent and the memory chip business made profits of nearly $30 billion on revenues of $55 billion, with some fabrication plants making as much as $1 billion in net profits each year.

This was all the more extraordinary as it seemed to defy a basic rule of the industry which was that as the power of the chips doubled (every 12 months according to industry experts) the price consequently halved. 'More power for less money' had been the industry's slogan. However, as the demand for PCs soared so the price of these chips rose to three times their costs of production and, furthermore, they stayed there. This gave chip manufacturers a tremendous opportunity to expand their business and to invest in new plant to produce even more chips.

Unfortunately, the picture has now changed, and with a vengeance. In December 1995 prices started to tumble from about $13 per chip by more than $1 per month. By March 1996 they were down to $9 each. The 'book-to-bill' ratio (a ratio that measures the ratio of production to sales) fell to 0.92. This meant that for every $100 worth of production there was only $92 worth of sales. This was the first time since 1989 that the ratio had fallen to below 1 and it got worse, falling to below 0.9 by March 1996. Manufacturers of chips, who had a few months earlier been planning big expansion programmes, were now scrambling to postpone them. Profit forecasts for the big chip manufacturers were revised downwards with one analyst estimating that the profits growth of the big five Japanese manufacturers would be reduced from 55 per cent to about 15 per cent.

Lower chip prices were of course good news for users of chips, from purchasers of PCs to car manufacturers and producers of mobile phones and pop-up toasters. Some of the big chip-makers had used the profits from their chip business as 'cash cows' to cross-subsidise their expansion plans into other unrelated businesses. For example, South Korea's Samsung Corporation and Japan's NEC had expanded into cars and aerospace as well as PCs. As the 'milk' from the 'cash cows' ran dry this would help those other firms who did not have this lucrative source of funds for financing their businesses.

The reasons why chip prices fell, and what makes this such a risky business to be in, are tied up with the economics of the industry. The chip market tends to be highly unstable, first because there are massive fixed costs associated with the production of chips and also because the demand for chips is itself highly unstable and affected by factors over which chip manufacturers have very little control. There is a long lead time (about one year to 18 months) to build the plant to fabricate these chips (the so-called 'fab' plants). It costs between $1 and $3 billion to build these 'fabs' and they can become obsolete within three years. The risks are therefore enormous. This is not an industry for the faint-hearted! No sooner does a 'fab' plant come on stream than the demand for chips changes. Normally a manufacturer can adjust production levels to match demand, but because of the need to keep the cost down and because of the high initial investment, new plant has to be big to spread the high R&D costs involved. Therefore, it is not always possible to adjust supply to changes in demand. In this respect the market conditions in this industry are not unlike the economic conditions that apply in a lot of agricultural markets where governments intervene to stabilise prices by market intervention, buying up surpluses when there is a glut, and selling out of intervention stocks when there is a shortage. While there have been attempts to smooth out the price cycles in the industry – with closer links being set up between 'fab' plants and their customers so that they can respond quickly to changes in market conditions and with PC manufacturers operating 'just-in-time' inventory control techniques – these measures have not proved to be effective in the recent downturn. While going up-market to produce the more expensive and higher value-added microprocessors has helped some American firms, it has not eliminated the basic volatility in this market nor significantly reduced the risks. Chip manufacturers are still almost exclusively tied to one industry with computer companies accounting for 60 per cent of the world-wide demand for chips. Mobile phones, another major customer, still only accounts for 10 per cent of sales of chips with other users coming nowhere near this figure.

The current crisis, it is argued, can be laid at the door of one company – Microsoft. Throughout the period the development of PCs has been by fits and starts. A lot of new PCs were sold on the back of developments in the chip pioneered by Intel which started with the 8086 microprocessor and subsequently developed the 80286 and the 80386, each new chip separated by a gap of about three years. However, up until the launch of Microsoft's Windows operating system in the late 1980s the number and value of these chips remained pretty much the same for each PC. With the arrival of Windows everything changed. To work effectively, Windows required about 4 megabytes of memory, about twice what was currently available in most PCs. This caused a surge in demand for more bigger chips and fuelled the boom period. New expansion plans were brought forward by 'fab' plants.

Then in 1995 Microsoft announced the world-wide launch of Windows 95 which needed twice as much memory again. Good news for the manufacturers of chips, you could be forgiven for thinking. Wrong! Companies and home PC users were slow to switch to Windows 95 partly because of the associated costs of replacing their existing hardware, partly because consumers were not entirely convinced they needed all this extra computing power, and partly because it was well known among consumers that Microsoft had another product waiting in the wings – Windows NT – which was even more powerful. Many consumers thus adopted a 'wait-and-see' policy, and this has had a disastrous effect even on the high-value end of the market, e.g. Intel's Pentium Pro microprocessor runs efficiently on only one of the new versions of Windows. In addition, chip-makers are now running up against the physical limits of the technology itself whereby it is becoming increasingly difficult to pack any more processing power onto a chip. The costs of doing so are becoming even more frightening and the increase in power is unlikely to be commensurate with the costs. Diminishing returns appear to have set in.

What can be done to reduce the risks of the 'fab' chip manufacturers? Is there a strategy that they can adopt that would in some way spread the risks? A number of strategies have been suggested. First, seek out a partner. One way to spread the risks involved in building expensive chip fabrication plant would be to team up with other manufacturers (or, indeed, with their customers the computer companies) and to have a series of joint ventures. IBM and Toshiba are building fabrication plant together as are Motorola and Siemens. Texas Instruments have a deal with the Italian government, Taiwan's Acer, Japan's Kobe Steel and a Singapore consortium. Secondly, computer firms are subcontracting the work of manufacturing chips. These companies are called 'fabless' companies. The companies that are in fabrication have the benefit of having a number of subcontracts from a variety of different computer customers. While it does not eliminate the risks entirely it does enable the fabricators to 'mix and match' the demands of their customers and to avoid becoming too closely tied to one PC manufacturer. Third, the chip fabricators can specialise and diversify. This would enable them to design variations of their basic chip for different specialist markets and hence not become so vulnerable to one segment of the market. For example, as Intel has begun to face increasing competition it has produced over 30 versions of its 486 chip and it is reported that Toshiba is doing much the same thing with its memory chips. Firms wanting to reduce their risks in this highly risky market may be forced to consider these types of strategy.

Adapted from *The Economist*, 23 March 1996.

Factor cost risk

This refers to the risk that the cost of a given factor of production is subject to some unexpected variations. Sudden and unanticipated changes to interest rates, for example, can significantly alter the economics of a given project. If the costs of borrowing money change dramatically then this can upset the calculations of a viable project. Equally, a sudden and unanticipated change in exchange rates can also alter the viability of a particular project. In the mid-1980s the economics of oil were based on a $40 price for a barrel of oil and a rate of exchange of £1 = $2.00. This implied a sterling price of approximately £20 per barrel. In the mid-1990s, however, the $ price of oil had fallen to about $18 per barrel while the rate of exchange was around £1 = $1.50 or about £12 per barrel. Investment appraisals carried out in the late 1980s on the viability of North Sea Oil wells now needed to be recalculated using the new lower sterling price. This has not only affected oil companies' revenues and profits but has also affected the government's own finances with significantly lower levels of taxation being yielded from the North Sea than had been previously calculated (the situation, of course, was made more difficult by the decline in production levels which was occurring simultaneously). The impact of exchange rate movements and the different mechanisms for stabilising exchange rates were discussed in Chapter 3. However, the key point to recognise is that the impact of sudden movements in factor costs can significantly increase the risks of any project.

Political risks

These arise from sudden 'discontinuous' change such as a change of government or a dramatic change in the political climate. The sudden and unexpected renewal of hostilities by the Irish Republican Army (IRA) in 1995 dramatically changed the climate for the tourist trade in London, especially after the capital experienced a renewal of the bombing. The change of government in 1997 meant an increase in the exposure of companies to political risk. This is not to imply that a Labour government would necessarily be any worse at managing the economy than its predecessor, but simply that the inevitable uncertainty caused by the changes of personnel at the top of the government would increase uncertainty and hence increase the risk factors associated with any given investment decision. There was evidence that in mid- to late 1996, business people were holding off major investment decisions until the political climate became clearer. Labour's plans over the privatisation of Railtrack have had an unsettling effect on investors in Railtrack shares. Labour was originally committed to 'a publicly owned, publicly accountable railway'. However, statements in 1996 seemed to call into question exactly what this will mean in practice with a Labour frontbench spokesperson indicating that returning the rail network to public ownership is not a high priority for an incoming Labour government and that this will remain a 'second order issue dependent on the availability of resources and as priorities allow.' As *The Economist* observed, 'Labour's current plans will merely depress the launch share price without adding much to investors' long-term risks.'[2] Finally, in a world of increasing international competition the attitudes of foreign governments can have a very significant effect on an industry as the ban of British beef by European governments in April 1996 demonstrated. Faced with falling consumer confidence and opposition from their own farmers to the importation of British beef, European governments imposed a ban on British beef which had a catastrophic effect on the livelihoods of British farmers and associated industries. Analysts were also forecasting that there could be a huge balance of payments crisis of up to £6.5 billion a year for several years, a slowdown in growth of GDP of about 1.2 per cent and an increased tax bill of up to £20 billion. While the exact size of these forecasts is subject to much debate there is little doubt that the increased political risks as a result of the BSE crisis will have far-reaching economic consequences.

PAUSE FOR THOUGHT 10

You are exporting electronic components to the Far East. What are the links between a possible change of government in the United Kingdom and the success of your business in that market?

Attitudes to risk

The way that firms cope with risk and the strategies they adopt depend on their attitude to risk and their objectives. For example, a firm may prefer a smaller but more certain outcome to one which is larger but less certain. To return to our previous example imagine that the choices facing the company are as follows:

➤ Option A: To give the existing product line (i.e. widgets) a 'face lift'.
➤ Option B: To launch the new gizmos.

The profitability of each option, however, depends on the state of the economy. Imagine for the sake of illustration that the economy can be described as having three possible outcomes, each with an associated probability:

➤ State 1 Recession (probability of 0.2).
➤ State 2 Flat economy (probability of 0.5).
➤ State 3 Boom (probability of 0.3).

The results can be summarised in Table 10.7.

Table 10.7
Evaluation of options taking account of risk

State	Probability	Option A	Option B	EVA	EVB
Recession	0.3	4,000	1,000	1,200	300
Flat	0.5	5,000	4,000	2,500	2,000
Boom	0.2	6,000	20,000	1,200	4,000
Total				4,900	6,300

Comparison of the risks

Option A

Outcome	EVA	Deviation (D)	D^2	Probability (P)	$D^2 \times P$
4,000	4,900	−900	810,000	0.3	243,000
5,000	4,900	100	10,000	0.5	5,000
6,000	4,900	1,100	1,210,000	0.2	242,000
Total					490,000

Standard deviation   700 ($\sqrt{490,000}$)
Coefficient of variation   0.142857 (standard deviation ÷ EVA)

Option B

Outcome	EVB	Deviation (D)	D^2	Probability (P)	$D^2 \times P$
1,000	6,300	−5,300	28,090,000	0.3	8,427,000
4,000	6,300	−2,300	5,290,000	0.5	2,645,000
20,000	6,300	13,700	1.88E+08	0.2	37,538,000
Total					48,610,000

Standard deviation   6972.087 ($\sqrt{48,610,000}$)
Coefficient of variation   1.106681 (standard deviation ÷ EVB)

As the table indicates, option B yields the best return. The expected value of option B (EVB) is £6,300 compared to the expected value of option A (EVA) of £4,900. However, the risks associated with option B are considerably higher. In order to measure the degree of risk we can calculate the coefficient of variation which is the standard deviation divided by the mean. In the case of option A the coefficient of variation is 0.143 compared with 1.107 for option B. In other words, option B is about ten times riskier than A and one would need to evaluate whether the prospect of £1,400 extra profit compensated for the increased risk. Individual managers will give different answers to this question depending on whether they are risk takers or risk averse.

Conclusions

We have now had a chance to look at a number of different techniques in the assessment of various investment projects and have examined the methods of incorporating risk and uncertainty into our evaluation. It is, however, important to bear in mind that investment appraisal is not just about the application of various techniques. It is also about judgement and assessing what are a business's key objectives as the following illustrative case study demonstrates.

Appendix

CASE STUDY 10.2

Highland Plastics (Inverness) plc[3]

In 1979 two men, John Semple and Derek Richards, decided to set up their own company producing polythene bags and PVC covers. Both men had for a number of years worked in the packaging industry. Since 1977, however, both had worked for British Plastics Limited (BPL). This was a London-based company. BPL had opened up a Scottish-based factory in Coatbridge, just outside Glasgow, and Semple and Richards had been appointed area sales manager and production manager respectively. However, both men, who were in their middle forties, had experienced increasing frustrations with BPL. They complained of BPL's lack of awareness of the Scottish market. BPL, they felt, was too big and impersonal. Richards also complained of increasing indiscipline on the factory floor and he blamed it to a large extent on intervention of unions. Semple too felt frustrated in so far as he was often unable to meet orders due to industrial disputes. Furthermore, head office in London was not allowing management decisions to be devolved to their Scottish factory and everything had to be referred to London for approval. Finally, the industrial Central Belt of Scotland was beginning to lose whatever appeal it may have had for the two men and their families. It has never failed to amaze them, however, that in spite of the inefficiency of BPL's operations in Scotland the company still continued to make huge profits.

So early in 1979 with the cash from savings, bank borrowing and the proceeds of the sale of two cars, they decided that they would set up on their own. They were resolved to ensure that their operations would be small and simple and that they would try to retain a 'family atmosphere' with their workers. They thus set up a factory in a small warehouse on the outskirts of Inverness. The local town council was extremely helpful and they also received a great deal of assistance from the Highlands and Islands Development Board. Furthermore, Semple was a keen fisherman and Richards and his family were keen skiers. The proximity of good rivers for fishing and Aviemore were two additional attractions. Both Semple and Richards had daughters – none of them was interested in the business.

Initially, they employed five people operating five second-hand polythene heat-sealers. They bought film in rolls of polythene tube. The heat-sealers would then weld bottom-welded bags. A guillotine knife was used to cut the bags at the appropriate length. However, the process was highly labour intensive. They also had no facilities or equipment for printing film and so they had to buy in reels of printed film and process it in the usual way. They also purchased one second-hand welder for converting the heavier PVC sheets into PVC packs, bags and covers. Although this was more profitable it was nevertheless a riskier line of business. Being more expensive, firms would often cut back on their demand for PVC in preference to polythene in times of slump. Thus the profits from PVC were much more subject to wide variations, and PVC was to form only a tiny fraction of their total turnover.

By 1983, their turnover was about £1 million and they were employing 20 people. Their current volume was about 5 million bags per annum or about 20,000 bags per eight-hour shift. After deducting all costs they expected to net a profit of 20 per cent of their turnover. Given that their initial capital to set up the company was about £100,000, they considered this an adequate return on their investment.

By 1985, their turnover had risen to £2.5 million and they were now employing 25 people. Their current volume was 12.5 million bags per annum (or 50,000 per eight-hour shift) and after deduction of all costs, the net cash flow was £250,000.

In 1986, however, they were faced with some awkward decisions. They were now reaching a size which meant they could begin to compete with the 'big boys' for some of the larger contracts such as in knitwear or the big potato merchants. However, their process was extremely labour intensive and they used mainly unskilled and semi-skilled, non-unionised female labour. Initially, the labour costs were only about 20 per cent of the total costs of their operations. But with inflation and equal pay legislation their labour costs now represented something like 40 per cent of the total costs. Nevertheless, the labour force had been extremely loyal and diligent and both Semple and Richards were quite happy to pay their workers well above union rates to keep the workers happy and the unions out of their factory.

If there was to be any further growth, however, Highland Plastics would need to invest in new capital equipment. After some deliberation they were faced with four options:

Option A: Buy an automatic polythene converter (APC) at a cost of £100,000. This machine had a capacity of 100,000 bags per eight-hour shift. It had an estimated economic life of five years. Richards and Semple calculated that the net cash flow over the next five years would be:

Year	1	2	3	4	5
(£)	50,000	50,000	100,000	50,000	25,000

However, they would have to lay off six women (or about 25 per cent of their labour force). Many of the women had been with the firm from its inception. Morale was high in the factory and both Semple and Richards were highly regarded by their workers. Likewise the two men had a high regard for their workers, all of whom they knew well.

Option B: Buy an automatic polythene converter and printer (APCP) at a cost of £550,000. The printer was bolted to the front end of the converter and converted unprinted film into printed film. There was thus a saving on printing costs since this cut out the need to buy print from outside sources. The capacity of the APCP was 250,000 bags per shift (or about five times the firm's current capacity). The net cash flow over APCP's five-year life were expected to be:

Year	1	2	3	4	5
(£)	200,000	200,000	200,000	200,000	200,000

However, this option would mean laying off ten workers, only about three of whom could be redeployed to other operations in the factory. Furthermore, they would now have to employ a qualified printer. (S)he has to be a member of a print union and so it would mean an end to Highland's 'no union' policy. (This salary, however, had been taken into account in calculating the anticipated net cash flows.)

Option C: Buy an automatic PVC converter (APVCC). This would entail diversifying away from polythene towards PVC. However, although it could be very profitable, it was regarded as the 'bread and butter' line with PVC being the cream on the cake. The cost of APVCC was £400,000 and over its five-year life the net dsh flows (assuming no fluctuations in demand) were expected to be:

Year	1	2	3	4	5
(£)	250,000	250,000	250,000	250,000	250,000

No increase in labour would be required as there could be some redeployment within the factory. Also there would be no redundancies. However, it would now mean that PVC would represent 65 per cent of the company's total output instead of its present 5 per cent. Very few big companies in the same business had more than 50 per cent of their capacity devoted to PVC.

Option D: Do nothing. Highland could not then expect any further substantial growth. Rising labour costs with virtually static or slow growth in turnover threatened profit margins which had come under some pressure in recent years.

Evaluation of options

There are a number of ways in which these projects can be evaluated.

1 The payback period (PBP) (i.e. the number of years it would take to pay back the investment).
2 The average rate of return (ARR)

$$= \frac{R - C}{C} \times 100 \div N$$

where R = sum of net revenues
C = capital costs
N = number of years

3 Net present value (NPV), where the cash flows are discounted by the cost of capital (20 per cent).
4 The internal rate of return (IRR), which calculates the rate of return on the project taking account of the timing of such flows. The IRR should exceed the cost of borrowing.

Question

Assuming the cost of borrowing to be 20 per cent, which option, if any, would you recommend Semple and Richards to choose? Using the table below set out the results of these measures:

Option	PBP (Years)	ARR (%)	NPV (£)	IRR (%)
A				
B				
C				
D				

Before reading the Postscript in the Solutions and Guidelines on page 439, what do you perceive to be the objectives of Highland Plastics and what long-term strategy would you recommend?

Notes
....

[1] Matthew Lynn (1990), in his book *The Billion Dollar Battle: Merck v. Glaxo*, describes the process as 'molecular roulette'. According to Lynn, at a rough average it was calculated that the chemists would find something interesting once in every 10,000 tries.

[2] *The Economist*, 6 April 1996, p. 36.

[3] The authors would like to thank John Brebner and Derek Taylor of Deeside Packaging (Stonehaven) Plc for their help in preparing this case study.

References and additional reading
....

Ferguson, P.R., Ferguson, G.J. and Rothschild, R. (1993) *Business Economics: The Application of Economic Theory*, Macmillan, London, esp. ch. 8, pp. 120–42.

Griffiths, A. and Wall, S. (1997) *Applied Economics*, Longman, London, esp. ch. 14, pp. 333–48.

Lynn, M. (1990) *The Billion Dollar Battle: Merck v. Glaxo*, Heinemann, London.

Reekie, W.D. and Crook, J. (1987) *Managerial Economics*, Philip Allan, Oxford, esp. ch. 12, pp. 321–66.

CHAPTER 11

Corporate strategy and business economics

Objectives

By the end of this chapter you will be able to:

➤ Define what is meant by 'corporate strategy' and identify the characteristics of corporate strategy.

➤ Understand and apply the various models which are used by corporate strategists for analysing the environment within which an organisation operates.

➤ Relate the principles of business economics to the strategic models for assessing the strategic choices facing organisations.

➤ Identify some of the costs and benefits of implementing strategic change.

➤ Outline the various options open to firms who wish to expand their activities into international markets and assess their costs and benefits.

➤ Critically analyse the theories of international business.

➤ Evaluate the extent to which globalisation exists.

Key concepts

Barriers to entry: various aspects and practices which might deter new firm entry to an industry or market.

Boston matrix: a device by which products can be rated according to sales growth and market share. Developed by the Boston Consulting Group in the USA, and involving categories such as 'problem children', 'stars', 'cash cows' and 'dogs'.

Focus strategy: in which the company identifies a segment in the market and tailors its strategy to serve that market excluding all other segments.

Generic strategies: Porter identified three such strategies, namely cost leadership (emphasis on cost reduction), differentiation focus (mixture of cost and revenue), and a focus strategy in which the company identifies a segment in the market and tailors its strategy to serve that market, excluding all other segments.

Globalisation: refers to the phenomenon whereby companies make decisions on location of production or sourcing of inputs or the sale of the product or service without reference to political or geographic boundaries.

Internalisation advantages: advantages that accrue to firms who undertake certain activities themselves as opposed to outsourcing or subcontracting these activities.

Location specific advantages: advantages from engaging in overseas production in specific locations, such as easier access to raw materials, to major markets, to cheaper labour/capital inputs, etc.

Multinational: a firm which owns, controls and manages assets in more than one country.

Ownership specific advantage: advantages held by multinational companies over firms in the host country via 'ownership' of certain characteristics, such as scale, market power, financial strength, human capital, etc.

PEST: an analysis involving the political, economic, social and technological environment in which the firm operates.

Porter's 'five forces': an analysis involving an assessment of the threat of (i) potential entrants and (ii) substitutes, as well as the power of (iii) suppliers and (iv) buyers, together with an exploration of (v) the degree of competitive rivalry.

Strategy: guiding 'rules' or principles influencing the direction and scope of the organisation's activities in the long term.

We have looked at a number of different elements in our discussion about business economics. It is now time to draw some of these together and to look at the way a business might use these elements in order to develop a strategy. As we shall see, there are considerable degrees of overlap between the areas of business economics and business strategy. (Is it a coincidence that many of the leading writers in the field of business strategy are, or were, economists?)

Corporate strategy defined

Strategy has been defined by Johnson and Scholes (1999) as follows:

> Strategy is the *direction and scope* of an organisation over the *long term*: ideally, which matches its *resources* to its *changing environment* and in particular its *markets*, *customers* or *clients* so as to meet *stakeholders*' expectations [our emphasis].

This stresses that strategic decisions are likely to affect the whole organisation rather than just a part of it. It concerns the range of activities that an organisation undertakes as well as the expectations of all the organisation's main stakeholders, as the following cases illustrate.

CASE STUDY **11.1** **Core competences – the cases of ITT and Hanson**

In 1920 Harold Geneen created ITT as a Caribbean telephone company. Under his ruthless financially driven approach, he slowly built ITT into one of the world's biggest multinational conglomerates acquiring a ragbag of hundreds of companies including Avis, Continental Baking, Rayonier, Sheraton and Hartford Fire Insurance. By 1970, Harold Geneen had control of 400 separate companies operating in 70 different countries.

Multinational conglomerates were regarded by investment analysts as the stock market's 'blue-eyed darlings' in the 1960s and 1970s. They were thought to be immune from the traditional swings of the trade cycle which seemed to afflict companies that were locked into a single national market with a limited product range. The skills of the managers were thought to be transferable from one industry to another no matter how different these industries were.

However, the mood of the markets swung against conglomerates as they struggled to perform as well as the markets expected. Disillusionment crept in as shareholders began to express their discontent at the way these companies were managed. Managers were encouraged to 'stick to the knitting' (according to Tom Peters and Robert Waterman) or, to borrow the words of Gary Hamel and C.K. Prahalad, to 'cultivate their core competences'. In short, companies were encouraged to concentrate on what they were good at and sell off those parts of the business that they knew little or nothing about.

As a prescription this simple injunction was sometimes quite difficult to implement because it was not always clear just exactly what was 'core' to a firm's main business. It required an analysis of the firm's value-chain and a very clear idea of which parts of the business added value and which did not, and which competences were unique to the firm and which were not. In the case of ITT it required a shift away from the previous philosophy of acquisitions to one of demerger. Thus when on 13 June 1995, Rand Araskog, ITT's boss, announced that ITT would be broken up it marked the end of an era.

ITT was to be formed into three easy-to-understand businesses. The biggest of the three was to be called ITT Hartford and it took over the sprawling insurance operations of the old ITT company. The new company was estimated to have a turnover of $11.1 billion and to generate an operating profit of $852 million. The second was to be called ITT Industries and took in the car, defence, electronics and fluid technology parts of the old ITT empire which in 1994 had sales of $7.6 billion and an operating profit of $418 million. Finally, the third element of the business was to be called ITT Corporation and included the hotels, entertainment and information-services businesses which accounted for sales of $6.5 billion and a projected profit of $875 million. The result of this restructuring was greeted enthusiastically by the stock market which raised the price of ITT shares by 30 per cent in the space of a few months. It was suggested that existing shareholders would get better value from now owning shares in three more clearly defined businesses. Separating out the businesses also would make it easier for the three businesses to get access to the cheapest capital.

In spite of the restructuring some critics believed that the process had not gone far enough. The company still covered a wide area and Mr Araskog found it difficult to decide where ITT's main focus or 'core competence' lay. To take just one example, ITT Corporation covered everything from sports teams (the New York Knicks and NY Rangers) to telephone directories and technical colleges and it was difficult to see where the industrial and commercial logic lay in this 'bundling' of firms.

The concept of 'core competence' has in recent years become very fashionable with a number of companies getting out of non-related businesses and demerging. In the UK, Courtaulds split itself into a textiles company and a chemical one; ICI has also split itself up into two, putting its drug and fertiliser business together to form a new company Zeneca. In addition, Hanson, the archetypal conglomerate, decided to demerge. For years Hanson's business strategy had been to act like an 'antique dealer' in companies, buying up old 'junk' companies in declining industries and by making them more efficient, selling them off at a profit. However, the day before its annual general meeting at the end of January 1996, Hanson, bowing to the pressure to concentrate on its 'core competence', announced that it was splitting up the company in order to acquire greater 'management focus'. It split into four separate quoted companies covering energy (Peabody Coal in the USA and Eastern Electric in the UK), chemicals (SCM in the UK and Quantum in the USA), tobacco (Imperial Tobacco in the UK) and bricks and building materials. City analysts at the time were not altogether surprised by this move as the rise in Hanson's share price has slowed down. For example, in 1995 Hanson's share price fell by 13 per cent while the market rose by 20 per cent. In the early 1990s Hanson's hitherto almost infallible touch as a supreme dealmaker seemed to desert the company. In 1991 ICI beat off a bid by Hanson to take it over and such was the ferocity of ICI's defence that Hanson backed off making high profile deals for a period. A year later in 1992, Hanson was outbid by a much smaller conglomerate for the takeover of RHM. This prompted questions to be asked about whether Hanson had lost its touch. Meanwhile, as indicated above, conglomerates were falling out of favour with investors on both sides of the Atlantic and 'core competence' became the guiding principle for a large number of companies. Hanson had already undergone something of a 'dress rehearsal' for demerging in 1995 with the floating of 34 Hanson businesses in the United States (such as Jacuzzi, Farberware cookware and Tommy Armour golf clubs) to create US Industries. This was clearly a defining moment according to then chief executive Derek Bonham. Talking of the reorganisation of Hanson's USA businesses (following the death of Lord Hanson's partner and right-hand man, Lord White, who handled the USA end of things for Hanson), Bonham said: 'We all knew the logic of what was going on. We learnt a lot from the demerger of USI.'

The way in which Hanson was managed changed when Mr Bonham became the chief executive. Instead of having a kind of arm's length relationship with its subsidiaries and being a 'strategic shaper' to use the Goold and Campbell classification*, Hanson found itself, under Bonham's direction, having to review or approve investment decisions of a large number of small and disparate divisions. The role of the 'centre' thus changed in its relationship with its subsidiaries from being a 'strategic shaper' to being a 'financial controller' with the centre taking on the role of 'banker/shareholder' (for details, see Johnson and Scholes, 1999, especially p. 426). Head office, therefore, was finding it increasingly difficult to assess the underlying performance of electricity and chemical firms in the group and hence making it difficult for Hanson to set realistic financial targets. As time went on it became increasingly difficult for Hanson to continue with its 'antique dealer' philosophy of company acquisitions. Quite simply there were fewer bargains to be found and the competition for buying the remaining 'bargain basement' companies was 'hotting up'. Hanson were not the only company able to spot 'golden nuggets on the compost heap'. The group tried for a while to develop a clear rationale for its strategy but commentators and analysts became unconvinced. As Andrew Campbell of the Ashridge Strategic Group commented: 'They [Hanson] picked out phrases like "energy" or "resources" or "consumer" and tried to stretch them like cling film over businesses that had nothing in common. It made no sense.'

Derek Bonham was only too aware of the problems facing big industrial conglomerates as they became 'dangerously cosy and before you know it they look like industrial museums'.

What the future holds for the separate Hanson companies remains to be seen. Imperial Tobacco (operating profit of £350 million on sales of £780 million) makes all its profit from the British market and it is shortly to acquire new plant which will make it even more efficient. This should make it an attractive acquisition for one of the bigger multinational tobacco companies such as BAT or American Brands. The chemical offshoot is small by international standards, although SCM does have a world leader in a whiting agent known as titanium dioxide. As a separate company it could become an inviting target for a big European or American chemical group. The future for the energy group is a bit more problematic as there is not much 'strategic logic' to a coal company in the USA and a small electricity company in the UK which uses gas as its method of generation! Further demerging is not out of the question.

Even firms that are reluctant to go the whole way to demerging, such as Kodak, have refocused themselves on their core business of 'imaging', and BP has become extremely focused by selling off most of its non-oil business, a policy being adopted by Royal Dutch/Shell. In Germany, Daimler-Benz was convinced at one time that it could achieve 'synergy' by producing freezers as well as aircraft and Volvo is retreating from food, drink and drugs to focus on its core areas of cars and lorries. Therefore, the attraction of having diversified businesses is diminishing. The arguments about the risk diversifying advantages of conglomerates are overplayed in a world where capital markets are increasing in their efficiency. Investors do not need to invest in conglomerates to diversify their risks; they can create a diversified portfolio of their own. Furthermore, breaking up companies helps to unlock value as managers focus their energies and attention on a narrower range of business interests.

Finally, it remains to be seen whether these ideas spell the end for conglomerates. There are still a number of successful conglomerates where the strategic logic and focus are not immediately apparent and yet who remain successful, for example General Electric. And in Asia the conglomerate is alive and well. Companies such as Malaysia's Sime Darby, Thailand's Charoen Pokphand and Taiwan's President Enterprises have their fingers in many pies from food to telecoms. How long they will continue to do so remains to be seen and already there are signs that a new breed of young managers in these companies are beginning to apply the philosophy of 'core competences'. Maybe ITT and Hanson might even become models of the new refocused multinational enterprise.

Notes:
* Goold, M. and Campbell, A., *Strategies and Styles*, Basil Blackwell, Oxford, 1987.
† Johnson, G. and Scholes, K, *Exploring Corporate Strategy*, Prentice Hall, London, 1999.

Based on information from *The Economist*, 17 June 1995 and 3 February 1996.

PAUSE FOR THOUGHT 1

Before you read on and from the cases outlined above, find links with previous chapters of this book. Can you find examples to illustrate how changes in the economic environment (Chapters 2 and 3) or changes to the structure of the economy (Chapter 4) or the way in which firms organised themselves (Chapter 5) have affected or are affected by the changes in corporate strategy indicated? Can you illustrate from the cases the links between a company's strategy and business objectives (Chapter 6), demand (Chapter 7), costs (Chapter 8), prices (Chapter 9) or investment decisions (Chapter 10)?

As can be seen from these examples in Case Study 11.1 some of our largest and best-known companies are having to redefine *the scope of the organisation's activities*. In particular, they are having to examine the way in which the firm is organised. As we saw in Chapter 5, a business can choose a variety of different ways to organise itself depending on the nature of the business, the type of product or service it is providing and the economic environment (both macro and micro) within which it is operating. As the case study illustrates, the environment within which these companies are now operating has changed and they are required to adapt to the new circumstances.

The second characteristic about strategy that Johnson and Scholes (1999) stress is the need to *match the activities of the organisation with the environment in which it operates*. In the 1960s and 1970s conglomerates were thought to be best in the sense that they did not have all their eggs in one basket. Indeed this was their defining strength. They often operated across international frontiers. They were multinational as well as conglomerate. However, as the case study illustrates, the environment changed. It was no longer thought necessary from a shareholder's point of view to diversify risk by investing in conglomerate companies. It also appeared that the phenomenal success that conglomerates enjoyed in terms of the rise in their share price was beginning to flag and companies which had a narrower focus seemed to be enjoying more success. The so-called synergy between different parts of a wide-ranging business did not appear to be taking place and a certain amount of disenchantment with the companies' performance set in. The companies therefore needed to match their resources to the environment within which they were operating.

Thirdly, Johnson and Scholes emphasise that strategy is to do with *matching an organisation's activities to its resources*. As recession hit some of the markets of the big conglomerates so there was a need to reassess the kinds of activities that the companies were engaged in and to decide which parts of the organisation's activities were still adding value. In this regard companies were having to look critically at their objectives and to ensure that the activities they were engaged in were still consistent with these objectives. Here there are strong links with Chapter 6. The emphasis on 'added value' and on the need to squeeze additional value from a company's resources can be regarded as a restatement of the profit maximisation principles outlined in that chapter. As we have seen with the case of BP there is a much greater focus on the 'bottom line', and the recent spate of exercises in 'downsizing' (or 'rightsizing' if one prefers a less pejorative term!) is a reassertion of the importance of profit as recession and increasing competition hit a number of firms.

Fourthly, Johnson and Scholes stress that *strategic decisions should have a major resource implication for the organisation*. Hanson's decision to demerge is therefore a 'defining moment' for the company as it represents a complete reversal of previous strategy and indeed of business philosophy. In the case of ITT, splitting up the main businesses and reorganising them into a more coherent structure has had significant resource implications. For example, a number of the central functions of administration, raising of finance and information technology may have to be duplicated in each of the main divisions. In the case of Hanson, the demerging strategy means that a number of businesses will have to be sold off and to become independent of the Hanson 'umbrella'. As with all umbrellas they provide protection from the bad weather. However, the newly demerged businesses will be required to find their own form of protection from the economic storms ahead by becoming more financially independent.

Fifthly, *strategic decisions affect operational decisions.* The distinction between the two types of decision is important. For example, the decision by BP to focus on more value added activities means that operationally it has to decide whether to operate in the same way as before (see case study on BP and profit maximisation in the appendix to Chapter 6). The strategy of becoming more focused on the oil business means that it no longer regards non-oil activities as a key element of its business. For example, in 1992 BP decided to outsource its finance function and to allow Andersen Consulting to undertake this function on behalf of the company. This was a major departure from established practice in the industry and affected the operation of its finance function in a fairly major way. The strategic decision to become more profit orientated led to significant changes in the operational decisions of the company.

Sixthly, strategy will be affected by *the expectations of those who have power and influence over the organisation's decisions.* In the case of both ITT and Hanson the expectations of the major shareholders played a big part in influencing the decision to demerge and focus on the companies' core competences. Shareholders were becoming disenchanted by the poor performance of these multinational conglomerates after years of spectacular growth in dividends and share prices. A change of leader at the very top of the organisation obviously has an impact on strategy. Indeed, organisations often deliberately choose a new leader to effect just such a radical change in direction. BP after years of continually disappointing results have clearly made just such a decision.

Seventhly, *strategic decisions will affect the long-term direction of the organisation.* In 1996 Nissan in the United States decided to change its marketing strategy. In a bold move, it decided to switch its emphasis from product marketing to brand marketing. Instead of advertising its cars, it decided in a radical departure to market the Nissan name which was not so well known in the United States. Using the tag line 'Life's a journey – enjoy the ride' it produced a two-minute 'Steven Spielberg-influenced' commercial which received its first screening in the US during the televising on American network television of the closing ceremony at the 1996 Olympic Games in Atlanta. It cost $2 million to produce but controversially made no reference at all to any of Nissan's current product range. The gamble was to change people's perceptions about the brand and to link it with what the advertisers perceive to be an American audience's preoccupation with seeking out 'the good life'. Nissan noted that people buy cars primarily because the brand allegedly makes a statement about the individual (BMW – expensive, up-market car for the 'newly arrived' business executive; Volvo – safe, reliable, dependable, middle-class, family car; Skoda – basic, no frills, 'anti-style' car for lower middle-class driver who is not interested in 'image'; VW Beetle – ultimate style icon for young, socially conscious, environmentally aware, upwardly mobile driver), and not principally because they have significant differences in performance or specification. Therefore, the Nissan strategy in the United States in 1997 was to reposition the brand and to give it an air of mystery, excitement and fun. The company was gambling that its $200 million budget would succeed in transforming the company's fortunes in one of the world's most demanding and competitive car markets. The advertising was therefore designed to entertain and amuse rather than necessarily to inform.[1]

These represent the key elements to defining strategy according to the leading writers in the field and as we have seen each of these elements has strong links with the elements of business economics described elsewhere in this textbook. The next section deals with the three key elements of business and corporate strategy.

Corporate strategy: analysis, choice and implementation[2]

There are three stages to understanding how corporate strategy operates. Each stage involves an understanding of the basic business economics of the situation. We will examine each of the stages in detail and link them to areas of business economics. First, we will examine the process of *strategic analysis*. Then we will examine *strategic choice* before concluding briefly with the *implementation of strategy*.

Analysis of the business environment

PEST analysis

In the first stage it is necessary to undertake an analysis of the business environment within which firms operate. To do this it is often necessary to undertake a PEST analysis. This involves examining the Political, Economic, Social and Technological environment within which firms operate. (Some writers refer to the analysis as PESTLE, with 'L' standing for the legal environment and the last 'E' referring to environmental factors such as pollution or destruction of important parts of our eco-systems. However, the present authors prefer to maintain the PEST framework and to consider such factors under the 'political' or 'social' categories.) To illustrate the kind of analysis required let us look at some recent examples in Case Study 11.2.

CASE STUDY **11.2**

PEST and multinationals

In deciding to set up business in a third world country, large multinational enterprises are increasingly having to undertake a detailed PEST analysis. (For more details of the reasons for firms becoming multinational see pages 331–5.) In the past, the multinational firms enjoyed unrivalled power over third world governments, especially in industries like oil and mining. The third world governments were often keen to attract foreign companies because they promised economic prosperity and a 'quick fix' of economic development for the underdeveloped country concerned. The MNEs held all the trump cards in so far as they possessed the technology and had access to the relevant markets. In addition, it was very attractive for the MNE to locate in third world countries because very often the rules and regulations governing the operations of business were fairly rudimentary. In other words, the political, economic, social and technological environment was very favourable to large MNEs operating in third world countries.

Not any more. Protesters have recently demonstrated against a number of companies and have been so successful that these companies have been forced to either abandon their previous strategies or modify them substantially.

Some recent examples emphasise the importance of undertaking a full PEST analysis before deciding on a strategy (or on the consequences of failing to take these factors into account in the first place).

➤ Unocal in the United States has encountered protests from political activists about its involvement (with Total in France) in an offshore gas field development in Myanmar (formerly Burma). The regime is being criticised for its poor record on human rights and for its flagrant violation of democratic rights. Carlsberg and Heineken have also pulled out of Myanmar.

➤ RTZ-CRA, which is a British company and the world's leading mining group, and Freeport-McMoRan, an American firm, are under attack from environmentalists for their involvement in a gold and copper mine operation in Irian Jaya, Indonesia. Although the company's financial performance was significantly better than in previous years, RTZ-CRA's last AGM was dominated by press reports of the protests of the tribespeople who turned up to disrupt proceedings.

➤ Royal Dutch/Shell had a miserable time in 1996 at the hands of protesters. Greenpeace and Shell clashed over the disposal of the Brent Spar oil platform and Shell was forced to back down in fairly humiliating circumstances over its original plans to dispose of the platform. It now appears that no oil company wants to be the next one to propose that one of its platforms is disposed of at sea. According to Richard LeCoyte of Greenpeace: 'There is a race [among the oil companies] to come second.' As if this was not bad enough protesters made huge political capital over Shell's relationship with the Nigerian government in the wake of the execution of nine political dissidents.

➤ Following a serious accident in a mine in Guyana which resulted in a serious spill of cyanide into the rivers, two American mining companies, Cambior and Golden Star Resources, came under relentless pressure from environmental groups.

➤ Finally, in Malaysia, ABB Asea Brown Boveri, a Swiss-based multinational, was the subject of widespread protests from environmentalists about its alleged destruction of the Malaysian rainforests.

To a large extent the multinationals have only got themselves to blame for this state of affairs. In order to show that they were not simply the greedy, money grabbing, economic imperialists that left-wing critics liked to portray them, a large number of MNEs have drawn up codes of ethics and signed international business charter-type agreements laying down certain ethical principles. This has made good commercial sense in that it has often 'spiked the guns' of environmental critics. It has also helped to reassure third world governments that they were dealing with responsible companies who had a clear understanding of their wider responsibilities. If, as sometimes appears to be the case, they fall short of these much trumpeted ideals, they should not be surprised if their critics have a 'field day'.

In addition, the groups that have traditionally been the MNEs' harshest critics have become extremely sophisticated in their campaigns. Greenpeace can no longer be dismissed as a bunch of cranks and their handling of the media in the Brent Spar incident showed that they have become extremely professional. Greenpeace, for example, now has offices in 33 countries including Latin America and Eastern Europe. Global communication means that MNEs' activities in previously remote locations are no longer 'out of sight' and, as some of the examples above illustrate, it is not beyond the resources of some environmental groups to transport the victims of so-called environmental crimes to the AGMs of the leading companies in order to extract the maximum political advantage. Protest groups are also using all the latest means of communication to spread their message. In South East Asia, for example, groups co-ordinate their activities using e-mail and the Internet.

In addition MNEs can no longer just shrug off the effects of the bad publicity as a 'storm in a teacup'. It was widely reported (and acknowledged by the company itself) that the possibility of a European boycott of Shell's products prompted the company to re-examine its policy on disposal of the Brent Spar platform. More recently, the state of Massachusetts in the United States has banned contracts with firms doing business in Myanmar.

All this means that the MNEs have to take account of the political and social dimensions involved in their strategies as well as the economic and technological aspects. Indeed, to ignore the first two is to put at risk the economic and financial benefits of these strategies. As one senior manager at Shell has indicated, they would have to 'think very carefully' before investing any further in Nigeria. Shell have already learned the recent lessons and are involving Greenpeace and Amnesty International in discussions on future strategy so that they can anticipate problems and try to accommodate protesters' fears rather than simply react to criticisms after the event. Shell are also paying more attention to the needs of indigenous tribes in the more remote parts of the world where the company is operating. In May 1996 before signing a deal with the Peruvian government to develop a gas field, Shell met and discussed the implications of the development with local tribespeople. Where once major multinational companies saw local political, social and environmental problems as the responsibility of the host government, they are now viewing these problems as their responsibility. This represents a significant sea-change in the way large multinational companies formulate strategy from the most recent past.

Adapted from *The Economist*, 20 July 1996.

Questions

1   What powers do host governments have to influence multinational companies to adopt 'good practice' as far as the environment is concerned?
2   Should multinational companies ever invest in countries with a poor record on human rights or who flout basic democratic rights?

Porter's 'five forces' analysis

In addition to undertaking a PEST analysis it is also necessary to undertake a structural analysis of the industry to gauge the strengths and weaknesses of the opposition and also to determine the competitive structure of a given market. One of the most utilised models for this type of structural analysis is Porter's 'five forces' model which has been developed by Michael Porter of Harvard University. Figure 11.1 outlines the main elements of his model (Porter, 1985, 1988).

This analysis relies very heavily on basic business economic concepts, which is perhaps not really all that surprising as Porter is an economist who has become one of the world's leading writers on business strategy.

The key elements in Porter's 'five forces' analysis allow us to make an assessment of the competitive structure of a given market and are a vital component in analysing the environment within which a firm operates. These can be identified as:

Figure 11.1
Competitive forces

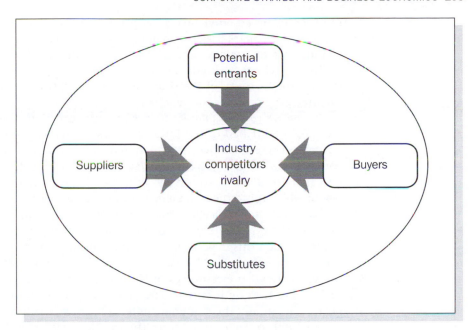

Source: Porter, M. E. (1985, 1988)

1 The threat of potential entrants.
2 The threat of substitutes.
3 The power of suppliers.
4 The power of buyers.
5 The degree of competitive rivalry.

First, let us look at the *threat of potential entrants*. The threat of new entrants coming into an industry depends on the barriers to entry. Barriers to entry, according to business economic principles, depend in turn on seven key factors which may be identified as follows:

1 Economies of scale.
2 Capital requirements of entry.
3 Access to distribution channels.
4 Cost advantages (sometimes referred to as incumbent advantages).
5 Expected reaction of existing firms.
6 Legislative intervention.
7 Differentiation of the product.

In some industries the economies of scale are such that firms need to be extremely large in order to be able to compete. This is particularly true of such markets as car and aircraft production as well as the pharmaceutical industry which require a huge investment in research and development.

PAUSE FOR THOUGHT 2 *Can you identify a number of other industries in which economies of scale play a significant part and which may act as a deterrent to enter new markets?*

The *capital costs* of entering retailing or of providing a home decorating service are clearly much less than those of entering the personal computer market or of setting up an ethylene cracker plant! Until recently it was also difficult to enter the beer market as the major brewers had *exclusive access to distribution* channels via tied public houses which meant that any new beer would find it difficult to gain access to the market. The Monopolies and Mergers Commission realised the inequity of the situation and forced the major brewers to divest themselves of a number of their 'pubs'.

Incumbent cost advantages often refer to the experience gained by firms who are long established in the industry. These firms have advantages over new entrants. The established firms may have the suppliers tied up in long-term contracts or they may have negotiated exclusive deals with a number of important retail outlets. Alternatively, they may have trained up a pool of skilled labour which it is difficult for a new firm to acquire in the short run.

The reaction of competitors may well deter new entrants. If it is well known, for example, that established firms will defend their market position by slashing prices then this may deter all but the most determined firms from entering the market. Rupert Murdoch's entry into satellite television required him to use virtually all the resources of News Corporation to go on sustaining the early losses that he incurred. The 'deep pockets' of News Corporation very nearly ran out and the venture required a massive financial restructuring package in 1990 to keep Murdoch in the satellite television business. However, what this demonstrated was that Murdoch and the News Corporation were not going to be deterred by the exceptionally high costs of entry and this gave a very clear signal to other potential entrants that they too would need to be prepared to spend millions of pounds to become a key player in this industry. British Airways was accused of 'dirty tricks' by a number of competitors, in particular Richard Branson of Virgin Atlantic when Virgin threatened to take a significant share of the transatlantic market. This was almost a re-run of the situation in the 1980s when the established airlines slashed their fares on the transatlantic routes and put Sir Freddie Laker's airline out of business.

Governments can dramatically change the competitive environment by legislation either by protecting state monopolies or by deregulating their activities through privatisation (see Chapter 12). In August 1996, the UK government suspended the Post Office's exclusive right to deliver letters charged at less than £1. The suspension was meant to give the Post Office a clear signal that the government was not prepared to tolerate a string of 24-hour stoppages and was contemplating opening up the market to private operators, a number of whom were already offering a mail delivery service.

Finally, firms can prevent entry by *product differentiation*, a tactic that has been employed successfully by the major soap detergent manufacturers, such as Unilever and Procter & Gamble.

PAUSE FOR THOUGHT 3 | *Identify as many different brands of washing powder as you can and indicate who the manufacturer is. Why do so few companies require so many different brands?*

All these factors come together to either increase or decrease the barriers to entry and hence to decrease or increase the threat of potential entrants.

Secondly, *the threat of substitutes* can alter the competitive environment within which firms operate. A new process or product may render an existing product useless. National Cash Register in Dundee was effectively finished with the advent of the silicon chip as virtually overnight electronic cash registers replaced the old-fashioned mechanical cash registers of the 1970s.

Case Study 11.3 illustrates the problems faced by one major company as the availability of substitutes made significant inroads into its market.

CASE STUDY **11.3**   **The threat of substitutes – Nintendo fights back**

In July 1996 Nintendo launched its new video game, the Nintendo 64. This was something of a 'make-or-break' decision in order to restore Nintendo's fortunes which had taken a dramatic slump since the dizzy heights of the late 1980s when the company was making more money than all the Hollywood studios put together. Nintendo suffered from a surfeit of substitute products which left it standing. Its sales suffered when Sega Enterprises seized the initiative in 1994 and launched a 32-bit game player called Saturn that had all sorts of clever graphics. As if that was not enough Sony entered the market with an even more exciting 32-bit machine called the PlayStation. The initial price for these two attractive rivals was ¥40,000 (or about £280) and although this was considered expensive Sega and Sony had little difficulty in stealing market share from Nintendo to such an extent that Sega overtook Nintendo's sales turnover, reaching ¥384 billion for the year ending March 1996. Sony's PlayStation contributed ¥195 billion to the company's Y4.6 trillion global revenue in 1997. Nintendo's new machine offered 64-bit memory and graphics described by industry watchers as 'dazzling', and in prelaunch trials it was claimed that games-hardened teenagers were agog at the effects created by the classic Super Mario played on the new 64-bit 'platform'. At this time Nintendo had a technological edge and its pricing reflected this short-term advantage. The new 64 retailed in Japan at ¥25,000 (£175) and it was said that the 64 was simply 'walking out the door' at that price with 300,000 sold in the first day alone. Industry analysts expected Nintendo to sell around 5 million machines by March 1997, by which time they would also be selling in the United States and Europe as well. Sega and Sony responded aggressively by slashing their prices. Sony reduced the price of its PlayStation from ¥24,800 to ¥19,800 (£174 to £139) and Sega immediately followed suit. It was thought that within a year Nintendo would have had to do the same and bring its price down to ¥20,000 (£140). As *The Economist* put it: 'the battle for the trigger fingers of 14-year-olds everywhere is set to become more brutal' (3 August 1996, p. 61).

It was also clear that the new competitive environment would have some casualties. Some of the smallest video game makers such as NEC and Sanyo, it was thought, would be forced to drop out. Even Sony and Sega would only be able to survive by making up the inevitable losses they would be forced to take by making profits from the sales of the games that run on their 'platforms'. The big problem that Nintendo had was that it did not possess the 'software' or games to show off its 64-bit memory and processing power to best effect. In addition, its first games were priced at ¥9,800 (£70) compared with ¥5,800 (£40) for the top-of-the-range Sega and Sony games. Because it was extremely complex to program new games for the Nintendo 64-bit machine and because of increasing competition from traditional PC machines as opposed to the games machine market, Nintendo found it difficult to plug this gap quickly. So not only had the environment for the games 'platforms' been transformed in recent years, so also had the market for the games themselves.

In August 2000 Nintendo moved to reassert its position by releasing details of its new games console, the GameCube, its replacement for the Nintendo 64. The new, smaller machine, which will offer 'superlative graphics and internet access', will only be available in July 2001 in Japan and October 2001 in the United States and Europe.

The GameCube, which is only the size of a shoebox, will play smaller, 3 inch (8 cm) game discs, and have an infrared, wireless television connection. Unlike the new Sony PlayStation2, it will not be able to play DVDs. Nintendo also revealed details of its new GameBoy Advance, a new version of its popular hand-held games console. It will have a new 32-bit graphics chip, eight times faster than the GameBoy, and a liquid crystal screen 50 per cent larger. The new GameBoy, which will be compatible with existing games, will be available in March 2001 in Japan and retail at approximately $90. Nintendo will also offer adapters to allow game playing via mobile phones. The launch of the new GameCube machine, originally code-named Dolphin and scheduled for Christmas 2000, was delayed by difficulties in obtaining enough computer chips, disappointing software makers.

The video game market, which is now reckoned to be larger than the movie industry, has been the subject of intense competition in recent years. Analysts said that Nintendo would secure its dominant position in the hand-held market, where it has sold more than 100 million units world wide. But it would have more difficulty in competing with industry heavyweights Sony and Microsoft in the video console market.

Sony, whose PlayStation has sold 73 million units, has already launched PlayStation2 in Japan, and plans to bring out the new console in Europe and America on 26 October. Rival Sega launched its Dreamcast one year ago, and Microsoft is planning to bring out its X-Box games console in the autumn of 2001.

Nintendo does have one advantage – its popular characters like Mario, Zelda and Pokemon, which particularly appeal to younger age groups. 'They still have a huge hold on the little kiddy market', said Zachary Liggett of WestLB Panmure in Tokyo. 'Those who are going to survive and really bang it out on the hardware market are Nintendo, Sony and Microsoft.'

Analysts believe that Nintendo was wise to stick to its strategy of being a games maker, and not try to directly challenge market heavyweights in building general home electronics devices. 'We don't have the motive of spreading our machines to the public so they will be later used as multipurpose audio-visual machines', said Genyo Takeda, who oversees research at Nintendo. 'We aimed for the best possible machine for playing games.'

Based on information from *The Economist*, 3 August 1996 and BBC News, 24 August 2000.

Questions

1 How would you describe the structure of this particular market?
2 What pricing strategy do you think is appropriate for this product?
3 Do you think that Nintendo can recapture the 'dizzy heights' it reached in the late 1980s?

Buyer and supplier power are also likely to have a significant effect on the competitive environment. As the Nintendo case illustrates, the 'suppliers' of the games are now in something of a strong bargaining position as the big companies attempt to produce ever more sophisticated games for their ever more powerful machines. The PC machine makers are also looking to software companies to supply them with the software that will help sell their machines, so the suppliers in this market have undoubtedly seen their market power increase in recent years and the prognosis is that it will increase even further. Another good example of the shift in bargaining power between manufacturers and distributors in recent years has been the brewing industry as Case Study 11.4 illustrates.

CASE STUDY **11.4** Supplier power – the case of the flat beer

The major brewers of beer used to enjoy considerable bargaining power in relation to the tied pubs. However, the Monopolies and Mergers Commission ruling in 1986 on tied pubs loosened the power of the brewers. For example, in 1986, 58 per cent of pubs were tied but by 1994 only 33 per cent were. The growth of the independent pub has put bargaining power into the hands of the pubs which is forcing rival brewers to compete for their business. We are also drinking less beer in our pubs as they transform themselves from traditional male beer-drinking establishments to becoming more family-orientated eating places complete with 'Bouncy Castles' . The growth in the sale of soft drinks and alcoholic alternatives to beer is also having an effect on the way pubs are viewed.

However, such has been the change in the bargaining power between the brewers and the pubs that the brewers have been forced to cut costs by seeking to make economies of scale, hence the logic behind the bid by Bass (market share 23 per cent) for Carlsberg-Tetley (market share 16 per cent) owned by Allied-Domecq. In addition, the second strategy of the brewers in the face of this switch in bargaining power has been to diversify into other retailing and leisure businesses such as hotels and restaurants. Whitbread, Britain's fourth largest brewer, for example, bought Pelican, a restaurant business. Scottish and Newcastle, which probably concentrates more heavily on brewing than other brewers, earns only a third of its profits from selling beer. The remainder comes from holiday resorts such as Center Parcs and Pontins. Allied-Domecq sold off Carlsberg-Tetley in order to reduce its dependency on beer and earns most of its profits from spirits, which account for 64 per cent of its profits, and food sales such as Dunkin' Donuts and Baskin Robbins ice cream which last year accounted for 28 per cent of its profits. Beer was therefore 'small beer' as far as its contribution to overall profits was concerned.

Adapted from *The Economist*, 3 August 1996.

Questions

1 Given the competitive environment now faced by the brewers, outline the two main strategies they are adopting and explain the rationale behind each.
2 What are the dangers of each of these strategies in your opinion?

CASE STUDY **11.5** Buyer power and supermarkets

In 1999 there was an investigation by the competition authorities into the way the supermarkets conducted their business. At the time of going to press the final report of this enquiry has yet to be published. However, the Competition Commission was looking at the power of suppliers and buyers as part of their enquiry. The following is an extract from the Competition Commission's Web page which highlights some of these issues and the proposed remedies.

1   *Competition Commission's areas of concern about the relationship of super-markets with suppliers*

The Commission has received evidence from both supermarkets and suppliers on their commercial relationships. It will wish to discuss whether supermarkets have excessive buying power or not, and if so, whether this:

(a)   lowers the price of products to consumers;

(b)   prevents efficient suppliers from earning a reasonable return;

(c)   leads to higher prices than otherwise of products sold by suppliers to other retailers;

(d)   damages the longer-term competitiveness of the grocery supply base, or some parts of it, in the UK; and

(e)   reduces consumer choice.

In particular, because the great majority of groceries are bought from supermarkets, fair and reasonable access to supermarket shelves may often be a precondition for an efficient supplier to survive and prosper. The Commission will therefore wish to focus specifically on the terms and conditions governing access to supermarket shelves and whether these are in any way unfairly discriminatory, either as between different suppliers or as between supermarkets' own-label products and those of other suppliers.

2   *Competition Commission's suggested solutions to the relations of supermarkets with suppliers*

In the event of any adverse findings in this area, the purpose of remedies would be to ensure no unreasonable use of excessive buying power, which might distort competition and which might in turn restrict consumer choice. This could occur through unreasonable terms, charges or costs being imposed on suppliers such that, for some at least, their competitiveness was adversely affected.

One possible solution to any such problems would be the drawing up of a code of practice governing such relationships to ensure that any supermarket found to have exploited excessive buyer power should no longer do so. Options include a voluntary code being issued by the supermarkets; an agreed code being established, using the good offices of one or more respected industry bodies; or the supermarkets being required to comply with a code drawn up by the competition authorities. The means of enforcement of a code would be a significant element in any such remedy. Here again the Commission invites views on whether the Director General of Fair Trading (DGFT) might monitor adherence to the code in the context of his powers under the 1998 Competition Act.

In general terms such a code would be designed to ensure that suppliers should have a reasonable degree of certainty as to the price they will receive (or the factors which can subsequently alter the price) when they accept orders; should not be required to vary the terms on which they are trading with supermarkets without reasonable notice, though the latter is likely to depend heavily on the nature of the products concerned; and should not face unreasonable or discriminatory trading terms or conditions.

In a properly functioning market, competition should ensure that these conditions are normally met. If the Commission were to conclude that excessive buyer power was inhibiting this and that a code of practice was required then its content might need to be quite specific. To assist those wishing to comment, the Commission has compiled a list of possible terms for inclusion in such a code, but reiterates that the list does not imply that any activities of any UK supermarkets have been found to be against the public interest:

(i) requiring reasonable notice (a) of any variation in the terms and conditions of supply (this to cover both standard terms and conditions of business and the terms of individual contracts, whether written or oral) and (b) of any requirement or invitation to contribute to the cost of promotions;

(ii) requiring reimbursement of costs imposed on suppliers as a result of variations of the terms and conditions of supply by supermarkets for which reasonable notice is not given;

(iii) prohibiting discrimination against suppliers because they are not prepared to participate in or contribute to certain promotions;

(iv) prohibition on supermarkets requesting or insisting that suppliers give them discounts from previously agreed prices other than where the basis for this has been identified and agreed in advance;

(v) prohibition on any penalty charges, fines or additional discounts for failure by suppliers to meet quality specifications, delivery quantity or times, etc., where the method of determining the payment is not agreed in writing in advance;

(vi) prohibition of any discrimination in the quality standards required as between one supplier and another for the same product;

(vii) no financial contributions to any third parties to be required or invited;

(viii) exclusive supply arrangements to contain identifiable benefits for suppliers to compensate for the restriction on their trading, and reasonable termination notice given to reflect this restriction;

(ix) agreeing with suppliers at the outset of a contractual relationship whether the cost of supplier audits by supermarkets are to be paid by the supplier, and means for ensuring that such costs are not excessive;

(x) no supplier to be given control of access to, or management of, supermarket shelf space;

(xi) listing fees, shelf access fees or other non-performance-related fees, or more generally fees payable as a condition for stocking, ordering or displaying products to be prohibited. Alternatively any such fees to be chargeable only where the supermarket subsequently guarantees to take a reasonable minimum supply of products. In the case of listing fees these might be required not to exceed the identifiable cost of assessing a supplier's suitability;

(xii) no interference with suppliers' other business activities, including prices charged by suppliers to other retailers;

(xiii) all arrangements with third parties involved in the supply of complementary goods or services, e.g. packaging or transport, to be transparent and agreed with the product supplier at the outset, in particular including any charges made by supermarkets to third parties which the latter might seek to reclaim from the supplier;

(xiv) prohibition of credit terms beyond a specific limit, e.g. 30 days or, alternatively, prohibition of credit terms which unreasonably discriminate between suppliers, or both.

Source: http://www.competition-commission.org.uk

Questions

1 From the *supermarkets*' point of view, what are the advantages and disadvantages of their buyer power?

2 From the *consumers*' point of view, what are the advantages and disadvantages of the supermarkets' buyer power?

3 From the *suppliers*' point of view, what are the advantages and disadvantages of the supermarkets' buyer power?

4 How would you evaluate the Commission's proposed remedies if it should be found that supermarkets are exercising monopsony (buyer) power?

Finally, *the extent of rivalry* between firms can influence the competitive environment within which firms operate. Rivalry is influenced by many of the things we have already discussed, such as the extent of the barriers to entry, the threat of potential entrants, and the availability of substitutes. It also depends on the number of firms in the marketplace, their relative market share and the extent of their interdependence. Case Study 11.6 illustrates the extent to which competitive rivalry influences the market for a product that barely existed before 1994.

CASE STUDY **11.6** **Competitive rivalry – the Navigator and the Explorer**

In 1994, a new company called Netscape was set up by Marc Andreessen, a young software engineer, and Jim Clark. In the space of two years it had distributed 38 million copies of its Internet 'browser' called the Navigator, a software package for negotiating your way around the millions of sites on the Internet. Without a 'browser' it is impossible to 'surf the Net'. The company had risen from nowhere to have a stock market valuation at the beginning of 1996 of around $6 billion and in the process made Andreessen and Clark extremely wealthy men. The astonishing rise of this previously little known company was a surprise given that the industry giants such as Microsoft pride themselves in being at the leading edge of new developments. It is fair to say that Microsoft was caught out by the speed of the developments in the Internet and, like IBM before it, found itself fixated by what it had previously made its reputation on. A number of analysts predicted that this was the beginning of the end for Microsoft in an industry with notoriously short product life-cycles. The barriers to entry into the software market are not particularly high and do not depend on access to expensive capital equipment. Thus Netscape was able to 'steal' a lucrative market from under the nose of Bill Gates and Microsoft and a number of industry watchers could not resist pointing out the irony of Gates being 'out-Gated' by a small software company in much the same way as he himself had taken on and defeated IBM.

In August 1996 Microsoft launched its answer, the Internet Explorer (version 3.0), a package which can do just as much as Netscape's Navigator, and battle was on for what is seen as the crucial market for 'Web browsers'. Netscape's 85 per cent market share was under serious threat and its stock market valuation fell dramatically.

All this is quite remarkable for a product which both companies give away for nothing! 'Browsers' are a classic loss-leader and the companies make their money not from the browsers but by selling 'server' software and services to people who run the web sites. These people are prepared to pay for this service simply because of the all-pervasiveness of the software. Thus to have dominance in this market is to open up a veritable treasure trove of other sources of revenue as more and more companies use the Internet to market and advertise their own products and services. Hence the need to convince the market that your 'browser' is the industry standard. Netscape, by stealing a march on Microsoft, was in danger of doing just that; hence Microsoft's retaliation.

The ferocity of Microsoft's onslaught began to become apparent. Bill Gates signed a series of deals with leading Internet-access companies to give their subscribers the Microsoft Explorer browser. These companies include American Online, Compuserve and of course Microsoft's own Microsoft Network. In addition, if you take the Explorer as the preferred browser, Microsoft will guarantee free access to a number of services for which consumers currently have to pay using the Navigator, such as the Wall Street Journal web site (currently costing $49 or £33 per annum which in effect Microsoft will pay). The really bad news for Netscape was that Microsoft has the best distribution channel of all – its own Microsoft operating software which is installed in just about every new PC. In 1996 Microsoft shipped over 46 million copies of its Microsoft Windows 95 which included the new Internet Explorer and it was planned that future versions of Windows would have the browser built in, eliminating the entire concept of a stand-alone browser programme, thereby threatening Netscape's very existence.

Thus Bill Gates moved in for a 'kill' rather than a knockout blow and by raising the stakes had also made it less likely that another new entrant would want to enter the Internet browser market. As Martin Haeberli, Netscape's director of technology, said at the time: 'Microsoft can afford to buy market share. We can argue about the fairness of that approach, but we can't compete in the same way.'

However, in 1999 the anti-trust authorities in the United States intervened and in a controversial verdict concluded that Microsoft's tactics were anti-competitive and ordered the company to be split up. In the meantime, Netscape, in order to survive, lost its independence to AOL, America's biggest online Internet service provider, in a takeover. AOL now provides all its customers with a free Netscape browser.

Based on information from *The Economist*, 29 June 1996 and 17 August 1996.

Questions

1 What advantages did Netscape have over Microsoft in 1997?
2 How did Netscape respond to the strategies of Microsoft?
3 How would you describe the structure of this market and what other factors could play a significant part in the way this market develops? (*Hint*: try a PEST analysis for Microsoft and Netscape.)
4 Were the anti-trust authorities right to intervene and order the break-up of Microsoft in your view? (*Hint*: you might like to visit a number of websites which will help you with this question; for example, try Microsoft's own web page at www.microsoft.com for the company's view. For a more objective view visit http://knowledge.wharton.upenn.edu/articles.cfm?catid=9&articleid=108 for views on whether the proposed remedies are a good idea.)

The Boston matrix

Having used the PEST framework to examine the environment in which the firm operates and also having looked at the competitive structure of the industry using Porter's 'five forces' analysis, we now complete the strategic analysis

Figure 11.2
Growth/share matrix

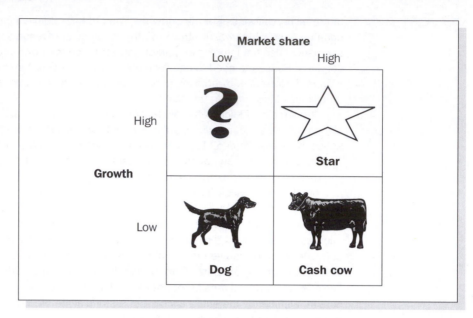

by examining the organisation's own competitive position. The most frequently employed framework for the analysis is the Boston Consulting Group's Growth/Share Matrix. Figure 11.2 gives the key elements of the model.

The organisation's portfolio of products or services is subjected to a detailed analysis according to two criteria. First, there is *market share of the organisation*. What percentage share of the market for each activity does the company possess? Is it high or low? Does it dominate the market in a way which makes its products almost an industry standard? Secondly, there is the *growth of the market as a whole*. Are the firm's products being sold in a fast-growing market? Or is the market a mature one with little evidence of growth? Each of these dimensions then can give rise to a fourfold classification.

➤ *The star*: Products or services in this category have high market share in a fast-growing market.
➤ *The cash cow*: Products or services in this category have a high market share in a slow-growing and mature market. They are very often the products and services for which the company is best known but from which the directors and senior managers are most reluctant to move away.
➤ *The problem child or query (?)*: Products or services in this category have the potential to become stars because they are in a high-growth market but have yet to establish market share. They need to have some care and attention devoted to them, for there is a danger that unless market share can be realised the market growth rate will eventually decline and the product or service will be transformed into a dog.
➤ *The dog*: This is a product or a service which is in a low (or no) growth market and for which the company has only a minimal share of the market. The company should get out of such markets and use the resources elsewhere.

PAUSE FOR THOUGHT 4 *Look back over the case studies outlined in this chapter so far and identify stars, dogs, cash cows and queries from the companies listed.*

Strategic choice

Porter's generic strategies

In discussing the strategic choices open to a firm we need to look at the work of Michael Porter (1980). Porter comes from an economics background and a lot of his recommendations are based on economic principles already encountered in this book. Writing in his pioneering book on *Competitive Strategy*, he identified three generic strategies open to firms. These are:

1 Cost leadership.
2 Differentiation.
3 Focus.

Cost leadership is described by Porter as requiring aggressive investment in efficient plant and machinery, tight cost controls avoiding taking on marginal high cost customers, cost minimisation in areas such as research and development, and advertising. Cost reduction becomes the dominant theme of the company's strategy and he quotes a number of firms in the United States, for example Texas Instruments, Black & Decker and Du Pont, for whom this was the key strategy in their success. The manufacturing process is simplified and economies of scale are sought. Higher value added is sought from the aggressive pursuit of cost reductions.

Differentiation stresses the revenue side and attempts to create something unique in the product. Using the concept of elasticity of demand, which was discussed in Chapter 7, the firm is attempting to make its demand inelastic so that it can charge a higher premium price. As Porter indicates: 'Differentiation provides insulation against competitive rivalry because of brand loyalty by customers and *resulting lower sensitivity to price*' [emphasis added].[3] This lowering of sensitivity to price is no more than the concept of elasticity restated. Differentiation can take many forms: for example, products can be differentiated by design through technology, or customer service or in the size and depth of its dealer network. In many ways the differentiation strategy may mean that market share targets are forgone in order to establish niche markets.

The final generic strategy described by Porter is called *focus* and involves elements of both. The key point about this strategy is that it is focused on a particular target market and serves their needs either by reducing cost or by differentiation. For example, a company may decide to serve only a few large customers and design its products to suit their individual needs, or design a product range specifically to meet the requirements of one market. This could be the case with a food distributor, for example, who decides to serve the fast food market and to limit its supply network to meeting the needs of the biggest four or five fast food companies. This would emphasise both the cost reduction aspects (they would stock only a limited range of products, not a complete range) and at the same time differentiate themselves from the usual food distributors by becoming known as the fast food's main distributor.

The main point about Porter's generic strategies is that it links in with the basic profit maximisation model which is outlined in Chapter 6. Although not made explicit in Porter's book, the strategies emphasise the revenue side (differentiation) and the cost side (cost leadership), the aim being to maximise the difference between the two. This is not to deny that other objectives may intervene and play their part. But the model of generic strategies can be seen as an extension of the basic profit maximisation objective.

The strategy clock

One model which has proved useful in discussing strategy is the strategy clock. This is set out in Figure 11.3. As can be seen, the two dimensions of strategy are identified as 'Quality' and 'Price'. It is the combination of these two dimensions which gives the company its competitive edge. The *perceived value* of the product or service is critical. It is not simply a matter of 'building in' additional features into the product in the hope of enhancing quality. The consumers must value these added features and what is more important be prepared to pay a premium price for them. In some cases in markets which are sensitive to price it may work in the opposite direction. Customers may not want to pay a higher price and prefer a 'cheap and cheerful option'. In terms of the strategic clock this strategy can be identified as 'route 1'. A good example of this type of strategy is provided by the case of easyJet. In the summer of 1996 a small airline was set up in the UK offering cheap flights to London. On one route from Aberdeen to London easyJet's price of £34 single was less than a third of the price of other scheduled airlines. The service was very basic (no inflight meals, which the company regarded as usually of a poor standard in any case and not much valued by customers). There was little spent on expensive corporate identifica-

Figure 11.3
Strategy clock

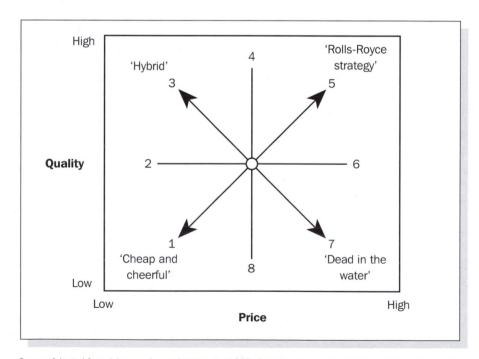

Source: Adapted from Johnson, G. and Scholes, K. (1997) *Exploring Corporate Strategy*, Prentice-Hall, London.

tion. For example, the cabin staff wore tee-shirts and jeans supplied by a local Benetton store! The airport that they used was Luton where the landing charges were less than at the more popular airports. This was clearly the cheap and cheerful strategy identified by route 1.

At the opposite end of the spectrum a company may choose a much more focused strategy where it charges its customers a premium price for a custom made 'Rolls Royce' service. This is known as focused differentiation in the jargon and is demonstrated as route 5 in the strategic clock. In terms of air travel this would be the equivalent of travelling Executive class on a transatlantic flight in Concorde. The premium price charged on the ticket reflects the value that consumers put on comfort and speed at this end of the market. In this context British Airways have a unique competitive advantage as they are one of the few airlines to possess a supersonic aircraft. The segment of the market they are aiming at is that part of the market which puts a premium on the three hours saved in a typical transatlantic flight and this is usually identified as the business market.

| **PAUSE FOR THOUGHT 5** | **1** *Can you identify other examples of companies that pursue strategies identified as route 1 and route 5 of the strategy clock?* |
| | **2** *Before reading on, what are the advantages and disadvantages of the 'hybrid strategy' identified as route 3 of the strategy clock?* |

There are of course intermediate positions between route 1, the 'cheap and cheerful' route, and the more focused upmarket route 5. These are known as 'hybrid' strategies and combine the elements of both price and value. Sainsbury's have a slogan which attempts to capture this strategy. 'Good Food Costs Less at Sainsbury's' is the tag line they use to sum up this strategy. On the face of it this may seem in some ways the best strategy as the company appears to be having the best of both worlds, namely a quality service at a cheap price. This, however, will only work if the company can sustain this price advantage. If, for example, other companies simply follow the same strategy and also cut their prices then the competitive advantage is eroded. There is no sustainable competitive edge. On the other hand, if a retailer has some advantage in terms of the use of technology to deliver large quantities of foodstuff to its retail outlets at speeds and in quantities that allow it to gain from the kind of economies of scale which its competitors cannot match, then it will have a sustainable competitive advantage. Unfortunately, it appears that in the retail sector in 1996 there is very heavy discounting, particularly in the food lines, and there is some doubt about the ability of a company like Sainsbury's to sustain its competitive advantage if it becomes 'stuck in the middle'. Thus the middle ground implied by the 'hybrid' strategy may not be the safe haven that it at first appears as companies in this position may find themselves under attack from both ends of the market spectrum (see Case Study 11.7).

CASE STUDY **11.7** New universities stuck in the middle?

In 1996, the government set up a committee under the chairmanship of Sir Ron Dearing to examine the funding of higher education in the UK. The problem of funding had become particularly acute with the expansion of higher education in the early 1990s. In 1992, for example, there was an increase in the number of new universities as the former polytechnics in England and Wales and a number of Central Institutions in Scotland were granted university status. These newer universities focused more on teaching than on research, which was the area where the older and more traditional universities had their strengths. In addition, there was increasing competition from the further education sector, which traditionally had run sub-degree courses only. This sector began to develop degree level work, often in collaboration with the newer universities, involving, for example, franchising out degree programmes to further education colleges. These could often be delivered at a fraction of the cost of degree programmes in the university sector. Meanwhile, as part of the lobbying process, those older traditional universities who already had a strong research base were pressing for a more selective approach to the distribution of research funding. Thus some of the newer universities, it was argued, were in danger of being 'stuck in the middle' and being squeezed at both ends of the spectrum (i.e. in teaching at one end and research at the other). There was also the possibility of some universities augmenting their income by charging additional fees to students and, by 1997, 20 universities were warning students in their prospectuses of this possibility. This would, for the first time, introduce an element of 'price competition' with the more popular universities able to charge a premium price for those courses where there was a heavy demand.

Questions

1   In terms of the strategy clock outlined above, what strategies would you advise the head of a new university to adopt? What are the advantages and disadvantages of each?

2   If the further education colleges are potential competitors, what is to be gained by collaborating with them?

The product/market matrix

Another alternative framework for looking at strategic choices facing a firm is the product/market matrix, which deals with three situations:

1   Related developments.
2   Related diversification.
3   Unrelated diversification.

Figure 11.4 outlines the options open to a company based on the matrix. In the cell identified as 'Present Market' and 'Present Product' the firm has three choices. It can decide to *withdraw* from that market altogether, *consolidate* its position or aim to achieve a greater market *penetration*. Each of these strategies needs to be carefully weighed up with an analysis of the costs and the benefits. Sometimes the greatest difficulty a company has is withdrawing from a market, especially one with which it has been closely identified.

In the cell identified as 'Present Market' and 'New Product' the firm is attempting *product development* in order to produce a new product to meet the existing market need.

PAUSE FOR THOUGHT 6   *Before reading on, can you identify, from cases in this chapter or elsewhere, examples of this type of strategic choice?*

Figure 11.4
Product/market matrix

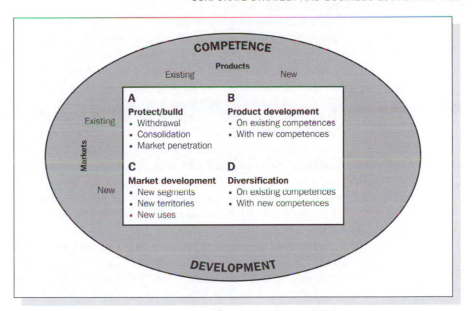

Source: adapted from Johnson and Scholes (1999)

One example is Microsoft's development of the Navigator web browser software package (see Case Study 11.6) which can be seen as an example of this type of strategy.

Another option is to develop a new market altogether for your existing product range. This type of *market development strategy* is currently the main strategic approach of the Scottish whisky companies. Traditionally whisky has been seen as a drink for the older (and perhaps more discerning, predominantly male!) market. The 1997 advertising campaign by Bell's Scotch Whisky attempted to break that mould by appealing to a younger (although it has to be said still predominantly male) market. In addition, new opportunities are opening up in the Chinese market which has hitherto not been seen as a market for whisky. Both of these strategies represent significant market developments for the whisky industry.

Finally, in the cell identified as 'New Market' and 'New Product' the strategic choice facing the firm is one of *diversification*, either in a related market by forward, backward or horizontal integration or more controversially by utilising the company's entrepreneurial flair, managerial skills or financial muscle and diversifying into unrelated fields, as the big conglomerate companies like Hanson and BTR did in the 1960s (but see Case Study 11.1).

CASE STUDY **11.8** **Sainsbury's strategic options – the product/market matrix applied**

J. Sainsbury has dominated the supermarket business for years and had been responsible for some radical changes to the way in which the retail business has been run in the past decade.

In a bid to 'reinvent' itself it has been quietly diversifying its retail portfolio covering several markets and countries in an attempt to develop other businesses capable of generating additional profits. The squeeze on profitability of the food retail business in the UK, which is already becoming fiercely competitive as Tesco and Asda fight to retain their position in the market, has forced Sainsbury to diversify its operations in a way which it is claimed distinguishes it from its competitors in the UK.

The diversification strategy began in the UK in 1977 when the first Savacentre store was opened. Savacentre is a hypermarket selling a whole range of clothing and other goods in addition to food. Homebase (a DIY store) followed in 1981 and the first investment was made in Shaws, a food retailer in the USA, in 1982 with full ownership coming five years later. These acquisitions moved Sainsbury away from its traditional food retailing business in the UK and according to figures published in 1994 accounted for 13 per cent of the group operating profit, rising, it is estimated by analysts, to 20 per cent over the next two or three years. In 1994, diversification took another step forward with the acquisition of a 16 per cent stake in Giant Foods in the USA.

The strategy appeared to be paying off as the group delivered a 10.2 per cent rise in operating profits in 1994, largely driven by the sparkling performance of its business outside food retailing. The then chairman, David Sainsbury, said that there was substantial common ground between these businesses and the core supermarket operations.

'They all use our key skills in buying, systems, property and own-brand development.'

'They also share the same business philosophy of offering value for money and quality.'

'We did not go into a discounting environment, as we felt we would not be comfortable with that.'

The strategy could not have come at a better time. The squeeze in the supermarket business has come and Sainsbury, unlike its rivals, was ready for this downturn, it was claimed.

'We thought we might start to see what we are now seeing in the industry and we always thought we could not go on growing at the same rate. The strategy was therefore to take the group's food retailing expertise abroad or move into other retail sectors in the UK but never to do both at the same time. We were determined only to *diversify in one dimension at a time*' [emphasis added].

Sainsbury's 1997 strategy can be analysed in terms of the matrix discussed above (see Figure 11.4). Figure 11.5 outlines the Sainsbury position.

Rival supermarkets were also trying to develop a similar strategy but to the extent that they had diversified at all they had come to it much later and with smaller diversification. Tesco succeeded in linking up with the Catteau supermarket chain in France and Global in Hungary. But these were quite small to have any impact on the group as a whole. In addition, by acquiring William Low, the Scottish retailer, Tesco had become even more tied to the UK. In addition in 1996 a number of supermarkets were looking to an alternative strategy of selling space in their superstores to other retail businesses such as banks and travel agents.

However in a reversal of strategy in August 2000 Sainsbury's confirmed it may sell its Homebase DIY stores. In a statement, the group said it was considering strategic alternatives for Homebase. These include 'an alliance, disposal or joint venture'. Sainsbury's has held discussions with a number of parties, the statement said.

Figure 11.5
Sainsbury's strategic choice

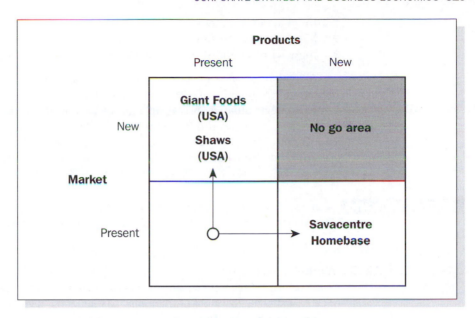

A sale could raise as much as £1 billion for the troubled retailer. Potential buyers or partners include Home Depot, the world's largest DIY retailer, and LeRoy Merlin, one of Europe's biggest home improvement groups.

By 2000, Sainsbury, once the top performer in the UK grocery industry, had slipped behind its rivals Tesco and Asda, which were considered to be more innovative and more responsive to their customers' needs. The challenge now for its new chief executive Sir Peter Davis, who joined from the Prudential at the beginning of 2000, is to turn the company around. He has warned shareholders the process could take three years but promised he would try to release more shareholder value from the retailer's assets. Previous speculation had centred on a possible sale of the company's banking arm or its Shaws grocery business in the USA.

So far, investors appear to have welcomed the possibility of a Homebase sale. One analyst said a sale would make sense. 'They need to focus on their core activities. Also DIY is scaling up in Europe and Homebase will need significant resources to compete', he said.

Based on information from *The Times*, 3 November 1994, and BBC News, 23 August 2000.

Questions

1 Why do you think that Sainsbury's were determined to diversify on only one dimension of the matrix at a time?
2 What is the synergy between a food retailer and a DIY store?
3 In terms of Sainsbury's pricing policy, where on 'the strategy clock' would you place them?
4 Why did Sainsbury's reverse the policy in the autumn of 2000?

Other strategies

Finally, firms may decide to look at wider alternatives to the ones identified so far. These may be identified as follows:

1   Internal development.
2   Mergers and acquisitions.
3   Joint ventures and strategic alliances.

A company that is breaking new ground may have no alternative but to go it alone. There may be no other company it can take over or with whom it can form a strategic alliance. It may also not be in a position to raise outside finance for its new venture and may therefore have to rely on internal funds for finance. In markets where there has been little change in market shares a new entrant might provoke a strong reaction from competitors. Hence a merger or takeover may be the best strategy. (See Case Study 11.9.)[4]

PAUSE FOR THOUGHT 7   *Can you identify any examples from the cases so far illustrated which fit the above description and where a merger might be the most appropriate strategy?*

CASE STUDY **11.9**   **'Auntie' in payTV deal**

As the number of television channels has increased in recent years with the advent of cable and satellite TV the BBC ('Auntie' to its friends) has found itself left behind. It is estimated that the BBC's share of the market (BBC1 and BBC2 audience figures) will drop from its current 43 per cent to about 33 per cent within the next decade. This would have a serious effect on the BBC's ability to find the necessary funds to finance its programmes. With audience figures of only one in three it becomes difficult to justify having a universal licence fee which provides 95 per cent of the BBC's total revenue. By continuing to ignore the growth of multichannel television the decline in the BBC, would become inevitable. However, in order to get into this market the BBC requires to have access to funds, distribution channels and knowledge and expertise about this new marketplace which it does not possess. The obvious solution to this dilemma is to seek out a suitable partner and set up a joint venture. During 1996, two partners pursued negotiations with the BBC, both anxious to utilise the BBC's single greatest asset – its brand name. The two suitors were BSkyB, owned by Rupert Murdoch's News Corporation, and Flextech, a subsidiary of Telecommunication Inc. (TCI), America's biggest cable-TV operator, which also owns Telewest, Britain's biggest cable company.

In September 1996, the BBC announced that it was discussing a joint venture with Flextech. There are a number of advantages to this deal. First, the BBC would have access to a source for the distribution of its programmes. TCI has a huge network of cable television channels in the USA and up until now the BBC has found it difficult to make any great headway there. It also allows the BBC to focus on the production of television programmes and to avoid the costly business of setting up a cable and satellite network. More importantly it will allow the BBC to have a foothold in the multichannel world of subscription TV. There will initially be six subscription channels each dedicated to a given sector (for example, drama, entertainment, documentaries, education, sport, and the weather). The BBC thus envisages that it will receive a steady stream of income from selling programmes rather than contemplating a huge cash outflow as it tried to set up rival distribution networks.

The deal if it proves successful will be a blow to BSkyB's plans to link up with the BBC. With the advent of digital TV BSkyB plans to launch 200 channels by 1997 and a joint venture with the BBC would have enabled BSkyB to fill its channels with top quality programmes and help it to shake off its somewhat 'naff' image.

The joint venture is not without its risks, however. The BBC's most precious asset is its brand name. How this is exploited by TCI is obviously something over which the BBC would need to exercise great care to ensure that Flextech provides the right 'showcase' for the BBC's programmes. In addition, there is obviously a potential clash of cultures. The BBC has a reputation of being unable to take commercial decisions quickly and sensibly, whereas TCI and its boss John Malone have a reputation of being entrepreneurial and risk-takers.

There is a further conundrum for the BBC. The more successful it is in becoming more commercial the less need is there for it to depend on the licence fee. They therefore need to strike a careful balance between being a commercial organisation funded from commercial revenue and a public broadcaster funded from the licence. Joint ventures are seen therefore as an integral part of this balancing strategy.

Question

What are the advantages and disadvantages, from the point of view of the BBC, of joint ventures?

Strategy implementation[5]

The final step in the strategy process is the implementation stage. This involves a variety of important elements such as planning how the firm is going to *allocate its resources* in order to achieve its strategies, ensuring that it has the right *organisational structure* in place in order to deliver the required strategy and being able to *manage the changes* in an appropriate manner. Each of these elements is dealt with briefly below.

Resource planning

In deciding how to allocate resources firms must decide first how much change they are proposing to implement. If the changes to strategy they are proposing are fairly small and to some extent are developments of existing strategies, the way in which the firm allocates resources may not have to be modified all that much. This can often be done by 'tweaking' the existing methods of allocating funds. Often the method is 'formula-driven'; that is to say each division or product is allocated a sum of money based on some formula which has previously been agreed. This may be based on turnover or profitability or even last year's budget figure plus a fixed percentage.

If the change is more fundamental and requires a significant shift then it may be necessary to depart from the formula driven approach and to either impose a new way of allocating funds internally or allow each of the divisions within the company to put their case for more funding. A further refinement is to have a combination of formula driven methods of allocating funding with an element of internal competition. Allowing an element of internal competition has the advantage of ensuring that the 'best' projects are considered and that the case for allocating funds away from some activities and towards others is considered on the basis of merit.

1 *What are the advantages and disadvantages of formula driven funding for allocating resources internally in a company?*

2 *What are the disadvantages of allocating funds internally purely on the basis of competition (i.e. each division or department competing internally for the funds)?*

Organisational structure

In implementing strategy it is necessary to examine whether the company has the most appropriate structure for delivering the policies. Different organisational structures were discussed in Chapter 6 and you should refer back to that discussion. Whether a company adopts the functional form, the multidivisional form, the holding company form or the matrix form will depend to a large extent on company culture, the type of market that the firm is in and the extent and speed of change that the company is required to implement.

CASE STUDY **11.10**
....

Hewlett-Packard and organisational structure

Carly Fiorina, chief executive of Hewlett-Packard (HP), is not just a new broom. Since she joined the computer and printer company in July 1999, she has been racing through the corridors of its world-wide operations, searching out dusty corners of inefficiency. Ms Fiorina has left nobody in doubt that change is the order of the day. Of HP's vaunted corporate culture – which stresses the advantages of autonomous business units and rejects traditional corporate hierarchy – she says her goal will be to 'preserve the best' and do away with the rest.

Her challenge is to sharpen HP's competitive edge and to improve its recent lacklustre financial performance. In fiscal 1999, ended 31 October, HP's revenues from continuing operations grew by just 7 per cent. That is a snail's pace compared with the 20 per cent growth recorded at Sun Microsystems, HP's strongest rival in the high-performance computer sector. IBM, the world's largest computer company, increased its revenues by more than 12 per cent during the first three quarters of 1999. HP's earnings growth has also been mediocre. Over the past five years earnings have grown at an average rate of 15.1 per cent, against an industry average of 25.6 per cent. Wall Street analysts are predicting a decline in HP's earnings in the first half of fiscal 2000.

Ms Fiorina makes no secret of HP's problems, most of which, she implies, are of its own making. The company's decentralised approach to management has created duplication and inefficiencies, she complains. In a significant change she quickly realigned the company's operations into four divisions – two that are 'customer focused' on the consumers and businesses that buy HP products, and two encompassing the company's broad computer and printer product lines.

This 'matrix management' approach has fallen out of favour at many large companies, yet Ms Fiorina sees it as the way to ensure that HP puts more of its energies into meeting the needs of customers, and balancing its engineering-led preoccupation with product development.

The new structure also ensures that divisions are interdependent, which she believes is vital. 'We have a lot of soloists in this company and what we need is an orchestra', she says. Her favourite example of the inefficiencies created is that HP has no fewer than 750 internal web sites for employee training. 'Now why do we have that?', she asks. The answer to Ms Fiorina's rhetorical question is that HP's business units have all created their own training programmes with little thought given to leveraging the efforts of other parts of the company. Similarly, product groups have created their own brand names, resulting in dozens of sub-brands that dilute HP's marketing efforts.

In a move that sends a strong message internally, as well as to the outside world, Ms Fiorina has launched a $200m corporate marketing campaign – the first for HP in more than a decade – that will replace much of the advertising traditionally controlled by product divisions. Yet internal web sites and advertisements are just the tip of the iceberg.

The independence of product divisions is deeply ingrained in HP's culture. It goes back to the company's founders. Bill Hewlett and David Packard 'feared the downside of big', says Ms Fiorina, 'and appropriately so. Sometimes that independence and ability to move quickly is a good thing. But it's not a good thing when we diminish our power in the marketplace. It's not a good thing when we're spending more money than we need to and not getting enough bang for the buck, and its certainly not a good thing when we're confusing our customers.'

Thus Ms Fiorina is now grappling with a problem that is all too common among leading high-technology companies: how to be big, yet nimble; efficient yet responsive to rapid changes in the market place. Ironically, she is doing so at a company that many industry observers thought had created the model for avoiding such problems.

So far, Ms Fiorina appears to have the support of HP employees. She has been well received during her whirlwind visits to HP's world-wide facilities, where she has tried to strike a balance between acknowledging accomplishments and demanding better performance.

'People need to intellectually understand the (need for) change first. They need to embrace it emotionally. And then they need to see some of it at work', she says. However, even as Ms Fiorina is working to boost employee morale, she is planning job cuts. Speaking to Wall Street analysts last week, Bob Wayman, chief financial officer, said the company would reduce operating costs by $1bn a year, within three years. Although much of the savings will come from rationalisation of facilities, there will be some workforce reductions, he acknowledged.

Source: *The Financial Times*, 7 December 1999.

Questions

1 What are the advantages and disadvantages of a decentralised approach to managing a company like Hewlett-Packard?
2 Outline the 'matrix management' approach which Hewlett-Packard is seeking to adopt.
3 What is wrong with 'a corporate culture which stresses the advantages of autonomous business units and rejects traditional hierarchies', particularly in the fast-moving business environment in which Hewlett-Packard operates?

In some cases, in order to effect significant change, the senior managers may set up special task groups outside the formal structures, which report directly to the chief executive officer, have wide-ranging powers to bypass existing managers and act as a kind of 'Trojan horse' for significant change. This is often an effective way of achieving significant change in an otherwise bureaucratic organisation which is heavily bound by rules and procedures.

Managing change

The process of managing change within organisations has received a great deal of attention in recent years and there is a growing literature on this important aspect of strategic management. (For a review of the most recent literature see references at the end of this chapter.) While a detailed discussion of this area takes us beyond the scope of a book on business economics, there are a number of points that can be made concerning the economic aspects of managing change.

The most obvious point is to consider the costs and the benefits of implementing any change. Managers, if they are acting rationally, need to assess the marginal benefits of the change and relate that to the marginal costs of implementing the change in question. Case Study 11.11 illustrates what can happen if change is not managed sensibly.

CASE STUDY **11.11** **Delta takes a nose-dive**

In 1994, Delta Airlines, America's biggest domestic airline, launched its 'Leadership 7.5' cost-cutting programme. Its aim was to reduce the cost per passenger mile to just 7.5 cents. Delta had been losing money to a number of low-cost competitors, in particular ValueJet and Southwest Airlines whose costs per passenger mile were some way below Delta's (7.5 cents compared to Delta's 9.3 cents). Delta decided to attack its cost base in order to reduce its prices and squeeze more profit from its existing routes. It also was anxious to recover lost market share. Hence the launch of its 'Leadership 7.5' programme.

Initially, the results were impressive. Delta cut $1.6 billion from its costs, reducing the cost per passenger mile to 8.3 cents. In addition, the operating profits for the fourth fiscal quarter of 1996 rose by 27 per cent to $569 million. The stock market price of Delta shares rose to 60 per cent above its 1994 level.

Unfortunately, there was a cost to all of this. The number of complaints received from Delta passengers rose dramatically. In 1990, for example, Delta was rated the best in terms of the number of complaints registered by passengers. By 1996 it had slipped to fifth out of the 10 biggest airlines. The main reason is not hard to find. The number of employees has fallen by 10,350 to around 60,000. The number of flight attendants has been reduced to the federally required minimum levels. In addition the number of staff used to clean the planes between flights has been reduced to such a level that there have been complaints about the standards of cleanliness on the flights. Flight attendant Deborah Thompson uses her own pillow and blanket on long haul flights. 'I don't dare put my head on one of our pillows', she says.

The Food and Drug Administration has warned Delta about 'unsanitary conditions' at its Cincinnati operations and it was claimed that coffee pots and lids were stored in dirty sinks used for cleaning mops. Frequent travellers have switched airlines after seeing filthy carpets and mildewed bathroom fittings on Delta planes. Rundown interiors made passengers think about the maintenance and safety of the planes and to raise concerns about these aspects.

All this is recognised by the company who acknowledge that they did not manage the change as effectively as they might. They failed to assess correctly the impact on staff morale of the savage cuts in the number of employees. Delta's chief executive officer Ronald Allen admits that service and morale suffered during the restructuring. He claims that Delta is now committed to a broader strategy that includes giving customers 'Delta-style' service and that the airline is working to improve its tarnished image.

Adapted from *USA Today*, 3 August 1996.

Change will become easier to manage if those who are likely to be affected can see the need for the change. Therefore a company facing extinction is often in a better position to make radical changes than a company that has been reasonably successful. Using a football analogy, it is often much more difficult to effect change to a team that is at the top of the league than to a team that is facing relegation. The costs (not to mention the risks) of tampering with success would appear to far outweigh the benefits for the table-topping team than for the team facing relegation. The really successful teams are the ones who manage to change dramatically and still remain at the top, as Liverpool Football Club did throughout the 1970s and 1980s. In terms of companies and corporations the 'trick' is to reinvent the successful formula that made them successful in the first place and still remain at the top of the tree while they effect the necessary changes to company culture, organisational structure and changing competitive environment. Often this involves 'head versus heart' dilemmas when a company has to decide to sell off a part of its business or an asset with which it has traditionally been associated. For example, in 1995 Colmans decided to sell off the division which made its world-famous mustard so that the company could refocus the business in more profitable areas.

In managing change managers must also be aware of the barriers that are put in the way of implementing change as these will increase the costs and delay the benefits of change. Often these are delaying tactics by those most likely to be affected by the changes proposed and can take a variety of forms. One of the best case studies in how to delay the implementation of any change can be seen in the classic comedy series '*Yes, Minister*' and '*Yes, Prime Minister*'. Sir Humphrey Appleby, the Permanent Secretary to Prime Minister Jim Hacker, exploits most of the delaying tactics to any change that he wishes to block and each of the tactics has its parallel in reality. These include such devices as setting up a working party to examine the proposal in more detail, introducing complexities and other factors which require more detailed consideration before a final decision can be taken, reducing the credibility of the person proposing the idea in the first place, or requesting a delay until some other piece of information (which is costly and time-consuming to obtain) becomes available. Alternatively, resisters to change may appeal to the manager's sense of insecurity, as Sir Humphrey does with Jim Hacker by describing the proposed change as 'courageous' or 'bold'! All these devices are likely to increase the marginal cost of implementing change.

Managers seeking to introduce radical change can of course employ a few tactics of their own to emphasise the marginal benefits of accepting change (or increasing the perceived marginal costs of not accepting change). A crisis can be 'manufactured' in which the company's prospects of continuing success are openly questioned by those senior managers who are proposing radical changes. Alternatively an external threat is 'played up' in order to get everyone focusing their energies outside the company rather than internally. It therefore becomes easier to effect changes if people believe that their jobs may be at risk or the very survival of the company is at stake. Clearly, this 'threat' must be credible to be effective and is a tactic that will lose its potency if it is repeated too often.[6]

Case Study 11.12 brings together a number of the ideas presented in this chapter.

CASE STUDY **11.12** **3M reinvents itself**

Minnesota Mining and Manufacturing (3M) is based in St Paul, Minnesota, USA, and has a reputation for being an innovative yet conservative type of company which rarely sacks its workers or engages in headline-making takeovers. It has made its reputation on the basis of its creativity, coming up with a constant stream of innovative products. It is estimated that it sells around 60,000 separate product lines from Post-it notes and saucepan scourers to surgical supplies and road signs. In 1995 alone it recorded 543 patents, 40 per cent more than in 1990. It has also been calculated that about $1 billion of 3M's 1994 sales of $15.1 billion were earned on products which have been developed in the previous 12 months and 30 per cent of its revenues come from products developed in the last four years. In addition 3M spends about 7 per cent of its revenues on research and development, which is about twice the American average.

However, behind its apparent success story there is another story to tell, one of expensive disasters and costly mistakes, such as the Floptical disc (which was aptly named as it was a flop!). 3M thought it would become the standard for the personal computer industry but it did not and it cost 3M very dearly. The Information, Imaging and Electronics (IIE) division responsible for the development of the Floptical disc swallowed up an astonishing $1.2 billion of the company's capital budget (about one-third of the total). This division, which accounted for over 30 per cent of 3M's sales, only contributed about 6.3 per cent to its profits, about a third of the margins earned by the two other divisions (consumer/industrial products and life sciences).

The biggest disappointment apart from the Floptical disc was the audio and video tape business. Here the lesson that 3M learned was that the market put price ahead of innovation. In the face of intense foreign competition and also escalating costs of raw materials (the price of cobalt, the basic raw material used in the production of tapes, tripled in three years) 3M simply could not compete. This was a business with which 3M had always been traditionally linked and therefore it was faced with a real 'head versus heart' dilemma. However, the chief executive officer, Livio DeSimone, did not flinch and sold the business off. The electronics bit of the IIE division is being retained and will be made an independent company and eventually sold.

Nevertheless, there was more pain ahead. The company lost about 5,000 of its 85,000 workforce, which represents the biggest cut in its history. The market conditions for its products remained unfavourable with stagnant selling prices and escalating costs (estimated at about 8 per cent per annum). What then were the strategic options open to 3M as a result of this fairly downbeat strategic analysis of their environment and how are they going to implement this change of strategy?

Mr DeSimone outlined a number of key strategies which he hoped would succeed. First, he pinned his hopes on 3M's core competence, its ability to produce more blockbuster products like the Post-it or the 3M adhesive tapes. To do this the allocation of resources would in future not be determined by formula but would be based on a careful assessment of which divisions came up with potential 'winners' which would enable 3M to stay ahead of the competition. In addition to the restructuring already mentioned of making three divisions go into two, the way it was proposed that the company should be organised internally would allow scientists in various disciplines throughout the company to keep in close touch via a company-wide database, thus giving them access to one another's expertise. Product development would follow a more 'market-centred' approach with new products serving the needs of existing markets and creating new markets. In addition, there has been a relentless focus on costs with Mr DeSimone reducing the number of managers by 20 per cent since he took over and increasing the financial goals set for the company by raising the target rate of return on capital employed to 27 per cent (currently at 21 per cent).

Managing this process was not at all easy. Pinning your hopes on coming up with innovative ideas was always going to be something of a hit or miss affair. The origin of the much vaunted Post-it product apparently stemmed from the fact that one of the 3M product researchers was trying to come up with a better bookmark for his hymn book! You cannot always plan for the next blockbuster. However, the best one can hope for is to try to create the type of business organisation which puts a premium on product development and which values innovation and 'mould-breaking'. Thus 3M is trying to reinvent itself. (For details of 3M and its innovations see its webpage at http://www.3m.com/us/about3M/innovation/)

Adapted from *The Economist*, 18 November 1995.

Questions

1 What 'external environmental factors' have influenced the change in strategy for 3M?
2 What choices face 3M and can you think of other options that they might have considered?
3 Why is this a company that has been reluctant to consider mergers, acquisitions and joint ventures as part of its strategic thinking?
4 Using any of the frameworks and models outlined in this chapter, discuss the strategic options that 3M has analysed. What do you understand by the term 'market-centred' approach in relation to product development and how can this be achieved?
5 As far as resource allocation within the company is concerned, how best do you think this should be done? What are the advantages and disadvantages of the methods discussed in the chapter and how might these methods of allocation work in the case of 3M?

International business strategies

As markets at home become more competitive and as companies seek to exploit their competitive advantages in new ways, so they begin to look at international business strategies. Why do companies 'go international'? Let us now look at the case of a company (Case Study 11.13) which is facing the problem of deciding how best it should serve its overseas markets.

CASE STUDY **11.13** **Mackbrew goes international**[7]

In 1873 two brothers, George and Jim McIntyre, formed a company in a small Scottish village outside Aberdeen that produced a soft drink called Mackbrew using a secret family recipe revealed to the brothers' father by an old Highland woman allegedly endowed with supernatural powers. The McIntyre brothers advertised it as having health-giving properties and it acquired a reputation locally as a drink to be given to elderly people who were convalescing from various illnesses like the common cold or influenza. For over a hundred years this family-run business continued to trade successfully to a limited market in the north-east of Scotland, the Northern Isles and in the Highlands and Islands and to make a respectable profit year after year. Their advertising and marketing could at best be described as 'quaint' and their slogan, 'Mackbrew maks ye new', was barely understood outside the confines of the local area. This did not stop people who drank Mackbrew claiming it gave them a surge of energy and a new zest for life.

In 1988, for the first time, the McIntyre family appointed an outsider, Roger Hartman, as managing director to head up the company while Sir Peter McIntyre, the great-great-grandson of one of the founding brothers, George, retained the post of chairman of the board. The McIntyre family was still represented at senior management level, however, as Sir Peter's daughter Louise, a recently qualified accountant, was appointed as head of finance. This was a considerable break from the past because the company had always resisted any attempts by 'outsiders' to take over the running of the company in spite of having received a number of offers from large soft drinks manufacturers over the years. However, Sir Peter recognised two things: first, there was no one within the family in his view who had enough experience to run and develop the company and, secondly, the company needed to change direction if it was to survive. These objectives, Sir Peter felt, could only be achieved by bringing in an outsider. What Hartman saw when he arrived was a company that was failing to exploit its full potential and for the next five years he endeavoured to reposition the brand and to advertise it more extensively outside the local area. By employing a good advertising agency, he completely revamped the product and opened up a new market among a younger age group. He wanted to position the product as a sports drink for athletes in the newly emerging sports drinks market. The 'Mackbrew' name was scrapped and replaced with the simple word 'Max' (splashed in red tartan letters across a black background) and to get away from its image as a drink for older people, a newspaper, poster and local radio campaign was mounted in which there were many images and sounds of young men and women having fun and living life to the full ('Live Life To The MAX!!' became the new slogan).

The local Premier League football team secured a sponsorship deal with the McIntyre company and the Max name was splashed across the front of their strip (which was changed to a predominantly black shirt with the red 'Max' logo on the front) and very soon the drink was becoming well known outside the local area. In 1990 a successful television advertising campaign in Scotland was followed by a successful national campaign. In 1992 the Scottish rugby team endorsed the product and within a very short period of time it was becoming well known outside the UK, particularly in those parts of the world where the Scottish Rugby team toured and where there was a strong ex-patriot Scottish community.

In 1995 Hartman was succeeded by Derek Segerfield, a London Business School MBA graduate, as managing director. Segerfield was something of an entrepreneur and he had experience in the drinks and leisure industry with a number of large international companies. He realised two things: first, that the company's brand name and image were its biggest assets; and, secondly, that this brand name could be exploited in a number of different markets in much the same way as Sir Richard Branson had exploited the Virgin name. So Segerfield set about to diversify the company and bought into a chain of hotels in Scotland using the Max name to market a range of outdoor adventure holidays in the Highlands of Scotland for the 18–35 age range (the MaxVax) still using the tag line of the original advertising campaign 'Live Life to the MAX'. Throughout the chain of hotels that Segerfield acquired, the Max drink was sold extensively.

In 1996 Segerfield launched a management development company using the Scottish Highlands as a training ground for developing leadership skills among senior company bosses. He was able to use the services of ex-Army personnel as the local regiment had just been disbanded. The management development company called MaxMan again utilised the Max brand name and the slogan 'Develop your potential to the MAX'. The captains of industry could be seen in adverts against a spectacular backdrop of mountains with cans and bottles of the Max drink endorsing the product and also the management training company. Segerfield had a whole series of ambitious plans to use the Max name in a variety of different ventures, from airlines (they were unfortunately prevented from using the name MaxFly as this was already owned by another company!) to life insurance (MaxLife), and to diversify into alcoholic drinks with a whisky-based lemonade drink aimed at the 18–35 age bracket, called the WhiskyMax.

However, Segerfield's long-term strategy crucially depended on getting the Max name known extensively outside the UK. 'Unless people buy into the Max image of fun and pleasure as well as healthy lifestyle then the strategy for diversification will remain a pipe dream', Segerfield announced. More controversially, while acknowledging that it had some marketing potential, Segerfield planned to try to shake off the 'Scottish' image of the product which he described as 'too parochial and a bit "naff" for a company with global aspirations. In some ways the dour Scots image can be seen as hindering our plans to make this company big internationally', Segerfield claimed. Therefore the red tartan lettering hitherto used in all the company's advertising was replaced with plain red lettering. However, the historical roots of the company were played up only in the slightly more 'tongue-in-cheek' style which it was felt would appeal to a younger and more cosmopolitan market.

The MaxVax holidays and MaxMan management development programmes had nevertheless slowly begun to attract a European clientele and through these ventures gradually the Max soft drink came to be known in a number of European countries, particularly in Norway, Sweden and Germany where the healthy image was well received. By 1994, 25 per cent of all sales of the Max drink were outside the UK. Europe accounted for about 10 per cent, the remaining 15 per cent being split between Australia and New Zealand (10 per cent) and South Africa (about 5 per cent). The hardest market to crack had been the United States, the home of the soft drink giants of Coca-Cola and Pepsi-Cola. Max had only achieved a very limited penetration there with some very modest sales in New England.

The success of the product abroad had to some extent taken the company by surprise. Nevertheless, it did prompt Segerfield to rethink some of his strategic priorities and to contemplate approaching the board with some ideas on how they could exploit the situation further. Segerfield had recently appointed a new business school graduate to his office and he asked the new appointee to prepare a report reviewing the options available to the company. 'We need to exploit the opportunities and the markets overseas if this company is to develop', Segerfield claimed.

The McIntyre board had in the past been reluctant to consider such radical plans ('We already have an overseas market', claimed one board member; 'we sell to Orkney and Shetland, don't we, and what could be more overseas than that?'). However, Segerfield, with Sir Peter's backing, knew that if the company was to develop in the way he wanted it would need to consider expanding its activities beyond simply exporting to predominantly English-speaking parts of the world. Segerfield felt that the European market was considerably untapped and wanted to exploit the Max drink's healthy living, fun loving image which it was slowly building up in the UK.

Task

Before reading on, review the options available to the McIntyre company if it wants to 'go international', analysing their advantages and disadvantages and the risks involved, and discuss the merits or otherwise of 'Max' going international in the soft drinks market.

In deciding to make the business international there are a number of options that can be considered:

1 Export from home base.
2 Set up an export agency.
3 License the product.
4 Set up a joint venture or strategic alliance.
5 Acquire or merge with a foreign company.
6 Set up a wholly-owned subsidiary.

Each strategy has its advantages and disadvantages and McIntyre would have to consider each of these carefully. However, the first step would be to consider whether or not they should 'go international' in the first place. There are a number of costs that the company would have to take into account which would require to be set against any potential benefits. First, even if the company limits itself to the present strategy of simply exporting to Europe there will be increased transport costs. Bottles and cans are bulky items to transport and the value added in the content would need to be high enough in relation to the costs of transportation. Also, there will be additional factors to take into account. Does the drink meet European Union (EU) standards regarding content, labelling and other health and environmental issues? The materials used in the bottle or can are subject to EU regulations and there are moves in some European countries to get companies to accept responsibility for the disposal of the packages in which their products are contained. The company may require to relabel the product to meet EU requirements, not least of which would be to print the labels in the language of the country in which the product is sold! There would be the risks involved in receiving payment in a foreign currency, especially if there should be fluctuations in the exchange rate. This would add a further risk to trading abroad and while there are ways in which this risk can be minimised (by using such devices as buying currencies in the forward exchange markets and currency options) these can be costly ways of reducing exchange rate risks. So the first questions to be asked are these:

➤ Are the market opportunities in the area concerned so good that they out-weigh the extra costs of doing business abroad?
➤ Have the market opportunities in the domestic market been fully exploited?
➤ Would resources be better deployed in aiming to get a greater market share in the home market?

We are not given information about the market share of Max in the domestic market. What we do know is that it is only relatively recently that the company launched a national campaign. Until then the product had only really had a presence in the Scottish market (and even then only in a region of the Scottish market). Segerfield's ambitions to turn this traditionally run family business into a global conglomerate may be premature and perhaps a degree of reality needs to be introduced into the strategic plans to be put to a fairly conservative and risk-averse board of directors.

Assuming, though, that the company has acquired a significant share of the domestic market and that it sees market potential for the Max soft drink in Europe, how best can it exploit this opportunity? One possibility is to appoint agents in the country concerned who have some knowledge of local market conditions, the language, the legal requirements and the best ways in which to market the product. This would be a relatively cheap way of establishing a presence in a foreign market. However, while this option has the advantage of cheapness and speed, it is not without risks. The agent may have other agencies and hence may not regard the promotion of the product as a high priority. It is true that the terms and conditions for one's overseas agent can be drawn up in such a way as to reward extra sales and that the agreement can be made exclusive. It also has the advantage in that if at any point the McIntyre company chooses to pull out of a given market its exposure in terms of the costs of withdrawal are fairly minimal. Nevertheless, it stops short of establishing a more permanent presence overseas and may appeal to a risk-averse board of directors. It is, however, unlikely to satisfy the ambitions of the managing director, Derek Segerfield, or possibly indeed Sir Peter McIntyre.

The next alternative to consider is setting up a licensing agreement with a manufacturer of soft drinks in the country concerned. This manufacturer would produce the drink under licence. There are a number of advantages with such arrangements. First, the McIntyre company would have none of the risks associated with setting up a manufacturing plant in a foreign country. All the risks associated with the production process would be borne by the licensee. They would pay McIntyre a fee for being allowed to manufacture and sell the product in the country concerned. Thus McIntyre would be relieved of the commercial risks associated with selling their product overseas. The extent to which McIntyre is insulated from these risks depends to some extent on the way the licensing agreement is drawn up. Some licensing agreements give the company that is licensing its product a share in any profits, in which case the risks are more evenly distributed between the two parties. In other cases a royalty-type payment may be made on the basis of output, in which case the income for the licencor is guaranteed and the risks are borne by the licensee. There are major drawbacks, however, with licensing agreements. The first and most obvious one relates to the risks that McIntyre will run if the company to whom they give the license fail to deliver the same quality of product that McIntyre produce themselves. There is a further complication. The formula on which the product is based is supposed to be a closely guarded secret. However, for the licensee to be able to produce the product they will need to know how to make it. Once the secret formula is made public it then becomes difficult to ensure that the company's main asset is not cloned by a number of rivals, costing McIntyre its competitive advantage. This is, of course, exactly why Coca-Cola has refused to allow anyone else to produce its product and why they have resisted forming partnerships with other companies to produce Coke.

To some extent the same arguments apply to joint ventures and strategic alliances. The attractions of joint ventures are that they are a more equal relationship between companies than licensing agreements. In a joint venture both parties undertake to put a certain amount of money into them and the rewards are normally divided up on the basis of the respective contributions. Both, therefore, share in the risks and rewards. Thus the McIntyre company may seek out, for example, a German soft drinks manufacturer as a partner and they may both agree to set up a new production plant in Germany. If we assume that the capital costs are equally divided then they may agree to split the profits in the same proportions. Alternatively, McIntyre may decide to form a strategic alliance with a major retail outlet (let us say a supermarket chain in France) to sell their product exclusively. This may not require the two companies to set up a separate company but merely to agree to co-operate in areas where there is mutual benefit. Where the arrangement is a joint venture then there is a risk of 'selling the family fortune' by sharing the information about how the product is made. There is clearly less of a risk in the type of strategic alliance that is outlined above, where the partners in the alliance are operating at different stages in the production process. This strategy would enable McIntyre to keep control of the production process but hand over the distribution and marketing to their strategic alliance partner.

It is the need for control which makes merger or acquisition of a foreign competitor an attractive proposition. With this option McIntyre would be able to control the production facilities themselves. They would also be able to set up relatively quickly as the production facilities already exist and they would therefore obviate the need to obtain the necessary planning permissions and to satisfy the various interest and pressure groups who become vocal when new building is proposed.

However, there are some disadvantages from foreign mergers and takeovers. Often the two companies have quite different cultures and it is sometimes difficult to get them to work harmoniously together. There is sometimes a tendency to duplicate functions and for there to be hidden costs in integrating two separate systems. This was recently demonstrated in the case of the BMW–Rover merger (Case Study 11.14).

A clash of cultures?

It was widely reported in the trade and business press that all was not well between BMW and its British partner, Rover. BMW had acquired Rover in 1994 essentially in order to take over the Range Rover product range of cars. BMW saw the four-wheel drive segment of the car market as an important area for development and was conscious that it did not have a product that could fill that niche in the market. The quickest and easiest way, it thought, to acquire this was to buy Rover from British Aerospace for whom it had always seemed an odd acquisition in the first place. The problem was that BMW also had to acquire other bits of the Rover empire as well, including the Mini, and it was over the development of the new Mini, due to be launched in 1999 and codenamed R59 (the original Mini had been launched in 1959), that there was a serious falling out between the partners. According to a widely leaked internal memo from BMW:

> the investment programme postulated by Rover and the management capacity needed to mastermind it, give reason for serious concern. If the financial and managerial drain continues at the present rate, BMW's own core projects will eventually come under threat.

> (Quoted in *The Sunday Times*, 11 August 1996)

It was also reported that several senior people in BMW expressed their dissatisfaction with Rover's performance in developing the new Mini. 'Rover need to get their act together', one BMW engineer was quoted as saying. 'Instead of making intelligent and beneficial contributions, Rover's strengths appear to be the creation of unnecessary friction, a disappointing no risk attitude and an amazing display of egoism', claimed another BMW manager.

Rover managers hit back, stating that there was no attempt by BMW to 'muscle in' and take over the Mini project, claiming that there was a good relationship between the two companies which had spent the past two years sorting out what was best for the group as a whole in terms of co-operative ventures.

In August 1996 Tom Purves, a former BMW manager who now headed up the UK division of BMW–Rover, appointed Martin Runnacles from BMW as Rover's marketing director, and the R59 project was redesignated the E50 project to be based on a BMW design, according to *Car* magazine. However, exasperated that Rover losses continued to mount, in 2000 BMW eventually closed its Rover plant at Longbridge, Birmingham.

Adapted from *The Sunday Times*, 11 August 1996.

As can be seen, mergers across national boundaries are not without their risks.

Another 'downside' of this type of arrangement is that foreign takeovers of national companies often excite the attention of host governments which are anxious to ensure that the national interest is being protected. It may be that in the case of soft drinks we should not exaggerate the importance that, say, the French or German governments attach to this industry. It is obviously not in the same league of importance as, for example, a major manufacturer of defence equipment (or indeed car manufacturing, which is often seen as a symbol of national prestige). But if the takeover of a French or German soft drinks company is seen by consumer groups as threatening to reduce competition and consumer choice, then host governments may be forced to intervene and to require there to be an investigation to ascertain whether the takeover is in the national interest. This may, therefore, increase the costs of this option for the McIntyre board and hence cause them to look at the final option.

The last option open to the board is to consider setting up production facilities in the country concerned by forming a wholly-owned subsidiary. The obvious advantage from this arrangement is that the McIntyre company would retain complete control over every aspect of the business. Also by entering the foreign market they are likely to increase competition, increase investment in the country concerned, add to employment and offer a greater choice to consumers. For these reasons they are likely to be welcomed by host governments which may even offer the company a generous package of aid to set up in their country in the first place.

Each of these strategies can be assessed against a set of criteria such as the degree of control that a firm can exercise, the resource implications and the risk that the firm may lose whatever competitive advantage it has in the market place ('selling a firm's Crown Jewels' or, to use more formal jargon, 'the risks of diffusing the firm-specific advantages'). These are set out in Table 11.1.

Strategy	Control	Resource implications	Risks of diffusion
Exporting	Low	Low	Low
Licensing	Low	Low	High
Joint ventures	Medium	Medium	Medium
Wholly-owned subsidiary	High	High	Low

Table 11.1
International business strategies: control, resources and risks

Adapted from Hill, Hwang and Kim (1990).

Table 11.1 indicates that there are low risks involved with exporting in terms of allowing a company's rivals to acquire its competitive advantages, which increase with joint ventures and are at their greatest with licensing. If firms are more interested in control then the wholly-owned subsidiary is by far the best strategy, although it is the option which requires the greatest resources. The best strategy for McIntyre will therefore depend on which factors the company regards as the most important. It has been argued that there are four major factors which influence the choice of entry mode:

1 The importance of economies of scale.
2 The degree of global competition.
3 Business 'environmental' factors such as the degree of country risk.
4 'Transaction' factors such as the value of firm-specific knowledge (i.e. how a company gains its competitive advantage).

If a firm wishes to pursue a global strategy and sell its product throughout the world it may favour having a high degree of control over its production processes and therefore favour the wholly-owned subsidiary. Equally, where the market structure is dominated by just a few firms, the firm may wish to pursue an international business strategy that gives it a high degree of control.

PAUSE FOR THOUGHT 9 *Why did Japanese car companies prefer to enter the European market by setting up wholly-owned subsidiaries as opposed to joint ventures or by acquiring indigenous firms?*

Theories of multinational business

As we have seen, one of the strategies that a firm can adopt is to set up production facilities in a number of different countries – in other words, to become a *multinational enterprise*. A multinational enterprise may be defined as a firm which owns, controls and manages assets in more than one country. It is normally the case that in order to do this, it sets up production facilities in a number of different countries and that it finances these operations by foreign direct investment (FDI). This definition implies that there must be direct investment (as opposed to simply taking an equity stake, i.e. buying shares in an existing company). In addition, there must also be a *transfer of resources* such as knowledge and enterprise, as well as money. Finally, the subsidiaries set up must be in more than one country. Some economists indicate that at least 25 per cent of a company's assets or turnover (sales) or profit must be earned outside its 'home' base before it can be classified as a multinational. For companies to be defined as 'global', the threshold for what economists call 'transnationality' is usually set at 50 per cent. The Index of Transnationality[8] attempts to measure what proportion of a company's assets, sales, employment or profitability is earned 'abroad' (i.e. outside the company's country of origin). Each of these measures will obviously give a different answer, depending on which variable is chosen. However, in order to try to take account of all of these indicators, an average is calculated using principally assets, sales and employment data. Where only one or two of these factors is measured, the average is calculated.

Table 11.2 gives the data for the top multinational companies for 1996 from the UNCTAD/Erasmus University database.

Why firms decide to become multinational in the first place can be answered by reference to three theories of multinational business. These can be classified as:

1   Ownership-specific advantages.
2   Location-specific advantages.
3   Internalisation advantages.

As the costs of setting up production facilities in a number of countries are likely to be quite considerable, it is argued that there must be considerable offsetting advantages for firms to 'go multinational'. In addition, these advantages must be even greater than the advantages that indigenous firms possess if the

Table 11.2

The world's top 50 TNCs ranked by foreign assets, 1996

Ranking by foreign assets	Transnationality index	Corporation	Country	Industry	Assets Foreign	Assets Total	Assets %	Sales Foreign	Sales Total	Sales %	Employment Foreign	Employment Total	Employment %	Transnationality Index	Global ≥50%	Global ≥75%
1	83	General Electric	USA	Electronics	82.8	272.2	30.4	21.1	79.2	26.6	84,000	239,000	35.1	30.7	No	No
2	32	Shell, Royal Dutch	UK/Netherlands	Petroleum explor., etc.	82.1	124.1	66.2	71.1	128.3	55.4	79,000	101,000	78.2	66.6	Yes	No
3	75	Ford Motor Company	USA	Automotive	79.1	258.0	30.7	65.8	147.0	44.8	a	371,702		37.7	No	No
4	22	Exxon Corporation	USA	Petroleum explor., etc.	55.6	95.5	58.2	102.0	117.0	87.2	a	79,000		72.7	Yes	No
5	85	General Motors	USA	Automotive	55.4	222.1	24.9	50.0	158.0	31.6	221,313	647,000	34.2	30.3	No	No
6	52	IBM	USA	Computers	41.1	81.1	50.7	46.6	75.9	61.4	121,655	240,615	50.6	54.2	Yes	No
7	79	Toyota	Japan	Automotive	39.2	113.4	34.6	51.7	109.3	47.3	34,837	150,736	23.1	35.0	No	No
8	49	Volkswagen Group	Germany	Automotive	a	60.8		41.0	64.4	63.7	123,042	260,811	47.2	55.4	Yes	No
9	71	Mitsubishi Corporation	Japan	Diversified	a	77.9		50.2	127.4	39.4	3,819	8,794	43.4	41.4	No	No
10	38	Mobil Corporation	USA	Petroleum explor., etc.	31.3	46.4	67.5	53.1	80.4	66.0	22,900	43,000	53.3	62.3	Yes	No
11	3	Nestle SA	Switzerland	Food	30.9	34.0	90.9	42.0	42.8	98.1	206,125	212,687	96.9	95.3	Yes	Yes
12	2	Asea Brown Boveri	Switzerland/Sweden	Electrical equipment	a	30.9		32.9	33.8	97.3	203,541	214,894	94.7	96.0	Yes	Yes
13	47	Elf Aquitaine SA	France	Petroleum explor., etc.	29.3	47.5	61.7	26.6	44.8	59.4	41,600	85,400	48.7	56.6	Yes	No
14	14	Bayer AG	Germany	Chemicals	29.1	32.0	90.9	25.8	31.4	82.2	94,375	142,200	66.4	79.8	Yes	Yes
15	34	Hoechst AG	Germany	Chemicals	28.0	35.5	78.9	18.4	33.8	54.4	93,708	147,862	63.4	65.6	Yes	No
16	57	Nissan Motor Co Ltd	Japan	Automotive	27.0	58.1	46.5	29.2	53.8	54.3	a	135,331		50.4	Yes	No
17	74	FIAT Spa	Italy	Automotive	26.9	70.6	38.1	19.8	51.3	38.6	90,390	237,865	38.0	38.2	No	No
18	8	Unilever	Netherlands/UK	Food	26.4	31.0	85.2	45.0	52.2	86.2	273,000	304,000	89.8	87.1	Yes	Yes
19	70	Daimler-Benz AG	Germany	Automotive	a	65.7		44.4	70.6	62.9	67,208	290,029	23.2	43.0	No	No
20	11	Philips Electronics NV	Netherlands	Electronics	24.5	31.7	77.3	38.9	40.9	95.1	216,000	262,500	82.3	84.9	Yes	Yes
21	9	Roche Holding AG	Switzerland	Pharmaceuticals	24.5	29.5	83.1	12.9	12.9	97.7	39,074	48,972	79.8	86.8	Yes	Yes
22	56	Siemens AG	Germany	Electronics	24.4	56.3	43.3	38.4	62.6	61.3	176,000	379,000	46.4	50.4	Yes	No
23	36	Alcatel Alsthom Cie	France	Electronics	23.5	48.4	48.6	24.6	31.6	77.8	118,820	190,600	62.3	62.9	Yes	No
24	40	Sony Corporation	Japan	Electronics	23.5	45.8	51.3	32.8	45.7	71.8	95,000	163,000	58.3	60.5	Yes	No
25	19	Total SA	France	Petroleum explor., etc.	a	30.3		25.8	34.0	75.9	a	57,555		75.9	Yes	Yes
26	20	Novartis	Switzerland	Pharmaceuticals,chem.	21.4	43.4	49.3	28.6	29.2	97.9	91,192	116,178	78.5	75.2	Yes	Yes
27	35	British Petroleum	UK	Petroleum explor., etc.	20.7	31.8	65.1	39.2	69.8	56.2	37,750	53,700	70.3	63.9	Yes	No
28	62	Philip Morris	USA	Food/tobacco	20.6	54.9	37.5	30.7	69.2	44.4	94,659	154,000	61.5	47.8	No	No
29	81	ENI Group	Italy	Petroleum explor., etc.	a	59.5		13.2	39.3	33.6	a	83,424		33.6	No	No
30	69	Renault SA	France	Automotive	19.0	42.2	45.0	19.4	36.0	53.9	43,381	140,905	30.8	43.2	No	No
31	31	BAT Industries Plc	UK	Food/tobacco	18.9	63.5	29.8	30.8	38.2	80.6	149,217	163,854	91.1	67.2	Yes	No
32	68	Du Pont	USA	Chemicals	18.4	38.0	48.4	20.8	43.8	47.5	34,000	97,000	35.1	43.7	No	No
33	30	Rhone-Poulenc SA	France	Chemicals/Pharmaceut.	a	27.1		13.3	16.8	79.2	41,818	75,250	55.6	67.4	Yes	No
34	1	Seagram Company	Canada	Beverages	18.2	18.6	97.8	12.2	12.6	96.8	a	31,000		97.3	Yes	Yes
35	42	BASF AG	Germany	Chemicals	17.9	28.2	63.5	23.8	32.4	73.5	42,339	103,406	40.9	59.3	Yes	No
36	46	Honda Motor Co Ltd	Japan	Automotive	17.8	33.5	53.1	26.4	42.3	62.4	a	101,100		57.8	Yes	No
37	43	BMW AG	Germany	Automotive	a	29.1		25.5	34.8	73.3	51,900	116,112	44.7	59.0	Yes	No
38	77	Mitsui & Co. Ltd	Japan	Trading	17.1	61.2	27.9	56.6	132.0	42.9	a	11,250		35.4	No	No
39	82	Nissho Iwai Corporation	Japan	Trading	15.2	47.2	32.2	49.6	153.5	32.3	1,997	6,684	29.9	31.1	No	No
40	93	Itochu Corporation	Japan	Trading	15.2	66.1	23.0	23.3	89.1	26.2	2,584	9,766	26.5	25.2	No	No
41	58	Hewlett-Packard	USA	Electronics	15.2	27.7	54.9	21.4	38.4	55.7	48,200	122,000	39.5	50.0	Yes	No
42	28	Ferruzzi/Montedison	Italy	Chemicals/agribusiness	14.9	21.6	67.1	11.8	15.5	76.1	17,570	29,564	59.4	67.8	Yes	No
43	51	Daewoo Corporation	Korea, Rep of	Diversified	14.9	32.5	45.8	10.2	26.4	38.6	37,501	47,609	78.8	54.4	Yes	No
44	27	News Corporation	Australia	Media	14.4	24.2	59.9	8.6	9.9	86.9	17,212	26,513	64.9	70.6	Yes	No
45	78	Chevron Corporation	USA	Petroleum explor., etc.	14.4	34.9	41.3	14.9	42.8	34.8	12,095	40,820	29.6	35.2	No	No
46	48	Dow Chemical	USA	Chemicals	14.4	24.7	58.3	11.3	20.1	56.2	21,039	40,300	52.2	55.6	Yes	No
47	37	Robert Bosch GmbH	Germany	Automotive	13.1	21.3	61.5	16.7	26.7	62.5	a	172,359		62.5	Yes	No
48	86	Marubeni Corporation	Japan	Trading	13.0	60.8	21.5	43.9	113.0	38.8	a	9,282		30.2	No	No
49	15	Cable & Wireless	USA	Telecommunications	13.0	15.5	83.9	7.0	9.7	72.2	29,613	37,448	79.1	78.4	Yes	Yes
50	4	Thomson Corporation	Canada	Printing & publishing	12.8	13.2	97.0	7.3	7.7	94.8	47,200	50,500	93.5	95.1	Yes	Yes

Note: a – where there is no data the transnationality index is calculated on the basis of the available data.
Source: UNCTAD/Erasmus University database (1999).

multinational firm is to compete and survive against the local competition. Some of these advantages may be grouped under the heading of *ownership-specific advantages*. Examples of the kinds of factors which prompt companies to become multinational relate to the advantages to be gained from being large. For example, economies of scale often result from being able to rationalise production on a global scale, with parts of the product being manufactured in one part of the world and other parts being made elsewhere, and with the final product assembled, marketed and distributed from another location. Other ownership-specific advantages could include access to raw materials which are not available to indigenous firms (for example, oil) or access to cheaper sources of capital (either because the firm is well known in the major financial centres or because it is large and diversified geographically and is perceived as less of a risk). Other ownership-specific advantages include the possession of important assets such as trademarks, patents and well-known brand names – for example, Coca-Cola or, in the case of Hoffman La Roche or Glaxo, the multinational pharmaceutical giants, the patents they had on the drugs they produced. Finally, we must not forget the managerial, marketing and organisational skills of the organisation (such those possessed by companies such as Hanson, Virgin and the Holiday Inn chain of hotels) as important ownership-specific advantages.

However, while ownership-specific advantages are undoubtedly part of the explanation they do not provide a complete picture. This explanation can help to answer the question of who becomes multinational but not necessarily why firms should choose to exploit their ownership-specific advantages by setting up production facilities in other countries.

Location-specific theories stress the importance of locational factors for attracting foreign multinational firms. Factors such as the fact that certain resources such as oil reserves are only located in certain parts of the world, or the existence of low labour costs to explain the attraction that some multinational firms have for third world locations, or the existence of tariff and non-tariff barriers, are often cited as reasons why firms become multinational. In addition the incentives offered by governments by way of grants and 'tax holidays' and help with infrastructure spending are also given as location-specific reasons for firms to become multinational. Finally, the possibilities of selling new products into growth markets and exploiting favourable market opportunities are seen as a powerful location-specific factor. As a result, it is often claimed that it was a combination of all these factors which made the United Kingdom an attractive location for Japanese car manufacturers setting up operations in the UK. Nevertheless, while location-specific factors play a part in a firm's decision-making process, they only address the question of where a firm should locate, not why it should decide to become multinational in the first place.

The final theory which is regarded by many economists as the most satisfactory explanation of why firms become multinational is referred to as *internalisation advantages*. This is based on the theories of the firm developed by Coase[9] and has led to the development of what is called *transactions cost economics*. According to this view, firms are faced with a choice in deciding how to develop and grow. They can either decide to expand their activities by going into the market place and buying such assets and resources as they require (for example, buying in supplies of raw materials and components from other firms who are in the market) or they can decide to undertake these activities themselves by either forward or backward vertical integration ('internalise the activities', to use the jargon). The decision to internalise is taken on the basis of the net benefits from doing so; in other words there must be tangible benefits from avoiding the use of the market place.

A number of internalisation advantages can be adduced. For example, by internalising activities it is possible to exercise greater control over the quality and the timing of the delivery of raw materials and components. Therefore an oil company, for example, by controlling the source of its raw material can plan the refining, production and the marketing of its product. By having control of upstream facilities (extraction of oil) it can control the downstream activities better (the refining, distribution and marketing of oil-related products). By controlling the supply of components, for example, a car company can better plan its operations. The car company would, however, have to continually weigh up the benefits of having a fully vertically integrated operation against the benefits of contracting out these services.

| PAUSE FOR THOUGHT 10 | *Why is it the case that the largest multinationals tend to be in just a few industries such as the oil industry (Royal Dutch/Shell, Exxon, British Petroleum) or cars (Ford, General Motors) or electronics (Asea Brown Boveri, Philips Electronics, Siemens)?* |

There is an area where the transaction costs model with its emphasis on internalisation advantages comes into its own. This occurs when the competitive advantage the firm enjoys is the result of its possession of an intangible asset for which no market exists. For example, one of the advantages that oil companies have is their ability to use their considerable managerial and organisational skills to extract oil from the ground and under the sea. It is difficult to imagine how a company could exploit this advantage other than by internalising it and doing the operations itself. It cannot license this 'asset' because it is intangible and it would be almost impossible to operate a satisfactory fee arrangement. A similar type of argument applies to such activities as the international hotel business. This is a business where any competitive advantage is almost entirely the result of superior managerial and organisational skills. It is difficult to imagine how these intangible assets can be exploited other than by the organisation setting up 'production' facilities in the country concerned. Exporting is impossible because of the nature of the 'product' and licensing and joint ventures risk passing over 'trade secrets' (the company's 'Crown Jewels') to third parties thereby diffusing its competitive advantage.

Another advantage claimed under the internalisation theory is that by undertaking these activities themselves firms eliminate some of the risks by controlling the price of raw materials. This can offer scope for tax planning as this internal transfer price can be used in such a way as to ensure that the profits occur in those parts of the world where the corporate tax rates are at their lowest. In addition, vertically integrated firms are often more able to erect barriers to entry, thereby reducing potential competition. This is regarded as a more plausible theory to explain *why* firms become multinational as opposed to *who* (ownership-specific advantages) or *where* (location-specific factors). However, it is probably fair to say that all three theories have a part to play in explaining the phenomenon of multinational enterprises. In essence, if firms are acting rationally they will be seeking to either *reduce costs* or *increase their revenues*. Multinational firms can *reduce costs* by vertically integrating their operations either backwards (like oil companies) or forwards (like a number of electronic and car companies setting up assembly plants in South East Asia). Alternatively, they can seek to *increase revenues* by extending the life-cycle of their products by setting up plant in other countries which are at a different phase of the product life-cycle. Thus American companies invaded Europe in the 1960s and 1970s, Japanese companies followed in the 1980s and 1990s with, for example, a whole range of consumer electronic products, while European companies sought to extend their product life-cycles by setting up production facilities in less developed third world countries.

Globalisation: myth or reality?

In recent years there has been much debate about whether or not multinational firms were becoming truly 'global' and that they were in fact not dependent on or linked with any specific country. This debate centred round two of the current most influential management thinkers, Kenichi Ohmae (1990) and Michael Porter (1989). According to Ohmae in his book *The Borderless World*, nations have become less important to companies, whether as a home base or as a source of identity. Cheap computing and communications, the lowering of tariff barriers against foreign direct investment, the spread of more homogeneous tastes, fashions and standards across national frontiers have pushed firms to compete in world markets rather than national ones. Thus old theories of how multinational companies were supposed to operate with a parent company located in a major economy and wholly-owned subsidiaries in an array of overseas markets have been replaced with 'global corporations' described by advocates as 'stateless world citizens' independent of their national origins.

Not so, claims Michael Porter. In order for companies to compete on a global scale they must first cut their teeth in competitive and demanding national markets and only by staying ahead of the competition in their own national markets will they be successful on a global scale.

In order to discuss the question of who might be right it is necessary to define what is meant by a *global company*. Globalisation can be defined as the phenomenon whereby companies make decisions on location of production or sourcing of inputs or the sale of the product or service without reference to political or geographic boundaries. There are three key propositions which can be said to characterise a global company and these are:

1 '*For the truly global company, the world is its market place.*' This means that it essentially sells a world product with only a few modifications to take account of local national circumstances. Coca-Cola and McDonalds are products that are sold in a more or less standard form throughout the world. Ford's launch of the Mondeo as a world car also typifies this approach.

2 *'For the global company the world is its production facility.'* This means that the company sets up production facilities anywhere in the world and it is not wedded to any particular national location. In addition it may source its inputs from anywhare in the world. As we saw in Chapter 4 the development of business-to-business (B2B) networks is now making this an increasing possibility.

3 *'In the global company the world is the place where its business functions are located.'* The truly global company ensures that its major business functions are not all located at its headquarters. The key functions are dispersed. Big firms can now raise finance anywhere in the world wherever it is cheapest. Marketing has also become more global, often with a single world-wide campaign, thereby saving on costs. In a few large firms, research and development, which has traditionally been kept close to a company's headquarters, has also become more global. IBM has a major R&D facility in Switzerland while ICI had a similiar facility in Japan.

PAUSE FOR THOUGHT 11   *Before reading on, what factors in recent years have made it easier for firms to become more global?*

There are a number of factors, which it is argued, increase the trend towards *globalisation* (see Case Study 11.15). First, cheaper computer and video networks improve international communications and this makes management and control across international frontiers much easier than it was a decade ago. In addition, the barriers against foreign direct investment and multinational enterprises have come down significantly in recent years as governments compete with one another to attract investment. There has also been a spreading of tastes across international frontiers with internationally recognised brand names that can be seen as a guarantee of quality (McDonalds in Moscow, Coca-Cola just about everywhere, and IBM and Price Waterhouse). As companies seek to reduce the risks of doing business, so globalisation as a strategy becomes attractive. Globalisation can also overcome trade barriers and be a response to the globalisation strategies of one's rivals.

However, when one comes to examine each one of the characteristics of a global company outlined above, then it is clear that few companies can be described as truly global. While companies try to 'think global' they invariably 'act local', to use Theodore Levitt's famous dictum (Levitt, 1983). There is compelling evidence that the multinational enterprise still retains a strong national identity. Table 11.2 above shows that of the top 25 non-financial multinational enterprises 19 had a transnationality index of over 50 per cent (meaning that over 50 per cent of their assets/sales/employment were in countries outside their country of origin). If one looked at the data for the next 25 MNEs in the top 50 then the number with more than 50 per cent drops to 15. Thus about 68 per cent of the top 50 MNEs have more than 50 per cent of their assets/sales/employment outside their home country. If one uses a more stringent statistical test by defining global companies as having a transnationality index of 75 per cent or over, the figures change dramatically. Only 24 per cent of the top 50 MNEs could be defined as global.

In addition, investment abroad by multinational firms still betrays strong regional bias with US multinationals favouring investments in Latin America, Japanese multinationals investing in Asia and European multinationals investing in Eastern Europe and the former Soviet Union. Thus there are still investment clusters of foreign direct investment along regional lines rather than the truly global lines that one might have expected.

Finally, it is still fairly clear that having a strong home base has been one of the main reasons why multinationals have been successful when venturing further afield. Moreover, trying to have a presence everywhere can be costly and, in spite of the considerable improvements in international communications, the costs of controlling the global company should not be underestimated.

The conclusion about whether we have truly attained globalisation must wait. As one senior manager of a large multinational commented:

> People who really believe that business is now borderless and that geography no longer matters do not get to the top of multinational firms. These days multinationals are not special because all businesses are to a greater or lesser extent international. Few, however, are global.[10]

CASE STUDY 11.15 Ford – a global company?

In July 1994, the world's most expensive car rolled off the production line in Ford's Kansas City assembly plant. Named the Ford Contour, it had cost Ford $6 billion to develop. The Contour was the North American version of the Mondeo world car which was launched in 1993 in Europe and achieved record sales of 470,000 cars and total dominance of the mid-sized car market. Ford was hoping that the Contour would achieve the same success in the States. Although the costs and time to develop this car were significantly greater than those of competitor firms, Ford had long-term goals in developing this car. Ford planned to use this model as the basis for a whole decade of new products. They planned to use the common platform of the Mondeo/Contour as the basis for developing their cars over the next ten years and Ford saw the Mondeo project as a 'cash cow' with the profits earned on this project financing Ford's ambitious plans to expand in Asia. In particular, Ford was aiming to make significant inroads into China, where it had some joint ventures, and India where it was lagging behind its great rival General Motors. Ford therefore planned to produce 800,000 Mondeo type cars each year.

In addition, Ford, headed up at that time by Scots born Alex Trotman who had spent over 40 years working his way up the company, was planning to reorganise itself along global lines in a project called Ford 2000. What this involved was a move away from its previous regional groupings to product groupings. Thus Ford had decided to merge its European business (with sales of $23 billion) with its North American operations (sales of $105 billion) and to create instead five product divisions (which in Ford-speak are called vehicle-programme-centres or VPCs). One such centre responsible for developing small front-wheel drive cars was to be split between Germany and Britain. Another which focused on large front-wheel drive cars, rear-wheel drive cars and pickup trucks and lorries was to be based in Dearborn, USA. All five divisions were to design and develop new models and were to be responsible for their manufacture, marketing and profitability.

As well as rationalising its production facilities, thereby reducing its engineering costs to match its Japanese competitors, Ford planned to rationalise its systems for ordering parts and to reduce the number of suppliers it had to deal with on a world-wide basis. Ford used an array of computer network and video links to allow people from around the world to work together, increasing the interchange of ideas and enhancing creative solutions to problems. Ford also believed that it could reduce the time it took to develop a new product from 37 months to 24 and reduce its order-to-delivery cycle to less than 15 days.

However, although at first sight it appeared that Ford had adopted the globalisation philosophy, it was apparent that not all of Ford's product range is 'going global'. It was recognised within the company that the only truly global part of its operations was in the mid-range cars. Europeans were not really into buying large Lincoln town cars and pickup trucks which were sold exclusively in the North American market. Some models developed by the VCPs were sold world wide. In addition, there was always a danger with major restructuring that the upheaval caused by adopting a radically different structure would cause the company to take its eye off the ball, which is of course to sell more cars world wide. General Motors spent years trying to recover from a major reorganisation in the late 1980s.

In fairness, Trotman went to considerable lengths to sell the concept of globalisation to the workforce and the transition from a regionally-based company to a product-based one organised on global lines appeared to have gone quite smoothly. The 'bottom line' of course is this: will Ford be more profitable as a result of the reorganisation? Recent results were a little disappointing with post-tax profits down by 22 per cent to $4.1 billion and the growth in market share coming to a halt. This may mean that Ford is repeating the mistakes of General Motors, although it may be too early to judge. Some analysts believe that Ford 2000 may only be the answer to yesterday's problems. John Lindquist of the Boston Consultancy Group observes: 'However worthy and sensible, all Ford 2000 is aimed at doing is solving a problem that they had created and that no one else had (except General Motors).'

Given that Ford's structure was based on regions it had no option, it is claimed, but to have a globalised structure just to stay in the game with the (mainly) Japanese competition which was more or less global in the first place.

Based on information from *The Economist*, 30 March 1996, 7 January 1995 and 23 July 1994.

Questions
1 What factors have propelled Ford to consider globalisation as a strategy?
2 From the three propositions of what a global company looks like, do you think Ford meets these tests?

CASE STUDY **11.16** **Globalisation and retailing**

Wal-Mart's £6.7 billion ($10.7 billion) bid for Asda, announced on 14 June 1999, was seen as a huge threat both to British supermarkets and to the rest of Europe's retailing élite. Unfortunately on the day it swooped on Asda, Bob Martin, Wal-Mart's long-standing international head, resigned unexpectedly, suggesting that the world's most powerful retailer was divided on how far and how fast to push globalisation.

Wal-Mart's British acquisition came at a time when retailers have become fixated by the strategy of globalisation. In 1999, for example, Royal Ahold, a Dutch supermarket operator, acquired supermarkets in Poland, four rival chains in Spain, one in America and two in Argentina. France's leading hypermarket, Carrefour, which is in 20 markets, had opened stores in Chile, Colombia, Indonesia and the Czech Republic and announced that it would move into Japan by the year 2000. Tesco, Britain's biggest food retailer, had moved into South Korea, its sixth overseas market. And Promodes, the French hypermarket group, had become the market leader in Argentina. Meanwhile, fast-growing clothes chains, such as The Gap, Sweden's Hennes & Mauritz (in 12 markets), and Spain's Zara (in 17), were opening a branch in a new country every few weeks.

However, in spite of this trend towards more globalisation, retailers seemed to be finding it hard to make a success of the transition from national to multinational. Although a few firms, such as IKEA, the Swedish furniture retailer, had done well, established international retailers still make most of their money and their highest returns at home (see table below). Carrefour's operating margins in France are more than 6 per cent of sales, whereas, after operating internationally for 30 years, it still loses money in much of Asia, Latin America and even some parts of Europe. Meanwhile Wal-Mart, which first went abroad in 1991, according to recent figures makes a return on capital of 5.8 per cent on its international business, far lower than in America. There is therefore some scepticism about just how successful these new global retailers will be.

One reason for scepticism is that retailers are being driven by slow growth at home as much as by the sight of opportunities abroad, according to Felix Barber of Boston Consulting Group (BCG) in Zurich. The small size of the Swedish market encouraged several of the country's retailers to move overseas as early as the 1970s. A few, such as IKEA and Hennes, have built strong international businesses, although they took years to do so. French retailers, such as Carrefour and Auchan, have gone into emerging markets to escape the constraints of national planning laws in their own countries. Even Wal-Mart, which is still producing sales growth in America, was going abroad partly because it already has a dominant share of the country's non-food market.

In addition, the opportunities abroad are dwindling. Many local retailers in Latin America, for example, have either been bought or are already in joint ventures. Because of the increased demand for new partners or acquisitions the price of those that remain is rising as multinationals seek to buy up partners all over the world. Carrefour's move into Japan in 1999 illustrates the point.

However, retailers assert that globalisation is about more than simply adding to their turnover. Sir Geoff Mulcahy, boss of Kingfisher, which launched an earlier, lower bid for Asda, argues that the main reason retailers want new sales is to exploit economies of scale and to spread the rising costs of marketing and technology. In Europe, international scope may also help retailers to cope with the single currency, which will make it easier for consumers to compare prices across borders.

In practice, however, international scale economies are hard to achieve. In the rush to acquire new markets, it is argued that many retailers forget that the crucial ingredient of their success at home is their relative size and market share. Without enough sales and profits in a particular market, even the most long-term management will find it difficult to justify the expense of setting up a large distribution network or installing the latest technology – and without these, so the argument runs, the international newcomer cannot compete with entrenched locals.

In America, Carrefour opened a mere three stores in Pennsylvania, and abandoned its investment before getting anywhere near the scale needed.

The secret may be to arrive in force. Ahold, which has bought itself a concentrated market share on America's east coast, is doing well. So is Carrefour in Spain, where the French firm is now the second-largest retailer. Ahold's frantic recent purchases in Spain are an attempt to catch up, though it still has less than 1 per cent of the market. Cross-border scale economies are particularly elusive in food retailing – precisely where overseas expansion has been most evident, according to economic analysts such as Goldman Sachs in London. The Boston Consulting Group argues that almost all retailers overestimate the scope for savings from aggregating lots of local orders for a product into a single worldwide contract. Few deals manage to produce even 1–2 per cent of sales in savings. The reason is partly that the biggest suppliers have not yet woken up to such 'global sourcing'. Meredith Prichard, J.P. Morgan's Latin American retailing analyst, argues that Procter & Gamble's priority in, say, Brazil is not going to be Wal-Mart, but CBD, the country's biggest retailer. 'P&G's managers negotiate locally, their goods are made locally and their internal targets are local', she adds.

In time, world-wide contracts will become more widespread – P&G announced plans to reorganise itself along global lines. However, the regional managers of suppliers are unlikely to embrace global sourcing with enthusiasm. Ira Kalish, a retail analyst at PriceWaterhouseCoopers, predicts that as suppliers succumb to pressure from retailers, perhaps a third of a supermarket's lines could be sourced globally or regionally in five years, up from less than 10 per cent now.

Yet global sourcing is not the whole answer, because it conflicts with the need to cater to local tastes. Stores in different countries stock very different goods, which undermines the point of global sourcing and complicates relations between local and global managers – of both the retailer and its supplier. Local taste crucially affects the way retailers sell their goods too. In 1996 Wal-Mart set up efficient, clean supercentres in Indonesia, only to find that Indonesians preferred Matahari, the shabbier shop next door, which reminded shoppers of a street market where they can haggle and buy the freshest fruit and vegetables. Two years later, Wal-Mart pulled out. Boots, a British pharmacy, found the number of visitors to its Thai shops soared after it started playing pop-music videos at full volume. Customers had found the shops too quiet. And when Boots opens in Japan this July, staff at the checkout will be standing up – its research has shown that Japanese shoppers find it offensive to pay money to seated staff. Even concepts that have global appeal need to be tailored to local needs. 'Act global but think local', as the well-known management dictum goes. For example, Jose Castellano, the chief executive of Zara, insists that 'as tastes for music and television have gone global, so has fashion'. Yet MTV, the epitome of a global media brand, decided to adapt its musical mix to local markets. Equally, Zara has lost sales in Britain, because its sizing is considered too small for the British figure.

If they are to overcome such obstacles, multinational retailers need to pay a great deal of attention to detail, and a willingness to do whatever local tastes dictate. Wal-Mart, for example, had to abandon its attempt to sell Brazilians (cheaper) Colombian coffee: they insist on drinking their own. IKEA tried to sell Americans its own beds, before discovering that they were the wrong size for their bedlinen; sales of its four-legged desks to Germans also flopped – five legs are preferred.

One way of getting an idea of the local tastes is to join a local partner, something that in many developing countries is required by law. But even that often leads to conflict, since many big Western retailers think they know better. In Brazil, Wal-Mart failed to tap the local knowledge of its joint-venture partner, Lojas Americanas. Failing to spot that most families have one car and shop at the weekends, Wal-Mart built car parks and store aisles that were too small to accommodate the weekend rush. Because many joint ventures fail, local firms are reluctant to give up trade secrets or surrender their best sites. After all, they could be competitors again within a few years.

Yet multinational retailers do have some advantages. Know-how is probably the greatest, according to Cees van der Hoeven, the chief executive of Ahold. At its heart, this is a sophisticated understanding of supply chains, beginning with electronic links to suppliers who can tell instantaneously what customers are buying at the checkout. The next, much trickier, stage is to persuade suppliers to share information with both retailers and rivals, so that they can minimise stocks and put more of what customers want on the shelves.

If cultures are similar or the retailer is established, it is relatively easy for suppliers to accept new buying systems and new technology, and this can lead to savings. Following a flurry of acquisitions in America, Ahold USA expects to save around $85m in 1999 and $115m in 2000. Similarly, Wal-Mart should be able to improve Asda's supply-chain management and make better use of its floor space. Meanwhile, 7-Eleven, a chain of convenience stores that is Japan's most successful retailer, is starting to apply its expertise to stores in Hawaii. However, even best practice is hindered by cultural differences. Wal-Mart has worked with Grupo Cifra, a Mexican retailer, since 1991 and has had a controlling stake for the past two years, but only recently introduced a modern till-information system (years after local rivals had installed one). So far, it has had little effect on margins, as employees are still learning how to use it. Because labour is so cheap, local managers are loath to announce the layoffs that the new technology allows. Similarly, new owners often meet resistance when they try to get their new subsidiary to cut links that were established with suppliers over many years.

Given that globalisation is fraught with such difficulties, which sort of retailers will make make a success of it? The leaders so far are 'category killers' with a strong focus, products with universal appeal and their own brands. The Gap, with its khakis and white shirts, and the IKEA furniture chain combine large volumes with higher margins and control over their design, distribution and sourcing. Some Internet retailers may turn out to fall into this group too, though maintaining a global brand over the long haul could prove cripplingly expensive for what are, after all, loss-making start-ups. And the international failures of Britain's Laura Ashley and Body Shop, and America's Toys 'R' Us, show what happens if expansion abroad is not carefully managed.

Food and general-merchandise retailers have a harder job. Crucially, they must dominate their home base, as do both Wal-Mart and Ahold – but as Promodes does not. Otherwise they will find it difficult to pay for their expansion. They also need to offer a variety of formats, from convenience stores to supermarkets and hypermarkets, in order to ensure market coverage.

Most important, a general retailer needs a strong brand if consumers are to trust it with their personal details or buy its higher-margin products and services. Tesco and 7-Eleven Japan have successfully used information from loyalty cards to adapt their stores, products and prices to local tastes and to move into services such as banking and bill payments. In 1999 a survey by CLK, a market-research group, showed that trusted retail brands have great power: a third of the 1,000 British adults surveyed said they would buy a house from an estate agent with a supermarket brand; 15 per cent would buy a supermarket-branded car. Boots is trusted by 85 per cent of young people in Britain (only 10 per cent have the same feeling for the royal family).

Yet, a well-known brand takes a great deal of time to create – partly because, unlike manufacturers whose products are promoted by shops, retailers must do all the promoting themselves. As Marc Berman, an analyst at Euromonitor in London, notes: 'Most retailers entering new markets are unknowns to suppliers and customers. Building trust takes years.'

Despite the time and the investment that will be needed, a small group of rich firms with skilled managers will probably succeed. They may even be able to pay over the odds for 'strategic' acquisitions – as Wal-Mart is doing with Asda – if this allows them eventually to dominate markets. British and continental European retailers are, in this sense, right to fear the arrival of Wal-Mart on their shores. But for many other retailers, the hoped-for economies of scale from globalisation will prove elusive. Local tastes will often get in the way; best practice will take frustratingly long to put into action. No doubt managers will persist in trying to go global. But too often they will be motivated less by the chance of creating value than by the fear of being left out and gobbled up themselves.

Adapted from *The Economist*, 19 June 1999.

Questions

1   What are the reasons for retailers 'going global'?
2   '… retailers seem to find it hard to make a success of the transition from national to multinational.' Why?
3   What do you deduce from the following table?

Retailer	Home country	Sales (1998 $bn)	% of sales overseas	No. of countries	Market capitalisation ($bn June 1998)
Wal-Mart	USA	150.7	17	10	199.7
Royal Ahold	Netherlands	37.1	71	17	22.0
Promodes	France	36.2	54	12	12.6
Carrefour	France	36.0	44	20	30.5
Home Depot	USA	30.2	neg	4	84.5
Tesco	UK	28.4	13	9	19.5
M&S	UK	13.3	16	34	16.8
Toys 'R' Us	USA	11.2	27	26	5.3
Pinault Printemps	France	10.0	30	23	19.3
Hennes & Mauritz	Sweden	3.4	82	12	17.9

Source: Quoted in *The Economist*, 19 June 1999.

Conclusions
• • • • • • • • • • • • • • •

This chapter has attempted to look at corporate strategy from a business economic perspective. In doing so it has drawn on the analysis–choice–implementation model developed by Johnson and Scholes, highlighting those economic aspects which are dealt with elsewhere in this book. For example, this chapter provides a useful synthesis between the economic principles outlined in earlier chapters which dealt with the economic environment within which firms operate, business organisation, markets, business objectives and pricing policies. It has also introduced a number of recent cases which illustrate the key concepts of this chapter. The final chapter will now look at the role governments play in business decision-making.

Notes
• • • • • • • •

[1] The authors are grateful to David Horncastle, advertising manager of Nissan (USA), for generously supplying information from which this example is drawn.

[2] This section is drawn from the work of Johnson and Scholes (1999).

[3] See Porter (1980), p. 38.

[4] For an alternative view of why mergers can go wrong see: 'How mergers go wrong', *The Economist*, 22 June 2000. One report by KPMG, a consultancy, concluded that over half of them had destroyed shareholder value, and a further third had made no difference!

[5] Strategy implementation takes in a wide range of issues which goes beyond the scope of this book. Students who wish to study this in greater depth are encouraged to read Johnson and Scholes (1999).

[6] For a detailed analysis of the tactics of managing change see Buchanan and Boddy (1993).

[7] Any similarity to any person, alive or dead, or any existing company is purely coincidental.

[8] One of the drawbacks of this index is that it takes no account of the spread of countries in which a company operates. Thus two companies may have the same transnationality index but one may be operating in more countries than the other.

[9] See R.H. Coase, 'The nature of the firm', *Economica*, Vol. 4, 1937, pp. 386–405.

[10] Quoted in *The Economist*, 27 March 1993.

References and additional reading
• •

Buchanan, D. and Boddy, D. (1993) *The Expertise of the Change Agent: Public Performance and Backstage Activity*, Prentice-Hall, New York.

Earl, P.E. (1995) *Microeconomics for Business and Marketing*, Edward Elgar, Aldershot, esp. ch. 11, pp. 340–403.

Ferguson, P.R., Ferguson, G.J. and Rothschild, R. (1993) *Business Economics: The Application of Economic Theory*, Macmillan, London, esp. ch. 12, pp. 219–48.

Grant, R.M. (1991) *Contemporary Strategy Analysis*, Blackwell Business, Oxford.

Hill, C.W.L., Hwang, P. and Kim, W.C. (1990) 'An eclectic theory of the choice of international entry mode', *Strategic Management Journal*, Vol.11, pp. 117–28.

Johnson, G. and Scholes, K. (1999) *Exploring Corporate Strategy*, Prentice Hall, London.

Kay, J. (1993) *Foundations of Corporate Success*: *How Business Strategies Add Value*, Oxford University Press, Oxford.

Levitt, T. (1983) 'The globalisation of markets', *Harvard Business Review*, May–June, pp. 92–102.

Mintzberg, H. (1979) *The Structuring of Organisations*: *a Synthesis of the Research*, Prentice-Hall, New York.

Ohmae, K. (1990) *The Borderless World*, Collins, London.

Porter, M. (1980) *Competitive Strategy*, Free Press, Collier Macmillan, London.

Porter, M. (1989) *The Competitive Advantage of Nations*, Collier-Macmillan, London.

CHAPTER 12

Government and business

Objectives

By the end of this chapter you will be able to:

➤ Appreciate why governments intervene in business matters.

➤ Examine the case for and against privatisation and other types of deregulation.

➤ Understand how monopolies, mergers and restrictive practices are affected by government policy.

➤ Assess the role of government in small firm policy.

➤ Identify the different types of regional and urban support available to firms.

➤ Understand how employment issues have been influenced by government policies.

➤ Assess the impact of EU institutions and regulations on various types of UK policy initiatives.

Key concepts

Acquisition: sometimes referred to as *takeover*, this occurs when the management of Firm A makes a direct offer to the shareholders of Firm B in seeking to acquire a controlling interest.

Deregulation: the replacement of government regulations by market forces; *privatisation* itself might be regarded as one form of deregulation.

Gateways: conditions of which one at least must be satisfied if a restrictive practice is to continue.

Merger: a combination of firms which usually occurs with the agreement of the management of the involved companies. Mergers may be *horizontal* (at same stage of production process), *vertical* (at different stages, either backwards towards the source of supply or forwards towards the retail outlet) or *conglomerate* (involving diversification).

Privatisation: the transfer of assets or economic activity from the public sector to the private sector.

Restrictive practices: practices in potential restraint of trade which must first be registered and ultimately abandoned unless deemed to satisfy at least one 'gateway' *and* to be in the overall public interest.

SMEs: small and medium-sized enterprises. Difficult to precisely define, but often regarded as businesses employing less than 250 employees.

Social chapter: specified minimum requirements involving labour markets agreed between members of the EU as part of the 1992 Maastricht settlement.

Introduction

The government, whether central or local, has a major impact on the day-to-day activity of businesses. In addition, the institutions and regulations of the EU provide further opportunities and restrictions on UK business activity. Earlier (Chapter 1) we looked at the *business environment* created by government monetary, fiscal and exchange rate policies and their rather general influence on firm activities. In this chapter we look in more detail at *specific policies* implemented by government. We then consider the impact of these 'supply side' policies on firm activities in the areas of privatisation, deregulation, mergers and acquisitions, monopoly and restrictive practices, small firm development, regional and urban location, terms of employment, etc.

Reasons for government intervention

In the perfectly competitive model of firm behaviour, firms and consumers possess complete information, selling and purchasing identical products on clearly defined markets which yield stable equilibrium solutions, in terms of both price and quantity. Any benefit or cost to the firm or consumer can in these circumstances be regarded as the equivalent benefit or cost to society. This is a world in which the term 'market failure' has no meaning and in which the price mechanism can be trusted to provide the appropriate 'signals' to both firms and consumers. All that firms and consumers need do is simply maximise profits and utility respectively, subject to the price signals conveyed by the market. The resulting allocation of resources will be efficient in terms of both *production* (output at minimum average cost) and *resource allocation* (no one can be made better off without someone being made worse off).

Of course such a 'perfect' economy has no need of government intervention. However, the real business environment in which firms actually operate bears little resemblance to the above. Information is fragmentary at best for both producers and consumers, the future is uncertain, markets may or may not exist and in any case often fail to reach stable and competitive equilibrium solutions. Private and social costs of production and consumption may diverge considerably with externalities, both positive and negative, widespread and price signals may be heavily distorted by all manner of uncompetitive practices. In other words, 'market failure' may be rampant, providing a host of reasons for governments to intervene to channel firm and consumer activities in particular directions. It is in the context of this more realistic type of business environment that we shall consider particular types of government intervention, starting with the issue of privatisation and deregulation.

Privatisation and deregulation

Nature of privatisation and deregulation

Privatisation means the transfer of assets or economic activity from the public sector to the private sector. Privatisation in the UK has reduced the number of nationalised industries in 2000 to a mere handful of enterprises accounting for less than 2 per cent of UK GDP, around 3 per cent of investment and under 1.5 per cent of employment. By contrast, in 1979 the then nationalised industries were a very significant part of the economy, producing 9 per cent of GDP, being responsible for 11.5 per cent of investment and employing 7.3 per cent of all UK employees. Indeed the public ownership of industries is now in retreat throughout the world as governments privatise. However, privatisation can often mean much more than denationalisation. For example, sometimes the government has kept a substantial shareholding in privatised public corporations (e.g. initially 49.8 per cent in BT), whereas in other cases a public corporation has been sold in its entirety (e.g. National Freight Corporation). Where public sector corporations and companies are not attractive propositions for *complete* privatisation then profitable assets have been sold (e.g. Jaguar Cars from the then British Leyland). Yet again many public sector activities have been opened up to market forces by inviting tenders, with the cleaning of public buildings and local authority refuse collection being examples of former 'in-house' services which are now put out to tender. Private sector finance and operation of facilities and services is also now established (e.g. in the prison service) and in a vast array of public/private finance initiatives. In other words, the many aspects of privatisation also involve aspects of *deregulation*, e.g. in allowing private companies to provide goods and services which could previously only (by law) be provided in the public sector.

Early privatisations, for example BT in 1984, were usually simple transfers of existing businesses to the private sector. Increasingly, privatisations have become much more complex, often being used to restructure industries by breaking up monopolies and establishing market-based relationships between the new companies. For example, the privatisation of British Rail involved separating ownership of the track (Railtrack) from the train operating companies and also from the train leasing companies. The train operating companies are in this case franchisees who have successfully tendered for contracts to operate trains for a specified period.

Market forces have also been introduced into the unlikely areas of social services, the health services and education – especially higher education. In health and social services this has been achieved through the purchaser/provider model in which, for example, doctors and 'primary care groups' use their limited budgets to buy hospital services needed by their patients. Funds, and hence the use of resources, are then controlled by *purchasers* rather than by *providers*. As a result, these 'purchasers' have an incentive to use hospitals offering, in their judgement, the 'best' service as described by some combination of quality and value for money. In higher education, the funding of universities has been closely linked to the numbers of students enrolling. It follows that any failure to enrol students, perhaps through offering unpopular courses, would drive a university into deficit and possible bankruptcy. Resources in this sector were previously allocated by administrators; now a market test is applied.

PAUSE FOR THOUGHT 1   *What factors other than receipts to the Treasury might you want to use in evaluating the 'success' or otherwise of privatisation?*

Arguments in favour of privatisation

A commitment to privatise wherever possible became established in the Conservative Party during Margaret Thatcher's first term. By 1982, the late Mr Nicholas Ridley, then Financial Secretary to the Treasury, expressed this commitment as follows:

> It must be right to press ahead with the transfer from state to private ownership of as many public sector businesses as possible. . . The introduction of competition must be linked to a transfer of ownership to private citizens and away from the State. Real public ownership – that is ownership by people – must be and is our ultimate goal.

Mr Ridley made a case for privatisation which focused on the traditional Conservative antipathy to the state. On this view the transfer of economic activity from the public to the private sector is, in itself, a desirable objective. By the early 1980s, privatisation was also supported by adherents of 'supply side' economics with its emphasis on free markets. Privatisation would expose industries to market forces which would benefit consumers by giving them choice, and also lower prices as a result of efficiency gains within the privatised companies.

Supply-side benefits

The breaking of a state monopoly via privatisation (e.g. Mercury competing with BT) would, in this view, enable consumers to choose whichever company provided the service they preferred. That company would then generate more profit and expand in response to consumer demand, whilst competitive pressure would be put on the company losing business to improve its service or go into liquidation. BT's reductions in telephone and Internet access charges in recent years have clearly been in response to competition. The pressure to meet consumer requirements should also improve internal efficiency (X-efficiency) as changes can be justified to workers and managers by the need to respond to the markets. The old public corporations were seen by those favouring privatisation as being producer led, serving the interests of management and workers rather than those of consumers and shareholders (in this case taxpayers). Privatisation was seen as introducing market pressures which would help to stimulate a change of organisational culture.

Trade unions can be expected to discover that previous customs and work practices agreed when in the public sector are now challenged by privatisation, as the stance taken by management changes from when it was a nationalised industry, with a new emphasis on raising corporate efficiency. In any case, competition in the product market will force moderation in wage demands and result in more attention being paid to manning levels, again raising efficiency. Privatisation contributes in these various ways to the creation of 'flexibility' in labour markets, resulting in higher productivity and reduced labour unit costs.

The stock market provides a useful market test for the now privatised companies. Poor performance in meeting consumer preferences or in utilising assets is likely to result in a share price which under-performs the rest of the market and undervalues the company's assets, ultimately leaving it vulnerable to takeover by a company able to make better use of the assets. Supporters of privatisation place more faith in these market forces than in the monitoring activities of a Department of State or a Parliamentary Committee.

Wider share ownership

Privatisation can also be expected to result in wider share ownership. By 2000, share ownership in the UK had spread to 22 per cent of the adult population, having been only 7 per cent as recently as 1981, with the total number of UK shareholders now about the same as the number of trade unionists. This increase in shareholding is largely due to privatisation. A new group of shareholders has become a participant in the 'enterprise culture'. As many as 90 per cent of the employees in the privatised companies have become shareholders in the companies they work for, at least initially. Share ownership by workers has long been advocated as a means of involving workers more closely with their companies and achieving improved industrial relations.

Reductions in PSBR

Privatisation has also been seen as a way in which the Public Sector Borrowing Requirement (PSBR) can be cut, at a stroke! The finance of external borrowing by the nationalised industries is regarded in accounting terms as being part of public expenditure, which then ceases when these industries become privately owned. Sales of assets or shares as a result of privatisation also increase government revenue, again reducing the PSBR in the year of the sale. Over the period 1979–99 the Treasury gained £70 billion from such asset sales. Privatisation has therefore made a very significant contribution to the budget surpluses of the late 1980s and to curbing the size of the budget deficits of the 1990s. It has been estimated that privatisation proceeds reduced the PSBR as a proportion of GDP by more than 1.5 per cent during the late 1980s, and by a still significant, if smaller, percentage in other years.

Managerial freedom

Other arguments in favour of privatisation include the suggestion that the activities of *state-owned* organisations are constrained by their relationship with the government. They lack financial freedom to raise investment capital externally because the government is concerned about restraining the growth of public expenditure. Privatisation is then seen as increasing the prospects for raising the necessary investment capital, thereby increasing productivity and lowering prices.

A further limitation on the nationalised industries has been the problems they have faced in seeking to diversify. In many cases diversification would be the sensible corporate response to poor market prospects, but it is not an option likely to be open to a nationalised concern. Since privatisation, however, companies *have* been able to freely exploit market opportunities. So, for example, most of the regional electrical companies have become suppliers of gas as well as electricity.

The 'globalisation' of economic activity also, in this view, leaves nationalised industries at a distinct disadvantage. For example, no private oil company would follow the nationalised British Coal in confining its activities to one country where it happened to have reserves. This international perspective is an important reason why the Post Office management has seen privatisation as 'the only (option) which offers us the freedom to fight off foreign competition'. In the postal services, increased competition is expected from the privatised Dutch Post Office and from further liberalisation of other national postal services expected within the European Single Market.

Privatisation, then, is seen by its supporters as a means of greatly improving economic performance.

Arguments against privatisation

Absence of competition

An essential aspect to the case *for* privatisation is the creation of competitive market conditions. However, some state-owned industries have faced stiff competition in their markets (for example, Post Office 'Parcelforce' from DHL etc.), so that privatisation of these industries might be considered irrelevant on the basis of this 'competitive market conditions' argument. This is but one of a number of arguments that can be made *against* privatisation.

The government also faces a dilemma as regards creating competitive market conditions when privatising public utilities which are monopolies; namely that it has another, and potentially *conflicting objective*, which is to raise money for the Treasury. Breaking up state monopolies in order to increase competition is likely to reduce the market value of the share offer; for example monopolies are likely to be worth more as share offers because they reduce uncertainty for investors. Critics would say that the government has allowed the creation of competition to be secondary to creating attractive share issues which sell easily. The result has been the transfer of public utility monopolies intact to the private sector, creating instead private sector monopolies.

The *natural monopoly* argument is also often made, namely that in some circumstances attempts to bring in competition might be regarded as counterproductive when average costs continually fall with size. In such cases an efficient market should, it is argued, contain only one, large scale, producer of the good or service. Many of the public utilities (electricity, gas and water), for example, have been regarded as 'natural monopolies' by those opposed to privatisation.

Nevertheless, competitive pressures are being applied to some of the previously public utility monopolies in their newly privatised form. For example, although at the time of privatisation, British Gas appeared to be a classic natural monopoly, since then consistent pressure from the regulatory authorities has created competitive market conditions in the supply of gas to industry, to such an extent that by 2000 the British Gas share of the *industrial* market was below 35 per cent and its share of the *consumer* market was under serious challenge from the 1998 decision to extend competitive supply to the domestic market for gas across the whole country. As regards BT, from the very beginning its monopoly position was challenged by Mercury. However, opportunities for new entrants created by rapid technological change have been even more significant in eroding the market dominance of BT. Cable TV companies can now provide highly competitive phone services using their fibre optic cable systems and the advances in 'third generation' mobile phone capabilities, such as WAP (wireless application protocol) telephony. Additionally, many large organisations have created their own phone networks and the Internet is creating still further opportunities for communication.

The technical and regulatory changes in the telecommunication and gas industries described above have benefited consumers, but consumers might well feel that these desirable outcomes could have been achieved under public ownership. If so, critics might then argue that consumers could have experienced *still greater benefit* from technical innovation because, under privatisation, lax regulatory regimes have allowed excessive levels of profit, to the benefit of shareholders and executives rather than consumers.

Presence of externalities

The rationale for privatisation is at its weakest when *externalities* exist. Indeed the former nationalised industries contained many examples of such externalities, which was one of the reasons for their original public ownership. Take the case of railways. The newly privatised rail companies are unable to charge road users for any benefits (e.g. less congestion) created by the lower levels of road usage which rail services create. Yet when the industry was in state ownership such 'positive' externalities could have been taken into account when financing British Rail. Similarly, in the now privatised water industry there is a vested interest in encouraging consumption to increase turnover, even if this means the need to build new reservoirs with a consequent loss of land, disruption to everyday life and dramatically changed landscapes. These 'negative' externalities are unlikely to be of major concern to the now privatised water companies. Yet again in the case of the electricity industry, the competitive market among the generators has had nearly fatal implications for the coal industry. New contracts for coal supplies to the privatised electricity generating companies were only secured by British Coal at world prices, well below the prices previously agreed. As employment in mining has plummeted, the cost has been borne by society. Miners' families and local communities have become much poorer, while public expenditure on unemployment and social security benefits has risen and tax revenues have been reduced by the rising unemployment. At a time of high unemployment, organisations which lower their *private* costs by making more workers redundant invariably create *social* costs (negative externalities).

Undervaluation of state assets

It is sometimes argued that valuable national assets have been sold during privatisation at give-away prices. In most cases public share offers have been heavily over-subscribed and large percentage profits have been made by successful applicants. Rolls-Royce shares, for example, were issued part-paid at 85p on 20 May 1987 and moved to 147p by the close of business that day, a profit of 73 per cent before dealing costs. British Telecom shares reached a premium of 86 per cent on the first day. Similarly, electricity privatisation has, to date, raised some £6.5 billion, but the assets involved had a value of £28 billion! Hardly surprisingly, the Regional Electricity Company shares had a first day premium of almost 60 per cent, and the Electricity Generating Companies shares a first-day premium of almost 40 per cent.

Underpriced issues have cost the Treasury substantial revenues and have also conditioned a new class of small shareholders to expect quick, risk-free capital gains. These expectations were encouraged by barrages of skilful advertising. Not surprisingly many of the new shareholders cashed in their windfall gains by selling their shares. As a result share ownership in the new companies quickly became more concentrated. For example, the 1.1 million BA shareholders at the flotation in February 1987 had reduced to only 0.4 million by early October.

Short-termism

The discipline of the capital markets may actually prove a very mixed blessing for some of the privatised companies if they become subject to the City's alleged 'short termism'. The large investment fund managers are often criticised for taking a short-term view of firm prospects. This would be particularly inappropriate for the public utilities, where both the gestation period for investment and the pay-back period tend to be lengthy.

Opportunity costs

It has also been argued that the flow of funds into privatisation offers has sometimes been diverted from other, more desirable uses. For example, it is reasonable to suppose that applicants for the newly privatised shares are using their savings rather than reducing their consumption. Large sums of money are therefore leaving the building societies during privatisations, and other financial institutions are also deprived of funds. This raises the possibility that what is merely a restructuring and change of ownership of state industry may be reducing the availability of funds for other organisations which would use them for real capital investment. In a similar vein, the contribution of privatisation to reducing the PSBR has been widely criticised as 'selling the family silver'. The sales involve profitable assets and, after privatisation, the Exchequer loses the flow of returns from them.

Burden on taxpayers

A final criticism of privatisation is sometimes made, namely that the public are being sold shares which, as taxpayers, they already collectively own. The purchasers of the shares benefit from the dividends paid by the new profit seeking enterprises, at the expense of taxpayers as a group. Those taxpayers who do not buy the shares, perhaps because they have no spare cash, are effectively dispossessed.

In these various ways, government encouragement for privatisation in its many forms has been regarded as a mixed blessing, providing benefits and costs to individuals, firms and society as a whole. Notice that many of these examples of privatisation involve deregulation, e.g. allowing private companies to provide goods and services which could previously only be provided in the public sector. However, in the public utilities, the fear of large (private) monopolies exploiting the consumer and intimidating other firms has also led to new regulations for electricity, gas, water, etc. It is hoped that, in due time, extra competition will remove the need for such regulations. An example of privatisation is given in Case Study 12.1.

CASE STUDY **12.1** **Privatisation in China**

The welfare of employees at Maanshan Iron and Steel, China's sixth largest steel producer located in central Anhui province, is the responsibility of Wang Rangmin. Mr Wang is in charge of 11 kindergartens, one for each factory; 15 primary and high schools employing 1,500 staff; a hospital with 900 beds and 1,200 workers; more than 56,000 apartments; numerous canteens; and the pensions of tens of thousands of retired workers. This is without counting the 10 schools in towns that mine Maanshan's ore, a technicians' school and a workers' university.

Despite these obligations, Maanshan still regards itself as one of the more fortunate Chinese State Owned Enterprises (SOEs). Three years ago it was picked by the central government as a candidate for a stockmarket listing in Hong Kong. Steel-making, the more profitable part of the business, was separated from the decrepit mining and iron-ore operations, and turned into a limited company. (The decrepit part, together with Mr Wang's welfare empire, became a new holding company.) The listing meant that it got $830 million in fresh capital, a fabulous sum, for expanding the factory.

The steel company's managers only pretend to use Western levels of accounting and management. They know that their company could produce as much with 35,000 staff as it now does with 50,000. But, despite the rigours of the stockmarket, they say they could not think of sacking their superfluous workers.

If Maanshan is having difficulty coping with 'the socialist market economy' that the country's leaders applaud so regularly, think of the bulk of China's SOEs which have no access to outside capital. They cannot afford to cut their bloated payrolls, or reduce the welfare obligations that many enterprises first contracted back in the 1950s. Several enterprises from that era have even had to build new factories just to employ the offspring of the first generation of workers.

According to some economists, state firms have cut their payrolls by 10 million people, to 90 million, in the past year alone. However, there is a huge problem: if state firms keep redundant workers on, they lose money: if they sack them, the jobless join a surly crowd who lack both training programmes and the dole.

State-owned enterprises still employ the bulk of China's 170 million-strong urban workforce. Yet they contributed less than one-third of industrial output in 1999, down from over three-quarters in 1978, when China started to free its economy. Even on official figures, the percentage of enterprises that lose money rose from 27 per cent in 1990 to 41 per cent in 1999; and for the first time ever, the state sector as a whole swung into a small loss during 1996.

Not all those state enterprises which are losing money are the industrial giants that the Soviet Union helped build 40 years ago. The loss-makers fall into different camps. Some are oil or coal companies, which are not allowed to charge world-market prices for their commodities. Others are trading houses. And quite a lot are rustbelt firms that built shiny factories over the past few years to make refrigerators, air conditioners and the like and are now in trouble in a cut-throat market.

Yet China's leaders keep on insisting that privatisation – at least for the 5,000 biggest state enterprises – would be tantamount to robber capitalism. More to the point, the government is underpinning its rhetoric with quantities of state money.

Perhaps 80–90 per cent of all the loans by state banks are made to state-owned enterprises, rather than to the vibrant private or collective parts of the economy. The money lent by banks to the state sector has risen, from 500 billion yuan ($80 billion) at the end of 1993 to over 1 trillion yuan ($120 billion) today. Conservative estimates put the increase in bad debts each year at 50–60 billion yuan. Total bad debts may be more than 25 per cent of the banks' assets. Last year banks increased their lending to state companies by 18 per cent, after inflation. Much of the borrowing went just to pay wages. So at present one part of the state – the SOEs – is massively supported by another part: the banks.

Were the music ever to stop, it could be disastrous. More than one-third of China's state enterprises, at an optimistic reckoning, have liabilities that exceed their assets. They are, in short, bankrupt by any standard definition.

Large SOEs are being encouraged to raise private capital, but state control is never to be surrendered. In the case of Maanshan, the steel company's listing has undoubtedly done some good: its supply of pig-iron is now secured by contractual obligations of price and quality. As a result, the holding company can no longer force it to take shoddy material. But extra capital can also allow failing companies to totter on for longer. With Maanshan, the intention is that, for years to come, the listed company will send a fat annual dividend to its parent, which will go partly to pay for all that welfare run by Mr Wang.

Smaller enterprises are encouraged to merge, or form 'shareholding co-operatives', where 'socialist production relations' are kept intact. For instance, workers at troubled enterprises are increasingly being urged to put up money to buy into the company. Some workers regard this frugal way to raise capital as a form of blackmail.

The truth is that no system of corporate governance is likely to work as long as these businesses belong to the state. Certainly, giving autonomy to managers might lead to better management. More likely, a system that encourages factories, their managers and workers to keep their gains when they do well, but to pass their losses back to the state when they do badly, will end in trouble.

Things may be about to change. One of the conditions of accepting China into the World Trade Organisation (WTO) in 2000 was that within two years foreign banks must be allowed to take deposits from, and lend to, *Chinese businesses*. Within five years of entry foreign banks must also be allowed to offer this same service to *Chinese individuals*. Commentators suggest that this additional competition for Chinese savings will make it more difficult for the Chinese government and banking system to support inefficient state industries.

Based on information from *The Financial Times*, 27 April 2000 and *The Economist*, 14 December 1996.

Questions

1 Identify and explain some of the points made in this article in *favour* of privatisation in China.
2 Identify and explain some of the points made *against* privatisation in China.

Mergers and acquisitions
••••••••••••••••••••••••••••••••

One of the most significant changes in the UK's industrial structure during this century has been the growth of the large-scale firm. Most of the growth in size has been achieved by merger or acquisition. In this section we consider the role the government has played in influencing merger activity and in regulating the activities of large firms (e.g. monopolies), including the use of restrictive practices.

A *merger* takes place with the mutual agreement of the management of both companies, usually through an exchange of shares of the merging firms with shares of the new legal entity. Additional funds are not usually required for the act of merging, and the new venture often reflects the name of both the companies concerned. A *takeover* (or *acquisition*) occurs when the management of Firm A makes a direct offer to the shareholders of Firm B and acquires a controlling interest. Usually the price offered to Firm B shareholders is substantially higher than the current share price on the stock market. In other words, a takeover involves a direct transaction between the management of the acquiring firm and the stockholders of the acquired firm. Takeovers usually require additional funds to be raised by the acquiring firm (Firm A) for the acquisition of the other firm (Firm B) and the identity of the acquired company is often subsumed within that of the purchaser.

Sometimes the distinction between merger and takeover is clear, as when an acquired company has put up a fight to prevent acquisition. However, in the majority of cases the distinction between merger and takeover is difficult to make.

Types of merger

Four major forms of merger activity can be identified: horizontal integration, vertical integration, the formation of conglomerate mergers, and lateral integration.

Horizontal integration

This occurs when firms combine at the same stage of production, involving similar products or services. Some 80 per cent of mergers in the 1990s have been of this type. The merger of Royal Insurance and Sun Alliance to form Royal Sun Alliance in 1996, and the Hong Kong and Shanghai Banking Corporation's acquisition of Midland Bank in 1992, were examples of horizontal mergers. Horizontal integration involving manufacturing firms may provide a number of economies at the level of both the plant (productive unit) and the firm (business unit). *Plant economies* may follow from the rationalisation made possible by horizontal integration. For instance, production may be concentrated at a smaller number of enlarged plants, permitting the familiar technical economies of greater specialisation, the dovetailing of separate processes at higher output, and the application of the 'engineers rule' whereby material costs increase as the square but capacity as the cube. All these lead to a reduction in cost per unit as the size of plant output increases. *Firm economies* result from the growth in size of the whole enterprise, permitting economies via bulk purchase, the spread of similar administrative costs over greater output, and the cheaper cost of finance, etc.

Vertical integration

This occurs when the firms combine at different stages of production of a common good or service. Only about 5 per cent of UK mergers are of this type. Firms might benefit by being able to exert closer control over quality and delivery of supplies if the vertical integration is 'backward', i.e. towards the source of supply. Factor inputs might also be cheaper, obtained at cost instead of cost + profit. The takeover of Texas Eastern, an oil exploration company, by Enterprise Oil in 1989 for £419 million, serves as an example of backward vertical integration. Of course, vertical integration could be 'forward' – towards the retail outlet. This may give the firm merging 'forward' more control of wholesale or retail pricing policy, and more direct customer contact. The purchase of the regional electricity company MANWEB by Scottish Power in 1995 was an example of vertical forward integration between a producer and a distributor of electricity.

Vertical integration can often lead to increased control of the market, infringing monopoly legislation. This is undoubtedly one reason why such mergers are so infrequent. Another is the fact that, as Marks & Spencer has shown, it is not necessary to have a controlling interest in suppliers in order to exert effective control over them. Textile suppliers of Marks & Spencer send over 75 per cent of their total output to Marks & Spencer which has been able to use this dependence to its own advantage. In return for placing long production runs with these suppliers, Marks & Spencer has been able to restrict supplier profit margins while maintaining its viability. Apart from low costs of purchase, Marks & Spencer is also able to insist on frequent batch delivery, cutting stockholding costs to a minimum.

Conglomerate merger

This refers to the adding of different products to each firm's operations. Diversification into products and areas with which the acquiring firm was not directly involved before, accounted for around 13 per cent of all mergers in the UK in the 1990s. The major benefit is the spreading of risk for the firms and shareholders involved. Giant conglomerates like Unilever (with interests in food, detergents, toilet preparations, chemicals, paper, plastics, packaging, animal feeds, transport and tropical plantations – in 75 separate countries) are largely cushioned against any damaging movements which are restricted to particular product groups or particular countries. The various *firm economies* outlined above may also result from a conglomerate merger. The ability to buy companies relatively cheaply on the stock exchange and to sell parts of them off at a profit later, became an important reason for conglomerate mergers in the 1980s. The takeovers by Hanson plc of the Imperial Group, Consolidated Goldfields and the Eastern Group in 1986, 1989 and 1995, respectively, provide good examples of the growth of a large conglomerate organisation. Despite these benefits of diversification, the recession of the early 1990s led many firms to revert to more familiar 'core' businesses. For example, the de-merger of Hanson plc in 1996 produced four businesses with recognisable 'core' activities, namely tobacco, chemicals, building and energy.

Lateral integration

This is sometimes given separate treatment, though in practice it is difficult to distinguish from a conglomerate merger. The term 'lateral integration' is often used when the firms which combine are involved in different products, but in products which have *some element of commonality*. This might be in terms of factor input, such as requiring similar labour skills, capital equipment, or raw materials; or it might be in terms of product outlet. For example, the takeover of Clerical Medical, the life assurance company, by Halifax Building Society for £800 million in 1996 involved the linking of companies with different products but within the same financial sector. The increase in savings by an ageing population, together with a reduction in mortgage business, meant that the Halifax had surplus funds which it could now direct into insurance policies using Clerical Medical's strong presence among independent financial advisers. These advisers could also act as distribution channels for other Halifax products as well as for those of its Clerical Medical subsidiary.

PAUSE FOR THOUGHT 2   *Can you list some recent examples of each of the above types of merger?*

Controls of mergers and acquisitions

United Kingdom legislation has been tentative in its approach to merger activity. This is because governments have recognised the desirable qualities of some monopoly situations created through merger and have therefore sought to examine each case on its individual merits.

Monopolies and mergers legislation

The 1965 Monopolies and Mergers Act updated an earlier 1948 Act and provided for the investigation of mergers or acquisitions which might produce or strengthen a unitary monopoly, defined as being where over 33 per cent of output was in the hands of a single firm. Such investigation could also occur where mergers involved assets in excess of £5 million. The Board of Trade (now the Department of Trade and Industry) could prohibit those cases found by the commission to be 'contrary to the public interest', and could set conditions under which certain mergers might be allowed to proceed. The effect of the 1965 Act was to slow down the trend towards greater industrial concentration rather than seriously to inhibit the growth of larger firms. Indeed, the vast majority of mergers and acquisitions proceeded unopposed. Since 1965, less than 3 per cent of mergers eligible for consideration by the Monopolies and Mergers Commission (now Competition Commission) have, in fact, been referred to it, with fewer than 1 per cent ruled against the public interest.

PAUSE FOR THOUGHT 3   *Why might the Monopolies and Mergers Commission (now called the Competition Commission) be reluctant to rule many mergers as being against the public interest?*

The UK's present legislation relating to mergers and acquisitions is mainly covered by the provisions of the 1973 Fair Trading Act. The 1998 Competition Act (which deals mainly with anti-competitive activity) also has implications for mergers, although these are relatively minor. The main aspects of merger control are as follows:

1   In order to *qualify for investigation* a merger must satisfy either the 'share of supply test' or the 'assets test'. In other words, the merger must result either in a situation where the merged firms would control 25 per cent or more of the market for a particular good or service in the UK as a whole or in a substantial part of the UK ('share of supply test') *or* the merger must involve gross world-wide assets exceeding £70m in value ('assets test').

2   In order to *enforce* merger control policy, the Office of Fair Trading (OFT) and the post of Director-General of Fair Trading (DGFT) were established in 1973. The Director-General heads the Office of Fair Trading (OFT) and advises the Secretary of State for Trade and Industry as to which mergers should be referred to a Competition Commission, which then decides whether or not the mergers are against the 'public interest'. (As we shall see, the lack of clear definition of the 'public interest' has led to some arbitrariness in the implementation of merger control policies.) The Competition Commission is an independent body with members drawn from industry, commerce and academic life. The Competition Commission investigates mergers submitted to it by the Secretary of State for Trade and Industry and reports its conclusions back to this Minister. Prior to 1999, the merger work of the Competition Commission was done by the Monopolies and Mergers Commission (MMC).

3   The procedure for referral can be followed in Figure 12.1. Some 28 per cent of all takeover bids are contested by the boards of the 'raided' companies (a) and in around 40 per cent of these cases the boards are able to defend themselves successfully (b) so that the proposals are abandoned. Of the cases that remain (voluntary mergers and unsuccessful defences by boards) only a small proportion (less than 3 per cent) are recommended for referral to the Competition Commission by the DGFT (c). As can be seen from Figure 12.1, the Secretary of State for Trade and Industry can overrule the DGFT's recommendation ((d) and (e)). After the Competition Commission has ruled on the merger, the Secretary of State has power to overrule such decisions ((f) and (g)).

The ability of the Secretary of State to use the 'public interest' test to overrule the Competition Commission's (previously MMC) recommendations has often created complaints of undue government involvement in decision-making. A few examples of the Secretary of State overruling the DGFT are considered below.

First, in February 1993, the DGFT advised the Secretary of State for Trade and Industry, Mr Michael Heseltine, to refer two takeover situations to the MMC, namely the GEC acquisition of Philips' infra-red components business and the hostile bid by Airtours for Owners Abroad. The Secretary of State rejected the DGFT's advice (d) on the grounds that the mergers might help to rationalise the industries concerned and create strong competitive companies. In the Owners Abroad case, it was felt that barriers to entry into the market were low and that the merger of these two companies would provide strong competition for the market leader, Thomson Holidays. The proposals were allowed to proceed.

Second, in August 1998, Margaret Beckett, the Secretary of State for Trade and Industry, overruled a decision by the MMC in a case relating to the Scottish bus industry. First Group, the transport company, had made a £96m acquisition of the Glasgow-based bus company SB Holdings in 1997. The acquisition was referred by the DGFT to the (then) MMC, which decided that such a merger might act against the public interest. It recommended that First Group should sell a division of its Scottish operations in order to reduce its market share

Figure 12.1

The referral procedure

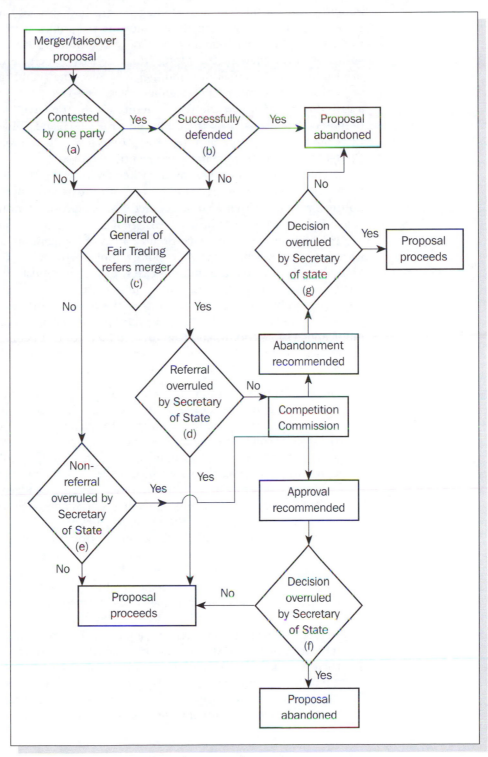

before the merger could be allowed to proceed. However, the Secretary of State overruled the MMC in August 1998 (g), arguing that soon after First Group had bought the bus company, a rival (Stagecoach) had entered the Glasgow bus market, thus increasing competition. Allowing the proposed merger to proceed *without* First Group having had to sell a division of its Scottish operations was contrary to the view of the MMC which felt that such deinvestment was needed to increase competition and thereby protect the 'public interest'.

Third, in November 1999, Stephen Byers, the Secretary of State for Trade and Industry, overruled the recommendation of the DGFT *not* to refer the proposed £8.5bn merger of the cable companies NTL and Cable & Wireless to the Competition Commission (e). The proposal was therefore referred to the Competition Commission (and subsequently approved).

Such complex manoeuvres by the Director-General of Fair Trading and the Secretary of State often give the impression of extensive behind-the-scenes political activity, rather than a detailed assessment of economic arguments when deciding whether to proceed with, or abandon, proposed mergers.

The MMC has been involved in most areas of competition policy, although its focus has broadened over time. For example, between 1950 and 1999, the MMC has investigated around 400 cases, of which almost 50 per cent were merger cases and around 35 per cent monopoly cases, with merger cases becoming increasingly more important. Most of the MMC reports over the 1950–96 period (54.3 per cent) involved Manufacturing, followed by Transport and communication (14.7 per cent) and Banking and finance (10.1 per cent).

Criticisms of the MMC (now Competition Commission) and of UK competition policy in general became stronger during the second half of the 1990s.

1   The MMC and its successor, the Competition Commission, have been criticised as lacking in both resources and professionalism. The Competition Commission has one full-time chairman, three part-time deputy chairmen, 31 part-time commissioners and fewer than 80 staff. Many argue that with such restricted resources, the commission is often 'out-gunned' by lawyers representing the firms under investigation. Further, the fact that detailed analysis of complex markets ultimately depends on the judgements of a few individuals for whom commission membership is only a part-time occupation is seen by some as unprofessional.

2   There is often an element of ideological inconsistency between government policy and subsequent MMC decisions. For example in 1995, Ian Laing, the Secretary of State, allowed through the Scottish Power (generator) bid for MANWEB (distributor) without referring it to the MMC. Yet in 1996, the Secretary of State *did* refer a similar (vertical) takeover bid by National Power (generator) for Southern Electricity (distributor). Even more surprising, when the MMC recommended the bid go ahead, the Secretary of State overruled the MMC and the proposal was abandoned.

3   There is arguably some strategic confusion in the implementation of competition policy. For example, blocking the National Power takeover of a regional electricity company arguably increases the likelihood of *overseas* bids for the power generating companies as well as the distribution companies.

More recent indications of the government's attitude towards mergers have appeared in a consultation document (August 1999) aimed at ensuring that merger policy should be geared to promoting UK competitiveness and the interests of the consumer. In other words, the 'public interest test' would now become more explicitly a 'competition test' taking into consideration many variables ranging from market power and dominance to efficiency gains for consumers. The consultation document also sought to reduce any potential political interference in the merger process. Two options were suggested in the document.

The first option broadly retains the present division between the OFT and the Competition Commission. The OFT would conduct preliminary investigations using the 'competition test' to determine whether or not an in-depth inquiry was merited. The DGFT would then make recommendations to the Competition Commission which could be overruled by the Secretary of State under the 'public interest test' only in very special circumstances (e.g. national defence issues). The Competition Commission would then be responsible for conducting a full investigation into the proposed merger and for reaching a conclusion as to whether or not a merger should be recommended. Again the Secretary of State would only be able to block this recommendation in the exceptional circumstances discussed above. This situation would be very similar to the procedure shown in Figure 12.1 but with the Secretary of State's power under (d), (e), (f) and (g) considerably curtailed, because the Minister could only overrule DGFT decisions through the now rather limited 'public interest' test but *not* through the 'competition test'.

The second option would remodel the UK along European Union lines, with the OFT undertaking a first stage investigation to determine whether a merger raises any 'serious doubts'. If the DGFT had any concerns after this initial investigation then the OFT would launch a second, more detailed investigation and come to a conclusion. Any appeals against this final decision would be referred to the Competition Commission which could confirm or overturn the decision. In this second option, the Competition Commission would act purely as an *appeals body* rather than as a decision-making body (as in the first option). Under this second option, as well as the current (asset and market share) criteria for measuring whether a merger qualifies for investigation, there is the suggestion of introducing a further threshold based on turnover, as is currently the case in the EU.

Restrictive practices legislation

The Restrictive Trades Practices Act of 1956 separated unitary monopoly investigations from *restrictive practices* operated by groups of firms. A restrictive practice operated by groups of firms had now to be registered with a Registrar of Restrictive Practices. It was his responsibility to bring cases to the Restrictive Practices Court, consisting of five judges and ten lay members with the status of a High Court. Such restrictive practices were deemed against the public interest unless they could satisfy at least one of seven 'gateways'.

1   That it protects the public against injury.
2   That it confers specific benefits on consumers.
3   That it prevents local unemployment.

4 That it counters existing restrictions on competition.
5 That it maintains exports.
6 That it supports other acceptable restrictions.
7 That it assists the negotiation of fair trading terms for suppliers and buyers.

Even having satisfied one or more of the 'gateway' conditions, the firms had still to show that the overall benefits from the restrictive practice were clearly greater than the costs incurred. This 'tail-piece' was largely responsible for the prohibition of many restrictive practices. Between 1956 and 1996 over 10,000 restrictive agreements have been registered. However, few of these have been brought before the court; the majority of such practices have been 'voluntarily' ended by the parties themselves in anticipation of an unfavourable decision by the court.

In 1968, 'information agreements' (i.e. agreements whereby information concerning prices, conditions, etc., are formally exchanged) were for the first time considered a restrictive practice. Also in 1968 an eighth 'gateway' was added, namely 'that the agreement neither restricts nor deters competition'. The Fair Trading Act of 1973 gave permission for restrictive practices legislation to be extended to cover *services* as well as the production of goods, though this was only implemented three years later. The 1976 Restrictive Practices Act consolidated previous legislation, with the Director-General of Fair Trading now responsible for bringing restrictive practices before the court.

Despite these changes, the adequacy of Restrictive Practices legislation has been questioned. For example, under the Restrictive Practices Act there are no financial penalties for failing to register a restrictive agreement. Again, because the powers of the Office of Fair Trading (OFT) to investigate suspected secret agreements are so limited, such agreements continue to abound.

EU legislation

Many European countries have long histories of state intervention in markets so it is hardly surprising that the European Commission accepts the case for intervention by member governments. Apart from agriculture, competition is the only area in which the EU has been able to implement effectively a common policy across member countries. The Commission can intervene to control the behaviour of monopolies, and to increase the degree of competition, through authority derived directly from the Treaty of Rome:

1 Article 81 prohibits agreements between enterprises which result in the restriction of competition (notably relating to price-fixing, market-sharing, production limitations and other restrictive practices). This article refers to any agreement affecting trade between member states and therefore applies to a large number of British industries.
2 Article 82 prohibits a dominant firm, or group of firms, from using their market power to exploit consumers.
3 Articles 87 and 88 prohibit government subsidies to industries or individual firms which will distort, or threaten to distort, competition.

A good indicator of the nature and intensity of merger and acquisitions activity in the EU can be gauged by a brief analysis of mergers/acquisitions which were notified to the European Commission between 1990 and 1999. These were mergers/acquisitions activities which were deemed by the European Commission as having the potential to exercise 'unacceptable power' within the EU. Although they do not represent the total number of mergers/acquisitions actually occurring in the EU, they do reflect merger activity involving the most important companies operating in the EU. From Table 12.1 we can see that 1,228 mergers were notified to the EU between 1990 and 1999 for preliminary investigation as to whether their likely impacts came under the scope of EU rules on merger activity. Some 458 or 37 per cent of the total involved companies located in different member states, while 370 or 30 per cent involved merger activity between EU and non-EU companies. Finally, some 273 or 22 per cent involved mergers between companies from the same country in the EU, i.e. 'home' mergers.

The word 'merger' is often used to cover a wider range of different types of concentrative activity. In Table 12.1 we can see that 'joint ventures' and 'acquisition of majority of assets' account for 84 per cent of notifications, while 'agreed bids' account for only 7 per cent of total activity. We can also see that five countries account for 68 per cent of all merger notifications within the EU, with the USA being the main non-EU country involved. Finally, the top five sectors most active in merger notifications account for a third of all cases. It is interesting to note that they are in the most technologically advanced sectors and in the increasingly competitive service sectors such as finance and insurance.

Table 12.1

Mergers and acquisitions activity between major companies, EU 1990–1999

Mergers and acquisition activity	1990–1999
Total number of notified cases	1,228
Borders of operations	
Cross-border: inside EU	458
Cross-border: EU – non EU	370
Cross-border: non EU – non EU	39
No cross-border: inside EU	273
No cross-border: outside EU	88
Type of concentration (% of total)	
Joint ventures	45
Acquisition of majority of assets	39
Agreed bid	7
Other mergers	9
Main countries involved in merger activity (% of total)	
Germany	21
UK	14
France	13
USA	13
Netherlands	7
Others	32
Top five sectors involved in merger activity (% of total)	
Chemicals and chemical products	10
Telecommunications	7
Financial intermediation	7
Insurance and pension funding	6
Manufacture of machinery and equipment	6

Adapted from European Commission (2000), *Statistics: European Merger Control* 1990–1999, Competition Directorate General.

European competition policy has been criticised for its lack of comprehensiveness but in December 1989, the Council of Ministers agreed for the first time on specific cross-border merger regulations. The criteria for judging whether a merger should be referred to the European Commission cover three aspects. First, the companies concerned must have a combined world turnover of more than 5 billion ECU. Secondly, at least two of the companies concerned in the merger must have a Community-wide turnover of at least 250m ECU each. Thirdly, if both parties to the merger have two-thirds of their business in the same member state, the merger will be subject to national and not Community controls.

The Commission must be notified of merger proposals which meet the criteria noted above within one week of the announcement of the bid and it will vet each proposed merger against a concept of 'a dominant position'. Any creation or strengthening of a dominant position will be seen as incompatible with the aims of the Community if it significantly impedes 'effective competition'. The Commission has one month after notification to decide whether to start proceedings and then four months to make a final decision. If a case is being investigated by the Commission it will *not* also be investigated by national bodies such as the British Competition Commission. Member states may prevent a merger which has already been permitted by the Community only if it involves public security, involves some aspects of the media or if competition in the local markets is threatened. The new policy took effect in September 1990 and has resulted in only 40 to 50 cases per year because the thresholds for investigations are so high.

There have been some reservations about the 1990 EU legislation on competition policy. First, a main aim of the legislation was to introduce the 'one-stop shop' which means that merging companies would be liable to either European *or* national merger control, but not both. However, we have noted that there are situations where national merger control can override EU control in certain instances, so that there may be a 'two-stop shop'. Secondly, it was not clear how the rules would apply to non-EU companies. For example, it was quite possible that two US or Japanese companies each with the required amount of sales in the Community, but with no actual Community presence, could merge. While such a case would certainly fall within the EU merger rules, it was not clear how seriously the Commission would pursue its powers in such cases. Third, it was not clear how the EU would deal with joint ventures which, as noted in Table 12.1, comprise some 45 per cent of concentrative activity in the EU.

In March 1998 a number of amendments were made to the scope of EU cross-border merger regulations, in effect increasing the number of mergers which can be referred to the EU Commission. The threshold (turnover) figures noted earlier had been criticised for being set at too high a level, so that only large mergers could be referred *exclusively* to the EU Commission, thereby meeting the 'one-stop shop' principle. Of course such an approach suited many individual member countries of the EU which did not want to cede to the Commission their own national authority to investigate mergers. However, by 1996 the EU Commission had suggested a 'middle road' whereby the old higher thresholds could remain but in which other thresholds would be introduced to allow more mergers to be dealt with exclusively by the EU Commission.

The result of these amendments means that the three original criteria for exclusive reference to the EU Commission still remain, but other criteria have been added to cover some mergers which would not be large enough to qualify under the ECU 5bn and ECU 250m rules described earlier. For example, the Commission can now assume exclusive jurisdiction for any merger if the following three new, and rather complicated, conditions *all* hold true. First, if the combined aggregate world-wide turnover of the undertakings concerned exceeds ECU 2.5bn *and* second, if in each of at least three member states, the combined aggregate turnover of the undertakings concerned is more than ECU 100m *and* third, if in each of the same three member states, the aggregate turnover of each of at least two of the undertakings concerned exceeds ECU 25m. The Commission believes that the new thresholds may result in more companies having the choice of making only one filing to the Commission instead of multiple national filings (i.e. there will now be more 'one-stop shop' opportunities). Of course the difficulty of calculating even more turnover figures than before will add to the complexity of the whole process. To date the Commission has handled around 80 merger cases per year since 1991, and the new legislation will perhaps increase this by another eight mergers per year. As regards joint ventures the new regulations make a distinction between 'concentrative' joint ventures and 'cooperative' joint ventures, with the new EU Commission rules applying to the first type (which was seen as concentrating power) but not to the second (which was merely seen as a method of coordinating competitive behaviour). The second type was to be covered by Articles 81 and 82 (formally Articles 85 and 86) of the Treaty of Rome, as before.

CASE STUDY **12.2** **Mergers and efficiency**

Few things have transformed American management as radically in the past couple of decades as mergers and acquisitions. The 1980s saw more than 55,000 companies change hands, for a total of just under $2,000 billion; and, after a cool spell in the early 1990s, the merger market heated up again, exceeding the 1980s figures in both volume and value of companies changing hands during the 1990s.

Is all this buying and selling good for companies? Michael Jensen, the most influential analyst of the phenomenon, thinks so. A professor at Harvard Business School, he argued that it discourages waste and forces managers to concentrate on their central task – creating value for shareholders. He even defends the $1,000 billion of debt accumulated in the buying frenzy of the 1980s on the grounds that, rather like a death sentence, it helped to concentrate the mind.

But others disagree. Another Harvard professor, Michael Porter, has demonstrated that the average acquisition fails to benefit the firm doing the acquiring. Two other academics at Columbia University, Matthew Hayward and Donald Hambrick, have shown that the premium that bosses pay for companies is determined more by the amount of coverage they get in the business press than by any possible synergies with their purchase.

One way to settle the argument is to look at the impact of acquisitions on innovation. The capacity to invent new products and processes in even the most mundane businesses is what keeps firms ahead; Rubbermaid leads the household-goods industry because it produces a relentless stream of new gizmos. Another American firm, Wal-Mart, has grown by getting its goods on the shelf faster and more cheaply than its rivals.

Unsurprisingly, the most frequently heard objections to the mergers and acquisitions frenzy of the 1980s and 1990s was that it would wreak havoc with R&D. A succession of economic studies – notably those of Bronwyn Hall, a professor at the University of California, Berkeley – found that it had no such effect. But these studies were based on too small a sample and too narrow a time scale to be definitive. A more recent study by Michael Hitt, a professor at Texas A&M University, which has neither shortcoming, offers powerful support to the critics of mergers.

Mr Hitt and his colleagues surveyed 776 industrial firms that reported R&D expenditure annually in 1985–91 and that also made available information on acquisitions, divestitures and financial performance. The authors measured innovation by looking at both R&D expenditure (measured against sales) and the introduction of new products and processes. The results were unequivocal: firms that adopted an aggressive acquisitions strategy spent less on R&D and produced fewer innovations than less active firms.

➤ Buying companies soaks up an enormous amount of money and management time. Not only does it take time to find and buy targets: managers also waste months or even years melding the two companies together and searching for those elusive synergies.

➤ Buying companies often creates debt. Servicing that debt siphons resources from internal projects – particularly as the rules imposed by creditors frequently discourage risky projects that tie up capital.

➤ Acquisitions force firms to discipline their managers with 'financial' controls rather than 'strategic' ones. This distinction was first popularised by Alfred Chandler, America's top business historian. Strategic controls are based on what the managers reckon will be good for the long-term health of the company. Financial controls concentrate on quarterly results and hard measures such as return on investment. Business managers who are subjected only to financial controls tend to reduce any new investments (notably in product development) that will pay off only in the long term (when they will have been moved to another job).

➤ Acquisitions can be seen as a substitute for internal innovation. Why risk inventing things yourself, the argument goes, when you can simply buy a firm that has already done so? Sometimes this works: America's General Electric has used this strategy to good effect. But the list of failed attempts to buy innovation is long: in software alone it includes Novell's purchase of WordPerfect and Borland's of Ashton Tate. Mr Hitt's paper speculates that one reason for such frequent failures is that acquiring firms tend to integrate innovative businesses into their organisations by imposing tight financial controls, effectively killing innovation.

A rather similar view of the impacts of merger activity was reported by the accountancy firm KPMG in the UK in 1999. In a major survey it reported that only 17 per cent of mergers added shareholder value, while as many as 53 per cent of mergers destroyed shareholder value. The report suggests that one of the factors driving the mergers 'boom', despite these harsh facts, has been the buoyancy of share prices. While the value of the targets has been rising, so too has the ability to pay of the predators, which have been able to issue new shares or rights issues of shares at high prices. In addition, many firms readily admit that their bids for rivals are partly motivated by the fear of otherwise dropping out of the FTSE 100 index, which usually has a substantial and negative impact on the share price. Indeed, smaller companies too are rushing to 'get married' in order to qualify in terms of size for the FTSE 250 list, according to John Kelly of KPMG's M&A department.

Based on information from *The Guardian*, 30 November 1999 and *The Economist*, 14 December 1996.

Questions

1 Identify and explain some potential *benefits* of mergers or takeovers considered in the case study.
2 Identify and explain some potential *costs* of mergers or takeovers considered in the case study.

The small firm
····················

As well as seeking to oversee and regulate the *growth* of companies through mergers and acquisitions, the government has sought to encourage new start-ups and *small firm* activity in general. Although the precise definition of a 'small firm' varies between countries, Table 12.2 suggests that small to medium-sized enterprises (SMEs) play an important role in UK economic activity.

Table 12.2 shows that there were some 3,658,000 businesses in the UK in 1998. The new category 'class size zero' includes enterprises which consist of one or more self-employed people with *no employees*. This category reflects the growth of self-employment in the UK, but while it accounts for 64 per cent of the total number of businesses it only accounts for some 12.7 per cent of total employment and 4.6 per cent of total turnover. Small businesses of fewer than 50 employees can be seen from the table to account for nearly half of total employment and over a third of total turnover. If we include small and medium-sized enterprises (SMEs), i.e. businesses employing fewer than 250 employees, then such businesses account for around 56 per cent of employment and 51 per cent of turnover. The total number of businesses in the UK rose from 2.4 million in 1979 to 3.7 million in 1998 and since most of the *new* businesses are small, this reflects a significant growth in the small firm sector.

PAUSE FOR THOUGHT 4   *As well as telling us much about the* small *firm, what does Table 12.2 tell us about larger firms?*

Table 12.2
Number of businesses, employment and turnover share by size band (1998)

Employment size band	Number of businesses ('000)	Share of total (%)		
		Businesses	Employment	Turnover
0	2,340	64.0	12.7	4.6
1–4	923	25.2	10.9	11.1
5–9	204	5.6	6.9	6.4
10–19	112	3.1	7.3	8.0
20–49	48	1.3	6.9	7.9
50–99	15	0.4	4.8	5.8
100–199	8	0.2	5.2	6.1
200–249	2	–	1.6	2.0
250–499	3	0.1	5.2	8.0
500+	3	0.1	38.5	40.1
	3,658	100.0	100.0	100.0

Adapted from Department of Trade and Industry (1999), Table 1.

The renewed interest in small firms

Empirical and other evidence began to accumulate in the late 1960s which challenged the views of many economists that large firms must be the engine of economic progress.

First, it began to be felt that large firms might not always be the most innovative. Instead of large firms growing still larger by capturing new markets as a result of product and process innovation, they often grew by taking over *existing* firms with established products and processes.

Second, evidence began to be published which indicated that small firms were themselves beginning to play an important role in innovation, such as developments in new products and processes.

Third, it was realised that the growth in size of firms (business units) was not, in the main, due to the growth in size of plants (production units). Concentration had often increased because firms had built or acquired *more* plants, not because they had built *larger* ones. Put another way, increasing concentration could not be explained by increased technical economies of scale at plant level. The small firm may therefore be able to compete with the large firm even though it produces in relatively small plants.

Fourth, evidence began to accumulate that acquisitions do not always have particularly beneficial effects on financial performances, such as profits or asset values. Again, such evidence gave grounds for optimism that the small firm may be at less of a disadvantage in terms of profitability than had earlier been thought.

Fifth, various surveys indicated that there is evidence that small firms have contributed a major part of the gains in employment while larger firms have been shedding labour. Birch (1979), in his study of changes in employment in the USA, concluded that small firms (those with 20 or fewer employees) generated 66 per cent of all new jobs in the USA in the period 1969–76. In the UK, Gudgin *et al.* (1979) showed that the main source of employment growth in the regions has been through the setting-up of new, small, indigenous firms, rather than through the inward migration of large firms. More recent studies have tended to confirm these earlier findings. For example, the European network for research on SMEs found that small and medium sized companies accounted for no less than 94 per cent of the UK *net* employment growth over the 1987–91 period. Keeble (1997) found that between 1990 and 1995 the number of people employed by small firms in the UK rose by as much as 19 per cent.

Sixth, the role of small firms in foreign trade has been shown to be more significant than was first thought. The study by Keeble (1997) also showed that the small firm sector as a whole was exporting an average of 12 per cent of its total turnover by the mid-1990s.

For all these reasons there has been a renewed interest in the small firm, which has been reflected in recent government policy. The Department of Trade and Industry introduced a new Enterprise Fund in 1998 designed to provide flexible support for those SMEs with growth potential. The fund has £180m to spend over the 1999–2002 period on the first three items listed opposite.

Measures to help small firms

As part of its policy of creating conditions favourable for sustained growth, the government has sought to stimulate the supply side of the economy, with special attention being paid to the small-firms sector. Specifically, action has been taken in four directions.

➤ Equity and loan capital.
➤ Tax allowances and grants.
➤ Less government interference (i.e. deregulation).
➤ Sources of advice and training.

Equity and loan capital

The flow of equity and loan capital to small firms has been improved by a number of schemes.

The Enterprise Investment Scheme

The Enterprise Investment Scheme (EIS) was introduced in January 1994 and is the successor to the former Business Expansion Scheme (BES) which had been operating since 1983. The EIS was introduced to encourage 'business angels' (outside investors with some business background) to invest in such companies. The scheme offers outside investors income tax relief at 20 per cent on annual investment of up to £150,000 a year in the ordinary shares (equity) of companies which qualify. In addition, any gains made on the sale of shares held for the full three years are exempt from capital gains tax. To qualify for EIS companies must have carried on an approved trade wholly or mainly in the UK for a period of three years after the date of issue of shares, but they need not be resident or incorporated in the UK. Most qualifying companies can normally raise up to £1 million a year through the scheme.

Small Firms/Loan Guarantee Scheme

This was introduced in June 1981 as a pilot scheme for three years. It was intended to cover situations where potential borrowers were unable to provide sufficient collateral, or where the banks considered the risk went beyond their normal criteria for lending. The government now encourages 'approved' financial institutions to lend to small firms by guaranteeing 70 per cent of each loan. This rises to 85 per cent of the loan being guaranteed for established businesses trading for two years or more. Loans of up to £100,000 (£250,000 for established businesses) can be guaranteed for between two to ten years. In return for the guarantee, the borrower pays the Department a premium of extra interest of 1.5 per cent a year for fixed interest loans. Overall, since the scheme began in 1981, some 69,000 loans valued at around £2.4 billion have been guaranteed.

Regional venture capital funds

These are public–private partnerships receiving government financial help from the DTI's Enterprise Fund. These partnerships are aimed at encouraging equity venture capital investment by the private sector in small firms across the English region. The first bids for government support were made in early 2000 and it is hoped that this will give total venture capital funds of nearly £500m to help to create a more dynamic SME presence in the regions.

Venture Capital Trusts

The Venture Capital Trust (VCT) was introduced by the Finance Act (1995) to encourage individuals to invest in smaller, unlisted trading companies. The VCT invests in a range of trading companies whose assets must not exceed £10 million, i.e. it invests in relatively small companies. VCTs are exempt from corporation tax on any capital gains arising on the disposal of their investments. Individuals who invest, i.e. buy shares, in a VCT are exempt from income tax on their dividends from ordinary shares and are also exempt from capital gains tax when they dispose of their shares. By April 2000 a total of 45 VCTs had invested £910m in small companies since the scheme began.

Alternative Investment Market (AIM)

This was opened in June 1995 to meet the demand for a low cost and accessible investment market for small and growing companies. Its trading rules are less demanding than those for a full listing on the Stock Exchange. For example, the cost of a full listing is often high because companies need to appoint mandatory 'sponsors' who check whether the listing rules have been followed. In the new market, the responsibility for the accuracy of the documents rests on the company directors alone. The new market would, in addition, be accessible to companies raising small amounts of capital and those with few shareholders. Investors in AIM companies benefit from the same tax breaks as apply to unquoted companies, including Inheritance Tax relief, Capital Gains Tax relief and relief under the Enterprise Investments Scheme and Venture Capital Trusts. Further, there would be no minimum or maximum limits set on the size of the company joining the market nor on the size of the issue. In brief, the Alternative Investment Market operates under rules which depend more on companies themselves disclosing the basic information rather than on their having to fulfil the strict suitability criteria for a full listing. The hope is that the market will be attractive to small companies, providing the finance and flexibility they need. By July 2000, there were 416 companies participating in the AIM, including football clubs (Preston North End plc), leisure and entertainment groups (Trocadero plc) and medical research and development companies (Electrophoretics International plc). Over £4.5bn has been raised on AIM since 1995, although with the cost of an AIM float as high as £250,000, many smaller firms have looked to other sources of funds.

Tax allowances and grants

In order to help small businesses, tax allowances have been modified, and grants offered.

Corporation tax

This has been made more generous for small firms – small companies in 2000 pay a reduced rate of 10 per cent on their profits (up to a profit limit of £10,000) compared to a standard rate of 30 per cent. Small firms can now set 40 per cent of the cost of investment in machinery and plant against corporation tax during the first year, after which this tax-free allowance falls to 25 per cent in each subsequent year. As a result, small firms are expected to pay some £140m less in 2000–2001. To qualify for such allowances a company must satisfy *at least* two of the following three conditions: a turnover of less than £11.2m, assets of less than £5.6m and employment of fewer than 250 workers.

Enterprise Grants (EG)
This is a scheme for firms employing fewer than 250 people in the new Enterprise Grant areas of England (see Figure 12.2 on page 377) introduced in November 1999 with some £45m committed to the EG scheme over the period 2000–2003. Under this scheme, companies investing up to £500,000 may apply for a once-and-for-all grant of 15 per cent of the fixed capital costs involved up to a maximum of £75,000. The scheme is administered by the Government Office for the Regions with advice from the Regional Development Agencies.

The Small Firms Merit Award for Research and Technology (SMART)
Under the SMART scheme individuals and independent small companies with fewer than 50 employees can submit proposals for funding 75 per cent of the total cost (up to £45,000) of feasibility studies into innovative technology. Larger independent businesses with fewer than 250 employees can apply for funding of up to 30 per cent of the total development cost of new products and processes.

In 1999 there was a major expansion of the scheme to cover R&D and consultancy costs for smaller projects undertaken by individuals or 'micro enterprises' with fewer than ten employees. Such grants are available to those who want to develop simple low-cost prototypes of new products which involve technological advance and/or novelty. The expenditure on such grants will average £33.3m per year between 1999 and 2002.

Critics of such schemes argue that civil servants are not the right people to pick 'winners' and that the schemes often do little to help firms exploit ideas commercially.

Less government interference (deregulation)

During the 1980s, successive Conservative governments were involved in various programmes to decrease government regulation of business activity. In late 1985, a White Paper entitled *Lifting the Burden* suggested that many burdens on business should be lifted. By the early 1990s many small businesses had benefited from these changes. For example, certain small firms were exempt from some of the requirements relating to industrial tribunals, maternity reinstatement and unfair dismissal procedures. Also small firms had the right to pay business rates by instalments. This process was speeded up by the government's *Deregulation Initiative* which had introduced some 450 measures to deregulate industry by 1994. Also in 1994, the statutory requirement that all companies should have their accounts audited was abolished altogether for companies with a turnover of less than £90,000. This meant that a large number of the smallest firms were saved the expense of the audit process. Since then further initiatives to reduce the regulatory burden on small firms have been announced by both Conservative and Labour governments. However, the complaints of small businesses remain, with 20 per cent of small firms in the annual Bank of England Survey in 2000 citing 'government regulations' as the most important problem they face.

Sources of advice and training

Training and Enterprise Councils (TECs)

The network of 82 TECs in England and Wales were charged with the responsibility of taking forward the government's strategy for training in the 1990s. These independent companies are run by boards of directors led by private sector business leaders and are contracted by the government both to provide the whole country with a skilled workforce and to support and coordinate local economic development. The TECs provide advice, counselling, training and consultancy facilities for small firms.

Chambers of Commerce

These also provide information and support services for small firms while the *Local Enterprise Agencies* (LEAs) offer advice and counselling to new and expanding businesses and often work under contract to the local TEC. There are now over 400 LEAs throughout the UK.

Business Links

These were established in 1993 and were intended to help small firms in particular. These are partnerships between the TECs, Chambers of Commerce, LEAs and local authorities, and bring together the most important business development services in a single, accessible location ('one-stop shops'). At the heart of each Business Link are the Personal Business Advisers (PBAs) who foster growth by helping to provide information and advice. The Business Links are designed for smaller companies with 20–200 employees and also specialise in services in the areas of export, consultancy, innovation, design and business skills.

Small Business Service (SBS)

Established in April 2000, the SBS is designed to act as an effective voice for small firms in government. It aims to simplify and improve the quality and coherence of government support for small firms and to ensure that such firms have the consultancy, advice and planning to help small businesses get online and invest in information technology. The SBS will establish a network of 45 local outlets based on a 'franchise model' so that the existing Business Links partners can submit proposals to deliver services on behalf of the SBS. People with considerable private sector experience will extend the Personal Business Advisers system introduced under the Links scheme, with each SBS outlet franchising professional organisations to deliver high-quality services. The aim of the new system is to help decrease 'red tape' and to standardise the information available to small firms. The new head of SBS will report to the Small Firms Minister and the Department of Trade and Industry Minister, as well as having access to the Prime Minister for consultation.

CASE STUDY **12.3** 'Show business angels'

Eight years ago Kathleen Williams, a middle-aged teacher from Sevenoaks in Kent, was left £1,000 by an aunt. Her husband Ken wanted to use the windfall to rebuild the garage, but Kathleen, an amateur dramatics enthusiast, had other ideas. Ken remembers, 'She took all the money and invested it in a West End show. She knew nothing about the commercial theatre and I mentally kissed goodbye to every penny.'

I was furious.' But not any more. Today that original investment is worth around £20,000 and Ken and Kathleen have proved that there's still no business like show business when it comes to making big money against all the odds.

They are angels, going where lesser mortals fear to tread, to finance theatre shows, sharing the smell of the greasepaint, the roar of the crowd – and the knowledge that nearly 40 per cent of West End shows flop within a fortnight. They also seem to have the vital secret of success when buying shares in the shows. . . luck.

'Our first investment was in *Cats*', says Kathleen. 'No one thought a musical based on T.S. Eliot poems had a hope in hell. Andrew Lloyd Webber even had to mortgage his house to produce it. Now the show has grossed over a billion – and we've made ten times our investment.'

While volatile public taste and soaring costs have made the production of a new show an increasingly hazardous business, never have so many people been so anxious to risk hard-won cash on theatrical speculation. According to the Society of London Theatres there are now at least 3,000 angels prepared to put up to £5,000 a year into new productions in the hope they will turn out to be the new *Cats, Les Miserables or Miss Saigon*, which together have grossed more than £2 billion.

It does happen. Blockbusters like *Me and My Girl* are giving investors a £400 return on every £100 risked, and wily angels who originally put up the cash for Agatha Christie's *The Mousetrap* have long since retired on the profits as the whodunit enters its world-breaking 48th year. In fact there couldn't be a better time to think about putting money into show business.

'Musicals are all the rage and making more money than ever before', says David Crosse, a West End actor-turned angel, who has backed over 20 shows in the past four years. 'There hasn't been a boom like this since before the war. Everyone wants big budget musicals and they cost anything from £750,000 to £3 million to stage. Now it's almost impossible to get government funding and loans, managements are relying increasingly on small private investors.'

Currently, about 20 managements are looking for small backers for straight plays and ten managements are soliciting money for musicals. But new angels are unlikely to get near big name producers who have their own long-term backers, and for a start will probably have to be content with stakes in new productions.

Details of shows needing backers are available from the Society of London Theatres, an organisation which liaises between potential angels and producers in need of cash. Investors are usually offered stakes based on units which can be anything from £250 upwards and are usually 1 per cent of the production costs.

So a £100,000 show would carry units of £1,000, while a unit for a £300,000 show would be as much as £3,000. But traditionally, units have been £1,000 or less – and small investors are resisting this price rise. They say they like to spread their limited capital over several shows and they can't do this if unit costs are high.

Most production companies work on a 60–40 basis, with 60 per cent of profit divided between the angels. But this can just be the start – most hit musicals tour the UK for at least a year. Then there's revenue from foreign transfers and possibly film and TV rights.

But never forget that showbiz investment is high risk, and chilling tales of disaster abound – investors in the flop musical *Rags* lost £25,000 each, and *Kelly* closed after one night, losing £400,000.

While there's big money to be made backing a hit, people should not become angels unless they can face the prospect of losing it, too. If a show flops, that will invariably happen. A short run, even in the West End, is unlikely to generate enough money to pay back the backers. Even rave reviews are often not enough to persuade theatregoers to buy tickets.

Questions

1 How do the 'angels' here compare with the 'business angels' of the Enterprise Investment Scheme?

2 What information might help investors in these shows be more aware of the risks involved?

Regional and urban policy

Government policy has, over many years, sought to influence the *location* of firms. This has usually been aimed at encouraging firms to move into *regions* or *urban areas* (e.g. inner cities) where there are above-average levels of unemployment and other types of deprivation (e.g. poverty). That such differences exist is beyond doubt. For example, unemployment in East Anglia in 2000 is 30 per cent below the national average while in the North East of England it is 56 per cent above that average. But is there really a need for government intervention to remove these geographical differences?

PAUSE FOR THOUGHT 5   *Find data in* Regional Trends *or in other sources to identify some of the differences between the main regions in the UK. Does there seem to be a 'regional problem'?*

The case for the free market

It has been argued that in a dynamic economy, regional or urban differences will be short-run, as in time market forces will tend to equalise the situation across regions and urban areas (*convergence*). This could occur through the movement of firms into the high-unemployment/low-income areas attracted by lower wage costs. At the same time there will be an outward migration of labour from the 'disadvantaged' areas to the relatively prosperous areas where demand, employment and wages are higher. It follows that if labour and capital are perfectly mobile, with no impediment to firms moving into and out of areas, then both regional and urban differences should disappear. For example, in the disadvantaged areas unemployment would fall and wages would rise as firms relocate themselves in these areas. Similarly, in the more prosperous areas unemployment would rise and wages fall as firms move out to the low-wage/low-cost areas. Given sufficient time, and no imperfections, this view suggests that there would be no need for government intervention to solve the 'regional or urban problem', since market forces will eventually cause these areas to converge.

The case for intervention

In practice, imperfections exist and even those who believe in the market mechanism may still advocate some form of regional and urban policy. First, neither labour nor capital is perfectly mobile. There may be a lack of knowledge on the part of employees or employers of opportunities in other areas; or there may be high 'costs' of movement, as with the need for rehousing, the breaking of social ties and the expensive relocation of plant and machinery. Secondly, there may be restrictions on the price of labour or capital, such as maximum or minimum wages, or limits on the dividends which firms can issue. These imperfections may reduce the incentives for both labour and capital to flow out of 'disadvantaged' and into 'advantaged' areas, and vice versa. Under these circumstances even the free-market supporter might admit the need for government intervention to offset these market imperfections. This may take the form of policies to promote labour mobility or to coax firms to move into more disadvantaged areas. Government intervention is then seen as necessary to *enhance* the workings of the market mechanism.

Another view of the regional problem sees a still more urgent need for government intervention (*divergence*). Market forces are regarded as acting in a way which will *aggravate* rather than smooth out geographical disparities. Intervention is no longer a supplement to market forces but must be strong enough to offset them. Any fall in output and employment in an area will reduce the size of the regional/urban market and erode economies of scale. Also labour migration from declining areas may consist of the younger, better educated, more adaptable component of the labour force, leaving behind a less productive labour force. New firms may no longer wish to locate production in such areas even if wages are lower. As regional/urban output declines and unemployment rises, local authority rates may become inadequate to sustain the basic infrastructure and services, further disadvantaging an area already in decline. In this view, government policy has to be strong enough to prevent regions/urban areas constantly 'diverging', with poor areas getting poorer and rich areas getting richer. Such a policy might seek to inhibit the movement of labour out of disadvantaged areas by giving firms incentives to locate there.

To sum up, if, as in the first view, the various regions/urban areas are seen as 'converging' over time, then government intervention need only strengthen the 'natural' market forces making for equality. However if, as in the second view, the regions/urban areas are seen as 'diverging' over time, then a greater degree of government intervention may be needed. Otherwise market forces will cause 'polarisation' between areas of very low output, employment and income on the one hand, and areas of very high output, employment and income on the other.

Regional policy in the UK

In the UK, the need for government intervention in the *regions* was accepted as far back as 1934, with the passing of the first of three Special Areas Acts. These aimed to help the depressed areas by setting up government trading estates, subsidising rents and providing low-interest loans. Since then legislation affecting the regions has been embodied in a variety of Industry and Finance Acts.

Economic planning in the regions is now based on the Government Offices for the Regions (GORs), which act as the regional arms of three government departments, namely the Department of the Environment, Transport and the Regions, the Department for Education and Employment and the Department for

Trade and Industry. Their role is to work in partnership with local communities, including local government, in order to promote economic prosperity in the regions as a whole.

The new GORs also became the basic geographic location for the eight new Regional Development Agencies (RDAs) set up in April 1999, followed by a further new RDA for London created in 2000 with the establishment of the Greater London Authority. They resemble the RDAs already in existence in Wales and Scotland and have the task of producing an economic strategy for each region while at the same time administering many of the government's regional and urban programmes.

During the 1990s three types of area were designated for regional assistance, namely Development Areas (DAs), Intermediate Areas (IAs) and 'split' areas which were a mixture of Development/Intermediate Areas. These areas were designated according to the degree of economic deprivation in those regions as measured by indices such as structural unemployment, long-term unemployment, economic activity rates, and so on. The degree of assistance given to these areas varied from those which needed most help (DAs) to those which needed less help (IAs), and in-between areas with pockets of localised problems ('split' areas). Once the assisted regions had been defined, then UK policy was designed to offer incentives to firms to move into those areas while controlling the expansion of firms outside those areas.

The latest decision to modify the coverage of the areas to be offered regional assistance began in 1999 when the government announced a review of the Assisted Areas of the UK in response to the new European Commission guidelines on regional aid introduced in 1997. This was part of the EU's drive to reduce the overall level of aid in the Community and prepare for the possible accession of new member states in the near future. It was hoped that the new areas will help to make the regional aid system both transparent and comparable across all EU member states. The UK government's latest proposals to the EU were made in 2000 and are shown in Figure 12.2. The *Tier 1* areas are those in which GDP per capita measured in purchasing power parity (PPP) is below 75 per cent of the EU average. These areas are automatically granted Assisted Areas status by the EU Commission. The *Tier 2* areas are more discretionary, being areas designated by the UK government using indictors which are acceptable to the EU (such as unemployment rates, labour participation rates, local dependency on manufacturing, etc.) which suggest significant disparities in economic conditions as compared to the rest of the country. Although the UK can propose the boundaries for Tier 2 areas, the EU can veto the national proposals. The new Tier 1 and Tier 2 areas cover about 29 per cent of the UK as compared to 34 per cent under the previous Assisted Areas regime. Firms in the Tier 1 areas will be eligible for grants of up to 40 per cent of the net project costs whereas firms in Tier 2 areas will be eligible for grants of up to 20 per cent of such costs. In addition, Figure 12.2 shows those areas covered by the new Enterprise Grant (see below).

A number of different types of financial and other incentives have been used by governments in support of regional policies.

Figure 12.2
The Assisted Areas
from July 2000

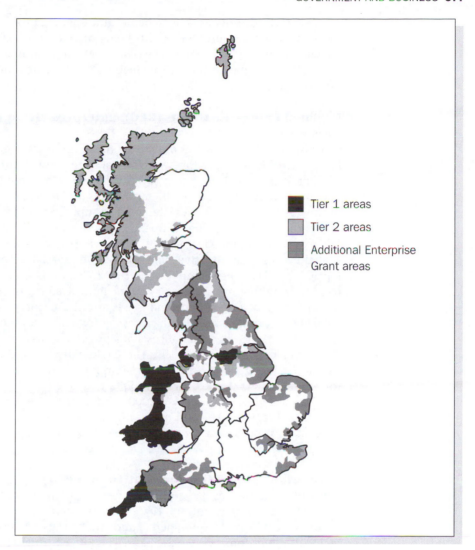

Tier 1 areas

Tier 2 areas

Additional Enterprise
Grant areas

Regional Selective Assistance (RSA)

This is a discretionary grant towards capital and training costs for projects which:

1 Have a good chance of paying their own way.
2 Create or safeguard jobs.
3 Benefit the local or national economy, but
4 Are unable to proceed without government money.

Regional Selective Assistance (RSA) is available for service as well as manufacturing companies, and most often is administered as a *capital-related* or a *job-related* project grant. Capital-related project grants are generally used to help cover the costs of land purchase and site preparation, or the acquisition of plant and machinery. Other costs, such as those incurred because of patent rights, professional fees or machinery installation, may also be covered. Job-related project grants are normally used to help cover the costs of hiring and training staff.

The DTI administers the scheme and spent £110m on RSA grants in 1999–2000, with around 850 grants being offered and 36,000 jobs created or safeguarded in that year alone. The cost per job was estimated at around £4,000 during this period with the scheme helping to stimulate around £1.3bn of total investment.

Regional Enterprise Grants (REG), Enterprise Grant (EG) and other assistance

Since April 1988, companies in Assisted Areas employing fewer than 25 people have been able to apply for two Regional Enterprise Grants. The first was an *investment grant* of 15 per cent towards the costs of fixed assets, subject to a maximum grant of £15,000. The second was an *innovation grant* of 50 per cent of the costs incurred which is designed to support product and process development in small companies with a maximum grant of £25,000. However, both REGs were discontinued in 1996/97 after evaluations of the scheme concluded that they were less effective than alternatives available through the RSA. To replace the REG, a new simplified *Enterprise Grant* (EG) was introduced in 2000 to stimulate the growth of small and medium sized firms in the newly created Enterprise Grant Areas of England (see Figure 12.2). Companies investing up to £500,000 in capital expenditure can apply for a once-and-for-all grant of up to 15 per cent of the fixed capital costs of a project, up to a maximum of £75,000. The scheme is administered by the GORs with advice from the Regional Development Agencies (RDAs) and £45m has been committed to the scheme for the period 2000–2003. In addition, a new Regional Innovation Fund (RIF) was introduced in the Budget of 2000 to support business clusters and 'incubators' in the regions. The aim of the RIF is to support collaborations and joint innovation projects among participating companies (e.g. universities and private companies).

European Regional Development Fund (ERDF)

Since 1973 the UK has had access to a further potential source of regional assistance, the EU. It was only in 1975, however, with the establishment of the European Regional Development Fund, that EU funds became available for regional support on a systematic basis. The ERDF is financed out of the general budget of the EU and allocates most of its funds to member countries on a quota basis rather than for specific regional projects. The funds are given directly to member governments, and are intended to be *additional* to regional aid already given by those governments. Unfortunately, there have been criticisms that these funds were used to replace rather than supplement regional expenditure by member governments. The ERDF is part of the wider *European Structural Funds* initiative which designated six objectives for European areas suffering from structural decline. Of these six, three objectives have been identified for regional enterprise initiatives, with Objectives 1 and 2 of particular importance. Objective 1 covers the most problematic regions lagging behind the rest of the EU, i.e. where GDP per capita is 75 per cent or less of the EU average (Tier 1 areas). From 2000 onwards, the Tier 1 areas in the UK have been identified as Merseyside, South Yorkshire, West Wales and the Valleys, Cornwall and the Isles of Scilly. The areas now outside Tier 1 status but previously included under the previous regime as most in need of assistance (i.e. Northern Ireland and the Highlands and

Islands) will receive transitional help for a further few years. Objective 2 covers regions which do not qualify as Tier 1 areas but which still exhibit symptoms of industrial decline, such as the North East, North West, Yorkshire and Humberside, West Midlands and South Wales (Tier 2 areas). Some 2.8 per cent of the UK's population is covered under Objective 1, and 26 per cent under Objective 2, thus covering some 29 per cent of the UK population in total (see Figure 12.2) compared to 34 per cent under the previous Assisted Areas regime. ERDF grants normally pay up to 40 per cent of the eligible cost of a project in Objective (Tier) 1 areas but less (20 per cent), in Objective (Tier)2 areas. The rest, i.e. 'matching funds', must be found by the prospective ERDF recipient from its own funds or from funds it can raise from other grant-awarding bodies. Over the period 2000–2006 the total allocated from the EU Structural Funds for all these areas will be £10 bn, with £3 bn for Objective (Tier)1 areas.

Use of controls

As well as various types of *incentives* to locate in the disadvantaged regions, the government has in the past made use of various *controls*. For example, it has used Industrial Development Certificates (IDCs) to prevent firms moving to 'overcrowded' regions. Only if an IDC was issued, for example, could the firm locate in, say, the South East of England. Unfortunately, firms refused an IDC were often unwilling to move to an Assisted Area, preferring to move to other parts of the UK, overseas or to abandon the project altogether. The government therefore abandoned IDC controls in 1981.

The effectiveness of regional policy

Various tax and investment incentives which have been at the heart of regional policy have been criticised as being too capital biased, encouraging more capital intensive processes in the Assisted Areas. Another criticism was that these incentives were often 'automatic', being available to all firms in the regions, whether they were creating new employment or not, although in recent years regional grants have become more selective. A number of studies here suggested that such grants have reduced unemployment in the Assisted Areas by around 0.5 per cent.

Certainly, disparities between the *traditionally* prosperous and disadvantaged regions seem to have narrowed. For example, during much of the 1990s the South East created fewer new businesses than the North or North West regions. It is for this reason that various types of assistance are now available to specific segments of the formerly more prosperous regions in the hope that modest assistance now will prevent them needing still greater assistance later.

Urban policy in the UK

There has been a continued drift of population and employment in the post-war period *away from* the major cities and conurbations and *towards* towns and rural areas. For example, the major cities and other metropolitan areas lost over 500,000 jobs between 1981 and 1999, whereas small towns and rural areas gained nearly 1.7 million jobs.

The government has sought to intervene actively in urban areas in a number of ways.

The Urban Development Corporations (UDCs)

These have been created (e.g. London Docklands) with special powers and resources to undertake substantial programmes of land acquisition and development. They can operate independently of local authorities in their areas and are given direct funding from the Treasury.

Enterprise Zones and Free Zones

These have been created to encourage firms to set up in the more derelict parts of inner-city areas. These *enterprise zones* have enjoyed a 10-year exemption on business rates, development land tax, etc. *Free zones* have been allowed to engage in trade without paying customs duties so long as the goods are to be processed prior to being exported out of the UK.

The Urban Programme

Broadly speaking, the aims of the Urban Programme include the following:

1 To promote the regeneration of local urban economies. This involves supporting projects which build new factory units or convert old ones and create training opportunities and jobs for the labour force in those areas.
2 To improve the physical environment of local urban economies. This involves modernising shops and other buildings while also improving parks, waterways and footpaths, etc.
3 To meet social and housing needs in urban areas directly. Social needs include the provision of community centres, sports facilities and health projects, while housing needs cover improvements in refuge accommodation and helping to improve conditions on housing estates which have environmental problems.

Much of this programme has been funded by the *Urban Development Grant (UDG)*, which has now been replaced by the *City Grant* (see below).

Derelict Land Programme

The Secretary of State for the Environment is empowered to pay grants to public bodies, voluntary organisations, private firms and individuals to enable derelict land to be reclaimed, improved or brought into use again. The grant varies between 50 and 100 per cent, depending on the location of the site and the institutions or persons applying.

City Grants

These have been designed to support capital investments undertaken by the private sector in property and business development, especially in the priority areas. The total project value must be above £200,000 and the private sector must convince the Department of the Environment that the project will provide jobs, private housing or other benefits. Further, to receive the grant the Department must be satisfied that the project is unable to proceed because the costs incurred in the development (including allowance for a reasonable profit) exceed the market value of the project. If the application is successful, then the grant would cover this deficit and would therefore allow projects which benefit the community to continue despite the apparent problems of covering all essential costs. The City Grant applications are made directly to the local offices of the DOE and appraisals of the projects are to be made within ten weeks. These procedures simplified and streamlined the grant system.

City Challenge

Local authorities in conjunction with the private sector submit *action plans* which must be environmentally imaginative while also helping to sustain economic activity in key inner city localities.

In these and other ways, the government has sought to help regenerate urban and inner city areas by direct policy action.

The effectiveness of urban policy

Although greater emphasis has been placed on urban policy over the last few years, it has not been without its critics.

First, it has been argued that resources directed to urban policies have been insufficient, accounting for only 4 per cent of the Department of the Environment's spending during much of the 1990s.

Secondly, it is claimed that urban policies have failed to ensure that new jobs created in the inner cities were filled by unemployed inner-city residents. Evidence suggests that higher-skilled commuters from outside the inner city areas often 'crowd out' inner city residents in the competition for employment.

Thirdly, the UDG was criticised for being more helpful in attracting renewal schemes to areas which already have a reasonable degree of economic activity. In a study of 41 UDG sponsored projects it was found that many of the schemes would have gone ahead even without UDG grants. In fact 64 per cent of the total employment generated by the UDG sponsored projects would have been created even without the government subsidy. In other words, companies were likely to have come to those areas even if they had not been offered subsidies.

Fourthly, there is a danger that urban policies could be detrimental to industrial growth as a whole. By limiting their aid to firms which locate in highly urbanised areas, governments may discourage production taking place in more suitable locations, leading to a less efficient allocation of resources. There is also the difficulty that inner cities may gain firms and employment at the expense of the suburbs, or other areas, so that there is no net gain to the economy as a whole.

Certainly, there is little evidence that the gap between inner cities and the major conurbations and more prosperous towns has closed significantly over the past two decades despite all these incentives.

Labour market policies

The government's role in the labour market is threefold: as an employer, as a legislator and as an economic and social policy maker.

The government is a major direct employer of labour, with central government employing 1.1 million persons, or 4 per cent of the workforce in 1999. It influences not only these pay settlements but also those of the local authorities and the remaining nationalised industries, in total an extra 4.1 million persons. The government can, through its position as a primary source of finance and by using cash limits, affect wage bargaining and employment levels in the local authorities and the nationalised industries.

As a legislator, the Conservative government of Margaret Thatcher was particularly active in using the law in an effort to reduce what it perceived as excessive union bargaining power, resulting in high UK wage costs and low labour productivity.

Closed shop

The closed shop is an arrangement whereby only members of specified trade unions can obtain or keep a job. A number of Acts made the closed shop unenforceable by trade unions during the 1980s.

Strikes and other industrial action

Since 1906 Parliament has protected trade unions from claims for damages resulting from strike action. However, the government has selectively removed that protection to discourage over-use of the strike weapon. For example, 'secondary action' (action against an employer not party to a dispute) was made unlawful in 1980, as was union picketing other than at the members' place of work. Since 1984 ballots must be held. Only if a majority of union members are in favour of strike action can a subsequent strike be declared legal, and this must occur within four weeks of the ballot result. Since 1993 these ballots must be fully postal and subject to independent scrutiny, thereby reducing the chance of undue pressure for strike in face-to-face union meetings.

Minimum wage

A National Minimum Wage (NMW) was introduced for the first time in the UK in April 1999. Adults were to receive at least £3.60 per hour with a lower 'development rate' of £3.20 per hour for 18–21 year olds. Until their abolition in 1993, certain industries had established voluntary agreements for minimum wages through the so-called Wages Council, but no national 'floor' for wages had existed before 1999.

Social Chapter

The Social Chapter was adopted in 1992 as part of the Maastricht Treaty. It established a number of *minimum* requirements for members of the EU involving hours and conditions of work. The idea was to provide 'equity', in terms of fair and reasonable employment rights, and a 'level playing field' in terms of competition between firms in member states. It was felt that if only some EU countries imposed better conditions of employment on its firms, then these countries would be at a competitive disadvantage. The UK, however, initially opted out of the Social Chapter and was not bound by its provisions, though some of its provisions (e.g. 48-hour maximum working week) were imposed under Health and Safety Directives which still applied to the UK. The incoming Labour government has abandoned the opt-out so that initiatives such as the

Working Time Directive (setting maximum working hours) in 1998 and the Parent Leave Directive (giving rights to paternity leave, etc.) in 1999 now apply to the UK.

Conclusions

The government has, in these various ways, sought to encourage, direct and control business activity. When markets are far from perfect, the government cannot rely on market forces alone to bring about the desired allocation of resources. The government instead must seek to provide incentives via tax and other allowances, to 'pump-prime' via selective government expenditure and to provide a broad framework for economic activity through government institutions and regulations. In doing all this the government must find a judicious blend of policies. For example, the advantages of markets in allocating resources efficiently via price signals must be harnessed, but potential excesses in the forms of monopolies, restrictive practices and other types of 'market failure' must be curbed.

References and additional reading

Birch, D.L. (1979) *The Job Generation*, MIT.

Griffiths, A. and Wall, S. (2001) Applied Economics (9th edn), Financial Times/Prentice Hall, Harlow, esp. ch. 4, 5, 8, 11 and 12.

Gudgin, G. *et al.* (1979) *New Manufacturing Firms in Regional Employment Growth*, Centre for Environmental Research.

Keeble, D. (1997) 'Small firms, innovation and regional development in Britain in the 1990s', *Regional Studies*, Vol. 31, No. 3, May.

Sources of information/data

Britain: an Official Handbook. Published annually by the ONS, this contains information and data on government and administration, external affairs, economic affairs, the environment, and social and cultural affairs.

Economic Trends. Published monthly by the ONS, this contains tables and charts illustrating trends in the UK economy.

Griffiths, M.A. and Wall, S.D. (2001) *Applied Economics*, 9th edn, Prentice Hall/Financial Times, London.

Labour Market Trends. Published monthly by the ONS, this contains data and articles on a wide range of labour market issues.

Regional Trends. Published annually by the ONS, this presents a wide range of economic, social and demographic indices on the regions.

Social Trends. Published annually by the ONS, this provides a detailed breakdown of patterns of household wealth, income and expenditure, together with demographic, housing and social trends.

Business economics and the Internet

Business Library Web pages (http://www.rgu.ac.uk/library/resource/manage.htm)
Those wishing to look for business and/or management information on the Internet may find this useful. Links are arranged under the headings Business (general), Business News, Marketing, Finance and Accounting, and Human Resource Management.

Business (general) links
If you are unsure where to start, try the Business (general) section. These highlight (and link to) the best collection of links on a range of business topics. The Business and Economy section of Yahoo (uk) includes links to company homepages, business sites and electronic journals.

Business News links
If you want to keep up to date with what's happening in the business world, use the Business News section. There is a link to the *Evening Standard*'s business pages which are updated four times a day! The link to *The Economist* provides access to a selection of articles and surveys from the magazine plus the opportunity to register for free weekly updates on the business world sent to your e-mail address.

CCTA Government information (http://www.open.gov.uk/)
This site will lead to most of the materials published by UK Government authorities, including the Departments of State and other Agencies.

The Economist (http://www.europe.economist.com/) and (http://www.economist.com.uk)
Very useful websites giving access to up-to-date material on the economy, business, the current week's issue of *The Economist*, book reviews and surveys. They also provide links to other related sites.

Financial Times (http://www.ft.com)
This covers current financial and business news. The user has to register (free) before using it but some of its services are not free.

HM Treasury (http://www.hm-treasury.gov.uk)
Press releases, ministers' speeches, lists of research papers, together with details of economic forecasts and budget measures are available on this site.

HMSO (http://www.the-stationery-office.co.uk)
This is a useful site to find out what is being published by HMSO.

The Institute of Fiscal Studies (IFS) (http//www.ifs.org.uk/)
The IFS gives details of the effects of taxation on individuals and companies.

Solutions and guidelines

➤ Answers and responses to Activities, Case Study questions, and Pause for Thought sections.

➤ All Activities, Case Studies and Pause for Thought sections are listed. We have put 'See text' where no solution or answer applies.

Chapter 1 The domestic economic environment

Pause for thought 1

The effect of freezing allowances is that more and more taxpayers would drift into the tax-paying bracket with the result that the Treasury would withdraw more and more income from the circular flow. This effect is called 'fiscal drag'. If earnings rise faster than the general level of inflation then much the same phenomenon will happen. For example, if average incomes rise by 10 per cent per annum and prices rise by 5 per cent per annum then more people will be dragged into the fiscal net.

Pause for thought 2

By abolishing the tax on domestic fuel and power the government would be injecting £1,900 million into the economy according to the figures. By imposing VAT on books and newspapers the Treasury would be withdrawing £1,300 million. The effect would be to increase injections by a net figure of £600 million. This would then circulate around the economy and would, depending on the size of the multiplier, increase aggregate demand by more than £600 million.

Pause for thought 3

There are a variety of factors that might affect the savings ratio. Firstly, there is the disposable income that households have. Generally speaking those with more disposable income save a higher proportion of their income than those on lower levels of income. Also age plays a part, with older consumers saving more proportionately than younger consumers. (This obviously is due to the correlation between age and income which, although far from being a perfect correlation, nevertheless shows that there is a positive relationship between the two.) The rate of interest will affect the savings ratio. A high rate of interest will encourage more savings than a lower one. Consumer confidence will also be critical here. If consumers have confidence in the way the economy is being run or there is a feeling that the economy will continue to grow, this will encourage spending. On the other hand, if there is a feeling that the economy is about to go into recession this will clearly have an impact on people's spending habits. There may also be regional or national differences in the propensity to save. (For example, it is alleged that the Scots are careful with their money and Aberdonians even more so!) A low savings ratio means that more income feeds through to aggregate demand than in economies with a high savings ratio. The fact that consumers in the USA currently (2000) have a low savings ratio means that there will be a rise in aggregate demand in the USA (and also the rest of the world as a result of American consumers' spending).

Case Study 1.1: UK manufacturing grows in confidence

1　The strength of sterling is a significant factor holding back firms. The prospect of another rise in interest rates would restrain economic growth and firms are anxious about the effects that this would have on their growth prospects. Consumer demand would be affected if the interest rate rises continued. These are the sorts of factors which affect business confidence.

2　Interest rate rises affect consumer spending. The costs of borrowing increase and this affects consumer spending. Higher interest rates also affect investment as this raises the cost of borrowing and means that firms would require to earn a higher rate of return to justify the higher costs of borrowing.

Pause for thought 4

The main reason that the savings ratio in the USA has fallen is because consumers in the USA have experienced a rise in disposable income coupled with a fall in the level of inflation. Interest rates have also been quite low and consumer confidence is high. The effect of this is to stimulate consumer spending and this will have a beneficial effect on the world economy as American consumers continue to spend. The circular flow of income from the UK's perspective will show that there is an increase in demand for UK exports which will add to aggregate demand and would generally speaking be beneficial to the UK economy.

Pause for thought 5

Figure 1.5 indicates that government revenue exceeds government expenditure in 2000/1. The implications are that there will be a withdrawal from the circular flow of income and that the level of aggregate demand will be reduced. What the chart is demonstrating, however, is what economists call the 'automatic fiscal stabiliser' effect. As the economy grows then government revenue will also increase as VAT and expenditure taxes rise in line with consumer spending. In addition, company profits rise and this will increase the revenues that the government receives from corporation tax. On the other hand, government expenditure will tend to fall as the economy grows as there will be fewer people who claim unemployment benefit, for example, and there is a corresponding fall in welfare payments.

Pause for thought 6

There has been a deficit in the trade in goods (which represents a withdrawal from the circular flow) whilst there has been a surplus in the trade in services (which represents an injection into the circular flow). The invisibles have been in surplus (injection) and we have been net importers of capital (injection).

Pause for thought 7

1   Of the various components of aggregate demand it is argued that it is easier for the government to make changes to its own expenditure (i.e. G). It can affect consumer spending by changing tax (e.g. by changing direct taxes like income tax or indirect taxes like VAT) or by changing interest rates. However, consumers' reactions to these changes are affected by their propensity to consume which in turn is affected by consumer confidence. Lower interest rates can give consumers more disposable income when mortgage interest falls. If consumers are worried about job security, for instance, then they may not be willing to spend and hence aggregate demand may not be greatly affected. Much the same argument applies to investment spending, which is very sensitive to levels of business confidence. Thus lower interest rates and lower corporation tax rates may give companies more profit but they may not necessarily invest more if they are not confident about the future. Exports and imports are also more difficult to influence directly as they depend on factors that are often outside a government's control, such as the growth of the world economy.

2   Reductions in income tax should affect consumption. They may indirectly affect exports and imports depending on whether there is a rise in inflation as a result of the increased aggregate demand. Lower corporation tax should give companies more profit and possibly affect investment (but see above for other factors to be taken into account). Changes to VAT should also affect the level of consumer spending. Lower interest rates have the potential to affect several components of aggregate demand (e.g. consumer spending, investment spending, exports and imports through the impact on exchange rates).

Pause for thought 8

The J curve will move from J_1 to J_2 if there is an increase in injections (i.e. an increase in investment, exports and government spending).

Pause for thought 9

The results in Table 1.4 indicate that as the size of the marginal propensity to withdraw income increases, so the size of the multiplier decreases.

Case Study 1.2: Japanese economy shows signs of recovery

1   Zero interest rates imply that there is no cost of borrowing. The intended effects are to encourage Japanese consumers to spend.

2   The intended outcome of this policy is to raise the aggregate demand function $(C + I + G + X)$ from AD_1 to AD_2. This causes the level of national income to rise from OY_1 to OY_2 (see the chart for details).

3   The multiplier process has failed because consumers are saving additional income. In short, the marginal propensity to consume is zero.

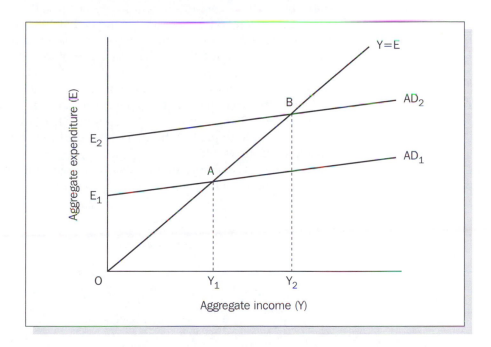

Case Study 1.3: Tax revenue ready reckoner and the 2000 Budget

1   There are many combinations that you could choose. For example, if you decided to focus on indirect taxes and cut VAT by 1 per cent then the effect would be to cost the government about £3.1bn. If, on the other hand, you wanted to focus the tax cuts exclusively on direct taxation, you could cut the income tax rates by 1 per cent and this would yield about £3.7bn (£390m + £2,650m + £720m). A 3 per cent cut in corporation tax rate would yield about £3.3bn.

2   The effects of the tax cuts will be a multiplier of this number because of the multiplier effects. The overall impact depends on which taxes are cut. Indirect taxes tend to affect those on lower incomes more than cuts in income tax. For example, if a household has a low income and hence does not pay income tax then income tax cuts will have no effect. On the other hand, cuts in VAT are more likely to impact on consumer spending directly. Cuts in corporation tax rates may feed through in terms of more investment but this is by no means certain. The effect on aggregate demand will therefore vary depending on which taxes are cut.

3   The dangers are that the increase in aggregate demand would exceed the capacity of the economy and cause inflation.

Activity 1.1: The aims of macroeconomic policy

1   As the data indicates, the economy has undergone a period of fluctuation and change in all of the macroeconomic variables in the period 1979–1999. Economic growth declined rapidly from 1979 to 1981. Inflation also fell but with a timelag in the period 1979–84, while unemployment rose to 3 million (again with a time lag). In addition, the balance of payments as measured by the current account surplus/deficit as a percentage of GDP showed an improvement. All this is pretty much as predicted by theory, namely, as the economy slows down inflation falls and unemployment rises. Also if you look at the data for the period 1983–89, there was significant economic growth resulting in a rise in inflation in 1990 to 9.5 per cent with unemployment falling to less than 2 million and the balance of payments on current account slipping into deficit. Again this is predicted by theory. More recently the economy has grown more consistently with low inflation and declining unemployment. However, there are differing time lags between changes in one variable and changes in others and it is not always possible to predict the exact relationship between the four main macroeconomic variables.

2   It is also pretty obvious from the data that the government has found it difficult to achieve all four objectives simultaneously.

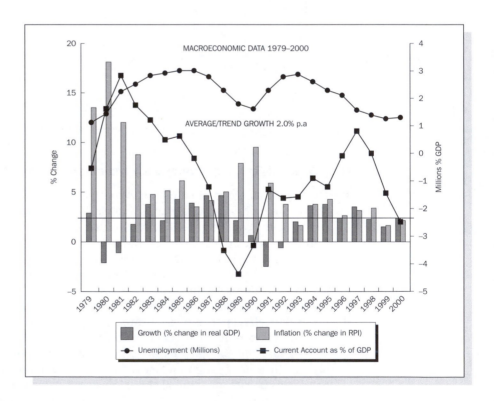

Pause for thought 10

It has been difficult to achieve these objectives because there are conflicts between these aims. For example, as can be seen when the government tries to achieve *full employment*, there is always the danger that the economy 'over-heats'. With 'too much money chasing too few goods' then aggregate demand outstrips aggregate supply and the effect is a rise in *inflation*. This can in turn affect our competitiveness and make it more difficult for the UK to remain competitive in international markets. This in turn adversely affects our *balance of payments*. The government is then often forced to slow down the economy by raising taxes and cutting spending and so this in turn affects *economic growth and full employment.*

Pause for thought 11

Types of unemployment	Examples
Seasonal	Ski instructors, Santa Claus 'workers', hotel workers
Cyclical	Construction workers, estate agents, car workers
Technological	Newspaper printers, unskilled workers, bank clerks
Frictional	Almost anyone who finds themselves 'between jobs'
Structural	Coal miners, shipyard workers, steel workers

Pause for thought 12

See text.

Pause for thought 13

The claimant measure does not include all those who are unemployed. It only counts those who are claiming unemployment benefit. It therefore tends to underestimate the numbers unemployed, particularly married women who when they become unemployed do not always claim unemployment benefit. The survey method therefore tends to produce a higher number of unemployed, but like all surveys it is subject to a margin of error.

Pause for thought 14

1 There is a chance for you to speculate here. Education has the potential to be transformed by such things as the Internet, e-mail and other computer-based innovations in learning. The model of the Open University may be replaced by the Virtual University and already in the Highlands of Scotland a number of agencies are working to make this a reality. Thus lectures and classroom lessons could be supplanted by downloading information directly to your PC at home, thus making it unnecessary for you to leave the comfort of your bedroom to study at school, college or university! (It also means that the lecturer/teacher could record his/her lecture on video and simply transmit it via satellite, cable or a CD-ROM with accompanying e-mailed material, thus allowing the tutor to remain in the comfort of his/her own home while teaching you!)

2   In medicine there is the possibility of surgeons and consultants in one part of the world being linked via satellite or cable to other more remote parts of the world and to be able to pass on their expertise to others. The technological revolution in world-wide communications opens up possibilities which can be seen as a threat or as an opportunity.

Pause for thought 15

1   Housing costs account for almost 20 per cent of average household spending (19.7 per cent). Therefore a 10 per cent rise in housing costs would feed through to a 2 per cent rise in the RPI (20 per cent of 10 per cent).
2   The biggest items of expenditure in the RPI are:
Food   13.0 per cent
Motoring expenses   13.6 per cent
Alcohol   7.1 per cent

Changes in the price of these goods will have a very significant impact on the RPI.

Pause for thought 16

The main weapons for reducing an inflationary gap are fiscal policy and monetary policy. With fiscal policy the authorities would reduce government spending and increase taxation, both direct (e.g. income tax) and indirect (e.g. VAT). With monetary policy the authorities (either the government directly or the central bank) would increase interest rates. This would have the effect of reducing consumer spending and investment spending, other things being equal.

Pause for thought 17

Any factors which raise costs in some way can be cited as a cause of inflationary pressure. If wages rise faster than productivity and the rise is independent of the level of demand in the economy then this can be said to be a major cost–push factor. The cause of such a rise is often put down to aggressive pay bargaining by a monopoly trade union. However, this has not been a significant cause of inflation for a number of years. A rise in the price of a key imported raw material such as oil in the early 1970s is an obvious cost factor. Devaluation or a downward float of the £ can also cause a rise in cost–push factors. Interest rate rises can, in the short term at least, cause costs to rise. The longer term effects of such an increase are more likely to cause a fall in inflation as there will be less spending and the costs of borrowing will also rise, causing a fall in investment.

Pause for thought 18

The case for an independent central bank is based on the fact that a number of economists believe that it is the best guarantee of price stability. The Governor of the Bank of England therefore sets monetary policy free from political interference. Not only is the Bank able to determine for itself the scope of any interest rate changes, but it is also free to determine their timing. Thus it is argued that there is no temptation for the Bank to time interest rate cuts to coincide with the party conference season, for example, or to time the cuts to occur before important elections. On the other hand, the question arises to whom is the Governor of the Bank of England accountable? At least if we do not happen to like the way that the government is running the economy then we can remove them at a General Election. What democratic control would we have over the Bank of England? There is also a fear that central bankers are by nature extremely cautious people and that there would therefore be a tendency to run the economy with spare capacity to avoid the slightest risk of inflation. The evidence on the success of those countries with independent central banks is mixed. Not all low inflation countries have an independent central bank and not all countries with independent central banks have low inflation. Central bank independence may be a necessary condition of price stability but it is not sufficient.

In order to overcome these difficulties it would be necessary to have some parliamentary accountability with the Governor possibly answerable to a select committee of Parliament. In addition, the appointment of the Governor and other senior officials in the Bank could be made subject to parliamentary scrutiny or approval for fixed periods. Failure by the Bank of England to meet its inflation targets requires the Governor to write to the Chancellor of the Exchequer explaining the reasons for the failure. This would be a fairly humiliating public exposure of failure and it is argued is a powerful incentive to meet the targets set.

Pause for thought 19

This is a complex question as there are a variety of factors which can affect an economy's ability to improve its underlying rate of growth. It is bound up with the quantity and the quality of a country's resources, the ways in which it deploys these and how it creates wealth. There may also be cultural factors at work, such as attitudes to risk-taking and the work ethic. Some see the role of the government as damaging in improving the economy's growth potential while others point out the benefits of the private and public sectors working together. A highly competitive home market may also produce world-beating firms able to innovate and develop new products and processes. Finally, some economists believe that it is the stability of the economic environment that is important in ensuring that firms have the confidence to invest in new plant and to develop new products.

Pause for thought 20

The controversial view in the 1980s was that the decline in our manufacturing base was linked to the discovery of North Sea oil. This discovery meant that the £ became a 'petrocurrency' and was much in demand in foreign exchange markets. The effect of this was to make the rate of exchange higher than it might have been. This in turn made it difficult for manufacturers of export goods to capture markets. In addition, the early 1980s saw a rise in interest rates as a result of the government's monetarist experiment, which also had the effect of causing the exchange rate to rise. These two effects therefore caused the demand for UK manufacturing exports to fall and hence, so the argument ran, caused the decline in the UK's manufacturing base.

Chapter 2 The international economic environment
....

Pause for thought 1

The reason why Alpha should trade with Beta relates to the law of comparative advantage. Alpha is four times more efficient at producing computers but only twice as efficient at producing cars. In these circumstances Beta would specialise in the production of cars (and gain all the advantages which accrue from such specialisation) while Alpha would benefit from specialising in the production of computers. Beta politicians could retreat behind tariff barriers, but consumers in Beta would lose out because they would be forced to produce both goods and, as indicated, they would be better to trade.

Activity 2.1

This example indicates that Omega is one-and-a-half times more efficient at producing both goods. Therefore strictly speaking there is no comparative advantage. However, it would pay for Omega and Gamma to come to some agreement about which products they were going to specialise in because there could still be gains from specialisation and trade.

Pause for thought 2

These are set out on pp. 36–7.

Pause for thought 3

It is not just the absolute level of wages which is important but the levels of productivity. In short it is the relative unit labour cost per unit (RULC) which is the important factor (see Chapter 4, Figure 4.2 and p. 100).

Pause for thought 4

See text.

Case Study 2.1: MerCoSur economies regain their footing

1   The major problems with MerCoSur are:
   ➤ Brazil's January 1999 devaluation of its currency, the *real*, heightened trade tensions between Brazil, Argentina, Paraguay and Uruguay. By making Brazil's exports cheaper the devaluation would have the effect of making it more difficult for the other countries in the customs union to export to Brazil.

➤ Tension about the trade imbalance with Brazil escalated when Argentina threatened to place import quotas on Brazilian shoes, clothes and textiles. Analysts say the tensions reflect a structural imbalance in the balance of payments between member countries that must be rectified to preserve MerCoSur.

2 MerCoSur cannot go on with the differential in currencies and economies between member states. If economies grow at different rates and have different rates of inflation and periodic currency realignments then it makes it very difficult to sustain any sort of customs union. Therefore a lack of 'convergence' between the economies of the member states poses one of the biggest threats to success.

Case Study 2.2: The beef over bananas

1 The WTO was set up to avoid trade wars. It should in theory have been able to adjudicate between the two major trading blocs but it has unfortunately been unable to do so in the case of bananas.

2 The underlying flaw appears to be the WTO's difficulty in enforcing its rulings. It has twice told the EU that its policy on the importation of bananas from the Caribbean at the exclusion of bananas from Latin America is illegal, but the EU still has to comply. In addition, the EU's ban on imported meat from the USA is also judged by WTO as against the rules, but no enforcement procedures seem to be effective. If the dispute is not settled then the role of the WTO as the main promoter of free trade is seriously impaired.

3 As the case study points out, the system had been effective. It has dealt with 163 disputes since the WTO was set up in 1995. America has brought the most cases, 53 in all, closely followed by the EU, with 43. America and the EU are also the most common defendants, the United States in 29 cases, the EU in 26. Developing countries have used the system too, both against each other and against rich countries. Most cases have been settled without the need for arbitration. And when the WTO has been called on to adjudicate, no government has yet defied any of its rulings.

4 The fear was that the WTO was seen as being so effective that it was encouraging countries to appeal to the WTO with cases which were to some extent at the limits of what the WTO should have been doing. For example, America tried to use the WTO to compel Japan to enforce its anti-trust rules. The EU complained to the WTO about America's Helms–Burton act, which penalises companies investing in Cuba, but later reached a bilateral settlement. Urged on by trade unions and green groups, America wants the WTO to impose tough and enforceable labour and environmental standards on developing countries.

5 Sometimes the two major trading blocs find it difficult to accept the rulings because of political pressures within their own countries. In the case of bananas there is a strong lobby for the EU to take bananas from the Caribbean because of the historical ties and also because of the economic damage that would be done to the local economies there. On the other side American multinational companies that supply bananas from Latin America are also lobbying the American government to take a tough line

with the EU. Thus we have a clash of powerful pressure groups within the EU and America. In the case of hormone treated beef there are also genuine anxieties from EU consumers about GM modified food which politicians believe would be unwise to ignore.

Pause for thought 5

The main reason is that critics see the WTO as promoting the interest of large multinational companies who, it is alleged, are more interested in profits at the expense of the environment. National governments are seen as being largely powerless to control these companies because their global reach and ability to move production around the world make them largely immune to national government control. The WTO is therefore seen as aiding and abetting a system of capitalism which critics believe is destroying the planet.

Case Study 2.3: China to join the World Trade Organisation

1   The *good news* is:
     ➤ Direct foreign investment in China may jump to $100bn (£68bn) a year by 2005, up from $40bn in 1999.
     ➤ Tariff cuts on many items, leading to
        – less obstruction on imports and exports,
        – reduced costs of raw materials,
        – cheaper prices.
     ➤ Companies from WTO member countries will enjoy improved access to restricted sectors such as telecommunications and insurance.
     Because of increasing competition from abroad, the *bad news* is:
     ➤ China's inefficient state-owned enterprises, in sectors like automotive, oil and steel, are expected to shed over 11 million workers into a crowded labour market.
     ➤ China's farmers, the majority of the population, may be hit even harder.
2   The dangers are that the Chinese economy may not be up to the challenges posed by exposure to international competition. It may also threaten the way that businesses in China are organised as small family-run businesses struggle to compete with large overseas multinational firms. Opening up an economy also has political consequences as consumers gain access to information from abroad. Buying goods over the Internet and seeing the variety of choice offered to foreign consumers may in the long term make it difficult for the Chinese government to control its people in the way it has done in the past. Thus liberalisation of trade may become a precursor to more political freedom.

Pause for thought 6

On the face of it, it would appear to be a 'bad thing' for UK companies to invest overseas by setting up plants there. It might be seen as 'exporting' British jobs abroad and should therefore be stopped. However, the short answer is no. Overseas investment results in interest, dividends and profits being 'repatriated' to the UK and so helps our balance of current account. In the short term there could be disadvantages if UK investment overseas is viewed as 'exporting jobs'. But in the long run it pays the UK to have a free flow of capital because we benefit from the investment made by foreign companies – for example, Japanese car manufacturers. There may be dangers if there were to be a wholesale exodus of firms to locate elsewhere as we would become totally dependent on imports of key products. If there were a threat that this might occur no government would stand idly by and allow it to happen. However, rather than 'banning' the export of capital it is more likely that a government faced with such a situation would examine the policies it was pursuing which were 'frightening off' firms and encouraging them to move abroad.

Pause for thought 7

There are many attractions in setting up plant in the UK. First, the UK's unit labour costs have not risen as fast as those of our international competitors. Wage increases have not outstripped labour productivity. As the UK is a member of the European Single Market, UK companies can sell their output to Europe without having to pay a common external tariff. Thus Japanese car companies are able to gain a competitive advantage from locating in the UK. Also the 'political climate' is fairly stable with a government which is sympathetic to foreign direct investment (FDI). One should also not underestimate the advantage of English as an international business language nor the aid packages that are put together by the development agencies (e.g. Locate in Scotland, which has been extremely successful in attracting high-tech inward investment to Scotland). The UK economy in recent years has also been able to combine steady economic growth with low inflation. However, there have been some arguments against the UK as a location for FDI. The longer the UK remains outside the single currency the longer that UK based firms have to face exchange rate risks. These extra risks are causing some firms to evaluate the UK as a base for their European operations. For example, in early 2000 it was claimed that Nissan were reviewing their long-term commitment to expand in the UK if there was no early sign that the UK would join the Single Currency.

Case Study 2.4: Japanese aircraft carriers

1   The 'invasion' of Japanese companies can benefit our balance of payments in a number of ways. First, if there is an import of capital into the UK this will represent positive benefit on our capital account. On the other hand, if initially the Japanese car companies have to import raw materials and are supplied from Japan then this will represent an increase in our import bill on the current account. If the output of these firms, however, is sold predominantly in Europe then there will be an increase in our exports and this will be a positive benefit to the current account. Finally, any profits, interest or dividends paid to Japanese investors will represent an outflow on the invisible part of the current account.

2   The effect of Japanese car companies on indigenous firms is likely to make them more competitive. In order to survive they are going to have to respond to the Japanese companies' reputation for high quality and

improved productivity. Some Japanese ideas such as 'quality circles' and 'just-in-time' will become adopted by UK firms. The expectation is that there will be indirect benefits to the indigenous firms as a result of the Japanese 'invasion'.

3   There are strong arguments on either side. The 'free trade' position stresses the benefits of competition from Japanese car firms and the spin-off in terms of the transfer of technology that such firms bring. The 'protectionist' position emphasises the damage that such competition could do to indigenous car companies. This is the position adopted by the French government towards protecting its own major car companies such as Renault and Citroën. It is hoped that by delaying competition from the Japanese the European car makers are able to 'get their act together' and to raise their standards of production and improve their productivity. The obvious danger is that having been shielded by protectionism they may be unable to compete effectively.

Pause for thought 8

One of the drawbacks of using floating exchange rates for resolving a balance of payments crisis is that in the short term it may actually make matters worse. There is a danger of the so-called J-curve phenomenon whereby the balance of payments gets worse as a result of a devaluation of the £. One of the immediate effects of a devaluation or a downward float is that imports become more expensive. In the short term this means that there is price inflation and as it is difficult to switch from imported goods to home-produced goods there is likely to be an increase in the import bill. On the export side there will be a fall in the price of exports as a result of a fall in the rate of exchange. However, it will take time before this feeds through to world markets. So the immediate impact of a downward float is for there to be an increase in the import bill and a decline in our export earnings, which is the exact opposite of the intended effect.

Case Study 2.5: Does devaluation provide a 'free lunch'?

1   The debate about whether we should have been inside the Exchange Rate Mechanism (ERM) or remained outside it is very similar to the arguments about whether we should join the single European currency. If the UK was inside the ERM we would benefit from the stability brought about by the mechanism. All the European Central Banks would support the £ and keep it within the agreed limits. This would remove to a large extent the instability and uncertainty caused by currency fluctuations. Businesses could price their products with some degree of certainty. In addition there would be a discipline imposed on businesses, workers and the government to do nothing that would jeopardise our competitiveness as we would not be allowed to take unilateral action regarding setting exchange rates under the rules of ERM.

     The disadvantages are that the UK government would be required to set its economic policies (fiscal and monetary) with reference to its partners in the ERM. For example, we could not simply cut taxes and allow the money supply to expand without it having an effect on our growth rates and inflation rates. This in turn would affect our balance of payments (which may slip into deficit). Outside the ERM the UK might simply let the exchange rate 'take the strain', an option which is closed off by our membership of the ERM.

There is also a critical question of the 'price' or rate at which a country joins the ERM. Too high a rate and the danger is that the UK's economy will plummet into a recession (this was the argument used by critics of our membership in 1990). Too low a rate and it may spark off an inflationary spiral and cause our economy to overheat. Also circumstances will inevitably change as our competitors will have differing rates of inflation and productivity growth. It may therefore be necessary to adjust rates of exchange. However, being part of a mechanism to reduce exchange rate movements means that other more painful ways of adjusting may have to be used.

2   Devaluation is only likely to work if there is spare capacity. Devaluation boosts the demand for exports which can only be met if spare capacity exists. If this is not the case then devaluation results in inflation which erodes the competitiveness of our exports. This in turn will cause a balance of payments crisis which will necessitate a further devaluation. Thus the policy is not costless. There is no 'free lunch'.

Chapter 3   Macroeconomic issues

Pause for thought 1

See text.

Pause for thought 2

1   The case for a minimum wage is controversial and has to do with the classical view about how labour markets work. It is argued that a minimum wage is needed to protect workers from being exploited in those sectors of the labour market where trade unions are weakest. Therefore it is seen as a way of counteracting the 'monopsony' (single buyer) power of large employers. It is also seen as an anti-poverty measure because of the need to make sure those at the lower end of the income scale have their earnings protected. However, there are dangers. If wages are fixed at a level above the 'equilibrium wage' (i.e. the wage rates at which supply and demand exactly match) there will be an excess of supply over demand for labour and hence a minimum wage will cause unemployment. There is also a view which says that if other workers try to maintain their differential wages between low paid workers and the rest, the effect of raising wages via a minimum wage will be to spark off a round of wage inflation which may make us uncompetitive abroad. However, none of this is inevitable. It critically depends on the level at which the minimum wage is pitched.

2   Those who argue for 'more flexible labour markets' (by which is meant that the forces of supply and demand should be allowed greater emphasis) are opposed to intervention by the state through a minimum wage. Labour market flexibility simply means ensuring that supply and demand factors can work more effectively in the labour market. However, the remedies are controversial. For example, reducing the monopoly power of trade unions, reducing the benefits/wages ratio to encourage workers to seek employment, abolishing wages councils (set up to protect the low paid) and removing the minimum wage can all be seen as introducing more flexibility into labour markets.

3   There are a number of ways in which mobility can be encouraged in the labour market. Training and education can give workers new skills and make them more employable. Grants to encourage workers to move to areas of high employment can also help. Change to the tax and benefit system can make it more worth while for workers to return to the labour market and get them out of the various poverty and benefit 'traps' which are sometimes unintentionally created by the tax and benefit system.

Case Study 3.1: Minimum wage, minimum impact?

1   There has been little impact because the minimum wage has been set at a level which has not resulted in job losses. Nor has there been much impact on differentials, as had been feared. Thus average earnings had not gone up by much as a result.

2   The Opposition had opposed the measure because of the fears that it would increase unemployment. As this has failed to materialise, the reason for opposing is much diminished.

Pause for thought 3

The argument for the Welfare to Work scheme is to encourage people on unemployment benefit to seek work. It therefore offers both 'stick and carrot' incentives to come off the dole and enter employment. The arguments against it are that it involves an element of compulsion and that if people do not join the scheme they will lose benefits.

Pause for thought 4

The classical remedies to solving unemployment rely on a view that the labour market is like any other market and if it is failing to clear (i.e. there is a surplus of supply over demand) then it is because the 'price' is too high. Price in this case means real wages. The controversial solution is that there should be a fall in real wages (i.e. for money wages to lag behind inflation). This can be achieved by making the labour market more competitive, removing the monopoly power of trade unions and abolishing any state intervention in the setting of wages (e.g. wages councils and a national minimum wage – see above).

Similarly, ways to reduce the non-accelerating inflation rate of unemployment (NAIRU) are also controversial, involving reducing unemployment and welfare benefits in order to 'encourage' workers to take up jobs, even low paid jobs which they might reject if unemployment benefits were seen to be too 'generous'.

Pause for thought 5

Microeconomic solutions refer to the classical remedies outlined in the Pause for Thought 4. The macroeconomic solutions are the Keynesian remedies of demand management. These fell into disfavour with the development of the rational expectations hypothesis, whereby it is asserted that workers will anticipate the effects of government policy to boost aggregate demand and simply appropriate the increases in expenditure that the government pumps into the economy and cause wages to rise. Governments cannot create jobs, the classical school asserts. Only firms can do that by being competitive. Also, increases in government spending will crowd out other types of spending (e.g. consumer spending and investment spending) and as a result there will be no net increase in aggregate demand, leaving wages higher but also creating more, not less, unemployment. The preferred remedies according to this view are therefore microeconomic ones.

Case Study 3.2: New millennium, new paradigm, new economy?

1 The rate of growth in the UK in 2000 is quite high by both historical standards (twentieth-century average about 2.0–2.5 per cent) but less so by international standards (see below). The latest figures put the rate at 3.6 per cent in the second quarter of 2000, which is up 3.1 per cent on the level of GDP from last year. The Misery Index puts the UK about fifth in this international league table! However, the Index is subject to wild short-term variations. For example, until recently the Japanese economy was in recession and would have had a much lower index than its current phenomenal score! Table Q1 gives the data for several key economies.

Table Q1

Country	GDP growth (%)*	Inflation (%)*	Unemployment† (%)	Misery Index‡	Current as % of GDP§
UK	**3.6**	**2.3**	**5.5**	**5.16**	**−1.7**
Australia	4.4	3.2	6.4	9.76	−4.7
France	2.8	1.7	6.8	−0.66	+2.3
Germany	4.7	3.0	9.5	9.59	−0.7
Japan	10.4	0.1	4.7	103.36	+2.6
Netherlands	3.0	3.2	2.6	3.20	+4.9
EURO 11**	**3.7**	**2.7**	**9.1**	**1.89**	**+0.5**
USA	5.3	3.1	4.0	20.99	−4.4
China	8.3	0.5	n.a.	n.a.	n.a.
Russia	6.7	18.8	n.a.	n.a.	n.a.

* Latest three months at an annual rate.

† ILO definition (except for UK claimant count).

‡ The Misery Index is calculated as follows: $(G^2 - I - U)$ where G, I and U refer to growth, inflation and unemployment rates.

§ *The Economist*'s poll of forecasters for 2000.

** For an up-to-date survey of Europe's economies see *The Economist*, 16 September 2000, p. 117.

Source: *The Economist*, 9 September 2000.

2 The two ways take into account all expenditure (RPI) and all expenditure less mortgage interest payments (RPI-X). The reason for RPI-X is because of the distorting effects that mortgage interest rate changes have on the RPI index itself. RPI is often referred to as the headline rate while RPI-X is the 'core' or underlying rate. The three factors are demand–push, cost–push and monetary factors. (Some economists list just two, arguing that monetary factors are in fact similar to demand–push.)

3 See Table Q1.

4 The Bank of England attempts to reach the target by setting interest rates and by controlling the money supply. There are a number of arguments in favour of central bank independence:

➤ No political interference.

➤ Policy is 'objectively set', not timed to coincide with political events.

There are some anxieties about independence of the central bank:

➤ Democratic accountability.

➤ Central bankers always err on the side of price stability and not on economic growth. (For more details see p. 392–3, Pause for thought 18 above.)

5 The two methods are the claimant count and the survey method, the differences arising from the fact that with the claimant count a number of unemployed people may be unemployed but not claim benefit (e.g. working women who are second income earners may not always claim unemployment benefit although they are unemployed). It is generally thought that the ILO survey method is a more reliable measure of unemployment.

6 See Table Q1.

7 Reasons why the UK might be able to combine growth with low inflation:

➤ Lowering expectations as a result of low inflation.

➤ Labour not as scarce as the figures imply.

➤ Insiders v Outsiders: '…Those in jobs face less competition from the long-term unemployed than those who have been out of work for just a few months, … long-term unemployment is tumbling.'

8 Three things need to be in place:

➤ Low import prices (low commodity prices + high £ helps) *but* will this last?

➤ Strength of the recovery. How fast?

➤ Supply of labour. Is there still some slack?

9 Latest forecasts (September 2000) show that there has been an upward revision of growth forecast for 2000 by all the independent forecasters from about 1.8 per cent in January to 2.25 per cent in August, also an upward revision of forecasts for inflation from 2.1 per cent to 2.7 per cent whilst unemployment forecasts are revised downwards from 1.8 million to 1.4 million on the claimant count.

Activity 3.1: The single currency: you decide

The articles outlined in note 9, p.89 to this chapter are the ideal starting point for a discussion. Two teams (4–5 per team) could undertake the research with one presenter per team taking about 10 minutes to outline the case for (or against). The rest of the group could form a 'Question Time' audience who can question any member of each team to explain and expand the points in the presentation. From the 'audience' you might select three people to act as 'rapporteurs' to summarise and comment on the strength of the arguments put forward. Then at the end a vote can be taken. Some of the key arguments would be those shown in Table 3.2.

Case Study 3.3: Economic and political pressure mounts on government to join the euro

The issue of our membership of the single currency is not going to be decided until after the next general election. The main reason is that at the moment (November 2000) public opinion is very much against entry, with opinion polls indicating that over 70% of those asked are against the UK's entry. Opposition has hardened since the Danish referendum in the autumn of 2000. The government is therefore anxious not to make the single currency an election issue. The government's position is that if it is returned to power there will be an evaluation on the five economic tests and a referendum on entry. What is not clear is (a) whether the five economic tests will be met and (b) the position the government will adopt in any referendum. There are clear tensions between those in government who want to adopt the 'wait and see' line and those who wish to actively campaign for entry to try to influence public opinion. For example, the Prime Minister was quoted in late October 2000 as indicating that if there were a referendum 'tomorrow' he would vote 'no' at the present time.

Chapter 4 The structure of the economy
··

Pause for thought 1

Using input and output measures will give different answers when looking at structural change. Those sectors which are capital intensive such as chemicals and pharmaceuticals will show up as being highly significant if measured by the value of their output but will have a lower level of significance when the percentage of the labour force employed in the sector is used as the measure.

Pause for thought 2

The answer is contained in the text. Strictly speaking, one should use constant prices to measure the impact of sectoral shifts, although even here there are some problems as indicated in the text. Make sure you understand the problems of using constant prices as well!

Pause for thought 3

The three reasons are as follows. Technological advances mean that a product or group of products can be produced cheaper and sold cheaper than before; if the same volume is sold (or there is not a significant increase in volume to compensate for the fall in the real price) one may infer incorrectly that the sector is declining in importance. Similarly, an increase in competition can reduce current prices and this can have a 'distorting' effect when analysing the importance of the sector. The third and most obvious reason is inflation which causes constant and current prices to diverge. If different sectors experience different rates of price inflation this can distort the picture.

In the 1970s, when OPEC kept the price of oil high, this would mean that we would tend to value the output of the oil sector (and also sectors which were big users of oil) at a higher level than might otherwise be the case. Subsequently, when the oil price fell dramatically in the mid-1980s the reverse would be true.

Pause for thought 4

This is a complicated question but can be answered by looking at both demand-side effects and supply-side effects. The *demand-side* effects are to do with the impact that the Internet can have on competition and market structures. As will be discussed later in the chapter, if the Internet leads to more competition as consumers go online, then it could lead to increasing demand for those sectors affected. It may also help to give manufacturing companies a competitive advantage if they set up Internet exchanges for suppliers. By streamlining the supply chain and reducing costs this too could stimulate demand for those companies able to reap the benefits of buying components online, for example. On the *supply side* it could obviously lead to the growth and development of new 'dot.com' companies in response to the Internet revolution. Thus one might expect there to be an increase in service companies and growth in this new e-business sector. It is, however, difficult to say whether it would result in a significant structural shift which would have been different from the trends already identified in the text. Certainly if manufacturers in the UK fail to become as 'wired' as their international competitors then there could be a significant structural shift away from manufacturing. At the present time the emergence of the 'new economy' is predominantly an American/European phenomenon and may, for the time being, have a significant impact on the service sector in these economies.

Case Study 4.1: The output of higher education

1   The problem in assessing the contribution of higher education to the economy is that there is no generally agreed way to measure its output. If one tried to value its output by multiplying the number of graduates by the starting salaries of the graduates, then there will be some double counting since this is already done in the national income statistics (using the income method to calculate this). One could measure the sector by valuing its inputs (i.e. how much is spent on the sector from all sources). This has the merit of being easier to measure but, as the case points out, for every £1 spent on higher education in the last ten years there has not been a corresponding increase in output as measured by the number of students through the system. Indeed, the aim is to achieve even greater efficiency

gains and so make each £1 work even harder. Thus a declining unit of resource may suggest that the higher education sector is less significant than it was five years ago while the increase in student numbers as a result of wider access points in the opposite direction.

2   The concept of 'value added' is used in the National Income accounts to value a sector's importance. Thus the value added of a car manufacturer is in principle easy to calculate as being the difference between revenue and costs after taking account of a return to the owners of the business (normal profit, to use the economist's jargon). Such a concept, while attractive in principle, becomes quite difficult to apply in practice to a university. What is an input? Are students an input? If a university takes on students with indifferent entrance requirements but produces 50 per cent of its graduates with First Class honours degrees, does it have a high value added? Presumably it does (although there are a number of fairly obvious problems with even this limited way of measuring value added). However, valuing this in a way that an economist could use to assess the sector's significance to the economy is fraught with difficulties. That is not to say that assessing the worth of a university by its output is not a good idea!

Pause for thought 5

Some economists fear the loss of manufacturing jobs will cause severe employment and balance of payments difficulties. There is also a danger that when demand picks up there will be less manufacturing capacity to be able to meet it and that this will cause inflation.

The jobs are being lost to third world countries and to the so-called 'tiger economies' of the Far East. Whether governments should do something about it is extremely debatable. Companies are less tied to given locations (for more details, see Chapter 11) and it may therefore be very difficult for governments to be able to affect any changes. In January 1997, for example, Ford announced that it would be closing its Halewood plant near Liverpool and focusing instead on its operations in Germany. Thus it could be argued that the UK was losing manufacturing jobs to a European competitor. It is, however, very hard in these circumstances for the UK government to influence the strategic decisions of a global multinational like Ford not to leave the UK. Having said that, the UK government has been successful in attracting Japanese car manufacturers with considerable assistance, so the 'trade' in manufacturing jobs is not all one way.

Pause for thought 6

If you define 'stars' as in the text as those economies that have been able to combine modest wage rises with significant rises in productivity (the result of which is a fall in the relative unit labour costs (RULC)), then the 'stars' are the United States and the United Kingdom (and more recently the French economy). The 'dogs', on the other hand, were Japan and Germany with a rise in their RULC of over 60 per cent and 30 per cent respectively.

Case Study 4.2: New Labour, old problems

1   The case for government intervention rests on the MISS (Manufacturing Is Special School of thought). It may be summarised as follows:
    (i)   Manufacturing jobs have higher productivity and higher wages; hence a shift to the service sector reduces the growth of GDP and incomes.
    (ii) Manufactured goods have a higher export content; thus a shift to services creates a balance of payments constraint on faster growth.
    (iii) The manufacturing sector possesses 'externalities' that create spin-off growth and jobs in other sectors, for example through economies of scale and greater rate of technical progress.

2   The arguments against such intervention are:
    (i)   There is a danger that the government will simply prop up 'lame ducks'.
    (ii) Governments have been very poor in the past at picking winners to support.
    (iii) The service sector can add value to GDP just as much as the manufacturing sector.
    It is argued that it becomes impossible for the government to 'second guess' the potential growth sectors and to subsidise these. In a world of increasing global competition it is almost impossible for governments to 'buck' market trends.

3   There are dangers in trying to manage the exchange rate to favour a given sector. Firstly, a single government may not be able to manage the exchange rate by itself. The exchange rate can be influenced by a whole host of factors over which individual governments may have little control. In the autumn of 2000 the € fell in value in relation to the £. This made it more difficult for UK manufacturing firms. Only by the concerted action of all the central banks were they able to stem the fall in the € temporarily. Also the solution of a cheap £ can set in motion inflationary pressures which may not restore the competitiveness of manufacturing in the long term. Nevertheless, there is a case to be made for joining an exchange rate mechanism which attempts to peg the rate of a currency to those of other countries. It was the main argument used for the UK's entry to the ERM in 1990 (although our experience of this was not a happy one with the rate being fixed too high initially and the UK government being forced out of the ERM two years later). Similar arguments are made about the UK's entry into the single currency.

Pause for thought 7

The arguments are similar to those outlined in Case Study 4.2 above.

Case Study 4.3: Productivity and the role of government

1   There are a number of factors which it is claimed affect productivity. One of these is *capital intensity*. This relates to the amount of capital to labour ratio. It is argued that the higher this number the greater the growth and

level of labour productivity. This in turn depends upon the *level of investment* in both process and product (for example R&D expenditure on new processes and new products can influence productivity). *Investment in human capital* in the form of education and training can enhance productivity. It is also argued that *increased competition and reduced regulation* coupled with incentives can act as a spur to improved productivity. (For a good source on this topic you should consult http:www.mckinsey.com features/uk/index.html for a report on 'Driving Productivity and Growth in the UK'.)

2   The evidence suggests that there is a productivity gap between the UK and our major international competitors in terms of output per worker. Even adjusting for the different length of time worked by workers in different countries and for the different capital quality and quantity, the gap remains. Reducing the gap is no easy matter. By offering tax incentives for firms to invest in R&D it is hoped to raise productivity. Increasing capital allowances also will affect the level of investment. Encouraging venture capital is also expected to improve investment and hence productivity.

3   There is scepticism about some of these measures. Firstly, the measures proposed are aimed at small firms, which are not the ones that undertake most of the investment. Secondly, tax breaks are only useful to firms that are making profits in the first place. However, it is when they are starting up (and usually in a loss making position) that new firms need the incentives, and tax breaks do not give them.

Case Study 4.4: Industrial policy in Finland

1   The case study illustrates briefly the idea of so-called 'new' industrial policy. It became fashionable in the 1980s in the UK to say that the government did not have an industrial policy. By that it usually meant the subsidising of industry and state intervention in the running and the location of certain key sectors. The experience of this type of industrial policy (practised by both Labour and Conservative governments) was not a happy one. The new type of industrial policy aims to make markets work better. Thus privatisation, monopolies and mergers legislation, trade union reforms and reform of the benefits system can all be viewed as ways of making markets work better (for more details see Chapter 12). In the case of Finland, the policy is described as active and market orientated and is not a 'hands off approach'.

2   'Political judgements and choice' clearly refers to the emphasis that different political parties put on the role of the state in influencing the decisions of firms. Those parties on the left in politics favour more state intervention than those on the right (although the distinction in the UK is becoming less clearly defined).

3   'Hands off' implies a *laisser faire* policy in which the market is left to determine things. An active policy which is market orientated is one that aims to remove market imperfections and to make the market work better.

Pause for thought 8

See text.

Pause for thought 9

Suppliers may be reluctant to join such exchanges for fear that they will have their prices beaten down by the power of the buyers and also by the fact that all of these business-to-business transactions will be seen on the Internet exchange. Suppliers may therefore feel exposed. (Some economists have called the Internet not so much 'New Economy' as 'Nude Economy'!) In addition there are also fears of collusion between suppliers to protect themselves from the full blast of competition via the web.

Pause for thought 10

The concentrated sectors are more suitable for hubs with the dispersed sectors more suitable for exchanges. Thus car manufacturers and supermarkets are likely to set up hubs, but hotels and restaurants, for example, are more likely to set up exchanges.

Pause for thought 11

See text.

Pause for surfing

This is an interactive exercise. There is no right answer!

Pause for thought 12

See text.

Case Study 4.5: Buying a car on the Internet

1   The main reason is that because of high prices charged in the UK it paid consumers to buy a car in the EU and import it into the UK. Both the Consumers Association and Richard Branson saw an opportunity to act as broker/distributor for new cars acquired in the EU. By October 2000 there were a number of other Internet companies in the same market, including broadspeed.com, carbusters.com, jamjar.com and theinternetcarcompany.co.uk.

2   The obvious limitation is that you cannot test drive the car or physically sit in the car. Nor can you get the smell of a new car from the Internet (at least not yet!).

3   The traditional car manufacturers have been offering a variety of deals designed to bring down the transaction cost of buying a car. These include pre-registering new cars and selling them as if they were 'second hand' at discount prices. In addition, they have used devices such as cash-back,

extended sales and time-limited offers, all designed to reduce the price. More recently Ford was the first major car manufacturer to announce in October 2000 that it was reducing its recommended prices. This was in response to pressure from the Competition Commission's recommendation to reduce prices.

Case Study 4.6: New business models and the Internet

1 There are a number of disadvantages. Firstly, consumers have a resistance to giving out credit card/bank details over the Internet. In addition, where the quality of the product is variable buying over the net without seeing or touching the item (the so-called high touch items) is a risk. There are some concerns about the efficiency of distribution and delivery.

2 There are a number of examples of each. A good example of 'disintermediation' would be Frederick Forsyth's recent move to sell his books chapter by chapter on the Internet. This move effectively cuts out whole swathes of the publishing, book retailing and distribution industries. Lastminute.com provides a good example of reintermediation, putting potential buyers and sellers in contact with one another. Navigation occurs with the creation of portal companies such as Yahoo or AOL who help consumers find the information they want on the Internet, whilst the example of the National Transportation Exchange (NTE) quoted in the case study provides a good example of infomediation.

Chapter 5 Organisation of firms and markets

Case Study 5.1: Moves to help people to set up in business

1 Essentially the setting up of a small business in the UK is not a difficult operation. The costs involved in actually forming a small business are relatively small. There is a direct relationship between the different types of organisational structure and cost of set-up, with the sole trader being the least expensive and the public limited company being the most costly. What needs to be done before commencement depends largely on the form of the organisation. For example, a sole trader has very little to do in legal terms, in contrast to the public limited company which must print prospectuses and give financial information and projections to prospective shareholders. In Germany, there is a large amount of resources being put into supporting small business start-up. It could be argued that the UK is also doing this through a number of different programmes such as the Enterprise Allowance Scheme, the Loan Guarantee Scheme, the Enterprise Initiative, and a concessionary rate of corporation tax for small businesses. Thus, it would appear that the UK and German governments are progressing along the same lines.

2 The Enterprise Allowance Scheme which pays the unemployed setting up a business £39 a week for the first year they are in business, and the Loan Guarantee Scheme which indemnifies small and medium-sized bank

lending to small firms. In addition, there is the Enterprise Initiative, which subsidises the provision of management consultancy services, and a concessionary rate of corporation tax for small businesses.

3 *Introduction of venture capital through banks* – this is obviously a good idea if it results in finance being available for business start-ups where previously it would not have been, or perhaps it may have been available but at an uneconomic rate of interest. This is somewhat similar to the Loan Guarantee Scheme identified above. Both systems seem to do largely the same task and the rationale behind both is to facilitate easier and more frequent business start-up.

Temporary liquidity finance – this is an excellent idea. One of the main reasons for small business failure is not lack of orders, but lack of money to pay bills in the short term, leading to creditors initiating bankruptcy proceedings. This would be a scheme that would be welcomed by businesses in the UK. The obvious concern would be one of financing, with the government being the obvious candidate to provide the money. This could possibly be raised by the company repaying the cash when it was performing at a certain level as measured by a number of predetermined criteria.

Tax breaks – again this is an excellent idea. It is to some extent replicated in the UK by the concessionary rate of income tax, but the German model is more wide ranging in its scope. There does not appear to be any reason (other than the funding of the scheme) as to why this would not be a success in the UK in enticing would-be entrepreneurs into taking the plunge into creating their own venture. The funding issue should not be a long-term concern as these ventures will create wealth for the economy, thus reducing benefit payments and government spending and increasing taxation income.

Less red tape and regulations – this is not really a concern for UK start-ups as the vast majority of businesses begin life as a small company where the red tape and regulations are largely insignificant.

Case Study 5.2: Report on liability law to be published

1 The winners will be the partners of the professional firms who no longer have the spectre of unlimited liability hanging over them. In future if they are deemed to have made an error and are subsequently sued, then the liability will be limited and payment met by the limited company, not the individual partners.

2 There exists the possibility that without the regulatory effect of the threat of unlimited liability being the ultimate sanction for professional accountancy firms if they make a fundamental error, then the standards of service that the clients receive will ultimately suffer.

3 *Advantages*: frees accountants from the threat of crippling court action in cases of alleged negligence; if the directors were negligent they can be sued rather than the auditors; the litigants in multinational disputes will find no advantage by taking auditors to court in the UK rather than the US.

Disadvantages: may not ensure the highest level of 'workmanship' in the profession – this is a somewhat weak argument as the profession has self-regulatory bodies that pride themselves in maintaining the highest of standards, with the fear of expulsion from these bodies seen as the severest punishment as it prevents them offering their services if they are not affiliated to the professional body, e.g. in the field of accountancy, bodies such as ICMA, ACCA, ICAEW and ICAS control professional standards in the UK. Overall this would appear to be a good idea taking the above advantages and disadvantages into consideration.

4   The system in the US would appear to represent greater fairness and to punish those that have been negligent, by an amount that is consistent with the degree of negligence that has taken place.

Case Study 5.3: KPMG *ends secrecy on partnerships*

1   KPMG believes that by making itself a limited company it will become more accountable to its clients. Its financial transactions will be available for all to see via Companies House and factors such as asset base and salaries will become known to the wider public audience. KPMG also believes that by doing this it will attract the best staff, who may have been more attracted by other careers where extensive liability for individuals was not an issue. If other firms do not follow suit then this gives KPMG a competitive advantage over its rivals.

2   The growing size of this profession has to a large extent shown that the argument relating to graduates shying away from accountancy because of the risk of auditor liability is false. The number of cases to date of successful court actions against accounting firms is such that this perceived recruitment deterrent has not in fact acted as such. If a large number of successful actions had taken place over the last 20 years, then this argument may have held some weight. At the moment it does not.

3   The main advantage would be that the fees, financial structure, salary payments, asset base, balance sheet, etc., of each firm would be available for scrutiny. Thus a more informed judgement on choice of firm could be made. In reality, there would probably be no disadvantage to the clients, as accountancy firms are regulated by their own professional bodies. It could, however, be argued that the amount of damages that could be claimed in court would not be as great as when unlimited liability status was in place.

Case Study 5.4: *Does who owns what matter?*

1   This largely depends on the individual, but to generalise if this is possible, the risk to the individual of making a strategic error when he works for a large organisation is that he may be reprimanded, demoted, overlooked for promotion in the future or, in the worst-case scenario, given the sack. If an error of the same magnitude is made by a sole trader this may result in his losing not only his business but also his house, car and other valuable belongings. It is clear that the trend may be towards risk avoidance if this were to be the case.

2   Based on the answer given to question 1, the answer to this would be yes. The ultimate sanction would be loss of employment, which is a situation that is more easily rectifiable than bankruptcy.

3   If the workers are part-owners of the company you would expect them to be more highly motivated as they will share in the profits of the firm. It is a straightforward motivational link to make between part-ownership of the business that you are working for and increased productivity and profitability. If the workforce works harder, this will have a direct impact upon the profit share-out at the end of the year. Whether this is likely to be a short-term phenomenon or not largely depends on the management of the business. It could be argued that it is more likely to be a long-term increase in productivity as workers discover that the benefits of putting in that little bit extra actually result in a quantifiable monetary reward to them. Thus, it is not likely to be short-term in nature.

Case Study 5.5: Brands Hatch takes fast track to the city

1   The rationale for expansion is that this company needs a large capital injection to fund expansion and restructuring. Some of the funds will also be used to repay debts.

2   In the short term, Nicola Foulston will probably remain in her position as chief executive, as she is the driving force behind the changes in the company. Her position in the long term is not quite so clear-cut now the company is being floated. It will largely depend on the performance of the share price and the company. If this is deemed unsatisfactory by the new shareholders she may be forced to move aside to allow a new chief executive to take control. This would not have been the case if the company had not changed status. In a family firm, the directors and chief executive do not have to respond to outside influences to the extent of a publicly quoted organisation.

3   It is difficult to see how the company could have raised sufficient financing to expand and to repay debt without converting to a public limited company. The only alternatives would have been to borrow the money, which increases the current debt, thus further increasing the interest payments of the firm. This would also reduce the amount of money available for expansion. Once shares are issued, then they do not have to be bought back from the shareholder, thus the money is invested on this basis. Another option may have been to merge with a company with cash to invest, but this would have resulted in a loss of autonomy for the firm and of control for the current chief executive.

Case Study 5.6: Changing ownership

1   The market in which Jessops operates is somewhat complex. It is competing with a number of different types and sizes of firms. This does give it rather a unique position which it has taken advantage of. It could be argued that it is rather vulnerable should one of the major players attempt to reorganise the market, or to become a more dominant force.

2   It is difficult to see how the company could survive in the long run in its current form. The nature of business today is for growth to achieve economies of scale and to facilitate innovation and product development. If Jessops remains a medium–small operator in the market place it would

appear to be an obvious candidate for takeover from one of the large firms in the industry. It needs to grow in order to prosper, and to achieve this it needs to raise extra capital. Thus, it would appear that the listing that Jessops is going for is appropriate to its strategic plan.

3   One of the pitfalls for the incumbent management team is that they may be removed by the new shareholders if they are not happy with the direction or performance of the company. In addition, the expansion may leave the company exposed to fluctuations in the economy.

Photography is an activity that can be curtailed in a period of economic downturn, thus the company may be rather exposed in a recessionary period and again be a takeover candidate. The company may also not be able to recruit the casual photographer as a consequence of its reputation for dealing more with the expert end of the market.

Case Study 5.7: Norwich leads float of insurers

1   In the early years of these companies they were offering one particular product and the profits of the firm were used to pay the life policies of those who had invested with them. As these firms have grown they have also diversified into a wide range of other products, broadly in the same field, but not related to the life policies held by the owners of the firm. In time, the growth of the non-life policy business has outstripped that of life policies, but only those with life policies were still technically the owners of the business – which is indeed a little odd.

2   Those that hold life policies with the company will be the winners as they will receive a payment for their part ownership of the company if they themselves vote to go in this direction. They will still hold their policies and they will have received a one-off additional payment. They will obviously be gainers. Those with other financial products will also benefit as the additional funds available via becoming a plc are likely to increase profitability and hence their payouts in the long run. In a wider sense these one-off payments are likely to stimulate demand in the high street, thereby raising aggregate demand with a consequent reduction in unemployment. It is difficult to pinpoint any losers at all in this particular situation, though possibly the increase in demand for goods and services may have some sort of impact on the rate of inflation in the short term.

3   It was thought at one point that this would be the trend and that all firms in this sector would move to this legal structure. However, in doing so they increase the likelihood of a hostile takeover from a larger financial institution such as a bank. This would result in rationalisations which would inevitably mean redundancies. It would seem unlikely that management of a company would vote for their own redundancies, thus this route may not be as popular as initially imagined. In addition, the new shareholders will be expecting dividends, thus the payout to policy holders may possibly be less as part of the profits generated will now have to be paid out to the shareholders.

Case Study 5.8: Windfalls or rates – the dilemma

1 There are a number of reasons why this is the case. It is perceived as being quite difficult to change from one provider to another. Thus, mortgage holders do not change because of this and also as a consequence of the complexity involved in presenting facts and figures to mortgage holders. Different rates are normally also accompanied with various other clauses. The terminology associated with this is often seen to be confusing and does not facilitate easy comparison between one mortgage and another. Additionally, borrowers often have been with an institution for a number of years, and after gaining from demutualisation feel a sense of loyalty, especially if by losing customers there is an impact upon the shares that they themselves own!

2 Short-termism is one of the most common features of individuals in this country and throughout the world. It is difficult to see the benefits of the long-term perspective when one is facing an attractive short-term gain. Investors also believe that they can invest the money themselves and make it grow.

3 The answer to this is relatively straightforward. Those organisations that have retained their mutual set-up have done so in the belief that the returns they can provide to their members are better under the current ownership structure. A plc has to make dividend payments to shareholders to retain their support and share price. A mutual organisation does not have to do this, thus its objectives are centred on providing the best deal for its members. One downside to this is that building societies do not have access to the vast sums that can be raised on the capital markets to offer a wide range of services, thus their expansion may be hampered in the long run.

Case Study 5.9: Ford infuriates competitors with Japanese adverts

1 Ford has caused anger by entering the market at a late stage and criticising the products of other manufacturers who have been in this particular market for a much longer period of time and have spent a lot of time and money cultivating the market to accept foreign car manufacturers. Ford has not contributed to this, and is now trying to enter the market after it has been established through a negative advertising campaign targeted at rival firms. Not surprisingly, this has not gone down too well.

2 Ford may have perceived entry into this market as being somewhat risky as Japanese consumers have in the past preferred home produced cars. However, it has monitored the situation and identified that a meaningful share of the population is willing to purchase foreign vehicles. A market does therefore exist and now Ford is attempting to infiltrate into it. So the answer to the question is yes – Ford has witnessed others entering the market and making high profits and has now chosen to follow.

3 The downside of this strategy is that others have gained a foothold in the market already and may have built up consumer loyalty which Ford may have difficulty breaking down.

4 This could also be incorporated within the answer to the previous question, in that this type of negative advertising is likely to induce similar retaliatory advertising from competitors. This will create a poor image for the Ford cars which are untested in the marketplace it is trying to enter. The competitors already have a foothold in the market, thus are less likely to be affected by the Ford campaign than vice versa.

5 This largely depends on whether the market has reached saturation point for foreign produced cars. If it has then the market is at its maximum size, thus if Ford is to enter the market it will be at the expense of at least one of the other competitors in the industry. This will result in a reduction in profit for all firms in the industry. In addition, firms will have to mount increased advertising campaigns to fight off the competition from Ford. This will increase expenses and reduce profitability, unless the market grows. Thus, profit levels within this sector of the market will be largely determined by whether there is more growth in the size of the market or not.

6 If profits are reduced then firms can either accept the situation or attempt to regain the ground they have lost. The disadvantage of trying to regain market share and profitability is that it can be extremely expensive – advertising campaigns, special promotional offers, etc. – and there is no guarantee of success. The market may evolve to a new equilibrium, with each of the competitors aware of this and happy to avoid confrontation and strategies such as price wars, which may in the end prove less profitable than acceptance of the new status quo.

Case Study 5.10: Torrid tales of tarot cards and topless darts

1 It is possible to argue this point from a number of angles – the owners have identified a demand and the structure of the industry is such that entry is not particularly difficult (assuming sufficient funds are available, together with technological knowhow, and talented presenters). The conduct is determined by the search for an audience. This has proved difficult because of the overall market in which it is competing, so to an extent conduct is being driven by market structure. In turn, what is determining performance of the company is the strategic decisions made by management on the basis of the market they find themselves in. It could be argued that this is, indeed, the case.

2 The decision was taken to enter into this market because it was identified through market research that there was scope to offer a certain brand of television that would generate an acceptable return on the investment that was needed to set it up.

3 This is an argument that can be forcefully made. It is quite true that the availability of large financial resources can often overcome barriers to entry. However, it does not always work. For example, in Case Study 9.1, p. 431 – The price of Tequila – there are two significant barriers which prevent other manufacturers distilling tequila and taking advantage of the large profits currently available. The first is legislation, preventing other producers using the name. It is not perhaps difficult to imagine how this could be overcome if a financial inducement were to be made. However, the second is the availability of the raw material, agave. These take eight years to produce. Thus, no amount of cash can speed up this process.

Chapter 6 Business objectives

Pause for thought 1

In general terms, mission statements are statements to do with the company's vision of itself. The Body Shop has perhaps the most explicit reference to values, being against animal testing and committed to campaigning for human rights and trading with indigenous people around the world. Goals are more specific and, in a sense, more 'measurable'. Thus Sainsbury's offers three things: value for money, competitive prices with the rest of the firms in the market and a wide choice. Objectives are much more detailed and are even more measurable. Thus in the case of Saatchi & Saatchi the objective was to obtain a 10 per cent trading profit, while Sainsbury's sought to maintain the real level of its capital expenditure over the next three years.

Case Study 6.1: Mission statements, goals and objectives

See text.

Case Study 6.2: The usefulness of mission statements

See text.

Pause for thought 2

If the price were to fall to £5.00 then the profit-maximising (or in this case loss-minimising) output would be between 200 and 300 shirts because the marginal cost at this output is £5 per shirt. The actual loss is about £500 which is less than at any other level of output.

Pause for thought 3

The most efficient level of output corresponds to the level of output where average cost is at its lowest which is 300 units (average cost £6.66).

Case Study 6.3: Executive pay and company performance – Mr Kipling's recipe?

See text.

Case Study 6.4: Maximising Attali's utility

1   The case highlights the fact that managers will often aim to maximise their own utility which includes, as the theory by Oliver Williamson highlights, 'emoluments' or what we would more commonly refer to as 'perks'. Mr Attali's departure coincided with a period when the bank was criticised for the number of poor loans and the way that these were 'turning sour'. Had Mr Attali kept the bank's major shareholders happy and not been quite so extravagant, then he might well have survived.

2 To some extent expenditure on things like a head office can be easy targets for criticism. As one investment analyst was heard to remark, 'When a company starts to spend money on its headquarters then sell the shares!'. However, there is a certain expectation that the style of the headquarters will reflect the status and the success of the organisation. If profit maximisation is seen as 'penny pinching' then this may give the wrong signals to customers and clients.

Pause for thought 4

Firms are more likely to be satisficers if they are achieving targets which are keeping their major stakeholders happy. These need not necessarily be maximising targets but certainly sufficient to give the shareholders a comfortable return on their investment. Small family businesses often display the characteristics of 'satisficers'. Other things apart from the relentless pursuit of profit may become important (e.g. the quality of life). It is sometimes suggested that if a firm is in a monopoly position then it is more likely to be a satisficer, although the evidence on this point is far from clear.

Pause for thought 5

Market share can be 'bought' at the expense of profit by simply selling at or near the cost of producing the product, thus creating a conflict between sales goals and profit goals.

Pause for thought 6

Behavioural theories suggest that the objectives of a firm depend upon the processes of decision making within the firm and the power and influence of the decision-makers. The theory suggests that there will be a trade-off between various powerful interest groups to arrive at a consensus on what are the key goals and objectives of the company. This theory is hard to test because it is almost impossible to predict how the company will react to a change in its economic environment. For example, if there is an increase in the demand for its products will it raise its prices? This may depend on whether it sees profit or sales as the key goal and the outcome could therefore depend on the complex process of interaction between the key decision-makers within the organisation.

Pause for thought 7

In applying Porter's 'five forces' you can look at each of the factors in turn and identify the key elements which influence them. The key factors are explained in more detail in Chapter 11.

If we take food retailing and try to identify *the threat of potential entrants* then there are undoubtedly barriers to entry which are high in this industry. There are considerable benefits from economies of scale, and the capital requirements to enter the market are high. There are problems in gaining access to distribution channels with suppliers. The present incumbents (Sainsbury,

Asda, Tesco, Safeway) enjoy considerable 'incumbent advantages', having been around for some time and built up a reputation, and they would react quickly to a perceived threat from a newcomer. In addition, the legal framework within which such companies operate makes it difficult to secure the necessary planning permission to build the kind of out-of-town superstores required.

As regards the *threat of substitutes* there are alternatives to superstores and these are becoming more prevalent. Specialist food retail outlets can obviously find a niche in the market place but these are not a very serious threat to the existing major retailers.

Buyer and supplier power are not really very significant here. The suppliers are not in a strong bargaining position when dealing with the major supermarkets. Customers are more discerning and supermarkets are very sensitive to the fact that customers will not stay loyal if they do not think that they are getting value for money. The introduction of loyalty cards is an attempt to keep hold of customers but also increases the barriers to entry of any new firm seeking to break into food retailing.

Finally, the *reaction of competitors* in this industry is fierce and each new move is almost immediately matched by the competition. For example, each of the major superstores has extended its services into petrol retailing (20 per cent of all petrol sold in the UK is sold through supermarkets with Sainsbury having 180 petrol stations, Tesco 254 and Asda 118), dry cleaning (Sainsbury has 36, Tesco 20, Asda 32), pharmacies (Sainsbury 54, Tesco 139, Asda 72), post offices (Sainsbury 6, Tesco 10, Asda 7) and florists (all stores for Sainsbury, Tesco and Asda).

Pause for thought 8

Poison pills, green-mailing and golden parachutes are all devices for thwarting the attempts of predators to take over companies.

A *Poison Pill* occurs when a target company seeks to acquire another company that would put it in direct competition with the 'raider'. The reason for this tactic is to provoke an investigation by the competition authorities. So, for example, if a car company is threatened with a takeover from a computer company, the car company might acquire another computer company so that if they were taken over the resulting combination would result in a monopoly situation in computers, provoking a reference to the Monopolies and Mergers Commission. This would make the deal unattractive to the computer company.

Green-mailing involves the target company offering to buy the predator's stock of your company's shares at a premium price with an agreement that the predator drops its takeover bid.

A *Golden Parachute* occurs when the company threatened with takeover, anticipating defeat for the senior managers, fixes up large severance compensation packages, in the event of their being removed following the takeover. This can increase the costs of winning for the predator and may make them back off.

(For more details of other tactics to thwart mergers, see R. Gilman and P.S. Chan, 'Mergers and takeovers', *Management Decision*, Vol. 28, No. 7, 1990, pp. 26–37.)

Case Study 6.5: Ownership and control, and business objectives – the case of Saatchi versus Saatchi

1 Whether you regard this as a good or bad example of corporate governance depends largely on whether you think that the case illustrates shareholder democracy in action. On the one hand, there was the apparently high-handed attitude of Maurice Saatchi towards the shareholders. The company's strategy of becoming a big global player was clearly not a success. It appeared that they had made a number of unwise acquisitions. They were failing to meet the minimum profit constraint that the shareholders required. The man responsible therefore had to 'carry the can' and go. Indeed there were some inside the company on the board of directors who felt that it should have come sooner rather than later.

On the other hand, there does appear to have been a concerted campaign by an aggressive fund manager, David Herro, to unseat Maurice Saatchi. This does not appear from this point of view to have been a kind of spontaneous uprising by disaffected shareholders at large. It appears, according to one view expressed in the case, that the motives were to make money on the shares by buying at the bottom of the market and engineering the removal of the chairman in order to get the benefit of the rise in the share price that such a move, it was hoped, would bring about.

2/3 This goes to the heart of the dilemma when one comes to discuss shareholder power and corporate governance. The answer is presumably yes, provided they command sufficient holdings to influence the board of directors, which in this case they did. It is important to note that David Herro's Harris Associates held less than 10 per cent but were able to influence the views of other significant US shareholders.

In a book published in February 1997 by Kevin Goldman called *Conflicting Accounts: The Creation and Crash of the Saatchi and Saatchi Advertising Empire*, the author relates how the financial advisers Warburg and UBS delivered sobering news to the board in December 1994. A poll of the largest shareholders had concluded that they wanted Saatchi fired and if the board did not do it then they (the shareholders) would. If one takes this evidence at face value then it does appear that it was not just one influential individual who held the fate of Maurice Saatchi in his hands.

The question of whether the intervention was 'helpful' is also debatable. By allowing Maurice Saatchi to leave along with other senior executives of the company and to set up a rival company, it undoubtedly damaged the firm. Some major clients defected to the new company and the resulting bad publicity injured the reputation of the Saatchi & Saatchi firm.

4 The case illustrates the importance of making sure that the firm earns the minimum profit to keep the shareholders satisfied. Failure to do so can result in senior managers being removed. It is this discipline which stops managers pursuing their own goals to the exclusion of the interests of the shareholders.

5 Saatchi & Saatchi disappeared as a company and changed its name to Concordat. Maurice Saatchi set up a new company called M. Saatchi.

Case Study 6.6: Directors' pay – a national lottery?

1 The most obvious way is to link executive pay to profitability. This could take the form of setting profits targets and increasing bonuses in line with these. Another technique is to have a share bonus scheme in which the senior managers are given shares and can benefit from the rise in share price that is brought about by their good management.

2 There is, however, a need to ensure that the targets set are not so modest that it is virtually certain that the senior managers will make them. A remuneration committee which has a number of non-executive directors from outside the company is one obvious mechanism. However, there has been criticism of this supposedly independent way of setting executive pay, as the non-executive directors are appointed to the board by those whose pay they are going to review and it is alleged that there can develop a too 'cosy' relationship between the non-executive directors and the senior managers of the firm. The evidence is that the pay of senior managers has outstripped average earnings.

3 The principal–agent theory looks at the relationship between owners and managers and discusses the difficult question of how agent/managers should be rewarded. A reward system which guarantees them an income no matter how well or badly the firm operates offers no incentive to improve, while a reward system which is based entirely on profit will be unattractive to the agent/manager. The case illustrates the difficulty of finding the right balance, with a number of critics suggesting that directors' pay should be more closely geared to realistic targets of performance.

Case Study 6.7: Profit maximisation – the case of BP (1992)

1 From the information provided in the case study it seems that while BP is going for profit maximisation Shell is focusing more on growth.

2 The risks with the BP strategy are that the company depends on a limited number of oil and gas fields and these tend to be concentrated in a limited geographic area with fields that are reaching maturity. The long-term growth prospects are more problematic than they are with Shell. The areas that BP is hoping to open up are expensive to develop at a time when the company is cutting back on its development expenditure.

Case Study 6.8: Business objectives: the case of BP (1998)

1 It would appear that BP's objectives have changed since 1992. Scale does matter in the case of oil companies. The earlier period was marked by a period of downsizing. However, it has been pointed out that you cannot downsize your way to becoming a world leader. BP recognises the importance of scale in gaining economies and in transferring its expertise across the whole range of its operations. Acquisitions also reduce the risks in terms of protecting it from being too dependent on a few key areas of the world. The costs of entry into certain parts of the world are increasing and so only very big players can afford to do this. The BP–Amoco merger allows the combined companies to pay for the ever-increasing costs of entry (e.g. infrastructure spending that is being demanded by host governments).

2 Size is seen as a means to an end – which is enhanced profitability, not as an end in itself. The company is clear in its public pronouncements that this is the case. However, one can never be entirely sure that senior managers do not view size as an important goal in its own right. As is pointed out elsewhere, there is a tendency for managerial rewards to be linked to size (although there are attempts to link rewards more to performance indicators which include measures of profit).

3 Size matters for the reasons outlined in **1** above.

Case Study 6.9: The division between owners and managers

1 The conventional view is that managers take a long-term view of the company's future while it is argued that the shareholders are more interested in short-term profits.

2 The research by Kochlar and David quoted in the case study challenges this assumption and turns the conventional wisdom on its head. The research by Hayward and Hambrick appears to provide powerful empirical support for Oliver Williamson's Managerial Utility Model, which suggests that managers are more interested in maximising their own satisfaction (or 'managerial ego' to use Hayward and Hambrick's phrase).

Case Study 6.10: The diminishing importance of size

1 There are a number of factors which have contributed to the lowering of barriers to entry into industries. The main driving force appears to be technology. Firms such as Microsoft and CNN have been able to challenge bigger rivals by taking advantage of new technology. In the case of Microsoft it was the development of clever software such as Windows 95 which enabled them to challenge such companies as IBM. CNN was able to use the new emerging technology to beam news via satellite links as it happened 24 hours a day from anywhere in the world.

In addition, increasing competition between financial institutions, because the rules governing the operation of the capital market were relaxed, meant that smaller firms now had access to the same sources of finance as their bigger competitors.

2 'Flexibility' presumably means the ability to quickly spot changes in the pattern of demand for the company's product or service and to meet it effectively. It implies a 'flat' organisational structure (see Chapter 5) so that decisions can be made and implemented quickly. It also implies a 'market-orientated' approach. This contrasts with 'economies of scale' where the driving force is size and the ability to combine production processes or to seek out 'synergies' by merging. This implies a more complex organisational structure and a 'production-orientated approach'. The argument being advanced is that in a world of fast-changing technology in which products and processes can quickly become obsolete 'flexibility' is valued more than 'economies of scale'.

3 In spite of the attractiveness of the arguments being advanced above, this view is challenged by a number of critics. In the case study a number of arguments are advanced against the 'small is beautiful' argument. First, not all big companies are unsuccessful. Secondly, large companies have 're-invented' themselves by restructuring or 're-engineering' themselves into smaller semi-autonomous divisions which focus on their core competences (for more details of this process see Chapter 11 and Case Study 11.1). Thirdly, the statistics on the job-creating potential of small firms have been exaggerated according to data published in the United States. Finally, many small firms rely on the big firms for their survival as the large companies 'contract out' some of their activities.

4   It is from the last two points that the idea about 'size being all in the mind' stems. Large companies are thus trying to achieve the kind of flexibility that small firms allegedly enjoy while at the same time trying to maintain the advantages of size. Thus large firms are restructuring themselves into semi-autonomous units responsible for achieving certain targets, while at the same time centralising and controlling those functions from which they can gain economies of scale. Each large firm will tackle this in a number of different ways. However, the essential point is that the clear distinction between 'large' and 'small' firms tends to disappear.

Chapter 7   Demand in theory and practice

Pause for thought 1

Another factor which could affect the demand for computer games is age, as the demand is likely to be greatest among those under 25. In addition there is clearly a seasonal factor which plays a significant part as demand is greatest at Christmas time. Technology can also play a part as new special 'platforms' are developed to run computer games which displace the traditional PC (for more details see Case Study 11.3).

Pause for thought 2

(a)   Assuming that the personal computer and the computer game can be seen as complementary goods then the relationship between the demand for the computer game and the price of the PC is an indirect one (i.e. as the price of the the PC rises so the demand for the game will fall). The sign of the beta coefficient would therefore be negative.

(b)   For competitive goods the relationship between the price of the competitive good and the demand for computer games is a direct one (i.e. as the price of CDs or cassettes rises so the relative price of computer games falls and they become more attractive to buy). The sign of the relevant beta coefficient will be positive.

Pause for thought 3

1   Nominal prices refer to prices expressed in money-of-the-day terms (i.e. the price that you observe today in the shops). A real price adjusts this price to take account of the general level of inflation.

2   If the price of computer games rises by 3 per cent in a year against a general rise in the level of inflation of 5 per cent then it can be said that there has been a fall in the real price of computer games by 2 per cent (5 – 3 per cent).

3   It clearly can as the above calculation illustrates.

4   There are plenty of examples to illustrate the relationship between real and nominal prices. For example in 1996 house prices rose by 8.4 per cent on average, the biggest jump since 1989. In 1990 nominal house prices fell for the first time in 20 years and continued to fall for the next three years. However, in real terms house prices actually fell for five years from 1990 to 1995. What this implied was that in the years 1994 and 1995, although the nominal price of houses recovered modestly, the 'gain' to sellers of houses was wiped out by the general rise in prices in that period. It was during this period that 'negative equity' (where a house was worth less than the mortgage on it) became a factor in the housing market. According to statistics published by the building societies about 1.7 million households in 1993 were in this position. A fall in the real value of houses also made them an extremely unattractive investment proposition and the housing market slumped with a sharp decline in the number of houses sold. 1997, however, was a good year in the housing market with a rise in house prices of about 8–9 per cent against a rate of inflation of 2–3 per cent, leading to a real rise in house prices of between 5 and 7 per cent. Thus the number of houses in 'negative equity' fell to below 100,000. (For more details, see *The Economist*, 19 January 1997, p. 27, 'Another housing boom?').

5   The price level relates to a given price, say £5 (or RPI of 100). A change in the price level refers to the percentage change, e.g. 5 per cent. In some cases the demand may be more sensitive to changes in the *price level* than to the *absolute price*.

Pause for thought 4

1   Setting Q = 0 and solving for P gives an answer of £30.

2   Setting P = 0 and solving for Q gives an answer of 300 units.

Pause for thought 5

This highlights the so-called 'percentage fallacy'. In calculating the percentage it all depends on where one starts. From £5 to £10 is a 100 per cent increase; from £10 to £5 is a 50 per cent fall. It is the same price change and this is why in elasticity calculations the formula will give you an unambiguous answer (see Box 7.1).

Nevertheless, percentages are still used to discuss elasticity concepts. For example, there has been much discussion about ways of reducing traffic congestion by using some price mechanism. One way is by road pricing. However, we are some way from achieving this, even assuming that it was politically acceptable. Another mechanism is to use petrol duties as a way of making it more expensive to run a car and hence it is hoped to cut down on the number of journeys that are made. Ideally the price elasticity of demand should be highly elastic so that a small increase in petrol duties would cause a significant drop in the amount of petrol usage. Critics of these measures have argued that raising petrol duties will have no effect on traffic growth. However, *The Economist* quotes a number of research studies which suggest that a 10 per cent rise in fuel prices would result in a 7 per cent fall in petrol use, thus implying a price elasticity of demand for petrol of –0.7 (see *The Economist*, 18 January 1997, p. 33–4, 'Jam tomorrow'). The implication of this is that demand for petrol is influenced by price but that it is not very sensitive and other more radical measures to reduce traffic congestion may have to be considered.

Box 7.1: The calculation of elasticity values: the 'arc' formula

The answer is $(10 - 8)/(10 + 8) \times (2 + 4)/(2 - 4) = -6/18 = -0.33$. The point about this answer is that the 'starting point' for the calculation makes no difference because using the arc formula will give you the same answer whether prices rise or fall.

Case Study 7.1: Cola war takes the fizz out of Cadbury profits

See text.

Case Study 7.2: The price of oil

See text.

Case Study 7.3: The demand for beer

1 The real price variable for beer is negative, indicating that as the real price of beer has risen so the demand for beer has fallen, other things being equal. As the real level of advertising has risen so also has the demand for beer. The weather variable and the real level of disposable income are also directly related to the demand for beer as one might have expected. The odd one out in the Reekie and Blight demand equation for beer is the real level of advertising for competing products. One would have expected that the more advertising on competing products the less the demand for beer. However, there are only two variables which are statistically significant and the model only 'explains' 57 per cent of the variation in demand ($R^2 = 0.57$).

2 There is no attempt to look at the influence of tastes (the influence of premium 'designer label' lagers), social class, age or gender on the demand for beer.

3 This depends on whether you think real or nominal prices are the key influence on demand. Real prices and real incomes take out the impact of inflation. Without this adjustment it is likely that the demand for beer and the actual price of beer will apparently rise together.

4 One possible explanation is that advertising on any kind of alcoholic drink is generic and has spillover effects for the demand for beer. Thus, speaking

from the personal experience of one of the authors, an advertisement in the run-up to Christmas 1996 by Gerard Depardieu for cognac reminded him to buy in the Christmas drinks which included no cognac (for which he has little taste) but did include beer (for which he has!).

5   One explanation is that there are some variables missing from the predictor equation. Another explanation is that the equation is incorrectly specified (see p. 180).

Pause for thought 6

The identification problem is less apparent with cross-sectional data because the data used is all collected at one point in time, hence any supply-side influences will have been mitigated.

Box 7.2: Impulse Ice Cream survey

See text.

Pause for thought 7

The text identifies two principal reasons. First, where the product or service is new then surveys are a better way of forecasting demand because no previous data is available and hence statistical methods are not practical. Secondly, surveys can gauge the influence of qualitative factors on demand as well as obtain information in a more disaggregated way (e.g. the demand for Caffreys beer as opposed to beer in general).

Pause for thought 8

The disadvantages relate to such factors as the sample size, its representativeness, the methods of sampling used and the time frame within which the survey is conducted.

Pause for thought 9

Surveys of your own salesforce suffer from the fact that there may be factors which can influence the answers that you may receive. The text identifies a number of these. As against that, the salesforce should be close to the market and can in theory give a quick and reliable forecast of demand.

Pause for thought 10

The question is asking you to review your understanding of all the techniques outlined in the text and to discuss the pros and cons of each. There is no 'right' answer to this and you are invited to discuss what factors might influence your choice of technique (e.g. time, costs, the risks of getting it wrong, etc.).

Pause for thought 11

The demand for higher education could be increased by the development of the Internet as a medium for delivering courses. It depends on the costs of access to the system for the customers. Some people will not be able to attend a 'campus-based' course and hence this method might prove attractive. It would mean that teaching materials which are print based may face competition from multi-media materials. Instead of reading about a given company in a textbook it is possible to have video case study material which can be replayed via a PC with supporting text. Companies that are producing traditional textbooks should therefore be prepared to extend their product range to include new electronically transmitted material. As the cost of the technology falls then so it will become more widely available and access to it will be increased.

Pause for thought 12

1   Simple extrapolation assumes that whatever factors affected demand in the past will continue to affect it in the future. However, in the field of forecasting the demand for higher education there are a number of changes which will affect future demand (e.g. the level of student support, the possibility of some universities charging additional fees, the level of support given by the government to fund certain courses, the demographic profile of the population), all of which could come into play in a way that they have not done in the past ten years. Thus extrapolation on the basis of past trends could give a very misleading picture.

2   The problems are compounded when one attempts to predict the demand for a given course such as business studies. The government may not wish to see an expansion in the numbers studying such courses and penalise universities if they exceed their target numbers in this area. Thus the 'environment' within which the forecasts have to be made has changed. As can be seen from the data in the table, the Business School in question experienced a significant increase in its total number of students in the early 1990s in response to government pressure to increase participation in higher education. Then the policy was reversed in 1994 and the brakes were put on further expansion. However, although intake numbers fell in 1994 and the rate of increase in total numbers slowed down, it proved difficult to get it right in 1995 and intake numbers shot up by 22.2 per cent. Making forecasts of intake for future years based on the erratic experience of previous years is therefore very hazardous.

Pause for thought 13

The demand for nursery school places based on the number of new births in a given area would be one example.

Case Study 7.4: Forecasting the demand for a new product – Windows 95

1 Forecasts of demand for a new software product such as Windows 95 are surrounded by a number of uncertainties. The big question is obviously the take-up rate of the new product which depends on the extra computing power required to run it. If to run Windows 95 requires consumers to buy a new PC or upgrade their existing PC then this adds substantially to the true costs of buying the new software. By identifying who has what computing power the forecasters are attempting to identify who could convert quickly and at what cost. The forecasters were, however, conscious that there had been an explosion in demand for new PCs in 1995 and that there would be considerable resistance from these consumers to add on extra computing power at an estimated cost of between £700 and £1,400 for what is essentially an 'invisible' item, namely the operating software as opposed to 'visible' software such as a multimedia package. Another uncertainty is the unwillingness of some consumers to buy a new software product for fear that it still has 'bugs' to be ironed out. The possibility of the launch of a new product such as Windows NT, which is a network based piece of software, is likely, according to some forecasters, to affect adversely the demand for Windows 95. Thus there are a whole host of 'qualitative' factors, any one of which the forecasters can take a different view of, that can affect the demand. Hence there was a wide variation in demand forecasts in 1995 (August–December) from 14 million to 29 million units.

2 The market is segmented according to a number of factors, for example business users versus home users. In addition the market is segmented according to the computing power that consumers already have.

Case Study 7.5: The National Grid and forecasting demand

1 There are a number of factors which can affect the demand for electricity at a given hour of the day. These can be summarised as:
  - ➤ Price: off-peak rates v peak rates.
  - ➤ Income: there is evidence that those on lower incomes spend less on heating, etc.
  - ➤ Price of substitutes: in the long term people may switch energy sources. In the short term there will be 'switching costs' to take into account. If cheaper and safe alternatives can be easily installed then there could be a switch to substitutes (e.g. stand-alone heaters that do not use electricity).
  - ➤ Time of day: demand will increase around meal times.
  - ➤ Temperature: obviously a key factor.
  - ➤ Special events: TV programmes such as football matches, 'cliff hangers' in soap operas, etc.

It is very difficult to model these special factors. Past data can be used as a guide to some extent. Intuitively factors such as time of day and temperature would seem to be the main drivers of demand. You could use correlations to try to 'explain' the variations in demand and to try to eliminate errors, but the margin for error can be upset by these special factors even if some can be anticipated (such as special TV programmes like a big football match.)

2 If the National Grid underestimates the demand then it will not have enough capacity to meet the demand and the risk is that there will be power shortages and power failures. If they overestimate demand they will have under-utilised capacity which is inefficient and costly. However, the balance of risk is likely to be greater with power shortages, so it is better for the National Grid to err on the side of overcapacity rather than undercapacity.

Chapter 8 Costs in theory and practice

Pause for thought 1

If a firm is covering all its variable costs, then any extra revenue will be making a positive contribution towards covering fixed costs, which will be incurred irrespective of production levels. If this is the scenario that the firm is faced with then it is worth continuing to operate in the short run. However, in the long run *all* costs must be covered to allow the company to report a profit. The advantage of calculating averages for costs is that it allows for comparison over different levels of production and over different time periods.

Pause for thought 2

Obviously this will depend on the area of the country in which you are located and the industries that are prevalent.

Pause for thought 3

The marginal costs would be significantly less if the second child were a girl and if the couple chose to use the clothes of the previous baby girl for the second baby girl. The toys for the first girl could also be used for the second. A number of items such as cots and car seats do not depend on the sex of the child, therefore it would not matter from a marginal perspective what the sex of the child was.

Case Study 8.1: The concept of marginal costs and benefits

1 This is a difficult question to answer. The most appropriate method would be to interview a large number of hospital administrators to find out about their understanding of marginal benefits as a result of increased spending. However, with the awareness that the NHS now has in relation to costs, it would come as no surprise if those in charge of operating the financial purse strings of a hospital were in fact extremely aware of the marginal benefits and costs of an increase or decrease in spending.

2 This obviously makes marginal analysis somewhat more complex. The concept is a relatively easy one to understand and to put into practical use in a company that only has a single product. However, problems such as the splitting of fixed costs and the amount of electricity that is used by each product, for example, make marginal analysis a much more difficult proposition.

3 This is probably the case because of the reasons cited in the answer above. It is difficult to think of a company today that makes a single product. Virtually all firms are involved in some sort of differentiation of their standard product and this makes marginal analysis cumbersome to put into practice. The use of average costs is more basic and may provide somewhat misleading information upon which to make decisions, but the information is freely and readily available to the managers to allow them to make decisions.

Case Study 8.2: Marginal analysis

1 When the marginal cost of the last student equals the marginal revenue he/she contributes.

2 The long-run viability of the MBA depends in part on the admission tutors accepting high calibre students that result in the value of the qualification being maintained. Altering the price of the product merely makes it more or less accessible depending on the funds that are at your disposal.

3 It would appear from this analysis that the university sector will find it beneficial to offer more and more courses on this basis. If there is a market demand for these types of qualifications, paid for directly by the customer, then educational establishments are likely to find it profitable to satisfy this demand. It means that the taxpayer has to fund less and less of the education system. This may allow tax cuts which will leave more cash in the consumer's pocket to allow him to make his own choice on educational provision. In the long term this system is arguably flawed, in that those from poorer backgrounds are denied the privilege of education that should or could be available to all.

Case Study 8.3: A marginal application

1 The information that is provided in the case study is at a very general level. Specific information such as problem areas for crashes and the impact and effect of each specific safety measure would ensure that the money is used as effectively as possible. At the moment the picture that is painted is of an overall nature which allows only a global strategic decision to be arrived at.

2 The evidence here suggests that it will. However, as new technological breakthroughs are found, some revolutionary device may be found that requires a small amount of capital expenditure, but would in fact increase road safety significantly. In all probability, however, the marginal benefit will continue to fall as additional expenditure will not be as effective as initial spending, since the main causes have been addressed.

Case Study 8.4: Marginal environmental analysis

1 The marginal analysis tells us that it is important to use marginal figures to pinpoint where the most effective policy response would be best directed. Simply using average figures does not indicate at what point the pollution would exceed the 'carrying capacity' of the river. If this point can be avoided then the anti-pollution policy is more likely to have been a success.

2　In the analysis of problems using a marginal approach the optimum point is usually where the marginal benefit from implementing a policy or decision is at its highest.

3　In the case of a river, reduced recreational facilities associated with the river such as swimming, fishing or canoeing. Pollution may get into the water supply causing illness. It may reduce the number of tourists coming to an area if the river is unsightly. It may lead to the river becoming a dumping ground, resulting in an increase in vermin in the area and a subsequent health risk developing.

Pause for thought 4

Some of the advantages are reduced administrative overheads, e.g. one admissions service, reduced number of receptionists, technicians and janitors. Also if both institutions have courses in the same subjects then not all lecturers will be needed as students can be put together and taught jointly, allowing for savings to be made in salaries, etc.

Case Study 8.5: The knowledge revolution

The nature of the business world of today is that there appear to be two types of organisation that are developing. There are very large corporations, and also small firms. This case study concentrates on the former. Firms are merging and creating huge organisations to benefit from economies of scale and to facilitate competitive operation on a global scale. This becomes more and more complex to manage as the data that is available to the strategic decision-makers in an organisation is huge. Consequently, knowledge management systems can act as a deciphering and filter mechanism to provide the relevant data. They can also be used to identify when there is repetition and when the same data is held in a number of different systems. If knowledge management systems operate effectively and are embraced by staff they are potentially a highly valuable tool in eradicating vast diseconomies of scale.

Case Study 8.6: What happens when companies combine?

1　This may have been because the new company would have only needed one board of directors and one management team. Therefore it is unlikely that individuals are going to vote to lose their jobs through choice. In addition the creation of such a large company would have resulted in an organisation that would have been difficult to control and may have resulted in even greater inefficiencies. Perhaps, the cultural differences between France and Sweden would not have made the merger a success. Possibly the destination of ultimate control was an insurmountable barrier, with both firms seeing themselves as the leading firm in the merger.

2　The company may have been so large that managerial diseconomies may have taken place. The very size of the organisation may have allowed managers to pursue non-maximising goals.

3 They are probably on the high side to convince the stock markets of the world and the shareholders of both companies that the proposed merger is an excellent idea and that they should support it.

Pause for thought 5

The implications for young people can be examined in two ways. The first is optimistic in that the kind of job that is being created today requires a high level of skill and training, thus the jobs will be interesting and varied. The more pessimistic view is that increased automation will reduce the total number of jobs available, in conjunction with a growing worldwide population which will result in a permanent imbalance between the number of people looking for jobs and the volume of jobs available.

Pause for thought 6

The advantage of humans is that they can interpret a situation and use common sense when a problem or request that has not previously occurred is presented in front of them. A fall in the price of labour relative to the price of capital is likely to result in more labour being used (substituted for capital) and less capital.

Chapter 9 Pricing in theory and practice
....

Case Study 9.1: The price of Tequila

1 The distillers would appear to be operating a simple process of average cost pricing. It is clear that the market conditions, i.e. increasing demand for the product, have had a significant impact on the amount of agave that is required by the distillers. The farmers cannot supply the amounts needed, therefore they have taken the opportunity of raising their prices. This in turn leads the distillers to increasing their prices as the cost of the raw materials has gone up. However, the key question that needs to be discussed here is: Is it the change in demand, or the inability of the farmers to supply increased volume of agave in the short run, that has resulted in the price of tequila spiralling? Or, perhaps more realistically, it is a little of both.

2 It could be argued that there are no groups that are suffering as a consequence of these price rises. If the tequila-drinking public are prepared to pay the increased prices, then this would suggest that all parties are happy with the situation. The distillers would prefer to have a lower agave price, which they have now negotiated. It will also be interesting to note whether or not they will pass lower production costs on to the consumer, or simply derive higher profit margins.

3 The price of tequila in the long run will be determined by the demand in the market place for the product. The purchasers of this commodity are notoriously fickle and fads come and go very quickly. If a new product gains popularity then the demand for tequila may drop dramatically and rapidly. If this were to be the case then a very high price would seem unsustainable.

Pause for thought 1

The conclusion that should be arrived at is that all television advertising is undertaken by firms operating within oligopolistic market structures. These firms have all undertaken product differentiation and other forms of non-price competition. It should also be noted that a number of industries will always be involved in some sort of price war, indicating that oligopoly theory does not always hold true.

Case Study 9.2: Competition under oligopoly – the Hoover free flight promotion

1   The Hoover campaign was a success in that it enticed a large number of people who might not otherwise have purchased a Hoover good, or any good at all, to purchase an item made by Hoover. This resulted in a huge increase in demand and market share. It was a failure in that Hoover received a huge amount of bad publicity, they had to spend an enormous amount of money purchasing expensive flights, and their reputation was damaged, making repeat purchases unlikely.

2   It is possible to argue that this may not have done Hoover any damage in the long run, even though their reputation has been dented in the short to medium term. If the consumers are satisfied with the products they have purchased, then if they come to replace them in, say, 3–4 years, the situation regarding the flights is unlikely to have a bearing on their choice.

3   It depends largely on the quality of the good being offered. Consumers may be enticed to buy a good as a result of a special promotion, and if they are satisfied then they are likely to make a repeat purchase. If, however, they are dissatisfied they will probably return to their original choice.

Pause for thought 2

The answer to this question is largely individual thoughts and opinions.

Pause for thought 3

The financial services industry has changed dramatically over the last 10–15 years. During this time the industry has been deregulated and liberalised. Along with this has been the demutualisation of building societies. This has resulted in all financial institutions moving into each other's markets and thus the level of competition has increased substantially. This has resulted in lower prices being offered to the consumer. A good example of this is the price of car insurance that during the early 1990s fell noticeably but is now very much on the increase. The market had too many players and to achieve economies of scale merger activity has taken place. This will result in a reduction in competition, thus choice for the consumer. Prices should consequently go up, thus increasing profits for the firms.

Pause for thought 4

Prices at petrol stations follow the predicted behaviour of oligopolistic markets quite closely. Firms attempt to entice you to their product through special offers and by offering attractive additional shopping facilities. The extent to which this breeds customer loyalty is open to debate. It is very much dependent on the individual and the offer that is being made.

Case Study 9.3: Miles more – a shake-up in UK domestic flights

1   British Airways do not see themselves in direct competition with the budget operator. They are offering a different service aimed at a different target audience. BA are aiming at the business traveller and provide a high quality travelling environment with top of the range meals and wines. The number of flights is frequent and at convenient times for business people. Budget operators are primarily concerned with leisure travellers. Thus BA can afford to charge higher prices.
2   This strategy would reduce profits in the short run. In addition, the market is large enough to cater for both types of operation as they are aiming at different niches. Thus both can quite happily operate together. There is also the risk of regulations being strengthened, or more strictly enforced.
3   Alternative modes of travel such as the bus industry and the rail industry, as people stop using these because of the low cost of flying.

Case Study 9.4: The price of compact discs

1   It would appear to be so. Traditionally, CDs have been charged at a higher price in the UK than in the US. Consumers are willing to pay this price, therefore suppliers are quite happy to go on charging this price.
2   Price benchmarking; average cost pricing.
3   It could be argued that there is. The costs of producing a CD in the UK are divided over a much smaller number of people than in the US. This results in a much higher unit cost. If the same mark-up is applied in both countries then the price of CDs in the UK will be much higher than in the US, which is in fact the case.

Pause for thought 5

The answers to the first three questions depend on the knowledge of the individual. The answer to the fourth is that it is the supplier who gains, in that income from sales is largely fixed and he can plan accordingly. The risk of profitability being damaged by price wars is reduced.

Case Study 9.5: Is this the end of sticky prices?

1/2   The answer relates to the conditions of a perfectly competitive market. The key reason why prices remain sticky in some markets and not others relates to the fact that prices will change when the cost of leaving them unchanged becomes bigger than the cost of adjusting them. It is costly to keep changing the price lists for hotel rooms on a daily basis. However, if by not changing prices in response to demand changes customers stop buying or switch to other products or services then the costs of leaving prices as they are will increase. One of the key features of a perfect market is supposed to be perfect knowledge of prices prevailing in the market. If there is perfect knowledge then it is unlikely that price differences for the same product will persist. The Internet gives consumers access to price information instantly and enables them to compare, thereby increasing the costs of leaving prices unchanged.

3   The article relates to three conditions where 'sticky' prices are likely to persist:

➤ When quality is hard to assess (some services when it is hard to determine quality before you sample it – by which time it is too late!).

➤ When consumers dislike frequent price changes (e.g. mortgage interest changes which tend to lag behind changes to other money market rates).

➤ When the market is monopolistic/oligopolistic.

Case Study 9.6: Pricing strategies in highly competitive markets

1   The make-up of the particular industry is such that it is extremely competitive with low margins and profitability, with little product differentiation. Increasing market share is difficult. Possibilities include takeover or merger with a rival firm, which would instantly increase market share and possibly bring some economies of scale. Alternatively, if large financial backing were available, then predatory pricing could be utilised in the medium term to try to drive rival firms out of the industry.

2   In the long term, probably yes. When there are low margins with fierce competition any downturn in trading conditions is likely to have a negative impact on the industry, making mergers almost inevitable.

3   The firms that use this industry are getting charged prices that are extremely low, thus keeping their costs to a minimum.

Pause for thought 6

It would appear to have very little use in strategic decision-making in a competitive environment because it is static and non-predictive. It indicates the situation that may occur at a specific period of time. In a competitive environment this is likely to be continually changing, with rivals attempting to increase market share through a number of different measures. The kinked demand curve is useful for describing a situation but not as a tool to assist in decision-making.

Case Study 9.7: Phones war may cut bills

1   It chose to enter because deregulation has now allowed it to enter, when previously it could not. There is also the opportunity to make significant profits in this market place, which is the motivating force behind all large corporations.

2   They started a price war to try to reduce the consumer loyalty that the UK population has towards BT and to try to build up a significant market share as quickly as possible. In this industry price is probably the most significant

factor in the choice of the consumer. It is also a focus for advertising material if they can undercut the incumbent. Price stability predicted by kinked demand is more relevant to existing firms' strategies, rather than those of new entrants such as AT&T.

3   *Price* – there will continue to be a price war in the short term, before moving back to approximately the level it is currently at in the long run as the market share settles down.

   New Entry – this will depend on the impact of the current batch of new entrants and how they perform, the financial backing of any potential entrant and the size of the market.

   Market Shares – this is somewhat difficult to predict. It depends on consumer loyalty, the extent of any new entry, the desire of any firm to try and increase their market share to the detriment of short-term profit, etc.

Case Study 9.8: A non-zero-sum game

1   Other factors may be related to what other firms are doing in the market place. Are there other firms who could be doing the same thing as these two? How would that impact upon this agreement? Has the company you are dealing with ever had an agreement of this type before? If so, did they hold to the agreement or did they cheat?

2   Yes. It does this by providing a range of outcomes that identify what will happen depending on their attitude to risk and the other firms' perception. The strategy selected itself reflects an attitude to risk; for example, maximin reflects a more pessimistic attitude than maximax, etc.

Pause for thought 7

The role of game theory in providing businessmen with a framework for decision-making is extremely limited. The examples commonly used are that of two firms in a zero-sum game. This is very unlikely to happen in practice in a dynamic and changing environment. It is useful in modelling firm behaviour and analysing possible outcomes from certain situations, but it is not particularly helpful as a predictive instrument.

Case Study 9.9: Indiscriminate pricing

1   That economic rationale for such a policy is that a firm is able to segment its market and charge the price that each market can bear. Thus as the article suggests, airlines can generate more revenue by having different prices for airline seats to the same destination. The demand from business travellers is inelastic as they want to get from A to B in the shortest period of time and are not too sensitive to the price charged. Tourists, on the other hand, are more price sensitive and there is likely to be more competition to fill seats from different airlines. Recently some airlines have realised that even the business markets may be 'soft' (i.e. price sensitive) and have set up services which are described as 'no frills'.

2   Firms make more money by charging different prices because they are able to segment the market. There will be some consumers who are willing to

pay more than the market price to obtain the good or service in question. Provided that there is no leakage from one market segment to another (i.e. the consumer buys at one price and sells at a profit in another market) then more revenue can be raised by price discrimination.

3   The answer is connected to the kind of market structure that the firm finds itself in. If, for example, the firm is in an oligopolistic market then there will be a tendency for its actions to affect the behaviour of other firms in the market. These are:

> There should be a *concentration of market power* (e.g. four firms with a total of 80 per cent market share and each with more or less the same market share).

> There should be *barriers to entry*.

> There should be a *high degree of interdependence*. This is more likely to happen when the first two conditions above apply and also when the costs of production and the state of technology are very similar between firms in the market place.

They will wind up worse off if they all discount together and so reduce prices. Also discounts offered to get customers to switch brands require the same discounts to be offered to existing customers. This can cause a loss of revenue even although sales may have increased.

4   This statement implies that it is sometimes better not to offer discounts in markets where there is a high degree of interdependence. The kinked demand curve can be used to demonstrate that there is no advantage to cutting prices as other firms in an oligopolistic market will simply follow suit.

5   The answer is 'not usually'. Some customers gain lower prices while others pay more. In those cases where companies agree not to discount it can be difficult to decide if they are doing so as the result of collusion (see reference to the Procter & Gamble case mentioned in the Case Study). If consumers are unhappy at the loss of discounts and *provided there is an alternative source of supply* then there should be no worries from the anti-trust/monopoly point of view. Only if there evidence of collusion (hard to prove) and monopoly power should the authorities intervene.

Case Study 9.10: The price of air?

There are a number of practical problems associated with this seemingly simple proposal. One problem concerns the way an auction of slots would be conducted. A given landing slot, say 08.05 at Heathrow, becomes valuable if an airline can also secure a take-off slot of say 08.55 to a European capital. Therefore, the valuation of one slot depends on securing other linked slots, so auctioning becomes extremely complicated. It is argued that there might be a partial remedy to this by a created 'after market' (i.e. the airlines trade slots with one another to get the best match for their schedules). However, unregulated, the potential for spoiling tactics could be great. Also it is argued that without some special concessions for smaller airlines they could simply be priced right out of the market, although 'free market' economists would argue against any type of protection for smaller airlines, arguing that 'if they can't stand the heat they should get out of the kitchen' and that once protected they would always need protecting.

Another aspect which would create some difficulties would be if the slots were sold but only for a limited period. Airlines would not know with any certainty if they would be able to retain the slot and this could deter them from developing the service by investing in facilities on the ground at given airports if there was the prospect of them losing the slot. Finally, there is likely to be strong political resistance to this proposal as national carriers lobby their respective governments to protect their position.

Chapter 10 Investment in theory and practice

Pause for thought 1

There are three main factors to take into account in evaluating a project. First, there is the capital cost of the project; secondly, there are the operating costs involved; and, thirdly, there is the likely income to be earned from the project. Low capital cost coupled with small running costs and a good stream of income over the life of the project will clearly make it viable.

Pause for thought 2

Looking at the net income – the net cash flows (NCFs) – after subtracting the initial capital outlay that the company will receive for the two projects, the figures are exactly the same (£35,000: see Table 10.1). So there does not seem to be much to choose between them. One might be tempted to look at the way the cash flows appear over the life of the project and conclude that widgets were a better bet because they offered a more steady stream of income. As against that, the gizmo project offers a quicker return because the capital costs are recouped more quickly. The point about this 'Pause for thought' is to start you thinking about the variety of ways one can look at capital projects.

Pause for thought 3

One of the main factors to take into account would be the risks associated with each project. Although both projects yield very much the same results there may be different risks involved. If, for example, there is more chance that the cash flows for gizmos will not be achieved, then you may prefer to go with the project in which the returns are more assured. To some extent this depends on how much of a gambler the management of the company is.

Pause for thought 4

The results are given in Table 10.2.

Pause for thought 5

The best combination with a capital budget of £75,000 is Projects B + C + F (total NPV = £32,000) whereas with a budget allocation of £100,000 the best combination of projects is B + C + D yielding a total NPV of £41,000.

Pause for thought 6

To some extent the same considerations that are mentioned in 'Pause for thought 3' also apply here. There are also strategic considerations to take into account. Does the firm wish to become a 'player' in the widget market? How realistic are the fears about the future of this market and should the firm diversify away from its traditional product base? The point here is that the techniques provide the manager with a starting point to discuss options. They are not an end in themselves and do not by themselves provide the whole answer.

Pause for thought 7

Using the weighted average method outlined in the text the answer is 13.5 per cent (15 per cent + 12 per cent divided by 2), given that debt and equity are used in equal proportions.

Pause for thought 8

A possible answer is:

Year	Widgets	Probability	ECF (widgets)
0	−100,000	1.00	−100,000
1	38,000	0.70	26,600
2	30,000	0.60	18,000
3	23,000	0.50	11,500
4	22,500	0.40	9,000
5	21,500	0.30	6,450
TOTAL			−28,450

What this reveals is that if managers take a more pessimistic view of the future then they will 'downgrade' the likely returns to the project.

Pause for thought 9

There are any number of examples of technological change which have affected both products and processes. National Cash Register (NCR) was hit in the 1980s with the advent of new electronically based cash registers and suffered as a result with the development of these new products. Fleet Street disappeared as the main centre for the production of newspapers as a result of new technology, thus doing away with the old 'hot metal' presses for producing newspapers. Direct banking is also having a similar effect on high street banks, affecting both the process and the products of financial institutions.

Case Study 10.1: When the chips are down

See text.

Pause for thought 10

A change of government could affect your export business if it results in a change in exchange rates. If, for example, there are fears that a new government might increase spending and increase the PSBR (see Chapter 1) then this may result in higher interest rates at home. This in turn could cause exchange rates to increase and make it more difficult to export. In 1979, for example, the new Conservative government raised interest rates to try to curb inflation. One of the consequences of this was for exchange rates to shoot up and this made life extremely difficult for exporters. In January 1997, the Labour party tried to reassure industrialists and City analysts that they would not 'take risks' with the economy in a bid to minimise the extent of the 'political risks' associated with a new government should the Conservatives lose the General Election.

Case Study 10.2: Highland Plastics (Inverness) plc

The results are as follows:

Option	Payback period (years)	ARR (%)	NPV (£)	IRR (%)
A	3.2	18.0	(469)	20
B	3.25	12.7	(35,210)	17
C	1.6	42.5	347,653	56
D	n.a.	n.a.	n.a.	n.a.

On the basis of the calculations it appears fairly self evident that the best option is Option C on all the criteria. However, the crucial question to ask is what are the key objectives of the two managers? With this option the PVC side of the business would account for 65 per cent of their output and as this is a more volatile market they would be more exposed to greater risks. (There is no assessment in the case of the risks associated with each option.)

There is a strong indication that both men are not risk-takers and they are not really 'profit-maximisers' either. They are in some senses between a 'rock and a hard place' and nothing they do is quite going to meet their aspirations. It is at this point that you might like to speculate on what you would recommend, which is not necessarily made explicit in the case, before reading the postscript which tells you what they actually did.

Postscript to Highland Plastics
In 1987 Highland Plastics was acquired by a company which was looking to diversify from its traditional pottery business in the Stoke-on-Trent area. The two directors Semple and Richards remained in position while the company Blackacre Potteries appointed a managing director. After three years both Semple and Richards took early retirement.

Two years later, Blackacre Potteries was itself taken over by a multinational company who decided to sell off Highland Plastics. Highland was then the subject of a management buy-out by the managers that Semple and Richards had brought in, so it reverted to a small private company.

In 1995, after years of successful trading, it was taken over by a large national packaging company. In 2000, after being taken over by a large multinational company, the factory was relocated back in the Central Belt of Scotland!

Chapter 11 Corporate strategy and business economics

∙∙∙

Case Study 11.1: Core competences – the cases of ITT and Hanson

See text.

Pause for thought 1

One of the ways that firms sought to reduce their exposure to the swings in the economy between boom and bust was to diversify internationally. In addition, by diversifying into many sectors of the economy it was hoped that they would also be immune from the ups and downs in any one market. Thus multinational conglomerates like ITT and Hanson diversified in order to take account of the changing domestic economic environment (see Chapter 2) and the shift in the structure of the economy (see Chapter 4). It is also clear that in the case of some of the larger conglomerates there were changes in objectives in the 1990s, moving away from growth and size and focusing more on value-added and profitability. The case also illustrates the changed way in which Hanson in particular organised itself internally (see Chapter 5) and how it reviewed the way in which it sanctioned investment decisions and how it viewed these (see Chapter 10). The case study looks at the benefits of size on costs (see Chapter 8) and highlights the debate about the benefits of size versus the more focused approach that these two companies appear to be trying to adopt.

Case Study 11.2: PEST and multinationals

1   Host governments can try to influence multinational firms to adopt 'good practice' as far as environmental protection is concerned. However, much depends upon the bargaining power that they can exert. If, for example, the resource that the multinational firm is trying to exploit is highly valued by the MNE and the host government has no desperate need to seek outside firms to exploit it, then the host government can hold some powerful cards and can therefore lay down stringent terms and conditions for allowing entry. On the other hand, the situation with some third world countries is often that they do not have the indigenous firms who can exploit the resource and they are therefore highly dependent on foreign multinationals to assist them. Nevertheless, as the case illustrates, some environmental groups have become very adept at embarrassing foreign MNEs with some bad publicity in their home markets.

2   This is a difficult question to answer. The 'absolutist' position is to say that MNEs should not do business with any regime which flouts basic democratic rights. However, it becomes quite difficult to know where to draw the line. How do you decide the 'good' and the 'bad' countries? What criteria do you adopt? There are many countries where the governments may behave in a way that we might not approve of but does this mean we should stop trading with firms from these countries? These firms may not approve of the regime either and be powerless to effect change. Trading

conceivably might be a way of trying to have some influence on the governments concerned. There are those who argue that the business of business is business and that foreign firms should not seek to interfere in domestic politics. Room for some debate here!

Pause for thought 2

A number of examples are given in the text and include the chemical industry, food retailing, and the manufacture of personal computers.

Pause for thought 3

If you can identify more than 20 brands of soap powder you are doing well. The point is that this type of proliferation of brands is designed to limit market entry.

Case Study 11.3: The threat of substitutes – Nintendo fights back

1 This would appear to be a classic oligopolistic market.
2 Given that Nintendo has a competitive advantage at the moment and it has the lead over its competitors, then it would appear that in the short term at least it can charge a premium price and undertake a bit of 'price skimming', seeking to maximise its profits in the short run while the demand for the new 64-bit games platform is inelastic. However, there is the complication that what the consumers want is sophisticated games to play on these new platforms. At the moment all this hand-held computing power is going to waste as Nintendo does not possess the games to show off its powerful platform. One technique would be to develop sophisticated games which it sells expensively on a high-powered platform which it sells cheaply. The games should be developed so that they could only run on the 64-bit platform and as they are a recurring item of expenditure (on which Nintendo can make money each time the consumer buys a new one) there is more chance of making higher profits from the games than from the platforms. The only problem with this strategy is that there does not appear to be the capacity to develop games software fast enough to plug this gap quickly.
3 This remains to be seen. Keep your eyes open for news of Nintendo in the financial press.

Case Study 11.4: Supplier power – the case of the flat beer

1 The two strategies are (a) try to achieve cost reductions by seeking economies of scale, hence the spate of mergers between brewers, and (b) diversification into other related businesses such as hotels and restaurants. Strategy (a) aims to work on the cost side of the equation and (b) seeks to enhance the income side.
2 The dangers are twofold. First, there is a limit to the gains in terms of cost reductions that can be made from economies of scale in the brewing industry. There could also be objections from the competition authorities to too much horizontal integration in the brewing industry. Secondly, the skills

required to run a successful hotel or restaurant chain are quite different from those of being a brewer. Diversification could therefore spread the necessary management skills and knowledge too thinly.

Case Study 11.5: Buyer power and supermarkets

1   From the supermarkets' point of view their buyer power can clearly secure low prices from suppliers. They are able to extract deals from suppliers because they have all the bargaining power. The disadvantage is that if they abuse this dominant position they could affect the profitability of other firms in the supply chain and thereby reduce the number of suppliers able and willing to supply supermarkets.

2   From the consumers' point of view the consumers in theory have the benefit of cheaper goods as a result of the supermarket power to buy goods cheaper than other retail outlets. However, there was a suspicion (which appears to have been unfounded according to the Competition Commission's latest report, October 2000) that the supermarkets failed to pass on these price reductions.

3   From the suppliers' point of view winning a supermarket contract gives them a huge outlet for their products. However, it is a 'two-edged sword' as the supermarkets can be very demanding customers. They can alter the terms of supply and if a supplier loses a contract then the damage can be severe as they will have few alternative outlets for their goods.

4   The Code of Practice proposed by the Competition Commission for regulating the relationship between suppliers and supermarkets is not legally binding and critics argue that it still gives the supermarkets enormous power. Also the main thrust of the Competition Commission's recommendations appears to have been 'kind' to the supermarkets in the face of some damaging allegations about abuse of market power. (For details of the Supermarket Report visit the Competition Commission's webpage at www.competition-commission.gov.uk.)

Case Study 11.6: Competitive rivalry – the Navigator and the Explorer

1   One advantage that Netscape had over Microsoft is what economists call an 'incumbent's advantage'. Being the first into the market with an Internet browser the company is able to make their product the standard for the industry. Just as in the early days the industry standard for computers was IBM so Netscape was able to swiftly establish a virtual monopoly position. They therefore became in essence the 'gatekeeper' to a whole new set of possible revenue streams based on products and services (particularly information services) sold via the Internet. Microsoft therefore had to decide whether to strike a deal with Netscape to include its 'browser' as part of Microsoft's package of software that would be loaded up on to your PC or whether to go to the expense of taking Netscape on 'head-to-head' by developing its own rival product. It chose the latter but initially had an uphill struggle to get itself established in the market place.

2 The long-term prospects for Netscape are somewhat daunting. They can try to compete 'head-to-head' but risk having the market taken from them. They are essentially a one-product company and they need to form strategic alliances with information providers to offer consumers a package of cheap (or free) access via the Navigator browser but make money on the subscriptions to information services, or offer to form an alliance with Microsoft (although it is probably a bit late for that now). Netscape could try to 'ape' Microsoft by developing its own operating system in which the browser is already installed to match Microsoft's strategy in this area, but this is a very expensive option and the risks of failure would be high. Microsoft, often portrayed as the small company that took on IBM and won, looks more of a predator in its battle with Netscape and is not planning on coming second in its 'Battle of the Browsers'.

3 The market for browsers is essentially monopolistic. It will become a duopoly for a period. Depending on the way the competitive rivalry develops, it may become a monopoly again. There are a number of other factors which will influence how this market develops. Political factors would include competition rules and how the various authorities regard the way competition develops in this market. Predatory pricing by Microsoft may attract the attention of anti-trust bodies in the United States. Economic factors include such things as rising disposable incomes and the real price of acquiring PCs with access to the Internet. There is much less resistance to computers and much less 'technophobia' as access to the technology becomes more affordable and more user friendly (social and technological factors). The biggest factor which will affect the way this market develops will of course be technological. As more services become available via the Internet then so the number of 'service providers' will increase. These companies may decide to integrate backwards and develop their own 'browsers' to allow consumers to gain access or they may strike deals with existing 'browser' companies. If the costs of developing the browser software fall then the first option could become very attractive and the market could be more competitive. On the other hand, if the service providers go the 'strategic alliance' route it could mean that the browser market remains monopolistic.

4 This is an interactive question with the answer depending on your point of view.

Pause for thought 4

Strictly speaking, one should identify products rather than companies. For example, as an illustration of a product which has a high market share in a growing market it is hard to find a better example of a 'star' than Netscape's Navigator. In the case of the multinational conglomerates of ITT and Hanson there were presumably a number of businesses which they sold off because they were 'dogs'. In the case of Microsoft its operating system, which is now in virtually every PC in the world, is to all intents and purposes its 'cash cow' because it is the vast income that this generates which is going to finance its other activities. Initially, its own product, the Explorer, could be viewed as a '?' (or 'problem child') because it currently has a low market share in a high growth market. But this situation is likely to change dramatically in the next year or so.

Pause for thought 5

1 You should look out for companies that sell on the basis of 'price' as opposed to companies that sell on the basis of 'quality' and also look at examples of companies that switch strategy. For example, in January 1997 it was reported by Verdict, the retail consultancy, that an all-out supermarket price war was now more likely than at any time in the past 15 years. This represents a switch in position for one of the four main players in this market, namely J Sainsbury. Essentially, Sainsbury had been operating a 'Rolls Royce' strategy. (However, this has often been the subject of much debate, notably between Michael Porter and Lord Sainsbury himself! Sainsbury claims that their slogan 'Good food costs less at Sainsbury's' implies that it is following a 'hybrid' strategy as is mentioned in the text, but they were not the cheapest in the sector and had traditionally sold on 'quality'.) Tesco, on the other hand, had the reputation of being the heavier discounter in this market ('Pile 'em high and sell 'em cheap' had been the motto of the founding father of the company, Lord Cohen). However, the market had moved on and Tesco had, by a combination of aggressive marketing and investment in new technology, stolen a march on Sainsbury and knocked them off the top as the UK's leading food retailer. Sainsbury aims to fight back according to *Verdict*.

'If Sainsbury's current policies do not succeed in restoring sales volume growth, the temptation to launch a broadside of wide-ranging and deep cuts will be acute', says the report. Thus in terms of the strategy clock, Sainsbury aims to move away from its previous 'Rolls Royce' position to a 'hybrid' position. To some extent, if Sainsbury does engage in price cuts to establish itself as the cheapest then it does imply that it was not strictly speaking operating a 'hybrid' strategy before.

2 The 'hybrid' strategy is criticised as being neither one thing nor the other. Companies that pursue such strategies are vulnerable to 'attack' on two fronts: from those 'below' them in the market who can sell cheaper and those 'above' them who can beat them on quality. Thus being stuck in the middle is thought to be unwise and Michael Porter is highly critical of firms that pursue such a strategy. The only unfortunate thing about this line of argument is that there is not a shred of evidence to support any of it!

In an article called 'On being stuck in the middle or good food costs less at Sainsbury's', published in the *British Journal of Management* in 1994, Michael Cronshaw, Evan Davis and John Kay analysed the rates of return on capital employed by a number of firms that pursue a mix of different price and quality strategies. The results of their research are set out below:

Rate of return on capital employed (per cent)

		Quality		
		Low	*Medium*	*High*
	Low	7.4	12.2	17.3
Price	*Medium*	5.2	9.9	16.1
	High	5.1	11.6	17.6

What this indicates is that those companies that were 'stuck in the middle' (i.e. who combined medium quality with medium price) had profitability levels which were better than those firms who pursue the 'cheap and cheerful' option of low price and low quality. In addition, the results indicated that 'low quality' strategies do worse irrespective of price and hence quality appears to matter more than price.

Case Study 11.7: New universities stuck in the middle?

1 The options to consider would be to become a top-class research-based university or to focus more on teaching and become instead a predominantly teaching university. In addition, if additional fees are charged then universities would be able to compete on price by offering a lower price with a lower quality (cheap and cheerful?) or more of a Rolls Royce premium price service. Some universities may decide to move away from 'hybrid' positions and become predominantly postgraduate institutions while others become niche players utilising their particular strengths with specialist degree programmes which are not offered by the competition. The reality is that it is not always easy to move from one position to another very quickly. For example, it takes time to build up research expertise and it is difficult in a knowledge based industry to acquire the expertise to develop internationally recognised specialisms. In addition, the competition is becoming more global as technology opens up the possibility of degree courses being delivered from anywhere in the world via electronic media.

2 It may be advantageous to have strategic alliances with local FE colleges as this allows a university to tap into markets either that they do not have the resources to reach themselves or that can act as a 'feeder' to other university programmes.

Pause for thought 6

There are numerous examples of new products for an existing market throughout the text from Sainsbury to Microsoft.

Case Study 11.8: Sainsbury's strategic options – the product/market matrix applied

1 The main reason was to reduce the risks involved in the diversification strategy and to limit the number of 'unknowns'.

2 The synergy is linked to the organisational, logistic skills that a food retailer brings to bear on a DIY business. This covers areas such as information technology and management information and financial control systems, stock control systems, purchasing and supply, marketing store layout, customer care, etc.

3 The case study, which is based on the situation in 1994, puts them at the 'Rolls Royce' end of the spectrum as it indicates that they were not comfortable with a discounting environment. This appears, however, to be about to be overtaken by events (see above solution to 'Pause for thought 5').

4 Investors feared that Sainsbury were moving too far from their 'core' business activities, which were draining their resources. The sale of Homebase would, it was argued, allow Sainsbury to reinvest the funds elsewhere, thereby 'releasing more shareholder value'.

Pause for thought 7

This is an open-ended question designed to provoke some discussion of why firms might choose to merge. Is it as a defence against a new upstart? Is it to acquire a foothold in a new and developing market? Is it, as in the case of conglomerates, to diversify the risks? Is it because 'going it alone' is too costly or too risky?

Case Study 11.9: 'Auntie' in pay TV deal

The main advantages to the BBC of a joint venture are of cost and speed to get into the multichannel satellite/cable market. The BBC simply does not have the resources to break into this market and it would take too long to set up the distribution network required to make this a commercial success. They are also extremely attractive to the 'distributors' because they have the reputation for producing quality television. The danger is to the BBC's own reputation because they may not have any control over the other programmes that are shown alongside the BBC's offerings. There is also the risk that the more commercially successful the BBC is, the harder it is to justify the retention of the licence fee.

Pause for thought 8

1 Formula driven funding gives the recipients some certainty on their budgets for the following year. If the formula has been agreed beforehand there is less acrimony in the way resources are divided up. The main disadvantage is that it is difficult to effect any radical changes in the priorities and objectives if the resources are allocated in this way. Some methods combine a sum which is allocated by formula (which gives some stability) but also has an element which is allocated by other criteria, including past performance, or some form of internal competitive bidding system.
2 Allocation purely by bidding produces the maximum uncertainty and runs the danger of there being 'strategic drift' with no centrally agreed plan of priorities.

Case Study 11.10: Hewlett-Packard and organisational structure

1 The advantage of a decentralised approach is that decision-making is speeded up. It also means that the division that is responsible for the decision is often 'closer' to the market and hence it is argued that decisions will be better informed. There is often a greater degree of 'ownership' of the decision and hence responsibility to make it work. The disadvantage is that sometimes there will be a clash between the division's goals and those of the organisation as a whole, leading to 'sub-optimal' decision-making. There is also the danger of duplication of some central functions.
2 The two dimensions of the matrix are: four divisions (2×2) that are based on products and customers. It appears from the case that the divisions are as follows:

Products:	Computers/Printers
Customers:	Domestic/Business

3 On the face of it there is nothing wrong with a corporate culture which stresses the advantages of business units and rejects hierarchies. However, it appears that too much autonomy to the divisions has created duplication and inefficiencies. It leads to too many 'soloists when what HP needs is an orchestra'. There is a danger of 'strategic drift' whereby each division goes off and does its 'own thing', leading to sub-optimal decision-making.

Case Study 11.11: Delta takes a nose-dive

See text.

Case Study 11.12: 3M reinvents itself

1 3M fell victim to changes in its external environment. It failed to gauge how the floppy disc market would develop. There were therefore unforeseen changes in technology. In addition, it got it wrong in the audio and video tape business, failing to anticipate the degree of foreign competition or to react swiftly enough to the rise in the price of cobalt (an external economic factor over which it had little control). In addition, the market conditions in 1995 for its main products also remained unfavourable.

2 Using the Ansoff matrix, 3M can try to develop a more 'market-centred' strategy. This implies that the options facing 3M are to innovate and to develop new products for existing markets (Post-it mark 2?), seek to develop new markets for their existing products or develop new products for entirely new markets. Secondly, 3M can sell off those bits of the business which are underperforming and focus on a narrower range of activities by identifying its 'core competences'.

3 This is a company that is fiercely independent with a philosophy and a style of doing business which it feels would be compromised by mergers or joint ventures. So long as the company continues to be successful then it can retain its independence and retain its philosophy.

4 See **2**.

5 Using the competitive bidding system allows 3M to back potential winners (assuming that those allocating the funds can spot them and those doing the bidding can deliver them). However, there is a danger that by turning everything over to the internal bidding system those divisions which are unsuccessful will go to the wall and lose staff and expertise. As the case illustrates, the way in which the hugely successful Post-it product was discovered and developed owes more to luck than good judgement. Spotting winners in the area of new product development is not an easy task and often companies have to be prepared to 'waste' millions of pounds or dollars before a new successful product is developed.

Case Study 11.13: Mackbrew goes international

The case provides an opportunity to explore some of the options discussed in more detail in the section which follows. However, the objective is to see how many of the six strategic options you could come up with before reading on. Try it. (No cheating!)

Case Study 11.14: A clash of cultures?

See text.

Pause for thought 9

The main reason hinges on the degree of control that they wish to exert. A joint venture means that they would have to relinquish some control to their partner. A takeover would reduce the number of firms in the industry and may excite the interest of the competition authorities as well as possibly provoke protests about 'foreign' takeovers. Wholly-owned subsidiaries increase competition, create new jobs and still leave the Japanese company managers in control.

Pause for thought 10

Reasons could relate to all three factors discussed in the text. *Ownership-specific factors* relating to all three industries suggest that they gain from economies of scale. As domestic markets are often too small to fully exploit these then the firms become multinational to gain the full benefits. In addition, there may be *location-specific factors* at work, most obviously in the oil industry. Finally, there are *internalisation* reasons. Rather than try to exploit the advantages that a firm has acquired in oil, cars and electronics by other means of 'going international' (e.g. licensing or exporting) the companies choose to keep the skills internally and to internalise the benefits by becoming multinational.

Pause for thought 11

Cheaper, easier and faster communications have assisted the process of globalisation. The reduction in the barriers to foreign direct investment and the spread of similar tastes across international boundaries have also helped to assist the process.

Case Study 11.15: Ford – a global company?

1   Ford was to some extent reacting to the competition which is global, particularly the Japanese car companies, and its main rival in the United States, General Motors. It is also under pressure to develop new models quickly, so the idea of using the same 'platform' worldwide to produce a variety of different models is attractive, given the time and the costs of developing new models.

2   The three tests are:
  ➤ World-wide market place.
  ➤ Production facilities located throughout the world.
  ➤ Business functions widely dispersed throughout the world (or HQ located in a country other than the country of origin).

Ford still has a strong regional structure but it probably passes the first two 'tests' above. However, in common with a large number of multinationals it still has a strong national identity. It can be argued that it still has some way to go before it is a truly global company.

Case study 11.16: Globalisation and retailing

1   There are several reasons why retailers go global:
    ➤ *Ownership-specific advantages*: These companies may have an expertise and an ability to deliver goods cheaply to consumers which they wish to exploit in international markets.
    ➤ *Location-specific advantages*: The companies may see opportunities in other markets such as rising disposable incomes, low barriers to entry, etc.
    ➤ *Internalisation advantages*: These relate to such intangibles as brands and know-how which the companies are unwilling to entrust to third parties (such as joint venture partners or licensees to exploit).
2   There are strong national and cultural factors which influence consumer choice. It is therefore difficult for companies to transform themselves into major international companies in a short period.
3   The table highlights the fact that in terms of the percentage of sales overseas only three companies have a figure in excess of 50 per cent and could be truly described as 'global'. All the other companies are more accurately described as 'international' as opposed to global.

Chapter 12 Government and business
....

Pause for thought 1

Many possibilities exist here, for example wider distribution of (share) ownership, increased productivity (of labour or capital), greater competition and more innovation.

Case Study 12.1: Privatisation in China

1   Clearly there is easier access to raise investment capital via privatisation, which could be used for modernisation, raising productivity and lowering unit cost. This certainty seems to be needed given the recorded fall in productivity of state-owned enterprises (SOEs), from over three-quarters of industrial output in 1978 to less than one-third in 1999, despite employing around the same number of workers.

    Other possible *favourable* aspects you might have commented upon include evidence that the small private sector is already vibrant, that many SOEs are effectively bankrupt, that the Maanshan steel company has benefited in terms of price/quality, and that the profits that it now makes can help support its various welfare services. The fact that Chinese entry into the WTO will mean greater competition for savings makes it even more important that Chinese firms become more efficient and profitable.
2   Some of the points *against* might include: danger of wide-scale liquidation of companies; collapse of employment and social disintegration; extra investment capital via privatisation might only be used to support inefficient practices; unwillingness of government to allow true change of ownership ('state control never to be surrendered'); and only *partial* discipline of market to be permitted (i.e. success rewarded but failure not penalised).

Pause for thought 2

Horizontal: NTL and Cable & Wireless (cable companies), Longman and Addison Wesley (publishing), and Renault and Nissan (motor vehicles).
Vertical: Powergen (electricity generation) and Norweb (electricity distribution) – an example of Forward Vertical Integration.
Lateral: Sea Containers (shipping) and Inter City East Coast (rail), etc.

Pause for thought 3

Desire to create UK 'winners' in a global market place, e.g. via fully utilising scale economies, even if some risk of non-competitive practices.

Case Study 12.2: Mergers and efficiency

1   Some of the *benefits* you might discuss include: threat of takeover as spur to management efficiency; sharper focus on creating shareholder value; possible synergies between merged firms; greater financial discipline; easy access to innovation already made by acquired firm.
2   Some of the *costs* you might discuss include: lack of benefit for acquiring company; few identifiable synergies actually discovered; negative impact on R&D and innovation; inefficient use of the scarce resource 'managerial time'; extra debt burden created; bias against 'strategic' thinking.

Pause for thought 4

For example, although only 0.2 per cent of businesses, by number, have over 250 employees, they contribute almost 44 per cent of all employment and over 48 per cent of all turnover in the UK.

Case Study 12.3: 'Show business angels'

1   These show-business 'angels' are largely amateur enthusiasts. 'Business angels' are outside investors with some business background encouraged via various tax incentives, etc, to bring their investments and expertise to small firms.
2   Many aspects here. Being aware of the 'break even figure' will help, i.e. the percentage occupancy figure per show agreed between the theatre and the entrepreneur (impresario) staging the show. Spreading risks by investing in different *types* of show, linking with management with a solid track record, checking that returns on subsidiary and other rights are available to investors, being aware of 'inside gossip' in theatre circles, etc., might all help, though risk is an inevitable part of such investments.

Pause for thought 5

You could look at data indicating some or all of the following by region: GDP per head; unemployment; consumer expenditure. You can also look at regional variations in the possession of various consumer goods (see also *Social Trends*).

Index